MANAGERIAL ACCOUNTING

MANAGERIAL ACCOUNTING

Second Edition

JAMES H. ROSSELL

WILLIAM W. FRASURE

Graduate School of Business
University of Pittsburgh

CHARLES E. MERRILL PUBLISHING COMPANY
A Bell & Howell Company
Columbus, Ohio

Copyright © 1972 by Charles E. Merrill Publishing Company, Columbus, Ohio. All rights reserved. No part of this book may be reproduced in any form, electronic or mechanical, including photocopy, recording, or any information storage or retrieval system, without permission in writing from the publisher.

International Standard Book Number: 0–675–09170–5
Library of Congress Catalog Card Number: 76–174156

1 2 3 4 5 6 7 8—77 76 75 74 73 72

Printed in the United States of America

Preface

This book presents in a logical pattern the basic considerations underlying financial and cost accounting data from a management point of view. Emphasis throughout is on how accounting aids management by providing financial information to allow control of current operations and to form a partial basis for formulating certain business policy decisions.

The book proceeds at a rapid pace with a highly conceptual and managerial approach. Understanding and use of accounting information, not design and construction, is the goal. Time-consuming involvement in the details, mechanics and techniques (debit and credit, journals, ledgers, trial balances and worksheets) is avoided through concentration on pertinent concepts which are meaningful and vital to management. Thus the approach throughout the book is on "how to use" accounting rather than "how to do it."

Throughout the book, the learning process is fortified by the presentation of examples taken from corporate annual reports to stockholders, references to current accounting and related literature, illustrations of actual applications, and information on relevant historical as well as current research. The questions, problems, and short cases at the end of each chapter have been classroom tested and have been selected because of their effectiveness in aiding the student to gain and retain mastery of important accounting concepts.

Managerial Accounting is divided into two major parts. The first part, Chapters 1 through 9, discusses financial statements and critically analyzes financial data from an interpretative and management-use point of view. The second part, Chapters 10 through 19, examines cost concepts and analyzes cost data that are pertinent to managerial control and the decision-making process.

As a college text, the book may be used as the basis of a one- or a two-term course, dependent upon the material selected for discussion and the depth into which various topics are probed. The organization of the book is such that each chapter may be used in numerical sequence or out of numerical sequence, or individual chapters or portions of chapters may be omitted. The sequence of the material selected and the depth to which various topics are studied will depend upon the individual using the book.

The second edition of this book combines a comprehensive revision and updating of original content with a substantial amount of new material. Additions or significant changes are provided for several important and timely issues, including:

>   Earnings per share
>   Reporting by lines of business
>   Statement of source and application of funds (Statement of changes in financial position)
>   Opinions of the Accounting Principles Board
>   Reporting of leases
>   The master budget
>   Mathematical and statistical techniques applied to accounting

The material in this book is the result of the experiences of the authors in teaching courses in managerial accounting at the undergraduate and graduate levels and in executive development programs at several universities and various in-company programs.

The authors gratefully acknowledge the helpful suggestions received from faculty at various colleges who used the first edition of this text. Special acknowledgment is due Professors Jacob G. Birnberg and Trevor Sainsbury of the University of Pittsburgh for their significant contributions to the content of Chapters 17 and 19. Grateful acknowledgment also is extended to the American Accounting Association, Financial Executives Institute, National Association of Accountants, and numerous publishers for permission to cite their various publications. Particular recognition is due to the many corporate officials who permitted us to use excerpts from their corporate financial statements and annual reports as examples to illustrate different concepts and practices.

Further acknowledgment is made to the American Institute of Certified Public Accountants, Inc., for the numerous citations from or references to *Accounting Trends and Techniques, Accounting Research Bulletins, Opinions of the Accounting Principles Board,* other Institute publications, and various Uniform CPA Examination problems.

October, 1972

James H. Rossell
William W. Frasure

Comment of Publisher

While this book was in the final stage of production, the Revenue Act of 1971 was passed by Congress. It was not possible to expand the book at such a late date to incorporate certain points contained in the Act, H.R. 10947, signed by the President on December 10, 1971. Instead, the principal points affecting this book are mentioned below and cross-referenced to the appropriate related material.

The Asset Depreciation Range (ADR) System, discussed in Chapter 6 on page 144, has now been codified. The Revenue Act of 1971 now makes it part of the "tax law"; formerly it was only a Treasury Department "regulation." One minor change was made concerning point c on page 144; the new law eliminates the provision by which a company could take a full year's depreciation for assets placed into service in the first half of a year.

The 7 percent investment credit, discussed in Chapter 7 on pp. 180–85, has been restored for equipment acquired, basically, after August 15, 1971. Also, in determining the amount of the "qualified investment," the useful life brackets have been shortened by one year. Thus the table on page 181, under the Revenue Act of 1971, is changed to the following:

If useful life is	Then the applicable percentage of the investment which qualified is	With a resultant effective investment credit of
Less than 3 years	None	None
3 or 4 years	33⅓%	⅓ of 7% = 2⅓%
5 or 6 years	66⅔%	⅔ of 7% = 4⅔%
7 years or more	100 %	7%

COMMENT OF PUBLISHER

It is interesting to note that the Revenue Act of 1971 specifically states that "—no taxpayer shall be required to use . . . any particular method of accounting for the credit." Thus the Act sanctions both the "flow through" and "deferral" methods discussed in Chapter 7. The Act goes on to state, "taxpayer shall disclose, in any such report, the method of accounting for such credit used by him for purposes of such report." With the restoration of the investment credit, several minor changes were made (*e.g.,* extension of the carryover period for unused credits under certain conditions; 4 percent credit only for eligible public utility property) which are beyond the scope of this book.

The reader is referred to the Revenue Act of 1971 for the various detailed technical points which relate to the above tax changes.

December, 1971 *Charles E. Merrill Publishing Company*

Contents

PART 1 FINANCIAL ACCOUNTING CONCEPTS, EVALUATIONS, AND PLANNING GUIDES

1 The Relationship of Accounting to Management 1

Definition of Accounting 1
Approach of the Book 2
Accounting: Technical Viewpoint Versus Managerial Viewpoint 2
Organizational Relationship of Accounting to Management 4
The Field of Accounting 6
Questions and Problems 7

2 The Balance Sheet 12

Assets, Liabilities, and Stockholders' Equity 13
Condensed Balance Sheet 13
Detailed Balance Sheet 16
Other Forms for the Balance Sheet 23
Forms of Business Organization 25
Uses of the Balance Sheet 25
Questions and Problems 26

CONTENTS

3 The Statement of Income   36

The Accounting Period 36
Title of Statement 37
Revenue and Expenses 37
Condensed Statement of Income 38
Classification of Revenues 38
Classification of Expenses 39
Earnings Per Share 44
The Accrual Basis of Accounting 46
The Matching Concept 47
Statement of Retained Earnings 47
Reporting by Lines of Business 50
Consolidated Financial Statements 50
Questions and Problems 60

4 Statement of Source and Application of Funds   73

Illustration of the Statement of Source and Application of Funds 75
Data for Preparation of the Statement of Source and Application of Funds 76
Source of Funds 79
Application of Funds 81
Summary 83
Questions and Problems 83

5 Measuring Management Performance, Return on Capital, Other Measurements   95

Percent of Net Income to Net Sales 96
Return on Capital 97
Summary—Return on Capital 112
Other Measurements 113
Significance of Measurements and Ratios 116
Conclusion 117
Questions and Problems 118

6 Property, Plant and Equipment: Acquisition, Depreciation, Disposal   134

Capital Expenditures and Revenue Expenditures 135
Depreciation 138
Depreciation Methods 145

Comparison of Principal Depreciation Methods 154
Revision of Estimated Useful Life 157
Disposal of Fixed Assets 158
Questions and Problems 162

7 Property, Plant and Equipment: Depreciation, Depletion, Amortization   172

Depreciation 172
Depletion 200
Amortization 204
Questions and Problems 215

8 Inventories and Inventory Management   224

Inventory 224
Inventory Management 250
Questions and Problems 255

9 Long-Term Debt, Stockholders' Equity   269

Long-Term Debt 270
Stockholders' Equity 281
Factors in Planning the Financial Structure 300
Questions and Problems 306

PART 2 COST ACCOUNTING CONCEPTS, CONTROLS, AND DECISION AIDS

10 Framework of Manufacturing Costs   331

The Elements of Manufacturing Cost 334
Process Costing and Job Order Costing 338
Accounting for Cost Elements 342
Questions and Problems 347

11 Behavior, Flow, and Classification of Production Costs   358

Cost Behavior 358
Cost Flow 360
Cost Classification 372
Questions and Problems 374

12 Flexible Budgeting — 384

Flexible Budgets 387
Questions and Problems 399

13 Manufacturing Cost Control Through Standard Costs — 407

Direct Material Standards 410
Direct Labor Standards 414
Manufacturing Overhead Standards 418
Product Standard Costs 426
Summary of Standard Costs 427
Questions and Problems 428

14 Direct Costing — 439

Direct Costing 441
Advantages of Marginal Income to Management 448
Considerations Underlying the Position of Direct Costing 451
Questions and Problems 454

15 Cost-Volume-Profit Relationships — 464

Break–Even Analysis 465
Profit–Volume Analysis 470
Differential Analysis 476
Summary 477
Questions and Problems 478

16 Cost Accounting Guides for Pricing Decisions — 486

Cost Pricing Methods 489
Summary 502
Questions and Problems 502

17 The Master Budget — 511

Limitations on Comprehensive Budgets 512
Steps in the Process 512
Budgeting Mechanics—An Overview 514
The Budgeting Process: An Illustration 518
New Planning Techniques 532
Questions and Problems 533

18 The Capital Expenditure Program 543

Capital Budgeting 543
Capital Expenditures Budget 544
Summary 556
Questions and Problems 557

19 Mathematical and Statistical Techniques Applied to Accounting 567

Economic Order Quantity Determination 568
Regression Analysis 572
Sampling 581
Control Chart for Variables 590
Linear Programming 598
Supplementary Readings 607
Questions and Problems 608

Appendices 615

Appendix A 617
Appendix B 633

Index 635

Part 1

Financial Accounting Concepts, Evaluations, and Planning Guides

1

The Relationship of Accounting to Management

Accounting has been called the "language of business." Business dealings of a financial or quasi-financial nature are expressed in accounting terms or in words substituted for accounting terminology. For example, an individual who purchases a residence for $30,000, paying $5,000 down and signing a mortgage for $25,000, does the following: he makes a "capital expenditure" for land and house of $30,000; he decreases his cash by a $5,000 "disbursement"; and he incurs a "long-term liability" of $25,000. Just as a law student must understand how to use legal terminology and a medical student must learn how to employ medical terminology, so a student of business must know how to use the terminology of accounting.

DEFINITION OF ACCOUNTING

There is a considerable degree of misunderstanding about the nature of accounting. Fundamentally, accounting is an information system by which financial data are recorded, accumulated, and communicated for decision-making purposes. Through financial reporting, information is provided concerning profitability, a vital element in our private enterprise economy. Accounting also provides data for the guidance and control of certain business operations.

The Committee on Terminology of the American Institute of Certified Public Accountants has defined accounting as follows:

Accounting is the art of recording, classifying, and summarizing in a significant manner and in terms of money, transactions and events which are, in part at least, of a financial character, and interpreting the results thereof.[1]

Recording is the mechanical process by which financial transactions and events are systematically placed in accounting records. Such transactions and events are analyzed so that they can be *classified* according to a predetermined system of accounting. Periodically, the information so recorded and classified is *summarized* by the preparation of financial statements and reports to the managers of an enterprise and to other interested parties. *Interpreting* basically refers to that utilization of the recorded, classified, and summarized data which reveals and emphasizes significant changes, trends, and potential developments in the affairs of an enterprise.

APPROACH OF THE BOOK

The foregoing definition delineates four facets of accounting. In general (as portrayed below), the first three facets refer to the "how to do" part of account-

recording classifying summarizing	interpreting
"how to do"	"how to use"

ing; the fourth, to the "how to use" aspect of accounting. It is to this fourth facet of the definition of accounting that this book is directed: principal emphasis will be placed upon the managerial significance of accounting facts, not on the facts themselves. Thus, the goal of this book is not to train accountants as such, but to enable those in or studying for a career in business to understand how accounting is used to formulate certain business decisions and to control certain business operations.

ACCOUNTING: TECHNICAL VIEWPOINT VERSUS MANAGERIAL VIEWPOINT

It is possible that the reader has heard accounting related to the sacred art of matching pennies, implying that accounting is merely a routine mechanical process of unvarying precision and petty detail. Or it may be that the reader has heard accountants called tinkerers of the records, indicating that it is possible for accountants to obtain different answers in a given situation for each differ-

---

[1] American Institute of Certified Public Accountants, Inc., Committee on Terminology, *Accounting Terminology Bulletin Number 1*, "Review and Résumé," (New York, 1953), p. 9. Copyright 1953 by the American Institute of Certified Public Accountants, Inc.

ent user of financial information. Rarely are such innuendoes justified. Much of the misunderstanding behind such comments may be traced to the repeated attempts made by accountants to adapt accounting to the diverse needs and objectives with which it is confronted. As an information system, accounting must be adapted to the environment it serves, but it cannot act as a substitute for sound judgment.

From the technical viewpoint alone, accounting must be flexible if it is to satisfy various kinds of needs. First, accounting must follow "generally accepted accounting principles" in the preparation of the financial statements for the annual report to stockholders and other interested parties, or the statements will not be given an unqualified opinion by an independent auditing firm of certified public accountants. (The reader is referred to the second paragraph of the accountants' reports or opinions attached to the financial statements in Appendix A, pages 619 and 625, in which reference is made to generally accepted accounting principles.) In addition, a company with stock listed on any of the stock exchanges must file with the Securities and Exchange Commission periodic financial statements which follow these accounting principles.[2]

Second, accounting must provide information which is vital and necessary for the proper preparation of various local, state, and federal tax returns. Accounting which follows generally accepted accounting principles for purposes of external reporting to stockholders and the SEC is inadequate for many tax purposes. For example, an item which is income for conventional accounting purposes—such as interest earned on bonds issued by states, municipalities, and other political subdivisions—is not taxable income for federal income tax. There are additional items of income and expense which may be treated in one manner for accounting purposes, but in an entirely different manner for tax purposes. Similarly, another item—such as depreciation expense or the depletion allowance—may be shown at a certain amount for accounting purposes, but at an entirely different amount for tax purposes. Thus, while accountants must record, classify, summarize, and present financial information in a manner which conforms with generally accepted accounting, they must treat some of the same information in an entirely different manner to satisfy tax requirements.

A third variation in accounting data is associated with certain industries. For example, the Interstate Commerce Commission requires railroad and pipe line companies to file periodic financial reports and statements prepared in a man-

---

[2] The term "generally accepted accounting principles" does not connote a rigid set of accounting rules and procedures by which minutely exact results may always be derived. On the other hand, these principles are far more than vague generalities. They are, in effect, generalizations from particular business practices. Like most principles, generally accepted accounting principles are the result of an evolutionary process: they change in response to changing business practices in a changing society, but usually change rather slowly.

It should be noted that in 1959 the Council of the American Institute of CPA's created the Accounting Principles Board. To date, the APB has issued 19 Opinions. Prior to 1959, the Committee on Accounting Procedure of the American Institute of CPA's issued 51 Accounting Research Bulletins.

ner specified by that commission. Similarly, governmental utility commissions control the financial reporting of utilities, and various governmental agencies exercise control over the financial reporting of insurance companies.

Thus, accounting must furnish financial reports and statements prepared in many different manners according to many different "rules." Yet, while satisfying these diverse obligations, accounting cannot ignore the chief reason for its existence.

The principal reason for the existence of accounting is the aid it provides to management. Accounting should aid management by furnishing information in reports and financial statements. It should provide a basis for financial interpretations which assist management in the formulation of certain policy decisions and in the control of current operations. Such internal reporting to management may—and often does—require the collection and presentation of financial information in a manner completely unlike that followed for external reporting. What is needed for reporting to the stockholders, what is legal for tax purposes, or what is required for various governmental agencies may be accounting information which is entirely unsatisfactory for the primary purpose of aiding management to direct the operations of a business. For example, management may wish the internal financial statements to reflect price-level changes to measure performance better over a period of time. Or direct costing may be desired to promote a clearer analysis of costs for pricing policies and future planning. Price-level adjustments to financial statements (to be discussed in Chapter 7) and the use of direct costing (to be discussed in Chapter 14) are considered unorthodox by many because they have not, as yet, been recognized as generally accepted accounting principles. Yet management may be convinced that such innovations are necessary if accounting is to maximize its value for decision-making purposes.

ORGANIZATIONAL RELATIONSHIP OF ACCOUNTING TO MANAGEMENT

The organizational structure necessary to guide the operations of a business differs with the type of business involved, the size and complexity of the company, and the varying philosophies and abilities of the individuals comprising the top management of the company. What may be an excellent organizational arrangement for one company could be almost unworkable for another. Thus, the location, duties, and responsibilities of the accounting function in the over-all organizational structure will vary somewhat from company to company. Usually this function is under the direction of an individual whose title is controller.[3]

Shown in the accompanying organization chart is the major segment of the top management organization of a hypothetical large industrial corporation. It

---

[3] Occasionally spelled comptroller, especially when related to governmental operations rather than business enterprises.

must be re-emphasized that the format of any such chart varies from company to company. The specific location of the controllership function is a variable. The chart indicates that both the controller and treasurer are on an equal plane, and that both report to the vice president in charge of finance. Probably the principal variant to this plan is that whereby both the treasurer and the controller are at the company staff level and report directly to the president of the company. Sometimes one individual has the title of Vice President and Controller; in such cases, the treasurer may report to this individual. Similarly, the reverse situation may occur when one person bears the title of Vice President and Treasurer. Again, the same individual may be both secretary and treasurer of a company. It is not uncommon to find, over a period of time, different combinations of these functions in the same company. This lack of uniformity in the location of the controllership function is not peculiar to that function alone. In practically all companies, the organization chart is molded to some degree by the abilities and personalities of the individuals comprising the management.

EXHIBIT 1-1

A Typical Organization Chart

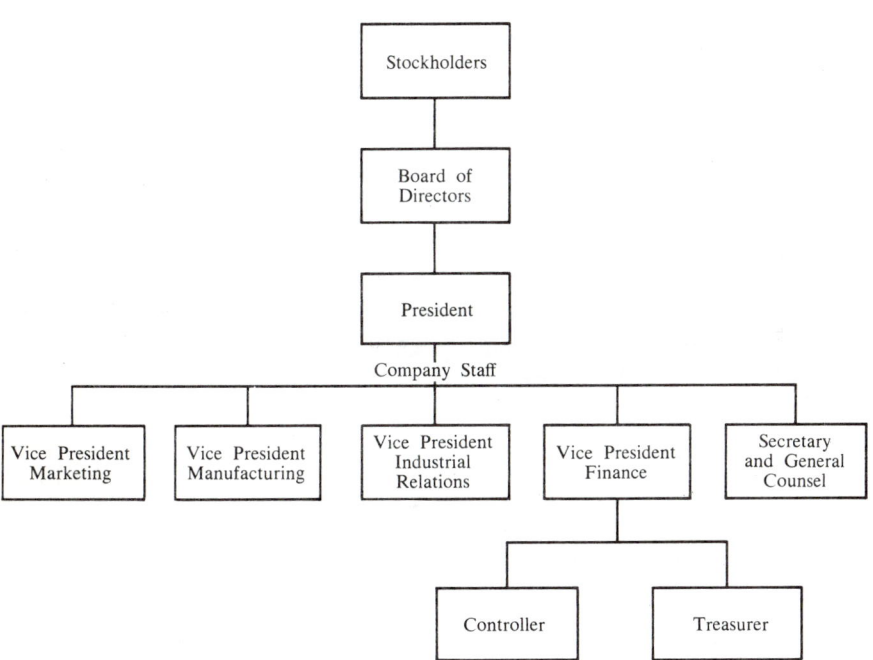

Assuming an organization chart like the one in Exhibit 1-1, with the controller and the treasurer both reporting to the vice president of finance, the controller is responsible for the over-all accounting function and the treasurer is responsible for the fiscal function.

In a broad sense, the functions allocated to the controller consist of:

> The collection, analysis, and interpretation of the financial information necessary for management use in the operation of the business.
>
> The maintenance of proper accounting records to provide proper reporting to various external groups (e.g., tax authorities, the Securities and Exchange Commission, governmental regulatory bodies).

Thus, the controller typically is responsible for the over-all system of accounting employed by the company; namely, the maintenance of internal control through the internal audit function, the preparation and explanation of financial analyses and reports, the budgetary control system, the various types of economic and profitability forecasts, and local, state, and federal tax returns.

The functions allocated to the treasurer in a broad sense ordinarily consist of:

> The planning of, and control over, the flow of cash as to sources and applications in conformance with the fiscal policies of the company.
>
> The protection and custody of funds and securities owned by the company.

Thus, the treasurer of the company typically is responsible for maintenance of a proper cash balance, preparation of forecasted cash flows, relationships with banks, investments of excess cash, credit and collection policies, procurement of capital and corporate financing, and the handling of corporate bank accounts.

An analysis of the responsibilities of the controller and the treasurer indicates that no fine line can be drawn between their functions. For example, the specific area of payrolls was mentioned neither under the functions of the controller nor the treasurer. In practice, the responsibility for the preparation and handling of payrolls may be included in the jurisdiction of either function. Whether it be under the duties of the controller or the treasurer, the controllership function must provide for the proper accounting and control of the payroll, and the treasury function must plan for the periodic out-flow of cash to meet the payroll. This illustrates the close liaison that must be maintained between these two separate functions.

THE FIELD OF ACCOUNTING

The field of accounting may be divided into four main categories: private, public, governmental, and institutional accounting.

Private accounting encompasses those persons employed by private business organizations. The preceding section of this chapter which concerned the controller's department provides the reader with an insight into the various facets comprising the area of private accounting. Though, basically, the materials in this book are presented from the point of view of private accounting as an aid to management, the principles discussed are generally applicable to the other three major divisions of accounting.

Public accounting, through independent practitioners, offers professional accounting services on a fee basis to business enterprises of all types, to governmental units and non-profit institutions, and to the general public. Among the varied services offered to clients by public accountants are audits, design and installation of accounting systems, income tax services, special investigations and reports, and management advisory services. To qualify as a certified public accountant, an individual must pass a uniform comprehensive written examination prepared by the American Institute of Certified Public Accountants and given by the individual states. In addition to the successful completion of the examination, many states require that the individual be registered or licensed to practice public accounting.

Governmental accounting consists of accounting activities performed at national, state, and local governmental levels. Examples of this area at the national level are the General Accounting Office of the United States and the Internal Revenue Service. Due to the wide scope of governmental activities, this division of accounting contains elements of both private and public accounting.

The area of *institutional accounting* refers to the accounting activities of non-profit organizations. Included in this category are charitable organizations, educational institutions, and churches.

Accounting serves many purposes. It often fulfills different needs with somewhat different answers obtained from the same information by following non-uniform but equally acceptable accounting methodologies. Because of its divided obligations, accounting at times appears to possess something akin to a split personality.

QUESTIONS AND PROBLEMS

1-1. Read the article "Horizons for a Profession: The Common Body of Knowledge for CPA's" in the September, 1966, issue of *The Journal of Accountancy,* and then choose the proper answer to each of the following six statements.

   a. The application of new methods in mathematics, statistics, and probability to problems in the management of formal organizations makes added mathematical capacity for tomorrow's CPA's:
      1. optional
      2. desirable
      3. mandatory
      4. too specialized to be worth the time

   b. A subject considered to be of highest importance in the common body of knowledge (for tomorrow's beginning CPA) is:
      1. written and oral English
      2. marketing

3. personnel relations
4. foreign languages

c. Accounting, while in truth a $\begin{Bmatrix} \text{a. deterministic} \\ \text{b. probabilistic} \end{Bmatrix}$ process, historically and to the present day is characterized by an appearance of $\begin{Bmatrix} \text{a. determinism} \\ \text{b. probabilism} \end{Bmatrix}$.

d. With respect to computers, it is recommended that tomorrow's beginning CPA have:
   1. a generalized acquaintanceship with what computers can do
   2. a knowledge of at least one computer language, ability to diagram an information system, and ability to prepare a program including debugging
   3. the knowledge to double as a computer expert

e. A knowledge of the fundamentals of behavioral science is:
   1. recommended
   2. considered desirable, though not specifically recommended
   3. not recommended

f. The oldest and best established of the quantitative techniques to aid in managerial decisions is:
   1. mathematics
   2. accounting
   3. statistics
   4. probability

1-2. Read the article "The New Financial Executive" in the February, 1965, issue of *The Journal of Accountancy,* and then choose the proper answer to each of the following four statements.

   a. The effect of electronic data processing (EDP) on the work of the financial executive has been to:
      1. make his job easier
      2. widen his horizon and responsibilities
      3. give him less time for planning because of his preoccupation with the mechanics of EDP

   b. The controller, comptroller, or treasurer, depending on what name each company calls its chief financial executive, performs basically the same task today as he did in 1915, only with a different title.
      1. True.
      2. False.

   c. The future financial executive will probably deal with such problems as working for better accounting principles, federal government relations, and labor relations.
      1. True.
      2. False.

   d. The area in the following list that is *not* the concern of the financial executive is:
      1. profit planning
      2. mergers and acquisitions
      3. insurance

[CH. 1] THE RELATIONSHIP OF ACCOUNTING TO MANAGEMENT 9

  4. research and development costs
  5. cannot choose one; all four areas are his concern

1-3. For both of the following statements, choose the proper answer to each.
  a. The members of the board of directors of most corporations are:
     1. appointed by the president of the corporation
     2. selected by management
     3. elected by the stockholders
     4. chosen by holders of preferred stock only
  b. The selection of a president for a corporation is made by:
     1. common stockholders
     2. preferred stockholders
     3. common and preferred stockholders
     4. the board of directors

1-4. If management believes that price-level adjustments to financial statements are necessary to make the statements more broadly meaningful, should generally accepted accounting principles be altered to permit the publication of such revised financial statements? Should Congress amend the Internal Revenue Code so that price-level adjustments on financial statements would be allowed?

1-5. What is your concept of the difference between bookkeeping and accounting?

1-6. Is accounting an exact science by which it is possible to measure business facts precisely?

1-7. Differentiate between the duties and responsibilities of the controller of a company and those of the treasurer.

1-8. The following news item (names of individual and company have been altered) appeared recently in the financial pages of a local newspaper:

  John Doe, plant accountant for X Co.'s Cleveland plant for six years, has been promoted to the newly created position of division controller, Special Products Division, with headquarters in Pittsburgh.
  Mr. Doe's duties will include internal functional control over plant accountants at special products plants located in four cities, and the establishment of selling prices and pricing policies for all special product items, parts, and accessories.

  Do you believe that "the establishment of selling prices and pricing policies" is encompassed in the responsibilities of a typical controller?

1-9. The Woltemar Company has operated profitably since its organization in 1935. Condensed financial statements of the Woltemar Company are reproduced below. Though twenty years apart and covering only two years out of two decades, 1952 and 1972 represent typical years for the company.
  Between 1952 and 1972, the Woltemar Company mechanized and modernized its plant. The principal reason for the improvement of the profit margin was the increased labor productivity attributable to the mechanization and modernization. As shown below, an increase in the dollar amount of all items has occurred over the years, and the company has improved its profit margin 20 percent. Moreover, it has always paid an annual $4 divi-

dend to its stockholders. Would you consider the Woltemar Company a "growth" company?

Balance Sheet
As of December 31

	1952	1972
Cash, Receivables, Inventories	$1,000,000	$2,000,000
Property, Plant and Equipment	2,000,000	4,000,000
Total Assets	$3,000,000	$6,000,000
Debts Owed	$ 500,000	$1,000,000
Stockholders' Equity	2,500,000	5,000,000
Total Equities	$3,000,000	$6,000,000

Statement of Income
For the Year

	1952	1972
Sales	$6,000,000	$9,000,000
Costs and Expenses	5,400,000	7,920,000
Net Income from Operations	$ 600,000	$1,080,000
Margin of Profit on Sales	10%	12%

1-10. The Runser Company manufactures and sells two products. The results of its operations for the year 1972 are shown below:

THE RUNSER COMPANY
Condensed Statement of Income
For the Year 1972

	Total	Product ABC	Product XYZ
Sales	$20,000,000	$10,000,000	$10,000,000
Costs and Expenses	14,000,000	6,000,000	8,000,000
Net Income	$ 6,000,000	$ 4,000,000	$ 2,000,000
Margin of Profit on Sales	$\frac{\$6}{\$20} = 30\%$	$\frac{\$4}{\$10} = 40\%$	$\frac{\$2}{\$10} = 20\%$

The year 1972 was a typical year in the operation of The Runser Company. There is a large unfilled demand for both of the company's products. Each product is independent of the other; neither is part of a product line. Total assets of the company amount to $20,000,000. $15,000,000 of this total is equitably allocated to Product ABC, and $5,000,000 to Product XYZ, as the capital necessary to manufacture and sell each product. Which product do you believe should have priority in a capital expansion program? State clearly any assumptions on your part and any additional information that you would desire.

1-11. Do you believe that accounting principles should be revised by a slow evolutionary process and thus appear somewhat antiquated at times, or do you prefer that accounting principles be revised periodically by the edict of some accounting group?

1-12. In a few countries a standardized set of accounting rules has been promulgated by an official body. All businesses, regardless of the industry or any peculiar circumstances within a given company, must follow a prescribed, uniform, stereotyped system of accounting. Discuss the advantages and disadvantages of such a procedure.

1-13. To become acquainted with certain available journals in the field of accounting, you are requested to read and submit a brief written summary of one article from a current issue of each of the following four publications:

    a. *Journal of Accountancy* (monthly publication)
       American Institute of Certified Public Accountants, Inc.
    b. *Accounting Review* (quarterly publication)
       American Accounting Association
    c. *Management Accounting* (monthly publication) (formerly *N.A.A. Bulletin*)
       National Association of Accountants
    d. *The Financial Executive* (monthly publication) (formerly *The Controller*)
       Financial Executives Institute (formerly Controllers Institute of America)

1-14. The following segment of a conversation was overheard recently:

> I'm the accountant for XYZ Company. I have complete charge of the books. Once a month, the auditors come in and adjust the books for me and prepare the monthly financial statements for our company.

    a. Do you believe the speaker is an accountant?

    b. Do you believe that the monthly work of the auditors represents auditing?

1-15. In 1914, the Interstate Commerce Commission prescribed a uniform accounting system containing uniform accounting rules for all regulated railroads. Inadequate revisions of the rules have rendered them largely out of date today.

    In addition to possible governmental inertia in periodic revision of such a system, do you see any additional dangers in the establishment of uniform accounting rules for American business by governmental decree?

2

The Balance Sheet

The balance sheet provides information which describes the financial standing of a company at a given instant. The time factor is especially significant because the statement conveys a financial message which is valid as of a given date only: yesterday's message would have been slightly different and tomorrow's message will be different. The statement might be visualized as a snapshot of the financial status of a company. Just as such a picture portrays an individual whose current image reflects the cumulative effect of physical change since birth, so a balance sheet presents a current image which reflects the cumulative effect of financial change throughout the lifetime of a company.

During the past 25 years there has been a change from the term "balance sheet" to "statement of financial position" and, in the past few years, a change back to the term "balance sheet." The table below shows selections taken from a yearly survey of annual reports issued by 600 industrial companies, which clearly indicate this change in terminology:[1]

Title of Statement

Terminology Applied:	1969	1965	1955	1946
Balance Sheet	512	470	466	578
Financial Position	61	94	92	12
Financial Condition	27	31	35	6
Other	0	5	7	4
Total	600	600	600	600

[1] American Institute of Certified Public Accountants, Inc., *Accounting Trends and Techniques in Published Corporate Annual Reports,* 24th ed., p. 43. Copyright 1970 by the American Institute of Certified Public Accountants, Inc.

ASSETS, LIABILITIES, AND STOCKHOLDERS' EQUITY

Basically, the balance sheet is divided into three sections: assets, liabilities, and equity of the owners. Assets are the resources owned by the company. Liabilities are the debts owed by the company; i.e., claims of creditors. Equity of the owners, usually referred to as stockholders' equity or net worth, is the excess of assets over liabilities. The relationship of the three components of the balance sheet may be expressed as:

$$\text{Assets} - \text{Liabilities} = \text{Stockholders' Equity}$$

or as:

$$\text{Assets} = \text{Liabilities} + \text{Stockholders' Equity}$$

To illustrate, assume that the assets of a company total $30,000,000 and that the liabilities amount to $10,000,000. The stockholders' equity is $20,000,000. The formal balance sheet is usually presented in one of three or four manners. The most common form of presentation is shown below.

THE FLEMING COMPANY
Balance Sheet
December 31, 1972

ASSETS		LIABILITIES	
		(Details)	
		Total Liabilities	$10,000,000
		STOCKHOLDERS' EQUITY	
(Details)		(Details)	
		Total Stockholders' Equity	20,000,000
Total Assets	$30,000,000	Total Liabilities and Stockholders' Equity	$30,000,000

Unlike the accompanying illustration, a published balance sheet shows details of the various items comprising total assets, total liabilities, and total stockholders' equity.

CONDENSED BALANCE SHEET

In presenting a balance sheet, the items constituting assets, liabilities, and stockholders' equity are classified under various headings. The number and type of such headings will vary, depending upon the situation of the company and the type of business. The following condensed balance sheet illustrates those primary classifications which are commonly encountered.

THE FLEMING COMPANY

Balance Sheet

December 31, 1972

ASSETS		LIABILITIES	
Current Assets	$12,000,000	Current Liabilities	$ 4,000,000
Investments	2,600,000	Long-term Debt	6,000,000
Property, Plant and Equipment	14,500,000	Total Liabilities	$10,000,000
Intangibles	400,000		
Deferred Charges	500,000		
		STOCKHOLDERS' EQUITY	
		Capital Stock	$ 2,500,000
		Additional Capital	4,500,000
		Retained Earnings	13,000,000
		Total Stockholders' Equity	20,000,000
Total Assets	$30,000,000	Total Liabilities and Stockholders' Equity	$30,000,000

Under each of the five classes of asset headings are listed the specific asset items which comprise that asset group. Likewise, each of the two categories of liabilities are subdivided according to the specific debts owed. The stockholders' equity section furnishes additional information concerning the capital stock, additional capital contributions, and the retained earnings. Before discussing the detailed items appearing on a statement of financial position, however, the principal classifications shown above must be clarified.

Classification of Assets

Current Assets are cash and other assets which are expected to be converted into cash or consumed in business operations within a relatively short period of time, usually one year or less. In addition to unrestricted cash, this category of assets includes such items as temporary investments in readily marketable securities or commercial paper, amounts due from customers for goods sold to them on credit, inventories on hand, and prepaid expenses. Prepaid expenses, shown last in the current asset section, usually represent services or benefits to be received and consumable supplies which will be used in the normal operation of a business instead of being converted into cash. As illustration, consider the company which two years ago paid in advance a three-year premium on the fire insurance policy covering its building. At the end of two years, the one-year unexpired premium represents an asset of the company. The company will realize this asset as a service or benefit (protection by insurance coverage) rather than in cash.

Reference to the detailed balance sheet on pages 18 and 19 will show that the current assets mentioned above are listed according to the order in which they are expected to be converted into cash.

The classification of Investments is provided for holdings owned of a relatively permanent nature. Included herein are securities of other corporations, advances to affiliated companies, and other long-term investments and equities. Temporary or short-term investments are not included in this classification; such investments are current assets.

Property, Plant and Equipment represents relatively long-lived assets of a tangible nature which are not intended for resale and are used in the operation of the business. These assets include land and depreciable assets such as buildings, machinery, and equipment. This class of assets is often called Fixed Assets.

Intangibles, as a class of assets, possess characteristics similar to those of property, plant and equipment items (fixed assets). Their value, however, does not derive from their physical nature but from the rights conferred by their ownership. Such intangible assets are patents, copyrights, and goodwill; sometimes they are shown under the classification Property, Plant and Equipment, rather than separately.

Deferred Charges represent expenditures made in one fiscal period which are not to be considered a cost of operations in that period, but which are carried forward to become an expense in subsequent periods. An example is an unusually large expenditure for moving and relocating factory machinery which is written off rateably over a period of years. As of any given date, that portion of the initial expenditure which had not yet been considered an expense would be a deferred charge.

Occasionally, additional classifications of assets are encountered, like "Other Assets." Such a category might include long-term receivables, special funds, or other assets not readily classified in one of the five preceding groups.

Classification of Liabilities

Current Liabilities are debts to be paid within a relatively short period of time, usually one year or less. Typical examples of current liabilities are amounts owed to trade creditors for materials, supplies, and services purchased on credit; amounts owed on promissory notes for funds borrowed from a bank; accrued or accumulated amounts owed but not yet due (as of the date of the balance sheet) for items such as salaries, taxes, and interest. Occasionally a different type of current liability is encountered when a company has collected or received income in advance of actually earning the amount; i.e., a magazine publishing company receiving a subscription accompanied by a check. Although the cash of the company is increased immediately, the company has not earned the income. It owes a debt to be paid by delivering magazines throughout the life of the subscription rather than by payment of cash.

Long-term Debt refers to liabilities which will not become due within the coming year. In fact, debts like mortgages and bonds may not come due for many years; the balance sheet usually indicates the maturity date of such long-term debts. Any portion of a mortgage or a bond issue that will come due within the coming year is shown as a current liability.

Classification of Stockholders' Equity

Stockholders' Equity, occasionally called net worth of the company, represents the excess of the company's assets over its liabilities. This "excess" is basically derived from two sources: capital contributions by the stockholders and accumulated net earnings which have not been distributed as dividends to the stockholders since the company was established.

The manner in which the capital contributed by the stockholders is presented in the balance sheet depends upon several factors: the type of capital stock, the value assigned to each share of stock, and the dollar amount for which each share of stock is issued. For example, the corporation, by its articles of incorporation, may have only one class of capital stock, or it may have both preferred stock and common stock. In addition, the capital stock may be par value stock or no par value stock. When shares of stock are issued, any consideration received above the par value of par shares or the stated value of no par shares is usually stated separately as Additional Capital, Paid-in Surplus, Capital Surplus, or Capital in Excess of Par Value or Stated Value. A complete discussion of these factors has been reserved until Chapter 9.

Retained Earnings represents the earnings of the company for all years to date which have not been distributed to the owners (stockholders), but reinvested and plowed back into the business. For example, The Fleming Company, since its organization in 1904, has had total net earnings over the years of $40,000,000. Of this, $27,000,000 has been used for dividend declarations and distributed to the stockholders; the remaining $13,000,000, which has been retained in the business, constitutes "Retained Earnings."

DETAILED BALANCE SHEET

The balance sheet illustrated on pages 18-19 is complete for most of the details shown on the typical published statement. Following is a brief explanation of each item appearing on the statement and the basis for the valuation of certain items.

Cash includes actual coin and currency on hand, such negotiable papers as money orders and checks for deposit, and unrestricted balances on deposit with banks.

Marketable Securities are readily marketable government obligations, commercial paper, and stocks or bonds of other corporations which are being held as short-term investments. The securities are listed at cost on the illustrative balance sheet, with a parenthetical note indicating that market prices of the securities exceed cost by a substantial amount. This "paper profit" is unrealized and is not considered profit until the securities are sold and a profit is actually obtained. On the other hand, if the securities had declined considerably below their cost, conservatism would usually require that the securities be written down to their present market value and the cost figure be shown parenthetically.

Accounts Receivable represents amounts due from customers for goods or services sold to them on open account (charge account).

Notes Receivable represents amounts due from customers evidenced by formal written promises to pay and amounts due from others on loans evidenced by signed promissory notes.

Reference to the illustrative balance sheet shows that $3,130,000 is due the business on both accounts and notes receivable, but, based on past experience, the company expects to realize $30,000 less than this amount. The $30,000 represents those receivables which will become bad debts if the company has estimated correctly. A majority of companies in business for some period of time have compiled an experience factor by which they are able to estimate accurately the anticipated amount of bad debts.

Inventories represents the goods and supplies on hand. The type or types of inventory which a company possesses depends upon the business in which the company is engaged. For example, if the company is a merchandising or trading concern, it purchases and sells essentially the same product. Examples of this type of company are F. W. Woolworth Co. and Federated Department Stores, Inc. In the current asset section on the balance sheet of each company is the item:

    Merchandise Inventories .... $ xxxxxxx

On the other hand, if the company is a manufacturing concern, it produces the finished product it sells. Raw materials are acquired and converted into a finished product by various manufacturing processes. Examples of this type of company are PPG Industries and United States Steel Corporation. The current asset item of "Inventories" on the balance sheet of PPG Industries is detailed in a note to the statements as follows:

    Inventories:
        Finished Products .... $ xxxxxxx
        Work in Process   xxxxxxx
        Raw Materials   xxxxxxx
        Supplies   xxxxxxx

The following is a brief explanation of each of the four types of inventory encountered in a typical manufacturing business.

Inventory of Finished Goods represents the stock of goods completely manufactured and on hand available for sale.

Inventory of Work in Process represents goods which are partially completed and still in the production process.

Inventory of Raw Materials represents the various materials acquired and on hand which have not yet undergone any manufacturing processes.

THE FLEMING
Balance
December

ASSETS

Current Assets:

Cash		$ 1,075,000
U.S. Government and Other Marketable Securities at cost (quoted market prices aggregate $1,800,000)		1,500,000
Accounts and Notes Receivable, less allowance for doubtful accounts of $30,000		3,100,000
Inventories, on last-in, first-out basis		6,300,000
Prepaid Expenses		25,000
Total Current Assets		$12,000,000

Investments:

Fund for Property Additions (U.S. Government Securities)	$ 1,800,000	
Investment in and Advances to Affiliated Companies	800,000	
Total Investments		2,600,000

Property, Plant and Equipment—*at cost:*

Land	$ 1,900,000	
Buildings	6,700,000	
Equipment	12,900,000	
	$21,500,000	
Less: Accumulated Depreciation to date	7,000,000	
Net Property, Plant and Equipment		14,500,000

Intangibles:

Trademarks and other intangible assets, less amortization	400,000
Deferred Charges	500,000
Total Assets	$30,000,000

Inventory of Supplies consists of those supplies used in the manufacturing processes, which either physically or economically are not considered a part of the finished product, like abrasives, lubricants, and similar items. In addition to manufacturing supplies, a company normally has an inventory of repair parts for machinery and equipment.

A comprehensive discussion of the determination of the cost assigned to the preceding inventories has been deferred to Chapter 8. It will suffice at this time to state that some of the more widely used methods employed for inventory valuation are various averaging methods, the first-in, first-out (FIFO) method, and the last-in, first-out (LIFO) method. The illustrative balance sheet on page 18 states that The Fleming Company is using the LIFO method.

COMPANY

Sheet

31, 1972

	LIABILITIES	
Current Liabilities:		
Note Payable to Bank		$ 850,000
Accounts Payable		2,400,000
Accrued Salaries, Wages, Taxes and Interest		250,000
Income Taxes Payable		500,000
Total Current Liabilities		$ 4,000,000
Long-term Debt:		
Debentures due 1980		6,000,000
Total Liabilities		$10,000,000

STOCKHOLDERS' EQUITY

Preferred Stock—4% cumulative, non-participating, non-convertible, par value $50.00 per share, authorized 50,000 shares; issued and outstanding 20,000 shares	$ 1,000,000	
Common Stock—par value $5 per share, authorized 500,000 shares; issued and outstanding 300,000 shares	1,500,000	
Capital in Excess of Par Value	4,500,000	
Retained Earnings	13,000,000	
Total Stockholders' Equity		20,000,000
Total Liabilities and Stockholders' Equity		$30,000,000

Under the LIFO method the goods "last-in" (most recently acquired) are, for costing and valuation purposes, assumed to be the "first-out": the first sold or used in production. Thus, the inventories physically on hand at a given date are valued at somewhat "ancient" or first-in costs, depending upon how long the company has been on LIFO and whether or not the quantity of inventory has changed materially over the years. It is not uncommon for companies which have been on LIFO for a number of years to show inventory amounts on the balance sheet which are considerably below current replacement costs because of rising price levels.

Prepaid Expenses represents those expenditures made for items like insurance premiums, certain taxes, and supply items which are chargeable against future revenues as operating expenses. As they are consumed, they become expenses of operations; until they are consumed, they represent current assets. Although a company may expect to convert all other current assets into cash, it anticipates only services or use from prepaid expenses.

Fund for Property Additions represents assets set aside to facilitate future property acquisitions. Although the illustrated financial statement shows a fund of U.S. Government securities, many funds contain securities of a non-governmental nature. The limiting feature of such a fund is the purpose for which the assets are set aside rather than the nature of the assets contained in it.

Investment in and Advances to Affiliated Companies indicates the amount of ownership that The Fleming Company has in the capital stock and/or bonds of affiliated companies plus loans made to such companies as advances. Through such investments, control may be exercised over other companies which may supply certain inventory items, provide important distributive outlets, or offer various benefits which are vital to the success of The Fleming Company.

Land is building sites and other ground owned and used in operating a business. The original cost of all such land, in our illustration, totals $1,900,000. In accordance with generally accepted accounting principles, the valuation of an asset in the United States is based upon historical cost. This means that the total price paid to acquire an asset represents the cost of that asset throughout its accounting existence. For example, a plot of ground which is owned and used in the operation of the business and which was purchased in 1934 at a cost of $200,000 is valued at $200,000 in the $1,900,000 amount shown for Land on the balance sheet as of December 31, 1972, even though the $200,000 plot of ground may today be worth $500,000.

Buildings of $6,700,000 shows the price paid for all factory buildings, office buildings, and warehouses which the company has acquired over the years, provided that they are still owned and used by the business as of December 31, 1972.

Equipment of $12,900,000 represents the amount paid for all machines, autos, and trucks, and other equipment which the company has acquired (regardless of the year of acquisition), provided that these items are still owned and in use as of December 31, 1972. Some companies prefer to segregate desks, chairs, showcases, cabinets, and similar items in a separate category titled Furniture and Fixtures on the balance sheet.

Accumulated Depreciation to date of $7,000,000 equals that portion of the $19,600,000 original cost of the tangible, long-life property now owned—except land—which has been written off rateably as an expense of operations through the year 1972. Estimated depreciation expense for each year is shown as one of the operating expenses in the statement of income (Chapter 3).

Net Property, Plant and Equipment of $14,500,000 represents the net *book* value or "undepreciated" cost of fixed assets. This dollar amount is not the current value or intrinsic worth of such assets. Instead, it represents that portion of the original price paid for such assets which has not yet been considered a cost of operating the business. For example, if an item of equipment purchased in early 1961 at a cost of $48,000 is still owned and used, the $48,000 is included in the $12,900,000 figure shown for Equipment. Assume that the item under consideration is depreciated over an eighteen-year life, two-thirds (12 years) of which has expired. The $7,000,000 amount shown for Less Accumulated Depreciation to date includes $32,000 for our hypothetical piece of equipment. Therefore, the Net Property, Plant and Equipment amount includes the remaining $16,000, which represents the undepreciated cost of the equipment. This is so, even though our item with a net *book* value of $16,000 may have a current market value of more or less than $16,000, and in spite of the fact that the item purchased 12 years ago for $48,000 may, today, have a replacement cost of $90,000. Historical cost figures shown on financial statements are usually at great variance with current values; this is attributable largely to the changing level of prices and the decreasing value of the dollar. This problem concerns not only the accounting profession but also those in management who use accounting information as an aid in formulating certain business decisions; the problem, and possible remedies for it, is discussed in Chapter 7.

The amount shown for *Trademarks and other intangibles, less amortization,* represents the net carrying value of the intangibles of the company. Intangible fixed assets are those which have no physical substance, like patents, copyrights, trademarks, franchises, and goodwill. However, ownership of any of these confers certain long-term rights upon the possessor. A patent granted to an inventor has a legal life of 17 years. Copyrights have a legal life of 28 years, with an additional 28-year renewal privilege. Theoretically, a trademark has an unlimited life. Privileges granted by a franchise may or may not have a determinable life. Goodwill, when it appears on financial statements, usually represents a "premium" amount paid to acquire another company or business. The amount of the goodwill purchased is that portion of the consideration paid for the acquired business in excess of the cost of the net tangible assets (assets purchased minus liabilities assumed). Many companies record intangibles as fixed assets at cost and then amortize (write-off) the cost of certain of these assets over a period of years. Other companies, recognizing the debatable value of such assets, either immediately charge off the costs of developing or acquiring intangibles like patents and trademarks as an expense of operations, or show their value at a nominal amount on the balance sheet.

Deferred Charges represent certain expenditures benefiting future years which are written off against income during such future periods. Typical deferred charges are costs of rearranging factory machinery, certain development and experimental costs, and any discount or expenses incurred upon the issuance of bonds by a corporation. Deferred charges, like prepaid expenses, represent certain future benefits to be received, but, unlike prepaid expenses, the actual services have been received or performed.

Note Payable to Bank is a written promise by the business to repay a bank loan of a certain sum at some fixed or determinable future date. Because the note is shown under current liabilities, it will mature within one year. Other notes payable may arise from credit purchases of goods or services from trade creditors when such debts are evidenced by formal written promises to pay.

Accounts Payable are debts owed to trade creditors for unpaid purchases of goods or services. Such debts are on "open account" to distinguish them from debts evidenced by promissory notes.

Accrued Expenses Payable are items such as salaries, wages, certain taxes, and interest—items which represent accumulating debts which have been incurred but not paid, usually because they are not yet due. For example, between pay dates, salaries and wages owed to employees accumulate day by day as a debt of the company. Another example, in some instances, is property taxes which accumulate or accrue on a *pro rata* basis until their due date. Yet another example might be the bonds shown under long-term debt on the illustrative balance sheet: unless the bond indenture called for an interest payment on December 31, 1972, interest has accrued on the bonds since the last interest payment date in 1972.

Income Taxes Payable is the estimated debt owed the government as of December 31, 1972, for payments not yet due on the corporate income tax liability.

Bonds Payable represent long-term borrowing by the corporation incurred by the issuance of bonds. The principal amount of a corporate bond issue, $6,000,000 in the case of The Fleming Company, is payable at the maturity date of the bonds. Interest, however, is usually payable semi-annually. There are many different types of bonds, two of the more usual being mortgage bonds and debentures. A mortgage bond issue is secured by a lien on certain property owned by the corporation. A debenture bond issue is not secured by any type of collateral; its security resides in the faith and credit of the corporation.

Preferred Stock is that portion of the ownership equity of the corporation which has certain designated rights which rank ahead of those belonging to common stock. The two preferences most frequently associated with preferred stock are the right to receive dividends before common stockholders and prior claim on assets upon liquidation of the corporation. The illustrative balance sheet shown earlier reveals that The Fleming Company has 4% cumulative preferred stock. This means that the annual $2 dividend (4% × par $50) payable on each share of preferred stock, if unpaid in any year, accumulates and must be paid with the current year's preferred dividend before any dividend can be declared on the common stock. The $2 per share is the maximum dividend on this preferred stock because it is non-participating; it cannot share with the common stock in any additional dividends. Also, it is not convertible into common shares.

Common Stock represents the residual portion of the ownership equity of the corporation. Although it ranks after the preferred stock in receiving designated privileges, it usually has the sole right to vote for the directors of a corporation.

Capital in Excess of Par Value, often called Paid-in Surplus or Capital Surplus, usually represents the amount received in excess of the par value of the shares of stock which have been issued by a corporation. For example, if some of the authorized—but as yet unissued—$5 par value common shares are issued at $25 per share, the $5 par value of each share is shown opposite Common Stock, and the remaining $20 received for each share is shown opposite Capital in Excess of Par Value. A typical additional source of Capital in Excess of Par Value is the capitalization of prior years' earnings by stock dividends; this point is discussed in Chapter 9.

Retained Earnings represents that amount of net earnings or profits which have not been distributed to stockholders out of the total net income earned by a company throughout its existence. It is often called Earned Surplus, Reinvested Income, or Earnings Retained for Use in the Business. Retained earnings are not in the form of cash or any other specific asset.

Bonds and other forms of long-term debt as well as the various items comprising stockholders' equity are illustrated and discussed in much more detail in Chapter 9.

OTHER FORMS FOR THE BALANCE SHEET

The balance sheet illustrated previously shows the assets on the left-hand side of the statement, and the liabilities and stockholders' equity on the right-hand side. While this represents the method most widely employed to present a balance sheet, two additional arrangements are often encountered. One of these lists the assets in detail and total, followed by the liabilities in detail and total, and shows the difference between the two totals as the amount of the stockholders' equity. Illustrated in condensed form by main categories only, it appears as follows:

THE FLEMING COMPANY
Balance Sheet
December 31, 1972

ASSETS

Current Assets	$12,000,000
Investments	2,600,000
Property, Plant and Equipment	14,500,000
Intangibles	400,000
Deferred Charges	500,000
Total Assets	$30,000,000

LIABILITIES

Current Liabilities	$ 4,000,000	
Long-term Debt	6,000,000	
Total Liabilities		10,000,000

STOCKHOLDERS' EQUITY

Preferred 4% Cumulative Stock	$ 1,000,000	
Common Stock	1,500,000	
Capital in Excess of Par Value	4,500,000	
Retained Earnings	13,000,000	
Total Stockholders' Equity		$20,000,000

The second procedure follows the working capital approach, whereby the statement begins with the subtraction of the current liabilities from the current assets to arrive at the working capital of the company. To the working capital, assets other than current assets are added and long-term liabilities are deducted to obtain net assets. Finally, the stockholders' equity is itemized and totaled. Obviously, the total of the stockholders' equity must agree with the amount of the net assets. Such a balance sheet, again in condensed form, is illustrated below.

THE FLEMING COMPANY
Balance Sheet
December 31, 1972

Current Assets	$12,000,000
Less: Current Liabilities	4,000,000
Working Capital	$ 8,000,000
Investments	2,600,000
Property, Plant and Equipment	14,500,000
Intangibles	400,000
Deferred Charges	500,000
Total Assets less Current Liabilities	$26,000,000
Less: Long-term Debt	6,000,000
Net Assets	$20,000,000
Stockholders' Equity:	
Preferred 4% Cumulative Stock	$ 1,000,000
Common Stock	1,500,000
Capital in Excess of Par Value	4,500,000
Retained Earnings	13,000,000
Total	$20,000,000

(For a specific illustration of this format, see the balance sheet in the 1970 annual report of The United States Steel Corporation.)

Although three different forms of the balance sheet have been illustrated, additional variations are employed for such specialized endeavors as insurance companies, banks, governmental units, railroads and utilities.

FORMS OF BUSINESS ORGANIZATION

With rare exceptions, businesses in the United States are organized as corporations, partnerships, or sole proprietorships.

A corporation may be defined as "a legal entity operating under a grant of authority from a state or other political autonomy in the form of articles of incorporation or a charter."[2] A partnership, as defined by the Uniform Partnership Act, is "an association of two or more persons to carry on, as co-owners, a business for profit." If a business is owned by one person, it is referred to as a sole proprietorship.

Though the number of businesses organized as sole proprietorships and partnerships greatly exceeds those organized as corporations, corporate business receipts constitute the major portion of the aggregate business receipts that are reported by all three forms of business organizations in this country. The importance of the corporate form of business organization is emphasized by the following figures.[3]

Type of Business Organization	Number of Businesses	Business Receipts
Sole Proprietorship	9,086,714	$ 207,477,000,000
Partnership	922,680	78,153,000,000
Corporation	1,468,725	1,224,370,000,000

The significant role of the corporation underlies the use of the corporate approach throughout this text. However, the reader is reminded that the same principles discussed for a corporation are, in the main, equally applicable to the other two forms of business organization.

USES OF THE BALANCE SHEET

The balance sheet of a company indicates to management the financial status of the company as of a given moment. Management uses subsequent statements to disclose, through comparison, changes in the various items which summarize the company's financial condition. An analysis of this and other statements enables management to obtain such vital information as changes in inventory levels, rapidity of accounts receivable collections, and rate of profit earned on the assets employed in the business.

Besides aiding management, other uses of the statement would include those made by creditors interested in the balance sheet as an aid for determining the security of their claims upon the company; stockholders who analyze the balance sheet (and the other financial statements) to determine the soundness

---

[2] Eric L. Kohler, *A Dictionary for Accountants,* 4th ed. (Englewood Cliffs, N.J.: Prentice–Hall, Inc., 1970), p. 121.

[3] U.S. Dept. of the Treasury, *Statistics of Income, 1966, U.S. Business Tax Returns,* U.S. Treasury Department Publication No. 438 (6–69), p. 3.

of their investment; potential investors who use the statement to guide their future activity; and labor union officials who analyze the financial statement to determine, among other things, the company's "ability to pay."

A governmental use of the statement exists whenever a corporation's stock is listed on one of the stock exchanges which require listed companies to file their financial statements periodically with the Securities and Exchange Commission. Another governmental use arises from one of the schedules on the annual federal corporate income tax return which requires the balance sheet of the company as of the last day of its fiscal year.

Although several important uses of financial statements, with emphasis on the balance sheet, have been summarized, many have not been described. Among others, a company's customers and the public in general are interested in the information disclosed by the financial statements. It is no wonder that today some are prone to criticize accounting statements like the balance sheet; too many different categories of people are attempting to use the identical balance sheet for many different purposes. For example, financial analysts, creditors, and stockholders may want to know what the corporation is currently "worth"; such information may require adjustments to a balance sheet based on the historical cost principle considered preferable or necessary for Securities and Exchange Commission requirements, federal income tax requirements, and generally accepted accounting principles. Therefore, to serve management best or for other special uses, certain items on the balance sheet are often changed or rearranged to facilitate current and meaningful interpretations.

Illustrative Balance Sheet

For illustrations of actual published financial statements, the reader is referred to Appendix A, the Consolidated Balance Sheet of Armstrong Cork Company and the Consolidated Balance Sheet of PPG Industries.

QUESTIONS AND PROBLEMS

2-1. For each of the following four statements, choose the best answer to each and indicate your choice on an answer sheet with the number 1 or 2 or 3.

   a. An inventory of store and office supplies on hand should appear on the balance sheet as a:
   1. prepaid expense
   2. portion of inventory of merchandise
   3. property, plant and equipment item

[CH. 2] THE BALANCE SHEET 27

b. On the balance sheet of a magazine publishing company, the amount for subscriptions collected in advance, but as yet unearned, will appear as:
  1. a prepaid expense
  2. a reserve fund
  3. the last current liability

c. Goodwill appears on a company's balance as the result of:
  1. its excellent established business reputation
  2. the excess paid for the net assets of other companies acquired
  3. the action of the board of directors to give recognition to the value of this item so that total assets represent the true value of all assets

d. Retained earnings is another term for:
  1. cash
  2. paid-in surplus
  3. earned surplus

2-2. The Property, Plant and Equipment section of the Balance Sheet of The Fleming Company shows a subtraction of $7,000,000 for Accumulated Depreciation to Date.

Does this $7,000,000 represent cash set aside to acquire new plant and equipment when the old is worn out? If your answer is yes, then explain why Cash, on the same statement, amounts to only $1,075,000. If your answer is no, then explain where the $7,000,000 is.

2-3. The illustrative Balance Sheet of The Fleming Company on page 19 shows Retained Earnings of $13,000,000.

If Retained Earnings are not in the form of cash or any other specific asset, *where* is the $13,000,000?

2-4. Many economists, accountants and businessmen criticize financial statements prepared in accordance with "generally accepted accounting principles." They claim such statements are misleading because they ignore the effect of the past two decades of inflation. To illustrate this point, they take the asset side of the Balance Sheet shown on page 18 and say, "What was done amounts to adding apples, oranges, peaches, pears, etc., and labeling the grand total Total Assets . . . Total Fruit would be more appropriate."

Refer to the Balance Sheet of The Fleming Company, and point out those items which underlie the above quotation. Justify or oppose the position of the critics.

2-5. The following statement appears on page 22 of the text: "Income Taxes Payable is the estimated debt owed the government. . . ."

Give at least three reasons why this liability may be an estimated, rather than an actual, amount.

2-6. Book value (or equity) per share of stock is that portion of the total stockholders' equity allocable to a particular class of stock, divided by the number of *outstanding* shares of stock in the same class. The 1969 annual report of PPG Industries discloses the following as of December 31, 1969:

Total stockholders' equity	$658,709,000
Portion of above equity applicable to preferred stock (No preferred stock issued by PPG Industries)	–0–
Stockholders' equity applicable to common stock	$658,709,000
Common shares issued	21,730,607
Less issued shares reacquired (treasury stock)	1,241,280
Common shares outstanding	20,489,327

Therefore, book value (or equity) per share of common stock on December 31, 1969, was

$$\frac{\$658,709,000}{20,489,327} = \$32.15$$

On this same date, the closing price on the New York Stock Exchange for common stock of PPG Industries was $35½.

Discuss the relationship, if any, between the book value and the market value of a share of stock.

2-7. The 1970 annual report of Armstrong Cork Company shows that the book value, per share, of the common stock on December 31, 1970, was $13.96.

a. Explain what this figure represents.

b. On December 31, 1970, the closing price on the New York Stock Exchange for the common stock of Armstrong Cork Company was $33¼ per share. Explain why book value and market value are not the same amount.

2-8. The following excerpt (Shareholders' Equity) is taken from the 1970 Balance Sheet of Aluminum Company of America:

Capital Stock:	Dec. 31, 1970	Dec. 31, 1969
Serial preferred stock, par value $100, authorized 1,000,000 shares: $3.75 cumulative preferred stock, authorized 660,000 shares, issued 659,909 shares	$ 65,990,900	$ 65,990,900
Common stock, par value $1.00(D), authorized 50,000,000 shares, issued: 1970—21,506,417; 1969—21,503,565	21,506,417	21,503,565
Additional Capital (E)	52,833,949	52,669,465
Retained Earnings (D)	1,108,675,622	1,054,364,618
Total Shareholders' Equity	$1,249,006,888	$1,194,528,548

Attached note E reveals that the entire additional capital increase of $164,484 was derived from the "excess of consideration received over par value of shares issued under employees' stock option plans and the excess of fair value over the aggregate par value of shares of common stock issued under the incentive compensation plan."

a. How many shares of common stock were issued during 1970?

b. What was the average amount of consideration received for each share issued in 1970?

2-9. In the 1969 annual report of Walt Disney Productions, the current liabilities section of the consolidated balance sheet appeared as follows:

	Sept. 27, 1969	Sept. 28, 1968
Installments due within year on notes payable	$ 1,568,000	$ 1,532,000
Accounts payable	12,375,000	7,562,000
Advance under contract	1,000,000	1,000,000
Payroll and employee benefits	3,681,000	2,983,000
Property, payroll and other taxes	3,305,000	2,897,000
Estimated taxes on income	9,792,000	9,057,000
Total current liabilities	$31,721,000	$25,031,000

a. Why do the fiscal years of the company end on the dates of September 27, 1969, and September 28, 1968?

b. Why is the estimated liability for income taxes as of each date less than the *expense* for each year ($16,700,000 and $12,516,000)?

2-10. The balance sheets for selected companies show the following as of December 31, 1969:

The Goodyear Tire & Rubber Company	
Goodwill, Patents and Trade-Marks	$ 1
Standard Brands Incorporated	
Goodwill	$ 50,458,572
Westinghouse Electric Corporation	
Goodwill and other acquired intangible assets	$ 56,218,217
R. J. Reynolds Tobacco Company	
Cost in excess of net assets of businesses acquired	$184,643,517
Brands, trade-marks and goodwill	$ 1
Kraftco Corporation	
Intangibles	$ 26,425,771

a. Why do some companies, such as Goodyear, "carry" goodwill at a nominal amount, while other companies, such as Standard Brands, show goodwill at a sizeable figure?

b. Would you consider the intangible assets of Westinghouse Electric Corporation to be *worth* more or less than those of R. J. Reynolds?

c. The amount shown for the intangible assets of Kraftco Corporation is less than 3 percent of the corporation's total assets. Do you believe a detailed breakdown of the figure is necessary?

d. On December 28, 1968, Kraftco Corporation showed intangibles at $23,458,481. The increase in intangibles is explained by the following note to the statement of financial position:

> Intangibles
>
> Intangibles represent the excess of the purchase prices paid over the net book values of the tangible assets of certain businesses acquired since 1955. The Company does not now intend to amortize items carried in this account.

Explain or illustrate, with assumed figures, using the first sentence of the above note, the increase in intangibles during 1969.

Note: The subject of intangible assets, especially goodwill, is more fully discussed in Chapter 7. Effective November 1, 1970, the cost of goodwill acquired in a merger accounted for as a purchase must be recorded and written off against earnings over a period not to exceed 40 years (Accounting Principles Board Opinion 17). Goodwill resulting from acquisitions of companies prior to November 1, 1970, is not subject to the mandatory amortization.

2-11. The Current Assets section of the Consolidated Statement of Financial Position of RCA Corporation (in the annual report for 1970) included the following:

Receivables
U.S. Government	$ 59,021,000
Other (less reserve of $21,233,000)	500,046,000

a. Interpret the meaning of the word "reserve" as it is used in connection with the above Receivables (which excludes Receivables from the U.S. Government).

b. All dollar amounts in the 1970 financial statements of RCA were rounded off to the nearest one thousand dollars. For a company of this size, do you have any objection to such a procedure?

2-12. In the 1969 annual report of Studebaker-Worthington, Inc., the Property, Plant & Equipment section of the Consolidated Balance Sheet appeared as follows:

PROPERTY, PLANT & EQUIPMENT, at cost:	Dec. 31, 1969	Dec. 31, 1968
Land	$ 9,987,093	$ 10,143,601
Buildings	92,660,005	88,547,415
Machinery and equipment	153,987,872	134,149,607
	$256,634,970	$232,840,623
Less: Reserve for depreciation	108,630,997	98,333,260
	$148,003,973	$134,507,363

a. What is your understanding of the term "Reserve for depreciation"?

b. To which of the items included in this section is the "reserve" applicable?

2-13. In a "twilight" area between the debt and the shareholders' equity sections of the consolidated balance sheet of The Procter & Gamble Company for the year ended June 30, 1969, appeared the following:

	June 30, 1969	June 30, 1968
Reserves:		
Self-insured risks	$4,220,000	$4,062,000
Foreign operations	1,400,000	1,400,000
	$5,620,000	$5,462,000

a. Interpret the two "reserves."

b. Can you justify such a "twilight" section? Are the two "reserves" a debt *or* a portion of stockholders' equity?

2-14. A special funds section of the balance sheet, located between the current assets and the investments sections of Erie-Lackawanna Railroad Company's 1967 annual report, appeared as follows:

	December 31	
	1967	1966
Special Funds:		
Sinking funds	$ 668	$ 868
Capital and other reserve funds	4,307,770	3,385,127
Insurance and other funds	343,143	334,386
Total special funds	$4,651,581	$3,720,381

What is your interpretation of the word reserve in the caption "other reserve funds"?

2-15. A partial condensed summary of the actual Consolidated Balance Sheet as of December 31, 1970, contained in the 1970 annual report of Bristol-Myers Company, is as follows:

ASSETS		LIABILITIES	
Current Assets	$443,673,000	Current Liabilities	$?
Investments and		Other Liabilities	?
Other Assets	?	Long-Term Debt	?
Property, Plant and Equipment	?	Total Liabilities	$347,657,000
Excess of cost over net tangible (etc.)	?	STOCKHOLDERS' EQUITY	
		5 items in proper order Total Stockholders' Equity	$376,011,000
Total Assets ...	$723,668,000	Total Liab. and St. Equity	$723,668,000

The following list contains the various asset, liability, and stockholders' equity items which actually appeared on the Consolidated Balance Sheet of Bristol-Myers Company, as of December 31, 1970:

Cash	$ 23,353,000
Land (at cost)	13,680,000
Accounts payable	59,148,000
Bank borrowings (short-term)	31,550,000
Buildings (at cost)	101,416,000
Machinery, equipment, fixtures, etc., (at cost)	141,749,000
Construction in progress (of plant, at cost)	33,392,000
Marketable securities (at amortized cost which approximates market) and time deposits	51,861,000
Capital in Excess of Par Value of Stock	47,183,000
U. S. and Foreign taxes on income (payable)	26,728,000

Inventories:

Finished stock	$83,079,000	
Work in process	27,276,000	
Raw material	28,701,000	
Packaging material	24,712,000	
Total:		163,768,000

Investments in and advances to unconsolidated subsidiaries and affiliates	3,301,000
Accrued expenses (payable)	50,411,000
Prepaid expenses	13,904,000
Prepaid taxes	17,519,000
Accumulated depreciation	94,407,000
Accounts receivable—customers (less reserves of $8,211,000)	159,640,000
Other receivables	13,628,000
Long-Term Debt	162,212,000
Other Liabilities	17,608,000
Miscellaneous investments and sundry assets	19,419,000
Excess of cost over net tangible assets received in business acquisitions	61,445,000
Preferred Stock, par value $1 per share Authorized: 10,000,000 shares Issued: $2 convertible series; 1,278,099 shares	1,278,000
Common Stock, par value $1 per share Authorized: 40,000,000 shares Issued: 29,681,248 shares	29,681,000
Retained Earnings	298,952,000
Cost of treasury stock: Common Stock: 21,645 shares	1,083,000

(Notes to the financial statements have been omitted.)

Required

Prepare the complete balance sheet as of this date in proper form.

2-16. The following items have been taken from the books and other records of Brown Corporation on December 31, 1972.

Delivery Equipment	$3,000	Building	$30,000
Land	4,000	Cash	6,000
Furniture and Fixtures	2,000	Mortgage Payable ...	6,900

Claims of creditors for amounts due them for merchandise 9,000
Rent collected in advance from tenant who is renting
    the third floor of the building 100
Claims on customers for merchandise sold on account 20,000
Long-term investment in XYZ Corporation common stock
    which cost $3,000 and has a current market value of 4,000
Promissory notes received by business from customers 5,000
Accrued interest due to business on notes 50
Interest paid in advance by business on notes 100
Accrued interest owed by the business on the mortgage 100
Inventory of merchandise which costs $20,000 and is
    marked to sell for 35,000
Promissory notes owed by the business 10,000
Trademarks 1,000
Prepaid Insurance 200
Unused stamps, stationery, and other office supply items 650
Estimated corporate federal income taxes payable 3,000
Accrued salaries owed to employees 400
Sales tax collected from customers but not yet remitted
    to state 200
Amounts withheld from employees' salaries but not yet
    remitted to federal government for:
        Income taxes 160
        F.I.C.A. taxes 40
Employer's unpaid payroll taxes consist of:
        F.I.C.A. taxes 40
        State and federal unemployment taxes 60
Capital stock 40,000
Retained earnings .... ?

Note: The liabilities for the various social security taxes may be listed individually or combined into one item under Current Liabilities on the balance sheet.
        Amounts for depreciable assets are net of accumulated depreciation to date.

Required

Prepare a classified balance sheet, *using proper accounting titles.*

2-17. The December 31, 1972, balance sheet of the business of E. G. Burbank (sole proprietor) showed:

$$\text{Assets} = \text{Liabilities} + \text{Owner's Equity}$$
$$\$100{,}000 = \$40{,}000 + \$60{,}000$$

An office desk was then purchased costing $400; payment was made with $200 cash and the issuance of a $200 note. The balance sheet would now show:

Assets = Liabilities + Owner's Equity
$ _____ = $ _____ + $ _____

2-18. For each of the following statements, choose the best answer and indicate your choice on an answer sheet by the number 1 or 2 or 3.

   a. If a company segregates and sets aside cash for a specific future use, the cash so segregated is referred to as a:
   1. fund (an asset)
   2. restriction on retained earnings
   3. retained earnings

   b. When a company prices its inventory on a LIFO basis, the dollar amount reported for inventory on the Balance Sheet represents:
   1. current replacement cost
   2. estimated selling price
   3. some amount below current replacement cost if costs have increased since the adoption of LIFO

   c. Book value per share of common stock of Armstrong Cork Company on December 31, 1970, was $13.96. This amount represents:
   1. market value per share on the New York Stock Exchange
   2. the net assets (A-L) per share of common stock per the books of Armstrong Cork
   3. the dollar amount each share would receive if the company were liquidated

   d. In general, it may be said that Retained Earnings represents the:
   1. net accumulation of annual net profits and losses over and above amounts declared as dividends to stockholders
   2. amount of cash and any marketable securities accumulated over the years
   3. excess of assets over liabilities

   e. Suppose the items listed below were either omitted or treated improperly (as stated) in the preparation of a balance sheet. Indicate in each case the effect of the errors on the equity of the owner (net worth).
   1. An asset was omitted.
      (a) Overstated
      (b) Understated
      (c) No effect
   2. The inventory of merchandise was overvalued.
      (a) Overstated
      (b) Understated
      (c) No effect
   3. A mortgage payable on the real estate was subtracted from (netted against) the total cost of the land and buildings.
      (a) Overstated
      (b) Understated
      (c) No effect
   4. Accrued wages at December 31 were ignored.
      (a) Overstated
      (b) Understated
      (c) No effect

5. A long-term permanent investment was shown as a current asset.
   (a) Overstated
   (b) Understated
   (c) No effect

2-19. The following items have been taken from the books and other records of T. Rhodes Corporation on December 31, 1972.

Promissory notes owed by the business to trade creditors	$ 10,000
Interest accrued on above notes	120
Bank loan payable in 90 days	12,000
Interest paid in advance to bank on above note payable	180
Cash	16,000
Delivery trucks	10,000
Land	15,000
Buildings	60,000
Merchandise inventory at cost	50,000
Unexpired insurance premiums	1,500
Due to creditors on open account for merchandise purchased	30,000
Due from customers on open account for merchandise sold	40,000
Unused store supplies (bags, cartons, boxes, etc.)	900
Furniture and fixtures	6,000
Goodwill	4,000
Patents	6,000
Accrued salaries owed to employees	600
Salaries paid in advance to employees	100
Dunkirk City bonds owned as temporary investment (market value $25,000), at cost	20,000
Interest accrued on above bonds	200
Mortgage payable on land and buildings	40,000
Interest accrued on above mortgage	400
Promissory notes received by the business from customers	15,000
Interest accrued on certain of the notes from customers	50
Interest collected in advance (unearned) on certain of the notes from customers	80
Unremitted income taxes withheld from employees' salaries	250
Unremitted F.I.C.A. taxes withheld from employees' salaries	50
Unremitted city wage tax withheld from employees' salaries	25
Employer's liability for unpaid F.I.C.A. taxes	50
Employer's unpaid state unemployment tax	25
Employer's unpaid federal unemployment tax	20
Estimated federal income tax payable	2,000
Capital stock	100,000
Retained earnings	?

Required

Prepare a classified balance sheet, *using proper accounting titles.*

3

The Statement of Income

The statement of income presents a financial review of the results of operations of a company over a specific period of time. It summarizes revenues and expenses in a manner which discloses whether a company's activities in a particular fiscal period have resulted in a profit or a loss.

The balance sheet shows the financial status of a company *as of* a given instant; the statement of income shows the profit earned or the loss sustained by a company *over a period* of time. The balance sheet is like a snapshot of a business; the statement of income resembles a moving picture. Just as a balance sheet may be prepared as of any given date, so a statement of income may cover any given period of time—a year, month, week, or even a day.

THE ACCOUNTING PERIOD

The time span between the preparation dates of financial statements is called the accounting or fiscal period. Such periods are normally uniform in length to facilitate management's use of comparative data, the calculation of federal and state income taxes, and conformance with the reporting requirements of various governmental agencies. To aid management, a majority of businesses prepare a statement of income for each month and a balance sheet as of the last day of each month. Consequently, the most common accounting period is one month.

In a broader sense and for most external reporting, the typical accounting period is one year in length. Annual statements are issued to stockholders; income taxes are determined annually; other reporting requirements are tied to a twelve-month period. In addition to comprehensive annual reports, a constantly increasing number of companies are furnishing stockholders with brief quarterly financial statements.

It is not ncessary that a fiscal year coincide with the calendar year. Although a majority of businesses have a fiscal year which coincides with the calendar year ending on December 31, there has been a movement, in recent years, to adopt a natural business year in preference to a calendar year. A natural business year is a fiscal year which ends on a date when business activity and inventory levels have reached their lowest point. Thus, many department stores have adopted a fiscal year of February 1 to January 31. The Internal Revenue Service discloses that, based upon corporate income tax returns filed during a recent year, approximately one-half of U.S. corporations have a fiscal year which agrees with the calendar year.

TITLE OF STATEMENT

The statement of income has several alternate titles, as shown by the yearly survey of annual reports issued by 600 industrial companies.[1]

Title of Statement

Terminology Applied:

	1969	1965	1960	1955	1946
Income	381	393	382	361	317
Earnings	182	174	152	135	10
Operations	30	24	35	30	10
All Others	7	9	31	74	263
Total	600	600	600	600	600

REVENUE AND EXPENSES

Basically, the statement of income compares the revenues with the expenses of a specific period. In a given period, revenue ordinarily represents the amount of goods sold and/or services rendered to customers; expenses represent expired costs incurred to produce those revenues. The relationship of the components of the statement of income may be expressed as follows:

Revenue − Expenses = Net Income for Period

Thus, a company with total revenues of $40,100,000 and total expenses of $37,100,000 during a period has a net income of $3,000,000.

---

[1] American Institute of Certified Public Accountants, Inc., *Accounting Trends and Techniques in Published Corporate Annual Reports,* 24th ed., p. 163. Copyright 1970 by the American Institute of Certified Public Accountants, Inc.

CONDENSED STATEMENT OF INCOME

In a statement of income, the revenue items are segregated by source of income, and expense items are categorized by type of expense. The sources of revenue and types of expense will vary depending upon the situation of the company and the nature of its business. The accompanying condensed statement of income illustrates revenue and expense classifications commonly encountered.

THE FLEMING COMPANY
Statement of Income
For the Year Ended December 31, 1972

Revenues:		
Sales (net)	$40,000,000	
Other Revenue	100,000	
Total Revenue		$40,100,000
Expenses:		
Cost of Goods Sold	$24,000,000	
Selling Expenses	7,800,000	
Administrative Expenses	2,200,000	
Other Expenses	200,000	
Income Taxes	2,900,000	
Total Expenses		37,100,000
Net Income for the Year		$ 3,000,000

This statement of income is presented in single-step form. One total amount is shown for revenue, and another total amount for expenses. The difference between the two is the net income (or loss) for the year.

CLASSIFICATION OF REVENUES

Sales represents those products, services, or merchandise which a company sells to its customers during a fiscal period. On financial statements and reports, the amount of sales is usually shown "net" after the subtraction of items such as:

  Sales returns, which represents the goods physically returned by customers;
  Sales allowances, which summarizes the deductions from original sales price permitted to customers for damaged goods, imperfect goods, or similar causes;
  Sales discounts, which is the deductions granted customers for payment of invoices within a stipulated period of time.
  This relationship may be summarized as follows:

Gross Sales − Sales returns, allowances, and discounts = Net Sales

Other Revenue is that income derived from sources other than the main source. Examples of such "other" sources for a manufacturing or merchandising company are dividends received on common or preferred stock held as an investment; interest earned on notes receivable, bonds, or savings accounts; rental income from property; and gains from the sale of fixed assets (as a gain on the sale of a piece of machinery).

CLASSIFICATION OF EXPENSES

Cost of Goods Sold summarizes the cost of the goods which a company has sold to its customers during a period. The determination of the cost of goods sold is discussed in detail later in the chapter.

The difference between net sales (the quantity of goods sold at selling price) and cost of goods sold (the same quantity of goods at cost) is often referred to as the gross margin. This point is also illustrated later in the chapter.

Selling Expenses, often referred to as marketing or distribution expenses, include such items as salesmen's salaries and commissions; payroll taxes on salesmen's salaries and commissions (typical payroll taxes are old-age benefits tax, state and federal unemployment taxes); advertising; depreciation, insurance, and property taxes on the assets of the company which are used in the marketing division of the business; delivery and shipping expenses; and traveling expenses of salesmen.

Administrative Expenses include such items as salaries of office force and company officers; payroll taxes on the above salaries; depreciation, insurance, and property taxes on the assets of the company which are used in the administrative or general office division of the business; directors' fees; expense of telephone and other utilities used in this division of the business; and printing and supplies, if used in the administrative division of the business.

The total of the selling and the administrative expenses is referred to as the *operating expenses.*

Other Expenses consist of those expenses not identified with the cost of the goods sold, nor with the marketing or administrative divisions of the business. Occasionally, these "other expenses" are called financial management expenses and losses. Examples of these expenses include interest expense on bonds payable; interest expense on notes payable; loss from the sale of assets owned (as a loss on the sale of investments held in other companies, or investments in government obligations); and fire or flood loss not covered by insurance.

Income Taxes, on the statement of income of a corporation, represent the company's income tax expense on the net income for the period.

Single-Step Form vs. Multiple-Step Form

The single-step form of the statement of income was illustrated by the statement presented on page 38. Although an increasing number of companies are using this simplified form in their annual reports, the slightly more complex multiple-step form is still widely used. While the single-step form has the distinct advantage of simplicity, the multiple-step form illustrated below more clearly indicates such important factors as the gross margin (often referred to as "gross profit on sales"), which denotes the spread between net selling prices and the cost of the goods; the average rate of gross margin for the year ($16,000,000 ÷ $40,000,000, or 40 percent); the ratio of $10,000,000 operating expenses to $40,000,000 net sales (25 percent); and the approximate 50 percent impact of the corporate net income tax rates upon the net income of the company. To show these analyses, many companies prefer the multiple-step statement. In most companies where weekly or monthly statements and operating reports are furnished to management for internal use, the multiple-step form is employed. However, to provide management with vital information which can aid the control of certain current operations and the formulation of certain business policy decisions, greater detail is required than that included on the statement illustrated.

THE FLEMING COMPANY

Statement of Income

For the Year Ended December 31, 1972

Net Sales		$40,000,000
Less: Cost of Goods Sold		24,000,000
Gross Margin on Sales		$16,000,000
Less: Operating Expenses:		
Selling Expenses	$7,800,000	
Administrative Expenses	2,200,000	10,000,000
Net Operating Income		$ 6,000,000
Other Expenses	$ 200,000	
Other Revenue	100,000	100,000
Net Income prior to Income Taxes		$ 5,900,000
Income Taxes		2,900,000
Net Income for the Year		$ 3,000,000
Net Income (Earnings) per Common Share (see page 45)		$10.03

Detailed Statement of Income

The typical details underlying each major item on the statement of income will be considered next without definition, since they are either self-explanatory or have already been identified. If reference is made to either the single-step or the multiple-step statement of The Fleming Company when the details of each summary item are introduced, their relationship to the statement of income should be readily apparent. It should be understood that these details rarely appear in published statements; to the extent possible, they are retained within the company and used for management guidance.

Net Sales of $40,000,000 is determined in the following manner:

Gross Sales			$40,600,000
Less: Sales Returns	$ 80,000		
Sales Allowances	25,000		
Cash Discounts	50,000		
State Sales Tax	250,000		
Federal Excise Tax	170,000		
Freight Out	25,000	600,000	
Net Sales			$40,000,000

To ascertain the Cost of Goods Sold ($24,000,000), a more involved analysis is required. This can be determined under two different assumptions.

Under the first assumption, The Fleming Company is a merchandising concern, which means that it sells substantially the same product that it purchases. To determine the cost of the goods *sold* during the period, it is first necessary to derive the cost of goods *available for sale* in that same period: that is, the sum of the inventory of merchandise on hand at the start of the period and the net cost of the merchandise purchased throughout the period. The next step is to subtract the cost of the goods not sold. Obviously, the cost of unsold goods is the inventory of merchandise on hand as of the end of the period. The difference between the cost of the goods available for sale and the cost of the unsold merchandise is the cost of goods sold. For a merchandising company, this information would be shown as follows:

Inventory of Merchandise, January 1, 1972			$ 5,500,000
Add: Net Purchases:			
Purchases		$24,775,000	
Freight In		225,000	
Less:		$25,000,000	
Purchase Returns	$ 50,000		
Purchase Allowances	25,000		
Purchase Discounts	125,000	200,000	
Net Purchases			24,800,000
Cost of Goods Available for Sale			$30,300,000
Less: Inventory of Merchandise, December 31, 1972			6,300,000
Cost of Goods Sold			$24,000,000

If, under the second assumption, The Fleming Company is a manufacturing company, the composition of the cost of goods sold section is slightly different. In lieu of beginning and ending inventories of purchased merchandise, the company has inventories of finished goods manufactured to be sold. And in place of "net purchases" of merchandise is the cost of goods manufactured. Considering these conditions, the cost of goods sold section of the statement of income appears as follows:

Inventory of Finished Goods, January 1, 1972	$ 5,500,000
Add: Cost of Goods Manufactured	24,800,000
Cost of Goods Available for Sale	$30,300,000
Less: Inventory of Finished Goods, December 31, 1972	6,300,000
Cost of Goods Sold	$24,000,000

The cost of the finished goods manufactured during the period consists of the costs of the raw materials used and the costs of the labor and manufacturing operations incurred at the factory to convert those raw materials into finished goods. A more comprehensive treatment of the determination of the cost of goods manufactured is presented in Chapter 10.

Selling Expenses ($7,800,000 for The Fleming Company) consist of the marketing, advertising, and distribution expenses which are listed below:

Salesmen's Salaries	$4,100,000
Salesmen's Commissions	700,000
Supervision Salaries	200,000
Vacation and Holiday Pay	450,000
Pension Expense	300,000
Compensation and Group Insurance	262,000
Social Security Taxes	300,000
Stationery	18,000
Telephone and Telegraph	83,000
Postage	69,000
Traveling Expenses	294,000
Branch Office Expenses	215,000
Convention Expenses	14,000
Sales Samples	80,000
Trade Publications	6,000
Catalogs and Price Lists	63,000
Displays and Exhibits	17,000
Radio and Television Advertising	225,000
Insurance on Property	98,000
Property Taxes	102,000
Depreciation	200,000
Miscellaneous	4,000
	$7,800,000

Administrative Expenses ($2,200,000 in our illustration) consist of office expenses, headquarters expenses, and certain general expenses as itemized below:

Officers' Salaries	$ 419,000
Office Salaries	635,000
Supervision Salaries	92,000
Vacation and Holiday Pay	100,000
Pension Expense	211,000

Compensation and Group Insurance	127,000
Social Security Taxes	60,000
Employee Publications	11,000
Stationery	3,000
Telephone and Telegraph	7,000
Postage	2,000
Traveling Expenses	75,000
Dues and Subscriptions	8,000
Donations	130,000
Bad Debts	62,000
Credit and Collection Expense	18,000
Legal and Other Professional Services	26,000
Light, Heat, and Water	16,000
Insurance on Property	42,000
Taxes on Property	55,000
Depreciation	100,000
Miscellaneous	1,000
	$2,200,000

Attention is directed to the several detailed expenses appearing under both Selling Expenses and Administrative Expenses; this condition exists because certain operational expenses apply to both divisions. To effect proper control of operations, certain items of expense should be prorated according to the extent to which each division is responsible for their incurrence. The $62,000 bad debts expense attributable to uncollectible accounts incurred by credit sales of merchandise is shown as an administrative expense because it is the administrative division, not the selling or marketing division, which passes on all credit applications.

Other Expenses ($200,000 for The Fleming Company) consist of the following:

Interest Expense on Bonds	$180,000
Interest Expense on Note	6,000
Fire Loss on Equipment	14,000
	$200,000

The preceding expenses are related neither to the cost of the goods sold nor to the selling or administrative activities of the business. Interest expense is not created through business operations, but arises from the financing of the business by outside sources. The loss item is non-recurring and not directly related to the company operations. Thus, on page 40, the category of other expenses is shown immediately after the determination of net operating income.

Other Revenue is derived from other than the main source of income for the company and does not enter into the determination of net operating income. For the year 1972, other revenue of The Fleming Company consists of:

Interest Earned on Investments	$ 85,000
Dividends Received on Investments	5,000
Gain on Sale of Land	10,000
	$100,000

Consideration of the various types of revenue and expenses thus far discussed indicates (as shown by the statement of income on page 40) a net income of $5,900,000 for The Fleming Company. However, this figure is the net income for the year *prior* to the expense for income taxes. As this is written, the United States federal corporate income tax rates are as follows:

Normal tax rate	22% of taxable net income
Surtax rate	26% of taxable net income in excess of $25,000

The over-all federal corporate tax rate is 48 percent of taxable net income minus $6,500 (26% surtax on the first $25,000 of income). Application of these tax rates to the $5,900,000 net income of The Fleming Company would produce an amount slightly different from the $2,900,000 expense shown on the statement of income. This is because net income (according to generally accepted accounting principles) and taxable net income (according to the Internal Revenue Code) are not necessarily the same. Certain items of income or expense may be treated in one manner for accounting determination of net income, but in another manner for the determination of taxable net income. We can use two examples to illustrate. Interest earned on bonds issued by a state, municipality, or other political subdivision, though income from an accounting point of view, is excluded in the determination of taxable net income. Depreciation expense may be computed by the straight-line method for accounting purposes, but by an accelerated method for tax purposes. Additional variations between the determination of accounting net income and taxable net income, when significant, are mentioned in the appropriate sections of the text.

EARNINGS PER SHARE

The Accounting Principles Board in its Opinion No. 15 (May 1969) stated that the earnings per share (or net loss per share) data should be "shown on the face" of the statement of income because of the "significance attached" to it by many people and as an aid in "evaluating the data in conjunction with the financial statements."

The amount of the earnings per share of stock, if a company has only one class of stock (and no securities convertible into stock or stock options or other rights which in the future could dilute earnings per share), is computed by dividing the net income for the period by the weighted average number of shares outstanding during the period. However, reference to the balance sheet of The Fleming Company on page 19 discloses that it has two classes of outstanding stock, non-convertible preferred and common. To calculate earning per share of *common* stock, the first step is to find the amount of net income for the year allocable to the *common* stock. This would be the net income for the year of $3,000,000 minus the *preferred* stock dividends (shown on page 48) of $40,000 ($2 per share times 20,000 outstanding shares). Therefore there is $2,960,000 allocable to the common stock. The second step is to compute the weighted average number of *common* shares outstanding during the year. Reference to page 19 shows that The Fleming Company had 300,000 shares outstanding at the end of the year. Reference to the balance sheet on page 49 discloses that only 290,000 shares were outstanding at the beginning of the year. Assume that the 10,000 additional shares were sold in the middle of the year. Thus, the weighted average number of common shares outstanding during the year is 295,000. The earnings per common share is derived as follows:

$$\frac{\text{Net income for the year } \$3,000,000 - \text{Preferred dividends } \$40,000}{\text{Weighted average number of common shares outstanding of } 295,000} = \$10.03$$

As in many corporations, the capital structure of The Fleming Company is a simple capital structure. However, if the corporation has a complex capital structure due to, for example, possible contingent issuances of common stock due to the future exercise of warrants or stock options, then two earnings per share amounts must be shown on the face of the statement of income. These two earnings per share amounts are referred to as the "primary earnings per share" and "fully diluted earnings per share." The primary earnings per common share amount is based on the average number of shares outstanding during the period, after preferred dividend requirements. The fully diluted earnings per common share amount assumes full conversion of such items as convertible debentures, exercise of outstanding stock options and issuance of shares under an incentive compensation plan. Presented below are two illustrations of such reporting on the statement of income.

BURLINGTON INDUSTRIES, INC.
For the Fiscal Year Ended September 27, 1969

Net Earnings per share:
Primary $3.01
Fully diluted 2.92

BULOVA WATCH COMPANY, INC.
For the Fiscal Year Ended March 31, 1970

Net income per average common share $1.92
Net income per share assuming full dilution 1.76

The detailed and complicated calculations behind these two earnings per share amounts are beyond the scope of this book; the interested reader is referred to Accounting Principles Board Opinion 15 on "Earnings per Share" and APB Opinion 9 on "Reporting the Results of Operations."

Earnings per share data has had increasing widespread usage in recent years. It is vital information for evaluating the trend in operating results over past years and for aid in forecasting the future. In addition, it is definitely necessary information to the financial analyst, the prospective investor, and present stockholders.

THE ACCRUAL BASIS OF ACCOUNTING

The balance sheet contained in the preceding chapter and the statement of income presented in this chapter were prepared in accordance with the accrual basis of accounting. Not all accounting records are maintained on an accrual basis. Instead, some records follow a methodology known as the cash basis of accounting. Although these two accounting bases have much in common, they possess some outstanding differences which should be understood.

Many small businesses and most professional men keep their records on the cash basis of accounting. By this basis, revenue is not recognized until cash is received, regardless of when the service was rendered or the income was earned. Similarly, an item of expense is ignored until cash is paid, regardless of when the actual expense was incurred. To illustrate, let us consider the determination of net income for an attorney in a given period. Determined on the cash basis, income from fees is not viewed as revenue when his services are rendered or when the bill is submitted to the client. Instead, the fee is recognized as revenue in the period when the cash is received, even though he may have rendered the service and "earned" the fee in a prior period. Likewise, his expenses are recognized in the period in which they are paid, regardless of when they were incurred.

Most businesses, due to the nature of their operations, cannot accurately determine their net income for a period by the cash basis of accounting. Take, for example, a company which purchases materials or merchandise with cash and on credit, maintains an inventory of goods on hand, and sells goods to customers for cash and on credit. Determining this company's profit on a basis of when cash is paid to creditors and when it is collected from customers would produce seriously distorted financial statements. Therefore, the company should use the accrual basis of accounting, which permits revenue to be recognized when earned and expenses to be established when incurred.

The illustrated statement of income of The Fleming Company shows gross sales for the year of $40,600,000. Under the accrual basis, the company recognizes revenue when the sale is made and title passes to the customer either upon delivery of goods to the customer or to a common carrier, depending upon the terms of the sale. Therefore, this method recognizes the revenue from a sale as being earned, whether or not cash has been received in payment by the end of the fiscal period. In fact, the balance sheet on page 18 indicates that The Fleming Company has over $3,000,000 of charge sales due from customers as of December 31. Similarly, expenses are recognized as incurred: the amounts shown on the statement of income for salaries and wages represent the actual expense throughout the entire year. Although a small portion of the total amount was not yet paid in cash by the company on December 31 (because the fifty-second weekly payroll period covered the last days of December and the first days of January of the next year), the portion for the last few days of December is not excluded from the total amount of expenses shown for the year. Expenses are recognized as incurred; not as paid. Of course, this situation creates a liability at the end of a fiscal period, shown in the current liabilities section of the illustrated balance sheet.

THE MATCHING CONCEPT

Since an accounting or fiscal period is a small segment of time in relation to the total life expectancy of a typical business, it is highly important that a statement of income properly matches expenses and revenue in a given period. An erroneous matching of expenses incurred to create the revenue which belongs to a given period will result in distorted financial statements. For example, if a fiscal period were fifty years long, the acquisition costs of buildings, machinery, and equipment would normally be expenses of producing the revenue of this period. Since fiscal periods are not of such length, the cost of such assets must be allocated equitably (by depreciation expense) throughout their useful life.

The matching concept is one of the justifications for the last-in, first-out method of pricing inventories. If the last goods acquired—regardless of physical flow—are considered the first goods used or sold, they will be expensed at the latest acquisition prices. Such costs would more closely match the related sales revenue of the period: recently incurred costs would be related to sales revenue on nearly the same cost-price level. This point is more fully discussed in the chapter on Inventories.

Today, one of the chief criticisms of accounting is that, because of inflation, the depreciation expense for many fixed assets is insufficient to match the real cost of capital consumed with the revenue produced by its use. For example, a building constructed in 1940 at a cost of $100,000 and with an expected life of 50 years might well have a $300,000 replacement cost today. Yet, since $100,000 was the *cost* of the building, $\frac{1}{50}$ of that cost ($2,000) is expensed each year on the statement of operations. Though the *cost* of the building is matched with revenue each year, it is debatable whether current costs and revenues are matched in an equitable manner. This point is more fully discussed in Chapter 7.

STATEMENT OF RETAINED EARNINGS

The third financial statement, the statement of retained earnings, may be viewed as the connecting link between the balance sheet and the statement of income. The statement of retained earnings discloses the changes during the year in the retained earnings portion of the stockholders' equity. These changes are attributable primarily to two things: the annual net income (or loss) of the company, and the amount of dividends declared to the stockholders throughout the year.

THE FLEMING COMPANY
Statement of Retained Earnings
For the Year Ended December 31, 1972

Balance, Retained Earnings, January 1, 1972		$11,540,000
Add: Net Income for the Year		3,000,000
		$14,540,000
Less: Dividends Declared		
On Preferred Stock	$ 40,000	
On Common Stock	1,500,000	1,540,000
Balance, Retained Earnings, December 31, 1972		$13,000,000

In this statement, the amount shown for retained earnings on January 1, 1972, agrees with that contained in the balance sheet as of December 31, 1971. The net income for the year 1972 ($3,000,000) is the amount shown by the statement of income (see page 40). The $13,000,000 amount of retained earnings as of December 31, 1972, agrees with that shown on the balance sheet (see page 19). This "tie-together" of the three financial statements may be seen more clearly in the statements on page 49.

During the past fifteen years, there has been a decided trend toward a combined statement of income and retained earnings. Instead of appearing as two separate statements, as discussed and illustrated so far in this chapter, they are often combined into one statement as follows:

THE FLEMING COMPANY
Statement of Income and Retained Earnings
For the Year Ended December 31, 1972

Net Sales	$40,000,000
Cost of Goods Sold	24,000,000
Gross Margin on Sales	$16,000,000
Operating Expenses	10,000,000
Net Operating Income	$ 6,000,000
Excess of Other Expenses over Other Revenue	100,000
Net Income prior to Income Taxes	$ 5,900,000
Income Taxes	2,900,000
Net Income for the Year	$ 3,000,000
Retained Earnings, January 1	11,540,000
Total	$14,540,000
Dividend Declared	1,540,000
Retained Earnings, December 31	$13,000,000

THE FLEMING COMPANY
Balance Sheet
As of December 31, 1972 and 1971

ASSETS			LIABILITIES		
	December 31			December 31	
	1972	1971		1972	1971
Current Assets	$12,000,000	$11,800,000	Current Liabilities	$ 4,000,000	$ 5,000,000
Investments	2,600,000	2,400,000	Long-Term Debt	6,000,000	6,500,000
Property, Plant and Equipment	14,500,000	14,165,000	Total	$10,000,000	$11,500,000
Intangibles	400,000	425,000	STOCKHOLDERS' EQUITY		
Deferred Charges	500,000	550,000	Preferred Stock	$ 1,000,000	$ 1,000,000
			Common Stock	1,500,000	1,450,000
			Capital in Excess of Par Value	4,500,000	3,850,000
			Retained Earnings	13,000,000	11,540,000
			Total	$20,000,000	$17,840,000
Total	$30,000,000	$29,340,000	Total	$30,000,000	$29,340,000

THE FLEMING COMPANY
Statement of Income
For the Year Ended December 31, 1972

Net Sales	$40,000,000
Cost of Goods Sold	24,000,000
Gross Margin on Sales	$16,000,000
Operating Expenses	10,000,000
Net Operating Income	$ 6,000,000
Excess of Other Expenses over Other Revenue	100,000
Net Income prior to Income Taxes	$ 5,900,000
Income Taxes	2,900,000
Net Income for the Year	$ 3,000,000

THE FLEMING COMPANY
Statement of Retained Earnings
For the Year Ended December 31, 1972

Balance, Retained Earnings, January 1, 1972	$11,540,000
Net Income for the Year	3,000,000
	$14,540,000
Dividends Declared	1,540,000
Balance, Retained Earnings, December 31, 1972	$13,000,000

Down to the point of net income for the year, this statement may be in either single-step or multiple-step form. Appendix A discloses that PPG Industries and Armstrong Cork Company employ somewhat separate statements.

REPORTING BY LINES OF BUSINESS

During recent years, there has been a pronounced trend by diversified companies toward voluntary disclosure of sales and profits by divisions or product lines or lines of business. Then, in October of 1970, the Securities and Exchange Commission revised Form 10-K. This form is the general form for annual reports to the SEC by companies having securities registered pursuant to the Securities Exchange Act of 1933. One of the revisions, effective for reports filed for fiscal years ending on or after December 31, 1970, is that the financial statements filed with Form 10-K *must* contain, by "lines of business," (i) sales and revenues and (ii) income before tax and extraordinary items, provided the "line of business" accounts for 10 percent or more of the total of each of the two amounts (15 percent, instead of 10 percent, if sales and revenues do not exceed $50,000,000 for the year). Since 10-K is a public document, the same information is being presented in annual reports to stockholders by an increasing number of companies. The SEC, as of the date this is written, has not attempted to define "line of business." It is their position that management of the company is in the most informed position to separate the company into "lines of business" for reporting purposes.

The breakdown shown in the 1970 annual report of Westinghouse Electric Corporation is presented below as an illustration. This company for years has reported to the stockholders more than just the necessary required financial data. This type of external reporting is similar to that which has been done internally for many years by companies appraising managerial performance by product lines or divisions, as discussed in Chapter 5.

CONSOLIDATED FINANCIAL STATEMENTS

The processes by which organizations grow or expand vary. And the methods by which business organizations do so must take into account various income tax, legal, regulatory, administrative, and financial considerations. One of the most common methods, the subject of this section of the chapter, is the acquisition by one company of the voting stock of another company. Assuming that enough stock is acquired to control the other company, the acquiring company is referred to as the parent company and the company whose stock was acquired as the subsidiary company. Even though both companies retain their separate legal entities, consolidated statements combining the net assets and operating activities of both companies are necessary to show the financial condition and operating results of the consolidated organization as a whole.

WESTINGHOUSE COMPANIES
Sales and Income After Taxes
(amounts in thousands of dollars)

| | Year Ended December 31, 1970 |||| | Year Ended December 31, 1969 ||||
| | Sales || Income After Taxes || Sales || Income After Taxes ||
	Amount	Percent Contributed	Amount	Percent Contributed	Amount	Percent Contributed	Amount	Percent Contributed
Power Systems	$1,351,500	31%	$ 25,230	20%	$1,107,018	28%	$ 50,624	33%
Consumer Products	716,591	17	195	—	708,670	18	9,449	6
Industry and Defense:								
Industry	1,392,186	32	64,215	51	1,248,664	32	58,912	38
Defense	466,339	11	6,732	5	505,594	13	6,420	4
Broadcasting, Learning and								
Leisure Time	307,080	7	25,496	20	288,034	7	27,478	18
Other	79,714	2	5,131	4	66,306	2	2,037	1
Total	$4,313,410	100%	$126,999	100%	$3,924,286	100%	$154,920	100%

Consolidated Balance Sheet at Date of Acquisition

To illustrate this discussion, the balance sheets of P Company and S Company as of December 31, 1972 are presented next. Up until this moment both have been completely independent companies. P company, in Phoenix, manufactures and sells generometers and has been in business twenty years. S Company, in St. Louis, manufactures and sells noskids and is a new (and quite profitable) company, having been founded only two years ago. At this point, please read carefully each company's balance sheet shown below—P Company, the first column *only* (labeled "Before") and S Company in the third column.

Now, on January 1, 1973, P Company acquires an 80 percent interest in S Company by acquiring 80 percent of S's outstanding capital stock in exchange for $440,000 of P's previously authorized but unissued preferred stock. The balance sheet of S Company is unchanged; the only factor that has

Balance Sheet

	P Company Before (Dec. 31, 1972)	P Company After (Jan. 1, 1973)	S Company Before and After
ASSETS			
Current Assets:			
Cash	$ 100,000	$ 100,000	$ 40,000
Accounts Receivable (net)	300,000	300,000	100,000
Inventories	400,000	400,000	100,000
Prepaid Expenses	20,000	20,000	10,000
Total Current Assets	$ 820,000	$ 820,000	$250,000
Investments:			
Investment in Company S (80%)		$ 440,000	
Property, Plant and Equipment:			
Cost less Accumulated Depreciation	$2,180,000	2,180,000	$350,000
Total Assets	$3,000,000	$3,440,000	$600,000
LIABILITIES			
Current Liabilities:			
Accounts Payable	$ 200,000	$ 200,000	$ 60,000
Accrued Expenses Payable	100,000	100,000	10,000
Income Taxes Payable	100,000	100,000	30,000
Total Current Liabilities	$ 400,000	$ 400,000	$100,000
Long-term Debt:			
Bonds Payable	$ 600,000	$ 600,000	-0-
Total Liabilities	$1,000,000	$1,000,000	$100,000

STOCKHOLDERS' EQUITY			
Preferred Stock of P Company:			
Issued and Outstanding	$ -0-	$ 440,000	
Common Stock of P Company:			
Issued and Outstanding	500,000	500,000	
Capital Stock of S Company:			
Issued and Outstanding			$200,000
Retained Earnings	1,500,000	1,500,000	300,000
Total Stockholders' Equity	$2,000,000	$2,440,000	$500,000
Total Equities	$3,000,000	$3,440,000	$600,000

changed is *who* owns its outstanding capital stock. Now note the two changes in the balance sheet of P Company as shown in the second column (labeled "After") on pages 52-53. The additional asset, Investment in Company S (consisting of 80 percent of the outstanding capital stock of that company), has been financed by issuance of shares of preferred stock (instead of by cash because of P Company's low cash position).

It is obvious that P Company (now known as the *parent* company) is in control of S Company (now known as the *subsidiary* company) due to its ownership of 80 percent of the voting stock of the latter company. Each company is and may well remain a separate legal entity. Such is the case, for example, with Westinghouse Electric Corporation's 77 percent ownership of Westinghouse Canada, Limited. And it is obvious that each company must continue to gather its own accounting and financial data in order to prepare their separate financial statements. However, because of the significant percentage ownership of P Company in S Company and the intent of long-term control, as well as their similarity in type of business, a set of *consolidated* financial statements should be prepared. A consolidated balance sheet, for example, would reflect the financial position of the over-all business enterprise at January 1, 1973. Such a consolidated balance sheet will now be shown.

At this point, it should be mentioned that the acquisition of S Company was by the "purchase" method. The reader is referred to Chapter 7, pages 210–11, for the distinction between the "purchase" and "pooling of interests" methods of accounting for business combinations. Likewise, it should be noted, that since S Company has been in business only two years, it is believed that their recorded asset amounts also reflect the fair value of each of them. Thus, any premium amount in the $440,000 amount paid by P Company for the acquisition of its 80 percent interest in S Company is *goodwill*. Again the reader is referred to Chapter 7, pages 212–13, for a discussion of goodwill, and for the requirement that it be amortized (effective November 1, 1970) over a life not to exceed 40 years.

In arriving at the consolidated balance sheet shown in column four on pages 54-55, little more is involved than cross-adding the items shown by the balance sheet of P Company in column one and the balance sheet of S Company in column two. Note that no formal accounting system exists which contains the combined amounts; the amounts on two separate sets of records simply are being cross-added to prepare the consolidated balance sheet. However, there are two complicating factors. First, there is a premium amount in the $440,000 amount paid by P Company for the 80 percent interest in the net assets of S Company. This excess amount paid over and above that paid for the 80 percent interest in the net assets acquired must be identified and shown as *goodwill* on the consolidated balance sheet. Second, P Company acquired only 80 percent of S Company. Thus, there is a *minority interest* of 20 percent by other owners in the *net* assets (assets minus liabilities) of S Company. This minority interest ownership must be indicated on the consolidated balance sheet. To handle these two factors, note the two sets of offsetting eliminations, labeled (a) and (b), in the third column on pages 54-55.

By issuing $440,000 worth of preferred stock, P Company purchased 80 percent of the *net* assets (assets-liabilities) or stockholders' equity in S Company. But 80 percent of the net assets ($600,000 assets − $100,000 liabilities) or stockholders' equity ($500,000), is only $400,000—$40,000 less than the $440,000 purchase price. And since it was previously noted that S Company's assets were on the statement at their fair value (especially since they were purchased only two years ago when the company was formed), the excess $40,000 represents the purchase of goodwill. Also, in cross-adding the separate balance

Balance Sheet

January 1, 1973

	Separate P Company	Separate S Company	Eliminations	Consolidated Balance Sheet
ASSETS				
Current Assets:				
Cash	$ 100,000	$ 40,000		$ 140,000
Accounts Receivable (net)	300,000	100,000		400,000
Inventories	400,000	100,000		500,000
Prepaid Expenses	20,000	10,000		30,000
Total Current Assets	$ 820,000	$250,000		$1,070,000
Investments:				
Investment in S Company (80%)	$ 440,000		−440,000 (a)	
Property, Plant and Equipment:				
Cost less Accumulated Depreciation	2,180,000	$350,000		$2,530,000
Goodwill			+ 40,000 (a)	40,000
Total Assets	$3,440,000	$600,000		$3,640,000

THE STATEMENT OF INCOME

LIABILITIES				
Current Liabilities:				
Accounts Payable	$ 200,000	$ 60,000		$ 260,000
Accrued Expenses Payable .	100,000	10,000		110,000
Income Taxes Payable	100,000	30,000		130,000
Total Current Liabilities .	$ 400,000	$100,000		$ 500,000
Long-term Debt:				
Bonds Payable	$ 600,000	-0-		$ 600,000
Total Liabilities	$1,000,000	$100,000		$1,100,000
Minority Interest in S Company			+100,000 (b)	$ 100,000
STOCKHOLDERS' EQUITY				
Preferred Stock of P Company:				
Issued and Outstanding ...	$ 440,000			$ 440,000
Common Stock of P Company:				
Issued and Outstanding ...	500,000			500,000
Capital Stock of S Company:				
Issued and Outstanding ...		$200,000	−160,000 (a) − 40,000 (b)	
Retained Earnings	1,500,000	300,000	−240,000 (a) − 60,000 (b)	1,500,000
Total Stockholders' Equity	$2,440,000	$500,000		$2,440,000
Total Equities	$3,440,000	$600,000		$3,640,000

sheets, there will be some double-counting that must be eliminated. Elimination (a) in the third column on pages 54-55 is designed to both set up the purchased *goodwill* and to eliminate this double-counting, by:

Against P Co. investment cost		$440,000
Offset S Co. equity purchased:		
80 percent of Capital Stock of S Co.	$160,000	
80 percent of Retained Earnings of S Co.	240,000	400,000
Goodwill purchased		$ 40,000

The consolidated balance sheet is designed to show the financial position of the consolidated business entity. In so doing, it must give recognition to equities of outsiders. The consolidated balance sheet on pages 54-55, obtained by cross-adding, contains *all* the assets and liabilities of S Company. But outsiders, the minority stockholders of S Company, have a 20 percent interest in the net assets of S Company. Elimination (b) in the third column above segregates this minority interest by:

Equity (net assets) retained by S Co. shareholders:
    20 percent of Capital Stock of S Co. .... $ 40,000
    20 percent of Retained Earnings of S Co. ... 60,000
Equals Minority Interest $100,000

In practice, this minority interest of others in a subsidiary usually is shown on the consolidated balance sheet as a separate item *between* the liabilities and stockholders' equity sections. Occasionally it will be shown as a liability and occasionally as a segment of stockholders' equity.

At this point, it would be possible to quickly terminate this brief overview of consolidated financial statements because the basic point has been made; namely, consolidated statements are designed to present the financial picture of the total combined business organization. In so doing, the effect of intraorganization transactions must be eliminated and the equities of any minority interests in any part of the over-all combined organization clearly indicated. However, it is worthwhile to discuss additional factors affecting consolidated financial statements that occur subsequent to the date of acquisition by one company of another. Therefore, next presented, on pages 57-59, are the Statements of Income and Retained Earnings for the next year, 1973, of P Company and S Company, and the Balance Sheet of each at the end of the next year, December 31, 1973.

Consolidated Financial Statements One Year After Acquisition

To prepare the Consolidated Statement of Income, note that the separate statements of income of each company have simply been cross-added down through the line for income taxes. This is possible because there have *not* been any financial transactions between the two companies during 1973 that affect the statement of income. (If there had been any such transactions, such as the sale of merchandise from one to the other, the reader can appreciate that the sale by one and the purchase by the other are offsetting items to be eliminated with a further possible adjustment for any resulting intercompany profit on the sale-purchase. On such complicating factors, the reader is referred to a standard book in the area of advanced accounting principles.) Note that the *consolidated* statement of income, down through the line for income taxes, contains 100 percent of the revenue items (net sales) of S Company and 100 percent of the cost and expense items (cost of goods sold, marketing and administrative expenses, and income taxes) of S Company. Thus, the consolidated statement includes all $60,000 of the net income of S Company. But 20 percent of the $60,000 net income does not belong to the consolidated organization, but to "outsiders"—the minority interest in S Company. Therefore, to arrive at the net income for the year of the consolidated organization, the $12,000 amount (20 percent of $60,000) must be removed. The $290,000 consolidated net income is the sum of the entire $242,000 net income of P Company and $48,000 (80 percent of $60,000) of the net income of S Company.

Statement of Income
For the Year Ended December 31, 1973

	Separate P Company	Separate S Company	Consolidated Statement of Income
Net Sales	$1,622,000	$510,000	$2,132,000
Cost of Goods Sold	900,000	300,000	1,200,000
Gross Margin on Sales	$ 722,000	$210,000	932,000
Marketing and Administrative Expenses	200,000	100,000	300,000
Net Operating Income	$ 522,000	$110,000	$ 632,000
Other Expenses: Interest Expense on Bonds	30,000	–0–	30,000
Net Income before Income Taxes	$ 492,000	$110,000	$ 602,000
Income Taxes	250,000	50,000	300,000
Net Income of Subsidiary Applicable to Minority Interests			$ 302,000 12,000
Net Income for the Year	$ 242,000	$ 60,000	$ 290,000

Changes in Retained Earnings
For the Year 1973

	P Company	S Company	Consolidated
Retained Earnings, January 1, as shown by January 1, 1973 balance sheet	$1,500,000	$300,000	$1,500,000
Net Income, 1973, as shown by above Statement of Income ...	242,000	60,000	290,000
80 percent of S Company net income to P Company*	48,000		
	$1,790,000	$360,000	$1,790,000
Dividends Declared	100,000	10,000	100,000
Retained Earnings, December 31, as shown by December 31, 1973 balance sheet	$1,690,000	$350,000	$1,690,000

* Could have been shown above on Separate P Company Statement of Income

The analysis showing the changes in retained earnings during 1973 contains the only intercompany transaction, namely, the dividend declared and paid by S Company. The $10,000 dividend has been distributed 20 percent ($2,000) to the outside minority interest and 80 percent ($8,000) to P Company.

Where is this receipt of $8,000 in cash reflected on P Company's statements? In the current asset, cash, of course, but also in retained earnings. Note that retained earnings includes *all* 80 percent of the $60,000, or $48,000, of the net income of S Company. To understand exactly what has taken place, an explanation is necessary of what is technically known as the equity method of accounting for intercompany investments. By the use of the equity method, the amount shown on the parent company's balance sheet as "Investment in Subsidiary" includes not only the initial purchase price, but also the parent company's pro rata share of the *retained* net income (or loss) of the subsidiary since the time of its acquisition by the parent company. In effect, the parent company each year takes up its full share of the subsidiary's net income as an

Balance Sheet
December 31, 1973

	Separate P Company	Separate S Company	Eliminations	Consolidated Balance Sheet
ASSETS				
Current Assets:				
Cash	$ 150,000	$ 60,000		$ 210,000
Accounts Receivable (net)	350,000	140,000		490,000
Inventories	550,000	145,000		695,000
Prepaid Expenses	50,000	5,000		55,000
Total Current Assets	$1,100,000	$350,000		$1,450,000
Investments:				
Investment in S Company (80%)	$ 480,000		−480,000 (a)	
Property, Plant and Equipment:				
Cost less Accumulated Depreciation	2,080,000	$320,000		$2,400,000
Goodwill			+ 40,000 (a)	40,000
Total Assets	$3,660,000	$670,000		$3,890,000
LIABILITIES				
Current Liabilities:				
Accounts Payable	$ 250,000	$ 80,000		$ 330,000
Accrued Expenses Payable	150,000	20,000		170,000
Income Taxes Payable	30,000	20,000		50,000
Total Current Liabilities	$ 430,000	$120,000		$ 550,000
Long-term Debt:				
Bonds Payable	$ 600,000	-0-		$ 600,000
Total Liabilities	$1,030,000	$120,000		$1,150,000
Minority Interest in S Company			+110,000 (b)	$ 110,000

STOCKHOLDERS' EQUITY				
Preferred Stock of P Company: Issued and Outstanding ...	$ 440,000			$ 440,000
Common Stock of P Company: Issued and Outstanding ...	500,000			500,000
Capital Stock of S Company: Issued and Outstanding ...		$200,000	−160,000 (a) − 40,000 (b)	
Retained Earnings	1,690,000	350,000	−280,000 (a) − 70,000 (b)	1,690,000
Total Stockholders' Equity	$2,630,000	$550,000		$2,630,000
Total Equities	$3,660,000	$670,000		$3,890,000

increase in its "Investment" and then reduces it by the amount it (the parent) actually receives in the form of dividends declared by the subsidiary. Thus, of the $48,000 net income allocable to the parent company, to date $8,000 has been "received" (in the form of dividends) while $40,000 technically has not as yet been received and is included in the asset "Investment in S Company" on the balance sheet of the parent company, as next explained.

On the two balance sheets for separate P Company, its Investment in S Company (80 percent) is shown at:

$$\begin{array}{ll} \text{December 31, 1973} \ldots\ldots\ldots & \$480,000 \\ \text{January 1, 1973} \ldots\ldots\ldots\ldots & 440,000 \\ \hline \text{Increase during 1973} \ldots\ldots\ldots & \$ 40,000 \end{array}$$

This $40,000 increase in the investment is P Company's $48,000 share of S Company's net income for 1973 less the $8,000 of it actually received as a dividend distribution from S Company. It should also be noted that exactly the same two eliminations are necessary to arrive at the December 31, 1973 consolidated balance sheet as were necessary a year earlier; only the dollar amounts are different because of the 1973 profit and dividend of S Company. Elimination (a) in the third column on page 58 is designed to both set up the same original $40,000 of purchased goodwill and offset the investment of P against 80 percent of the stockholders' equity of S, by:

Against P Co. investment		$480,000
Offset S Co. equity:		
80 percent of Capital Stock of S Co.	$160,000	
80 percent of Retained Earnings of S Co.	280,000	440,000
Goodwill originally purchased		$ 40,000

And, again, elimination (b) sets up the 20 percent minority interest of the "outsiders" in the net assets of S Company, by:

S Co. equity (net assets) of outsiders:
20 percent of Capital Stock of S Co.	$ 40,000
20 percent of Retained Earnings of S Co.	70,000
Equals Minority Interest	$110,000

Note the $10,000 increase in the minority interest since January 1. This is their share of the net income of S Company for 1973 (20 percent of $60,000) of $12,000 less the $2,000 of it received as their share of the dividend (20 percent of $10,000) declared by S Company.

Obviously, this abbreviated discussion of consolidated statements has avoided many complicating factors that arise in actual business dealings. However, the goal has been met of presenting the general principles by which consolidated statements are derived and the reasoning for so doing. The reader interested in an in-depth study of the subject is referred to the several chapters on the subject that will be found in the usual advanced accounting principles book.

QUESTIONS AND PROBLEMS

3-1. Answer the following three statements true or false:
  a. The exact earnings of a business entity cannot be definitely determined before the end of the life of the business.
  b. The Statement of Income is a more useful statement to those in management than the Balance Sheet.
  c. For the full year of 1972, Marshall Company shows the following data for Heat and Light Expense:

Total for services rendered by the utility companies	$1,000
Cash payments to the utility companies	900
Accrued utility expenses payable	100

  If Marshall Company is on the accrual basis, Heat and Light Expense on the Statement of Income will be $1,000.

3-2. For each of the following six statements, choose the best answer to each and indicate your choice on an answer sheet with the number 1, 2, or 3.
  a. Cost of goods sold represents the volume of goods sold during the year at:
     1. selling price
     2. cost
     3. value
  b. One of the "key" dollar amounts readily shown by a multiple-step statement of income that is not separately set out on a single-step statement is:
     1. cost of goods sold
     2. net operating income
     3. depreciation expense

c. An uninsured tornado loss on a factory building should appear on the statement of income as:
   1. a part of cost of goods sold
   2. an operating expense
   3. an "other expense" item
d. Dividends on common stock declared during the year reduce:
   1. the net income for the year
   2. retained earnings at the date declared
   3. federal income tax expense of the corporation
e. When a company costs its inventory on a LIFO basis, the $ amount reported for cost of goods sold on the Statement of Income represents:
   1. most recent costs
   2. the oldest costs
   3. some amount below current replacement cost if costs have increased since the adoption of LIFO
f. Cash dividends to stockholders are:
   1. an expense on Statement of Income
   2. a distribution of corporate profits to stockholders
   3. a return of the capital investment

3-3. The 1970 annual report of Kraftco Corporation (formerly National Dairy Products Corporation) presented the Consolidated Statement of Income for the 52 weeks ended December 26, 1970, in the single-step form, similar to that illustrated on page 38. The following list contains the various items of "Income" and "Costs and Expenses" which actually appeared on the statement:

Cost of products	$2,103,405,060
Interest on long-term debt	4,339,832
Net sales	2,751,129,371
Delivery, selling, and administrative expense	484,058,356
Provision for federal and foreign taxes on income	81,331,000
Other income	9,613,980
Miscellaneous charges—net	5,603,437

Net income per share of common stock and common equivalent shares, based on average number of shares outstanding, was $2.93 (and $2.92 assuming conversion of convertible bonds).

Required

Prepare the consolidated statement of income in single-step form. The "Net Income for the Year" was $82,005,666. (Notes to the financial statements have been omitted.)

3-4. The 1970 annual report of Arvin Industries, Inc., presented the Consolidated Statements of Operations and Retained Earnings for the 53 weeks ended January 3, 1971, in the multiple-step form, similar to that illustrated on page 40. The annual report contained a combined statement of income and retained earnings. The following list contains the various items which actually appeared on the statement:

Selling, general, and administrative expense	$ 16,973,065
Net sales	165,765,561
Other deductions (including interest of $2,906,382)	3,504,448
Retained earnings, beginning of year (Dec. 28, 1969)	25,902,749
Cash dividends paid	2,733,867
Cost of goods sold	140,700,455
Federal and state income taxes	2,780,238
Other income	868,699

Earnings per share amounted to $.98

Required

Prepare the Consolidated Statements of Operations and Retained Earnings. The balance of retained earnings on January 3, 1971, was $25,844,936. (Notes to the financial statements have been omitted.)

3-5. The financial statements contained in the 1969 annual report of AMAX (American Metal Climax, Inc.), show the following assets, liabilities, and shareholders' equity items as of December 31, 1969, and the income and expenses for the year 1969:

Cash	$ 18,670,000
Investments in AMAX Credit Corporation and 50%-owned companies	17,400,000
Accounts payable and accrued liabilities	87,920,000
Federal and foreign income taxes (payable)	16,900,000
Accumulated depreciation and depletion	248,540,000
Inventories	127,590,000
Dividend income	22,230,000
Short-term marketable securities, at cost (approximates market)	106,250,000
Investments in other companies	54,790,000
Interest income and net profit on investments	12,450,000
Interest on notes payable	10,810,000
Notes payable	12,590,000
Net sales	753,490,000
Cost of sales, exclusive of items shown separately	591,250,000
Prepaid expenses and other current assets	9,200,000
Federal and foreign income taxes (expense)	27,420,000
Long-term receivables, loans, and charges	27,110,000
Accounts receivable, less allowance for doubtful accounts of $3,330,000	126,380,000
Time deposits and certificates of deposit	14,060,000
Notes payable (non-current)	201,210,000
Deferred income taxes, reserves, etc. (non-current liability)	58,940,000
Common stock, par value $1 a share; authorized 35,000,000 shares; issued 23,699,333 shares	23,670,000
Retained earnings, December 31	361,060,000
Selling and general expenses	48,830,000

[CH. 3] THE STATEMENT OF INCOME 63

Preferred stock, par value $1 a share; authorized
  5,000,000 shares; issued and outstanding 790,891
  shares 790,000
Depreciation and depletion 27,210,000
Taxes other than federal and foreign income taxes 13,560,000
Capital surplus 168,100,000
Cost of treasury stock (common; 17,205 shares) 540,000
Production payments, unearned treatment charges, etc.
  (current liability) 10,280,000
Retained earnings, January 1 324,420,000
Dividends declared for the year:
  Preferred stock 1,150,000
  Common stock 31,300,000
Property, plant and equipment, at cost 688,010,000
Net earnings per common share $2.92

Required

Prepare in proper form:

a. Consolidated Statement of Financial Position (Balance Sheet).

b. Consolidated Statement of Income (multiple-step form).

c. Consolidated Statement of Retained Earnings.

(Notes to the financial statements have been omitted.)

3-6. The MBA Corporation was organized three years ago by three energetic young college graduates. You are employed as "business manager." Since the chief accountant of the company resigned two weeks ago and has not been replaced yet, your most pressing need is for financial statements for the year just ended. You decide to prepare the statements yourself.

The following amounts are disclosed by the records:

Cash .... $ 8,000
Accrued Expenses Payable 500
Land, Buildings, and Equipment 76,000
Accounts Receivable 9,300
Net Sales 159,000
Paid-in Surplus 7,500
Common Stock (Par $10) 30,000
Gain on Sale of Marketable Securities 2,800
Accounts Payable 3,000
Accumulated Depreciation to date 12,000
Mortgage Payable (includes installments totaling $4,000
  due in 1973) 40,000
Prepaid Expenses 300
Inventory, January 1, 1972 30,000
Estimated Doubtful Accounts 100
Purchases (net of returns and discounts) 90,000
Retained Earnings, December 31, 1972 19,500

Permanent Investments (present market value $4,500), at cost	3,000
Retained Earnings, January 1, 1972	11,300
Dividend Income	400
Inventory, December 31, 1972	23,500
Estimated Income Taxes Payable	7,500
Selling, General, and Administrative Expenses	37,500
Income Tax Expense	7,500
Dividends Paid	10,500
Interest Expense on Mortgage	2,000

Required

Based upon your few weeks of instruction to date, prepare in proper form:

a. Balance Sheet, as of December 31, 1972.

b. Statement of Income and Retained Earnings, for the year ended December 31, 1972. (Use multiple-step form for portion pertaining to statement of income.)

3-7. For each of the following statements, choose the best answer to each and indicate your choice on an answer sheet with the number 1, 2, or 3.

a. As of December 31, 1970, The Aluminum Company of America had 21,506,417 shares of $1 par value common stock outstanding. Mr. Jones owns 100 of these shares. Through his broker, he sells the 100 shares at $56 per share (on the New York Stock Exchange) and the shares are purchased by Mr. Smith at $57 through his broker. The effect of this transfer of ownership of 100 shares upon the financial statements of ALCOA is:
1. none
2. changes Balance Sheet but not the Statement of Income
3. varied effect on the financial statements

b. When a corporation originally issues stock at a price in excess of par (if par value stock) or in excess of stated value (if no par value stock), this excess amount, per the corporate records, results in:
1. "Other Income" on the Statement of Income
2. an increase in Capital or Paid-in Surplus on the Balance Sheet
3. Earnings Retained in the business

c. The primary responsibility for presenting fairly the financial statements (indicating the financial position and the results of operations) contained in the company's annual report is that of:
1. the C.P.A. firm which does the audit and attaches its opinion to the statements in the annual report
2. the company itself
3. the SEC (Securities and Exchange Commission)

d. Assume a mercantile business employs the accrual basis of accounting. The cost of goods sold figure is the same as:
1. the total cash paid for merchandise purchased
2. the total cash paid for merchandise purchased plus amounts still owed for merchandise purchased
3. the total cost of merchandise purchased, increased, or decreased by the net change in the inventory of merchandise from the beginning to the end of the fiscal period

e. On the balance sheet, the amount representing the difference between the cost of the property, plant and equipment and the accumulated depreciation to date is:
   1. estimated current value
   2. estimated liquidation value
   3. estimated unexpired or unrecovered cost

3-8. The accounting records of Texas Products Corporation show the following assets and liabilities *as of* December 31, 1971, and the income and expenses *for the year* 1971.

Cash	$ 10,000	dise, December 31, 1971	19,000
Accounts Receivable	12,000	Prepaid Insurance	470
Notes Receivable	6,000	Inventory of Office Supplies	300
Accrued Interest Receivable	30	Inventory of Merchandise, January 1, 1971	14,500
RCA Common Stock (market value $11,000)	10,000	Purchases	140,000
Land	4,000	Freight In	1,500
Building	30,000	Purchase Returns and Allowances	1,000
Accumulated Depreciation	6,000	Purchase Discounts	1,000
Furniture and Fixtures	5,000	Sales Salaries	16,000
Accumulated Depreciation	1,000	Advertising	2,400
Goodwill	5,000	Transportation Out	2,000
Accounts Payable	14,290	Store Expenses	512
Notes Payable	4,000	Social Security Taxes—Sales Salaries	1,344
Accrued Property Taxes Payable	700	Office Salaries	14,000
Estimated Federal Income Taxes Payable	5,000	Office Expenses	350
Federal Income Taxes Withheld	200	Insurance	600
F.I.C.A. Taxes Withheld	60	Depreciation of Building	750
F.I.C.A. Taxes Payable	60	Depreciation of Furniture and Fixtures	400
Federal Unemployment Tax Payable	240	Property Taxes	1,200
State Unemployment Tax Payable	150	Utilities Expense	916
Rent Collected in Advance	100	Bad Debts	200
Mortgage Payable	10,000	Social Security Taxes—Office Salaries	1,176
Capital Stock	40,000	Interest Earned (on Notes)	150
Retained Earnings, January 1, 1971	11,098	Cash Dividends Received	400
Dividends Paid	5,000	Rent Earned	800
Sales	199,000	Interest Expense (on Notes)	200
Sales Returns and Allowances	1,000	Interest on Mortgage	400
Sales Discounts	2,000	Loss on Sale of Plant and Equipment	1,000
Inventory of Merchan-		Estimated Federal Income Taxes	5,000

Note: Social security taxes (showing rates as this is written) consist of the following:

Federal Old Age and Survivors Insurance Tax
(F.I.C.A.), including Medicare 5.2%

Federal Unemployment Tax 4%

State Unemployment Tax (maximum rate is dependent on state law; actual rate may be lower due to merit rating based on company's employment experience) 2.8%

Thus 8.4% of salaries equals the company's social security taxes (no employee earned in excess of the amount subject to the various payroll taxes).

Required

Prepare the three financial statements in proper form.

Notes: The operating expenses of the business may be presented in one category as "Operating Expenses" or segregated between "Selling Expenses" and "General and Administrative Expenses."

The final amount arrived at on the Statement of Retained Earnings must agree with the amount shown for Retained Earnings on the Balance Sheet as of December 31, 1972.

3-9. Prepare in proper form for the T. Cobb Corporation:

a. Balance Sheet, as of December 31, 1972.

b. Statement of Income and Retained Earnings, for the year ended December 31, 1972. (Use multiple-step form for portion pertaining to statement of income and also show the earnings per share of common stock.)

The following amounts (in thousands of dollars) are disclosed by the records:

Cash	$ 3,000
Land, Buildings, and Equipment, at original cost	60,000
Net Sales	100,000
Accounts Payable	4,000
Inventory, January 1, 1972 (on FIFO basis) at cost	15,000
Purchases (net of returns and discounts)	57,500
Estimated Income Taxes Payable	5,000
Income Tax Expense	10,000
Marketing Expenses	11,000
Inventory, December 31, 1972 (on FIFO basis) at cost	12,500
Retained Earnings, January 1, 1972	30,000
Retained Earnings, December 31, 1972	?
Estimated Doubtful Accounts	100
Prepaid Expenses	100
Accumulated Depreciation to date	20,000
Accounts Receivable	8,000
Accrued Expenses Payable	800
Interest Expense	240
Investment (10%) in Foreign Company, at cost	4,000
Intangible Assets (principally goodwill)	500

[CH. 3] THE STATEMENT OF INCOME 67

6% Preferred Stock, Par $100; 10,000 shares issued and outstanding	?
Capital in Excess of Par and Stated Value	8,000
Dividends from Foreign Company	700
Notes Payable to Bank (short-term)	1,000
3% Debentures, due 1978	7,000
Common Stock, No Par, at stated value of $5; 800,000 shares issued and outstanding	?
Administrative Expenses	9,000

Dividends Paid:
    On Preferred .... 6% ($6.00 per share)
    On Common ....$4.00 per share
    (No additional shares were issued in 1972.)

Note: Neither the preferred stock nor the bonds are convertible into common stock.

3-10. Prepare in proper form (including headings) for the Wrangall Corporation:

    a. Balance Sheet, as of December 31, 1972.

    b. Statement of Income and Retained Earnings (combined), for the year ended December 31, 1972. (Use multiple-step form for portion of the combined statement pertaining to statement of income.) Compute the earnings per share of common stock.

Cash	$ 3,000
Land, Buildings, and Equipment, at original cost	60,000
Net Sales	100,000
Freight In	500
Accounts Payable	4,000
Inventory, January 1, 1972 (on FIFO basis) at cost	15,000
Purchases (net of returns and discounts)	57,000
Estimated Income Taxes Payable	5,000
Income Tax Expense	10,000
Marketing Expenses	11,000
Inventory, December 31, 1972 (on FIFO basis) at cost	12,500
Retained Earnings, January 1, 1972	30,000
Retained Earnings, December 31, 1972	37,240
Estimated Doubtful Accounts	100
Prepaid Expenses	100
Accumulated Depreciation to date	20,000
Accounts Receivable	8,000
Accrued Expenses Payable	760
Interest Expense	450
Permanent Investment (10%) in Affiliated Company, at cost	4,000
Intangible Assets (principally goodwill)	500
6.5% Preferred Stock, Par $20; 200 shares issued and outstanding	4,000
Capital in Excess of Par and Stated Value	3,000
Dividends from Affiliated Company	950
Notes Payable to Bank (short-term)	1,000

7% Debentures, due 1988	4,000
Common Stock, No Par, at stated value of $5; 1,200 shares issued and outstanding	6,000
Administrative Expenses (including bad debts)	9,000
Dividends Paid:	
On Preferred .... 6.5% ($1.30 per share)	260
On Common .... $2.50 per share	3,000
(No additional shares were issued in 1972)	
Mortgage Payable (including installments of principal totalling $500 due in 1973)	3,000

Note: Neither the preferred stock nor the bonds are convertible into common stock.

3-11. Select three assets on the balance sheet of the company in problem 3-9 or 3-10 (whichever was assigned) and state some other cost or "valuation" basis which might have been used to determine the dollar amount (gross or net) of the assets.

3-12. Read the two articles mentioned below and answer the four questions.
Questions a and b are based upon the article, "How's the Annual Report Coming?" from *Fortune,* January, 1964.
Questions c and d are based upon the article, "The Development of Accounting Principles" from *The Journal of Accountancy,* September, 1964.
Choose the number 1, 2, or 3 of each of the four questions to indicate the selection of the proper answer to each, according to the articles.

  a. From a *logical* point of view, the annual report to the stockholders of a company *should* be a report from:
    1. the members of the board of directors
    2. the president of the corporation
    3. the controller and treasurer of the corporation

  b. Honest financial reporting, in large part, by major American corporations:
    1. has become a way of life
    2. lags behind such financial reporting found in European countries
    3. is the exception rather than the rule

  c. The development of accounting principles should be by:
    1. a co-operative effort of industry, the Institute, various other professions, trade associations, and government
    2. edicts of the Accounting Principles Board ratified by the Institute
    3. legislation

  d. Complete uniformity in accounting practices is:
    1. the ultimate goal of the Accounting Principles Board
    2. possible within the next five years
    3. not attainable

3-13. As sole owner, R. E. Lee started a merchandising business on July 1, 1971, called The Virginia Merchandise Mart. The following facts were taken from the books and records as of June 30, 1972, the end of his first year in business. The fiscal year of the business is July 1 to June 30.

[CH. 3] THE STATEMENT OF INCOME 69

Cash	$ 9,675	Office Equipment	4,000
Sales	110,700	Office Supplies Expense	514
Rent Collected in Advance	100	Interest Earned	190
Transportation In	2,170	Miscellaneous Selling Expenses	321
Transportation Out	1,109	Repair Expenses	401
Prepaid Insurance	400	Purchases	72,310
Insurance on Merchandise	420	Inventory of Merchandise, July 1, 1971	28,000
Insurance on Office Equipment	80	Inventory of Merchandise, June 30, 1972	32,500
Cash Dividends Received	350	Property Taxes	1,200
U.S. Grant Corporation Capital Stock (permanent investment)	7,150	Accrued Property Taxes Payable	600
Store Equipment	8,000	Miscellaneous General Expenses	123
Depreciation of Store Equipment	600	Delivery Truck Expenses	1,780
Bad Debts	280	Federal F.I.C.A. Taxes Withheld	100
Fire Loss on Office Equipment	1,500	Federal F.I.C.A. Taxes Payable	100
Gain on Sale of Investments	2,800	Depreciation of Office Equipment	400
Purchase Returns and Allowances	1,180	Advertising	697
Sales Salaries	10,000	Sales Returns and Allowances	1,200
Social Security Taxes—Sales Salaries	600	State Unemployment Tax Payable	140
Building	30,000	Mortgage Notes Payable	17,500
Accrued Salaries Payable	485	Accrued Commissions Receivable	200
State Income Tax Withheld	27	Commissions Earned	200
Prepaid Advertising	75	Sales Discounts	1,027
Inventory of Store Supplies	125	Delivery Equipment	6,500
Store Supplies Expense	422	Accounts Receivable	16,525
Heat, Light and Water Expense	972	Depreciation of Delivery Equipment	1,000
Sample Expense	487	Office Salaries	5,000
Notes Payable	1,500	Social Security Taxes—Office Salaries	300
Federal Unemployment Tax Payable	50	Rent Earned	350
Notes Receivable	4,000	Accrued Interest Receivable	40
Purchase Discounts	512	Accounts Payable	6,883
Interest Expense	82	Telephone and Telegraph Expense	196
Insurance on Delivery Equipment	290	Trademarks	100
Federal Income Tax Withheld	200	Depreciation of Building	600
Interest on Mortgage	700	Insurance on Store Equipment	70
Insurance on Building	396	R. E. Lee, Capital	?
Land	5,000		
Accrued Interest Payable	15		

On July 1, 1971, R. E. Lee made an initial capital investment in the business of $79,500. During the fiscal year ended June 30, 1972, he made added investments of $10,000 and withdrawals of $6,445.

Required

a. Prepare the following three financial statements in proper form:
   1. Balance Sheet as of June 30, 1972. The amounts listed above for depreciable plant and equipment items are net amounts after depreciation to June 30, 1972, was deducted.
   2. Statement of Income for the year ended June 30, 1972.
   3. Statement of Owner's Equity (or Capital) for the year ended June 30, 1972.

b. Prepare the following financial analysis:
   1. Current ratio as of June 30, 1972.
   2. Working capital as of June 30, 1972.
   3. Rate (%) of gross profit for the year ended June 30, 1972.
   4. Rate (%) of net operating income for the year ended June 30, 1972.

c. What amount (in dollars) has been *paid* for each of the following expenses during the year? (Assume no other facts.)
   1. Total Salaries of $15,000.
   2. Property Taxes of $1,200.
   3. Total Interest Expense of $782.

d. What amount (in dollars) has been *collected* for each of the following income items during the year? (Assume no other facts.)
   1. Interest Earned of $190.
   2. Commissions Earned of $200.
   3. Rent Earned of $350.

3-14. The "natural business year" of a company coincides with the company's annual cycle of activity. The natural business year ends when inventories on hand, receivables from customers, and loans owed to banks are at their lowest point in the annual activity cycle.

Required

a. What are the advantages of using a natural business year rather than the calendar year for a company's fiscal year? Name some possible disadvantages.

b. Suggest logical fiscal closing dates if the concern is a:
   1. manufacturer of automobiles
   2. brewery
   3. refiner of gasoline
   4. manufacturer of wallpaper
   5. publisher of school and college books
   6. department store
   7. college

3-15. Company P acquired 90 percent of the capital stock of Company S on January 1, 1973 at a cost of $110,000. The following data are submitted at December 31, 1973:

	Company P	Company S
Capital Stock (Par $100)	$500,000	$75,000
Retained Earnings, January 1, 1973	180,000	45,000
Net Income for Year 1973, from *own* separate operations	45,000	5,000
Dividends Paid during 1973	30,000	4,500

Required

What amounts should appear on the Consolidated Balance Sheet as of December 31, 1973 (assuming the equity method which was the method used in the chapter) for:
1. Minority Interest
2. Goodwill
3. Consolidated Retained Earnings

3-16. Parent Company owns an 80 percent interest in Subsidiary Company. Their *separate* financial statements reveal the following:

Parent Company retained earnings, January 1, 1973	$40,000
Parent Company net income for the year 1973	60,000
Subsidiary Company net income for the year 1973	70,000
Subsidiary Company dividends during year 1973	25,000
Parent Company dividends during year 1973	–0–

Required

On the December 31, 1973, Consolidated Balance Sheet, what will be the amount for Consolidated Retained Earnings?

3-17. If Parent Company in Problem 3-16 paid $114,000 for the stock of Subsidiary Company on January 1, 1973, what would be the amount shown for "Investment in Subsidiary" on Parent Company's separate balance sheet at December 31, 1973?

3-18. Old Beulah Corporation was incorporated in 1946. The balance sheet disclosed the following stockholders' equity section at December 31, 1972.

6 percent Cumulative, Non-Participating, Non-Convertible, Preferred Stock, Par $100; 400,000 shares authorized; 100,000 shares issued and outstanding	$ 10,000,000
Common Stock, Par $50; 1,000,000 shares authorized; 600,000 shares issued, of which 100,000 are in the treasury	30,000,000
Capital in Excess of Par	15,000,000
Retained Earnings (total)	55,000,000
	$110,000,000
Less: Treasury Stock, Common (100,000 shares @ $70 cost)	7,000,000
Total Stockholders' Equity	$103,000,000

During 1972 no shares of either class of stock were sold or purchased. The treasury stock was purchased in 1967. There are no dividends in arrears on the preferred stock.

The Statement of Retained Earnings for 1972, disclosed the following:

Retained Earnings, January 1, 1972				$52,600,000
Net Income for the Year 1972		$5,000,000		
Dividends during 1972:				
On Preferred Stock				
($6 per share)	$ 600,000			
On Common Stock				
($4 per share)	2,000,000	2,600,000		2,400,000
Retained Earnings, December 31, 1972				$55,000,000

Required

Compute the 1972 earnings per common share.

4

Statement of Source and Application of Funds

The balance sheet, the statement of income, and the statement of retained earnings are the principal financial statements which historically have been presented. Within a company, they guide the decision-making process of management; externally, they provide information to creditors, stockholders, potential investors, and other interested parties. In addition to these statements, most companies make extensive use of various types of reports, supplementary schedules, and additional statements as aids in planning and controlling operations. Of these, the most frequently encountered is the statement of source and application of funds. Although not a new statement, it has not appeared with any frequency in the annual reports of corporations until recently; it has been widely used by various companies over many years as a pertinent tool of internal analysis. In October of 1970, the Securities and Exchange Commission revised Form 10-K. This form is the general form for annual reports by companies having securities registered pursuant to the Securities Exchange Act of 1934 and the Securities Act of 1933. One of the revisions, effective for fiscal years ending on or after December 31, 1970, is that the financial statements filed with Form 10-K *must* contain the statement of source and application of funds. Then, in December of 1970, an exposure draft of the proposed Accounting Principles Board Opinion titled "Reporting the Sources and Uses of Funds" said in its opinion "such a statement (funds statement) should be included as one of the basic financial statements in financial reports of a business entity." Thus, this financial statement now should be considered one of the principal financial statements along with the balance sheet and statement of income and retained earnings. Accounting Principles Board Opinion No. 19, dated March 1971, and titled "Reporting Changes in Financial Position," requires (for fiscal years ending after September 30, 1971) such a statement to accompany both the balance sheet and statement of income and retained earnings. The statement of source and application of funds is also identified by titles such as source and use of funds, funds flow statement, statement of changes in financial position, and other similar titles.

The word *funds* has several different connotations. To illustrate the various connotations of the term, using some simple examples, assume that it is 11:00 A.M. on a Wednesday morning, and someone says to you: (1) "Do you have enough funds for lunch today?" In this case you will think only in terms of the very very short run, an hour, and you will probably base your reply on the amount of your most liquid current asset. In this case *funds* means cash to you.

However, if the person should say: (2) "Do you have enough funds for an evening out tonight?" the time period has been slightly lengthened. In this case you will think in terms of the very short run, eight hours or so, and could base your reply on your present cash position *plus* any amount you might expect to receive this afternoon from liquidating (selling) readily marketable securities owned (as cashing in your Series E Bonds). In this case *funds* means the *sum* of your first two *current assets*.

But, if the person should say: (3) "Do you have enough funds for skiing this weekend?" the time period has again been lengthened. Though still thinking in terms of a relatively short run, now you will probably base your reply on the sum of your first three current assets; cash, readily marketable securities, and any accounts receivable you expect to collect from some of your friends within a few days.

On the other hand, if the person should say: (4) "Will you have enough funds for the big dance in a few weeks?" you will think in terms of a slightly longer time period. Considering this intermediate length time period, you will probably base your reply on the sum of the three current assets (cash, readily marketable securities, and accounts receivable) *minus* accounts payable for your charge account purchases which will come due within the next few weeks.

Finally, if the person should say: (5) "Will you have enough funds to purchase an automobile within the next six months to a year?" you will now base your reply on a somewhat "long run" time period perspective. In this case you will probably consider the effect of the change that will occur in the intervening time period in your net working capital, the total of your current assets (cash, readily marketable securities, receivables, *and* inventory) *minus* your total current liabilities (accounts and notes payable, taxes payable, etc.).

It is obvious that additional meanings for the word *funds* are possible. And it is apparent that all the usages of *funds* are important when considered in their particular context. However, the material which follows in this chapter is limited to the fifth meaning above for *funds,* namely, net working capital.

The statement of source and application of funds reports the source and the disposition of funds which have flowed through a business during a particular period of time. Some have referred to it as a "where-got" (source), "where-gone" (application) statement. The term *funds* is used here in a relative, rather than a general, sense. These funds consist of more than cash alone or even cash plus readily marketable securities. Instead, they refer to the composition of the net working capital of the company; i.e., current assets minus current liabilities. A business is concerned with its cash position and cash flow; it is also vitally concerned with the broader picture presented by the flow of net working capital, as this is represented by the total of such items as cash, readily marketable securities, receivables, and inventories minus claims against the current assets in the form of current liabilities.

To illustrate the importance of a statement of source and application of funds, let us assume that a stockholder, a creditor, or some executive of a company is furnished the following financial statements (reproduced on pages 77 and 78):

Comparative Balance Sheet, As of December 31, 1971 and 1972
Statement of Income, For the Year 1972
Statement of Retained Earnings, For the Year 1972

After studying the above statements, our hypothetical reviewer might muse as follows:

> I think that I understand these financial statements, but I'm still puzzled. I see that the company had a net income during 1972 of $3,000,000. In addition, $700,000 was received from issuing common stock. This is a total of $3,700,000. Of this, $1,540,000 went for dividends. This leaves $2,160,000. Then, by comparing the amounts on the balance sheet at the end of each year, I can see that working capital was increased by $1,200,000. This still leaves $960,000 unaccounted for. Where is it?

In answering such questions, the statement of source and application of funds is invaluable for it shows the specific sources from which funds were derived and the various applications or uses to which the funds were placed during the year.

ILLUSTRATION OF THE STATEMENT OF SOURCE AND APPLICATION OF FUNDS

While there is no stereotyped form for the statement of source and application of funds, the statement on page 76 is arranged in a typical manner. This statement, covering the year 1972, has been prepared for The Fleming Company from the following: comparative balance sheets as of December 31, 1971 and 1972, specific items from the statement of income and statement of retained earnings for the year 1972, and an analysis of certain supplementary data.

THE FLEMING COMPANY
Statement of Source and Application of Funds
For the Year Ended December 31, 1972

Working Capital (Funds), January 1, 1972			$6,800,000
Source of Funds:			
Operations:			
Net Income for the Year, per Statement of Income		$3,000,000	
Plus expenses which did not require use of funds:			
Depreciation of plant and equipment	$1,640,000		
Amortization of intangible assets and deferred charges	75,000		
Fire loss on equipment	14,000		
	$1,729,000		
Less profit on sale of land included below in proceeds from sale	10,000	1,719,000	
Funds provided by operations		$4,719,000	
Proceeds from issuance of common stock		700,000	
Proceeds from sale of land		275,000	
Proceeds from insurance on equipment destroyed by fire		46,000	
Total Sources		$5,740,000	
Application of Funds:			
Declaration of dividends:			
On preferred stock	$ 40,000		
On common stock	1,500,000	$1,540,000	
Retirement of bonds		500,000	
Addition to fund for property additions		200,000	
Purchase of building		1,700,000	
Purchase of equipment		600,000	
Total Applications		$4,540,000	
Increase in Working Capital			1,200,000
Working Capital (Funds), December 31, 1972			$8,000,000

DATA FOR PREPARATION OF THE STATEMENT OF SOURCE AND APPLICATION OF FUNDS

The following condensed financial statements and an analysis of certain supplementary data were used to determine the *sources* and the *applications* of funds, as illustrated in the preceding Statement of Source and Application of Funds for The Fleming Company.

THE FLEMING COMPANY
Comparative Balance Sheet
As of December 31, 1972 and 1971

ASSETS	December 31, 1972	December 31, 1971	Increase or (Decrease)
Current Assets:			
Cash	$ 1,075,000	$ 1,280,000	$ (205,000)
Marketable Securities	1,500,000	1,500,000	—
Receivables	3,100,000	3,500,000	(400,000)
Inventories	6,300,000	5,500,000	800,000
Prepaid Expenses	25,000	20,000	5,000
Total	$12,000,000	$11,800,000	$ 200,000
Investments:			
Fund for Property Additions	$ 1,800,000	$ 1,600,000	$ 200,000
Affiliated Companies	800,000	800,000	—
	$ 2,600,000	$ 2,400,000	$ 200,000
Property, Plant and Equipment:			
Land	$ 1,900,000	$ 2,165,000	$ (265,000)
Buildings	6,700,000	5,000,000	1,700,000
Equipment	12,900,000	12,400,000	500,000
	$21,500,000	$19,565,000	$ 1,935,000
Accumulated Depreciation	(7,000,000)	(5,400,000)	1,600,000
Net	$14,500,000	$14,165,000	$ 335,000
Intangibles, less amortization	$ 400,000	$ 425,000	$ (25,000)
Deferred Charges	$ 500,000	$ 550,000	$ (50,000)
Total Assets	$30,000,000	$29,340,000	$ 660,000
LIABILITIES			
Current Liabilities:			
Note Payable	$ 850,000	$ 1,300,000	$ (450,000)
Accounts Payable	2,400,000	2,900,000	(500,000)
Accruals Payable	250,000	200,000	50,000
Income Tax Payable	500,000	600,000	(100,000)
Total	$ 4,000,000	$ 5,000,000	$(1,000,000)
Long-term Debt:			
Debentures	$ 6,000,000	$ 6,500,000	$ (500,000)
Total Liabilities	$10,000,000	$11,500,000	$(1,500,000)

STOCKHOLDERS' EQUITY

Preferred Stock (Par $50)	$ 1,000,000	$ 1,000,000	—
Common Stock (Par $5)	1,500,000	1,450,000	50,000
Capital in Excess of Par Value	4,500,000	3,850,000	650,000
Retained Earnings	13,000,000	11,540,000	1,460,000
Total Stockholders' Equity	$20,000,000	$17,840,000	$ 2,160,000
Total Liabilities and Stockholders' Equity	$30,000,000	$29,340,000	$ 660,000

THE FLEMING COMPANY
Statement of Income
For the Year Ended December 31, 1972

Revenues:

Sales (net)	$40,000,000	
Other Revenue	100,000	
Total Revenue		$40,100,000

Expenses:

Cost of Goods Sold	$24,000,000	
Selling Expenses	7,800,000	
Administrative Expenses	2,200,000	
Other Expenses	200,000	
Income Taxes	2,900,000	
Total Expenses		37,100,000
Net Income for the Year		$ 3,000,000

Note: $1,640,000 of depreciation of buildings and equipment, $25,000 amortization of intangible assets, and $50,000 amortization of deferred charges are included in the expenses shown above.

THE FLEMING COMPANY
Statement of Retained Earnings
For the Year Ended December 31, 1972

Balance, Retained Earnings, January 1, 1972		$11,540,000
Add: Net Income for the Year		3,000,000
		$14,540,000
Less: Dividends Declared		
On Preferred Stock	$ 40,000	
On Common Stock	1,500,000	1,540,000
Balance, Retained Earnings, December 31, 1972		$13,000,000

[CH. 4] STATEMENT OF SOURCE AND APPLICATION OF FUNDS 79

The way in which the principal financial statements of The Fleming Company and supplementary data were used to prepare the Statement of Application of Funds on page 76 will be explained by a description of the composition of the statement's two major divisions.

SOURCE OF FUNDS

The typical sources of funds in a business are:

> Funds generated by operations,
> Sale of additional capital stock,
> Increase in long-term debt,
> Disposal of non-current assets, and
> Decrease in working capital.

Reference to the financial statements of The Fleming Company (pages 77 and 78) will reveal whether funds were provided by each of the above sources, although the exact amount provided cannot be determined until each source is examined and modified for any changes required by an analysis of supplementary data. The actual amount of funds provided by each source was determined as follows:

Funds generated by operations was the result of the current year's operating activities. The statement of income indicates a net income of $3,000,000 for the year, but the company's operations generated funds which exceeded this figure. This difference is because the net income was computed by subtracting expenses from revenues, and certain expenses did not require the use of funds. For example, the footnote to the statement of income states that $1,640,000 of depreciation expense on buildings and equipment is included in expenses. This amount does not represent an outward flow of funds this year. The actual outflow of funds occurred in prior years when the fixed assets now being depreciated were acquired. The $1,640,000 of depreciation expense represents the current year's allocation of a portion of the total original cost of those fixed assets. Thus, to determine funds provided by operations, this type of expense must be added back to the previously determined net income for the year. Similarly, the $25,000 current year's amortization or write-off of intangible assets and the $50,000 amortization of deferred charges must also be added back to net income for the year.

During the year 1972, a fire destroyed some of the company's equipment which had been acquired several years ago at a cost of $100,000. To the date of the fire, the equipment had been depreciated a total of $40,000, leaving $60,000 as the undepreciated balance or unrecovered cost of the equipment. Since the company does not completely insure its equipment against fire hazards, only $46,000 was collected from the insurance company. Therefore, a $14,000 fire loss was incurred by the company. In summary:

Cost of equipment destroyed by fire	$100,000
Accumulated depreciation to date	40,000
Undepreciated balance	$ 60,000
Proceeds received from insurance company	46,000
Amount of fire loss	$ 14,000

The fire loss of $14,000 is one of the items contained in "Other Expenses" on the statement of income. Although this amount is definitely a loss to the company, no funds were expended (actually $46,000 of funds were received). Consequently, this $14,000 represents another expense which must be added back to the previously determined net income to ascertain the funds provided by operations during the year.

The comparative balance sheets show that the land amount was reduced during 1972. The supplementary data reveals that land, originally acquired at a cost of $265,000, was sold for $275,000. Since the entire proceeds of $275,000 is shown as a source of funds on the statement of source and application of funds, the $10,000 profit on sale of land, which had been included in the net income for the year, must now be subtracted from net income to determine the funds provided by operations. This adjustment provides a more accurate figure for funds provided by operations, for the sale of land is not directly related to the usual operations of the company.

An alternative method for determining the *funds generated by operations* is possible; perhaps it may be more logical. Actually, the previously calculated $4,719,000 source of funds from operations is a "net" source. Reference to the statement of income shows that:

Funds came in from business operations as follows:	
Sales revenues	$40,000,000
Other revenues (excluding $10,000 profit on sale of land)	90,000
Funds in from operations	$40,090,000
Funds went out due to business operations as follows:	
Cost of goods sold	$24,000,000
Selling *and* Administrative *and* Other Expenses totaled $10,200,000, but included $1,729,000 of expenses which didn't use funds (depreciation of $1,640,000, amortization of $75,000 and the loss of $14,000)	8,471,000
Income Taxes	2,900,000
Funds out due to operations	$35,371,000
Net Funds from operations	$ 4,719,000

Either this method or that previously discussed of adjusting the net income for the year are acceptable for determining the funds provided by operations. Obviously, both methods should give the same result.

Sale of additional capital stock provided funds when 10,000 shares of the $5 par value common stock were sold at $70 per share. The $700,000 of funds provided from this source is reflected on the balance sheet by increases in the following two items:

Common Stock (10,000 shares @ $5)	$ 50,000
Capital in Excess of Par Value (10,000 shares @ $65)	650,000
Funds provided by sale of common stock	$700,000

Consequently, the statement of source and application of funds must show $700,000 of funds provided by the sale of common stock.

Increase in long-term debt provides funds for a company. No such source of funds occurred during the current year for The Fleming Company.

Disposal of non-current assets by The Fleming Company occurred twice during the year. Both of these entered into the adjustments which were previously made to the funds provided by operations. The exact amount of funds provided by each of these disposals must be shown on the statement of source and application of funds. The sale of land provided $275,000 of funds. And the fire, which inadvertently "disposed" of some of the company's equipment, provided $46,000 of funds from the insurance company. Additional analysis of the comparative balance sheet does not indicate any other disposals of non-current assets, any decrease in investments, or any sale of buildings or equipment. Moreover, the decreases in intangibles and deferred charges have already been reconciled to the amounts written off during the current year as amortization expense.

Decrease in working capital provides funds; no such source of funds exists for The Fleming Company for the current year.

APPLICATION OF FUNDS

The typical applications or uses of funds in a business are as follows:
>Declaration of cash dividends,
>Reduction of long-term debt,
>Purchase of outstanding capital stock,
>Acquisition of non-current assets, and
>Increase in working capital.

Reference to the financial statements of The Fleming Company (pages 77 and 78) will reveal whether funds were utilized for each of the preceding applications. Although the financial statements may not readily disclose the exact amount of funds that have been applied, an examination of each indicated application can determine the exact amount of each use of funds. The actual amount of funds employed by each application was determined as follows:

Declaration of cash dividends are disclosed by the statement of retained earnings: $1,540,000 of funds were used during the year for dividends to stockholders.

Reduction of long-term debt in the amount of $500,000 is shown by the comparative balance sheet. An examination reveals that, although the debenture bonds were not scheduled to mature for several years, funds were used during the year to retire prematurely a portion of the bonds by purchasing them at par on the open market.

Purchase of outstanding capital stock did not occur, as reference to the comparative statement of financial position indicates that neither preferred stock nor common stock was reacquired during the year. Instead, additional common stock was issued.

Acquisition of non-current assets did occur, as an analysis of the supplementary data underlying changes in these assets (shown by the comparative balance sheet) discloses that funds were applied during the year to increase investments, acquire a plant building, and purchase new equipment.

The fund for property and plant additions (to be used to acquire additional facilities in approximately five years) was increased $200,000 by the purchase of U.S. Government bonds. An additional plant building was purchased for $1,700,000, and new equipment was also purchased for $600,000. However, the comparative balance sheet shows a net increase of only $500,000 for equipment, since $100,000 of equipment was destroyed by fire.

To prepare a source and application of funds statement, it may be necessary to analyze the amount of net change in the accumulated depreciation to date. In the present case, the net increase of $1,600,000 shown on the comparative balance sheet is readily accounted for as follows:

	Accumulated depreciation to date on		
	Buildings	Equipment	Total
Balance, December 31, 1971	$1,500,000	$3,900,000	$5,400,000
Depreciation expense for 1972 per statement of income	200,000	1,440,000	1,640,000
Total	$1,700,000	$5,340,000	$7,040,000
Removal of portion allocated to equipment destroyed by fire	—	40,000	40,000
Balance, December 31, 1972	$1,700,000	$5,300,000	$7,000,000

Increase in working capital in the amount of $1,200,000 is indicated by the comparative balance sheet. Though only the net amount of change is shown on the source and application of funds statement on page 76 in this chapter, certain companies prefer to detail the change, item by item, for each of the

	Current Assets	minus	Current Liabilities	equals	Working Capital
December 31, 1972	$12,000,000		$4,000,000		$8,000,000
December 31, 1971	11,800,000		5,000,000		6,800,000
Increase in Working Capital					$1,200,000

current assets and current liabilities. (Reference to page 625 of Appendix A will reveal that Armstrong Cork Company shows the amount of the net change in working capital and, on page 618, PPG Industries takes the same approach.)

SUMMARY

The most important use of a source and application of funds statement is that made by management to indicate the sources and uses of funds of the company, to show financial changes not apparent by the traditional analysis of the balance sheet and statement of income, and to aid those responsible for financial decisions and future planning.

Although a large majority of companies prepare the statement for internal use only, there is a decided trend toward its inclusion in the annual report, since it furnishes considerable financial information to stockholders, financial analysts, and other interested parties.

QUESTIONS AND PROBLEMS

4-1. The following information was prepared by the G. Edwards Corporation. There were no disposals of fixed assets during 1972.

G. EDWARDS CORPORATION
Balance Sheet

	December 31 1972	December 31 1971
Current Assets	$20,000,000	$18,000,000
Current Liabilities	9,000,000	8,500,000
Working Capital	11,000,000	9,500,000
Property, Plant and Equipment	50,000,000	45,000,000
Accumulated Depreciation to date	22,000,000	20,000,000
Net Property, Plant and Equipment	28,000,000	25,000,000
Stockholders' Equity	$39,000,000	$34,500,000

	December 31	
	1972	1971
Stockholders' Equity Evidenced By:		
Capital Stock, Par $50	$15,000,000	$15,000,000
Capital in Excess of Par	4,000,000	4,000,000
Retained Earnings, January 1	15,500,000	13,500,000
Net Income for the Year	6,000,000	3,000,000
	21,500,000	16,500,000
Dividends during the Year	1,500,000	1,000,000
Retained Earnings, December 31	20,000,000	15,500,000
Stockholders' Equity	$39,000,000	$34,500,000

Required

Prepare a source and application of funds statement for 1972.

4-2. The balance sheets of the Mart Merchandising Corporation at December 31, 1972 and 1971, were as follows:

	December 31, 1972	December 31, 1971
ASSETS	(Amounts represent thousands of dollars)	
Current Assets		
Cash	$1,000	$ 1,650
Accounts Receivable $5,400		$3,800
Less: Allowance for		
Doubtful Accounts 100	5,300	90 3,710
Notes Receivable	500	250
Inventory of Merchandise .	8,100	7,800
Prepaid Expenses	225	250
Total Current Assets .	$15,125	$13,660
Land, Building and Equipment		
Land	$ 2,100	$ 2,100
Building $9,150		$8,000
Less: Accumulated Depreciation 1,250	7,900	800 7,200
Furniture and Fixtures ... $ 850		$ 620
Less: Accumulated Depreciation 90	760	60 560
Net Land, Building and Equipment ...	$10,760	$ 9,860

	December 31, 1972	December 31, 1971
ASSETS	(Amounts represent thousands of dollars)	
Intangible Assets (at cost less amortization)		
Patents, Goodwill, Trademarks, etc	$ 435	$ 750
Total Assets	$26,320	$24,270
LIABILITIES		
Current Liabilities		
Accounts and Accruals Payable	$ 9,500	$ 8,300
Long-term Debt		
Bonds Payable	2,000	1,000
Total Liabilities	$11,500	$ 9,300
STOCKHOLDERS' EQUITY		
Contributed Capital		
Capital Stock (Par $100)	$10,000	$12,000
Premium on Capital Stock	600	1,000
Total	$10,600	$13,000
Retained Earnings	4,220	1,970
Total Stockholders' Equity	$14,820	$14,970
Total Creditors' and Stockholders' Equity	$26,320	$24,270

During 1972:

A new roof which cost $150,000 and a $1,000,000 addition to the building were added to the Building amount.

Some of the old fixtures and furniture having a total cost of $170,000 and accumulated depreciation to date of $20,000 were sold for $125,000. New modernistic furniture was purchased for $400,000.

The Depreciation Expense on furniture and fixtures for 1972 was $50,000.

Bonds in the amount of $1,000,000 were issued at par.

20,000 shares of capital stock were retired during the year at a cost of $2,400,000. The $400,000 excess of redemption price over par value was charged against the Premium on Capital Stock.

The only two items directly affecting the Retained Earnings during the year were net profit or loss for the year and dividend declarations of $250,000.

Required

Prepare a statement of source and application of funds for 1972.

4-3. The following column appeared on page one of the Wall Street Journal on August 4, 1969.

The Outlook

Appraisal of Current Trends In Business and Finance

Trying to assess the behavior of the stock market is a bit like trying to assess the behavior of the fairer sex. In each instance, the endeavor can be highly hazardous.

Women, we of course know, are intrinsically fascinating, exasperatingly complicated and wildly unpredictable. But they also are magnificently simple, at least according to an older and wiser colleague here. The simplicity, he says, is not readily apparent to the dazzled male eye—until one recognizes that women are composed of fat, muscle and bone, precisely the same ingredients (though the arrangement differs slightly) that go into the far less mystifying male form. This fact of science, our colleague claims, tends to be overlooked by men who are bewildered by female behavior.

The parallel, to be sure, is less than perfect. But it is a fact that the stock market is intrinsically fascinating, exasperatingly complicated and wildly unpredictable. Is it also magnificently simple? Few stock market observers would say so. But most would at least agree that there are some fat-muscle-and-bone fundamentals in the composition of the market that tend to be overlooked in times such as this—when the Dow-Jones industrial stock average has fallen 14.6% in the last 2½ months.

When a person buys a share of stock, this normally enables him to gain a share in the profits of the particular company, through dividend payments. If the company's profits picture happens to be bright, a share of its stock would normally be expected to sell at a relatively high price, in terms of earnings. Conversely, the stock of another company whose profits picture happens to be bleak would normally be expected to sell at a relatively low price, in terms of earnings.

In short—and there is nothing very mysterious about it—the price of a stock normally reflects the health of the particular company's earnings.

The relationship between the price of a share of stock and the earnings that underlie the share is usually expressed as a "price-earnings ratio." If a particular stock sells at $15 per share, and the company earns $1 per share annually, the stock carries a price-earnings ratio of 15-to-one, or simply 15 in the jargon of Wall Street.

The relationship of price to earnings provides a simple means of gaining perspective not only on the price of a single stock but on many stocks taken as a whole. For example, it is possible to compute a price-earnings ratio for the 30 stocks that make up the Dow-Jones industrial average. At the end of last week, the Dow-Jones industrial average, at 826.59, was 13.9 times the $59.38 combined per-share earnings of the 30 Dow-Jones stocks for the 12 months ended March 28.

The table below attempts to place the latest price-earnings ratio for the Dow-Jones industrial stocks into post-World War II perspective. Figures for past years are based on the Dow-Jones average at each year's end and on full-year earnings.

The table shows that the Dow-Jones stocks are selling at prices that are relatively low in terms of earnings. The price-earnings ratio generally was higher than at present through most of the current decade, as well as through a considerable part of the 1950s. Indeed, the only period in the postwar years in which the ratio was consistently lower than now was the pre-1954 era. The current ratio seems positively depressed when compared

Year	Ratio		Year	Ratio
1948	7.7		1960	19.1
1950	7.7		1962	17.9
1952	11.8		1964	13.6
1954	14.4		1966	13.6
1956	15.0		1968	16.3
1958	20.9		1969	13.9

with the levels that prevailed in the 1958-64 period. In the third quarter of 1961, the ratio reached nearly 25-to-one, almost twice last week's level.

Another way of gaining perspective on the current price-earnings level is to see how it compares with ratios that prevailed near the finish of past periods of expanding business, shortly before a recession.

There have been four major recessions in the postwar era, and in each corporate profits declined substantially. Just before the first of these recessions, in 1948-49, the price-earnings ratio of the Dow-Jones stocks stood at 8.5, far less than at present. Before the second, in 1953-54, the ratio was at 10.0, also below the present level. But before the 1957-58 recession, in which profits fell especially steeply, the ratio was 14.4, higher than now. And before the 1960-61 setback, it stood at 18.2, far higher than now.

Still another way of assessing the current price-earnings level is to observe the "quality" of the earnings that go into the ratio. Besides actual profits, companies also gain funds through depreciation. These depreciation funds represent sums deducted each year by corporations from pre-tax profits for the depreciation of such fixed assets as machine tools.

While they don't show up as profits in company earnings reports, these depreciation funds are nearly as good as profits, in the view of many analysts. Cash from depreciation can be plowed into new facilities, and the more a company can finance such spending out of depreciation, the more its current earnings can be freed for dividend payments.

Currently, for each dollar of after-tax profits, U.S. corporations produce more than 90 cents in depreciation money. Through all the 1960s and nearly all the 1950s, depreciation funds have amounted to well over 50 cents per dollar of earnings. But in earlier postwar years, there was relatively little depreciation money backing up each dollar of earnings. In 1948, when the price-earnings ratio stood at 7.7, depreciation amounted to only 30 cents per dollar of earnings.

The unpredictability of today's stock market is plainly apparent. Will the economy soon enter a recession? If so, will profits shrivel? Can companies continue to produce depreciation funds at a high rate? But it is also a very simple fact that in terms of earnings stocks generally are selling at prices higher than in early postwar years but lower than in most recent years. In this inflationary time, that's quite a distinction.

—Alfred L. Malabre Jr.

Required

After rereading paragraphs 12, 13, and 14 in the above 15 paragraph column, discuss what you believe is meant by:

a. actual profits

b. depreciation funds

c. depreciation funds are nearly as good as profits

d. cash from depreciation can be plowed into new facilities

4-4. The Management Planning Committee of Fineview Corporation has finalized plans for next year. Included in their planning are the following items:

a. Funds are to be obtained by issuing debenture bonds at the beginning of the year due in ten years in the amount of $2,500,000 with interest payable semi-annually at the rate of 8 percent a year.

b. Securities held as "permanent" investments in a fund for plant expansion (a non-current asset) and having a cost of $500,000 are to be sold for $800,000.

c. Within current assets is a short-term investment in U.S. Government Securities, at a cost of $100,000. This will be sold at cost.

d. Capital expenditure projects costing $3,000,000 are to be undertaken.

e. Working capital should be increased by $600,000 because of the contemplated capital expenditure program.

f. Continue making quarterly dividend payments of $.37½ a share on the 1,000,000 shares outstanding.

g. The controller has prepared the following projected statement of income for next year:

FINEVIEW CORPORATION
Estimated Statement of Income
For Next Year

Net Sales		$16,000,000
Cost of Goods Sold		9,000,000
Gross Margin on Sales		$ 7,000,000
Marketing and Administrative Expenses	$3,000,000	
Depreciation Expense	1,000,000	4,000,000
Net Operating Income		$ 3,000,000
Interest Expense on Bonds (debentures)		200,000
		$2,800,000
Gain on Sale of Permanent Investments		300,000
Net Income Before Income Taxes		$ 3,100,000
Income Tax Expense		1,600,000
Net Income After Income Taxes		$ 1,500,000

Required

Prepare an estimated statement of source and application of funds for next year. Because the amounts are estimates based on plans rather than actual results of what has already happened, the statement will not "balance." Therefore, "balance" the statement by an item indicating the dollar amount by which the objectives of the Management Planning Committee will fall short or be more than fulfilled if all the estimates turn out to be fact.

4-5. A major stockholder of Nunnery Hill Company, when he received the company's annual report on March 20, 1972, stated that something definitely had to be wrong with the financial statements. The Statement of Income for 1971 reported a net loss for the year of $40,000; yet, a comparison of the December 31, 1970 and December 31, 1971 Balance Sheets showed that working capital increased by $25,000.

During the year 1971, the company paid $15,000 for new equipment. Depreciation expense of $50,000 was deducted on the Statement of Income. In 1971, $30,000 was borrowed (new long-term debt) from the Prudential Insurance Company for 10 years.

Required

Prepare a statement of source and application of funds to show whether the stockholder is right or wrong.

4.6. Consecutive balance sheets of Allegheny Equipment Company contained the following:

	December 31, 1972	December 31, 1971
Property, Plant and Equipment, at cost:		
Machinery and Equipment	$350,000	$300,000
Accumulated Depreciation to date	165,000	170,000
Unrecovered Cost	$185,000	$130,000

During the year 1972, machinery and equipment was sold at a gain of $2,000 (shown as "other income" on the Statement of Income). New machinery and equipment was purchased at a cost of $80,000. Depreciation expense on machinery and equipment in 1972 (per the Statement of Income) amounted to $20,000.

Required

Calculate the proceeds received from the sale of the machinery and equipment.

4-7. The Marin Manufacturing Corporation commenced business on December 31, 1969. On that date, its initial balance sheet appeared as follows:

Balance Sheet
December 31, 1969

Working Capital (Current Assets less Current Liabilities)	$ 2,000,000
Property, Plant and Equipment (at cost)	8,000,000
Net Assets	$10,000,000
Capital Stock (Par $50)	$10,000,000
Capital in Excess of Par Value	–0–
Retained Earnings	–0–
Stockholders' Equity	$10,000,000

During the first four years of business, the Marin Manufacturing Corporation operated at exactly the break-even point each year. The statements of income for the four years appeared as follows:

Comparative Statements of Income
For the Years Ended December 31

	1973	1972	1971	1970
Net Sales	$8,000,000	$6,000,000	$7,000,000	$5,000,000
Costs and Expenses	8,000,000	6,000,000	7,000,000	5,000,000
Net Income for Year	–0–	–0–	–0–	–0–

During this time, there were no acquisitions of additional fixed assets nor disposals of any of the original items owned on December 31, 1969. Each year's depreciation expense amounted to $500,000 ($8,000,000 cost of plant ÷ average composite life of 16 years); this expense was included in the costs and expenses amounts shown by the above statements of income. No dividends were declared during the four years.

Required

a. Prepare a balance sheet as of December 31, 1973.
b. Prepare a single statement of application of funds covering the four-year period of January 1, 1970, to December 31, 1973.
   Note: Assume that all "funds provided (net)" were used to increase working capital.
c. Why was not a portion of the funds provided by operations used for dividends to the stockholders?
d. Assume that annual depreciation expense was $1,000,000 (average composite life of plant only 8 years) instead of $500,000 (thus each year indicates a $500,000 net loss), and:
   1. redo requirements a and b.
   2. explain why increased depreciation expense did not "provide" additional funds.
e. Assume that annual depreciation expense was $250,000 (average composite life of plant is 32 years) instead of $500,000 (thus each year indicates a $250,000 net income before tax), and:
   1. redo requirements a and b. Assume a corporate income tax rate of 50 per cent.
   2. explain why operations which resulted in an annual "net income after tax" of $125,000 provided less funds than operations at break-even point or at a net loss.

4-8. The following is the final portion of a conversation which took place in the office of A. C. Van Dusen, Vice-President—Finance, in late January of 1973:

M. A. ROBINSON, DIVISION MANAGER OF PRODUCT CHAMP: "Look, don't give me such a hard time. I'm working *for* the Company. Either I get $10,000,000 for our capital expansion program to increase our output and competitive position for Champ, or Champ perishes. It's our biggest profit maker at present, but Octopus, Inc., and Noodles, Ltd., are not only increasing capacity but making rapid technological advances. Although we are presently on top, we can't stand still. Remember what happened to Tippetts Company with its generometers when they stood pat with a winning hand several years ago."

A. C. VAN DUSEN: "But, we just don't have the funds. Available funds are already committed."

H. E. DAER, TREASURER: "And look at our overall cash position. It is $1,000,000 less than one year ago."

J. HUDSON, C.P.A., CONTROLLER: "Money is limited, you know. We just don't grind the printing press to make more."

M. A. ROBINSON: "Look, you fellows are only concerned with the sacred art of matching pennies. I've thoroughly analyzed our proposed $10,000,000 capital expansion program. It's a low risk program. It betters all your benchmarks by any of your fancy schemes: payback, MAPI formula, or rate of return computed by the discounted cash flow method."

J. HUDSON: "Your program may be a worthy one, but it will have to wait at least one year before we can embark on it. If you want to see where our cash came from and where it went in the past year, Mr. Daer can draw up a cash flow statement for you."

M. A. ROBINSON: "No, that isn't necessary. Thirty years ago, as an engineering student in college, I learned the basics of accounting. They still haven't changed: debits are still on the left. I know that 'cash' flows constantly among the various items constituting working capital and other items. I even understand the difference between the cash and the accrual basis of accounting. I've completely analyzed our 1972 statements (attached). We made a profit of $10,000,000 and only paid out $2,000,000 in dividends. Furthermore, we issued additional capital stock during the year. Yet cash goes down and working capital remains almost the same. You number jugglers haven't convinced me that funds are tight."

J. HUDSON: "I can see what is causing the confusion. Now look at our 1972 financial statements while I take ten minutes and prepare a 'where got' and 'where gone' analysis for you. Technically this is known as a source and application of funds statement."

THE VAN DUSEN MANUFACTURING COMPANY
Comparative Balance Sheet

	December 31 1972	December 31 1971
Current Assets:		
Cash	$ 3,000,000	$ 4,000,000
United States Government Bonds, at cost	3,100,000	3,000,000
Accounts Receivable (less estimated doubtful accounts)	22,900,000	19,000,000
Inventories	50,000,000	51,000,000
Prepaid Expenses	1,000,000	1,000,000
Total Current Assets	80,000,000	78,000,000

Less: Current Liabilities:		
Accounts Payable	29,000,000	27,000,000
Accrued Expenses Payable	3,000,000	2,000,000
Estimated Income Taxes Payable	7,000,000	9,000,000
Total Current Liabilities	39,000,000	38,000,000
Net Working Capital	41,000,000	40,000,000
Investments in Foreign Companies, at cost	5,000,000	3,000,000
Property, Plant and Equipment:		
Land	12,000,000	10,000,000
Buildings	40,000,000	35,000,000
Accumulated Depreciation to date ...	18,000,000	17,000,000
	22,000,000	18,000,000
Machinery and Equipment	79,000,000	70,000,000
Accumulated Depreciation to date ...	29,340,000	25,000,000
	49,660,000	45,000,000
Net	83,660,000	73,000,000
Goodwill; and Patents less Amortization to date	900,000	3,000,000
Total Assets, less Current Liabilities	130,560,000	119,000,000
Bonds Payable	17,560,000	21,000,000
Stockholders' Equity	$113,000,000	$ 98,000,000
Stockholders' Equity represented by:		
Capital Stock (Par $100)	$ 40,000,000	$ 35,000,000
Paid-in Surplus	22,000,000	20,000,000
Reinvested Earnings	51,000,000	43,000,000
	$113,000,000	$ 98,000,000

THE VAN DUSEN MANUFACTURING COMPANY
Statement of Income and Retained Earnings
For the Year Ended December 31, 1972

Net Sales		$200,000,000
Cost of Goods Sold		140,000,000
Gross Margin on Sales		60,000,000
Marketing and Administrative Expenses	$31,900,000	
Depreciation of Plant, Machinery and Equipment and Amortization of Patents	7,100,000	39,000,000
Net Operating Income		21,000,000

[CH. 4]   STATEMENT OF SOURCE AND APPLICATION OF FUNDS   93

Other Income:		
Dividends from Foreign Companies ..		2,000,000
		23,000,000
Other Expenses:		
Loss on Disposal of Machinery and Equipment	$ 938,000	
Interest on Bonds Payable	800,000	1,738,000
		21,262,000
Income Taxes		9,262,000
Net Income prior Extraordinary Charges		12,000,000
Write-off of Goodwill		2,000,000
Net Income for the Year		10,000,000
Retained Earnings, January 1, 1972		43,000,000
		53,000,000
Dividends, 1972		2,000,000
Retained Earnings, December 31, 1972 .		$ 51,000,000

Additional analysis discloses:

a. A portion of the long-term debt was retired at par (face) in 1972.

b. The 1972 capital expansion program resulted in acquisitions of land and buildings. No land or buildings were disposed of during 1972. A considerable amount of new machinery and equipment was acquired during 1972; part was for expansion purposes and part was to replace technically obsolete equipment.

c. No patents were acquired or sold during 1972. The patents had a remaining life of 10 years on January 1, 1972, and are being amortized over this life.

d. Goodwill, which had appeared on the balance sheet at a fixed constant amount for several years, was written off in its entirety in 1972, as an extraordinary charge against earnings.

e. Technologically obsolete machinery and equipment was disposed of as follows during 1972:

  1. Machinery and equipment with an unrecovered cost (book "value") of $1,100,000 was sold for $200,000.

  2. Machinery and equipment with an unrecovered cost (book "value") of $40,000 was scrapped; the scrap was sold for $2,000.

f. On January 1, 1969, the company changed its inventory pricing method from FIFO to LIFO. In 1972 alone, it is estimated that this saved the company $1,000,000 in income taxes.

Required

Assume that you are Mr. J. Hudson, Controller. Using the above financial statements and additional supplementary data, prepare a source and application of funds statement for 1972. As a check on the amount of one of the sources of funds, namely the amount provided by operations, determine that amount by both the regular method and the alternative method. Support clearly, by supplementary schedules or calculations, the amount of new machinery and equipment purchased in 1972.

4-9. The letter—with editor's comment thereon—reproduced below is from the November 15, 1962, issue of *FORBES*.[1]

Depreciation

Sir: You mention U.S. corporations dipping into their "depreciation accruals" (*FORBES*, Oct. 1, p. 7) to raise money for plant and equipment.

Your magazine and many other business periodicals consistently make this error. No funds are *provided* by depreciation; the funds had already been expended when the capital asset was acquired.

A greater disservice is being done by statements about funds being provided through depreciation. Some businessmen actually have the impression that the more equipment they purchase, the more funds they will generate as their depreciation climbs.

The fact remains that internal funds—some of it profits, some of it depreciation money—are providing the capital dollars.

—Ed.

Required

In not more than 100 words, reconcile the views of the author of the letter and the editor of *FORBES* with respect to "depreciation provides funds or money."

---

[1] *FORBES* Magazine, November 15, 1962, copyright Forbes Inc., 1962. Used by permission.

5

Measuring Management Performance, Return on Capital, Other Measurements

The primary objective of a private enterprise concern is profit. Management is charged with the responsibility to plan and direct the affairs of a company toward the attainment of this goal.

In Chapter 1, the principal reason expressed for the existence of accounting was the aid it provides to management. Thus, attention should be focused upon the managerial significance of the data provided by the accounting information system which reveals changes and indicates significant developments in the affairs of an enterprise.

One of the functions of the interpretive area of accounting should be the proper appraisal of the results of past business activities for measurement of performance: financial statements and supplementary data should be analyzed for significant relationships to measure performance in relation to the profitability of the enterprise. The aim of any such analytical review is to provide a guide for future actions.

When judging the degree of success or failure of a business, the paramount question is how to measure performance. Traditionally there has been reliance, in varying degrees, on certain time-honored and generally useful financial analyses and ratios like working capital, current ratio, net earnings per share of outstanding stock, rate of profit on stockholders' equity, percent of profit to sales, turnover of inventories, ratio of stockholders' equity to liabilities, and many others. The selection of the measurements to be used often depends upon the category of the individual making the analysis; e.g., stockholder, creditor, financial analyst, plant manager of the company, or director of the corporation. And, all too often, numerical ratios or rates are themselves used as answers for measurement of performance rather than as initiators of further analysis and future planning.

PERCENT OF NET INCOME TO NET SALES

Historically, the percentage margin of profit on sales, expressed as the relationship of the net income to the net sales for the period, has been the ratio most widely employed to measure past performance and to plan future actions. This ratio is computed as follows:

$$\text{Margin Percentage} = \frac{\text{Net Income for the Period}}{\text{Net Sales for the Period}}$$

With rare exceptions, internal reports to management and external reports to stockholders and the public always indicate the percentage margin of profit. For example, the 1970 Annual Report of Caterpillar Tractor Co. contains two pages of "Significant Trends Since Incorporation" (April 15, 1925), which include the following (dollar amounts expressed in millions):

Year	Sales	Profit Amount	% of Sales	Year	Sales	Profit Amount	% of Sales
1925	$ 13.8	$3.3	23.68%	1948	$218.0	$17.5	8.00%
1926	20.7	4.3	20.86	1949	254.9	17.2	6.74
1927	26.9	5.7	21.28	1950	337.3	29.2	8.67
1928	35.1	8.7	24.86	1951	394.3	15.8	4.01
1929	51.8	12.4	23.96	1952	480.8	22.7	4.72
1930	45.4	9.1	20.05	1953	437.8	20.6	4.71
1931	24.1	1.6	6.50	1954	406.7	25.9	6.37
1932	13.3	(1.6)	(12.23)	1955	533.0	36.0	6.76
1933	14.4	.4	2.46	1956	685.9	55.5	8.09
1934	23.8	3.8	15.98	1957	649.9	40.0	6.16
1935	36.4	6.2	17.15	1958	585.2	32.2	5.51
1936	54.1	10.2	18.90	1959	742.3	46.5	6.27
1937	63.2	10.6	16.72	1960	716.0	42.6	5.95
1938	48.2	3.2	6.71	1961	734.3	55.8	7.60
1939	58.4	6.0	10.28	1962	827.0	61.9	7.49
1940	73.1	7.8	10.71	1963	966.1	77.3	8.00
1941	102.0	7.7	7.60	1964	1,216.6	129.1	10.61
1942	142.2	7.0	4.93	1965	1,405.3	158.5	11.28
1943	171.4	7.6	4.42	1966	1,524.0	150.1	9.85
1944	242.2	7.3	3.03	1967	1,472.5	106.4	7.22
1945	230.6	6.5	2.82	1968	1,707.1	121.6	7.12
1946	128.4	6.1	4.76	1969	2,001.6	142.5	7.12
1947	189.1	13.5	7.13	1970	2,127.8	143.8	6.76

[CH. 5] MEASURING MANAGEMENT PERFORMANCE, RETURN ON CAPITAL

Many regard the margin percentage as the key measurement of management's performance. This measurement is important to indicate the spread between revenue and expenses of the period, and it is conceded that without a margin of profit a company "has nothing." But the percent of net income to net sales is not *the* principal measurement of performance. Consider these percentages of profit, based on figures taken from the 1969 annual reports of:

	Percentage of profit (after income tax) on sales
Weyerhaeuser Company (Year Ended December 28, 1969)	10.96%
Procter & Gamble Company (Year Ended June 30, 1969)	6.92%
United States Steel Corporation (Year Ended December 31, 1969)	4.50%
The Kroger Co. (Year Ended December 27, 1969)	1.11%

It is incorrect to conclude from these figures that Weyerhaeuser Company is the most profitable company or that it is about one and one-half times as profitable as Procter & Gamble Company. And it is erroneous to assume that United States Steel Corporation is about four times as profitable as The Kroger Co. These margins of profit disregard the amount of capital employed by each company to produce the volume of sales on which the margin of profit has been earned.

RETURN ON CAPITAL

Used alone, the possible inadequacy of the percentage margin of profit on sales as a measurement of performance may be illustrated by assuming a company with sales of $1,000,000 and a net income of $100,000. On the surface, its 10% margin of profit indicates a highly profitable business. But, if the capital employed in this same company is $2,600,000, the profit on capital employed is only 3.8%, about equal to that earned on a savings account at a bank.

In the determination of return on capital for a business, the term "capital" may not be employed in the usual accounting or financial usage of the word; namely, to indicate the excess of assets over liabilities. From an economic point of view, the use of total assets as the "capital" of a business is more broadly meaningful for measuring the performance of management. It is the *total* assets of a company, not some smaller amount, which are available to management in the operation of a business. Thus, for measuring the performance and effectiveness of management, the total of all assets entrusted to its use appears to be a valid base and return on capital may be computed as follows:

$$\text{Return on Capital} = \frac{\text{Net Income for the Period}}{\text{Total Assets}}$$

Reference to the preceding four companies whose 1969 percentages of profit on sales were cited reveals the following returns on total assets (based on their annual report figures):

	Percentage return (after income tax) on capital (total assets)
Weyerhaeuser Company	8.45%
Procter & Gamble Company	11.07%
United States Steel Corporation	3.31%
The Kroger Co.	5.57%

Though Weyerhaeuser Company had a margin of profit on sales of about one and one-half times that of Procter & Gamble Company, the latter has a return on capital about 30 percent *larger*. And United States Steel Corporation, which had a margin of profit on sales four times that of The Kroger Co., has a rate of return on capital which is about 40 percent *smaller*.

The rate of return on capital depends upon two factors. The first of these, the margin percentage of profit on sales, has been illustrated. The second factor is turnover of capital employed. Using total assets as the capital employed, the turnover of capital employed is determined as follows:

$$\text{Turnover of Capital} = \frac{\text{Net Sales for the Period}}{\text{Total Assets}}$$

The turnover of capital is an indication of management's effectiveness in using the total capital of the business to generate sales volume. In a sense, it indicates how diligently management is working the assets to generate the sales volume. Obviously, as shown by our four illustrative companies, the turnover depends in part upon the type of business.

	Turnover of Capital
Weyerhaeuser Company	.772
Procter & Gamble Company	1.60
United States Steel Corporation	.736
The Kroger Co.	5.02

Both Weyerhaeuser Company and United States Steel Corporation have a capital turnover of less than once a year. But Kroger Co., has a turnover in excess of five times a year.

Before proceeding into the controversial areas embodied in the concept of return on capital, a summary of the pertinent points already discussed is in order. Return on capital, though not a new concept, has been widely accepted by management as a tool for measuring performance. Today, the top managements of many companies feel that performance should be measured by the profit earned on capital employed.

	This performance depends upon:	This performance is measured as follows
	Percentage of profit on sales × Turnover of capital =	Return on Capital
	$\dfrac{\text{Net Income}}{\text{Sales}} \times \dfrac{\text{Sales}}{\text{Total Assets}} =$	$\dfrac{\text{Net Income}}{\text{Total Assets}}$

The rate of return on capital employed may be determined directly, without resort to the two dependent factors, by dividing the profit earned by the capital employed. However, to prevent overlooking the two dependent factors which produce the return on capital, it is advisable to compute separately the percentage of profit on sales and the turnover of capital. Then, the multiplication of these two factors will give the rate of return on capital. The procedure, applied to the four companies, is:

	Percentage of profit on sales	×	Turnover of capital	=	Percentage return on capital
Weyerhaeuser Co.	10.96%	×	.772	=	8.45%
Procter & Gamble Co.	6.92%	×	1.60	=	11.07%
U.S. Steel Corp.	4.50%	×	.736	=	3.31%
The Kroger Co.	1.11%	×	5.02	=	5.57%

It must be remembered that different types of businesses cannot be validly compared on a single basis, like percentage of profit on sales or turnover of capital. Return on capital, the result of both factors, is the common denominator necessary for comparative purposes, since it equitably compares a company which has a high profit margin on sales and low turnover, with another which has a low margin on sales but a high turnover. The concept of return on capital employed uses sales, capital, and profit to provide an index to a company's performance.

Today, many single companies are diversified to the extent that their range of items sold is almost as varied as if our four illustrative companies were in reality only one company with four separate divisions selling timber, soap, steel, and food. For example, in 1970, PPG Industries, Inc. had the following distribution of its net sales: glass 42 percent, chemicals 29 percent, coatings and resins 22 percent, fiber glass 6 percent, and other 1 percent. As a result, return on capital has become a prime tool or common denominator for measuring and comparing performance by product lines, divisions, and plants within a company. Where decentralization of management and operations allows each division, plant, or product line to be treated as if it were a separate business, it is not uncommon to find year-end bonuses based on the performance of individual segments of the business, with performance measured by the return on capital employed.

Return on Capital—Illustrative Case

Using the financial statements for Holliday Corporation, an assumed company, the complexities involved in the determination of a rate of return on capital employed may be clearly illustrated.

HOLLIDAY CORPORATION
Statement of Income
For the Years Ended December 31, 1972 and 1971

	1972	1971
Net Sales	$29,000,000	$25,000,000
Cost of Goods Sold	19,000,000	16,000,000
Gross Margin on Sales	$10,000,000	$ 9,000,000
Selling, General, Administrative Expenses	7,000,000	6,400,000
Net Operating Income	$ 3,000,000	$ 2,600,000
Other Income:		
Interest Income	17,000	16,000
Other Charges:		
Interest on Long-term Debt	(90,000)	(90,000)
Net Income prior Income Taxes	$ 2,927,000	$ 2,526,000
Income Taxes	1,427,000	1,226,000
Net Income for the Year	$ 1,500,000	$ 1,300,000

Note: Depreciation included in costs and expenses amounted to $600,000 in 1972 and $550,000 in 1971.

Determination of the Capital Base (Denominator)

Total Assets vs. Other Bases. The amount of capital, the base on which the rate of return is calculated, is usually the total assets of a company. On Decem-

Holliday Corporation—Summary Balance Sheet

Various Assets	$15,000,000	Current Liabilities	$ 3,000,000
		Long-term Debt	3,000,000
		Stockholders' Equity	9,000,000
	$15,000,000		$15,000,000

Competitor Corporation—Summary Balance Sheet

Various Assets	$15,000,000	Current Liabilities	$ 3,000,000
		Long-term Debt	—0—
		Stockholders' Equity	12,000,000
	$15,000,000		$15,000,000

HOLLIDAY CORPORATION
Balance Sheet
December 31, 1972 and 1971

ASSETS	1972	1971
Current Assets		
Cash	$ 350,000	$ 400,000
U.S. Government and Other Marketable Securities	500,000	550,000
Accounts Receivable	2,400,000	2,200,000
Inventories (LIFO basis)	2,500,000	2,400,000
Prepaid Expenses	50,000	50,000
Total Current Assets	$ 5,800,000	$ 5,600,000
Property, Plant and Equipment		
Buildings and Equipment (cost)	$12,200,000	$11,300,000
Less: Accumulated Depreciation to Date	4,700,000	4,200,000
	$ 7,500,000	$ 7,100,000
Land (cost)	1,100,000	1,000,000
Construction in Progress	600,000	300,000
Total Property, Plant and Equipment	$ 9,200,000	$ 8,400,000
Total Assets	$15,000,000	$14,000,000

LIABILITIES	1972	1971
Current Liabilities		
Accounts Payable	$ 1,100,000	$ 1,200,000
Accrued Wages and Salaries	200,000	150,000
Income Taxes Payable	1,100,000	850,000
Miscellaneous Payables	600,000	300,000
Total Current Liabilities	$ 3,000,000	$ 2,500,000
Long-term Debt		
Debentures, Due May 1, 1985	3,000,000	3,000,000
Total Liabilities	$ 6,000,000	$ 5,500,000
STOCKHOLDERS' EQUITY		
Capital Stock, $10 par value Authorized 500,000 shares Outstanding 300,000 shares	$ 3,000,000	$ 3,000,000
Capital Contribution in Excess of Par	1,000,000	1,000,000
Reinvested Earnings	5,000,000	4,500,000
Total Stockholders' Equity	$ 9,000,000	$ 8,500,000
Total Equities	$15,000,000	$14,000,000

Note: The last-in, first-out basis of stating inventories was adopted by the company on January 1, 1955. Accordingly, the carrying value of these inventories was approximately $1,500,000 below current replacement cost at December 31, 1972, and $1,400,000 below current replacement cost at December 31, 1971.

ber 31, 1972, the balance sheets of both Holliday Corporation and Competitor Corporation show that the management of each company has $15,000,000 of total capital or assets for use in business operations. Though the balance sheets show that the financial policies of the two companies differ on the utilization of sources of funds to raise capital, the fact remains that the management of each company has the same amount of total capital to use in the operation of the business. While these financial policies are vital factors in the long-run stability of the company and the return accruing to the stockholders, return on capital employed measures performance of management in everything entrusted to its control, namely total assets, regardless of the source of the assets. Thus, though the stockholders of both companies may be interested in the earnings based on the respective $9,000,000 and $12,000,000 investments, and though creditors, bankers, and financial analysts may be interested in the respective 1:1:3 and 1:0:4 ratios of current debt to long-term debt to stockholders' equity, the performance of each company's management should be judged according to the profit earned on the $15,000,000 of capital available to each. The business manager should be measured in terms of the yield earned on that total capital irrespective of the source of the resources, be it from equity of owners, by long-term debt, or through current liabilities. The accompanying table from a study of forty-two companies which use return on capital to measure past performance confirms this assertion by showing that 32 of them base rate of return on assets.[1]

Table 5-1

Investment Base Use in Evaluating Past Performance for a Company as a Whole

Investment Base	Number of Companies Reporting Use of Each Base
Total assets available	28
Total assets employed (i.e., excess or idle assets eliminated)	4
Stockholders' equity plus long-term debt	6
Stockholders' equity	7
Total	45

Note: The total exceeds the number of companies interviewed because some companies use more than one base for computing rate of return.

Average Total Assets. Because a balance sheet indicates total assets as of a given instant, many companies use some method of averaging total assets to obtain the capital base. An averaging procedure lessens the effect caused by an

---

[1] National Association of Accountants Research Report No. 35, *Return on Capital as a Guide to Managerial Decisions* (New York, 1959), p. 8.

unusual event which might temporarily distort total assets. Likewise, the period-end total asset amount includes the effect of the current period's profit not distributed as dividends; averaging will reduce the factor of attempting to earn profit this period on a porton of this period's profit. Also, whenever return on assets is used internally to measure management performance at the plant or divisional level, the use of other than a year or month-end amount will lessen the temptation of the local manager to improve temporarily his rate of return by some unsound method of decreasing the asset base as of a given moment.

The limited financial information given for Holliday Corporation permits a simple average of assets as of the beginning and end of 1972. Such an average, $14,500,000 in this case, theoretically appears more valid for a capital base than does the midnight December 31, 1972, amount of $15,000,000. For internal reporting, management would have month-end and quarter-end total asset amounts available for determining an average total asset base. As the base against which to measure earnings at each division and plant monthly, one company, for example, uses a progressing two-month to thirteen-month average of the assets at each location for the months of January through December each year.

Omission of Specific Assets from Capital Base. In certain instances, management may deem it appropriate to remove specific assets from the total asset amount to arrive at a more realistic capital base against which to measure the profit earned for the period. Thus, if the management of Holliday Corporation believes that performance should be measured by the profit earned on the assets *used,* the temporarily idle capital tied up in construction in progress could be removed in the determination of average total assets. In this case, the average capital base would be $14,050,000, as follows:

$$\text{Average Assets Used} = \frac{(\$15,000,000 - 600,000) + (14,000,000 - 300,000)}{2}$$

This procedure recognizes that nothing can be earned on this asset until the plant is completed and in operation.

An additional complicating factor involved in the determination of an equitable capital base occurs when one of the company's assets is an investment in foreign subsidiaries. Consider the case of ABC Company, with assets in excess of $300,000,000 and annual profits in excess of $30,000,000, which has shown the accompanying information for wholly owned foreign subsidiaries during the past six years. By December 31, 1973, the balance sheet asset at cost has increased $2,000,000, because added investments have been made in the foreign subsidiaries. The equity of ABC Company in these same subsidiaries on December 31, 1973, exceeds cost by $1,100,000, since that amount of earnings has not been "withdrawn" in the form of dividends. Though exactly 50% of such earnings have been distributed to the parent company over a six-year period, by individual years the percentage has been 33⅓ percent, 25 percent, 12½ percent, 200 percent, 66⅔ percent, and 10 percent. Thus, total assets per the balance sheet (as of a specific date) include only the cost of this particular asset, and the final profit earned by ABC Company for a par-

	BALANCE SHEET ASSET	STATEMENT OF INCOME	NOTE TO FINANCIAL STATEMENTS	
	"Investment in Wholly Owned Foreign Subsidiaries, at Cost"	"Dividends Received from Wholly Owned Foreign Subsidiaries"	Equity in Foreign Subsidiaries	Earnings of Foreign Subsidiaries
1968	$3,000,000	$ 100,000	$3,200,000	$ 300,000
1969	3,000,000	100,000	3,500,000	400,000
1970	3,500,000	50,000	4,350,000	400,000
1971	4,000,000	600,000	4,550,000	300,000
1972	4,500,000	200,000	5,150,000	300,000
1973	5,000,000	50,000	6,100,000	500,000
		$1,100,000		$2,200,000

ticular year is influenced by the dividends received rather than actual earnings. To determine the rate of return on capital employed for ABC Company as a whole, this inequity is usually handled by one of three procedures. The first of these is to do nothing and use the figures exactly as shown by the balance sheet and the statement of income. The usual arguments advanced for this approach are that the amounts involved are usually immaterial to the totals; and that the more the actual figures are modified or changed, the less their reliability in the minds of those whose performance is being measured. A second method is to eliminate the cost of the asset from the capital employed denominator and remove the dividend income from the profit earned numerator. Those supporting this procedure state that it will more fairly evaluate performance of two completely unlike operations, foreign and domestic. Furthermore, relative instability is inherent in many foreign investments because of fluctuating foreign currency rates, exchange restrictions, and possible expropriation of U.S. foreign subsidiaries. The third alternative is to adjust the total assets by replacing the cost of the investment with the equity amount and modifying the profit earned by substituting the earnings of the subsidiaries for the dividends received.[2] This procedure is an attempt to appraise performance on a more current worth basis than on a cost basis. The greater the materiality of the dollar amounts involved, the greater the deliberation management should give to the situation to appraise fairly the performance of the company as a whole.

Reference to Table 5–1 will show six companies which use stockholders' equity plus long-term debt for the capital base. In effect, capital employed in such cases is total assets minus current liabilities. On this point, the N.A.A. study states:

> The six companies using equity plus long-term debt as their investment base reason that, since current liabilities are temporary in nature,

---

[2] Dated March 1971, Accounting Principles Board Opinion No. 18, titled *The Equity Method of Accounting for Investments in Common Stock,* recommends the equity method of presentation in the financial statements.

management should not be expected to earn a return on assets supplied by short-term creditors.[3]

Valid as such reasoning may be, the theory which holds management responsible for earning a return only on current assets in excess of current liabilities is somewhat at odds with the concept that management's performance should be judged on all capital entrusted to its control. However, any business using such a base for capital employed will find itself in accord with the method of General Motors Corporation, Armco Steel Corporation, and Westinghouse Electric Corporation. Some companies use more than one base for computing rate of return; General Motors, for example, in addition to calculating the rate of return on total assets minus current liabilities, calculates the rate of return on total assets.

Addition of Specific "Assets" to Capital Base. In certain instances, it may be necessary to add "missing assets" to the total asset amount already shown to arrive at an equitable base for capital employed in the business. A distorted and unrealistic rate of return may occur in the case of a company which does not own, but instead leases, a portion of its tangible fixed assets. At present, under generally accepted accounting, usually only assets *owned* appear on the balance sheet; usually disclosure of *rented* property is shown by a note to the financial statements.[4] Thus, when a company leases a considerable amount of its fixed assets, either the total asset amount used as capital employed must be increased to show a realistic rate of return on a company-wide basis, or some discount factor must be applied to a rate predicated upon an abnormally low asset base. The problem is far more critical when comparative performance of management is attempted on a plant-by-plant basis. For example, divisional statements may show that Plant A owns $10,000,000 of tangible fixed assets, whereas Plant B, of comparable capacity and producing the same product, owns only $2,000,000 of tangible fixed assets and rents the remainder under long-term leases. Direct comparison of the profits earned on the capital employed for both plants is impossible unless an adjustment is made to the divisional balance sheet of Plant B for the assets it uses but does not own; no method of adjustment satisfactory to all has yet been developed. One method used, as reported in the N.A.A. study, is:

> Where, as is often the case, lease arrangements are merely forms of borrowing, some companies capitalize the interest factor imputed in rental payments to develop a capital value for inclusion in rate of return calculations.[5]

---

[3] *Ibid.*, p. 9. Copyright © 1971 by the American Institute of Certified Public Accountants, Inc.

[4] Under certain circumstances a rented asset is included among the tangible fixed assets of a company. This can occur when the lease agreement is in reality an installment purchase contract. See Chapter 7.

[5] N.A.A. Research Report No. 35, *Return on Capital as a Guide to Managerial Decisions*, p. 11.

A variation of this same procedure would be to capitalize as an asset, with an offsetting liability, the present value of future payments to be made under long-term leases. In any case, those in management should be cognizant of the possible distortion in rates of return when attempting to evaluate performance of a plant which leases a portion of its assets. Some companies, for example, include all purchased *and* leased assets in the base to arrive at total assets used in the business by various divisions.

Adjustment of Specific Assets in the Capital Base. It is possible that the effect on a particular company's capital employed base of the factors mentioned in the preceding sections may be minor in comparison to the effect caused by inequities in the valuations used for the property, plant, and equipment owned. Consider the amount shown by the balance sheet of Holliday Corporation on page 101 in this chapter. Should the base amount of capital employed in the business reflect the buildings and equipment at their depreciated cost of $7,500,000 as of December 31, 1972, or at some other amount? These amounts

Buildings and Equipment (cost)	$12,200,000
Less: Accumulated Depreciation to date	4,700,000
	$ 7,500,000

include fixed assets and their accumulated depreciation to date in all types of dollars, dependent upon when the assets were acquired. In addition, the amount shown for accumulated depreciation to date may reflect the effect of accelerated depreciation.[6] Therefore, it may be extremely difficult to determine an equitable dollar amount for the property, plant, and equipment in the total assets of $15,000,000 shown by the balance sheet in the determination of a capital employed base.

The non-comparability of similar items is extremely critical when the rate of return for one plant or division of the company is compared against another. For example, the figures above may include a building constructed for Division A of Holliday Corporation in early 1948 at a cost of $1,000,0000 and a building of identical type and size constructed in early 1968 for Division B at an inflated cost of $3,000,000. Assume that each building, when constructed, had an estimated useful life of 50 years and that straight-line depreciation is used. The balance sheet prepared as of December 31, 1972, will reflect, among Division A's various assets, a building which has been depreciated $20,000 annually ($1,000,000 cost ÷ 50 years) for the past 25 years. Total assets of Division A will include a $500,000 building." On the other hand, the balance sheet as of this same date for Division B will reflect, among that division's total assets, a building which has been depreciated $60,000 annually ($3,000,000 ÷ 50 years) for the past five years. Total assets of Division B will include a $2,700,000 building," a figure 5⅖ times larger than that for Division A. Not only will the denominator—capital employed—be disappor-

---

[6] A detailed analysis of the various methods of depreciation is presented in Chapter 6, and the effect of a changing price level is discussed in Chapter 7.

tionately higher for Division B, but the numerator—profit earned—will reflect a charge for three times as much depreciation expense. If divisional managerial performance is measured by the profit earned on the capital employed and no adjustment is made for the above distortions, obviously Division A is the place to work.

DIVISION A—HOLLIDAY CORPORATION
Balance Sheet
December 31, 1972

ASSETS

Cash		$ xxxxxxxx
Accounts Receivable		xxxxxxxx
Inventories (LIFO basis)		xxxxxxxx
Property, Plant and Equipment:		
Building, at cost	$1,000,000	
Less: Accumulated Depreciation to date ($20,000 × 25 years)	500,000	500,000
Other plant & equipment items, net of accumulated depreciation		xxxxxxxx
Total Assets		$x + 500,000

DIVISION B—HOLLIDAY CORPORATION
Balance Sheet
December 31, 1972

ASSETS

Cash		$ xxxxxxxx
Accounts Receivable		xxxxxxxx
Inventories (LIFO basis)		xxxxxxxx
Property, Plant and Equipment:		
Building, at cost	$3,000,000	
Less: Accumulated Depreciation to date ($60,000 × 5 years)	300,000	2,700,000
Other plant & equipment items, net of accumulated depreciation		xxxxxxxx
Total Assets		$x + 2,700,000

To compensate for such inequities, three possible courses of action will be suggested. The first of these is to do nothing with the dollar amounts based upon original cost: use the figures exactly as shown by the divisional balance sheets, then compensate for inequities by recognizing that divisions like A and B, though producing the same product by the same process, cannot possibly earn the same rate of return. One method of such compensation establishes different target rates of return for Divisions A and B. This first course of action, using fixed assets in the capital base on an "as is" basis of original cost less accumulated depreciation thereon, is the method at present employed by Armstrong Cork Company and Westinghouse Electric Corporation. A strong argument for such a procedure, though directed at company rather than divisional level as previously shown, is the following statement by I. Wayne Keller, former Vice President of Armstrong Cork Company:

> Personal experience has demonstrated that, where assets reflected in the published financial statements are used as the capital employed at the company level, there is a ready acceptance of the figure. When other values are used, confusion is created which detracts from the true purpose of effective use of the ratios.[7]

Keller continues:

> The prime danger in departing from the published financial statements is that management time, which should be devoted to holding and improving the ratios, will be diverted to attacks upon the validity of the amount of capital used in determining the ratios.[8]

Note that these statements argue against *any* modification of the actual conventional accounting figures. Admitting the validity of Keller's point, it is difficult to believe that, if it were applied at the divisional or plant level, there would not be as much confusion among the plant managers as to why they need not obtain identical rates of return.

A second possible remedy for distortion is to include all fixed asset amounts in the capital base at replacement value. For example, one company using this method developed a series of index numbers with the period 1947–1949 equal to 100. Then the fixed assets at each division were listed by year of acquisition and converted to common like-type dollars by index numbers. The N.A.A. study indicates that two of the 42 companies in its report make adjustments for changing price levels.

> One of these companies revalues its fixed assets by use of currently published indexes of construction prices in an attempt to approximate replacement cost. The other company uses such indexes in addition to insurance figures.[9]

While this method of adjusting fixed assets provides for equalization of dollar values, it makes no provision for older facilities and equipment that may be less efficient and require greater maintenance expense. And, though most index numbers move in a somewhat common direction, there is always an argument over the validity of the particular index number(s) used for any such adjust-

---

[7] I. Wayne Keller, "The Return on Capital Concept," *N.A.A. Bulletin* (March, 1958), p. 15.
[8] *Ibid.*, p. 17.
[9] N.A.A. Research Report No. 35, *Return on Capital as a Guide to Managerial Decisions*, p. 11.

ment. Because of rapidly changing prices during the past 20 years, it may be more equitable to adjust fixed assets by index numbers, imperfect as the method may be, than to do nothing.

A third method of modifying the fixed asset amounts is to add back the accumulated depreciation to date; i.e., include the fixed assets in the capital base at original cost, rather than cost less accumulated depreciation to date. Thus, the capital employed base for Division A of Holliday Corporation would include the building at $1,000,000 (rather than $500,000), and the capital base for Division B would include the building at $3,000,000 (rather than $2,700,000). The buildings would then be in the respective divisional capital bases in a 1 to 3 ratio, rather than the former 1 to 5⅖ ratio. There are three predominate arguments advanced for such a procedure. First, it is a rough adjustment for the changing value of the dollar, and it provides some equalization between older plants constructed at relatively low cost and newer plants built at high cost. While the newer plants still appear to be penalized to some degree (e.g., the 1 to 3 ratio in Divisions A and B for identical buildings), the newer plant should be more efficient and require less maintenance expense. The second argument for including fixed assets in the base at gross (original cost) is that the conventional accounting procedure of writing down such assets by periodic depreciation is intended to amortize the cost of the fixed assets systematically and has little to do with any change in the efficiency of such assets. Regardless of the portion of original cost amortized, a 25 year old building is nearly as efficient for production as one five years old. A seven year old turret lathe is relatively efficient compared to one a year old; otherwise, action should be taken to replace the seven year old lathe. And a new truck will not deliver the goods any better or faster than a three year old truck kept in a proper state of repair and maintenance. The third argument is more subtle in its implications. Because floor space is one of the most costly operating factors in business today, the inclusion of the fixed assets in the capital base at cost attempts to force the divisional manager to get rid of "junk." For example, consider the equipment and machinery portion of the fixed assets per the balance sheet of Division A:

Equipment and Machinery at cost	$2,100,000	
Less: Accumulated Depreciation to date	1,100,000	$1,000,000

Included is a fully depreciated 15 year old drill press which had originally cost $100,000. Thus, the above amounts include:

Drill press, at cost	$ 100,000	
Less: Accumulated Depreciation to date	100,000	$ –0–

Though it was replaced two years ago by a new, modern, more efficient piece of equipment, the old drill press still stands idly in one corner of the plant "just in case" or because "you never know." After all, it is fully depreciated. Thus, it is not costing anything—only valuable floor space! The add-back of accumulated depreciation to date means that the division manager must measure his profit earned against a capital base which includes the original $100,000 cost of the old drill press, or dispose of it. Among companies which, for various reasons, include fixed assets at original cost in the capital employed base is E. I. duPont de Nemours & Company.

An additional asset, inventories, may merit consideration in the determination of an equitable capital base. This is especially the case if the company has been on LIFO for some time. For example, the balance sheet on page 101 in this chapter indicates that if Holliday Corporation had not adopted LIFO, the December 31, 1972, amount for inventories would be $4,000,000 instead of $2,500,000. When measuring performance, management should be charged with earning on the $4,000,000 current cost of the inventories, rather than on a lower figure resulting from a change in an accounting method 20 years ago.

In summary, the points made in the preceding five sections indicate that judgment must be used to decide whether to include, exclude, or modify certain assets or their stated amounts in the determination of an equitable capital base. In part, the materiality of amount is a factor. The particular uses to be made of the measure of performance must be considered. And consistency should be maintained to minimize any charge of "number juggling."

Determination of the Profit Earned (Numerator)

The determination of the amount of profit earned, the numerator with which the rate of return is calculated, is subject to many judgmental factors. Reference is again made to the financial statements of Holliday Corporation; specifically, the statement of income on page 100. Consider whether the "profit earned" should be viewed as:

> Net income for the year ($1,500,000 per the statement of income),
> Net income prior income taxes ($2,927,000),
> Net operating income ($3,000,000), or
> Some other meaure of profit earned.

Conventional accounting fairly presents the fact that Holliday Corporation has a net profit of $1,500,000 for 1972. This is the resultant amount based on overall performance of the company. And, if the rate of return of Holliday Corporation is to be measured against that of Competitor Corporation or that of the industry as a whole, a numerator of $1,500,000 as the profit earned appears equitable. From this point of view, profit after all income and expense factors (including income taxes) is a fair measure of profit earned. Basically, all companies are subject to the same tax rates in a given period.

However, if Holliday Corporation intends to compare its overall performance in 1972 with that of preceding years, it may be more equitable to use a profit earned amount which is not influenced by changing tax laws and tax rates. The effect of changing tax laws and rates, over which management has no control, may be illustrated from the following information selected from the annual reports of Armstrong Cork Company:

[CH. 5] MEASURING MANAGEMENT PERFORMANCE, RETURN ON CAPITAL 111

FROM ANNUAL REPORTS[10]

Representative Years	Earnings before income taxes	Income taxes	Net Earnings	Income taxes as % of earnings before tax
1970	$31,563,000	$13,750,000	$17,750,000	43.6%
1968	69,241,000	34,350,000	34,891,000	49.6%
1965	63,693,000	30,000,000	33,693,000	47.1%
1963	55,162,000	28,100,000	27,062,000	50.9%
1961	37,331,012	18,825,000	18,506,012	50.4%
1956	27,020,380	13,700,000	13,320,380	50.7%
1951	18,648,831	10,119,231	8,529,600	54.3%
1947	15,803,429	6,154,837	9,648,592	38.9%
1944	11,763,658	7,544,660	4,218,998	64.1%
1939	5,470,006	1,029,812	4,440,194	18.8%

These figures reflect fairly constant federal income tax *rates* (approximately 48 percent to 52 percent) since the excess profits tax was repealed on January 1, 1954. However, these *dollar* amounts for income taxes have been affected by changing federal provisions for such items as depreciation, the investment credit, and tax surcharges for several of the years from 1954 to date, as well as by changes in foreign income tax laws and rates. Also, the amounts for any one year could be distorted due to various other factors, such as the extensive production interruptions which occurred in 1970. Note the effect of the excess profits tax during World War II (e.g., 1944) and again during the Korean War (e.g., 1951). In between these two wars—"the good old days"—the prevailing tax rate was approximately 38 percent. And, prior to 1940, income taxes were a comparatively small cost of doing business. Thus, it is evident why some companies, in measuring the performance of management on a comparative basis, prefer to use a profit earned amount which is prior to income taxes. If this is the preference of the management of Holliday Corporation, a profit earned amount of $2,927,000 may better measure those factors which are under the control of management.

Theoretically, if rate of return is based upon total assets, interest expense should not be deducted when determining the profit earned numerator. In this respect, interest expense is a payment to creditors who have supplied short-term and/or long-term capital, just as dividends are distributions to the owners who have supplied capital. Should this concept be utilized by Holliday Corpora-

---

[10] As mentioned in Chapter 3, in any specific year, net income for tax purposes usually differs from net income for accounting purposes. And over the years, both accounting principles and tax laws have changed. But the above figures are sufficiently representative to illustrate the effect of increasing and decreasing tax rates.

tion, a profit earned of $3,017,000 before income taxes and interest on debt should be measured against total assets employed.

When return on capital is used for measuring the performance of management in the *operation* of the business, the best measure of profit earned may be the net operating income. For 1972, Holliday Corporation had a $3,000,000 net income from operations; i.e., from the production and sale of its products. For Holliday Corporation, this procedure would exclude the other income item of interest earned during the year. Consideration also should be given to the exclusion of the asset, the securities on which the interest was earned, from the asset base. Consistency should be maintained in the determinations of "capital" and "income."

In the determination of the profit earned numerator, there is much to recommend the exclusion of non-recurring items which may occasionally appear as Other Income or Other Charges or as Extraordinary Gains or Losses. For example, a gain on the disposal of plant and equipment items is unrelated to the basic purpose for which a business is operated. And a casualty loss attributable to a flood or fire is outside the normal operations of the usual company. Such non-operating income and expense items should not be permitted to distort a measure of operating performance.

SUMMARY—RETURN ON CAPITAL

Normally, profits do not just happen, but are the result of operations properly planned. Management needs proper criteria for appraising past operations and planning future operations; in recent years, management has come to rely rather heavily upon return on capital for the common denominator to measure effectiveness of past operations so that intelligent decisions can be made with respect to future operations.

The calculation of a numerical rate of return on capital does not provide an "answer." Investigation and analysis of the causes of the calculated numerical rate is vital if the tool is to be useful. In the final analysis, return on capital can be improved only by management action to increase sales volume, decrease costs, reduce or minimize assets employed, or some combination of these three factors.

In recent years, the increased size and the widely diversified operations of many companies have resulted in a trend toward a decentralized form of business organization. Thus, performance of management in terms of profit responsibility has also been localized, and return on capital has assumed increasing importance as a method of measuring performance at the divisional, plant, or product-line level. Therefore, in addition to the basic problems concerning which assets to include in the base, how to value these assets, and how to determine net income, there is the added problem of equitably allocating certain assets to the divisions, plants, or product lines. For example, should the capital invested in a headquarters office building be allocated to the divi-

[CH. 5]   MEASURING MANAGEMENT PERFORMANCE, RETURN ON CAPITAL   113

sions, and if so, how?[11] In principle, the problem of equitable allocation of common assets to divisions is the same as the equitable allocation of common costs and expenses to divisions, plants, and the departments within a plant.[12]

In this chapter, the discussion of return on capital has concerned only the appraisal of past operating performance. This performance may be measured at the company level, division or plant level, and by product lines. Evaluations of such performance may be made by comparisons with competitor companies, industry-wide statistics, with all businesses as a whole, and with the company's own predetermined goals. All of this should aid the planning of future actions. In Chapter 18, return on capital will be discussed as a tool for capital planning which appraises proposed acquisitions of capital assets.

OTHER MEASUREMENTS

Many specific ratios and measurements may be determined from an analysis of financial statements. Most accounting principles texts contain a chapter on statement analysis, and there are several books devoted entirely to this area; such sources are replete with the determination and significance of various ratios and measurement devices. However, the majority of these measurements deal with specific segments of the basic return on capital formula. The common segmented ratios and measurements are listed below under the appropriate portion of the return on capital formula. Each of these measurements will be illustrated using the financial statements of Holliday Corporation on pages 100 and 101. Though the overall rate of return on total assets contains the detailed measurements and ratios discussed below, the analysis of component factors aids the determination of why the overall rate is a given amount.

RETURN ON CAPITAL		
Percentage of net profit on sales ×	Turnover of capital =	Return on capital
Related segmented measurements		
(1) Percentage of gross margin on sales	(1) Turnover of receivables	(1) Return on stockholders' equity and the leverage factor
(2) Percentage of operating profit on sales	(2) Turnover of inventory	

---

[11] For a discussion of methods used in practice, the following two reports published by the National Association of Accountants are recommended: N.A.A. Research Report No. 35, *Return on Capital as a Guide to Managerial Decisions*, Chapter 4; N.A.A. Accounting Practice Report No. 14, *Experience with Return on Capital to Appraise Management Performance*, pp. 11–14.

[12] See Chapters 12 and 13 for the allocation of common manufacturing costs.

Percentage of Profit

The percentage of net profit for the year on sales (5.17%) measures the rate of return on net sales after all costs and expenses. In effect, each $1.00 of

$$\frac{\text{Net Income for the Year}}{\text{Net Sales}} = \frac{\$\ 1,500,000}{\$29,000,000} = 5.17\%$$

net sales produced approximately $.05 of profit. All other profit percentages are segments of this overall profitability ratio.

The percentage of gross margin on sales (34.48%) measures the relationship of gross margin to net sales. In effect, each $1.00 of net sales represents

$$\frac{\text{Gross Margin on Sales}}{\text{Net Sales}} = \frac{\$10,000,000}{\$29,000,000} = 34.48\%$$

a recovery of the cost of the goods sold of approximately $.65½ and produces a gross margin of $.34½ to cover operating expenses and provide net income.

The percentage of operating profit on sales (10.34%) measures the basic profitability of sales, Holliday Corporation's primary purpose in business.

$$\frac{\text{Net Operating Profit}}{\text{Net Sales}} = \frac{\$\ 3,000,000}{\$29,000,000} = 10.34\%$$

This ratio excludes the effect of the somewhat unrelated items of other income and other charges.

Turnover

Turnover of capital, with capital defined as total assets, was discussed and illustrated beginning on page 97 in this chapter. The turnover of average total assets, unadjusted for any of the reasons previously discussed, was twice for Holliday Corporation during the year 1972.

$$\frac{\text{Net Sales}}{\text{Average Total Assets per books}} = \frac{\$29,000,000}{\$14,500,000} = 2\ \text{times}$$

Usually, all other turnover figures in general use by companies for analysis are segments of this overall turnover figure.

The turnover of accounts receivable, nine times in 1972, is determined by dividing the net credit sales (total net sales of $29,000,000 minus cash sales

$$\frac{\text{Net Sales on credit}}{\text{Average Accounts Receivable}} = \frac{\$20,700,000}{\$\ 2,300,000} = 9\ \text{times}$$

of $8,300,000) by the average accounts receivable. In this illustration only the amount of accounts receivable at the beginning and end of the year were available; a more representative average could be computed by using month-end balances. The turnover figure is a measure of the liquidity of receivables. A turnover of nine times means that the accounts receivable as of a given date will be collected in approximately one and one-third months. The usual ex-

[CH. 5] MEASURING MANAGEMENT PERFORMANCE, RETURN ON CAPITAL   115

pression of the average collection period is in days, in this case approximately 41 days, computed as follows:

$$\frac{\text{Average Accounts Receivable}}{\text{Net Sales on credit}} \times \text{Number of Days in period}^{13} = \frac{\$2,300,000}{\$20,700,000} \times 366 = 41 \text{ days}$$

The turnover of inventories, assuming that Holliday Corporation is a merchandising concern and not a manufacturer, would be computed by dividing the cost of the merchandise sold by the average inventory at cost. However, the "cost" of these two items is not comparable for Holliday Corporation. Because the inventories are on a LIFO basis, their amounts are stated in somewhat ancient costs; the cost of goods sold amount basically represents current costs. To secure a realistic inventory turnover figure for Holliday Corporation, one should use similar "costs," which is possible in this case because of the footnote to the balance sheet (see page 101). The inventory turnover of almost five times a year, computed below, means that the company has sold and

$$\frac{\text{Cost of Goods Sold}}{\text{Average Inventories at replacement cost}} = \frac{\$19,000,000}{\tfrac{1}{2}(\$4,000,000 + \$3,800,000)} = 4.87 \text{ times}$$

replaced its overall average inventory almost five times a year.

Return

Return on capital was discussed and illustrated beginning with page 97 of this chapter. Recognizing all the limitations subsequently mentioned concerning the data to be used in such a calculation, it is assumed that Holliday Corporation computed its rate of return on capital as follows:

$$\frac{\text{Net Income for the Year}}{\text{Average Total Assets}} = \frac{\$1,500,000}{\$14,500,000} = 10.35\%$$

The return of 10.35% for 1972 represents rate of profit earned on all of the capital available for use by management.

From the view of the stockholders of the company, the rate of return on only the stockholders' equity is of primary interest. Based upon the financial statements on pages 100 and 101, the rate of return on stockholders' equity (17.14% for 1972) is determined by dividing the net income for the year by the average stockholders' equity.

$$\frac{\text{Net Income for the Year}}{\text{Average Stockholders' Equity}} = \frac{\$1,500,000}{\$8,750,000} = 17.14\%$$

From the overall viewpoint of measuring the management's performance, this particular measurement is limited, because it measures profit against only a portion of the total capital used. The rate of return on stockholders' invest-

---

[13] Number of days in the period, in this case the year 1972.

ment, while of prime concern to groups like investors, is of limited overall use, because it is only a segment of the total; it is more akin to a measurement of financial management than to a measurement of the management based on operations of the company. This may be seen more clearly when it is realized that Holliday Corporation is trading on the equity. Trading on the equity occurs whenever a business finances a portion of the total assets owned with sources of funds other than those provided by the equity of common stockholders. These additional sources of funds are principally of three types:

1. Preferred stock with a fixed dividend rate (Holliday Corporation has not issued preferred stock.)
2. Long-term debt with a limited return (Holliday Corporation issued $3,000,000 of debentures due in 1985.)
3. Short-term debt with a limited or no return (Holliday Corporation had $2,500,000 of current liabilities as of December 31, 1971, and $3,000,000 of such short-term debt as of December 31, 1972. Since none of this debt includes interest bearing notes payable, the assets provided by such funds are employed without cost to Holliday Corporation.)

If the cost for use of such funds is less than the return their use earns for the common stockholders, the leverage factor is favorable; a reverse situation would indicate unfavorable leverage. In the case of Holliday Corporation, the leverage factor is favorable: the return on the average stockholders' equity is 17.14%, while the return on average total assets is 10.35%. This is attributable to the leverage factor, the ratio of assets to stockholders' equity (1.658), computed as follows:

$$\frac{\text{Assets (average)}}{\text{Stockholders' Equity (average)}} = \frac{\$14,500,000}{\$ 8,750,000} = 1.658$$

The leverage factor of 1.658 times the return on assets of 10.35% equals the return on stockholders' equity of 17.14%.

SIGNIFICANCE OF MEASUREMENTS AND RATIOS

Any measurement or ratio is meaningless unless it is analyzed for cause and related to other relevant data.

Much data is available for comparison; for example, Dun & Bradstreet, Inc., annually publishes 14 ratios for many lines of business. If Holliday Corporation were a paper box and container manufacturer, it could compare its yearly and five-year averages with those published by this source. A rate of net profit on net sales for 1969 in excess of 3.36% would indicate that the company was above the median point on margin for this year. And since the median collection period by paper box manufacturers for receivables was 38 days during this period, Holliday Corporation could compare its collection experience against this median.[14] If Holliday Corporation were in the petroleum industry, the *An-*

---

[14] Amounts reprinted by special permission from *Dun's Review*. Dun & Bradstreet Publications Corp.

nual *Financial Analysis of a Group of Petroleum Companies* published by The Chase Manhattan Bank, N.A., would indicate that in 1969 it should have earned in excess of 11.3 percent on stockholders' equity and in excess of 10.6 percent on borrowed and invested capital to be above the probable average of the over-all industry. And, if Holliday Corporation were a manufacturer of primary nonferrous metals. *The Quarterly Financial Report for Manufacturing Corporations* for the third quarter of 1970, compiled jointly by the Federal Trade Commission and the Securities and Exchange Commission, would enable the company to compare its figures for the third quarter of 1970 to the following for that industry:

Profit per dollar of sales, before federal income taxes	7.4%
Profit per dollar of sales, after taxes	5.4%
Profit on stockholders' equity, after taxes	9.1%
Current assets to current liabilities	2.21

and to such as the following for all manufacturing corporations.

Profit per dollar of sales, before federal income taxes	6.6%
Profit per dollar of sales, after taxes	3.9%
Profit on stockholders' equity, after taxes	9.0%
Current assets to current liabilities	1.98

These are but a few of the examples of the comparative data available for comparison and analysis.

Any resultant numerical ratio must be viewed in its proper context. A given numerical answer may be good in one situation and poor in another, or it may be both from different points of view. For example, a high inventory turnover may be excellent because it indicates a minimum investment of funds in this asset, but a high turnover could also indicate the possibility of lost sales attributable to an insufficient quantity of goods on hand.

CONCLUSION

Management judgment should pre-empt any ratio or measurement. No group of ratios answers a problem any more than a computer can think: ratios can only indicate areas for investigation. Intelligent managerial use of such ratios is required to unearth cause and effect.

In addition, all ratios and financial measurements must be viewed in their proper perspective. First, no two companies, even those in the same business, are exactly alike in their operations or in products produced and sold. Second, generally accepted accounting principles permit alternative methods of treating items. Third, though the dollar sign is a common denominator, it is subject to changing value. Fourth, though history does repeat itself, it is always difficult to compare past results with future plans. In effect, only general, not specific, conclusions should be drawn from comparative financial data.

QUESTIONS AND PROBLEMS

5-1. Following are the condensed financial statements of Fala Corporation:

Balance Sheet
as of December 31, 1972

Cash	$ 10,000	Accounts Payable	$ 10,000
Marketable Securities	5,000	Accrued Expenses Payable	20,000
Accounts Receivable (net)	20,000	Total Current Liabilities	$ 30,000
Inventories	25,000	Long-term Debt (mortgage)	20,000
Total Current Assets	$ 60,000	Total Liabilities	$ 50,000
Investments	30,000	Capital Stock $50,000	
Plant & Equipment (net)	60,000	Retained Earnings 50,000	100,000
Total Assets	$150,000	Total Equities	$150,000

Statement of Income and Retained Earnings
for the Year 1972

Net Sales		$300,000
Cost of Goods Sold		160,000
Gross Margin on Sales		$140,000
Operating Expenses		90,000
Net Operating Income		$ 50,000
Other Income (from securities and investments)	$2,800	
Other Expenses (interest on debt)	1,800	1,000
Net Income Before Tax		$ 51,000
Income Taxes		21,000
Net Income for Year		$ 30,000
Retained Earnings, January 1, 1972		40,000
		$70,000
Dividends on Capital Stock		20,000
Retained Earnings, December 31, 1972		$ 50,000

Required

a. Margin of profit on sales (net income for year as a percentage of sales)
b. Turnover of "capital" (capital defined as total assets as of December 31)
c. Return on "capital"
d. Leverage factor
e. Return on stockholders' equity (use Stockholders' Equity at December 31)

5-2. The following conversation took place in the office of A. Schreib, President of Harvey Corporation:

A. SCHREIB, PRESIDENT OF HARVEY CORPORATION: "Summarizing our two meetings of last month, I think that the possible acquisition of Young Corporation by us would be no bargain. True, our management consultant, Mr. Malloy, says that we can probably acquire Young Corporation at a reasonable price. But, as I recall the tenor of our previous meetings, we thought we might well be acquiring a mediocre company."

E. WOODS, TAX MANAGER OF HARVEY CORPORATION: "I'm still confused. What's being considered? Are we thinking of the purchase of Young's total assets or the acquisition of their outstanding capital stock? The tax consequences are different."

E. B. MALLOY, MANAGEMENT CONSULTANT: "I say first things first. Are you or aren't you interested in acquiring Young Corporation? It isn't often that such a solid company is available; it was only through an unusual contact that I unearthed the possibility. To my way of thinking, tax possibilities should be considered only after a decision to acquire has been made."

M. K. EVANS, EXECUTIVE VICE-PRESIDENT: "Don't fail to consider one vital point: while their basic product is similar to ours, it really isn't competitive. In fact, it would be an excellent item to supplement our own line."

J. HOWARD, CONTROLLER: "Frankly, I'm not impressed by the whole idea. Look at their profit margin. It's only 5% on sales; ours is 8%. They started business at approximately the same time we did, yet their sales volume is 80% of ours. Their assets and their annual net profit each are one-half of ours. They certainly are not a growth company like us. To my way of thinking, acquiring Young Corporation would be acquiring long-term trouble."

A. SCHREIB: "Basically, I must agree. And I know that your comparative figures are not distorted; for example, they use accelerated depreciation as we do, and they also adopted LIFO at the same time we did. Frankly, I think their problem is management. I've never been impressed by their deadpan attitude and lack of sparkle. They don't give their company a good image. Now, what do you think of this—let's buy them out, fire their management, and rattle-shake-and-roll their operation so it produces a decent margin of profit?"

E. B. MALLOY: "Now wait a minute; let's unscramble three points. First, larger numbers don't prove growth. There is a difference between true growth and mere expansion. Second, I think that their management are sound people. To lose them could be disastrous: what do you know about manufacturing their basic product? Third, and most important, I believe their company is at least as profitable as yours; thus, it would be a wonderful acquisition. Throughout your discussion, you have been looking at only one thing, percentage margin of profit on sales. True, yours is better. But you are comparing unlike things. Their product is different from yours. For example, a service station couldn't expect the same percentage margin on a gallon of gasoline and a quart of oil. You are ignoring the turnover of capital investment which is needed for an overall appraisal. Now look at these comparative figures I've worked out which consider both margin and turnover. Together they give the whole picture, the return on capital concept, which I think is a fairer manner to appraise the performance of the company and its management. First, let me show you the 1973 comparisons and explain what they imply."

Required

Assume that you are E. B. Malloy, Management Consultant. Using the attached financial statements of both companies, prepare the comparative figures which you believe he presented to the management in accordance with the comments above concerning margin, turnover, and return on capital. Indicate clearly your basis and determination of each item.

HARVEY CORPORATION
Balance Sheet

	As of December 31 1973	As of December 31 1972
ASSETS		
Current Assets	$ 5,500,000	$ 5,000,000
Property, Plant and Equipment:		
Cost	15,500,000	14,000,000
Accumulated Depreciation to Date	8,500,000	7,500,000
Net	7,000,000	6,500,000
Total Assets	$12,500,000	$11,500,000
LIABILITIES AND STOCKHOLDERS' EQUITY		
Current Liabilities	$ 3,000,000	$ 2,500,000
Long-term Debt—4% Bonds	1,000,000	1,000,000
Stockholders' Equity	8,500,000	8,000,000
Total Equities	$12,500,000	$11,500,000

HARVEY CORPORATION
Statement of Income and Retained Earnings

	For Year Ended December 31 1973	For Year Ended December 31 1972
Net Sales	$10,000,000	$ 9,600,000
Less Costs and Expenses	8,400,000	8,064,000
Net Income before Income Taxes	1,600,000	1,536,000
Less Income Taxes (50%)	800,000	768,000
Net Income for the Year (8%)	800,000	768,000
Retained Earnings, January 1	3,184,000	2,816,000
	3,984,000	3,584,000
Dividends	400,000	400,000
Retained Earnings, December 31	$ 3,584,000	$ 3,184,000

YOUNG CORPORATION
Balance Sheet

	As of December 31 1973	As of December 31 1972
ASSETS		
Current Assets	$ 2,100,000	$ 2,100,000
Property, Plant and Equipment:		
Cost	8,300,000	7,500,000
Accumulated Depreciation to Date	4,200,000	3,800,000
Net	4,100,000	3,700,000
Total Assets	$ 6,200,000	$ 5,800,000

LIABILITIES AND STOCKHOLDERS' EQUITY

Current Liabilities	$ 1,000,000	$ 800,000
Long-term Debt—4% Bonds	2,500,000	2,500,000
Stockholders' Equity	2,700,000	2,500,000
Total Equities	$ 6,200,000	$ 5,800,000

YOUNG CORPORATION
Statement of Income and Retained Earnings

	For Year Ended December 31	
	1973	1972
Net Sales	$ 8,000,000	$ 7,500,000
Less Costs and Expenses	7,200,000	6,750,000
Net Income before Income Taxes	800,000	750,000
Less Income Taxes	400,000	375,000
Net Income for the Year	400,000	375,000
Retained Earnings, January 1	1,175,000	1,000,000
	1,575,000	1,375,000
Dividends	200,000	200,000
Retained Earnings, December 31	$ 1,375,000	$ 1,175,000

5-3. The Regular Department Store typically sells 95% of its volume on regular 30-day charge account and 5% for cash; installment time-payment sales are insignificant. In the most recent year, $75,000,000 of sales were on regular charge account.

The store has always earned a profit, but sales volume has been declining each year for the past several years. The Board of Directors and top management of the company are under pressure from disgruntled stockholders.

Attached are the most recent financial statements of the Regular Department Store.

Required

a. Compute, for the most recent year, the following ratios for Regular Department Store:
  1. Current ratio
  2. Average collection period for accounts receivable
  3. Inventory turnover
  4. Margin of profit (net income for the year as percentage of sales)
  5. Return on investment (net income for year as percentage of average stockholders' investment)

b. Based upon your evaluation of results obtained from the above five ratios, you, as a management trainee in the company, are requested to give your impression of the performance of the present management of the Regular Department Store. In your answer, comment upon the result of each of your five computations.

REGULAR DEPARTMENT STORE
Balance Sheet

	As of January 31 1973	As of January 31 1972
ASSETS		
Current Assets:		
Cash	$ 2,000,000	$ 2,000,000
United States Government Securities (short term)	27,000,000	19,000,000
Accounts Receivable (net of estimated doubtful accounts)	15,000,000	17,000,000
Merchandise Inventories (priced at the lower of cost or market)	24,000,000	31,000,000
Supply Inventories and Prepaid Expenses	2,000,000	2,000,000
Total Current Assets	70,000,000	71,000,000
Properties and Equipment (at cost):		
Land	600,000	670,000
Buildings, Fixtures and Equipment	6,750,000	7,000,000
Less: Accumulated Depreciation	4,450,000	4,400,000
Net	2,300,000	2,600,000
Leasehold Improvements (less amortization)	200,000	230,000
Net Properties and Equipment	3,100,000	3,500,000
Total Assets	$73,100,000	$74,500,000
LIABILITIES AND STOCKHOLDERS' INVESTMENT		
Current Liabilities:		
Accounts Payable	$ 6,400,000	$ 8,200,000
Accrued Expenses and Miscellaneous	1,400,000	1,660,000
Income Taxes Payable	1,600,000	2,000,000
Total Current Liabilities	9,400,000	11,860,000
Stockholders' Investment:		
Preferred Stock		
Authorized, issued, and outstanding: 20,000 shares of no par value, non-callable, $7.00 per share cumulative dividends; stated at liquidating value	2,000,000	2,000,000
Common Stock		
Authorized 1,000,000 shares of no par value; issued and outstanding: 650,000 shares, at stated value	21,000,000	21,000,000
Earned Surplus—representing earnings reinvested in the business	40,700,000	39,640,000
Total Stockholders' Investment	63,700,000	62,640,000
Total Liabilities and Stockholders' Investment	$73,100,000	$74,500,000

REGULAR DEPARTMENT STORE
Statements of Income and Earned Surplus

	For the Years Ended January 31	
	1973	1972
Net Sales	$80,000,000	$95,000,000
Deductions:		
Cost of Merchandise Sold	55,000,000	65,400,000
Wages and Salaries	14,600,000	16,500,000
Other Expenses—net	3,000,000	4,000,000
Rents	1,000,000	1,100,000
Depreciation on Buildings and Equipment	300,000	300,000
Property, Social Security, and State Taxes	1,100,000	1,200,000
Total Costs and Expenses	75,000,000	88,500,000
Net Income before Income Taxes	5,000,000	6,500,000
Income Taxes	2,500,000	3,300,000
Net Income for the Year	2,500,000	3,200,000
Retained Earnings, February 1	39,640,000	37,880,000
Total	42,140,000	41,080,000
Cash Dividends:		
Preferred Stock—$7.00 per share	140,000	140,000
Common Stock—$2.00 per share	1,300,000	1,300,000
Total Dividends	1,440,000	1,440,000
Retained Earnings, January 31	$40,700,000	$39,640,000

5-4. Compare the result of each of your five computations in problem 5-3 with those of other department stores *and* give your evaluation of Regular Department Store versus other department stores. Financial data is available from many sources for department stores, one of which is published in *Dun's Review* under the caption "The Ratios of Retailing."

5-5. The following are the most recent financial statements of Springfield Corporation:

SPRINGFIELD CORPORATION
Condensed Balance Sheet
December 31, 1972

ASSETS

Current Assets (Schedule A)	$ 800,000
Investments	50,000
Property, Plant and Equipment (Net)	650,000
Total Assets	$1,500,000

LIABILITIES

Current Liabilities	$300,000	
Long-term Debt	100,000	
Total Liabilities		400,000

STOCKHOLDERS' EQUITY

Capital Stock (Par $100)	$800,000	
Retained Earnings	300,000	
Total Stockholders' Equity		$1,100,000

SPRINGFIELD CORPORATION
Condensed Statement of Income
For the Year Ended December 31, 1972

Net Sales		$2,500,000
Less: Cost of Goods Sold (Schedule B)		1,700,000
Gross Margin on Sales		$ 800,000
Less: Operating Expenses		500,000
Net Operating Income		$ 300,000
Other Expenses	$6,000	
Other Revenue	3,000	3,000
Net Income before Income Taxes		$ 297,000
Estimated Income Taxes		147,000
Net Income for the Year		$ 150,000

SPRINGFIELD CORPORATION
Statement of Retained Earnings
For the Year Ended December 31, 1972

Retained Earnings, January 1, 1972	$ 210,000
Add: Net Income for the Year	150,000
Total	$ 360,000
Less: Dividends	60,000
Retained Earnings, December 31, 1972	$ 300,000

Schedule A
CURRENT ASSETS

Cash	$ 190,000
Accounts Receivable	175,000
Notes Receivable	5,000
Marketable Securities	47,000
Inventory of Merchandise	380,000
Prepaid Expenses	3,000
Total Current Assets	$ 800,000

Schedule B

COST OF GOODS SOLD

Inventory of Merchandise, January 1		$ 420,000
Purchases	$1,710,000	
Transportation In	20,000	
Gross Cost of Merchandise Purchased	$1,730,000	
Less:		
Purchase Returns and Allowances . $30,000		
Purchase Discounts 40,000	70,000	
Net Cost of Merchandise Purchased		1,660,000
Cost of Merchandise Available for Sale		$2,080,000
Less: Inventory of Merchandise, December 31		380,000
Cost of Goods Sold		$1,700,000

Required

From the foregoing data for the Springfield Corporation, you are asked to determine and explain the significance of:

a. The working capital as of December 31, 1972.

b. The current ratio (working capital ratio) as of December 31, 1972.

c. The acid test ratio as of December 31, 1972.
   Note: Acid test ratio = Cash, Receivables and Marketable Securities to Current Liabilities.

d. The merchandise turnover during the year 1972 in number of days.

e. The average number of days' sales uncollected as of December 31, 1972. (The amount of cash sales during the year was insignificant.)

f. The profit earned in 1972 per share of capital stock. (No change in outstanding capital stock took place during the year.)

g. The rate of gross margin for 1972.

h. In recent years, there has been a marked increase among companies using rate of return on capital employed to measure performance. A company's performance, for example, may be measured by the profit earned (net income) on the capital (total assets) employed. This performance is measured as follows:

$$\text{Return on Capital Employed} = \frac{\text{Net Income}}{\text{Total Assets}}$$

This performance is dependent upon:

$$\text{Margin of Profit} = \frac{\text{Net Income}}{\text{Net Sales}}$$

and

$$\text{Turnover of Capital} = \frac{\text{Net Sales}}{\text{Total Assets}}$$

126   FINANCIAL ACCOUNTING CONCEPTS   [CH. 5]

The interrelationship of the components may be expressed as follows:

$$\frac{\text{Return on Capital Employed}}{} = \frac{\text{Margin of Profit}}{} \times \frac{\text{Turnover of Capital}}{}$$

$$\frac{\text{Net Income}}{\text{Total Assets}} = \frac{\text{Net Income}}{\text{Net Sales}} \times \frac{\text{Net Sales}}{\text{Total Assets}}$$

Compute the 1972 rate of return on the capital employed for the Springfield Corporation supported by its two components.

5-6. The following is a comparative statement of income for Walter Good Company:

	For the Year Ended		
	Dec. 31, 1972	Dec. 31, 1971	Percentage Change
Net Sales	$1,070,000	$1,000,000	+ 7%
Cost of Goods Sold	693,000	700,000	− 1%
Gross Margin	$ 377,000	$ 300,000	+26%
Operating Expenses	57,000	60,000	− 5%
Net Income before Income Taxes	$ 320,000	$ 240,000	+33%

Sales revenues have increased 7%, while cost of goods and operating expenses have decreased 1% and 5%. As a result, net income (prior income taxes) has increased 33%; 1972 has been a banner year! However, further investigation reveals that in 1972 selling prices were 10% higher than in 1971.

Required

a. What was the sales *volume* percentage change from 1971 to 1972?

b. Indicate what change took place in *unit* cost of goods sold in 1972 as compared to 1971.

c. Comment on the trend of operating expenses.

5-7. Using the financial statements of Harvey Corporation given in problem 5-2:

a. Determine the following as of the last day of the fiscal year:
   1. Working capital
   2. Current ratio (also known as working capital ratio)
   3. Book value per share of common (or capital) stock. The average number of shares outstanding during 1973 was 45,000.

b. Determine the following for the fiscal year:
   1. Margin of profit (net income as a percentage of sales)
   2. Turnover of capital, with capital defined as total assets (sales divided by total assets)
   3. Return on capital (net income divided by total assets, i.e., your answer to b.1 multiplied by your answer to b.2)
   4. Leverage factor (assets divided by stockholders' equity)
   5. Return on stockholders' equity (net income divided by stockholders' equity, i.e., your answer to b.3 multiplied by your answer to b.4)

5-8. Harvey Corporation (see problem 5-7) is a manufacturer of paper and allied products. Compare the results of six of your eight calculations (ignore a.1 and a.3) for Harvey Corporation with those for the industry. Industry data is available from many sources, one of which is the *Quarterly Financial Report for Manufacturing Corporations,* compiled jointly since 1947 by the Federal Trade Commission and the Securities and Exchange Commission.

Required

How, in your opinion, does Harvey Corporation as an individual company compare with companies in its industry?

5-9. Using the annual report of a company furnished to you by your instructor:
   a. Determine the following as of the last day of the fiscal year:
      1. Working capital
      2. Current ratio (also known as working capital ratio)
      3. Book value per share of common (or capital) stock
   b. Determine the following for the fiscal year:
      1. Margin of profit (net income as a percentage of sales)
      2. Turnover of capital, with capital defined as total assets (sales divided by total assets)
      3. Return on capital (net income divided by total assets, i.e., your answer to b.1 multiplied by your answer to b.2)
      4. Leverage factor (assets divided by stockholders' equity)
      5. Return on stockholders' equity (net income divided by stockholders' equity, i.e., your answer to b.3 multiplied by your answer to b.4)

5-10. For the past several years, *Fortune* has published an annual "Fortune Directory" of the 500 largest U.S. industrial corporations (ranked by sales). Using the most recent issue, compute profit as a percentage of assets for the first five companies in the list. Then, compare this ratio with two given percentages, profit to sales and profit to "invested capital." Does the comparison suggest any relationships? As an added assignment, you may wish to extend your calculations and comparisons beyond the first five companies and employ appropriate statistical techniques to reveal any possible correlation of size of company, return on assets, margin of profit, and return on invested capital.

5-11. The chief postulate of our private enterprise system is that the individual's quest for gain maximizes the public welfare. As regards capital, for example, prospective returns are presumably highest from those uses currently most favored by consumers and, of these, from those in which additional capital represents the least cost means of production. Capital allocation in response to profit expectations occurs at two levels: first, by investor selection among enterprises; and, second, by management selection among projects. The motivations and competitive conditions essential to smooth functioning of this allocation system are not always fully realized. Nevertheless, by the criteria of material output and public acceptance, it works quite well.

Does accounting contribute to effective operation of the allocation system? Discuss.

5-12.   **EARLE WRIGHT CORPORATION**
              (Case in abbreviated form)

Earle Wright Corporation of Arkansas City, Kansas, has manufactured a complete line of widgets for many years. During these years, both sales volume and capital invested in the business have *steadily* increased. For example:

Year	Net Sales	Net Earnings (per Statement of Income)	Total Assets (per Balance Sheet)
1947	$150,000,000	$10,000,000	$ 95,000,000
1952	200,000,000	9,000,000	135,000,000
1957	250,000,000	11,000,000	170,000,000
1961	302,800,000	18,500,000	213,000,000
1965	374,700,000	33,700,000	277,700,000
1969	552,300,000	58,100,000	487,700,000

One director of the company recently raised the question, "Is ours *really* a *growth* company?" His concern arose from his recent reading (see attached references on pages 132–133) and his application of the "rate of return on capital employed" concept to the financial data of Earle Wright Corporation. This particular director feels (along with an increasing number of those in the managements of many companies) that a company's performance should be measured by the *profit earned* on the *capital employed*.

This performance is measured as follows:

This performance is dependent upon:

$$\frac{\text{Return on Capital Employed}}{} = \frac{\text{Margin of Profit}}{} \times \frac{\text{Turnover of Capital}}{}$$

$$\frac{\text{Profit Earned}}{\text{Total Assets}} = \frac{\text{Earned Profit}}{\text{Sales}} \times \frac{\text{Sales}}{\text{Total Assets}}$$

When the director applied this "formula" to the financial data of the Earle Wright Corporation for the past 19 years, he obtained the following results:

	Return	=	Margin	×	Turnover
1951	11.59%		9.10%		1.27
1952	11.66%		9.54%		1.22
1953	12.01%		9.61%		1.25
1954	12.67%		10.78%		1.18
1955	14.88%		11.91%		1.25
1956	12.46%		10.56%		1.18
1957	10.16%		8.93%		1.14
1958	12.03%		11.04%		1.09
1959	15.53%		13.29%		1.17
1960	12.13%		11.00%		1.10
1961	13.03%		12.00%		1.09
1962	13.68%		12.67%		1.08
1963	16.44%		15.51%		1.06
1964	17.00%		16.50%		1.03
1965	16.05%		16.16%		.993
1966	14.05%		14.33%		.985
1967	10.01%		10.57%		.947
1968	11.80%		11.95%		.988
1969	9.80%		10.93%		.896

Note: Amounts may not exactly cross-multiply due to rounding of numbers.

Note: Over the years, the amounts are not exactly comparable, due to:
> Change in the method of accounting for wholly owned foreign subsidiaries.
> Change in the method of accounting for the investment credit.
> Acquisition of other companies.
> Sale of certain businesses.

"See," he said, "our rate of return in 1969, though satisfactory, is less than ever. Though our margin is excellent, our turnover of capital keeps deteriorating."

When questioned by the other directors about discrepancies between his numbers and those based upon the company's financial statements, he replied, "Oh, I adjusted the raw financial data. For example, I used profit before income taxes and exclusive of miscellaneous income and other expenses. And I used 'gross' total assets by adding back accumulated depreciation to date, plus a few other minor adjustments." When accused of juggling the numbers, the director's defense was, "This is what some other companies do, companies that are larger and more profitable than ours."

This director then went on to get a few other things off his chest: "The typical corporate annual report—ours included—is likely to convey the impression that the reporting corporation is a growth company. Normally, the president's letter to the stockholders speaks of the year's financial results in glowing terms. It indicates that sales have increased over the preceding year or why they will be improved in the immediate future; that earnings per share are improved or should be in the coming years; that specific costs have been controlled effectively; and that dividends have been maintained or slightly increased. Along with the president's letter, the typical annual report contains narrative, pictures, and graphs concerning new products introduced, other companies purchased or acquired, increased emphasis on research and development, additional outlays for capital expenditures, improved employee benefits, and other favorable indicators. Finally, the financial statements are presented. Often a quick glance or cursory examination is all that the typical reader of an annual report affords to the financial statements. He is convinced that the company is in fine shape; the financial statements are certified, and, in the main, this year's dollar amounts for items like total assets, net income, sales, etc., are greater than the amounts of the preceding year. Obviously, this is another growth company.

"But is it a growth company? Perhaps it is only an expanding company; is there a difference? Those who provide information to aid management in formulating certain policy decisions and in controlling current operations are —or should be—aware of the distinction. A growth company is to be desired; an expanding company to be challenged. Measuring the performance of management to determine whether or not a company is a growth company may conceivably differ from measurements employed by analysts, bankers, investors, or lenders.

"When judging the degree of success or failure of a business firm, the first question is: how do you *measure* a business? Traditionally, there has been general reliance, in varying degrees to be sure, on certain standard and generally accepted financial analyses and ratios like working capital, current ratio, acid test, net earnings per share, rate of profit on stockholders' equity, net profit on sales, gross profit on sales, turnover of inventories, ratio of stockholders' equity to total liabilities, and others.

"At this point it is pertinent to ask, 'Why not *measure* a business firm in the same manner that many companies today are measuring themselves?' The concept of Return on Capital Employed is a measuring tool that uses sales, invested capital, and profit as an index to a company's performance. Today, management is conscious of how effectively it is using its available capital. Until recently, most businesses emphasized the rate of profit on sales. The possible inadequacy of this measurement, when used alone, may be illustrated by assuming a company with sales of $1,000,000 and a net profit of $100,000. On the surface, a 10% margin of profit indicates a profitable business; but if the capital employed by this same company is $3,300,000, the profit on capital employed is only 3%, less than that earned on Series E Bonds. Return on Capital Employed, though not a new concept, has been widely accepted by management in recent years as a tool for measuring performance. Today, the top managements of many companies feel that a company's performance should be measured by the *profit earned* on the *capital employed* in the business.

"Rate of return appears to be a relatively stable measurement device when measuring the performance of a company over a period of years. It should be an aid in determining whether a company is a growth company or merely an expansion company. Over a period of time, an increase in the dollar amounts shown on the financial statement of a company may indicate expansion in the sense that the company is larger. However, the company may not be a growth company; it may be simply 'fatter.' This point was emphasized by T. G. Mackensen when he was a special studies analyst for the H. J. Heinz Company: 'True growth comes from the ability of management to employ successfully additional capital at a satisfactory rate of return. The company that is merely expanding at declining rates of return on investment will eventually be brought to a stop by lack of expansion capital.'[15]

"Based on an application of the return on investment concept to various industries and several companies within these industries, Harvey O. Edson summarized his study as follows:[16]

1. For the total company return, a range of 20 percent–35 percent before taxes would be considered quite satisfactory.
2. Within protected product lines, a 30 percent–40 percent experience would be quite adequate over an extended period of time.
3. Your ROI should be better, certainly, than that of the related industry experience indicated on our table. Remember, these are over-all averages, and the ratios are depressed by the poor, below-average performers. Possibly your industry average might be the low point in your desirable range.
4. Develop individual ROI ratios for the best companies within your industry. Conceivably that factor would become the high point of your ROI range.
5. The more competitive the general conditions within your specific industry are, the narrower and lower the probable range of ROI will be.

---

[15] "Modern Techniques of Financial Analysis for Management Planning: An AMA Symposium," *Journal of Accountancy* (February, 1954), p. 175. (Copyright © 1954, by the American Institute of Certified Public Accountants, Inc.)

[16] Harvey O. Edson, "Setting a Standard for Your Company's Return on Investment, *The Controller* (now *Financial Executive*) (September, 1958).

[CH. 5] MEASURING MANAGEMENT PERFORMANCE, RETURN ON CAPITAL 131

6. Well-protected product lines, i.e., (a) special arts and methods not known to the general trade, or (b) patent protected, should show higher rates of return than more competitive lines."

Case Considerations

a. As an illustrative experiment, use the summary annual report figures of Earle Wright Corporation to determine how the director calculated the 1969 return, margin, and turnover.

b. Do you believe that Earle Wright Corporation is a growth company?

c. Should the "profit earned" be the:
   1. Net Income for the Year
   2. Net Income prior Income Taxes
   3. Operating Profit before Income Taxes
   4. Some other measure of "profit earned"

d. Should the "capital employed" be the:
   1. Total assets, per the balance sheet
   2. Average total assets
   3. Gross total (or average) assets—add back depreciation to date
   4. Net Worth (Stockholders' Equity)
   5. Net Worth plus Long-term Debt (Assets minus Current Liabilities)
   6. Some other measure of "capital employed"

e. Should the rate of return be determined for:
   1. The company as a whole
   2. The product lines (or divisions or plants) within the company

f. Should the rate of return be compared with:
   1. Past experience within the company
   2. A predetermined goal of the company
   3. Current budget forecast of the company
   4. Other companies in the same industry

EARLE WRIGHT CORPORATION
Balance Sheet
As of December 31

	1969	1968
ASSETS		
Current Assets (cash, receivables, inventories, etc.)	$193,800,000	$186,000,000
Long-Term Notes Receivable	36,700,000	–0–
Property, Plant and Equipment (at cost)	398,600,000	409,200,000
Less: Accumulated depreciation to date	(145,600,000)	(162,400,000)
Miscellaneous Assets	4,200,000	2,800,000
Total Assets	487,700,000	435,600,000

LIABILITIES

Current Liabilities (Payables due within one year)	85,000,000	72,300,000
Miscellaneous Liabilities	16,100,000	15,800,000
Long-Term Debt	10,800,000	7,300,000
Total Liabilities	111,900,000	95,400,000

STOCKHOLDERS' EQUITY

Capital Stock Outstanding	39,600,000	29,900,000
Contributed Capital in Excess of Par	38,600,000	50,500,000
Earnings Retained in Business	297,600,000	259,800,000
Total Stockholders' Equity	375,800,000	340,200,000

EARLE WRIGHT CORPORATION
Statement of Income
For the Year

	1969	1968
Net Sales	$552,300,000	$570,500,000
Gain from Sale of Businesses	26,200,000	–0–
Miscellaneous Income (net)	1,600,000	1,100,000
	580,100,000	571,600,000
Costs and Expenses	491,900,000	502,400,000
Net Earnings before Income Tax	88,200,000	69,200,000
Income Tax Expense	30,100,000	34,300,000
Net Earnings for Year	58,100,000	34,900,000

References

1. "Annual Report on American Industry," *Forbes*. The January 1, 1971 issue rates 659 major companies.
2. National Association of Accountants, Research Report No. 42, *Long Range Profit Planning,* December 1, 1964.
3. Robert Morris Associates, *Annual Statement Studies.*
4. "Watch That Waistline!", *Forbes,* May 15, 1970.
5. Keith Powlison, "Obstacles to Business Growth," *Harvard Business Review,* Vol. 31, No. 2, (March–April 1953), 48–56.
6. F. J. Muth, "Return on Capital Employed—A Measure of Management," N.A.C.A. *Bulletin,* Vol. XXXV, No. 6 (February, 1954).
7. R. B. Read, "Return on Investment—Guide to Decisions," N.A.C.A. *Bulletin,* Vol. XXXV, No. 10 (June, 1954).
8. "Return on Investment: Gist of a Technical Service Survey," N.A.C.A. *Bulletin,* Vol. XXXV, No. 6 (February, 1954).
9. "How H. J. Heinz Manages Its Financial Planning and Controls," *Financial Management Series 106,* American Management Association.

10. National Association of Accountants, Research Report No. 35, *Return on Capital as a Guide to Managerial Decisions,* December 1, 1959. This 107-page booklet contains much excellent source material. Part I, Rate of Return for Measuring Periodic Profit Performance, discusses how various companies calculate rate of return, how it is analyzed and used, and the use of return on capital as a guide in pricing. Part II, Using Rate of Return in Capital Planning, analyzes many methods including the discounted cash flow method.
11. National Association of Accountants, Accounting Practice Report No. 14, *Experience with Return on Capital to Appraise Management Performance,* February 1962.

6

Property, Plant and Equipment: Acquisition, Depreciation, Disposal

Property, plant and equipment, often called fixed assets, comprise a significant portion of the total assets of most companies; on the next page the survey of the 1970 annual reports of some typical large industrial companies illustrates this fact. Because of the relative importance of fixed assets, this chapter and the one following contain an examination of the accounting principles and practices which apply to this category of assets.

Property, plant and equipment represent relatively long-lived assets having a tangible nature which are used in the operation of the business and not held for sale. Examples of these assets are building site land; depreciable assets like buildings, machinery, and equipment; and depletable natural resources like oil, timber, and mineral deposits. Occasionally, the scope of the term *property, plant and equipment* (or *fixed assets*) is broadened to include intangibles. Intangible fixed assets, as a class, possess characteristics similar to those of tangible property, plant, and equipment items. Their value, however, does not originate in their physical substance, but is attributable to the rights conferred by their ownership. Examples of such intangible assets are patents, copyrights, trademarks, and goodwill.

Each accounting period should be systematically charged with its share of the cost of fixed assets (tangible and intangible) possessing a determinable life.[1] The terms regularly employed to identify the allocation of such costs to the applicable accounting periods are:

---

[1] Building site land does not have a determinable life. Certain intangible assets like trademarks, goodwill, and some franchises may not have a determinable life.

[CH. 6] PROPERTY: ACQUISITION, DEPRECIATION, DISPOSAL

Depreciation ...... the periodic charge for tangible assets other than natural resources.
Depletion .... the periodic charge for natural resources.
Amortization ...... the periodic charge for intangible assets.

Company	Property, Plant and Equipment[2] Cost	Accumul. Deprec.	Net	Total Assets	Net P. P. & E. as % of Total Assets
(amounts in millions of dollars)					
General Motors Corporation ...	13,545	8,132	5,413	14,174	38%
General Electric Company	3,651	1,902	1,749	6,310	28%
U.S. Steel Corporation	9,471	5,548	3,923	6,311	62%
DuPont (E. I.) de Nemours ...	4,942	3,019	1,923	3,567	54%
Gulf Oil Corporation	10,212	4,870	5,342	8,672	62%
Swift & Company	685	324	361	825	44%
General Dynamics Corporation .	757	440	317	1,096	29%
Kraftco Corporation	782	393	389	1,031	38%
RCA Corporation	1,406	625	781	2,936	27%
Continental Can Company, Inc.	1,322	639	683	1,535	45%
United Aircraft Corporation ...	853	531	322	1,546	21%

This chapter and the first portion of the next chapter discuss property, plant and equipment and the related facets of depreciation. The last two sections of the next chapter discuss natural resources and their depletion and intangible assets and their amortization.

An understanding of the distinguishing characteristics of two types of expenditures is necessary for a discussion of fixed assets and their depreciation. Presented next are the fundamental concepts necessary for such understanding.

CAPITAL EXPENDITURES AND REVENUE EXPENDITURES

An expenditure is the contracting of a liability for the acquisition of an asset or the incurring of an expense. An understanding of the basic differences between *capital* and *revenue* expenditures is a prerequisite to the determination of the cost of fixed assets, which costs may be ultimately depreciated, depleted, or amortized.

A capital expenditure benefits future fiscal periods as well as the current one; it results in an increase in the carrying value of an asset, usually a fixed asset, on the balance sheet. A revenue expenditure benefits only the current fiscal period; it results in the increase in an item of expense on the statement of

---

[2] Exclusive of intangibles where separately stated.

income.[3] These are concise explanations of the two terms; neither term can be defined to coincide perfectly with the various treatments given expenditures under practical implementations in business. The differentiation between capital and revenue expenditures will be illustrated by examples.

First, ABC Company purchases a second-hand delivery truck and incurs the following four expenditures in connection with this acquisition:

Invoice from X Company for second-hand truck	$2,000
Invoice from Z Company to have the truck completely overhauled prior to placing the truck into service	300
Cost of gasoline and oil for the first week's operation of the truck	50
Driver's salary for the week	150

Which of these four expenditures should be capitalized? One of the guiding principles underlying the classification of expenditures is that expenditures made to place a fixed asset in condition, in position, and ready for use should be capitalized. Accordingly, the capitalized cost of the above truck is $2,300. This amount represents the cost of the newly acquired fixed asset as an addition to existing property, plant and equipment. The other two expenditures, totaling $200, are revenue expenditures; they represent expenses concerned with the operation of the acquired asset and should be deducted from revenue on the statement of income.

A second example is used to illustrate an extension of the guiding principle already established. DEF Company, located in Buffalo, N.Y., purchases a piece of machinery and incurs the following expenditures:

Cost of machine, f.o.b. Cleveland, Ohio	$6,000
State sales tax	200
Freight charges to Buffalo	150
Insurance on machine while in transit	25
Cost to install machine in plant	200
Cost to break-in machine	125
Total	$6,700

Theoretically, the total cost of $6,700 may be capitalized as an addition to property, plant and equipment. All six of the expenditures are incurred in acquiring the machine and placing it in condition, in position, and ready for use: no usable asset is acquired until $6,700 has been expended. Also, if the terms of purchase with the vendor in Cleveland were f.o.b. Buffalo, installed and ready to operate, the vendor's invoice for the machine would be approximately $6,700. To some degree, however, actual company practice may differ from the concepts embodied in accounting theory. Many companies have established a policy of charging to revenue all expenditures which are less than a stated amount—for example, $100. If this were the situation with the company in the second example, the $25 for insurance included in the above

---

[3] Revenue expenditures are often referred to as operating expenditures.

total could be expensed rather than capitalized. Also, in practice, many companies capitalize installation costs but expense breaking-in costs. This practice is followed when it is considered impractical to segregate breaking-in costs when the break-in operations are performed by the company's own employees. The pertinent point involved here is that the company follows a *consistent* policy for all expenditures which concern similar property acquisitions.

When considering what treatment a given expenditure should receive, it is entirely possible to arrive at one answer which is in accord with accounting theory, a second that conforms with company policy, and a third which complies with federal income tax regulations and related court decisions. For example, the state sales tax on the purchase of the above machine could be viewed in theory as a capital expenditure, but it may be treated as a revenue expenditure if it is deductible for purposes of federal income tax.[4] Due to the borderline nature of certain expenditures, such as major repairing and overhauling of equipment, the area of capital versus revenue expenditures results in much tax litigation.

One of the most concise and clear summaries of the differences between capital and revenue expenditures was that made some years ago by the Board of Tax Appeals in the Illinois Merchants Trust Company case, in which the Board said:

> In determining whether an expenditure is a capital one or is chargeable against operating income, it is necessary to bear in mind the purpose for which the expenditure was made. To repair is to restore to a sound state or to mend, while a replacement connotes a substitution. A repair is an expenditure for the purpose of keeping the property in an ordinarily efficient operating condition. It does not add to the value of the property, nor does it appreciably prolong its life. It merely keeps the property in an operating condition over its probable useful life for the uses for which it was acquired. Expenditures for that purpose are distinguishable from those for replacements, alterations, improvements or additions which prolong the life of the property, increase its value, or make it adaptable to a different use. The one is a maintenance charge, while the others are additions to capital investment which should not be applied against current earnings.[5]

Management should adhere to sound policies in distinguishing between capital and revenue expenditures; mishandling of these items will distort certain amounts in the balance sheet and prevent the matching of applicable costs with related revenue on the statement of income. In addition, management should be aware in its planning that many borderline cases, for tax purposes,

---

[4] There is a general state sales tax in all but a few of the 50 states. In the majority of such states, owing to the wording of the state statute, the tax may be deducted in the year incurred for federal income tax purposes; but in a few states the tax must be capitalized as a portion of the cost of the capital asset and recovered through depreciation.

[5] *Illinois Merchants Trust Company, Executor, Estate of William B. Manierre,* CCH December 1952, BTA 103 (acq.).

are subject to a degree of control. For example, a deferred maintenance policy which causes the replacement of a worn-out motor on a large piece of machinery with a new motor costing $600 probably is a capital expenditure; but, a continuing maintenance policy which results only in periodic *repairs* and minor replacements of the parts to the original motor probably constitutes revenue expenditures.

DEPRECIATION

Concept of Depreciation

The term *depreciation* is employed in the periodic write-off of the cost of all items of property, plant, and equipment except such tangible assets as land and natural resources and certain long-lived intangible assets. The term *depreciation* denotes the periodic cost allocation against revenue of such tangible assets as buildings, machinery, and equipment. These fixed assets have a limited useful life; physically, they deteriorate from use and from the action of the elements. An adequate repair and maintenance policy may slow, but cannot halt, this deterioration. In addition, such tangible fixed assets gradually become obsolete as a result of improved models, new inventions, and changes in consumer demand. The term depreciation includes both concepts: loss of serviceability from physical deterioration and loss of utility from gradual obsolescence.

Equitable methods must be used to write off the cost of fixed assets like buildings, machinery, and equipment items as their useful lives decrease. If the length of an accounting period exceeded or at least equalled the life of the fixed assets owned by a company, the depreciation problem would not exist. Thus, if a fiscal period were 50 years, practically all fixed assets would be an expense of the 50-year period. However, the one-year fiscal period is customary in business. Therefore, each fiscal period should be systematically charged with its proportionate share of the cost of fixed assets so that such cost will be fairly allocated as expense to each fiscal period throughout the estimated useful lives of the assets. In effect, the cost of each fixed asset is a long-term prepaid expense which, by some equitable method, must be prorated over its useful life as an expense to be matched against revenue during each period.

Definition of Depreciation

An explanation of the term depreciation is contained in a release by the Committee on Terminology of the American Institute of Certified Public Accountants:

> Depreciation accounting is a system of accounting which aims to distribute the cost or other basic value of tangible capital assets, less salvage (if any), over the estimated useful life of the unit (which may be a

group of assets) in a systematic and rational manner. It is a process of allocation, not of valuation.[6]

Depreciation accounting must be recognized as a process of allocation of cost, not as a process of constantly valuing or revaluing fixed assets according to what they are currently "worth." In accounting usage, depreciation does not attempt to measure the decline in value of a fixed asset. Instead, depreciation is a process by which the cost of a fixed asset is equitably distributed over the years of its estimated useful life.

The Three Unknowns

The determination of that portion of the cost of a tangible fixed asset which is to be allocated to each fiscal period as depreciation expense requires decisions with respect to three factors: the cost (or other basic value) of the fixed asset, its salvage value (if any), and the estimated useful life of the asset. In varying degrees, the determination of these three factors is a matter of judgment, experience, fact, and educated guess. Rarely are all three of the unknowns capable of exact determination at the time a fixed asset is acquired. In fact, it may not be until years later, when the fixed asset is disposed of, that all three factors are finally capable of precise calculation. The necessity of resolving these unknowns at the time a fixed asset is acquired—coupled with perfect vision when using hindsight—has produced much litigation in the tax courts. Therefore, a résumé of the pertinent points that should be considered in making decisions concerning each of these three factors is presented next.

Cost (or Other Basic Value)

Basically, cost is the sum of the actual expenditures involved in acquiring and placing a fixed asset in operating condition. As discussed earlier in this chapter, such cost is often in excess of that paid to the vendor. A piece of machinery purchased f.o.b. shipping point has an acquisition cost in excess of that paid to the seller of the machine. The total cost of the asset, the amount to be depreciated, frequently includes items like freight charges, installation costs, and break-in expenditures. These points were discussed earlier, but there are additional factors which must also be resolved in certain instances.

Consider the case of a company which purchases land and a second-hand factory building for a lump sum price of $500,000. What is the cost of the building, which is subject to depreciation; what is the cost of the land, which is not subject to depreciation? If the purchase agreement does not explicitly specify the portion of the $500,000 purchase price allocable to each, an equit-

---

[6] American Institute of Certified Public Accountants, Inc., Committee on Terminology, *Accounting Terminology Bulletin Number 1*, "Review and Resume" (New York, 1953), p. 25. Copyright © 1953 by the American Institute of Certified Public Accountants.

able allocation must be made. One possible method of allocation is to use the values at which each is assessed for property taxes, as follows:

	Assessed Value	Percent of total	Apportionment of purchase price
Land	$100,000	¼	$125,000
Building	300,000	¾	375,000
Total	$400,000		$500,000

Another method of apportioning the total purchase price is by an independent appraisal of the land and the building. In addition to the $375,000 cost apportioned to the building, additional capital expenditures may be incurred in getting this second-hand fixed asset into condition and ready for use.

Another situation in which the cost of a fixed asset is not readily determinable is in the case of a company constructing a fixed asset itself for its own use. Without getting involved in the details, the reader can easily appreciate that, while the material costs could be identified without too much difficulty and the labor costs might be readily segregated equitably, the proration of many of the appropriate general overhead expenses like heat, light, telephone, and administrative salaries would require careful analysis and would not be capable of precise apportionment. If all applicable costs are not equitably allocated between the fixed asset under construction and the goods being produced for sale, distorted financial information will result which could seriously mislead management if the dollar amount involved is material.

Occasionally a basis other than cost is used for establishing the dollar amount assigned as the value of the asset acquired. This situation occurs when land and buildings are donated to a company to induce it to establish a plant in a specific locality. In such an instance, the fixed assets may be shown on the financial statements at market value at the time of acquisition. Another situation is presented when fixed assets are acquired through the issuance of the company's own capital stock. Should such assets be shown at their own market value or at the value of the shares issued to acquire the assets?[7]

Cost (or other basic value) is not always readily determinable, nor is it always subject to precise measurement. Nevertheless, the determination must be made in as equitable a manner as possible.

Salvage (If Any)

The amount to be depreciated over the estimated useful life of a fixed asset is the difference between the cost and the salvage value of the asset. Salvage value, as used in the determination of depreciation, is the estimated amount which will be realized from a tangible fixed asset at the time it is sold or otherwise disposed of at the end of its estimated useful life. To ascertain the total amount to be depreciated, salvage value must be determined at the time the

---

[7] This point is discussed in Chapter 9.

asset is acquired; yet it may be many years before the exact salvage amount is actually ascertainable. In the case of some assets, salvage value might represent a substantial portion of the original cost, as new automobiles purchased by automobile rental agencies which dispose of them after only a very limited period of use. However, in the case of other assets, salvage value may be negligible or non-existent; for example, the cost of scrapping an asset may approximate its junk value. Often this is the case with a building; a similar situation occurs with certain machinery in industries where technological or style changes are very frequent. Past experience is usually the most valid basis for estimating salvage value. If there is no past experience available for new types of fixed assets like an atomic power plant or Disneyland, judgment appears to be the best basis for estimating salvage value. Rather than salvage value, a company may wish to use *net* salvage value (salvage value reduced by the estimated cost of removing, dismantling, or junking the asset). A company should be consistent in its use of either salvage value or net salvage in determining its depreciation allowances.

Estimated Useful Life

The third factor to be predetermined to allocate depreciation expense equitably is the estimated useful life of the asset. Estimated useful life is not necessarily the useful life inherent in the asset; rather, it is the period over which the asset is expected to be useful in the business of the particular company. Identical depreciable assets may conceivably have different estimated useful lives for different companies.

If someone were to ask, "What is the estimated useful life of an automobile?" his question could not be answered properly until answers had first been furnished for several other questions, among which would be these:

> What is the repair and maintenance policy for the automobile? Is it a scheduled program of adequate maintenance, or is it of the bare minimum necessity type?
>
> Is the automobile kept in a garage, or does it stand out in all kinds of weather?
>
> How many miles is the automobile driven per year?
>
> Assuming that the usual operator is a skilled and experienced driver, are there occasions when young, inexperienced operators drive the car? If so, how frequently do such occasions occur?
>
> Is the automobile viewed as simply a means of transportation or in some other manner? In other words, do model changes and innovations which cause gradual obsolescence mean that it will be more quickly disposed of than would otherwise be the case?

From the foregoing, it is apparent that estimated useful life is dependent upon many factors, chief among which are the company's policy on repairs and maintenance; wear and tear from operations, climatic and other local conditions; human behavior; economic changes; inventions; and normal obsolescence. Estimated useful life is a matter of judgment and should be forecasted according to past experience and all other pertinent data. An estimated life for a depreciable asset, once determined, should be changed if at some time in the future conditions clearly warrant such a change. Many companies review such estimates periodically.

From 1934 through July 11, 1962, the only guide to useful lives for depreciable assets justifiable for income tax purposes was Bulletin "F," issued by the Treasury Department. Last completely revised in January, 1942, Bulletin "F" listed estimated useful lives for approximately 5,000 types of assets. Illustrative items included in the list were:

Item Description	Life (Years)
Factory buildings	50
Office buildings	67
Warehouses	75
Apartment buildings	50
Brick kilns	25
Hotel carpets and rugs	6
Blast furnaces (iron and steel industry)	25
Passenger automobiles	5
Salesmen's automobiles	3
Office desks	20
Generators, large units above 3,000 kv.-a	28
Aircraft engines	6,000 flying hours

For two reasons, the estimated lives listed in Bulletin "F" were not to be accepted as final answers. First, the average useful life figure was intended only as a rough guide or starting point from which a company should estimate life based upon the period over which the depreciable asset was expected to be useful in the business of that particular company. Second, the accelerated pace of technological innovation and increasingly rapid changes in economic conditions rendered the list somewhat antiquated since it was released in January of 1942. Bulletin "F" was intended only as a guide; in reality, however, it acted as a "par" against which the Internal Revenue Service compared the depreciable lives used by companies. And, in addition, the burden of proof for deviations from Bulletin "F" lives was placed on the taxpayer.

On July 11, 1962, the Treasury Department issued *Depreciation Guidelines and Rules,* officially known as "Revenue Procedure 62–21." Instead of establishing lives on individual items of depreciable property, as did Bulletin "F," the guideline lives contained in Revenue Procedure 62–21 apply to only about 75 broad classes of assets. Each class is assigned a guideline life for tax purposes. These 75 broad classes are enumerated as subdivisions of the following four groups of depreciable assets used in business:

Group One: Assets used by business in general
Group Two: Non-manufacturing activities (excluding transportation, communications, and public utilities)
Group Three: Manufacturing
Group Four: Transportation, communications, and public utilities

Group One contains assets in common use by all businesses, like office furniture, automobiles, trucks, and office machines. The other three groups contain all the equipment and productive machinery used by a specific industry. The following examples are selected at random from the four groups and 75 classes of depreciable assets enumerated in Revenue Procedure 62–21.

Group	Class	Class Description	Life (Years)
One	1	Office Furniture, Fixtures, Machines, and Equipment	10
	2	Transportation Equipment:	
		(b) Automobiles, including taxis	3
		(d) General-purpose trucks:	
		Light (actual unloaded weight less than 13,000 pounds)	4
		Heavy (13,000 pounds or more)	6
	4	Buildings (other than special purpose structures)	
		Type of Building (four of thirteen):	
		Apartments	40
		Factories	45
		Office Buildings	45
		Warehouses	60
Two	1	Agriculture:	
		(a) Machinery and Equipment (including fences)	10
		(d) Farm Buildings	25
	6	Recreation and Amusement (other than land improvements or structures)	10
	7	Services (Personal and Professional)	10
Three	4	Chemicals and Allied Products	11
	5	Electrical Equipment:	
		(a) Electrical Equipment	12
		(b) Electronic Equipment	8
	8	Glass and Glass Products	14
	17	Petroleum and Natural Gas:	
		(c) Petroleum Refining	16
	19	Primary Metals:	
		(a) Ferrous Metals	18
		(b) Nonferrous Metals	14
	28	Tobacco and Tobacco Products	15
Four	3	Electric Utilities	
		(a) Hydraulic production plant	50
		(b) Nuclear production plant	20

	(c) Steam production plant	28
	(d) Transmission and distribution facilities	30
	Each guideline class includes the related land improvements.	
7	Pipeline Transportation	22

Note that the guideline life for the entire class of office furniture, fixtures, machines, and equipment is ten years. Under Bulletin "F" each individual item in this category had a separate life, ranging from five years for a typewriter to fifty years for an office safe. The new and shorter lives contained in the "guideline lives" are intended to give recognition to factors like more rapid obsolescence caused by changing technology, new inventions, and foreign competition. While the shorter lives have been referred to as "equivalent to a tax cut" and a "stimulus to continued economic growth," ultimately such lives had to be justified by the business utilizing them. The guideline lives, or possibly even shorter lives being used by a business at present, had to be consistent with the actual practice of the business in retiring and replacing its depreciable assets. The reasonableness of the lives used were gauged by a technique known as the "reserve ratio" test; i.e., the comparison of the ratio of accumulated depreciation to date to the cost of the assets in the particular guideline class, with a predetermined range within which the ratio should fall.

On January 11, 1971, President Nixon announced, effective January 1, 1971, three important changes with respect to depreciation allowances on business *equipment* (e.g., machinery and equipment; but *not* buildings and real estate improvements). They are:

a. the introduction of the Asset Depreciation Range (ADR) System, which permits business equipment to be depreciated over lives that are not more than 20 percent shorter nor 20 percent longer than the "guideline lives" established by the Treasury Department on July 11, 1962 (see pages 142–44).
b. the termination of the complex "reserve ratio test" effective December 31, 1970, so that the life over which business equipment is written off need no longer be consistent with actual practice in retiring and replacing such depreciable assets (see page 144).
c. a modified "convention" under which a full year's depreciation may be taken for assets placed into service in the first half of a year and one-half year's depreciation for those acquired in the second half of the year.

In describing these changes, the literature abounds with such terms as "promote economic growth," "increase the competitiveness of U.S. goods in world markets," "create new jobs," "offset the toll inflation has taken in the value of depreciation deductions," "stimulate the economy in 1971," and "adjust the imbalance in tax distribution attributable to the Tax Reform Act of 1969." At the time of this writing, there is debate in Congress as to whether or not this liberalization of depreciation should be repealed or modified.

When the triumvirate of unknowns, cost (or other basic value), salvage value (if any), and estimated useful life has been resolved, an answer must, in turn, be supplied to an involved question: what method of depreciation should be used?

DEPRECIATION METHODS

The objective of any depreciation method should be to allocate the cost less salvage value of a depreciable fixed asset over the estimated useful life of that asset in a manner which is both systematic and rational. The depreciation methods used today by a majority of the firms located in the United States may be divided into the following two categories:

(1) Those methods characterized by the cost minus salvage divided by life procedure:
  (a) Straight-line method
  (b) Units-of-production method
(2) Those methods characterized by the accelerated depreciation procedure:
  (a) Declining balance method
  (b) Sum-of-the-years' digits method

To illustrate and explain the various methods of depreciation, assume the following facts for a new machine purchased on January 1, 1971:

Cost (invoice price plus other applicable capital expenditures)	$8,000
Estimated salvage value	250
Estimated useful life:	
In years	5
In units of production	25,000

Straight-Line Method

The method of depreciation most commonly used for many years has been the straight-line method. The theory underlying this method of apportionment is that depreciation is a function of time. The straight-line method produces a uniform annual depreciation expense for each year of the asset's life. The annual depreciation charge is obtained by dividing the amount to be depreciated, cost minus salvage value, by the number of years of estimated useful life. Applying this method to the facts provided above, the annual depreciation expense amounts to $1,550, computed as follows:

$$\text{Annual depreciation} = \frac{\text{Cost} - \text{estimated salvage value}}{\text{Estimated life (in years)}}$$

$$\text{Annual depreciation} = \frac{\$8,000 - \$250}{5 \text{ years}}$$

$$\text{Annual depreciation} = \$1,550$$

Assuming no changes or revisions during the four years in cost, estimated salvage value, or estimated useful life for the above piece of machinery, the table below summarizes the effect on the financial statements of the resulting straight-line depreciation.

Year	Statement of Income For the Year Depreciation Expense	Cost	−	Balance Sheet As of December 31 Accumulated Depreciation to date	=	Cost less Accumulated Depreciation
1971	$1,550	$8,000	−	$1,550	=	$6,450
1972	1,550	8,000	−	3,100	=	4,900
1973	1,550	8,000	−	4,650	=	3,350
1974	1,550	8,000	−	6 200	=	1,800
1975	1,550	8,000	−	7,750	=	250*
	$7,750					

* Estimated salvage value

An alternative manner of expressing estimated life when straight-line depreciation is used is by a percentage rather than actual years. In the above illustration, the amount to be depreciated (cost minus salvage value) may be multiplied by 20 percent rather than divided by five to obtain the annual depreciation allocation. Similarly, a depreciable fixed asset with a four-year life would have a depreciation rate of 25 percent, and an asset with a 12-year life would have a depreciation rate of 8⅓ percent. The multiplier is obtained by dividing 100 percent by the number of years in the estimated useful life of an asset.

The principal advantages of straight-line depreciation are the relative simplicity of computation and the ease with which the concept is understood. The disadvantage advanced by most critics is that this method of depreciation does not give recognition to fluctuations in the actual use made of the asset. If the asset is a building, the effect of such fluctuations probably would be minor. But, if the asset is a machine whose usage might be expected to fluctuate widely from period to period, straight-line depreciation may not be realistic. Also, in the later years of life, when efficiency of operation of the asset may be somewhat lower and repair and maintenance expenses may tend to increase rather sharply, a constant straight-line depreciation charge plus an increasing repair and maintenance expense may produce an unreasonably high total for the two operating expenses.

Units-of-Production Method

The units-of-production method allocates the depreciable basis of a fixed asset according to the use made of that asset during each period. It recognizes that assets which receive irregular use, like certain machinery or trucks, should be depreciated according to their usage rather than by the passage of time. Units of production or output may be expressed in an estimated number of working hours or the number of units of goods to be produced by a machine. In the case of an automobile or truck, units of production or output may be expressed in an estimated number of miles that may be expected from the vehicle. The unit depreciation charge is calculated by dividing the fixed asset's life (expressed in the estimated total number of measurement units) into the acquisition cost less anticipated salvage value of the asset. Applying this method to the assumed facts stated on page 145, the unit depreciation expense for the machine amounts to 31¢ per unit produced; it is computed as follows:

$$\text{Depreciation expense per unit} = \frac{\text{Cost} - \text{estimated salvage value}}{\text{Estimated life (in units)}}$$

$$\text{Depreciation expense per unit} = \frac{\$8,000 - \$250}{25,000 \text{ units}}$$

Depreciation expense per unit = 31¢

Assume that there are no changes in the basic facts employed in the original unit depreciation charge, and that the machine's output during the ensuing years is as follows:

1971	6,000 units
1972	4,000 units
1973	7,000 units
1974	5,000 units
1975	3,000 units
	25,000 units

From the above information, the depreciation expense for each period, in this case each year, can be readily obtained by multiplying the previously computed unit rate of 31¢ by the number of units produced during each period. For example, the depreciation expense for 1971 would be 31¢ × 6,000 units or $1,860. The following table summarizes the effect on the financial statements of depreciation determined by the units-of-production method.

	Statement of Income For the Year		Balance Sheet as of December 31		
Year	Depreciation Expense	Cost	− Accumulated Depreciation to date	=	Cost less Accumulated Depreciation
1971	$1,860	$8,000	− $1,860	=	$6,140
1972	1,240	8,000	− 3,100	=	4,900
1973	2,170	8,000	− 5,270	=	2,730
1974	1,550	8,000	− 6,820	=	1,180
1975	930	8,000	− 7,750	=	250*
	$7,750				

* Estimated salvage value

The chief advantage of the units-of-production method of depreciation is that the cost of the asset is allocated as expense in proportion to the use made of the asset in securing its related revenue. To some extent in the case of certain depreciable assets, this method makes possible a more accurate matching of expenses with revenue than does the straight-line method of depreciation. Though the arithmetic calculation of depreciation is elementary when the units-of-production method is used, the method does require that a record be maintained of the unit output or the hours worked by a particular asset or group of assets.

To compensate for unusual situations which might occur when highly abnormal operating conditions prevail, certain companies which use a units-of-production method establish both minimum and maximum amounts for the depreciation expense in any one year. For example, if an asset is idle throughout an entire year, it does depreciate to some extent. If, on the other hand, a machine is required to produce 10,000 units instead of the 2,000 units normally produced in a year, the machine has not necessarily depreciated five times as much.

Background of Accelerated Depreciation

Prior to 1954, the straight-line method of depreciation was used almost to the complete exclusion of all other methods in the determination of periodic depreciation expense. In 1953, one source, in comparing the use of various methods of depreciation, stated with respect to the straight-line method:

> This is by far the most common method, and is used by more than 90% of all taxpayers entitled to the deduction.[8]

Then, as today, some companies used the units-of-production method for selected assets. In a few instances, a limited version of the declining balance method of depreciation was used for rental housing. But the straight-line method of depreciation was by far the preferred method.

The foregoing is not intended to imply that the straight-line method was the only method of depreciation thought to be justifiable at the time; but, with few exceptions, it was the only method used. Nevertheless, for many years preceding 1954, literature in accounting and related areas devoted considerable attention to a discussion of other methods of depreciation. Among the other methods proposed were the accelerated methods of depreciation known as the declining balance method and the sum-of-the-years' digits method.

Accelerated methods of depreciation provide greater charges in the early years of the asset's life and progressively smaller charges in later years. Theoretically, the continually decreasing periodic depreciation expense will be counter-balanced by an increasing expense for repairs and maintenance as the asset ages. Thus, the total of these two operating expenses, depreciation plus

---

[8] *Prentice-Hall 1954 Federal Tax Course, Students Edition* (Englewood Cliffs, N.J.: Prentice-Hall, Inc., 1953), p. 2009.

repair and maintenance expense, would approximate an equal amount for each year of the life of the asset. In theory, the situation might be illustrated as follows (amounts not related to previous examples):

Year of Life	Depreciation Expense	Repair and Maintenance Expense	Total of the Two Operating Expenses
1st year	$1,000	$ 0	$1,000
2nd year	800	200	1,000
3rd year	600	400	1,000
4th year	400	600	1,000
5th year	200	800	1,000

In theory, it is not difficult to justify this method for many assets. For example, the trends illustrated above for depreciation expense and repair and maintenance expense typically represent the operation of a privately owned automobile. Similar conditions prevail with certain depreciable assets used in business.[9] In fact, an additional argument favoring a depreciation method which produces decreasing annual charges can be advanced. Assets having revenue-producing possibilities which are considerable at the time of their acquisition and shortly thereafter could conceivably lose this advantage long before the end of their estimated useful life because of the inability to forecast accurately the long-range market demand for the products produced by such assets. Thus, heavy depreciation in the early years of the life of an asset might produce a more rational allocation of its cost.

Despite long-standing arguments favorable to accelerated depreciation, prior to 1954 business almost completely rejected the use of any method of accelerated depreciation. Why did this condition exist? Probably because such methods were not acceptable for income tax purposes. But, on August 16, 1954, the President signed into law a new income tax code containing provisions pertaining to accelerated depreciation retroactive to January 1, 1954. Reaction by accountants and the business community was immediate. In fact, what had been largely interesting theory suddenly became common practice. Even the Committee on Accounting Procedure of the AICPA reacted quickly when in October, 1954, it stated:

> The declining-balance method is one of those which meets the requirements of being "systematic and rational" (*Accounting Terminology Bulletin No. 1,* paragraph 56). In those cases where the expected productivity or revenue-earning power of the asset is relatively greater during the earlier years of its life, where maintenance charges tend to increase during the later years, the declining-balance method may well provide the most satisfactory allocation of cost. The conclusions of this bulletin also

---

[9] There have been a few studies which tend to discredit this idea. They indicate that maintenance costs have varied little with the age of the asset.

apply to other methods, including the "sum-of-the-years' digits" method, which produce substantially similar results.[10]

Declining Balance Method

The declining balance method of depreciation is one of two commonly used methods which provide larger depreciation charges during the first years of the asset's life and steadily decreasing charges over the estimated useful life of the asset. By this method, a fixed rate is applied to the *cost* (*not* to the cost minus salvage value) of the asset in the first period to determine that period's depreciation expense. In each subsequent period, the depreciation expense is computed through application of the same fixed rate to the remaining balance (cost minus accumulated depreciation to date) of the asset.

In theory, the fixed rate is determined by extracting the root, equivalent to the estimated life, of a quotient which is obtained by dividing the salvage value by the cost of the asset. Using the same assumed facts as those shown on page 145, the fixed rate is calculated as follows:

$$\text{Fixed rate of depreciation} = 1 - \sqrt[n]{\frac{\text{Salvage value}}{\text{cost}}}$$

$$\text{Fixed rate of depreciation} = 1 - \sqrt[5]{\frac{250}{8,000}}$$

$$\text{Fixed rate of depreciation} = 50\% \text{ [11]}$$

The first table on page 151 summarizes the effect that the theoretical fixed rate used to calculate declining balance depreciation would have on the resulting financial statements.

There are at least two reasons which explain why the theoretical fixed rate is seldom encountered in practice. First, this rate involves rather complex calculations. Second, the Internal Revenue Code of 1954 states that the maximum rate that may be used is twice the straight-line rate. Thus, for the machine in our example, the effective fixed rate that would actually be used for tax purposes is twice the straight-line rate of 20 percent, or 40 percent[12]; thus, it is commonly referred to as the double declining balance method of depreciation. Use of this rate can lead to a few complications. For example, if the permissible maximum tax rate of 40 percent (twice the straight-line rate) is

---

[10] American Institute of Certified Public Accountants, Inc., *Accounting Research Bulletin No. 44*, "Declining-Balance Depreciation" (October, 1954) paragraph two. Copyright © 1954 by the American Institute of Certified Public Accountants, Inc.

[11] Figures were purposely chosen which would simplify arithmetic and add to clarity of presentation. Rarely would the rate equal an even percentage. For example, if cost is $1,000, salvage is estimated at $100, and life is 10 years, application of the formula would give a fixed rate of 20.5672%.

[12] Similarly, if an asset had a six-year life which would produce a straight-line rate of 16⅔ percent, the permissible effective fixed percentage rate for declining balance depreciation would be 33⅓ percent.

Year	Cost less Accumulated Depreciation on Machine on January 1		Fixed Rate		Depreciation Expense	Cost		Accumulated Depreciation to date		Cost less Accumulated Depreciation
1971	$8,000	×	50%	=	$4,000	$8,000	−	$4,000	=	$4,000
1972	4,000	×	50%	=	2,000	8,000	−	6,000	=	2,000
1973	2,000	×	50%	=	1,000	8,000	−	7,000	=	1,000
1974	1,000	×	50%	=	500	8,000	−	7,500	=	500
1975	500	×	50%	=	250	8,000	−	7,750	=	250*
					$7,750					

*Estimated salvage value

used, the results shown in the preceding table would be changed to the following (rounded to the nearest dollar):

Year	Cost less Accumulated Depreciation on Machine on January 1		Fixed Rate		Depreciation Expense	Cost		Accumulated Depreciation to date		Cost less Accumulated Depreciation
1971	$8,000	×	40%	=	$3,200	$8,000	−	$3,200	=	$4,800
1972	4,800	×	40%	=	1,920	8,000	−	5,120	=	2,880
1973	2,880	×	40%	=	1,152	8,000	−	6,272	=	1,728
1974	1,728	×	40%	=	691	8,000	−	6,963	=	1,037
1975	1,037	×	40%	=	415	8,000	−	7,378	=	622*
					$7,378					

* More than estimated salvage value of $250.

Note that, at the end of the estimated useful life, the remaining carrying value or undepreciated cost of $622 exceeds the estimated salvage value of $250. Similarly, total depreciation is $7,378, not $7,750. For these reasons, the income tax law permits a change during the life of the asset from the double declining balance method to the straight-line method so that unrecovered cost less salvage value may be depreciated over the remaining estimated useful life. Presumably, if no such switch to straight-line is made and the asset is continued in use beyond the fifth year, depreciation at the permissible fixed rate on the unrecovered cost of the asset can be continued until it has been depreciated down to the salvage value. Conversely, sometimes the application of twice the straight-line rate will depreciate an asset down to salvage value before the end of its originally estimated useful life. Then, depreciation charges should cease before the termination of estimated useful life, for in no case should an asset be depreciated below its estimated salvage value.

Sum-of-the-Years' Digits Method

The sum-of-the-years' digits method of depreciation, like the declining balance method, produces gradually decreasing depreciation charges over the estimated useful life of the asset. This method, unlike the declining balance method, is somewhat easier to compute and avoids the problem of a possible remaining excess of unrecovered cost at the end of estimated useful life. Under the sum-of-the-years' digits method, the depreciation expense for any given year is computed by multiplying the total cost less salvage value by a changing fraction. In any year, the fraction used requires a numerator which corresponds to the remaining years of estimated life of the asset and a denominator which equals the sum of the numerical sequence formed by the years in the asset's total life. Using the original example of a machine with a five-year life, the numerator of the applicable fraction for the first year would be 5, for the second year 4, and so on until it reached 1 for the last year of life. The denominator of the fraction each year would be 15, the sum of the numbers designating the years in the total life; that is, $1 + 2 + 3 + 4 + 5$. Thus, the depreciation expense for the first year would be $5/15$ of the cost minus salvage value of the machine, for the second year, $4/15$ of the cost minus salvage value. Using the assumed facts on page 145, the following table summarizes the effect of the sum-of-the-years' digits method of depreciation on the information provided by the financial statements.

Year	Cost less Salvage Value	× Fraction =	Depreciation Expense (Statement of Income For the Year)	Cost	−	Accumulated Depreciation to date	=	Cost less Accumulated Depreciation (Balance Sheet As of December 31)
1971	$7,750	× $5/15$ =	$2,583	$8,000	−	$2,583	=	$5,417
1972	7,750	× $4/15$ =	2,067	8,000	−	4,650	=	3,350
1973	7,750	× $3/15$ =	1,550	8,000	−	6,200	=	1,800
1974	7,750	× $2/15$ =	1,033	8,000	−	7,233	=	767
1975	7,750	× $1/15$ =	517	8,000	−	7,750	=	250*
			$7,750					

* Estimated salvage value

Any company intending to use either of the two accelerated methods of depreciation for federal income tax purposes should be aware of the provisions of Section 167(c) of the 1954 Internal Revenue Code and the changes made by the Tax Reform Act of 1969 which state, generally, that the tangible fixed asset, to be eligible for such depreciation, must have a useful life of three years or more, be acquired after December 31, 1953, and be an unused new asset (second-hand assets are not eligible).

In recent years, some of the accelerated depreciation provisions have been suspended, reinstated, altered, or repealed for income tax purposes. An awareness of these changes is necessary when planning for new capital expenditures.

The Investment Credit and Accelerated Depreciation Suspension Act, P.L. 89-800, signed by the President on November 8, 1966, contained the following two principal provisions:

1. The 7 percent investment credit, to be discussed in Chapter 7, was suspended on property acquired or constructed during the period of October 10, 1966, through December 31, 1967.
2. Accelerated depreciation (both double declining balance and sum-of-the-years' digits methods), discussed in this chapter, was prohibited on *buildings* (but *not* on machinery, equipment, etc.) if ordered or if construction was started during the period of October 10, 1966, through December 31, 1967.

The aim of these two provisions was to discourage capital expenditures and thus decrease or restrain one of the inflationary pressures on the economy. There were certain minor exceptions to the above two provisions, designed chiefly to benefit the small businessman, which are beyond the scope of this book. These two provisions were not "repealed"; rather they were to have been "suspended" for approximately 15 months. When the economy suddenly turned down, due to many factors, the suspension was quickly terminated, ahead of schedule, effective principally with property acquired after March 9, 1967.

The Tax Reform Act of 1969, P.L. 91-172, signed by the President on December 30, 1969, contained the following principal provisions, which are still in effect as of the date of this writing:

1. Repealed the 7 percent investment credit, to be discussed in Chapter 7, effective April 18, 1969.
2. Reinstituted the concept of rapid amortization, to be discussed in Chapter 7.
3. The only accelerated depreciation method permitted for new real business property (office buildings; not machinery, equipment, etc.) purchased or constructed after July 24, 1969, is the 150 percent declining balance method. In effect, for new buildings, the maximum rate is 1½ times the straight-line rate. If a new building with an estimated life of 50 years is acquired, the 150 percent declining balance method would result in annual depreciation rate of 3 percent (1½ times the 2 percent straight-line rate) on the diminishing balance. Note that the double declining balance and the sum-of-the-years' digits method are *still available* for new personalty business (machinery, equipment, etc.) property.
4. The above deceleration of accelerated depreciation does *not* apply to *new* real property which is principally new residential rental property, e.g., a new apartment building. Both the double declining balance method and

the sum-of-the-years' digits method may still be used on new residential rental property.
5. A 125 percent declining balance method may be employed to depreciate *used* residential rental property with a life of 20 years or more at acquisition.

The aim of the repeal of the investment credit and the deceleration of accelerated depreciation was to aid in curbing the inflationary aspects of the economy. The chief aim of the other provisions is to better environmental conditions and housing.

COMPARISON OF PRINCIPAL DEPRECIATION METHODS

The summary presented below of the preceding detailed tables clearly indicates the effect of the various methods on the information provided by the financial statements. When the units-of-production method is used, the depreciation expense for the period varies directly with the use made of the asset. When the straight-line and the accelerated methods of depreciation are used, passage of time, rather than usage, usually determines the depreciation expense for the period; the amount of expense is the resultant of the specific method

Annual depreciation expense on the Statement of Income

Year	Straight-Line	Units-of-Production	Declining Balance[13]	Sum-of-Years' Digits
1971	$1,550	$1,860	$3,200	$2,583
1972	1,550	1,240	1,920	2,067
1973	1,550	2,170	1,152	1,550
1974	1,550	1,550	691	1,033
1975	1,550	930	415	517
	$7,750	$7,750	$7,378	$7,750

selected. A comparison of results for the first two years, based upon our assumed facts, reveals that, of the $7,750 amount (cost less salvage value) to be allocated over the five-year life of the asset in a "systematic and rational manner," 40 percent is distributed as expense in the first two years by the straight-

Method of Depreciation

Year	Straight-Line	Declining Balance	Sum-of-Years' Digits
1971	$1,550	$3,200	$2,583
1972	1,550	1,920	2,067
	$3,100	$5,120	$4,650
% of $7,750	40%	66%	60%

---

[13] Using the tax method of double the straight-line rate.

line method; the declining balance and the sum-of-the-years' digits methods distribute 66 percent and 60 percent of it in the same time period. A reverse situation prevails in the later years of life. What, then, should determine the method of depreciation selected?

Selection of a Depreciation Method

The selection of a depreciation method should be based, theoretically, on the premise that one method will most fairly provide the proper information for management guidance. A depreciation method should allocate the cost of an asset equitably over its useful life so that the closest possible matching occurs each period between expired costs and related revenue. Thus, each company must base its selection of the method or methods of depreciation to be employed upon the kind of information it needs for management guidance, the nature of its business, and the types of depreciable plant and equipment items which are involved. It is not uncommon for a given company to use different depreciation methods for the various classifications of depreciable property it owns.

An additional factor must also be considered in selecting proper depreciation methods. While the above approach may be fine theory from the point of view of financial reporting, the effect of a federal corporate income tax rate of approximately 50 percent should not be ignored. If the accelerated methods of depreciation, rather than straight-line, are used, the impact of income taxes may be reduced. Both accelerated methods provide greater depreciation expense in the earlier years of an asset's life; this reduces, in these years, the net income subject to tax. The amount of the decrease in taxes payable during such years is approximately 50 percent of the amount by which accelerated depreciation exceeds straight-line depreciation on the assets involved. For a company of any size, the dollar amount involved may be material. In 1960, for example, it resulted in a tax deferral of $4,667,936 for The Procter & Gamble Company, $4,827,559 for The Detroit Edison Company, and $4,530,-000 for American Can Company. This current tax deferral conserves additional funds which can be alternatively employed in the business; but what of the future—those later years when accelerated depreciation is less in amount than straight-line depreciation? Discussion of this point is reserved for the next chapter.

As with so many decisions required of management, a policy concerning depreciation methods must be resolved with an awareness of tax consequences. Each company must make its decision based on past experiences, present status, and expected future results. Any decision based solely on a gamble that tax rates will move one way or another could be disastrous. Many companies have resolved the dilemma concerning depreciation methods by adopting one or more methods to present fairly the financial results and a different method or methods for income taxes. For example, Reynolds Metals Company uses straight-line depreciation for financial accounting and the declining balance method for income taxes. But, while this procedure solves one problem, it creates another. The financial statements will be distorted if the statement of income shows a smaller depreciation expense and a larger net income than does the tax return; because of the excess depreciation deducted on the tax return, the actual federal income taxes for the year will be less than the amount that would be allocable to the net income shown by the financial statement of income. To prevent such distortion, a provision for deferred income taxes should be provided for in the financial statements; this point is discussed at the beginning of the next chapter. As an example of such a situation, in the 1970 Annual Report of Armstrong Cork Company, note 7 to the financial statements states:

>*7. Deferred income taxes:*
>The company generally uses straight-line depreciation for financial reporting purposes and accelerated depreciation as permitted by the Internal Revenue Service for tax purposes. Provision ($2,229,000 in 1970) has been made in the accounts for future income taxes applicable to depreciation and other minor items reported differently for tax and financial reporting purposes.

Group and Composite Rate Depreciation

For clarity, the theory underlying the depreciation methods explained and the facts employed to illustrate such theory in examples have been limited to the depreciation of a single asset. Many companies, regardless of the depreciation method or methods selected, apply these methods to homogenous groups of fixed assets rather than to specific units. For example, a delivery service might depreciate, upon acquisition, a fleet of trucks as a group rather than individually. Similarly, a department store might depreciate its showcases as a group; another business might use group depreciation for its office typewriters.

When the group method of depreciation is used, useful life is estimated for the group as a whole to establish a depreciation rate. This rate of depreciation is then applied to the total cost of the group for the previously determined life or until the group of assets is fully depreciated. Use of the group method assumes that early retirement of a specific item will be offset by late retirement of another in the same group. Any unduly large variation in this predicted pattern of retirements would necessitate an adjustment in the group rate of depreciation.

The composite method of depreciation differs from the group method in that the composite category contains depreciable assets unlike each other in form, but like each other in that they are all used in a specific segment of the business. For example, the composite may be an open hearth unit, the overall life of which is 25 years; the composite may contain everything in it from the building with a 50 year life, charging machines with a 20 year life, and ingot molds with a 5 year life. A composite life of 15 years may be used for office equipment; but whenever the office equipment is segregated into groups, group lives could be:

Furniture, fixtures, and filing cases .... 20 years
Mechanical equipment .... 8 years
Safes .... 50 years

The averaging technique used by a composite rate will be a time saver if the rate does not require frequent revisions. Accuracy of a composite rate is always subject to greater debate than the more commonly employed group method.

REVISION OF ESTIMATED USEFUL LIFE

The periodic depreciation expense for a fixed asset may be changed because of a revision in the asset's originally estimated useful life. Usually, such revisions are not made unless the amount involved is material.

As an illustration of the problems created by the revision of estimated useful life, assume that a machine costing $30,000 was originally estimated to have a useful life of ten years and no salvage value. At the end of five years, it is ascertained that the machine still has ten years of useful life remaining: the machine has an overall useful life of fifteen years instead of ten. The company uses the straight-line method of depreciation. What action, if any, should be taken to adjust the financial statements for the excess depreciation taken during the first five years? What should the revised annual depreciation charge be for the next ten years?

Theoretically, $2,000 instead of $3,000 depreciation should have been expensed in each of the past five years. The past overstatement of this expense has understated net income each year by $1,000 and has produced a cumulative effect of a $5,000 understatement in retained earnings reinvested in the business. Similarly, assets are also understated by $5,000. As shown below, the property, plant and equipment section of the balance sheet at the end of the fifth year indicates that $15,000 of unrecovered cost remains to be depreciated, while the amount would be $20,000 if useful life had been correctly anticipated. In principle, the correction of this situation would require that retained earnings reinvested in the business be increased $5,000 to adjust for the $1,000 understatement of net income each year for five years, and that the assets of the company be increased $5,000 by changing the amount

	Based upon an estimate of	
	10-year life	15-year life
Machinery (at cost)	$30,000	$30,000
Less: Accumulated depreciation to date	15,000	10,000
Unrecovered cost	$15,000	$20,000

shown for "Less: Accumulated depreciation to date" from $15,000 to $10,000. In this manner, unrecovered cost of $20,000 would be equitably allocated over the remaining ten years of life as an annual $2,000 charge against revenue.

In practice, a more realistic method is usually followed. By this method, the remaining unrecovered cost of $15,000 is divided by the revised estimated remaining life of ten years to derive a $1,500 annual depreciation charge against revenue. This procedure has the effect of letting bygones be bygones. By either method, the full $30,000 of original cost will be allocated over fifteen years.

Accounting theorists are not in agreement about the proper procedure to be employed when a revision of estimated useful life is necessary. Many of their arguments center around sophisticated distinctions, as whether the error in establishing useful life was routine and mechanical or an error in judgment, and whether the events leading to a revision of life were of an unusual nature. Those in management should be aware of the effect of any revisions in estimated life upon the financial data which they employ in the guidance of the business.

Management should also be aware of the necessity of revising the estimated useful life of depreciable assets whenever conditions warrant such adjustments. Such periodic reviews may either increase or decrease estimated remaining life. For example, in 1959 Walt Disney Productions increased the remaining life of Disneyland from its life of seven years originally established in 1955. On the other hand, many companies have found it necessary to revise downward the estimated remaining life of many assets. A period of rapid technological changes produces more rapid obsolescence of certain depreciable assets than originally anticipated. In addition, certain depreciable assets like machinery may have their remaining useful life shortened by extraordinarily heavy usage (i.e., daily plant operations may increase from one to three eight-hour shifts). Management should consider possible complications with the Treasury Department when contemplating any redetermination of estimated remaining useful life of depreciable assets. Such contemplated revisions should be made only when the change in useful life is significant and there is a clear and convincing basis for the redetermination.

DISPOSAL OF FIXED ASSETS

Disposals of depreciable fixed assets create problems which must be resolved correctly to insure the proper effect upon periodic financial statements; inaccurate solutions may unwittingly mislead both internal management and outside reviewers of the company's financial reports. To illustrate the typical problems which arise through such disposals, the following facts are assumed to apply to a piece of machinery which was purchased by a company on January 5, 1970:

```
Cost:
    Invoice price ............................ $ 9,800
    Freight (capitalized) ......................    300
    Installation (capitalized) ..................    100
                                                 ───────
        Total cost of machine ................. $10,200
                                                 ═══════
```

[CH. 6]   PROPERTY: ACQUISITION, DEPRECIATION, DISPOSAL   159

> Estimated salvage value .... $ 200
> Estimated useful life .... Five years
> Depreciation method:
>   Regular straight-line
>   Computed to nearest full month
>   Neither group nor composite methods used
>   Fiscal year of company coincides with calendar year

The December 31, 1972, balance sheet of the company showed for this particular asset:

> Machinery $10,200
> Accumulated depreciation to date[14] 6,000
> Cost less accumulated depreciation .... $ 4,200

Three different types of situations are created by making the following three assumptions about the manner by which the machine is disposed of on March 31, 1973:

(1) Sold the machine for $5,000 cash.

(2) Sold the machine for $3,500 cash.

(3) Traded in the piece of machinery for another machine priced at $12,000. Received a trade-in allowance of $3,500 (the amount for which it could have been sold for cash) and paid the balance of $8,500 in cash.

Under all three assumptions, recognition first must be provided for the additional depreciation which accumulated between December 31, 1972, and the date of the disposal in 1973. Since the company computes depreciation to the nearest full month, depreciation for three months, one-fourth of a year, of 1973 will amount to $500.[15] Thus, total accumulated depreciation to the date of disposal is $6,500.

Under the first assumption, there is a $1,300 gain on the sale of the piece of machinery, computed as follows:

> Cost (total) of machine $10,200
> Less accumulated depreciation (6,000 + 500) 6,500
> Cost less accumulated depreciation .... $ 3,700
> Cash received from sale 5,000
> Gain on disposal .... $ 1,300

Under the three assumptions provided, the summary tables which follow indicate the effect of the sale on the financial statements. Using the first assumption, the balance sheet as of March 31, 1973, reflects the increase in the cash balance

---

[14] Annual depreciation of $\dfrac{\$10,200 - \$200}{5 \text{ years}}$ or $2,000 times three full years to date.

[15] To simplify depreciation computations, many companies charge one-half a year's depreciation in the year of acquisition and one-half a year's depreciation in the year of disposal, regardless of the actual specific dates.

attributable to the $5,000 cash receipt. The property, plant and equipment section of the statement reflects a $3,700 net decrease attributable to the removal of the $10,200 machine and its contra item of accumulated depreciation to date of $6,500 (actually $6,000 as of January 1 plus $500 additional for the first three months of 1973). The statement of income for the first three months of the year, of course, includes the $500 of depreciation expense allocated to this period of time. In addition, the non-operating section of the statement of income discloses the $1,300 gain on disposal of the machinery. The resulting overall net income for the period which is not distributed as dividends increases the retained earnings of the company.

Under the second assumption (if the machine is sold for $3,500 cash), there is a loss of $200, since the cash received is $200 less than the $3,700 amount which represents the cost of the machine less accumulated depreciation. Reference to the following tables indicates that the effect of this sale upon the pertinent items contained in the financial statements would be similar to that explained under the first assumption.

The third assumption (if the old machine is traded in for a new machine) also results in a $200 loss on disposal of the old machine, as indicated below:

Cost (total) of old machine	$10,200
Less accumulated depreciation (6,000 + 500)	6,500
Cost less accumulated depreciation	$ 3,700
Trade-in allowance received	3,500
Loss on disposal	$ 200

As in the second assumption, $3,500 is "received." However, under the second assumption, the machine was disposed of by an outright sale and the receipt

Balance Sheet
As of March 31, 1973

	First Assumption	Second Assumption	Third Assumption
Current Assets:			
Cash	+ 5,000	+ 3,500	− 8,500
Property, Plant and Equipment:			
Machinery	−10,200	−10,200	{+12,000 / −10,200}
Less: Accumulated depreciation	− 6,500	− 6,500	− 6,500
Net	− 3,700	− 3,700	{+12,000 / − 3,700}
Stockholders' Equity:			
Retained Earnings		The gain or loss on disposal becomes a portion of the net income for the period retained and reinvested in the business	

Statement of Income
For the Three Months Ended March 31, 1973

	First Assumption	Second Assumption	Third Assumption
Operating Expenses:			
Depreciation of Machinery	+ 500	+500	+500
Other Income:			
Gain on Disposal of Fixed Assets ..	+1,300		
Other Expenses and Losses:			
Loss on Disposal of Fixed Assets ..		+200	+200

was in cash; under the third assumption, the receipt is a trade-in allowance. Thus, the new machine, priced at $12,000, requires a cash outlay of only $8,500 as follows:

Cost of new machine	$12,000
Less trade-in allowance received	3,500
Cash disbursed to acquire new machine	$ 8,500

Reference to the preceding tables indicates the effect of the trade-in of the old machine for a new machine upon the financial statements. The balance sheet reflects the decrease in the cash balance attributable to the $8,500 disbursement for the new machine. The property, plant and equipment section of the statement reflects a net increase of $8,300 produced by the $12,000 increase for the acquisition of the new machine and a $3,700 net decrease attributable to the disposal of the $10,200 old machine and its accumulated depreciation to date of $6,500. The statement of income for the period, as for the second assumption, includes the $500 of current depreciation expense on the old machine and the $200 loss on the disposal of this machine.

While the theory followed above regarding the trade-in of one asset for a similar type of new asset is sound as theory, it does not agree with the income tax provisions regarding trade-ins. Federal income tax provisions require that, for the typical trade-in situation just illustrated, no gain or loss be recognized when property used in business is exchanged for property of a like kind.[16] Because the tax provisions prevent such gains or losses on trade-in from being recognized as income or expense, the cost of the new asset acquired must be adjusted in the following manner for tax purposes:

$$\text{Basis of new asset} = \text{Cost of new asset} \begin{cases} + \text{ Non-recognized loss} \\ - \text{ Non-recognized gain} \end{cases}$$

Thus, the $12,000 new machine acquired by trade in our third assumption would have a tax basis of $12,200 because of the addition of the $200 non-recognized loss on the disposal of the old machine. And for taxes, depreciation of the new machine would be based upon $12,200 rather than $12,000. Rather than use one method for general accounting and another for taxes in such situ-

---

[16] Internal Revenue Code, Section 1002.

ations, many companies simply follow the tax method for general accounting purposes when the dollar amount involved is not significant. In such a case, the balance sheet under the third assumption would indicate an increase in Machinery of $12,200 instead of $12,000, and the Loss on Disposal of Fixed Assets of $200 on the statement of income would be eliminated.

Those in management who are responsible for decisions regarding acquisitions and disposals of items of property, plant, and equipment should be aware of the foregoing principles. The disposal of a fixed asset by *sale,* accompanied by the purchase of a similar fixed asset, normally will produce a gain or loss situation for both general accounting and tax purposes. On the other hand, the acquisition of a similar new fixed asset resulting from disposal of the old asset by *trade-in* normally will not produce a taxable gain or deductible loss. Proper planning will provide the method to be employed to maximize company interests.

The businessman should also be aware of the fact that normally, when the group or composite method of depreciation is used, no gain or loss is recognized for either general accounting or taxes when an asset is sold, scrapped, or traded in. Under normal circumstances, when specific assets which are a part of a group are retired, it is assumed that any individual gains and losses on such disposals will offset each other.

QUESTIONS AND PROBLEMS

6-1. Letter an answer sheet from a through f and then for each of the following expenditures, place a "C" if the item is a capital expenditure or if it can be capitalized; place an "R" only if the item is definitely a revenue (operating) expenditure.

  a. The cost of a new battery and battery cables for the company's second-hand delivery truck purchased two days ago. The other cables were worn through in one spot and the battery (apparently original equipment) was worn out.

  b. The cost of a new battery for a company auto used by salesmen. The company purchased the auto two years ago and depreciates it over four years; the original battery, now being replaced, wore out.

  c. The cost to the University of Bellevue for putting in stone and concrete sidewalks where students had worn paths over the years across the grass lawn.

  d. The cost to the University of Bellevue for reseeding portions of the lawn worn by student traffic, student recreational activities, and ROTC drills. The original cost of the lawn had been capitalized in "Land."

  e. The cost of a set of basic medical encyclopedias needed in the office library of a doctor.

f. The cost of the annual one-year subscription to the American Medical Journal needed in the office library of a doctor.

6-2. Van Sickle Merchandising Company purchased a used delivery truck for $2,500. Prior to placing the truck in use, it sent the truck to the Butler Garage for overhauling and reconditioning. The itemized bill received from the Butler Garage disclosed:

Overhauling motor	$150
Reconditioning chassis	100
New delivery truck body	500
Two new tires to replace "bald" ones	70
Spotlight	30
Gasoline and oil	15
Anti-freeze (non-permanent)	10
State inspection sticker (semi-annual)	5
Total	$880

What portion of the $880 should be capitalized and what portion should be expensed? Prepare your answer in accord with accounting theory rather than company policy or tax considerations.

6-3. At December 31, 1972, the balance sheet of the Beulah Corporation disclosed:

Property, Plant and Equipment, at cost:		
Land	$ 500,000	
Buildings	2,000,000	
Machinery	700,000	
Automobiles (10 @ $4,000)	40,000	
Total	$3,240,000	
Accumulated Depreciation to date	1,000,000	
Unrecovered Cost		$2,240,000

During 1973, the following events affecting the various property, plant and equipment items occurred:

a. To increase its employee parking area, the corporation purchased adjacent land for $100,000 and a building on it for $50,000. It cost $3,000 to raze the building and $2,000 to level the land.

b. An air-conditioning unit was purchased and installed in each of the ten company automobiles, cost $500 each. The autos had never been air-conditioned.

c. Each automobile received its usual 10,000 mile tune-up and had new spark plugs and points installed at a cost of $15 each.

d. A piece of machinery (original cost $100,000) with an estimated life of 10 years was completely rebuilt at a cost of $40,000 during the eighth year (1973) of its life, extending its estimated useful life for seven more years from January 1, 1973. For this item, see the explanation of "CA" at the beginning and end of problem 6-4.

e. The buildings were painted at a cost of $25,000. The corporation's maintenance policy includes painting its buildings every fifth year. The corporation last painted them in 1968.

f. Depreciation expense (total) for the year as shown by the statement of income was $350,000.

Required

At December 31, 1973, the balance sheet of the Beulah Corporation would show:

```
Property, Plant and Equipment, at cost:
    Land .......................... $
    Buildings .......................
    Machinery .......................
    Automobiles (10 autos) ..........    _____
        Total .......................  $
    Accumulated Depreciation to date ...  _____
    Unrecovered Cost ............................... $_____
```

6-4. For each of the items below, you are to indicate the preferred accounting treatment. Letter your answer sheet from a through j, and opposite these letters place:

"C" if the item is a capital expenditure and increases an asset.

"CA" if the item is a capital expenditure but is chargeable against accumulated depreciation to date.

"R" if the item is a revenue expenditure and increases an expense item on the statement of income.

a. The Talbot Co. spent $8,600 during the year for experimental purposes in connection with the development of its product. This is approximately the same amount that the company has been spending for this purpose annually for many years.

b. In April, the West Co. paid cash of $2,800 because a suit was lost in defense of a patent infringement case.

c. The Miller Co., plaintiff, paid $5,000 for legal fees in December, in connection with a successful infringement suit on its patent. No damages were awarded. (See page 206.)

d. The Placey Company recently purchased land and two buildings for a total cost of $35,000 and entered the purchase on the books. Razing costs of $1,200 were incurred in removing the smaller building, which had an appraised value at acquisition of $6,200, to make room for new construction.

e. On June 1, the Geneva Hotel installed a sprinkler system throughout the building at a cost of $13,000. As a result, the insurance rate was decreased by 40 percent.

f. A motor in one of Company B's trucks was overhauled at a cost of $600. It is expected that this will extend the life of the truck for two years.

g. An improvement, which extended the life but not the usefulness of the assets, cost $6,000.

h. Joe Donald and Frank Rice, maintenance repair men, spent five days in

[CH. 6]   PROPERTY: ACQUISITION, DEPRECIATION, DISPOSAL   165

unloading and setting up a new $6,000 precision machine in the plant. The wages earned in this five-day period totaled $240.

i. The Edison Electric Utility Company recorded the first six months' interest on 6 percent, $100,000 ten-year bonds sold six months ago. The bonds were sold to finance the construction of a hydroelectric plant. Six months after the sale, the construction of the hydroelectric plant was completed and operations were begun.

j. The Hiway Supermarket Co. paid a special "tax" assessment. The special assessment provided funds for the construction of public streets in the area in which the market was located.

Note: This problem has been adapted from a problem on the Uniform CPA Examination.

"CA" represents a capital expenditure, but one that is chargeable against accumulated depreciation to date rather than shown as an addition to cost. This is a procedure often used when a major replacement of a component part or an improvement in effect "makes good" prior years' depreciation or extends life; e.g., a new roof installed on a ten-year-old brick kiln.

6-5. The Finance Committee of Unocheck Corporation is debating the proper treatment of a contemplated $300,000 renovation cost of its $1,000,000 25-year-old office building (new roof, new elevators, new front on first three floors, complete new plumbing and wiring, etc.). While the expenditure may lengthen the life of the building, it might also be viewed as either making good prior years' depreciation, or a property addition, or merely bringing the building back to its original condition. If the renovation is undertaken, paid for, and completed in December of the current year, show how the current year's estimated statements would be changed if the expenditure is:

Statement of Income		(1) An Addition to Buildings	(2) A Restoration of Prior Depreciation	(3) A Revenue Expenditure
Net Sales	$10,000,000	$10,000,000	$10,000,000	$10,000,000
Costs and Expenses	7,000,000			
	$ 3,000,000	$	$	$
Income Tax (50%)	1,500,000			
Net Income	$ 1,500,000	$	$	$
Balance Sheet				
Current Assets	$ 8,000,000	$ 7,700,000	$ 7,700,000	$ 7,700,000
Building	$ 1,000,000	$	$	$
Accumul. Depreciation	−500,000			
	$ 500,000	$	$	$
Other Assets	3,000,000	3,000,000	3,000,000	3,000,000
	$11,500,000	$	$	$

Current Liabilities	$ 4,500,000	$	$	$
Stockholders' Equity	7,000,000			
	$11,500,000	$	$	$

Note: Ignore any possible depreciation on the $300,000.

Note: For the second alternative, see the explanation of "CA" at the beginning and end of problem 6-4.

6-6. The Roddy Manufacturing Corporation decided to construct a new plant on the outskirts of Erehwon, Ohio, and incurred the following expenditures:

Purchase price of land including an old farmhouse		$ 250,000
(Approximate apportionment of expenditure is $235,000 to land and $15,000 to house)		
Net cost of clearing land:		
Razing house $1,000		
Less sale of scrap 200		
	$ 800	
Removing trees, stumps, brush	3,200	4,000
Leveling land (cut down small hill and filled ravine)		32,000
Cost of building (paid to contractor)		2,000,000
Cement driveways and walks		6,000
Fence around property		3,500
Landscaping (grass, trees, shrubbery, etc.)		4,500
Total		$2,300,000

Required

a. What portion of the $2,300,000 should be capitalized as the cost of the:
   Land?
   Land Improvements (attachments)?
   Building?

b. Should any portion of the $2,300,000 be treated as an operating expenditure?

6-7. Letter an answer sheet from a through t and then for each of the following expenditures, place a "C" if the item is a capital expenditure or if it can be capitalized; place an "R" only if the item is definitely a revenue (operating) expenditure.

   a. The cost of moving old machinery from several old plants to another much larger building and cost of reinstalling the machinery; object was to consolidate the company's operating activities.

   b. Purchase and installation of an excellent quality vinyl-asbestos floor in the reception office of a steel company. The flooring covered a hardwood floor so badly worn that it couldn't be refinished.

   c. Landscaping expenditures incurred in the construction of a shopping center.

[CH. 6]   PROPERTY: ACQUISITION, DEPRECIATION, DISPOSAL   167

   d. Cost of installing a police signaling system by a jewelry store.

   e. Repairs on the main office building of a steel company to the gutters which were damaged by a heavy snow storm.

   f. Interest, during construction, on funds borrowed to finance new capital projects by Sacramento Municipal Utility District.

   g. The cost of a new engine (motor) in the company's delivery truck.

   h. Interest paid to MNBT Bank by ABC Department Store on funds borrowed to carry excess inventory needed during the fall-Christmas season.

     BNP Bank purchased a membership in the Wildwood Country Club, to be used by officers of the bank in the bank's business:

   i. The initiation fee of $300 and the required purchase of stock, $800, in the country club.

   j. The monthly dues in the club.

   k. Cost of a new battery for the salesman's auto; the old battery was ruined by neglect during a sub-zero cold wave.

   l. Architect's fee for plans for a new office building just constructed.

   m. Special tax assessment for prorata share of the cost of a sewer line, replacing septic tanks.

   n. Painting the office building of the company; it had not been painted for seven years.

   o. Annual termite inspection fee of $100 paid for inspection of the company's various buildings in Florida.

   p. Firman Company purchased an ancient three-story building in the old French quarter of New Orleans. Though the architects retained by Firman Company recommended that the company demolish the building, permission could not be obtained from local authorities because of the historical and architectural value of the building. Therefore, the company expended $50,000 to place the building in condition so that it could again be used for revenue producing purposes.

   q. Dental fees paid by an actor for necessary new bridgework to replace bridgework broken when he made a series of TV prize fight pictures.

   r. Expenditure of $100, to State Department of Revenue, for license plates for delivery truck.

   s. Title search on a tract of ground purchased as a building site.

   t. Cost of tuition for a college program of study (for the typically successful, full time, day school candidate for a degree).

6-8. On July 1, 1971, M. L. Thompson Corporation traded in an old piece of machinery for a new but similar machine. The old machine had cost $7,900 when purchased January 2, 1961. Estimated life of 15 years and salvage value of $400, both established at the date of acquisition, had never been changed for old machine. The December 31, 1970, balance sheet showed for this particular old asset:

     Machinery $7,900
     Accumulated depreciation to date 5,000 $2,900

The company uses straight-line depreciation but does not use either the group or composite methods. When the trade-in occurred on July 1, 1971, the corporation received a trade-in allowance of $950 for the old machine (the amount for which it could have been sold for cash) and paid the balance of $8,100 in cash for the new machine, which was priced at $9,050.

Required

a. Compute the gain or loss on the disposal of the old machine.

b. For tax purposes, such a gain or loss is not recognized. Therefore, compute the depreciation basis of the new machine for tax purposes.

6-9. ROC Corporation purchased a piece of new machinery on January 2, 1971. ROC Corporation is the original user of the machinery: cost $60,000; estimated salvage value $5,000; estimated useful life 10 years. (The corporation did *not* elect to use the 20 percent additional one-shot first-year depreciation allowance as discussed in Chapter 7 on this acquisition.) Compute the *1971 and 1972* expense for depreciation if ROC Corporation uses the:

a. Straight-line method

b. Declining balance method (tax method—twice straight-line rate)

c. Sum-of-the-year's digits method

6-10. Assume the information given in problem 6-9, except that the machinery purchased was second hand machinery.

Required

Compute the *maximum* allowed depreciation expense for both 1971 and 1972.

6-11. For each of the following statements, choose the best answer to each and indicate your choice on an answer sheet with the number 1, 2, or 3.

a. Depreciation accounting is the process of:
   1. revaluing the asset on the balance sheet as it wears out
   2. expensing the cost of the asset in a systematic manner as a charge against revenues so as to determine an accurate profit for the period
   3. providing for replacement of the asset when its useful life is ended

b. Accelerated depreciation, approved by the Revenue Act of 1954, was an attempt by Congress to:
   1. update generally accepted accounting principles
   2. "stimulate" the economy
   3. give recognition to a long established business practice with respect to depreciation methods used in business

c. The "guideline lives" are the result of:
   1. an Act of Congress
   2. a Treasury Department release
   3. a study by the American Institute of CPA's

d. Accelerated depreciation:
   1. usually expenses the total cost (less any salvage) of the asset in a shorter number of years than straight-line depreciation

[CH. 6] PROPERTY: ACQUISITION, DEPRECIATION, DISPOSAL 169

    2. is available on all fixed assets, except land, acquired since January 1, 1954
    3. is not mandatory; straight-line depreciation may still be elected

6-12. Assume the following facts with respect to a new machine purchased by Fairbanks Manufacturing Company on January 2, 1971:

    Cost:
        Invoice price $110,000
        Transportation charges   2,000
        Installation charges   4,000
            Total cost of machine $116,000
    Estimated salvage value .... $ 4,000
    Estimated life:
        In years .... Ten
        In units-of-production 100,000

The company did not use the 20 percent depreciation allowance discussed in Chapter 7.

Required

Determine for each of the two years, 1971 and 1972, the depreciation expense per year by each of four methods. Units produced are: 10,000 in 1971; 20,000 in 1972. Present your answers in the form of the following chart (round to nearest dollar if necessary).

Year	Straight-line	Units-of-Production	Sum-of-Years' Digits	Declining Balance (Tax Method)
1971				
1972				

6-13. Assume the following facts for a new machine purchased by Richmond Products, Incorporated, on January 2, 1971:

    Cost:
        Invoice price $22,500
        Transportation charges 500
        Installation charges 1,000
            Total cost of machine $24,000
    Estimated salvage value .... $ 600
    Estimated Life:
        In years .... Three
        In units-of-production 93,600

Required

Determine the depreciation expense per year for each of the three years and the accumulated depreciation at the end of the third year by each of the following methods:

a. Straight-line
b. Units-of-production

c. Sum-of-years' digits

d. Declining balance (tax method)

Notes: Units produced are: 30,000 in 1971; 32,000 in 1972; 31,600 in 1973. The company did not use the initial 20 percent depreciation allowance discussed in Chapter 7.

6-14. A new type of machinery, a generometer, was purchased by Whittier Company on January 1, 1968, at a cost of $31,000. It was estimated that the generometer would have an estimated useful life to the company of approximately ten years and salvage value of approximately $1,000. Because of the invention of a new high-speed and extremely efficient type of generometer which was recently developed and sold to Whittier's competitors, it became reasonably certain early in 1972 that, by the end of 1973, the old style generometer would have to be junked and replaced by the new style generometer and that salvage value would be negligible rather than $1,000. Such rapid obsolescence was not anticipated in estimating the useful life of Whittier's present generometer. Compute the depreciation expense for the year 1972, assuming that the company uses straight-line depreciation (and did not use the initial 20 percent depreciation allowance discussed in Chapter 7).

6-15. A building purchased on July 1, 1953 (thus straight-line depreciation), for $800,000 with no salvage and a life of 20 years, was sold on December 31, 1965, for $430,000 cash. Compute the gain or loss on sale of the building.

6-16. A building purchased in January 1950 (thus straight line depreciation) for $600,000 with no salvage and a life of 30 years was sold on July 1, 1963, for $300,000 cash. Compute the gain or loss on sale of the building.

6-17. The depreciation policy and procedures of Willetts Manufacturing Company for its various types of depreciable assets (for both book and income tax purposes) are as follows:

a. For depreciable assets acquired prior to January 1, 1954:
  1. Straight-line depreciation for all buildings, machinery, equipment, and furniture and fixtures.

b. For depreciable assets acquired since January 1, 1954:
  1. Accelerated depreciation on new depreciable assets acquired with an estimated life of three years or more, as follows:
     (a) Declining balance (tax method) on all buildings.
     (b) Sum-of-the-years' digits method on all machinery, equipment (including trucks), and furniture and fixtures.
  2. Straight-line depreciation on used depreciable assets acquired; also on new depreciable assets which have an estimated life of less than three years.

c. For depreciable assets acquired since January 1, 1958:
  Same policy as for those acquired since January 1, 1954. The 20 percent initial depreciation allowance is *not* used. (See Chapter 7 for discussion of 20 percent initial depreciation allowance.)

d. In all cases, the company computes depreciation to the nearest full month. All amounts are rounded to the nearest dollar.

[CH. 6] PROPERTY: ACQUISITION, DEPRECIATION, DISPOSAL 171

Required

Complete a depreciation schedule for selected depreciable assets of the Willetts Manufacturing Company by stating the following for each asset shown below:

a. Method of depreciation used.

b. Amount of accumulated depreciation to date, as of January 1, 1971.

c. Amount of depreciation expense for the year 1971.

Item	Date Acquired	Cost	Salvage	Life (Years)
Brick factory building	Jan. 3, 1952	$305,000	$5,000	50
Machinery (turret lathe)	July 1, 1953	18,500	500	18
Machinery (drill press)	Jan. 2, 1967	36,800	800	8
Furniture and Fixtures	Jan. 2, 1968	20,000	500	10
Machinery—used	July 2, 1968	16,000	1,000	5
Office building	Jan. 2, 1969	500,000	–0–	50
Fixtures—used	Oct. 1, 1969	14,000	–0–	10
Plant building	Jan. 2, 1971	500,000	–0–	50
Machinery (lathe)	Jan. 2, 1971	74,000	2,000	8

Note: Problem 6-17 does not consider the "guideline lives" (effective July 12, 1962).

7

Property, Plant and Equipment: Depreciation, Depletion, Amortization

DEPRECIATION

Depreciation and Deferred Income Taxes

In the discussion in Chapter 6 concerning the selection of a depreciation method, it was stated that many companies use the straight-line method for financial reporting and adopt an accelerated method of depreciation for income tax purposes. This practice raises two problems: first, the alleviation of any possible distortion in financial reporting; and second, the extent to which the resulting deferred tax liability actually will become payable in future years. These two points will now be given necessary additional explanation.

The first problem concerns the distortion that might occur in financial reporting when the statement of income shows a smaller amount for depreciation expense than the tax return does, and when the statement also indicates a reduced expense for the year's federal income tax payments because of the excess depreciation deducted on the tax return. To alleviate such possible distortion, the AICPA's Committee on Accounting Procedure recommended that:

> There may be situations in which the declining-balance method is adopted for income-tax purposes but other appropriate methods are used for financial accounting purposes. In such cases, accounting recognition should be given to deferred income taxes if the amounts thereof are material, except in those rare cases, such as are mentioned in paragraph 8,

where there are special circumstances which may make such procedure inappropriate. The foregoing provision as to accounting recognition of deferred income taxes applies to a single asset, or to a group of assets which are expected to be retired from service at about the same time; in this case an excess of depreciation taken for income-tax purposes during the earlier years would be followed by the opposite condition in later years, and there would be a tax deferment for a definite period. It applies also to a group of assets consisting of numerous units which may be of differing lengths of life and which are expected to be continually replaced; in this case an excess of depreciation taken for income-tax purposes during the earlier years would be followed in later years by substantial equality between the annual depreciation for income-tax purposes and that for accounting purposes, and a tax deferment would be built up during the earlier years which would tend to remain relatively constant thereafter. It applies further to a gradually expanding plant; in this case an excess of depreciation taken for income-tax purposes may exist each year during the period of expansion in which event there would be a tax deferment which might increase as long as the period of expansion continued.[1]

Though this statement refers to declining balance depreciation, it is equally applicable to sum-of-the-years' digits depreciation.

To illustrate the application and effect of the principle involved, assume the following facts covering the four-year period of 1971 through 1974 for The Static Corporation:

Sales, each year $1,000,000
All expenses prior income taxes except depreciation on special lathes, each year 800,000
For ease of illustration, a federal corporate income tax rate of 50%.
Purchase in January 1971 of special lathes at a cost of $225,000, scrap value of $25,000, and life of four years. For depreciation of these lathes, the company has decided to use straight-line depreciation for financial reporting purposes and sum-of-years' digits depreciation for tax purposes. Thus depreciation charges will be:

	Straight-line depreciation on financial statements	Sum-of-years' digits depreciation on tax return
1971	$ 50,000	$ 80,000
1972	50,000	60,000
1973	50,000	40,000
1974	50,000	20,000
	$200,000	$200,000

---

[1] *Accounting Research Bulletin No. 44* (*Revised*), "Declining-balance Depreciation," paragraph 4. Copyright (1958) American Institute of Certified Public Accountants, Inc.

Except for depreciation on the special lathes, all items of income and expense are identical for financial reporting and tax purposes.

The accompanying illustrative segments of the condensed financial statements reflect the effect of these assumed facts over the four-year period.

THE STATIC CORPORATION
(amounts in thousands of dollars)

Statement of Income

	1971	1972	1973	1974
Sales	$1,000	$1,000	$1,000	$1,000
Less all expenses except depreciation on special lathes ..	800	800	800	800
	$ 200	$ 200	$ 200	$ 200
Straight-line depreciation on special lathes	50	50	50	50
Net income prior tax	$ 150	$ 150	$ 150	$ 150
Provision for federal income tax	$60	$70	$80	$90
Provision for deferred federal income tax	15 75	5 75	(5) 75	(15) 75
Net Income for the year	$ 75	$ 75	$ 75	$ 75

Corporate Tax Return Calculation

	1971	1972	1973	1974
Sales less expenses (per above) ...	$200	$200	$200	$200
Sum-of-years' digits depreciation on special lathes	80	60	40	20
Taxable income	$120	$140	$160	$180
Corporate income tax, assuming 50% rate	$ 60	$ 70	$ 80	$ 90

Balance Sheet

	Dec. 31, 1971	Dec. 31, 1972	Dec. 31, 1973	Dec. 31, 1974
Liability section: Deferred federal income tax ..	$15	$20	$15	$ 0

Reference to the above statements reveals that the actual income tax liability for 1971 is $60,000. However, if the straight-line depreciation used on the statement of income for financial reporting had also been used on the tax return, the tax would have been $75,000. Therefore, tax of $15,000 has been postponed or deferred until later years. This deferred income tax is shown on the balance sheet as a liability, usually following the current liabilities and any long-term debt, but prior to the stockholders' equity section.[2] To alleviate possible distortion in the reported profits shown by the statement of income, the provision for federal income tax expense is shown at an amount representing the tax that would have been incurred if the straight-line amount of depreciation shown by the statement of income had been deducted on the tax return. On most published statements of income, only the total $75,000 income tax provision or expense is shown, not the segregation into expense currently payable and expense payable at some indefinite future date.

In 1972, the deferred tax liability increases in a similar manner but by a smaller amount; namely, $5,000, which is equal to 50 percent (the assumed tax rate) of the excess of accelerated depreciation of $60,000 over straight-line depreciation of $50,000.

In 1973, the situation is reversed. Straight-line depreciation shown on the statement of income exceeds the amount for accelerated depreciation deducted on the tax return. Thus, a portion of the previously expensed but deferred tax liability becomes payable. The tax expense on the income statement is $75,000, but $80,000 is payable, $5,000 of which represents previously deferred income tax. By the end of 1974, the end of estimated useful life of the special lathes, the deferred tax liability has been eliminated.

The Static Corporation, over the four-year period, has paid the same amount of federal income taxes that it would if it had never used accelerated depreciation for taxes. Despite this apparent "breakeven" answer in overall tax payments, the company has received one definite benefit: by deferral of tax payments, it has had extra monies for three years to use in the business on which it should expect to earn a return. Unless there are extenuating circumstances, a company is practically forced to use accelerated depreciation, at least for taxes, to take advantage of this free use of money.

Furthermore, the situation illustrated has been for an absolutely static type of company. All other things have been held equal to simplify the illustration; no new equipment, for example, has been purchased for four years. This is unrealistic, since practically all businesses are constantly acquiring new depreciable assets. These new assets, as acquired, are similarly available for accelerated depreciation. This is the gist of the other problem raised in the preceding chapter, the long-run effect of accelerated depreciation. It is a matter of conjecture whether, in future years, the deferred tax liability actually will become payable. Barring a change in the tax code, it is possible that the majority of businesses will continue to acquire new depreciable assets in a quantity at least sufficient to offset continually the effect of decreasing accelerated depreciation deductions on older assets. It is also possible that an expanding com-

---

[2] Reference to pages 622 and 620 of Appendix A will reveal like treatment on the Consolidated Balance Sheets of Armstrong Cork Company and PPG Industries.

pany might build up a deferred tax liability of gigantic proportions. Experience to date with accelerated depreciation for taxes precludes any definite answer to these possibilities.

Special Amortization of Emergency Facilities

Closely akin to the problems raised by accelerated depreciation are those arising from the rapid amortization of emergency facilities. During World War II, the Korean conflict, and for a period thereafter, certificates of necessity were issued by the government to permit those fixed assets certified as necessary for the war effort or national defense to be written off for tax purposes in 60 months. This special amortization privilege meant that these assets could be "depreciated" over a period much shorter than their probable useful life. Any portion of a facility not so certified would be eligible for only normal depreciation. For example, assume a plant building completed in early January, 1951, at cost of $10,000,000, on which a 75 percent certificate of necessity is obtained. Also assume that it has no salvage value and a normal estimated useful life of 40 years. Three-fourths of the building ($7,500,000) would be "amortized" over five years, and one-fourth would be "depreciated" over forty years. Thus, the total allocation to expense, at least for income taxes for the years 1951 through 1955, would amount to $1,562,500. But, for the next 35 years,

Year	Amortization of 75% of building $7,500,000 ÷ 5 years	Depreciation of 25% of building $2,500,000 ÷ 40 years	Sum of yearly amortization and depreciation
1951	$1,500,000	$ 62,500	$ 1,562,500
1952	1,500,000	62,500	1,562,500
1953	1,500,000	62,500	1,562,500
1954	1,500,000	62,500	1,562,500
1955	1,500,000	62,500	1,562,500
1956	0	62,500	62,500
1990	0	62,500	62,500
	$7,500,000	$2,500,000	$10,000,000

1956 through 1990, it would amount to only $62,500. Some companies have reflected rapid amortization on the financial statements in the same amount as that deducted for income taxes. Other companies have shown the equivalent of normal depreciation, $10,000,000 divided by 40 years ($250,000), on the financial statements while deducting on the tax return the amounts shown in the last column of the above table. The American Institute of Certified Public Accountants, through its Committee on Accounting Procedure, has attempted to bring some standardization into practice.[3]

It is interesting to note that the term amortization, rather than depreciation, has been employed to denote the write-off of such tangible fixed assets as buildings, machinery, and equipment when these are covered by certificates of necessity.[4] Such practice conflicts with the usual usage of the term amortization which is ordinarily reserved to indicate the write-off of intangible fixed assets.

Though no new certificates of necessity have been issued since 1959, this discussion is pertinent for several reasons. First, the financial statements of many companies still show the effect of such rapid amortization. The 1960 annual report of Union Carbide Corporation contained the following note to the financial statements:

> The cost of facilities constructed by the Corporation under Certificates of Necessity issued by the United States Government is amortized for tax purposes over a period of 60 months from the date of completion and is charged against income over the same period. During the year 1960, such amortization amounted to $11,640,000, including normal depreciation of approximately $5,424,000. After the year 1960, the remaining amount to be amortized is approximately $8,109,000.

Reference to the 1960 annual report of PPG Industries would disclose that the company was still amortizing emergency facilities but that, unlike Union Carbide Corporation, charged to income only normal depreciation and established a deferred tax liability in a manner identical to that previously discussed in connection with accelerated depreciation. A second reason for a review of what at present may appear to be past history is to alert the reader to the possibility that a portion of the net fixed assets, cost less depreciation to date, of some companies may be somewhat understated owing to their rapid write-off for financial reporting purposes as well as for tax purposes. A third reason for a review of rapid amortization is to point out the weakness in any management policy decision which overemphasizes present tax consequences at the sacrifice of possible long-run effects. Consider the case of a company which received a certificate of necessity on a new facility near the close of World War II. For a short period, while income tax rates were exceedingly high because of the excess profits tax, the company benefited substantially from a tax standpoint owing to rapid amortization. But shortly after the close of the war, the repeal of the excess profits tax reduced the effective tax rate to only 38 percent. Continued rapid amortization at this tax rate produced a much smaller tax savings.[5] Then, just as the facility was fully amortized, the Korean conflict

---

[3] For details, see *Accounting Research Bulletin No. 27; Accounting Research Bulletin No. 43*, p. 76.

[4] Even building site land is subject to rapid amortization if covered by a certificate of necessity.

[5] Some companies availed themselves of the provision to abandon special amortization and to write off any unamortized balance by regular depreciation over remaining normal useful life.

began in June of 1950. Regular tax rates quickly rose to 52 percent, and an excess profits tax was reimposed. The company now found itself at a distinct disadvantage, because little, if any, of the depreciable base of the World War II facility remained for write-off at a much greater tax savings. Moreover, the substantially reduced asset base provided an additional handicap when the company used this base to determine its excess profits. While managers must consider tax consequences in their planning, they should not attempt to outguess future tax changes at the sacrifice of sound planning. A fourth reason for the review is that the concept of rapid amortization recently has been resurrected and made applicable to four widely diverse types of property.

The Tax Reform Act, signed into law by President Nixon on December 30, 1969, contains three provisions for rapid amortization and one for rapid depreciation. First, rapid amortization over 60 months, instead of the regular depreciation allowance, may be elected for certified pollution control facilities placed in service between January 1, 1969, and December 31, 1974, on plants in operation before January 1, 1969. Second, rapid amortization over 60 months, instead of regular depreciation over the usual 14 year life, may be elected for new rolling stock of railroads placed in service between January 1, 1970, and December 31, 1974. Third, rapid amortization over 60 months, instead of regular depreciation allowance, may be elected for certified coal mine safety equipment placed in service between January 1, 1970, and December 31, 1974. And, fourth, within specified dollar limits, capital expenditures between July 25, 1969, and December 31, 1974, for the rehabilitation of slum and substandard housing rented to low or moderate income persons may be written off by rapid depreciation over five years using the straight-line method.

Initial Depreciation Allowance

A new concept of depreciation was introduced to United States businessmen by the Small Business Tax Revision Act of 1958. Though a discussion of the technical income tax provisions concerning depreciation is beyond the scope of this book, an appreciation of the basic factors is necessary to a proper evaluation of alternative courses of action and a correct interpretation of resulting financial facts. For these reasons and for a possible indication of the future course which income tax provisions concerning depreciation may take, an understanding of the additional first-year depreciation allowance is important. Though a part of the Small Business Act, the new provision applies to all businesses, large or small.

In addition to regular depreciation, straight-line or accelerated, this provision in the tax Code permits an initial 20 percent one-shot depreciation allowance in the year during which qualifying property is acquired. To be eligible for this allowance, the depreciable asset must be tangible personal property (i.e., machinery and equipment, not buildings) with a remaining useful life of at least six years at the date of acquisition. The tangible personal property may be either new or used. However, the application of the initial 20% allowance is limited to a maximum of $10,000 of such property acquired by a corporation in any one year. (It is possible for sole proprietorships and partnerships to receive slightly greater benefits than corporations.) The initial allowance is applied to $10,000 maximum of the cost of such assets, not cost less salvage value. The regular first-year depreciation is then computed on cost minus the 20 percent initial allowance (and minus salvage value unless the double declining balance depreciation method is used). Regular depreciation may be straight-line or accelerated depreciation if the property qualifies as new property; only straight-line depreciation may be employed if it is used property.

To illustrate this concept, assume that a corporation purchases a piece of new machinery in January for $45,000. The machine has an estimated useful life of ten years and a salvage value of $3,000. The company elects to use its maximum $10,000 annual amount available for the 20 percent initial allowance on this asset. Sum-of-the-years' digits depreciation is regularly employed by this company for this type of fixed asset. The depreciation expense for the first year would be $9,273, computed as follows:

Initial allowance, 20% of $10,000	$2,000
Sum-of-the-years' digits depreciation:	
$10/55$ of $40,000$[6]	7,273
Depreciation expense for the year	$9,273

The obvious question at this point is why one should be so concerned with one tax provision which can at best increase the total depreciation expense of a corporation by $2,000 in any one year. The most important reason is the implication of things to come. The concept of an initial depreciation allowance, while new to United States businessmen, is established practice in certain other countries. For example, Great Britain permits a similar type of initial depreciation allowance of 60 percent on the cost of machinery and 40 percent on the cost of plant buildings (and at times has allowed a 50 percent rate on vessels) in order to enable business to amortize a larger portion of the cost of the property more quickly. These varying rates are applicable to the *total* cost of the assets, not to a limited $10,000 of total cost for all fixed assets acquired in any one year. The Congress of the United States has already considered bills to liberalize the present initial depreciation allowance. Tax laws, once envisioned solely as a means of raising revenue, now appear to be taking on additional "duties." It is interesting to note that the last four federal income tax changes which liberalized depreciation allowances occurred during the "recession" years of 1954, 1958, 1962, and the "recovery" year of 1971. In 1954, an attempt was made to increase industrial activity through greater expenditures for *new* plant, equipment, and machinery. In 1958, an attempt was made to aid small businesses. In 1962, the new guideline lives were hailed by Secretary of the Treasury Dillon as "a major stimulus to our continued economic growth."

---

[6] Cost of $45,000 minus $2,000 initial depreciation allowance minus $3,000 salvage value.

Then, in January of 1971, these guideline lives were modified by the ADR System as discussed in Chapter 6. There is the possibility that, if such additional depreciation provisions like initial depreciation allowances of varying rates on different types of plant, machinery, and equipment should be adopted in the United States, such periodic revisions in the tax structure could greatly influence the flow of capital into or out of specific industries.

Credit for Investment in Certain Depreciable Property

The Revenue Act of 1962 and the Revenue Act of 1964 contained a new and far-reaching concept known as the 7 percent investment credit. The announced aim of the investment credit was to encourage modernization and expansion of productive facilities and thereby increase productivity and profitability. The amount of the credit was based upon new capital investment and in the form of a reduction in the income taxes otherwise payable.

The 7 percent investment credit was repealed effective April 18, 1969, by the Tax Reform Act of 1969 signed into law on December 30, 1969. However, the salient features of the investment credit will be presented in a condensed fashion for several reasons. First, the impact of the credit from 1962 to 1969 will affect the financial statements of many companies for many years into the future. Second, the affect of the investment credit on financial statements has been material because of the major dollar amounts involved. Third, the possibility exists that history would repeat and the credit would be restored some time in the future; in seven years, the credit has been an on-again off-again item and altered five times by Act of Congress.[7] And, fourth, an awareness of the credit is believed desirable so that one may be knowledgeable about one of the methods that has been used in an attempt to tune the economy.

The application of this tax concept had widespread effect on many management decisions, including the decisions to consider leasing buildings, but buying machinery and equipment; to determine when to buy and when to sell certain depreciable assets; to consider the acquisition of new assets instead of used ones; to contemplate, if reasonable, the assigning to newly acquired property a useful life of at least eight years; to study the advantages and disadvantages of capitalizing borderline items as a portion of the cost of certain newly acquired depreciable assets; and to weigh the different accounting methods for the investment credit because of the possible impact on net earnings for the year.

---

[7] For example, the Investment Credit and Accelerated Depreciation Suspension Act, P.L. 89–800, signed by the President on November 8, 1966, suspended the 7 percent investment credit on property acquired or constructed during the period of October 10, 1966, through December 31, 1967. See page 185 below.

One of the aims of this provision was to discourage capital expenditures and thus decrease or restrain one of the inflationary pressures on the economy. There were certain minor exceptions to this provision, designed chiefly to benefit the small businessman. The investment credit was not "repealed"; rather it was to have been "suspended" for approximately 15 months. When the economy suddenly turned down, due to many factors, the suspension was quickly terminated, ahead of schedule, effective principally with property acquired after March 9, 1967.

The underlying reasons for the effect of the investment credit upon these decisions will be apparent from a short presentation of the salient points comprising this tax "benefit."

The investment credit was based upon the amount of certain new and used tangible depreciable property acquired after December 31, 1961. Normally, all personal tangible property qualified for the credit; e.g., machinery, equipment, trucks, and office furniture. Non-personal tangible property such as buildings did not qualify.

The credit was equal to 7 percent of the "qualified investment" made during the year. An investment was not fully qualified for the 7 percent credit unless it had a useful life of at least eight years. Thus, the effective percentage was less for assets with a shorter life, as follows:

If useful life was	The applicable percentage of the investment which qualified was	With a resultant effective investment credit of
Less than 4 years	None	None
4 or 5 years	33⅓%	⅓ of 7% = 2⅓%
6 or 7 years	66⅔%	⅔ of 7% = 4⅔%
8 years or more	100 %	7%

These percentages applied to the *total* cost of all *new* eligible property acquired. But the maximum qualified investment in *used* eligible property acquired in any one year which was eligible for the credit was $50,000 (for most corporations; the limitation was different for some other types of business entities).

To illustrate these considerations in determining the investment credit, assume that a cement manufacturing corporation acquired and placed into service the following six assets in 1968:

Asset	Years of Life	Cost	Applicable Percentage	Qualified Investment
Automobiles (new)	3	$ 25,000	(1) None	$ -0-
Tractor units, over-the-road (new)	4	60,000	33⅓%	20,000
Company airplane (new)	6	150,000	66⅔%	100,000
Machinery (new)	20	80,000	100 %	80,000
Machinery (used)	10	80,000	(2) 100 %	50,000
Office building (new)	45	500,000	(3) None	-0-
Total qualified investment				$250,000
				.07
Investment credit				$ 17,500

(1) Life less than 4 years
(2) Applicable only to $50,000 maximum on used assets
(3) Buildings not eligible for the credit

Several technical points must be mentioned about the investment credit of $17,500 for the sake of accuracy. First, the credit reduced the corporate tax liability that would otherwise have been payable. Second, in general, the maximum credit allowed against the tax liability was the lesser of the amount of the actual tax liability itself, or $25,000 plus one-half of the tax liability in excess of $25,000. Third, any excess credit not used in a given year could be carried back or forward against tax liabilities of other years under certain conditions. Fourth, if any properties were prematurely disposed of (e.g., a ten-year life asset is sold after five years), a portion of the tax credit may have had to be repaid. Fifth, the investment credit was not 7 percent but 3 percent on property acquired for use in a public utility business.

The provision for the investment credit in the Revenue Act of 1962 required that the basis of the property be reduced by the amount of the credit. For example, *if* the $80,000 of new machinery in the illustration had been acquired in 1962 or 1963 (instead of 1968), the basis for depreciation would have been only $74,400; i. e., $80,000 minus 7 percent of $80,000. This meant that $5,600 less of depreciation could be expensed over the 20-year life of the machinery. Therefore, at an assumed 50 percent tax rate, subsequent income taxes would have been increased by $2,800 (50 percent × $5,600) during the 20 years. The long-run benefit was not a tax savings of $5,600, but only 50 percent of that amount, or $2,800. This is illustrated by the following summary:

	1962	Next Nineteen years	Twenty-year total
Tax *reduction* because of credit	$5,600	$ –0–	$5,600
Tax *increase* because of reduced depreciation expense (50% × $280 smaller annual depreciation)	140	2,660	2,800
Tax savings	$5,460	($2,660)	$2,800

The provision for the investment credit in the Revenue Act of 1964 eliminated the requirement that the basis of the property must be reduced by the amount of the credit before depreciation is calculated. Thus, the long-run benefit starting with 1964 was the full amount of the credit and not one-half of it as just illustrated, *if* the asset was purchased on or after January 1, 1964. For example, the $80,000 of new machinery in the above illustration, since it was acquired in 1968, had a basis for depreciation of the full $80,000. Therefore, the entire $5,600 credit was a tax savings.[8]

Among the various possibilities of accounting for the investment credit, the two methods which are predominant will be presented. One method regards the investment credit as simply a tax reduction in the current period when the

---

[8] The Revenue Act of 1964 also contained a provision for adding back to basis for subsequent depreciation charges over remaining life, the tax credit reductions made to property acquired in 1962 and 1963.

[CH. 7] PROPERTY, PLANT AND EQUIPMENT 183

assets are acquired (the "flow-through" method). The other method regards the credit as a benefit to be recognized prorata over the productive life of the assets acquired (the "deferral" method) rather than all in the year of acquisition. It should be remembered that the over-all long-run effect will be identical regardless of which of the two procedures is used. However, the year to year effects will differ. To illustrate the two methods of financial reporting for the investment credit, assume the following for a given company:

1. New machinery with a guideline life of ten years is purchased in January, 1968, at a cost of $100,000. Salvage value is negligible.
2. Company uses straight-line depreciation method for both external financial reporting and income tax purposes. The company does not use the 20 percent initial depreciation allowance.
3. State corporate income taxes are not a factor.
4. Maximum amount of investment credit can be utilized as a reduction of the federal income tax liability. The company does not exceed the various limitations on the use of the investment credit.
5. The investment credit is $7,000 (7 percent × $100,000).
6. Annual depreciation expense is $10,000 ($100,000 ÷ 10) on the *full* cost of the new machinery.
7. Total 1968 depreciation is $500,000 ($490,000 on old assets + $10,000 on the new machinery).
8. $400,000 of the 1968 tax liability has been paid by December 31, 1968.
9. The company keeps this particular piece of machinery at least eight years and thus does not lose any portion of the maximum credit of 7 percent. In other words, none of the original $7,000 credit is "recaptured" by the government because of early disposition of the machinery.

The flow-through method, which views the investment credit as a tax reduction in the current period, results in the acquired machinery being reflected on the statement of financial position at its original full cost, $100,000, and annual depreciation expense, $10,000, based on this full cost as a charge against revenues on the statement of income. The $7,000 investment credit is reflected as a reduction in the current liability for federal income taxes payable as a result of the reduction of federal income tax expense of the year. This procedure results in the following statement presentation.

Balance Sheet
As of December 31, 1968

Property, Plant and Equipment:		Current Liabilities:	
Machinery, at cost	$100,000	Federal Income Taxes	
Less: Accumulated depreciation	10,000	Payable ($100,000 less $7,000 credit)	$93,000
	$90,000		

Statement of Income
For Year Ended December 31, 1968

Net Sales	$10,000,000
Cost of Goods Sold	6,000,000
Gross Margin on Sales	$ 4,000,000
Operating Expenses (except Depreciation)	2,500,000
	$ 1,500,000
Depreciation ($490,000 + 10,000)	500,000
Net Income before Federal Income Taxes	$ 1,000,000
Federal Income Taxes of $500,000, less $7,000 credit	493,000
Net Income for the Year	$ 507,000

The deferral method, which views the investment credit as a benefit to be recognized prorata over the productive life of the acquired machinery, results in the asset being reflected in the statement of financial position at only $93,000 ($100,000 full cost less the $7,000 "discount" or government subsidy on purchase), and annual depreciation expense, $9,300 ($93,000 ÷ 10), based on this *net* cost as a charge against revenues on the statement of income.[9] The $7,000 investment credit is reflected as a reduction in the current liability for federal income taxes payable. However, federal income tax expense for the year is not reduced by the credit of $7,000; the expense remains at its original $500,000.[10] Thus, the net income for the year is $700 higher annually for ten years than it otherwise would be because of a charge of only $9,300 for depreciation expense instead of $10,000. This procedure results in the following statement presentation.

Balance Sheet
As of December 31, 1968

Property, Plant and Equipment:			Current Liabilities:	
Machinery, at cost	$100,000		Federal Income Taxes	
Less: Credit	7,000		Payable ($100,000	
	$ 93,000		less $7,000 credit)	$93,000
Less: Accumulated				
depreciation	9,300			
	$ 83,700			

---

[9] Another method is to show machinery at $100,000 and a Deferred Investment Credit of $7,000; then write off depreciation at $10,000 annually while amortizing the investment credit as a reduction of income tax expense.

[10] Depreciation for tax purposes is still based on the full cost amount of $100,000.

Statement of Income
For Year Ended December 31, 1968

Net Sales	$10,000,000
Cost of Goods Sold	6,000,000
Gross Margin on Sales	$ 4,000,000
Operating Expenses (except Depreciation)	2,500,000
	$ 1,500,000
Depreciation ($490,000 + 9,300)	499,300
Net Income before Federal Income Taxes	$ 1,000,700
Federal Income Taxes	500,000
Net Income for the Year	$ 500,700

Regardless of which of the two methods is used, the long-run effect, over ten years in this case, will be identical. The first method, which views the investment credit as a tax reduction in the year in which the asset is acquired, recognizes the full benefit in the first fiscal period. The second method, which views the investment credit as a reduction in the cost of the asset, recognizes the benefit prorata over the life of the acquired asset. The difference in the timing of the tax benefit is illustrated by the following summary:

Investment credit recognized as a benefit:	1966	Next nine years	Ten-year Total
In year asset is acquired	$7,000	$ -0-	$7,000
Prorata over years of asset's life	700	6,300	7,000

Thus the investment credit has caused further diversification in the manner in which a given financial situation may be handled for reporting purposes. Evidence indicates that the majority of companies used the flow-through method. However, those companies which used the deferral method will still have the effect of the amortization of the investment credit on their financial statements for many years, as witness this statement from the 1970 annual report of PPG Industries: "The unamortized investment credit of $14,005,000, deferred from years prior to 1969, will be added to earnings over the next eight years." Also, it is interesting to note that Congress is now (October 1971) debating whether or not to restore the 7 percent investment credit.

Possible Transition to Price-Level Depreciation

All of the discussion to this point, both in the preceding chapter and in this chapter, has been based upon the concept of allocating the *cost* of fixed assets to operations as an expense of doing business. At times, it has been necessary to discuss certain facets of the problem which appear to deviate somewhat from this idea. In fact, there exists in the United States today a strong minority opinion favoring change in one of the basic conventions of accounting; namely, that the basis for depreciation, original cost, should be replaced by a basis which makes allowances for changes in the price level.

The concept of depreciation based on current costs rather than on actual original cost, though at present not generally accepted, might well become "generally accepted" in the future. In this connection, it is interesting to note the pattern of changes which have occurred in depreciation practices. Accelerated depreciation methods such as declining balance and sum-of-the-years' digits were commonplace in many European countries long before their general acceptance in the United States in 1954. Japan, Sweden, Britain, and a few other countries have long made considerable use of variations of initial depreciation allowances, the first limited application of which did not occur in the United States until 1958. And now, in countries where inflation has been somewhat severe, various methods of price-level depreciation have become effective.[11]

After approximately two decades of inflation, and notwithstanding a few recessions, there is need to question whether long-term assets should be depreciated on the basis of historical cost or whether depreciation amounts and the related assets should be adjusted to reflect changes in price levels. The discrepancy between replacement and historical cost exists because monetary units cease to be a reliable measure when prices are changing rapidly.

Effect of Changing Price Level on Property, Plant and Equipment

Approaching the problem first from the point of view of the balance sheet, how significant is the following information shown by the 1970 annual report of Bethlehem Steel Corporation?

Property, plant and equipment, at cost	$4,909,538,000
Less: Accumulated depreciation	2,839,200,000
Net	$2,070,338,000

These amounts include assets and their accumulated depreciation to date in terms of all types of dollars. These figures might well include non-depreciable land acquired at the inception of the corporation in 1905; a building still in use which was acquired in 1935 when a dollar was worth $2.28; another building purchased in 1946 when the dollar was worth $1.51; machinery purchased in 1950 when a dollar was equal to $1.15; and equipment purchased in 1959 when the dollar was worth $0.99.[12] Bethlehem Steel Corporation has followed the generally accepted accounting principle of stating the property, plant, and equipment items at historical cost less accumulated depreciation and amortization to date based upon those costs. Thus, the total figures are a conglomeration of all different types of past dollars.

---

[11] Some such countries are Italy, Formosa, Brazil, Argentina, and The Netherlands.

[12] Based upon purchasing power of the dollar expressed in terms of reciprocals of the wholesale price index compiled by the Department of Labor, Bureau of Labor Statistics. Average of base period 1957–1959 equals 100.

[CH. 7] PROPERTY, PLANT AND EQUIPMENT 187

The non-comparability of similar items is clearly illustrated by analyzing the following situation. A company constructed a brick building in 1950 at a cost of $1,000,000; in 1966, a second brick building, identical to the first was constructed at a cost of $2,000,000. Each building, when constructed, had an estimated useful life of 40 years. Annual straight-line depreciation on the first building was $25,000, but was $50,000 on the identical second building. Thus, the property, plant and equipment section of the balance sheet as of December 31, 1970, would contain the following:

Building	$1,000,000	
Less: Accumulated depreciation to date ($25,000 × 20 years)	500,000	$ 500,000
Building	$2,000,000	
Less: Accumulated depreciation to date ($50,000 × 5 years)	250,000	1,750,000

This information is presented fairly in terms of historical cost. But because the statement contains dollars unadjusted for price-level changes, such information may be meaningless to the user of financial statements; or it may be misleading if he assumes that the second building is "worth" three and one-half times the first building. The confusion stemming from the non-comparability of reported financial data has been partially responsible for a decreasing usefulness of the traditional balance sheet to the point where it may be that the assets shown thereon represent only unabsorbed dissimilar costs not yet charged to operations.[13]

One suggested method of alleviating the situation is to adjust the figures by an index number.[14] Of the various index numbers available, one possibility would be the Construction Cost Index published by *Engineering News Record*, which uses a base year of 1913. Calculations based on these records would indicate that if 1950 = 100, then the index was approximately 200 in 1966 when the second building was constructed, and it reached 271 by 1970. Expressed in current dollars, the amounts stated for the two buildings could be restated as follows on December 31, 1970:

---

[13] The following statement contained in the Price Level Study section of the 1960 annual report of The Reece Corporation fairly summarizes the situation presented above:

This Company's relatively heavy investment in inventory and fixed assets, including machines leased to customers, requires constant awareness of the effects of price level changes. In periods of inflation, a large share of reported earnings must be reinvested in the business to overcome erosion of capital and provide for reasonable growth. This thought is best illustrated by the fact that during the last 10 years the book value of the Company's fixed assets has increased 22% in Historical Dollars but only 2% in Uniform Dollars.

[14] No index number exists with which some weakness cannot be found. The two used in this portion of the chapter are used solely for illustrative purposes and not because *their* specific use is recommended.

Building	$2,710,000	
Less: Accumulated depreciation to date ($67,750 × 20 years)	1,355,000	$1,355,000
Building	$2,710,000	
Less: Accumulated depreciation to date ($67,750 × 5 years)	338,750	2,371,250

The significance of these amounts is readily apparent because of the deliberate simplification in the original facts selected to illustrate the principle. The actual conversion of an item to current prices may be achieved by multiplying its original cost at date of acquisition by a fraction whose numerator is the current index number and whose denominator is the index number at the time of the asset's purchase. Accumulated depreciation to date is similarly converted by applying the fraction to accumulated depreciation based on the original cost.

The chief criticisms advanced against price-level adjustments to balance sheet amounts are definitely worthy of comment. One criticism is that if the basis of historical cost dollars is abandoned, no completely objective data remain as the basis for accounting, because any revaluations made or index numbers employed are estimates based upon judgment. Furthermore, such adjustments may be more misinterpreted by those using financial statements than are the present statements based upon original cost. Another argument advanced against price-level adjustments is that the degree of inflation in this country is not sufficient to warrant such adjustments. One should not ignore the reverse situation which occurred during the depression of the 1930's when many assets purchased in the 1920's had to be written down, not up! In addition, how can management appraise past performance if accounting does not furnish financial information based upon past costs? Though portions of these opinions may be valid, they do not resolve the problem or provide much aid in the solution of a greater problem not yet discussed: the effect of price-level changes upon the statement of income.

Effect of Changing Price Level on the Statement of Income

As an introductory illustration of the effect of the changing value of the dollar upon reported profit, assume the following facts:

In 1950, land is purchased at a cost of $10,000. The general price index is 100.

In 1970, the land is sold for $20,000. The general price index is 200.

Using the historical cost convention for profit measurement results in an apparent profit of $10,000; however, there is no real profit, because the general price index has doubled. An additional complication could be added by assuming the existence of an index of land values of 100 in 1950 and 250 in 1970. If the land was sold for only $20,000, orthodox accounting would show a book profit of $10,000, whereas there is a $5,000 real loss in current dollars based on an index of land values; rather than a $10,000 profit, management may be responsible for a $5,000 loss.

Many accountants, economists, and businessmen argue persuasively that reported profits reflecting historical cost depreciation are grossly overstated and that, as a result, the consumption of productive capital is being taxed. This occurs, it is contended, because the failure to measure depreciation in present cost prevents matching current costs against current revenue in determining reported profits. Orthodox depreciation computed on original cost of assets acquired at prices substantially lower than those currently prevailing involves matching depreciation allowances computed in one monetary unit against current income expressed in another or less valuable unit.[15] This leads to overstatement of profit and overpayment of income taxes; it may result in impairment of capital, inability to replace existing plant facilities, and the distribution of dividends from an income that is partially fictitious. These points are developed in the following illustration.

Illustrative Case

In the first column of the following statement of income, prepared in an orthodox manner in accordance with generally accepted accounting principles, the reported net income for the year is $100,000. Of this amount, 60 percent is distributed to stockholders by dividends, and 40 percent is plowed back into the business.

Statement of Income
For the Year 1972
(in thousands of dollars)

	Column One Per generally accepted accounting	Column Two Per price-level depreciation
Net Sales	$1,000	$1,000
Less: Cost of Goods Sold	600	600
Gross Margin	$ 400	$ 400
Less: Selling and Administrative Expenses	150	150
	$ 250	$ 250
Less: Depreciation Expense	50	100
Net Income prior Income Taxes	$ 200	$ 150
Less: Income Taxes (50% rate)	100	100
Net Income for the Year	$ 100	$ 50
Disposition of Net Income for the Year:		
To stockholders	$ 60	$ 60
To retained earnings	40	−10
	$100	$ 50

---

[15] See Benjamin F. Fairless, "Steel's Depreciation Problem," 64th general meeting of the American Iron and Steel Institute, May 24, 1956.

Depreciation expense is segregated from cost of goods sold and from selling and administrative expenses so that total depreciation expense of the year may be isolated for analysis. Inventories are priced on a LIFO basis, which results in an amount which closely approximates current costs for the cost of goods sold during the year. Thus, in both Column One and Column Two of the statement of income down to the item of depreciation expense, current or recent costs are fairly matched with current revenue: to this point, net income is measured in units of approximately equal purchasing power.

Reference to the contrasting statements of income presented in parallel columns above indicates different amounts for depreciation expense. Column One shows $50,000 of depreciation expense based on the historical acquisition cost of depreciable property, regardless of changing price levels, and is in accordance with generally accepted accounting principles. Column Two sets forth the depreciation expense at $100,000 to give effect to the changing value of the dollar; it is not in accordance with generally accepted accounting principles.[16] Many would argue that the $200,000 amount shown in Column One as the net income for the year prior to income taxes is not accurate as the statement no longer matches current costs with current revenue; the $50,000 of depreciation expense is based on past historical costs rather than current costs. On the other hand, the $150,000 amount shown in Column Two as net income for the year prior to income taxes does fairly present the results of operations, because current costs have been matched with current revenue; income determination is in units of approximately equal purchasing power. Basically, this is the same argument that is advanced to justify LIFO.[17] From a theoretical point of view, it is difficult not to embrace price-level depreciation for depreciable fixed assets when the LIFO concept is accepted for the pricing of goods.

On these statements of income, income taxes will approximate $100,000 in both cases, because price-level depreciation is not an allowable deduction for tax purposes. Therefore, Column One shows net income for the year of $100,000 and follows generally accepted accounting, while Column Two indicates net income of only $50,000. Since dividends of $60,000 have been distributed to shareholders during the year, the $40,000 of remaining "profits" is retained and reinvested in the business, as reflected by Column One. On the other hand, Column Two indicates that such dividend payments, out of a "real" profit of only $50,000, have impaired capital to the extent of $10,000. Thus, proponents of price-level depreciation maintain that depreciation on a basis of historical cost overstates profit and results in an effective tax rate in excess of 50 percent. In turn, this may cause an impairment of capital, an inability to replace existing plant facilities, and the payment of dividends from a dollar income that is partially fictitious.

---

[16] The arbitrary selection of a multiple of two for depreciation expense will be supported by comments in the next paragraph.

[17] See Chapter 8; also brief references in Chapters 2 and 3.

The effect of recalculating depreciation on a current basis varies among industries. The percentage reduction in net income, when depreciation is adjusted to reflect changes in price levels, will be less in a company with a preponderance of such short-lived depreciable fixed assets as the tools, dies, and patterns used by an automobile manufacturer than in a company owning a substantial amount of long-lived assets, such as a steel producer and a public utility. *Engineering News Record* shows that the Construction Cost Index rose from 100 in 1940 to 273 in 1955. Based upon this trend, it has been stated that

> Over the 15-year period the rate (of cost increase) was approximately 7 percent per annum compounded. . . . By using this 7 percent per annum figure, we can get an indication of the over-all inadequacy of depreciation on facilities which have a life of 25-years, and which have been bought in equal physical amounts each year. . . . In short, to recover purchasing power under these assumptions, our regular depreciation allowance needs to be multiplied by 2.15 . . . . If the average life of facilities were ten years, instead of 25, the multiple of 2.15 would drop to 1.42. . . . If the life averaged only five years . . . the multiple would drop to 1.22 . . .[18]

It should be remembered that acceptance of depreciation computed on a current basis for income tax purposes would increase expenses and reduce reported profits, thus decreasing the income tax paid. This might necessitate increasing the general tax rates. Such a combination of factors, dependent upon amount of and variation in the average life of long-term assets, would affect various companies and industries differently. In turn, this could lead to a redistribution of the overall tax burden among such companies and industries.

Price-Level Depreciation (and other price level adjustments)

As of yet, there is no "official" sanction in the United States of price-level depreciation (or any other accounting price-level adjustments). The American Institute of Certified Public Accountants, through its Committee on Accounting Procedure, stated, back in 1953:

> It has been suggested in some quarters that the problem be met by increasing depreciation charges against current income. The committee does not believe that this is a satisfactory solution at this time. It believes that accounting and financial reporting for general use will best serve their purposes by adhering to the generally accepted concept of depreciation on cost, at least until the dollar is stabilized at some level. An attempt to recognize current prices in providing depreciation, to be consistent, would require the serious step of formally recording appraised current values for

---

[18] Benjamin F. Fairless, "Steel's Depreciation Problem," p. 4.

all properties, and continuous and consistent depreciation charges based on the new values. Without such formal steps, there would be no objective standard by which to judge the propriety of the amounts of depreciation charges against current income, and the significance of recorded amounts of profit might be seriously impaired.[19]

The American Accounting Association, through its Committee on Concepts and Standards Underlying Corporate Financial Statements, has stated:

> In periodic reports to stockholders, the primary financial statements, prepared by management and verified by an independent accountant, should, at the present stage of accounting development, continue to reflect historical dollar costs.[20]

The Securities and Exchange Commission, which has authority to police the financial reporting of a large segment of our economy attributable to business corporations, in 1948 and again in 1954 denied requests of registrants to reflect depreciation on replacement cost in financial statements filed with the Commission.[21]

The decade of the 1960's saw several significant moves in the direction of price-level adjustments on published financial statements. In addition to many excellent articles in the various professional journals, several significant studies were made on the subject of price-level adjustments, among which are those cited in the following four paragraphs.

In 1961, the Accounting Principles Board of the American Institute of CPA's authorized a research study concerning the potential effect of price-level adjustments on financial statements. The study was published in 1963 and recommended that supplementary financial statements should be presented by companies giving effect to changes in the general price level.[22] As shown later in this chapter by the illustrative statements of Indiana Telephone Corporation, historical dollar amounts are converted to general purchasing power dollars. Thus, for example, assets are stated at cost (in terms of general purchasing power) and *not* at "current value."

As a result of Accounting Research Study No. 6, *Reporting the Financial Effects of Price-Level Changes,* the Accounting Principles Board prepared a research draft of a proposed pronouncement which included an illustrative set of supplementary price-level statements. On the basis of this research draft, a

---

[19] *Accounting Research Bulletin No. 43,* "Restatement and Revision of Accounting Research Bulletins," p. 68. Copyright (1953) American Institute of Certified Public Accountants, Inc.

[20] *Accounting Concepts and Standards Underlying Corporate Financial Statements, Supplementary Statement No. 2,* August 1951, American Accounting Association; reaffirmed in 1957 by the Committee.

[21] Securities and Exchange Commission, 14th Annual Report, p. 111, and 20th Annual Report, p. 107.

[22] American Institute of Certified Public Accountants, Inc., Accounting Research Study No. 6, *Reporting the Financial Effects of Price-Level Changes,* (New York, 1963).

field test was conducted on 18 companies which restated their financial statements by making general price-level adjustments. This field test, sponsored by the Accounting Principles Board, seems to confirm the viewpoint of Accounting Research Study No. 6. Following is the opening paragraph of the article by Paul Rosenfield (who is a project manager in the accounting research division of the American Institute of CPA's) describing the field test on the financial statements of the 18 companies:

> Eighteen companies recently participated in a field test of general price-level accounting and many of the participants were surprised with the results. In spite of the modest rate of inflation in the United States in recent years, differences between financial statement amounts before and after restatement for general price-level changes were significant for many of the companies. The differences varied widely from company to company and even between years for the same company. Net income was a larger amount after restatement than before restatement for some companies and a smaller amount for others.[23]

In 1969, the Accounting Principles Board issued Statement No. 3, "Financial Statements Restated for General Price-Level Changes." In commenting on Statement No. 3, George C. Watt stated ". . . (Statement No. 3) . . . is commendable, for it represents standby capacity ready for either, at some subsequent date, mandatory supplemental disclosure or, in the event of runaway inflation, mandatory application in the preparation of the primary financial statements."[24] Statement No. 3, (an APB Statement, not an APB Opinion), 71 pages in length, suggests supplementary information (statements) restated for general price-level changes using the Gross National Product Implicit Price Deflator and "provides recommendations on how to prepare and present" such supplementary information.

It should be noted that *A Statement of Basic Accounting Theory,* published by the American Accounting Association in July, 1966 (prepared by a Committee to Prepare a Statement of Basic Accounting Theory), recommends that current cost financial statements be shown along with historical cost statements. Though not an "official" statement of the American Accounting Association, the publication of the *Statement* was approved by its Executive Committee.

None of the foregoing precludes any company from including in its reports paragraph explanations, graphs or tables, and supplementary schedules or statements to enhance the explanation of the effect of price-level changes. Many companies have done so.

Thus, depreciation based upon the historical cost of depreciable property, regardless of changing price levels, remains a generally accepted accounting

---

[23] Paul Rosenfield, "Accounting for Inflation—A Field Test," *The Journal of Accountancy,* Volume 127, Number 6, (June, 1969), 45.
[24] George C. Watt, "Price-Level Accounting Americanized," *The Price Waterhouse Review,* Volume 14, Number 3 (Autumn, 1969), 50.

principle in the United States. Such principles are resistant to change, and changes occasionally require a lengthy process of establishing substantial recognition of the need. Although the three organizations cited above exercise considerable leadership in striving for better methods of financial reporting, they do not have sole responsibility. Corporate financial statements are representations of the reporting corporation, and corporate management has the primary responsibility for its own statements.

Possible Progression Toward Price-Level Depreciation

Next presented is a summary of references to, and present applications of, price-level depreciation in the financial statements and supplementary data used for external reporting. They indicate a possible movement, as yet of untested strength, toward price-level depreciation.

Shortly after the close of World War II, many companies were concerned with the inadequacy of depreciation allowances attributable to the rapid increase in costs then being experienced. United States Steel Corporation, in its annual report for 1947, attempted to give partial effect to increasing replacement costs by showing on the statement of income, in addition to regular depreciation expense, an amount of $26,300,000 titled "Added to Cover Replacement Cost." The next year, 1948, page 5 of the annual report of United States Steel Corporation contained the following statement:

> However, in view of the disagreement existing among accountants, both public and private, and the stated position of the American Institute of Accountants, which is supported by the Securities and Exchange Commission, that the only accepted accounting principle for determining depreciation is that which is related to the actual number of dollars spent for facilities, regardless of when or of what buying power, U.S. Steel has adopted a method of accelerated depreciation on cost instead of one based on purchasing power recovery.

Because of the unacceptability of a depreciation basis other than original cost, most companies have limited themselves to devices such as comments, graphs, and charts in their annual reports to reflect the effect of a changing price level. Typical is the following from the Financial Review portion of the 1952 annual report of Westinghouse Electric Corporation:

> Operating costs for 1952 included $21,836,000 for depreciation and amortization of facilities. This computation, conforming with generally accepted accounting practice and federal income tax regulations, is based on the original cost of facilities. However, because of the reduced purchasing power of the dollar, this amount of depreciation does not provide adequate funds for replacement of obsolete or worn-out facilities which were bought over a period of several decades. The annual amount of depreciation computed on the basis of current replacement costs of existing facilities and using present depreciation rates is estimated to be

$29,580,000. This compares with depreciation actually allowed on such facilities of $21,836,000.

In the Financial Summary section of its 1960 annual report, United States Steel Corporation made the following statement:

> Under the tax code the depreciation allowable in the calculation of taxable income must be based on the prices often paid years ago—25 years or more in the case of United States Steel—for the items subject to depreciation. But amounts so determined cannot at today's inflated prices possibly have buying power equivalent to that originally expended and thus be sufficient to meet current needs if the enterprise is just to "stay even." The deficiency amount which should realistically be regarded as depreciation is thus treated as income and on that pretense over half of it taxed away. This is more than inimical to growth; it puts a tax on just keeping even.
>
> Illustrative of the seriousness of these matters are the facts of United States Steel. For the post-war years, 1946–1960, United States Steel's recorded wear and exhaustion—sometimes called depreciation—aggregated $2,872,000,000. Of this amount, $2,671,000,000 was deductible in determining taxable income. If, each year, depreciation had been sufficient to recover the appropriate *buying* power—not just the number—of dollars originally expended, the total would have been $4,276,000,000. The deficiency from this amount needed to stay even was $1,605,000,000, on which taxes were levied as though it were income.

In its 1970 report, immediately following the financial statements, Gulf States Utilities Company presented the following information:

Value of Original Plant Dollars Declines

> The Company's utility facilities were constructed over a period of many years and consequently "Net Plant" as stated on the books represents the investment of dollars of widely different value. Because of this fact, the "Total plant less accumulated provision for depreciation" shown on the Balance Sheet on pages 10 and 11 of this report which is stated as "Original Cost" does not reflect the effect that the declining purchasing power of the dollar has had on the current valuation of the Company's property.
>
> The effect of such dollar depreciation on the Company can be illustrated by applying the Consumer Price Index, as published by the Bureau of Labor Statistics, to the original cost dollars shown as "Total plant less accumulated provision for depreciation." By doing this, the figure would become $1,188,200,000, which is $308,700,000 or 35.1 percent greater than the amount as shown on the Balance Sheet.
>
> The management will continue to strive for regulatory recognition of such decreases in the value of the dollar and the need for consideration of this factor in rate making.

Until recently, the only formal recognition given price-level problems in published financial statements per se was a very limited adoption of the method employed by a few companies such as Bristol-Myers (through 1962). This method involves earmarking a portion of retained earnings as an allocation for higher plant replacement costs. It is an attempt to place the reader of the financial statements on guard against the fact that a portion of retained earnings may be partially phantom in nature. Replacement of plant facilities is contemplated at higher price levels. Depreciation expense on the statement of income and fixed assets on the balance sheet are still shown at amounts based on historical cost.

In 1952, after four years of work on the problem of determining business income, a "Study Group on Business Income," composed of business executives, economists, labor leaders, government officials, lawyers, and accountants, released its deliberations. Approximately 70 percent of the 44 members recommended eventual determination of income in units of approximately equal purchasing power. One of the conclusions of the study group was:

> For the present it may well be that the primary statements of income should continue to be made on bases now commonly accepted. But corporations whose ownership is widely distributed should be encouraged to furnish information that will facilitate the determination of income measured in units of approximately equal purchasing power, and to provide such information wherever it is practicable to do so as part of the material upon which the independent accountant expresses his opinion.[25]

A step in this direction was taken by the Indiana Telephone Corporation beginning with its 1954 annual report, in which contrasting financial statements were presented in parallel columns. A minor portion of the financial statements is shown below to illustrate the publication of dual statements.

Column A amounts are based upon generally accepted accounting principles. Column B figures are restated for changes in the purchasing power of the dollar. The conversion of the fixed assets (and a minor dollar amount of certain other assets) into current dollars, as shown by Column B of the balance sheet, causes an adjustment of stockholders' equity. While a presentation of this type is an obvious aid to a utility seeking a fair return on the fair value of its property, the statements also are a pioneering attempt to show the effect of the changing value of the dollar upon financial statements.[26] Because of the current interest in price-level depreciation, the complete financial statements of Indiana Telephone Corporation, the notes thereto, and the opinion of the independent public accountants are reproduced in full in Appendix A-3.

---

[25] American Institute of Certified Public Accountants, Inc., *Changing Concepts of Business Income,* (New York: The Macmillan Company, 1952), p. 105. Copyright (1952) American Institute of Certified Public Accountants, Inc.

[26] The first comprehensive writing in this area is a book by Henry W. Sweeney, *Stabilized Accounting* (New York: Harper & Brothers, 1936).

Statement of Income
Year 1970

	Column A Historical Cost	Column B Historical Cost Restated for Changes in Purchasing Power of Dollar
Depreciation provision, Note 2	$1,541,560	$1,950,962
Net Income, Note 1	$1,637,288	$1,188,779

Statement of Assets and Capital
December 31, 1970

	Column A Historical Cost	Column B Historical Cost Restated for Changes in Purchasing Power of Dollar
Telephone Plant, at original cost, Note 1:		
In service	$30,292,769	$38,010,120
Less: Accumulated depreciation	9,166,697	12,062,598
	21,126,072	25,947,522
Plant under construction	1,068,349	1,088,113
	22,194,421	27,035,635
Total Investment in Telephone Business	$23,759,100	$28,530,587
Common Shareholders' Interest:		
Common stock, no par value, authorized 500,000 shares, issued 492,086 shares	4,251,785	6,237,301
Retained earnings	4,751,675	2,413,070
	9,003,460	8,650,371
Less: Treasury stock, 4,336 shares, at cost ..	(5,192)	(7,590)
Stock discount and expense	(78,368)	(118,246)
Total common shareholders' interest ..	8,919,900	8,524,535
Unrealized effects of price level changes, Note 1 .	—	5,166,852
Total Investment in Telephone Business	$23,759,100	$28,530,587

Notes to Financial Statements (below is portion of Notes 1 and 2)

1. *Explanation of financial statements.* In the accompanying financial statements, costs measured by the dollars disbursed at the time of the expenditure are shown in "Column A—Historical Cost." In "Column B—Historical Cost Restated For Changes in Purchasing Power of Dollar" (where the amounts in A and B differ), these dollars of cost have been restated in terms of the price level at December 31, 1970, as measured by the Gross National Product Implicit Price Deflator. Since 1954, the Corporation has presented supplemental financial information recognizing the effect of the change in the purchasing power of the dollar relating to telephone plant and depreciation expense in the annual report to shareholders.

In computing the amounts set forth in Column B of the accompanying financial statements, the Corporation has followed the methods set forth in Statement No. 3 released in June, 1969, by the Accounting Principles Board of the American Institute of Certified Public Accountants, except that, contrary to Statement No. 3, the effects of price level changes on long-term debt and preferred stock have been reflected as income in the year in which the debt and preferred stock are retired as required by the specific instruments under which they were issued. The Accounting Principles Board has tentatively taken the position that all such amounts should be taken into income in the year of price level change. In the opinion of the Corporation's management and of its independent public accountants, such tentative viewpoint of the Accounting Principles Board does not result in a proper determination of income for the period. "Unrealized Effects of Price Level Changes" recognizes the excess of adjustments on the Statement of Assets over the adjustments of Common Stock and Retained Earnings.

2. *Recovery of capital and return on capital.* Under the law of Indiana, the Corporation is entitled to recover the fair value of its property used and useful in public service by accruing depreciation based on the "fair value" thereof and is entitled to earn a fair return on such "fair value." The amount shown in Column B for telephone plant approximates the fair value of the property as determined based on the principles followed by the Public Service Commission of Indiana in an order dated September 1, 1967, authorizing the Corporation to increase its subscriber rates.

In the accompanying financial statements, Column A includes depreciation expense based on historical cost and Column B includes depreciation expense, *as well as other expenses,* on the basis of historical cost repriced in current dollars to reflect the changes in the purchasing power of the dollar. Also, the annual reports to the Indiana Commission are in the same basic form shown herein.

A similar procedure, though not so complete with respect to presentation in the financial statements, was adopted, beginning in 1957, and used consistently each year through 1969, by the Sacramento Municipal Utility District. On its operating statement of net revenue for the year 1969, operating expenses include:

    Provision for depreciation:
        Computed on historical cost $5,748,333
        Additional provision to reflect increase in
           price level (Note 3) 1,973,000

The only change from the orthodox presentation of a balance sheet is found in its capitalization section, which shows:

Accumulated price-level depreciation (Note 3) $12,064,000

Note 3 to the financial statements reads as follows:

> The District provides for depreciation on the historical cost of the electric properties on a straight-line basis at rates determined by engineering studies. Beginning in 1957 additional amounts were provided representing the difference between depreciation computed on property adjusted to current price levels and depreciation based on the historical cost. In 1969 and 1968 such additional provisions amounted to $1,973,000 and $1,516,000, respectively.

The opinion of the independent public accountants is interesting. A middle paragraph has been placed in the "Certificate" between the two typical stereotyped paragraphs comprising the standard auditor's opinion. It reads as follows:

> As set forth in Note 3 to the accompanying financial statements, the statements of net revenue and funds reflect additional charges for depreciation of $1,973,000 and $1,516,000, respectively, for the years 1969 and 1968; these charges are equivalent to the amount by which depreciation computed on the cost of depreciable property, adjusted to reflect current price levels, exceeds depreciation computed on cost. Although generally accepted accounting principles presently provide that depreciation shall be based upon cost, we approve of the practice adopted by the District since it results, in our opinion, in a fairer statement of net revenue. In other respects, the financial statements, in our opinion, were prepared in accordance with generally accepted accounting principles.

A few other companies have taken similar approaches to reveal the effect of price-level depreciation upon the results of their operations.[27]

Summary: Price-Level Depreciation

The argument concerning price-level depreciation is not settled; much information developed through research studies and various publications concerning the pros and cons of the situation is available for the person who wishes to pursue the subject further.[28]

---

[27] See annual report of Iowa-Illinois Gas and Electric Company for 1970.
[28] Especially recommended are the following studies published by the American Accounting Association:
"Price Level Changes and Financial Statements, Case Studies of Four Companies," by Ralph C. Jones.
"Price Level Changes and Financial Statements, Basic Concepts and Methods," by Perry Mason.
"Effects of Price Level Changes on Business Income, Capital and Taxes," by Ralph C. Jones.
"A Statement of Basic Accounting Theory," by the American Accounting Association (1966).
Many current articles concerning price level depreciation are available in the various business, financial, and accounting journals.

It should be remembered that the objective of price-level depreciation, like that of historical cost depreciation, is not founded upon the concept of replacement of tangible capital, but the recovery and maintenance of tangible capital; the amount recovered may be reinvested in anything or in nothing. Inflation cannot be cured by any form of accounting. The objective of price-level depreciation is to prevent the loss of capital through inflation by permitting the recovery of capital in an amount equal to the dollars of purchasing power originally invested in the facilities.

If management believes that the effect of price-level changes warrants the recasting of the financial information which it needs to control operations and to formulate certain business policies, such adjustments should be made. There is no requirement that internal financial reporting must follow generally accepted accounting principles. Financial reports using a constant (rather than a fluctuating) dollar may well aid management in comparing operating results of one plant with another and in comparing the operating results of a specific division today with its performance of some years ago. In some instances, such adjusted information may prove invaluable as an aid in the formulation of pricing policies and in decisions regarding capital expansion programs. Realistic dividend policies may be more equitably established, and the information could prove useful in labor-management discussions. Thus, although price-level depreciation is not valid for tax purposes or external financial reporting, it may be the method which best fulfills the chief purpose for which accounting exists, namely, as an aid to management.

DEPLETION

Depletion is the term employed to describe the write-off or amortization of fixed assets characterized as natural resources. As timber or coal, oil, ore, and other mineral deposits are removed or extracted from their natural position, the costs applicable to the removed portion of these natural resources, often called wasting assets, are expensed against revenue of the period. Depletion and depreciation are similar in that both refer to the systematic process of allocating the cost, less salvage value, of tangible fixed assets over their estimated useful life as charges against revenues of the periods benefited by such assets. Depletion and depreciation differ in that depletion is primarily related to the physical removal or diminution of a fixed asset, while depreciation is not ordinarily related to an actual reduction of the physical properties of a fixed asset.

Depletion expense is customarily determined in the same manner that depreciation expense is calculated under the unit of production method. For illustrative purposes, assume that in January, 1971, the Berkeley Oil Corporation purchases oil lands in a single tract at a cost of $15,300,000.[29] It is

---

[29] For simplification of the illustration which follows, it has been assumed that the company purchases the oil lands. More frequently, natural resources like oil deposits are acquired for development through leasing.

estimated that the residual value, or surface rights, of the land is $300,000. Recoverable oil reserves are estimated to be 50,000,000 barrels. Therefore, the "unit" (per barrel) depletion charge is determined as follows:

$$\text{Unit depletion charge} = \frac{\text{Cost of natural resource} - \text{residual value}}{\text{Recoverable reserves}}$$

$$\text{Unit depletion charge} = \frac{\$15,300,000 - \$300,000}{50,000,000 \text{ barrels}}$$

Unit depletion charge = 30¢ per barrel of oil

If 2,000,000 barrels of oil are extracted and sold in 1971, the depletion expense for the year will be determined as follows:

Depletion expense = Unit depletion charge × number of barrels recovered
Depletion expense = 30¢ × 2,000,000 barrels
Depletion expense = $600,000

In future years the unit depletion charge must be revised if a material change occurs in any of the factors employed in the original determination. For example, a material change in the estimated quantity of recoverable reserves would require an adjustment in the unit depletion charge.

As of December 31, 1971, the fixed assets section of the balance sheet should contain the following explanation:

Property, Plant and Equipment (on the basis of cost):
Oil Properties	$15,300,000	
Less: Accumulated depletion to date	600,000	$14,700,000
Plant and Equipment	$........	
Less: Accumulated depreciation to date	......	....
Net Property, Plant and Equipment		$........

A complete statement of income for the year is presented next. The $600,000 depletion expense shown is the allowance previously computed and is based upon *cost* factors. However, the $425,500 amount for federal income

BERKELEY OIL CORPORATION
Statement of Income
For the Year Ended December 31, 1971

Net Sales		$5,000,000
Less:		
Cost of Goods Sold, Selling, Administrative and General Expenses	$2,850,000	
Intangible Drilling Costs	200,000	
Exploration and Development Expenses	50,000	
Depreciation Expense	100,000	
Depletion Expense	600,000	3,800,000
Net Income before Federal Income Taxes		$1,200,000
Less: Federal Income Taxes		425,500
Net Income for the Year		$ 774,500

taxes is not based upon the $1,200,000 net income figure shown on the operating statement. This is attributable to the special provision in the federal income tax code which provides for a percentage depletion allowance to the owner of an economic interest in a natural resource. While a detailed discussion of the income tax factors applicable to depletion is definitely beyond the scope of this text, recognition of the highlights of this tax provision will provide a better understanding of the related accounting practices.

A brief historical review of federal income tax provisions affecting depletion discloses a constant liberalization in the amount of depletion allowed as a tax deduction. The Revenue Act of 1913 limited depletion, based upon the cost of the natural resource, to 5 percent of gross income. World War I caused depletion to become a congressional favorite. Congress fostered the discovery and development of underground natural resources by the introduction of the discovery value method of depletion for mines, oil, and gas. Then, the Revenue Act of 1926 introduced percentage depletion on oil and gas by providing for a depletion deduction of 27½ percent of gross income (changed to 22 percent in late 1969), with a maximum limitation of not more than 50 percent of taxable income of the taxpayer computed without the allowance for depletion, but in no case less than if computed on cost. In 1932, Congress introduced percentage depletion on mines at varying rates for different minerals and eliminated the discovery value method for those mines permitted to use the percentage method. Between 1932 and 1954, periodic revenue acts passed by Congress extended percentage depletion to additional natural resources and further reduced the application of the discovery value method as a basis of depletion. In addition, the percentage rates were increased for many minerals. The Code of 1954 extended percentage depletion to practically all natural resources and completely eliminated the discovery value method of depletion from the tax code. The Tax Reform Act of 1969 reduced some of the percentage depletion rates. Today, the depletion allowance or deduction for federal income taxes is the greater of the:

1. Cost method
2. Percentage method (percentage of the gross income from the producing property). However, the percentage depletion allowance must be limited to 50 percent of the taxable income computed with the depletion allowance excluded.

At present, percentage depletion rates are applicable to over one hundred natural resources and minerals. Some illustrative rates are:

22%	oil and gas, sulphur, uranium.
22%	if from deposits in the U.S.: asbestos, bauxite, mica, cobalt, lead, manganese, nickel, zinc, etc.
15%	if from deposits in the U.S.: gold, silver, copper, iron ore.
14%	ball, china, and sagger clay; refractory clay, borax, potash, granite, limestone, etc.
10%	coal, sodium chloride, lignite, etc.

7½%	......	clay and shale, if used or sold for use in manufacture of sewer pipe or brick.
5%	......	gravel, peat, sand, etc.

Since 1926, when the principle of percentage depletion was first established, volumes have been written on the pros and cons of the subject; often the factual economic considerations are confused by political considerations. The usual justification for different depletion percentages is the varying degrees of risk involved in locating and extracting the different types of natural resources and the relative importance of the different resources to the national defense and welfare.

By continuing with the Berkeley Oil Corporation illustration used previously in this discussion, the federal income tax allowance for depletion expense can be determined. To stress the principles involved in the tax calculations, assume that the item of income and all of the expenses—except depletion—shown on the preceding statement of income are identical for company accounting and for taxes. Similarly, assume that the net sales amount ($5,000,000) agrees with the definition of gross income as prescribed by the tax regulations; namely, the amount for which the company sells the oil in the immediate vicinity of the well.

Cost depletion, as previously determined, amounted to $600,000. The unit depletion charge of 30¢ was multiplied by the number of barrels of oil extracted and sold. The percentage depletion allowance is .22 times the gross income of $5,000,000 derived from the property, or $1,100,000. For tax purposes, the greater of cost depletion or percentage depletion must be used in any given year. However, in the case of Berkeley Oil Corporation, the deduction cannot be $1,100,000, because this amount exceeds the limitation placed upon percentage depletion: 50 percent of taxable net income determined prior to the deduction for depletion. Reference to the statement of income discloses that the limiting net income figure is $1,800,000 ($5,000,000 of gross income less $3,200,000 of expenses except depletion). Fifty percent of this net income is $900,000, the maximum allowance for percentage depletion.

In summary, the periodic depletion allowance for income taxes, which is not necessarily the same amount for general accounting, is the larger of (1) or (2) below unless (3) is smaller than (2), in which case the allowance is the larger of (1) or (3).

(1) Cost depletion method:
   Unit depletion charge × barrels sold
       30¢   × 2,000,000   = $600,000

(2) Percentage depletion method:
       %   × gross income
       22%   × $5,000,000   = $1,100,000

(3) Limitation on percentage method:
       50%   × taxable net income prior depletion deduction
       50%   × $1,800,000   = $900,000

Cost depletion, like depreciation, ceases when the cost of the property has been recovered. However, percentage depletion continues as long as gross income is obtained from the property and the results of operations yield a net income for the period. By percentage depletion, it is not unusual for a taxpayer to recover an amount greater than the cost of the property.

Those charged with management responsibilities of a financial nature in an extractive industry should be aware of the interrelationship of percentage depletion and accelerated depreciation. A considerable number of companies purposely have not availed themselves of the opportunity to employ accelerated depreciation, since percentage depletion is limited to 50 percent of taxable income before the depletion deduction and accelerated depreciation might reduce this base to such an extent as to reduce also the percentage depletion allowance.

AMORTIZATION

Intangible fixed assets possess characteristics which are similar to those of tangible property, plant and equipment items. However, intangibles have no bodily substance: their value is attributable to the rights conferred by their ownership.

Similar to the process by which tangible fixed assets are depreciated, the cost of intangible fixed assets possessing a determinable life should be systematically charged against revenue during each fiscal period by a process referred to as amortization. Unlike tangible fixed assets, where the accumulated depreciation to date is shown as a contra item subtracted from the original cost of the assets, intangible fixed assets are usually directly reduced by each period's amortization. The Consolidated Balance Sheet of Textron, Inc. as of January 3, 1970, illustrates this procedure.

Property, plant and equipment, at cost:	
Land and buildings	$110,831,000
Machinery and equipment	362,678,000
	$473,509,000
Less accumulated depreciation and amortization	240,546,000
	$232,963,000
Amount paid over value assigned to net assets of companies acquired, less amortization	$ 34,911,000
Patents, at cost less amortization	$ 18,566,000

Usually intangible fixed assets like leasehold improvements, leases, and leaseholds are shown at cost less amortization to date. However, it is common practice to show intangibles like patents, goodwill, trademarks, and brand names at a nominal value, usually one dollar.[30]

---

[30] For illustration, see the December 31, 1969, balance sheet of The Goodyear Tire & Rubber Company.

The Committee on Accounting Procedures of the American Institute of Certified Public Accountants stated that intangibles may be classified into the following two types:

1. Those having a term of existence limited by law, regulation, or agreement, or by their nature (such as patents, copyrights, leases, licenses, franchises for a fixed term, and goodwill as to which there is evidence of limited duration);
2. Those having no such limited term of existence and as to which there is, at the time of acquisition, no indication of limited life (such as goodwill generally, going value, trade names, secret processes, subscription lists, perpetual franchises, and organization costs).[31]

This same reference also indicated the preferred procedures to be followed for the amortization of these two broad classes of intangible assets.

Type (a) The cost of type (a) intangibles should be amortized by systematic charges in the income statement over the period benefited, as in the case of other assets having a limited period of usefulness. If it becomes evident that the period benefited will be longer or shorter than originally estimated, recognition thereof may take the form of an appropriate decrease or increase in the rate of amortization or, if such increased charges would result in distortion of income, a partial write-down may be made by a charge to earned surplus.

Type (b) When it becomes reasonably evident that the term of existence of a type (b) intangible has become limited and that it has therefore become a type (a) intangible, its cost should be amortized by systematic charges in the income statement over the estimated remaining period of usefulness. If, however, the period of amortization is relatively short so that misleading inferences might be drawn as a result of inclusion of substantial charges in the income statement, a partial write-down may be made by a charge to earned surplus, and the rest of the cost may be amortized over the remaining period of usefulness.[32]

The above two references from APB No. 43 were superseded on November 1, 1970, by APB Opinion No. 17. The conclusions contained in APB Opinion No. 17 are:

The Board concludes that a company should record as assets the costs of intangible assets acquired from others, including goodwill acquired in a business combination. A company should record as expenses the costs to develop intangible assets which are not specifically identifiable. The Board also concludes that the cost of each type of intangible asset should be amortized by systematic charges to income over the period

---

[31] *Accounting Research Bulletin No. 43,* "Restatement and Revision of Accounting Research Bulletins," p. 37. Copyright (1953) American Institute of Certified Public Accountants, Inc.

[32] *Accounting Research Bulletin No. 43,* "Restatement and Revision of Accounting Research Bulletins," pp. 38–39. Copyright (1953) American Institute of Certified Public Accountants, Inc.

estimated to be benefited. The period of amortization should not, however, exceed 40 years.[33]

With this background of long-term intangibles, the methods of their presentation, and the methods for their amortization, a brief description of each of the more commonly encountered intangibles is presented next.

A *patent* is an exclusive right granted by the United States Patent Office to an inventor, permitting him to use, sell, or manufacture his invention. The legal life of a patent is 17 years and is not renewable. Thus, the cost of a patent is amortized over its legal life or its estimated economic useful life, whichever is shorter.

The amortization basis of a patent depends upon several factors. If a patent is purchased from another party, the basis is the amount paid for it. However, if a patent is developed (in effect, acquired from the government), its cost would include items such as legal and filing fees, the cost of drawings and working models, and the research, experimental, and development expenditures which have led to the patent. The major portion of these costs of developing a patent are normally the costs for the research, experimental, and development work. Many companies operate large research laboratories which continually work on a variety of projects, including ideas which may lead to the procurement of patents. Some companies capitalize such expenditures as a portion of the cost of patents obtained, and then periodically amortize such costs against revenue. More often, due to the considerable dollar amount which may be involved and the opportunity to expense such costs immediately for tax purposes, companies charge such research and development expenditures to operations as they are incurred. This latter procedure also eliminates the problem of deciding how much overall research and development cost should be allocated to each specific patent obtained as a capitalized cost.

Often it is said that a patent has no proven worth until it has stood the test of an infringement suit. Thus, the costs involved in successfully defending the first infringement suits may properly be capitalized as a part of the cost of the patent; the cost of unsuccessful suits plus the cost of the then valueless patent would be expensed.

A *copyright* is an exclusive right granted by federal law to an author or artist permitting him to use, sell, or reproduce his literary or artistic creation. The legal life of a copyright is 28 years, with a renewal privilege of an additional 28 years. Because of the short revenue-producing life of most copyrighted items, their cost is usually amortized over a relatively few years rather than over their legal life.

The costs of developing a copyrighted item and the copyright fee are usually nominal and thus are expensed in the period incurred. However, a copyright

---

[33] American Institute of Certified Public Accountants, Inc., *Opinion of the Accountting Principles Board, Number 17,* "Intangible Assets," p. 334. Copyright (1970) by the American Institute of Certified Public Accountants, Inc.

may be purchased at a considerable cost; then the purchase price is capitalized and systematically amortized as a periodic charge against revenue.

A *franchise* is an exclusive privilege granted by the federal, state, or other governmental unit to a company permitting the use of certain public property. Such franchises are usually associated with public utility companies and grant exclusive privileges like the use of rights-of-way for transportation purposes and the use of public property for the laying of gas mains.

The life of a franchise may be a definite number of years, an indefinite number of years, or perpetual. If life is a definite number of years, the cost (if any) should be amortized over the shorter of its contract life or estimated economic useful life. If life is for an indefinite number of years, any cost involved in obtaining the franchise should be amortized fairly rapidly, since the franchise could be revoked at any time. Theoretically, the cost of a perpetual franchise (e.g., franchises by the federal government granting rights-of-way to the land-grant railroads west of the Mississippi River) need not be amortized as long as the franchise possesses income-producing value.

Normally, the acquisition cost of a franchise is nominal unless an existing franchise has been purchased from another company. Those using financial statements should be aware that any dollar amount appearing on a balance sheet for franchises may be completely unrelated to its worth.

Franchises may require periodic payments like yearly license or rental fees to a governmental unit; any such expenditures should be expensed as incurred.

Occasionally, dealer franchises are encountered whereby a manufacturer of a product grants a dealer the privilege of marketing a product within a given territory. Such business agreements require analysis and treatment as those granted by governmental agencies.

A *leasehold*, acquired by a contract called an operating lease, is an agreement giving the lessee the right to use the property of the lessor, or owner, for a prescribed period. In return he must make a series of regular payments on dates specified in the contract. Unless the lessee makes a lump sum deposit at the outset of the contract, nothing appears in the balance sheet of the lessee to indicate the existance of the lease. The periodic rental payments made by the lessee are included in his operating costs. Thus it is possible for a company to lease (rather than purchase) a considerable amount of fixed assets and thereby indicate on the balance sheet no dollar amount for fixed assets, leasehold, or obligation for future rentals. However, if the amount is material, Accounting Principles Board Opinion Number 5 requires that adequate disclosure be made.[34] This would be done through footnotes to the financial state-

---

[34] American Institute of Certified Public Accountants, Inc., Accounting Principles Board Opinion No. 5, *Reporting of Leases in Financial Statements of Lessee,* (New York, 1964). For additional information on leases, the reader is also referred to APB No. 7.

American Institute of Certified Public Accountants, Accounting Principles Board Opinion No. 7, *Accounting for Leases in Financial Statements of Lessors,* (New York, 1966).

ments. Typical of the disclosure required is the following footnote from the 1969 annual report of the Cook Paint and Varnish Company:

> Note F: *Long-Term Lease Commitments*—At November 30, 1969, the Company had approximately 154 leases expiring on various dates to 1981, with present minimum annual rentals of approximately $697,500.

Also note the following from the 1969 annual report of F. W. Woolworth Co.:

> Note 1—Long-Term Leases: Minimum annual rentals under more than 4,000 property leases in effect at December 31, 1969 amounted to $96,045,108, which is summarized according to lease expiration periods: 1970–1974, $17,222,987; 1975–1979, $24,260,045; 1980–1989, $45,404,080; 1990–1999, $7,057,800; and subsequently $2,100,196.
>
> Total rent charged to expense for the year including rentals based on a percentage of sales but excluding payments of real estate taxes, insurance and other expenses required under some leases amounted to $104,970,373 in 1969, $93,908,618 in 1968.

In some instances the lease agreement is, in fact, an installment purchase contract. These leases are called financing leases. The various payments under the agreement are in reality debt payments rather than rental payments. In such instances accounting principles dictate that the substance rather than the legal form of the agreement must be reflected in the financial statements; it should be recorded as a purchase agreement. While it can be difficult in practice to ascertain if a lease is an operating lease or a financing lease, the characteristics of each can be described. Under an operating lease the agreement is for only a portion of the asset's life. The lessor pays all the costs usually associated with ownership, such as property taxes. The agreement does not provide for the transfer of title from the lessor to the lessee. The lease may or may not be cancellable. In contrast, a financing lease is noncancellable by either party except under the most unusual circumstances. Should the term of the lease be less than the life of the asset, then the agreement gives the lessee an option to purchase the leased asset on or before the termination of the lease for a nominal amount relative to the property's expected value at time of purchase. Under a financial lease the lessee rather than the lessor pays those costs usually borne by the owner, e.g., taxes, insurance and maintenance.[35] The payments required under the lease are discounted at the interest rate the lessee pays for its long term debt. This amount is shown as an asset on the balance sheet, indicating that the property right is acquired by a lease agreement. The liability is included among the long term liabilities. (See Chapter 9, page 272). Typical of the format for disclosure of the property rights in a balance sheet is that found in the 1969 annual report of Century Electric Company:

---

[35] The financing lease is discussed in Accounting Principles Board Opinion Number 5. See sections number 9, 10, 11, 12.

Plant Property and Equipment
  Property rights under leases $5,016,485

The cost of the property right is amortized over its useful life as any other comparable asset would be. Thus, under certain financial leases where a purchase option exists, the cost of the property right will be amortized over a period longer than the term of the lease.

A company enters into financing lease agreements so as to minimize the portion of its capital tied up in fixed assets. In the typical case it minimizes capital investment by avoiding the need to raise additional capital through borrowing (e.g., bonds, mortgages) or equity capital (e.g., a new stock issue). In some cases it minimizes its investment in fixed assets by selling off properties currently owned and then immediately leasing them for a substantial period. Such a transaction is called a sale and leaseback. By entering into a sale and leaseback agreement the managers of the company are able to free capital previously invested in fixed assets for other activities. It is important to note that the accounting procedures specified in A.P.B. 5 do *not* alter the financial liquidity advantages of the financial lease. However, it does require the balance sheet to reflect the effects of the event as if the company had borrowed the necessary funds. Thus, it does alter the desirability of leasing assets relative to purchasing them in those instances where the disclosure of the asset and the debt on the balance sheet would significantly alter the picture presented of the firm's financial position, e.g., the calculation of the rate of return or the ratio of total debt to total equity.

Leasehold Improvements consist of any improvements or alterations made by the lessee to leased property. Since such additions revert to the lessor at the termination of the lease, leasehold improvements usually are amortized over the life of the improvement or the period of the lease, whichever is shorter. Consider the properties section of the December 31, 1970, Balance Sheet of F. W. Woolworth Co.

Properties, at cost	1970	1969
Land and buildings	233,495,014	212,975,894
Furniture, fixtures and equipment	358,657,521	332,315,700
	592,152,535	545,291,594
Accumulated depreciation (Note C)	189,250,981	177,484,850
	402,901,554	367,806,744
Buildings on leased grounds, less amortization ...	30,941,525	26,491,030
Alterations to leased and owned buildings, less amortization	105,863,417	92,967,714
	539,706,496	487,265,488

Observe that the last two items, excluding the portion constituting alterations to owned buildings, represent leasehold improvements subject to amortization.

Goodwill is a term which conveys different meanings to different people. To the layman, the term may imply a successful company which has fine facilities, markets excellent products, and has outstanding customer relations. To the accountant, the term usually means the capitalized value of any expected future excess profits to be earned by the company, possibly, but not necessarily, as a result of the intangibles considered by the layman. In any case, goodwill, as an intangible fixed asset appearing on a balance sheet, normally represents the amount actually paid, in the acquisition of a going business, in excess of the value of the net tangible assets acquired. But, to the businessman who has paid this excess amount to acquire another company, the use of the term goodwill as a caption representing the excess payment could be completely misleading. While the motivating factor for the premium payment by the businessman might be expected future excess earnings, the acquisition of another company could be undertaken to assure a source of supply of raw materials, as part of a diversification program, to secure a tax advantage, or for some other reason. Practically, regardless of the "goodwill" of a company, this intangible asset should never appear as a recorded asset unless it has been purchased.

There are two methods of accounting for business combinations. They are known as the "purchase" method and the "pooling of interests" method. A detailed analysis of the criteria for each method is beyond the scope of this book. APB Opinion No. 16, effective November 1, 1970 spells out the rules for each and the interested reader is referred to this 47 page source for any in depth study desired. The conclusions of APB Opinion No. 16, in full, are:

> The Board concludes that the purchase method and the pooling of interests method are both acceptable in accounting for business combinations, although not as alternatives in accounting for the same business combination. A business combination which meets specified conditions requires accounting by the pooling of interests method. A new basis of accounting is not permitted for a combination that meets the specified conditions and the assets and liabilities of the combining companies are combined at their recorded amounts. All other business combinations should be accounted for as an acquisition of one or more companies by a corporation. The cost to an acquiring corporation of an entire acquired company should be determined by the principles of accounting for the acquisition of an asset. That cost should then be allocated to the identifiable individual assets acquired and liabilities assumed based on their fair values; the unallocated cost should be recorded as goodwill.[36]

As an illustration, assume the following condensed balance sheet of Kenneweg Corporation immediately prior to its acquisition of Wilson Company:

---

[36] American Institute of Certified Public Accountants, Inc., *Opinions of the Accounting Principles Board, Number 16,* "Business Combinations," p. 283. Copyright (1970) American Institute of Certified Public Accountants, Inc.

Various Assets	$22,000,000
Various Liabilities	$12,000,000
Stockholders' Equity:	
Outstanding Preferred Stock, Par $100	-0-
Outstanding Common Stock, Par $100	4,000,000
Additional Capital Contributions by	
Stockholders in Excess of Par	1,500,000
Reinvested Earnings	4,500,000
	$22,000,000

Kenneweg Corporation, bent upon a program of expansion and diversification, is interested in acquiring the Wilson Company. The Wilson Company has been in business for many years, has a fine established business reputation, and manufactures an excellent staple product which appears to have outstanding future prospects. It is anticipated that the pattern of above-average profits generated by Wilson Company will continue if the company is acquired by Kenneweg Corporation. Continued negotiations end with the acquisition of Wilson Company by Kenneweg Corporation. Kenneweg Corporation acquires the net tangible assets of Wilson Company for $2,000,000. These net tangible assets consist of:

Various assets acquired and fairly valued at	$1,900,000
Liabilities assumed of	200,000
Net tangible assets	$1,700,000

The excess payment of $300,000 is for goodwill purchased. This business combination should be accounted for by the "purchase" method.

Settlement of the $2,000,000 purchase price might be by a cash payment of that amount. However, in this illustration assume that Kenneweg Corporation issues preferred stock in exchange for the business of Wilson Company. In the exchange, 20,000 shares of the $100 par stock are issued. The resultant condensed balance sheet of Kenneweg Corporation would now reflect the following factors:

Various Assets:		
Original amount		$22,000,000
Tangible assets acquired from Wilson Company		1,900,000
Goodwill purchased		300,000
		$24,200,000
Various Liabilities:		
Original amount	$12,000,000	
Liabilities of Wilson		
Company assumed	200,000	$12,200,000

Stockholders' Equity:
Outstanding Preferred Stock, Par $100	2,000,000
Outstanding Common Stock, Par $100	4,000,000
Additional Capital Contributions by Stockholders in Excess of Par	1,500,000
Reinvested Earnings	4,500,000
	$24,200,000

Assets have been increased $2,200,000; $1,900,000 of tangible assets have been acquired, and $300,000 of goodwill has been purchased. Liabilities have increased by $200,000 of debts assumed. The $2,000,000 settlement made by the issuance of 20,000 shares of preferred stock has increased stockholders' equity that same amount.

Since the term *goodwill* conveys various meanings to those using financial statements, many companies have avoided it by employing more descriptive alternatives. One such term is that shown by the Consolidated Balance Sheet of Westinghouse Electric Corporation. At December 31, 1967, it showed:

Purchase price of going businesses acquired in excess of their net tangible assets $46,975,695

Purchased goodwill may appear to have an unlimited life. By theory, then, it might be maintained that, once paid for, goodwill should remain intact on the balance sheet at its purchase price. This was the recommended procedure previously quoted for such a "type b" intangible asset. However, this same reference provided for the amortization of such "type b" intangibles when subsequent events justify their write-off. Because the unlimited life of goodwill is debatable and its subsequent value is highly questionable, many companies do systematically amortize the asset. A review of published financial statements indicates that many companies carry this intangible asset at a nominal value, like one dollar. However, per APB No. 17, goodwill acquired on or after November 1, 1970, *must* be amortized over a life not to exceed 40 years. Generally speaking, under the present federal income tax code, no amortization of goodwill is deductible for tax purposes; only at the date of sale or liquidation of a company may such an item be considered for income tax purposes.

The examples which follow are intended to illustrate the varying terminology and procedures used in accounting for goodwill acquired prior to November 1, 1970. From the 1970 annual report of National Distillers and Chemical Corporation:

	December 31	
	1970	1969
Goodwill—at cost	15,199,000	15,199,000

And from the 1970 annual report of Warner-Lambert Company:

	December 31	
	1970	1969
Goodwill and Unamortized Cost of Patents (Note 5)	23,866,000	22,125,000

Note 5 Goodwill and Unamortized Cost of Patents: Goodwill arose in connection with certain acquisitions and represents the excess of the purchase price (including the fair value of the Warner-Lambert stock issued) over the value of the net tangible assets acquired. Generally, the goodwill so acquired is not being amortized since the value thereof is expected to be retained or increased. If a reduction in the value of the goodwill becomes evident, it is amortized until such time that no further diminution of its value is apparent. The cost of patents is being amortized over their legal lives.

Likewise, from the 1970 annual report of Ford Motor Company:

	December 31	
	1970	1969
Excess of Cost of Investments in Consolidated Subsidiaries Over Equities in Net Assets	279,200,000	279,200,000

The excess of cost of investments in consolidated subsidiaries over equities in net assets at the date of acquisition is not being amortized because, in the opinion of management, there has been no decrease in value.

And, from the 1970 annual report of PPG Industries, Inc., an alternative treatment:

	December 31	
	1970	1969
Excess of Cost of Investments in Consolidated Subsidiaries Over Equities in Net Assets—Unamortized Balance	5,442,000	8,327,000

Note Amortization of Intangible Assets: The Corporation purchased several companies in prior years for prices in excess of book values of the net assets acquired. The excess, treated as goodwill, is being amortized over a 10 year period. During 1970, the amount amortized against net earnings was $2,874,000, equivalent to $.14 per share. The amount of goodwill at December 31, 1970, of $5,442,000 will be charged against earnings over the next two years.

Note 5 to the financial statements in the 1969 annual report of American Home Products Corporation reads as follows:

Intangible assets at December 31, 1969 consist of $73,625,828 of goodwill, trademarks, formulae, etc., acquired since January 1, 1954, which is not being amortized since the Company believes there has been no diminution in value of these assets, and $1,520,659 for patents and patent rights acquired since January 1, 1950, which are stated at cost less amortization. In accordance with generally accepted accounting practice at the time, goodwill, trademarks, formulae, etc., acquired prior to January 1, 1954, aggregating approximately $40,000,000, were written down to $1 by charges against retained earnings and capital surplus; however, such amount should be recognized in any determination of total invested capital.

In August of 1970, Opinion No. 17 of the Accounting Principles Board was issued, making amortization of goodwill mandatory effective November 1, 1970. Such goodwill acquired in a merger accounted for as a purchase must be recorded and written off against earnings over a period of up to 40 years. This Opinion is applicable only to acquisitions on and after November 1, 1970. Thus, alternative methods of accounting for goodwill acquired prior to that date may persist for several years.

Organization Costs consist of those expenditures incurred at the formation of a corporation for items such as incorporation and charter fees, legal and accounting fees, printing of stock certificates, underwriting fees, and expenses incident to the sale of the stock. In theory, this "type b" intangible has an unlimited life because such organization costs benefit all future years of corporate life. In practice, because the total dollar amount involved is not usually a considerable sum and the asset is of uncertain worth, organization costs are customarily written off in the first year, or the first few years, of business. Prior to 1954, organization costs were deductible for federal income taxes only in the year of dissolution. The Internal Revenue Code of 1954 allows corporations an election to deduct certain organization costs ratably over a period of 60 months or more, beginning with the month the corporation commences business. This election applies only to the expenditures incurred before the end of the corporation's first taxable year and does not apply to organization costs as expenditures involved in the issuing of securities.

A trademark is a distinctive symbol (a drawing or an emblem) which is used to distinguish a company's product or products from those of other companies. The trademarks of many companies are most valuable assets. Yet, trademarks seldom appear on a balance sheet at other than a nominal figure. The costs involved in developing a trademark are often expensed as incurred, because the useful life of a trademark is so indefinite. Trademarks may be registered with the federal government for an indefinite life.

The preceding sections have presented the salient points with respect to those intangible fixed assets most often encountered. Other intangibles occasionally shown by financial statements are brand names, formulas, designs, research and development costs, subscription lists, scripts, film rights, mining or timber rights, and licenses.

[CH. 7] PROPERTY, PLANT AND EQUIPMENT 215

QUESTIONS AND PROBLEMS

7-1. For each of the following statements, choose the best answer and indicate your choice on an answer sheet.

a. If a company's balance sheet shows an amount for goodwill, such an amount represents:
1. the purchase price of going businesses acquired in excess of their net tangible assets (less amortization to date)
2. the arbitrary value the company has assigned to its own established business reputation generated through excellent customer relations and by marketing profitably well accepted products
3. the excess of the appraised value of the company over and above the amount actually shown by stockholders' equity

b. Price-level depreciation is:
1. shown on 20 percent of United States published financial statements
2. a tax gimmick
3. an attempt to match current costs against current revenues and thus maintain capital investment intact

c. Petroleum companies usually don't use accelerated depreciation because:
1. percentage depletion gives them enough of a tax advantage
2. of the limitation on percentage depletion
3. it isn't generally accepted accounting

d. Increased depreciation expense to reflect current costs was first shown on the operating statement of:
1. Indiana Telephone Company in 1955
2. Sacramento Municipal Utility District in 1957
3. U.S. Steel Corporation in 1947

e. Many companies show goodwill at $1 because of:
1. income tax advantages
2. conservatism and the debatable dollar amount to the reader of financial statements
3. its negligible development cost

f. Any permission, by a change in the Revenue Act, to use price-level depreciation for income tax purposes would be least advantageous to:
1. public utilities
2. steel companies
3. auto manufacturers

g. Wiggle Manufacturing Corporation's new lathe (problem 7-3) cost $31,000 more than the old one because of:
1. price-level changes
2. its being a better piece of machinery
3. both a and b

h. A majority of accountants believe that any company using price-level depreciation for external reporting:

1. should write up fixed assets
2. should show that long-term debt will be paid off in cheaper dollars
3. is not following generally accepted accounting principles

i. Percentage depletion:
   1. gives oil and gas companies abnormally high profits
   2. is based upon equity, risk, necessity to national defense, and welfare of the nation
   3. resulted from the Oklahoma-Texas oil lobby in 1926

j. A patent:
   1. has a life of 28 years
   2. is an intangible fixed asset
   3. is a guarantee of an invention

k. Price-level depreciation is somewhat similar to LIFO in its effect on the:
   1. Statement of Income
   2. Balance Sheet
   3. income taxes

l. The suspension of the investment credit from October, 1966, to March, 1967, was accompanied by the suspension of accelerated depreciation on buildings.
   1. True
   2. False

m. Coats Manufacturing Company in 1970 purchased a brand new office building to expand its operations. Which of the following provisions apply to the $700,000 cost of the building:
   1. 20 percent initial one-shot depreciation
   2. 7 percent investment credit (on all or part)
   3. accelerated depreciation (DB at 150 percent of S-L rate)
   4. accelerated depreciation (SYD)
   5. all of the above
   6. 1 and 2
   7. 1 and 3
   8. 2 and 3
   9. 1, 2, and 3
   10. 1, 2, and 3 or 4
   11. 3 or 4
   12. none of the above

n. The Tax Reform Act of 1969, signed by President Nixon on December 30, 1969:
   1. repealed the investment credit
   2. repealed accelerated depreciation on personalty (machinery, etc.)
   3. repealed all accelerated depreciation on realty (buildings) except for rental property and except for 150 percent DB depreciation on other new buildings
   4. 1 and 2
   5. 1, 2, and 3
   6. 2 and 3
   7. 1 and 3

7-2. If the company in problem 6-12 uses straight-line depreciation for its financial statements and double declining balance depreciation for tax purposes, what will be the approximate dollar amount of its deferred income tax liability on the Balance Sheet prepared at *December 31, 1972?* Assume a 50 percent tax rate and no other facts.

7-3. The Harrison City plant of Wiggle Manufacturing Corporation is preparing the next issue of its local house organ (company newspaper for employees). Among the usual news items, the company plans a very short educational story for its employees to be titled, "Why 'Depreciation Dollars' Don't Go Far Enough." The article will be supplemented by pictures of two turret lathes. The planned textual draft of the article, submitted to company headquarters for approval, is as follows:

> In 1955, the Harrison City plant bought a turret lathe (picture above) for $8,000. Last year, 1971, when it came time to replace this lathe, the plant had $8,000 (set aside in depreciation allowances) and $200 from the sale of the old lathe. But the cost of the new lathe (picture below), same model, was $21,000. With attachments needed to do more advanced work, total cost was $39,000. The added $31,000 had to come from only one place—our profits. At Wiggle's rate of profit last year, it would take nearly a million dollars in sales to make enough profit to replace one lathe that keeps one employee per shift on the job. "Depreciation" just isn't enough.

Required

Criticize the script.

7-4. H. C. Carlson Corporation purchased a piece of machinery on January 2, 1971, at a cost of $15,000. Estimated useful life is eight years and estimated salvage value is $400. The machinery purchased was new, not used. The corporation *did* elect to use the total annual $10,000 amount allowed for 20 percent initial one-shot depreciation on this particular acquisition.

Required

Compute the *maximum* allowable depreciation expense for 1971. The company wishes to "recover" the investment in this new machine as quickly as possible.

7-5. Assume the information given in problem 6-9 except that:
   a. The machinery purchased was second-hand used machinery.
   b. The corporation *did* elect to use the total annual $10,000 amount allowed for 20 percent initial one-shot depreciation on this particular acquisition.

Required

Compute the *maximum* allowable depreciation expense for both 1971 and 1972.

7-6. The Ft. Yukon Oil Company purchased oil lands in January, 1972, at a cost of $100,000,000 containing approximately 1,000,000,000 barrels of recoverable oil. 40,000,000 barrels of oil were produced and sold in 1972. Gross income (Sales) from the property amounted to $30,000,000 in 1972 and total deductions (Expenses) except for depletion amounted to $18,000,000.

Required

a. What amount normally would be shown for Depletion Expense (on cost) on the company's Statement of Income?

b. On the company's tax return:
   1. What is the maximum depletion deduction for federal income tax purposes?
   2. If the deductions were $24,000,000 instead of $18,000,000 what is the maximum depletion deduction?
   3. If the deductions were $10,000,000 instead of $18,000,000, what is the maximum depletion deduction?

7-7. Based upon your study of the annual reports of Sacramento Municipal Utility District (portions reproduced in Chapter 7) and Indiana Telephone Corporation (reproduced in Appendix), both of which show price-level depreciation in the financial statements, but in different manners, answer each of the following by inserting check marks at *all* the proper places:

	S.M.U. District	I.T. Corp.
Fixed Assets are shown at:		
Cost less accumulated depreciation	_____	_____
Cost of property repriced in current dollars less accumulated depreciation to date on current dollar basis	_____	_____
Long-term Debt is shown:		
In the traditional manner	_____	_____
At an adjusted amount to reflect the fact that "good" dollars were borrowed and the debt will be repaid in "cheap" dollars ...	_____	_____
Net Income for the year, as shown by the Statement(s) of Income, reflects depreciation expense:		
Based upon original historical cost	_____	_____
Based upon current price levels	_____	_____

7-8. Scranton Coal Company purchased a coal mine which contained approximately 20,000,000 tons of recoverable coal in January, 1972, at a cost of $5,000,000. 1,000,000 tons of coal were mined and sold in 1972. Gross income from the property amounted to $8,000,000 in 1972, and total deductions (expenses) except for depletion amounted to $6,000,000.

Required

a. What amount would be shown for Depletion Expense on the company's Statement of Income?

b. On the company's tax return:
   1. What is the maximum depletion deduction for federal income taxes?
   2. If the deductions were $6,800,000 instead of $6,000,000, what would be the maximum depletion deduction?

[CH. 7] PROPERTY, PLANT AND EQUIPMENT 219

3. If the deductions were $7,600,000 instead of $6,000,000, what would be the maximum depletion deduction?

7-9. If not previously assigned, problem 2-10 may be used at this point. This problem is concerned with intangible assets.

7-10. Assume that Flamingo Corporation, a manufacturer of electrical household appliances, acquired the following fixed assets on January 3, 1971:

	Cost	Estimated Salvage
New items:		
Automobiles	$ 20,000	3,000
Light general purpose trucks	30,000	5,000
Heavy general purpose trucks	60,000	7,000
Office furniture, fixtures, equipment, and office machines	50,000	2,000
Machinery, equipment, dies, jigs	400,000	15,000
Office building	1,000,000	–0–
Used items:		
Office machines; estimated useful life remaining is five years	60,000	–0–
	$1,620,000	

Required

a. Prepare and complete a columnar schedule containing the following column headings:

1. Item (list the seven acquired fixed assets)
2. Cost
3. Guideline Group and Class
4. Life (years) (per Revenue Procedure 62–21)
5. Eligibility for 20 percent Initial Depreciation
6. Estimated Salvage
7. First Year Depreciation Choices:
7a. Straight-line
7b. Sum-of-Years' Digits
7c. Declining Balance (Tax Method)

Column 5 should be filled in with the word "Yes" or "No" for each of the seven fixed assets acquired. *Select* the machinery and equipment for the 20 percent initial allowance.

In columns 7a, 7b, and 7c, compute the 1971 depreciation expense for each of the seven fixed assets by every method allowable for the particular asset. For any item where the arithmetic becomes involved, show only the arithmetic equation by which the amount would be computed.

b. If the Asset Depreciation Range (ADR) System (effective January 1, 1971; see discussion in Chapter 6, page 144) had been elected to modify the guideline lives listed in column 4 for requirement a, what are the *shortest* lives over which each of the seven assets could have been depreciated? (Note: Years should be rounded to the nearest half year.) Would the adoption of ADR have changed the depreciation *method* used on any of the seven depreciable assets?

7-11. There has been a good deal of criticism of the traditional "historical" cost records and the data which they reflect, especially during times of inflation or deflation. In order to assist in the interpretation of accounting reports as normally prepared, many accountants have suggested that the recorded cost data be first utilized in the preparation of the conventional financial statements, and then, as a supplementary technique, these statements be converted into dollars having a uniform purchasing power through the application of price indexes to the recorded dollar amounts. There has been some considerable difference of opinion among these accountants as to whether to use a "general" price index, such as the wholesale commodity price index, or the cost of living index, or, on the other hand, to use a more "specific" price index that is more applicable to the industry involved, or to the particular items being converted (for instance, using a construction index for the conversion of plant and equipment items, or using a special price index constructed for a specific industry).

Required

Give arguments for and against each of these two types of indexes.
(Uniform C.P.A. Examination problem.)

7-12. The comments below are from a footnote supplementing Justice Jackson's separate opinion in a Supreme Court case, Power Comm'n vs. Hope Gas Co. (1944), 320 U.S. 591.

> "To make a fetish of mere accounting is to shield from examination the deeper causes, forces, movements, and conditions which should govern rates. Even as a recording of current transactions, bookkeeping is hardly an exact science. As a representation of the condition and trend of a business, it uses symbols of certainty to express values that actually are in constant flux. It may be said that in commercial or investment banking or any business extending credit, success depends on knowing what not to believe in accounting. Few concerns go into bankruptcy or reorganization whose books do not show them solvent and often even profitable. If one cannot rely on accountancy accurately to disclose past or current conditions of a business, the fallacy of using it as a sole guide to future price policy ought to be apparent. However, our quest for certitude is so ardent that we pay an irrational reverence to a technique which uses symbols of certainty, even though experience again and again warns us that they are delusive. Few writers have ventured to challenge this American idolatry, but see Hamilton, Cost as a Standard for Price, 4 Law and Contemporary Problems 321, 323–25.***"

Required

Give your recommendations to alleviate the causes which create situations of the type portrayed in the above comments of Justice Jackson.

7-13. The Wabash Corporation purchased a brand new piece of machinery on January 2, 1971; cost $87,500; estimated salvage value $4,500; estimated useful life 9 years. The 20 percent one-shot initial depreciation allowance for the year is used on this acquisition. Compute, for 1971, the *total* depreciation expense (*include* one-shot amount), by:

a. straight-line
b. sum-of-year's digits
c. declining balance (tax method)

7-14. The Canyon Corporation purchased a brand new piece of machinery on January 2, 1971; cost $100,000; estimated salvage value $3,000; estimated useful life 10 years. The 20 percent one-shot initial depreciation allowance for the year is used on this acquisition. Compute, for 1971, the *total* depreciation expense, by:

a. straight-line
b. sum-of-year's digits
c. declining balance (tax method)

7-15. If the machinery in problem 7-14 had been *used* machinery, what would have been the *maximum* depreciation permitted in 1971 for "generally accepted accounting" and "income tax" purposes (same amount for both).

7-16. Assume that the Whittier Construction Corporation acquired the following fixed assets on January 3, 1969:

New, Unused:	Cost	Estimated Salvage	Life (Years)
Office furniture and fixtures	$ 50,000	$ 2,000	10
Machinery—all purpose	100,000	5,000	10
Office building	400,000	–0–	45
Equipment and Machinery	200,000	20,000	15
Used, Second-Hand:			
Equipment and tools	100,000	–0–	10

Required

Compute the amount of the investment credit. (The Company had an income tax expense for the year of $1,000,000.)

Note: The investment credit is applicable to eligible acquisitions made or ordered prior to April 18, 1969. The U.S. Congress is now, 1971, in the process of restoring the investment credit.

7-17. Skadden, Inc., a retailer, was organized during 1966. Skadden's management has decided to supplement its December 31, 1969 historical dollar financial statements with general price-level financial statements. The following general ledger trial balance (historical dollar) and additional information have been furnished.

1. Monetary assets (cash and receivables) exceeded monetary liabilities (accounts payable and bonds payable) by $445,000 at December 31, 1968. The amounts of monetary items are fixed in terms of numbers of dollars regardless of changes in specific prices or in the general price-level.
2. Purchases ($1,840,000 in 1969) and sales are made uniformly throughout the year.
3. Depreciation is computed on a straight-line basis, with a full year's depreciation being taken in the year of acquisition and none in the year of retirement. The depreciation rate is 10 percent and no salvage value is an-

SKADDEN, INC.
Trial Balance
December 31, 1969

	Debit	Credit
Cash and receivables (net)	$ 540,000	$
Marketable securities (common stock)	400,000	
Inventory	440,000	
Equipment	650,000	
Equipment—Accumulated depreciation		164,000
Accounts payable		300,000
6% First mortgage bonds, due 1987		500,000
Common stock, $10 par		1,000,000
Retained earnings, December 31, 1968	46,000	
Sales		1,900,000
Cost of sales	1,508,000	
Depreciation	65,000	
Other operating expenses and interest	215,000	
	$3,864,000	$3,864,000

ticipated. Acquisitions and retirements have been made fairly evenly over each year and the retirements in 1969 consisted of assets purchased during 1967 which were scrapped. An analysis of the equipment account reveals the following:

Year	Beginning Balance	Additions	Retirements	Ending Balance
1967	—	$550,000	—	$550,000
1968	$550,000	10,000	—	560,000
1969	560,000	150,000	$60,000	650,000

4. The bonds were issued in 1967 and the marketable securities were purchased fairly evenly over 1969. Other operating expenses and interest are assumed to be incurred evenly throughout the year.
5. Assume that Gross National Product Implicit Price Deflators (1958 = 100) were as follows:

Annual Averages	Index	Conversion Factors (1969 4th Qtr. = 1.000)
1966	113.9	1.128
1967	116.8	1.100
1968	121.8	1.055
1969	126.7	1.014

Quarterly Averages			
1968	4th	123.5	1.040
1969	1st	124.9	1.029
	2nd	126.1	1.019
	3rd	127.3	1.009
	4th	128.5	1.000

Required

a. Prepare a schedule to convert the Equipment account balance at December 31, 1969 from historical cost to general price-level adjusted dollars.
b. Prepare a schedule to analyze in historical dollars the Equipment—Accumulated Depreciation account for the year 1969.
c. Prepare a schedule to analyze in general price-level dollars the Equipment—Accumulated Depreciation account for the year 1969.
d. Prepare a schedule to compute Skadden, Inc.'s general price-level gain or loss on its net holdings of monetary assets for 1969 (ignore income tax implications). The schedule should give consideration to appropriate items on or related to the balance sheet and the income statement.
(Uniform CPA Examination)

8

Inventories and Inventory Management

Inventory

Inventory represents the cost of goods owned as of a specific date. The type of inventory which a company owns depends upon the company's business: if the company is a merchandising concern, it purchases and sells the same product. For example, in the Balance Sheet of F. W. Woolworth Co. as of December 31, 1970, the inventory appeared as follows:

    Merchandise inventories (Note B) $525,380,119

On the other hand, a manufacturing concern produces the finished product which it sells. Its inventories consist of raw materials not yet placed into production, work in process (partially completed goods in production), and finished goods available for sale. In addition, a manufacturing company usually has inventories of manufacturing supplies, repair parts, containers, and packaging supplies; usually it also maintains an inventory of finished parts which it has produced or purchased. A typical presentation of inventories by a manufacturing-type company is contained in Note 3 to the Balance Sheet of Ingersoll-Rand Company as of December 31, 1970:

    Note 3: Inventories: Inventories are valued at the lower of cost less allowances for obsolescence, principally on the first-in, first-out basis, or market and include:

Raw materials and supplies	$ 25,978,000
Work in process	86,036,000
Finished goods	196,348,000
	$308,362,000

Variations from the two examples presented above will be encountered in businesses differing from typical merchandising or manufacturing endeavors. For example, in the current asset section of the Balance Sheet of The Detroit

[CH. 8] INVENTORIES AND INVENTORY MANAGEMENT 225

Edison Company as of December 31, 1970, the inventories appeared as follows:

Inventories, at average cost—
Fuel $39,051,000
Construction and maintenance materials 27,288,000
Merchandise for resale 1,179,000

Various analyses of published financial reports indicate that inventories comprise a major segment of total current assets as well as a considerable portion of total assets. Examine the accompanying survey of the 1970 annual reports of eleven large industrial companies.[1] For comparison, one utility company and two retail merchandising companies are also shown. Because of the sizeable investment which inventories represent in the typical company, this chapter discusses the major principles and practices which apply to cost determination, valuation, and management of inventories.

| | Amounts in millions of dollars ||| Inventories as percentage of ||
Company	Inventories	Current Assets	Total Assets	Current Assets	Total Assets
General Motors Corporation	4,115	6,235	14,174	66%	29%
General Electric Company	1,555	3,335	6,310	47%	25%
U.S. Steel Corporation	923	1,770	6,311	52%	15%
Du Pont (E. I.) de Nemours	752	1,525	3,567	49%	21%
Gulf Oil Corporation	533	2,448	8,672	22%	6%
Swift and Company	177	408	825	43%	22%
General Dynamics Corporation ...	71	735	1,096	10%	7%
Kraftco Corporation	362	599	1,031	60%	35%
RCA Corporation	409	1,481	2,936	28%	14%
Continental Can Company, Inc. ..	356	594	1,535	60%	23%
United Aircraft Corporation	206	1,106	1,546	19%	13%
Utility:					
Detroit Edison Company	67	133	1,984	50%	3%
Merchandise:					
F. W. Woolworth Co.	525	690	1,436	76%	37%
Federated Department Stores, Inc.	236	701	1,166	34%	20%

Cost Determination

The determination of the cost of a company's inventory as of a specific date, except in unusual and isolated situations, is *not* a simple matter. Many valid

---

[1] These are the same eleven companies that were used in Chapter 6 for a comparison of fixed assets to total assets. Reference to both of these tables discloses that the total of inventories *and* net property, plant, and equipment comprise from 34 percent to 77 percent of total assets for the typical company. Similarly, the total of inventories and net property, plant, and equipment comprise 95 percent, 74 percent, and 55 percent of total assets for Detroit Edison, F. W. Woolworth, and Federated Department Stores. The above percentages are intended only to convey a general panorama of the relative components of total assets. Unusual situations in any one company may skew comparative figures. In utility companies, fixed assets normally predominate (i.e., 92 percent of total assets in Detroit Edison).

and logical methods are available to a business enterprise. To illustrate, assume the following set of elementary facts for a company that commences business to buy and sell a single product on July 1 and has the following flow of goods during July:

July 1—Purchase of one item	$100 cost
July 20—Purchase of one item	110 cost
July 30—Sale of one item	180 selling price

What is the cost of the one item of inventory on hand at July 31? If it is assumed that the one sold was the first one purchased, the first-in, first-out (FIFO) concept, then the inventory cost of the one on hand is $110. But, if it is assumed that the one sold was the last or most recent one purchased, the last-in, first-out (LIFO) concept, then the inventory cost of the one on hand is $100. A third answer is possible by computing an average cost for both items purchased. In this simplified example, the average cost of each of the two items purchased is $105 (total cost of $210 divided by the quantity of two items); thus, the inventory cost of the one on hand is $105.

At this point, recall that one of the objectives of accounting is to present fairly the operating results of the period. The method used to determine the cost of an inventory at the end of a fiscal period should not be viewed principally as a means of determining a dollar amount to be presented as a current asset on the balance sheet. To present fairly the operating results of the period, attention must be directed to the cost determination of the goods sold during the period. The diagrams presented next reflect the effect resulting from the three methods of cost determination on the operating statements.

If the first-in, first-out (FIFO) method is used, then, *theoretically,* the oldest unit of inventory has been sold. As shown below, matching the $100 cost

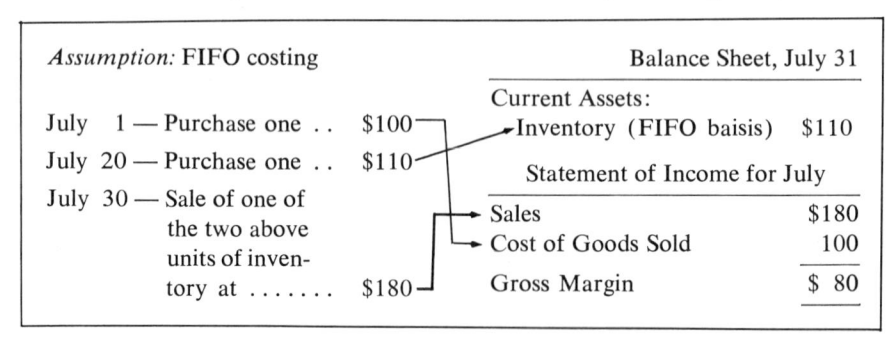

Assumption: FIFO costing	Balance Sheet, July 31	
	Current Assets:	
July 1 — Purchase one .. $100	Inventory (FIFO baisis)	$110
July 20 — Purchase one .. $110	Statement of Income for July	
July 30 — Sale of one of		
the two above	Sales	$180
units of inven-	Cost of Goods Sold	100
tory at $180	Gross Margin	$ 80

against the $180 revenue results in a gross margin of $80 when a FIFO flow of costs is assumed. If the last-in, first-out (LIFO) method is used, then, theoretically, the most recently acquired unit has been sold. As shown, matching the $110 cost against the $180 revenue results in a gross margin of $70 when a LIFO flow of costs is assumed. When an average cost method is used, theoretically no particular unit is assumed to have been sold or retained in inventory. As shown below, matching the $105 of cost against the $180 of revenue results in a gross margin of $75 when the total cost of the

[CH. 8] INVENTORIES AND INVENTORY MANAGEMENT 227

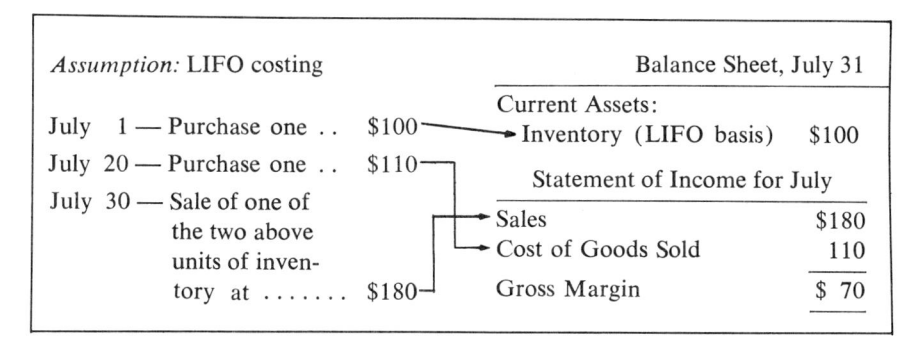

Assumption: LIFO costing   Balance Sheet, July 31

July 1 — Purchase one .. $100
July 20 — Purchase one .. $110
July 30 — Sale of one of
         the two above
         units of inven-
         tory at $180

Current Assets:
Inventory (LIFO basis) $100

Statement of Income for July

Sales	$180
Cost of Goods Sold	110
Gross Margin	$ 70

---

two units is averaged. An analysis of these three diagrams indicates the effect of an assumed flow of costs on both the portion of acquisition costs identified with goods in inventory and the portion of acquisition costs assigned to the goods sold during the period. It should be emphasized that the selection of any method of cost determination of inventory is *not* predicated upon the

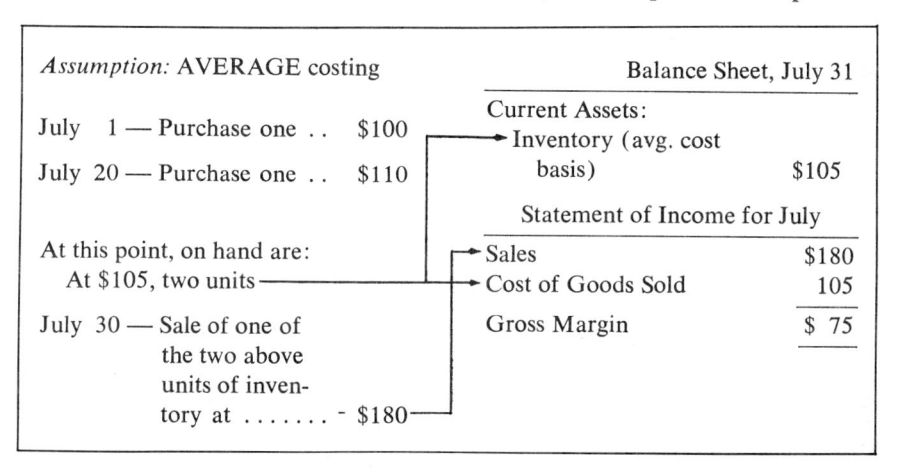

Assumption: AVERAGE costing   Balance Sheet, July 31

July 1 — Purchase one .. $100
July 20 — Purchase one .. $110

At this point, on hand are:
   At $105, two units

July 30 — Sale of one of
         the two above
         units of inven-
         tory at .... - $180

Current Assets:
Inventory (avg. cost basis) $105

Statement of Income for July

Sales	$180
Cost of Goods Sold	105
Gross Margin	$ 75

---

actual manner by which the goods physically move into and out of an inventory. For example, a company may use the LIFO method of cost determination even though, as a matter of policy, it attempts to physically dispose of its goods on the FIFO basis. A more comprehensive treatment of the methods of the cost determination of inventory and cost of goods sold is presented in succeeding pages.

To determine the cost of an inventory item, additional factors must be considered. For example, if a retail concern purchases an item for its inventory from a vendor at an invoice price of $50, this amount usually will not represent the full or total cost of the item. In addition to the invoice cost, consideration should be given to related direct costs (e.g., transportation and insurance during transit) and related indirect costs (e.g., storage and handling). Whether such costs are allocated to items of inventory as a portion of cost or immediately expensed against revenue of the period depends upon the policy of the particular company. For a manufacturing company, the determination of the total cost of inventory items is complicated further by various alternative cost accounting methods employed to allocate manufacturing costs to specific products.[2] Those who use financial information for comparative analyses (e.g., between companies) should be aware that, in addition to possible non-comparability of figures determined by FIFO, LIFO, or average cost, the cost determination policy, under any of these methods, will vary from company to company even within the same industry. Failure to consider related direct and indirect costs in addition to the actual invoice cost may lead to erroneous managerial decisions.[3]

Cash discounts on purchased goods should be considered in the cost determination of inventory items. Assume that the $50 inventory item mentioned in the preceding paragraph is purchased by the company with terms of 2 percent discount if paid for within thirty days. While a majority of companies appear to view the $1 discount as a savings with a resulting inventory cost of only $49, other companies view the $1 discount as an item of miscellaneous income earned by the company and cost the inventory item at $50. From a theory point of view, the latter method is debatable, because nothing is earned by simply paying invoices in time to take advantage of cash discounts; income is recognized only when items are *sold* at a profit, not when purchased at a reduced cost.

Perpetual and Non-Perpetual Inventory Systems

Inventories may be accounted for by a perpetual inventory system which requires continuously maintained records indicating the amount of each individual item of inventory on hand at any given time. Or inventories may be accounted for by a non-perpetual inventory system which necessitates a physical count of the items to determine the amount of the inventory at a specific date. The non-perpetual system is often referred to as a periodic inventory system. A perpetual inventory system may be maintained only in terms of physical quantities of items or in terms of both physical quantities and dollars of cost.

Even though a business maintains its inventory records on a perpetual basis, it is necessary to verify the accuracy of these records by actual physical counts of the various inventory items. Such physical counts may be made at periodic intervals for selected inventory items during the year, or by a systematic continuous method which verifies each item of inventory at least once a year, or

---

[2] See Chapter 12.

[3] For example, a review by The Comptroller General of the United States of selected activities in the management of food supply by the Military Subsistence Supply Agency disclosed that transportation costs of approximately $600,000 annually which were applicable to perishable foods furnished to commissary stores were not being added to the prices charged such stores but, in effect, were being absorbed by the Government; see Report to The Congress of the United States by The Comptroller General of the United States, *Review of Selected Activities in the Management of Food Supply by the Military Subsistence Supply Agency, Department of Defense,* November 1961.

by complete annual physical count as of a given date. Regardless of the safeguards imposed by internal control systems to prevent inaccuracies and despite the advances in inventory control made possible by electronic computers, discrepancies do occur between an inventory quantity kept by perpetual records and the quantity obtained by a periodic physical count. The causes of such discrepancies, due to the "people" element in any system, range from clerical error to theft. The auditing standards of the public accounting profession require verification of inventories. To implement this standard, certain auditing procedures are followed, including the physical count or measurement of a sample of the company's inventory to test how well the company itself has performed the periodic physical count function.[4]

Illustrative Facts

To present more fully the underlying theories involved in
(1) the determination of the cost to be deferred in inventory as of a specific date, and
(2) the determination of the cost applicable to the goods sold or used during a specific period of time,
the accompanying facts are assumed to present and compare the results under various cost determination methods for a single item (#156) of inventory.

		Item #156	
July 1	....	Inventory of 300 units, each at a cost of $50	
		Purchases at varying costs as indicated	Sales; all at the price of $80 per unit
July 5	....	200 @ $52	
10	....		100
20	....	200 @ $55	
25	....		400
30	....	200 @ $57	
Totals		600 purchased	500 sold
July 31	....	Inventory of 400 units	

For clarity of comparison, the beginning inventory of 300 units is costed at $50 per unit for each inventory method illustrated. Though many methods of cost determination for the pricing of inventories are in use, only three methods are used extensively.[5] They are: first-in, first-out; average cost; and last-in, first-out.

---

[4] For a detailed discussion and illustration of how statistical sampling is employed to attest to the fairness of an amount, see the section on sampling in Chapter 19.
[5] For a comprehensive survey relative to the frequency with which the various methods of cost determination are used in practice, see the latest annual edition of *Accounting Trends and Techniques in Published Corporate Annual Reports*, by the American Institute of Certified Public Accountants, Inc.

First-In, First-Out (FIFO) Method

The FIFO method of cost determination is based upon a flow of costs in which the first or earliest costs incurred are the first costed out of inventory. The method only assumes that the first items purchased or received are those items which are first sold or issued. The FIFO method of cost determination may be used regardless of the manner or order in which the actual goods are physically removed from inventory. Reference to the perpetual inventory record that follows clearly illustrates the issuance of 100 units on July 10 and

First-in, First-out Cost Determination Method   Item #156

DATE	RECEIVED (or purchased)			ISSUED (or sold)			BALANCE ON HAND		
	Quantity	Unit Cost	Amount	Quantity	Unit Cost	Amount	Quantity	Unit Cost	Amount
July 1							300	$50	$15,000
5	200	$52	$10,400				{300 / 200}	{50 / 52}	25,400
10				100	$50	$ 5,000	{200 / 200}	{50 / 52}	20,400
20	200	55	11,000				{200 / 200 / 200}	{50 / 52 / 55}	31,400
25				{200 / 200}	{50 / 52}	20,400	200	55	11,000
30	200	57	11,400				{200 / 200}	{55 / 57}	22,400
Totals	600	—	$32,800	500	—	$25,400			

400 units on July 25 from the oldest priced units on hand at the time of each issuance. Thus, the net income for July, as shown by the statement of income, matches the earliest incurred costs with current revenue. And, since the goods are theoretically removed and costed from inventory in the same sequence as acquired, the ending inventory, shown as a current asset on the balance sheet at July 31, reflects the cost of the last 400 units acquired.

The FIFO method has been subject to much criticism because of its apparent failure to match current costs with current revenue. For example, the above inventory record indicates a cost of goods sold amount of $25,400 for the 500 units issued during July. The earliest costs of $50 and $52 are matched against revenue of the period. But the latest incurred and most current cost is $57 per unit. Because management is inclined to compare the most recent or current costs with the current selling price for decision-making purposes, the FIFO concept (as used for income determination) may be at variance with management's thinking when costs are not relatively stable.

The first statement of income (FIFO-perpetual) on page 238 shows a gross margin of $14,600. In a period of rising cost prices, as in our illustration, the FIFO method may somewhat overstate the income of the period, because it does not match current costs with revenue. Though the most current cost incurred is $57 per unit, the period's income has been determined by matching the oldest costs of $50 and $52 against current revenue of $80 per unit. And, in a period of falling cost prices, the reverse situation would occur: FIFO would tend to understate income of the period by matching the older higher costs against revenue.

The use of FIFO for the cost determination of inventory presented in balance sheets is not subject to the same degree of criticism. Because the first goods "in" are assumed to be the first goods "out," the last goods "in" are presumed to be those on hand at the balance sheet date. Reference to the preceding inventory record reveals that the ending inventory of 400 units consists of the most recent acquisitions totaling 400 units. Thus, the inventory amount of $22,400 reflects the most recent costs of $55 and $57 per unit. Similarly, in a period of declining cost prices, the inventory amount would reflect the most recently incurred acquisition costs; as will be discussed shortly, there is a procedure whereby such declining costs may be written down to current replacement cost in case this amount is less than the most recently incurred acquisition costs. As shown by the diagram below, the FIFO method of cost determination allocates the total $47,800 cost of available goods (opening inventory of $15,000 plus purchases of $32,800) by charging the earliest acquisition costs against revenue of the period and deferring the most recent acquisition costs in inventory.

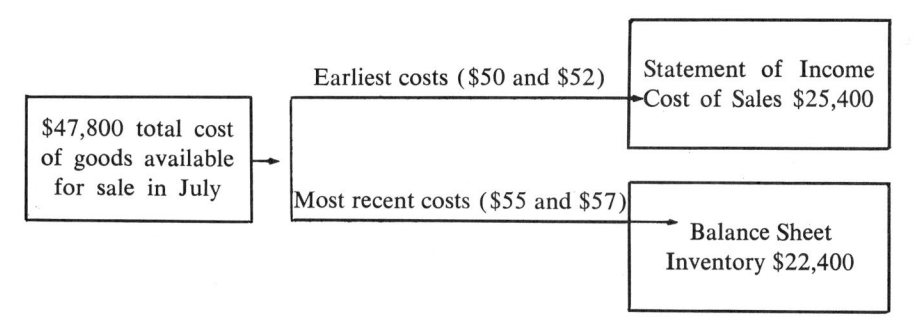

```
                                    ┌─────────────────────────┐
            Earliest costs ($50 and $52)  │ Statement of Income     │
         ┌──────────────────────────────┐ │ Cost of Sales $25,400   │
┌──────────────────┐                     │ └─────────────────────────┘
│ $47,800 total cost│                    │
│ of goods available│ ──►                │
│ for sale in July  │    Most recent costs ($55 and $57)
└──────────────────┘ └──────────────────────────────┘
                                              ┌─────────────────────────┐
                                              │ Balance Sheet           │
                                              │ Inventory $22,400       │
                                              └─────────────────────────┘
```

The analysis of the perpetual inventory record and the first statement of income on page 238 reveal the effect of FIFO on the financial statements.

The preceding discussion assumed that a perpetual inventory record of both quantity and dollars was maintained for inventory item #156. Now, consider the FIFO method under a non-perpetual or periodic inventory system. The company's records still indicate the following minimum information about the opening inventory and acquisitions during the period:

July	1	....	Inventory of 300 units @ $50	......	$15,000
	5	....	Purchase of 200 units @ 52	......	10,400
	20	....	Purchase of 200 units @ 55	......	11,000
	30	....	Purchase of 200 units @ 57	......	11,400
			900		$47,800

A physical inventory count at July 31 reveals that there are 400 units on hand. The FIFO method of inventory assumes that the ending inventory consists of the latest 400 units acquired. Thus, the ending inventory is costed at the latest unit costs incurred to acquire the number of units presently on hand, as follows:

$$\begin{array}{ll} 200 \text{ units} \times \$57 = \$11,400 & \text{(last acquisition)} \\ 200 \text{ units} \times \$55 = 11,000 & \text{(next to last acquisition)} \\ \hline 400 \phantom{\text{units} \times \$55 =} \$22,400 & \end{array}$$

When the ending inventory is stated at the latest incurred costs, the remaining (and earliest) portion of incurred costs is allocated to the units disposed of during the period, as follows:

July 1	Cost deferred in inventory of 300 units	....	$15,000
During July	Cost incurred for purchase of 600 units	....	32,800
	900 units	....	$47,800
July 31	Cost deferred in inventory of 400 units	....	22,400
For July	Cost charged against sales of 500 units	....	$25,400

It should be noted from this presentation and the second statement of income (FIFO-periodic) shown on page 238 that the FIFO method of cost determination gives identical results regardless of whether a perpetual or periodic inventory system is in use.

Last-In, First-Out (LIFO) Method

The LIFO method for the cost determination of inventory as of a specific date and for the cost of the goods sold or used during a specific period is somewhat the reverse of the FIFO method. The LIFO method is based upon a flow of costs whereby the last costs incurred are the first costed out of inventory as stock items are issued. The method assumes that the last items purchased (or received) are the first to be sold (or issued), regardless of the actual order in which the goods are physically issued from inventory. Reference to the perpetual inventory record below reveals that 100 units were issued on July 10 and 400 units were issued on July 25 from the latest priced units on hand at the time of each issuance. On a statement of income for July, current revenue would be matched with costs which are more current than those resulting from the FIFO method.

The LIFO method has been the subject of much discussion and wide adoption since World War II. It should be remembered that these years have been characterized by increasing costs and rising selling prices. From a theoretical point of view, LIFO is advocated for this type of situation, because it results in a more realistic net income by matching more current costs (usually higher) against revenue. For example, the below inventory record indicates a cost of goods sold of $26,400 for the 500 units issued during July. Except when the inventory level (on July 25) temporarily fell under the opening July 1 quantity on hand, the recent costs of $55 and $52 are matched against revenue of the period. The revenue from the first 200 units to be issued in August will be matched with the most recent acquisition cost of $57 per unit on July 30. It is contended that this is how management actually makes plans; i.e., by matching the current or most recent costs with current revenue.

Last-in, First-out Cost Determination Method — Item #156

DATE	RECEIVED (or purchased) Quantity	Unit Cost	Amount	ISSUED (or sold) Quantity	Unit Cost	Amount	BALANCE ON HAND Quantity	Unit Cost	Amount
July 1							300	$50	$15,000
5	200	$52	$10,400				{300 / 200}	{50 / 52}	25,400
10				100	$52	$5,200	{300 / 100}	{50 / 52}	20,200
20	200	55	11,000				{300 / 100 / 200}	{50 / 52 / 55}	31,200
25				{200 / 100 / 100}	{55 / 52 / 50}	21,200	200	50	10,000
30	200	57	11,400				{200 / 200}	{50 / 57}	21,400
Totals	600	—	$32,800	500	—	$26,400			

Past costs, while important as a guide in planning, are secondary to current costs in decision-making.[6]

The third statement of income (LIFO-perpetual) on page 239 shows a gross margin of $13,600. In a period of increasing costs, as in our illustration, the LIFO method will result in a smaller net income than will the FIFO

---

[6] A logical extension of this reasoning would lead to a NIFO (next-in, first-out) concept. A sale of a unit normally leads to the purchase of another unit for inventory. Thus, it is the cost of the next unit "in" which should be compared with the revenue from the present unit sold to more perfectly match costs with revenue.

method. This is because the higher, more recent costs are matched against current revenue of $80 per unit. By theory, the reduced margin of $1,000, which results from the use of LIFO, may be defended on the basis that the lower margin is more realistic: it matches more current costs with current revenue in income determination.

From a practical standpoint, tax considerations exert an even greater influence than the theoretical aspects mentioned so far. For example, when R. J. Reynolds Tobacco Company adopted LIFO in 1957, it reduced its earnings before taxes for that year by $26,897,049 and, accordingly, its income taxes by approximately $14,555,000. Because LIFO assumes that materials and other cost elements used in production or sold are the most recent acquisitions, LIFO boosts production costs and the subsequent cost of the goods sold in periods of rising costs. So long as costs continue to increase, the tax advantage continues. Presumably, R. J. Reynolds did not expect their cost prices to drop below their January 1, 1957, level.

While LIFO is logical from the standpoint of stating the results of current operations by charging against revenue the more recent and current costs, it may seriously distort the dollar inventory amount shown by the balance sheet. Because the last goods "in" are assumed to be the first goods "out," the old first goods "in" are presumed to be those on hand at the balance sheet date. Reference to the preceding inventory record discloses that, though 500 units are sold during July, 200 of the 300 old $50 units on hand at the start of the period are assumed to be still on hand. In fact, all 300 of the old units would be presumed to be still on hand if the inventory level had not dropped below 300 units on July 25 (a point which the LIFO-periodic system ignores, as will be shown). Thus, the inventory amount of $21,400 reflects the somewhat ancient cost of $50 for half of the units. That $50 cost will remain as long as at least 200 units are on hand, regardless of the time that may elapse or the amount of the increase in current replacement cost. This resulting understatement of the current asset is sometimes called the "LIFO cushion" or "LIFO reserve."

The preceding discussion assumed that a perpetual inventory record showing both quantity and dollars was maintained for inventory item #156. Now, consider the use of the LIFO method under a non-perpetual or periodic inventory system. The company's records would still indicate the following minimum information concerning the opening inventory and acquisitions during the period:

July	1	....	Inventory of 300 units @ $50	......	$15,000
	5	....	Purchase of 200 units @ 52	......	10,400
	20	....	Purchase of 200 units @ 55	......	11,000
	30	....	Purchase of 200 units @ 57	......	11,400
			900		$47,800

A physical inventory count at July 31 reveals that there are 400 units on hand. The LIFO method assumes that the ending inventory consists of the earliest 400 units acquired; the ending inventory is costed at the earliest unit costs incurred to acquire the number of units presently on hand, as follows:

    300 units × $50 = $15,000 (earliest acquisition)
    100 units × 52 =   5,200 (next to earliest acquisition)
    ——— $20,200
    400

When the ending inventory is stated at the earliest or oldest costs, it is the remaining and most recent portion of incurred costs ($27,600) which is allocated to the units disposed of during the period. It should be noted from this

July 1	Cost deferred in inventory of 300 units	$15,000
During July	Cost incurred for purchase of 600 units	32,800
	900 units	$47,800
July 31	Cost deferred in inventory of 400 units	20,200
For July	Cost charged against sales of 500 units	$27,600

presentation and the fourth statement of income (LIFO-periodic) shown on page 239 that the LIFO method of cost determination will not give identical results for the perpetual and the periodic system whenever the inventory quantity level decreases, *during* the period, so that some of the older cost layers are assumed to have been issued prior to the acquisition of additional goods. The application of LIFO by the periodic system more aptly parallels the underlying theory of LIFO, because it ignores fluctuating inventory levels *during* the period. Thus, the LIFO base of 300 units at $50 each will never be reduced until the inventory quantity drops below 300 units as of the close of the fiscal period.

As shown by the diagram below, the LIFO method of cost determination

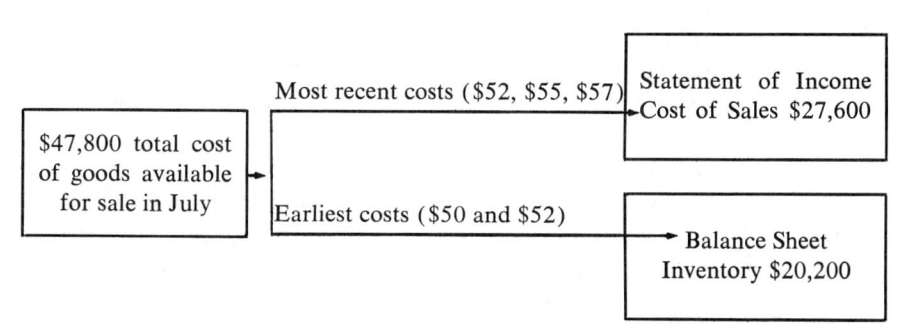

```
┌─────────────────┐     ┌──────────────────────────────┐   ┌──────────────────────┐
│ $47,800 total cost│   Most recent costs ($52, $55, $57)│   Statement of Income  │
│ of goods available│──→│                              │──→│ Cost of Sales $27,600│
│  for sale in July │   ├──────────────────────────────┤   └──────────────────────┘
│                   │   │Earliest costs ($50 and $52)  │   ┌──────────────────────┐
└─────────────────┘     └──────────────────────────────┘──→│ Balance Sheet        │
                                                           │ Inventory $20,200    │
                                                           └──────────────────────┘
```

allocates the total $47,800 cost of available goods (opening inventory of $15,000 plus purchases of $32,800) by charging the most recent costs against revenue of the period and deferring the earliest or oldest costs in inventory.[7]

---

[7] These comments regarding LIFO have been presented for an uncomplicated situation: no trouble is encountered in applying the theory and following the cost flow for one stock item. However, consider a company with many different items of inventory, or a diversified company that manufactures everything from light bulbs to appliances,

This analysis is based upon the periodic system of LIFO discussed immediately above and shown by the fourth statement of income (LIFO-periodic) on page 239.

Average Cost Methods

Though there are several variations in the method by which an average cost may be determined, the most common procedure determines the average unit cost by weighting the calculation in relation to the differing quantities of goods acquired at varying costs. The weighted average unit cost is determined by dividing the total dollar cost of units available for sale or issue by the total number of such units.

Moving Average Method

If a perpetual inventory record is maintained showing both quantity and cost price, a new weighted average unit cost must be determined at the time of each acquisition if the unit purchase price differs from the unit cost of those items already on hand. When the weighted average method is used in conjunction with such a perpetual inventory system, it is called the moving average method. Reference to the assumed facts on page 229 and to the perpetual inventory record and accompanying unit cost calculations on the next page reveals the determination of cost by the moving average method. On July 5, when the month's first purchase of stock item #156 is made, the 200 units purchased increase the balance on hand to 500. Dividing the $25,400 total cost by the 500 available units results in a weighted average unit cost of $50.80. This unit cost is used for the cost determination of all units on hand *and* all units issued or sold until additional units are acquired at a cost other than the present $50.80; in this case, on July 20.

The moving average method is affected by both past costs and most recent costs in the determination of both the July 31 inventory amount and the cost of the goods sold during July. To a degree, the averaging procedure levels out a fluctuating unit cost; the amount of cost deferred in inventory as of a given date and the amount of cost allocated to the units sold during the period usually fall between the amounts as determined by FIFO and LIFO. Com-

---

motors, and generators. Similarly, think of the complications when a company changes models of an existing product or drops a product line but adds a new line in its place. And, in a manufacturing concern, the difficulty of tracing the various factors of cost through succeeding stages of production to finished goods inventory may be quite complex. An analysis of such complicating factors is beyond the scope of this book and is not necessary for an understanding of the LIFO concept. It is sufficient to say that such complicating factors have been overcome without an impossible amount of clerical work. Illustrations later in this chapter reveal actual companies with such complications which are on LIFO. Among the procedures in use to minimize LIFO difficulties is the grouping of many inventory items into a few "pools" and the use of the "dollar value" method by the application of index numbers to year-end inventories.

	Moving Average Cost Determination Method						Item #156		
	RECEIVED (or purchased)			ISSUED (or sold)			BALANCE ON HAND		
DATE	Quan-tity	Unit Cost	Amount	Quan-tity	Unit Cost	Amount	Quan-tity	Unit Cost	Amount
July 1							300	$50.00	$15,000
5	200	$52	$10,400				500	50.80	25,400
10				100	$50.80	$ 5,080	400	50.80	20,320
20	200	55	11,000				600	52.20	31,320
25				400	52.20	20,880	200	52.20	10,440
30	200	57	11,400				400	54.60	21,840
Totals	600	—	$32,800	500	—	$25,960			

Computation of weighted average unit cost:

$$\frac{\text{Total cost}}{\text{Total units}} = \underbrace{\frac{\$25,400}{500} = \$50.80}_{\text{July 5}} \qquad \underbrace{\frac{\$31,320}{600} = \$52.20}_{\text{July 20}} \qquad \underbrace{\frac{\$21,840}{400} = \$54.60}_{\text{July 30}}$$

parison of the fifth statement of income (moving average-perpetual) with the preceding four statements on page 239 illustrates this point. In a period of rising costs indicated by our assumed facts, the moving average unit cost will lag and be less than most recent costs. In a period of falling costs, this same lag will result in a moving average unit cost which exceeds most recent costs.

Weighted Average Method

The weighted average method involves the same basic concepts and results in the same general effects as the moving average method. The weighted average method is used when an averaging effect on costs is desired by the company which uses the periodic inventory system or employs the perpetual inventory system only for quantities. At certain intervals, as at the end of each month when financial statements are prepared, a weighted average unit cost is computed. This unit cost is then used to determine both the cost of all units on hand in inventory at that date and the cost of all units sold or issued during the period. Using the assumed data on page 229, the weighted average unit cost of $53.11 may be determined as follows:

July 1 ..... Opening inventory 300 units @ $50 = $15,000
     5 ..... Purchased 200 units @ 52 = 10,400
    20 ..... Purchased 200 units @ 55 = 11,000
    30 ..... Purchased 200 units @ 57 = 11,400
                                            900                    $47,800

$$\text{Weighted average unit cost} = \frac{\text{Cost of units available for sale}}{\text{Number of units available for sale}}$$

$$\text{Weighted average unit cost} = \frac{\$47,800}{900} = \$53.11$$

The 400 units on hand at July 31, as determined by a physical count or by a perpetual inventory record maintained for quantities only, multiplied by the weighted average unit cost of $53.11, defers $21,244 of cost in inventory as a current asset. The 500 units sold during July, multiplied by the same $53.11 unit cost, results in a cost of goods sold of $26,556 to be charged against the July revenue. A comparison of the diagram below with the two preceding diagrams for FIFO and LIFO shows the effects of the different methods upon the determination of costs deferred in inventory and costs charged against

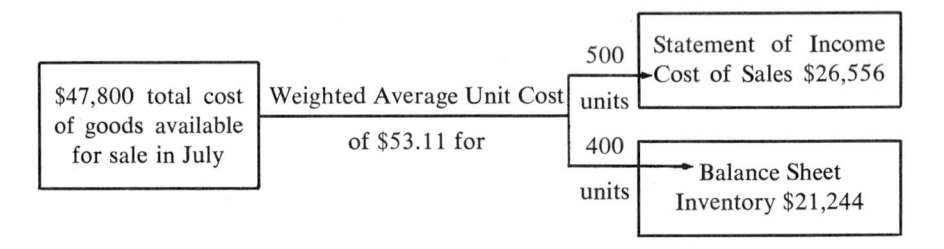

```
                                                500    Statement of Income
                                                units  Cost of Sales $26,556
$47,800 total cost   Weighted Average Unit Cost
of goods available        of $53.11 for
for sale in July                                400
                                                units  Balance Sheet
                                                       Inventory $21,244
```

revenue of the period. An analysis of the sixth statement of income (weighted average-periodic) below reveals the same general effect upon gross margin, when compared to FIFO and LIFO, as that caused by the moving average method.

Illustrative Comparison of Cost Methods

The six illustrative statements of income shown below have been referenced repeatedly regarding the comparative effects of the three principal methods of

Statement of Income (through Gross Margin)
Month of July

	Units	FIRST-IN, FIRST-OUT (Perpetual)	FIRST-IN, FIRST-OUT (Periodic)
Sales	500	$40,000	$40,000
Cost of Goods Sold:			
Inventory, July 1	300	$15,000	$15,000
Purchases	600	32,800	32,800
Available for Sale	900	$47,800	$47,800
Inventory, July 31	400	22,400	22,400
Cost of Goods Sold	500	25,400	25,400
Gross Margin on Sales		$14,600	$14,600

	Units	LAST-IN, FIRST-OUT (Perpetual)	LAST-IN, FIRST-OUT (Periodic)
Sales	500	$40,000	$40,000
Cost of Goods Sold:			
Inventory, July 1	300	$15,000	$15,000
Purchases	600	32,800	32,800
Available for Sale	900	$47,800	$47,800
Inventory, July 31	400	21,400	20,200
Cost of Goods Sold	500	26,400	27,600
Gross Margin on Sales		$13,600	$12,400

	Units	MOVING AVERAGE (Perpetual)	WEIGHTED AVERAGE (Periodic)
Sales	500	$40,000	$40,000
Cost of Goods Sold:			
Inventory, July 1	300	$15,000	$15,000
Purchases	600	32,800	32,800
Available for Sale	900	$47,800	$47,800
Inventory, July 31	400	21,840	21,244
Cost of Goods Sold	500	25,960	26,556
Gross Margin on Sales		$14,040	$13,444

cost determination. A study of these statements, the summary presented below, and a review of the underlying principles of each inventory method are suggested at this point.

COST DETERMINATION METHOD	INVENTORY SYSTEM	BALANCE SHEET JULY 31 Current Asset Inventory	STATEMENT OF INCOME FOR JULY		
			Sales	Cost of Goods Sold	Gross Margin on Sales
First-in, first-out	Perpetual	$22,400	$40,000	$25,400	$14,600
First-in, first-out	Periodic	22,400	40,000	25,400	14,600
Last-in, first-out	Perpetual	21,400	40,000	26,400	13,600
Last-in, first-out	Periodic	20,200	40,000	27,600	12,400
Moving average	Perpetual	21,840	40,000	25,960	14,040
Weighted average	Periodic	21,244	40,000	26,556	13,444

Before proceeding further, a few points basic to all of the preceding discussion should be reiterated to prevent possible misinterpretations. First, to clearly isolate the varying effects of the different cost determination methods, an opening inventory of $15,000 (300 units at $50 each) was assumed for each of the six illustrations. Normally, this would not occur unless this is the first month of business and the beginning inventory constitutes a portion of the initial capital investment or the business is a going concern now changing its inventory method from a plan whereby in the past each item of inventory always has been specifically identified with its own individual acquisition cost. In fact, if a zero opening inventory is assumed, the varying effects of the three principal cost determination methods would be as discussed. Whatever the inventory method selected, the July 31 current asset amount listed in the table immediately above will become the August 1 amount of opening inventory and thus continue the effect of the method used in July. Second, a period of rising costs was selected for the illustrative examples and the rate of the cost increase condensed into the one-month illustration might better be viewed as a panorama of a longer period of time. Even a one-year period can result in a significant change. It has already been mentioned that the use of LIFO reduced the net income of R. J. Reynolds Tobacco Company by $26,897,049 before tax and by $12,342,049 after tax. Similar results were experienced by Westinghouse Electric Corporation during 1956, its first year on LIFO; increasing costs were charged against revenue rather than deferred to year-end inventory, and net income was reduced $25,000,000 before tax and $12,000,000 after tax. Third, the effects of the various cost determination methods of inventory should be considered for increasing, decreasing, and stable cost levels. In general, an increasing cost level has been characteristic of the past twenty years. The long-run effect of LIFO upon income determination, in a period of increasing cost levels, is indicated by the excerpts taken from the annual reports of companies shown on pages 247–248. Decreasing cost levels would give opposite effects. Such an experience occurred in the late 1950's when copper prices decreased sharply. Companies with copper inventories on LIFO were forced to match lower, not higher, current costs against revenue. For an illustration of the effects of such a situation, see page 245. If cost levels were stable over a considerable period of time, any of the three inventory cost determination methods theoretically would produce identical results. Fourth, even if it were assumed that over a long period of time what goes up comes down, the aggregate income of the business entity for this lengthy period would not necessarily be identical regardless of its inventory method. Federal and state income tax rates change. And even if tax rates were stable over a long period of time, the company that pays a lower tax in year one which is offset by a higher tax in year ten has benefited by the "time-value" of the additional funds it has had for use in the business during the intervening years.

The Lower of Cost or Market

To this point, all of the discussion has centered on the principal methods employed to determine the *cost* of inventory for the balance sheet and the *cost* of goods sold for the period's operating statement. Market conditions may occur so that the *cost* of the items contained in an inventory exceeds that at which the goods currently can be replaced. Competitive conditions often force selling prices down when replacement costs decrease. Therefore, it may be unrealistic to defer in inventory a cost amount in excess of current replacement cost. Such a decline might logically be charged against revenue in the period when the decline occurred rather than in a succeeding period when the goods are sold. The use of cost or market, the lower, recognizes this concept in the valuation of inventories.

The recommendation of the AICPA concerning the application of the lower of cost or market with respect to inventory pricing is as follows:

> A departure from the cost basis of pricing the inventory is required when the utility of the goods is no longer as great as its cost. Where there is evidence that the utility of goods, in their disposal in the ordinary course of business, will be less than cost, whether due to physical deterioration, obsolescence, changes in price levels, or other causes, the difference should be recognized as a loss of the current period. This is generally accomplished by stating such goods at a lower level commonly designated as *market*.[8]

For the meaning of the term market, the AICPA states:

> As used in the phrase *lower of cost or market,* the term *market* means current replacement cost (by purchase or by reproduction, as the case may be) except that:
> (1) Market should not exceed the net realizable value (i.e., estimated selling price in the ordinary course of business less reasonably predictable costs of completion and disposal); and
> (2) Market should not be less than net realizable value reduced by an allowance for an approximately normal profit margin.[9]

Not all accountants completely agree with certain of the details stated immediately above by the AICPA with respect to the upper and lower limits used to determine market figures. Because these theoretical details are unnecessary for a basic understanding of the lower of cost or market, the issue will be avoided in the forthcoming example by assuming that market falls within these limits.

The concept of the lower of cost or market should not be viewed as another method of cost determination of inventory. First, cost must be determined by one of the three principal methods which have been discussed. Then, cost should be compared to market. For federal income tax purposes, a business may value its inventories either at cost or at the lower of cost or market. Once

---

[8] *Accounting Research Bulletin No. 43, Restatement and Revision of Accounting Research Bulletins,* p. 30. Copyright (1952) American Institute of Certified Public Accountants, Inc.

[9] *Ibid.,* p. 31.

the valuation method has been selected, it may not be changed without the permission of the Internal Revenue Service. However, a business may not value its inventory at the lower of cost or market for tax purposes if it determines the cost of the inventory by the use of the LIFO method.

When a company values its inventory by the lower of cost or market, its application may be on an item by item basis or on the inventory total as a whole or on a basis of separate groups of the inventory. The table below illustrates the determination of inventory at the lower of cost or market by the first procedure. If the company values its ending inventory at cost, on a FIFO basis, its valuation is $6,500. But, if the company has selected the lower of cost or market as its valuation basis, the inventory will be shown at

		Unit Price		Inventory at		C or M,
Item	Quantity	Cost (1)	Market (2)	Cost	Market	Lower
AB	100	$ 9.00	$8.50	$ 900	$ 850	$ 850
CD	400	10.00	9.40	4,000	3,760	3,760
EF	300	2.00	2.10	600	630	600
GH	200	5.00	5.30	1,000	1,060	1,000
				$6,500	$6,300	$6,210

INVENTORY AT DECEMBER 31, 1971

(1) As determined, for example, by FIFO.
(2) Meaning current replacement cost.

$6,300 if market is applied to the inventory as a whole, since that amount is $200 less than cost. And if the application of the lower of cost or market is made to the inventory on an item by item basis, the inventory will be shown at $6,210, because that amount is $290 less than cost. Again, the company must be consistent from year to year in the procedure by which the lower of cost or market is determined.

The use of the lower of cost or market, which allows inventory to be shown at an amount below cost, is consistent with the principle of conservatism. As noted in other chapters, many accounting procedures are based on this principle, which never anticipates profits but always anticipates and provides for losses. If the company with the assumed facts of the preceding paragraph values its December 31, 1971 inventory at the lower of cost or market amount of $6,210, the write-down of the inventory by $290 will constitute a charge against revenue for the year 1971. Thus the reduction of net income is made in the year of the decline, not in 1972 when the goods are sold. Regardless of the direction in which selling prices of the goods actually may move in 1972, the charge against the revenue realized from such sales will be the $6,210 of "cost" deferred in inventory, not the actual cost of $6,500.

As previously stated, an analysis of methods used by companies for determining cost of inventories showed that the great majority used FIFO, LIFO, or average cost. However, this same analysis reveals that, as a basis of pricing, the use of the lower of cost or market very greatly exceeds the use of cost as a basis.[10]

Examples of the use of the lower of cost or market illustrate the concepts just presented. The balance sheet of Fruehauf Corporation at December 31, 1970 showed:

Current Assets:
  Inventories (Note C) $89,756,334

The notes to the financial statements contained the following disclosure as to the determination of both "cost" and "market."

> Note C: Inventories—Inventory amounts are based upon physical determinations during the year and have been stated at the lower of cost or market prices. Cost prices are determined by the first-in, first-out method, and market prices represent the lower of replacement cost or estimated net realizable amount.
>
> A summary of inventories follows:
>
> | | |
> |---|---:|
> | New trailers | $17,907,062 |
> | Production parts, work in process, and raw materials | 44,305,029 |
> | Service parts and orders in process | 18,155,320 |
> | Used trailers | 9,388,923 |
> | Total | $89,756,334 |

The 1970 annual report of Ingersoll-Rand Company discloses the fact that cost has been reduced by an allowance for obsolete inventory. It is not un-

Current Assets:
  Inventories $308,362,000

> Note 3: Inventories are valued at the lower of cost less allowances for obsolescence, principally on the first-in, first-out basis, or market and include:
>
> | | |
> |---|---:|
> | Raw materials and supplies | $ 25,978,000 |
> | Work in process | 86,036,000 |
> | Finished goods | 196,348,000 |
> | | $308,362,000 |

usual to use different cost determination methods for different segments of inventory as shown by the Statement of Financial Position of American Metal Climax, Inc., at December 31, 1970.

---

[10] See latest edition of *Accounting Trends and Techniques*.

Current Assets:
   Inventories (Note 4) $141,600,000

Note 4:
   Metals refined and in-process at the lower of cost (primarily last-in, first-out) or market (at December 31 market quotations: 1970, $113,510,000) .... $ 57,570,000
   Metal fabricated products, etc., at the lower of cost (first-in, first-out) or market 52,950,000
   Ores, concentrates, and chemicals, at the lower of average cost (primarily) or market 13,710,000
   Operating supplies, at average cost, less reserves 17,370,000
                                                            $141,600,000

The valuation basis is somewhat different for each of the four classes of inventory, and three different cost determination methods are employed.

As shown by the Balance Sheet of Weyerhaeuser Company at December 28, 1969, both FIFO and LIFO are used as cost determination methods and both are valued at the lower of cost or market.

Current Assets:
   Inventories (Note 2) $153,696,000

Note 2: Inventories are stated at the lower of cost or market, with approximately 20 percent of the cost determined on a last-in, first-out method and the remainder on a first-in, first-out method. At December 28, 1969, inventories consisted of: logs and chips, $23,413,000; work in process and finished goods, $101,626,000; and materials and supplies, $28,657,000.

While the use of LIFO coupled with the lower of cost or market is mandatory for external reporting, federal income tax regulations specifically prohibit the use of the lower of cost or market when cost is determined by LIFO. The paramount reason for this restriction on the use of LIFO can be shown by a simplified illustration. Assume a time period of rising cost levels followed by a time period of falling cost levels. Ignoring factors such as a changed tax rate, the total profit earned over the sum of *all* time periods should be identical

      Time period one:
         First purchase .... 1 unit @ $4 cost price
         Second purchase ...... 1 unit @ $6 cost price
         Then, first sale .... 1 unit @ $10 selling price
      Time period two:
         On hand .... 1 unit @ $6 FIFO; $4 LIFO
         First purchase .... 1 unit @ $3 cost price
         Then, first sale .... 1 unit @ $10 selling price

whether FIFO or LIFO is used. As shown by the summary results for two time periods, LIFO has resulted in a higher total margin of $1. And the ending in-

Time period one:

Statement of Income	FIFO	LIFO	Balance Sheet	FIFO	LIFO
Sale of 1 unit	$10	$10	Ending Inventory of 1 unit at a cost of	$6	$4
Cost of 1 unit	4	6			
Margin	$ 6	$ 4			

Time period two:

Statement of Income	FIFO	LIFO	Balance Sheet	FIFO	LIFO
Sale of 1 unit	$10	$10	Ending Inventory of 1 unit at a cost of	$3	$4
Cost of 1 unit	6	3			
Margin	$ 4	$ 7			

Sum of periods one and two:

Statement of Income	FIFO	LIFO
Margin	$10	$11

ventory at LIFO is overstated because current replacement cost of $3 per unit is below the old LIFO base of $4 per unit. The regulations of the Treasury Department prohibit the write-down of the LIFO inventory from $4 to $3, with the resultant $1 market decline loss charged against income of the second period. The net effect of such a lower of cost or market concept coupled with LIFO would constitute a return to FIFO: the ending inventory would be reduced to $3 and the margin of the second time period would be reduced to $6. If it is assumed that over the life of the business entity, all other things remain

Time period three:
On hand .... 1 unit @ $ 3 FIFO; $4 LIFO
Final sale .... 1 unit @ $10 selling price
No ending inventory

Statement of Income	FIFO	LIFO
Sale of 1 unit	$10	$10
Cost of 1 unit	3	4
Margin	$ 7	$ 6

Sum of periods one, two, and three:

Statement of Income	FIFO	LIFO
Margin	$17	$17

equal (they never do), total margin will be identical. If the business entity is liquidated in an assumed third time period, the counteracting effects in the three periods will result in identical total margins, because total costs of $13 have been matched against the sale of three units for $30. While the long-run concept may be theoretically sound, it is no satisfaction to a company on LIFO which encounters the situation shown at the end of the second time period. The penalty for matching current costs against current revenue in the second time period is an overstated ending inventory—and an overstated profit for the period for income tax purposes according to those who have actually encountered such a periodic down-swing of cost levels.

Illustrative Results of FIFO vs. LIFO

Those who use financial information as a guide to planning and as a basis for certain business decisions must be alert to the varying effects of the different inventory methods and to consequent possible distortions in the financial information produced from these methods.

Partial non-comparability of financial data, even between companies in the same industry, is possible for many reasons already discussed in preceding chapters. In addition to the varying methods of accounting for items such as depreciation, intangible assets, and the carrying value of unconsolidated foreign subsidiaries, the user of financial information should be cognizant of the varying methods of cost determination of inventories. As an example, consider the following from the December 31, 1969, consolidated balance sheets of:

Ford Motor Company

Current Assets:
Inventories, at the lower of cost (substantially first-in, first-out) or market $2,285,900,000

Chrysler Corporation

Current Assets:
Inventories $1,225,193,676

Note to financial statements:
Inventories are stated at the lower of cost or market. The last-in, first-out (LIFO) method is used for determining costs for 58 percent of the total inventory. Cost of the remaining inventories is determined using the first-in, first-out or average cost methods.

Because of their different methods of cost determination of inventories, it is inaccurate to state that Ford's inventory exceeds Chrysler's by approximately $1,060,000,000. Chrysler's inventories, in part, have been on a LIFO basis for thirteen years. In the first year alone, 1957, LIFO resulted in their December 31, 1957 inventories being stated at $10,000,000 less than if they had remained on FIFO as in preceding years. Similarly, the companies' net incomes are not directly comparable in any one year. Again, in the first year of LIFO, 1957, Chrysler's net income was approximately $5,000,000 less than if they had remained on FIFO. And Chrysler's cash flow was improved by nearly $5,000,000 in 1957 by that amount of reduction in its income taxes for the year; only the future can decide whether this tax savings is temporary or permanent. At least the company will have had the interest-free use of these funds in the intervening years. It is interesting to note that in 1970, Chrysler, with permission of the Treasury Department, switched from LIFO to FIFO, resulting in a $20,000,000 increase in profits (actually, a smaller net loss for the year 1970).[11]

A person using financial information must have the ability to understand financial accounting data at least to the point where he can ask the proper question when he encounters a point as clearly presented as the following, which was shown by the balance sheet in the 1970 annual report of Caterpillar Tractor Co.:

> Current Assets:
> Stated on basis of cost using principally "last-in, first-out" method:
> Inventories $678,100,000
>
> Note: A major portion of the inventories is stated on the basis of the "last-in, first-out" method of inventory accounting adopted in 1950. This is a generally accepted accounting method designed to allocate incurred costs in such a manner as to relate them to revenues more nearly on the same cost-price level than would the "first-in, first-out" method used prior to 1950. The general effect is to determine reported profits without including therein a major portion of the increases in inventory costs which result from rising price levels.

His question should be, "After 21 years, by how much?" Should the trend of rising cost levels continue, it may well be that the materiality of the amount involved will necessitate a reference as to the amount by which LIFO inventories are below present cost levels. A few companies now present such information. Such a disclosure was given on the December 31, 1970 balance sheet of Crane Co., when that company presented its inventories as follows:

> Current Assets:
> Inventories, less LIFO reserve of $32,540,704, at lower of cost or market:
> Finished goods .... $ 68,239,222
> Work in process 51,063,708
> Raw materials and supplies 17,511,686
> $136,814,616

---

[11] The effect of such a material accounting change must be (and was by Chrysler) fully disclosed. See paragraph 9 of Opinions of the Accounting Principles Board, No. 20, *Accounting Changes.* Copyright (1971); American Institute of Certified Public Accountants, Inc.

Likewise, on the January 31, 1971 balance sheet of Federated Department Stores, Inc., when that company showed:

> Current Assets:
> Merchandise inventories (note 1) $235,746,092
>
> Note 1: Merchandise inventories are substantially all valued by the retail method and stated on the LIFO (last-in, first-out) basis which is lower than market. They are $43,839,000 lower than they would have been had the first-in, first-out basis been used.

Many companies which adopted LIFO many years ago, still have a considerable portion of their inventory stated at cost levels as of the date of their adoption of LIFO. Generally speaking, only quantity increases in year-end inventories since the adoption date of LIFO enter into inventory at a current cost level. One of the few times when the old LIFO base costs can be liquidated occurs when a company has a lower year-end inventory quantity this year than it had last year. Fluctuating inventory levels *during* a particular year may be ignored by using LIFO only at year-end to cost quantities.

The foregoing discussion definitely is not intended to belittle certain accounting methods. The past 30 years have produced a tremendous improvement in accounting methods and procedures. The tolerance range of variations in acceptable procedures has been greatly narrowed, and future years will see additional improvement. External forces such as inflation and high tax rates coupled with changing tax laws have also plagued accounting methodology. From an income determination point of view, LIFO does more accurately match current costs with current revenue for many companies. Constant revisions in the tax code since 1939, when LIFO was first introduced, today permit any taxpayer who has an inventory to use the LIFO method upon the approval of the Internal Revenue Service. Because of rising costs and high tax rates, LIFO has become increasingly advantageous to companies. Thus, the "cost" of the inventory shown by the balance sheet is often only an indication of outdated past costs deferred for a given quantity of goods. In the future, as accounting becomes less a tool of management and more a measurement of management's performance (as discussed in Chapter 5), it is believed that the balance sheet will reassert its importance on a level equal to that of the statement of income; that it will be less a *balance* sheet and more an indicator of financial position.

Effect of Differing Inventory Methods

The managerial significance and use of accounting data in the area of inventories is of prime importance with respect to many decisions which must be made in the management of any business. No repetition of the differing effects of the inventory cost determination methods, under alternative conditions, will be restated at this point. It is sufficient to say that the selection of a particular method has ramifications far beyond the determination of what portion of the total cost of goods is to be deferred in inventory as an asset and what portion is to be allocated as a charge against revenue of the period.

While an understanding of the differing cost flows possible under the various cost determination methods is important, those in management should be fully cognizant of all the resultant effects produced by the method selected. If a company uses LIFO, total assets may need restating prior to their use as an amount of capital employed for the determination of profit earned on capital employed as a measure of performance. Working capital amounts and ratios may be distorted; comparisons in the same company from period to period or between like companies in the same industry at a given moment may be misleading. Inventory turnover ratios are affected by the choice of the cost determination method. The impact of income taxes on the net income for the year will affect the flow of funds of the company. The cost of an item of inventory, per the records of the company, may be completely useless as a possible aid in management's deliberations concerning the establishment of an equitable selling price. To the extent that such ramifications mentioned are not understood, they may lead to improper decisions by those in management who use financial data for planning.

One partially redeeming factor to these comments is that, whatever the method of inventory costing and inventory valuation selected, it must be used consistently from year to year. Otherwise, any set of comparative financial data would be practically worthless. Consistency in method is required for both income tax purposes and for external reporting. In this respect, it should be remembered that the certificate of the independent public accountant concludes with an opinion on the company's published statements that they "were prepared in conformity with generally accepted accounting principles applied on a basis *consistent* with that of the preceding year." While this does not preclude a change in a company's inventory method, as from FIFO to LIFO, the effect of such change must be disclosed for that year. When Westinghouse Electric Corporation changed its inventory method in 1956, the accountants' report or "certificate" by the independent certified public accountants concluded with:

> . . . in conformity with generally accepted accounting principles applied on a basis consistent with that of the preceding year, apart from the change to the LIFO (last-in, first-out) method of inventory valuation, which we approve. As a result, approximately $25,000,000, representing rising inventory cost levels during 1956, was excluded from valuation of year-end inventories, which had the effect of reducing net income after taxes by about $12,000,000.

In addition to the factors which have been discussed, the selection of an inventory cost determination method should be partially influenced by the company's type of business. For example, LIFO is more advantageous to a company in an industry characterized by the large inventories in relation to total assets. Companies in certain of the metal industries fall into this category and thus find LIFO advantageous, during rising cost levels, because of their relatively slow inventory turnover. On the other hand, many retail stores, drug companies, and beverage companies are on FIFO or average cost methods because of a relatively low quantity of inventory in relation to total assets or because of a high turnover rate.

INVENTORY MANAGEMENT

Management of inventory encompasses a wide range of varying activities within a business. In scope, these activities range from the actual planning for purchases of materials and goods, through scheduling and control in all stages of production for a manufacturing business, to the ultimate delivery of the product to the customer. Excess inventory results in idle capital and often increased expenses. Lack of sufficient inventory results in lost sales and often increased expenses. Increasingly today, more scientific approaches are being employed in the management of inventory as businesses strive toward the utopian goal of having just the right amount of goods on hand in exactly the right places at precisely the time they are needed.

Carrying Costs of Inventory

Reference to the table on page 225 indicates the considerable capital investment which most companies must tie up in inventories. The cost which must be incurred to carry such inventories is not so obvious. Without attempting to make an all inclusive list, carrying costs include expenses such as:

> Handling costs—upon receipt and issuance of goods plus any intervening handling due to sorting, inventory counting, and relocation.
> Storing costs—for depreciation, maintenance, property taxes, utilities (or lease or rent expense) and other operating expenses of storage areas and warehouses.
> Financial costs—for paper work relating to all phases of inventory maintenance from purchase orders for raw materials to accounting costs for perpetual record of finished goods; local taxes on inventory balances; and insurance covering inventory.
> Risk costs—as obsolescence on certain items, possible physical deterioration, breakage, theft, and price declines.
> Capital costs—for interest on loans needed to carry inventory; imputed cost of interest at prevailing rate of funds tied up in inventory.

While such carrying costs will vary from company to company, reliable estimates indicate that these costs usually range from 15 percent to 25 percent annually on the original inventory cost. One manufacturing company with a fairly short production cycle has stated that its carrying costs amount to 20 percent. Another company involved in domestic production for foreign shipment and sale estimates its carrying costs at 34 percent. Regardless of the percentage, the multiplication of even a minimum percentage by the inventory amounts shown for selected companies earlier in this chapter results in a staggering total dollar cost for maintenance of inventories. Instances are encountered in which such costs approach the annual net income after taxes for a company. Thus, the concern of companies with respect to the maintenance of proper inventory levels is understandable.

Basic Objectives of Inventory Management

Present business practices validate the premise that some irreducible minimum amount of inventory is mandatory. Theoretically that amount would be predicated, in a manufacturing company, upon a perfect blend of timing in the receipt of previously ordered raw materials based on the length of the production cycle so that the finished goods are completed on exactly the date necessary to ship them to the customer for arrival of his required delivery date—all at the most efficient level of activity in order to minimize costs. As long as people are involved, such perfection will not be possible. Yet, the theoretical concept contains the basic objectives of inventory management: it emphasizes the attempt to maintain an inventory amount where its carrying cost is properly equated with the gain to be derived from having the inventory available.

One of the basic objectives, then, is customer satisfaction. Availability of finished goods for proper delivery date must not be forfeited by maintaining too small a finished goods inventory. Profits result only from the *sale* of goods at an amount in excess of cost. Yet, to maximize this profit, additional costs to carry an excessive quantity of inventory must not be incurred. In addition to matching customer requirements to inventory size, management must maintain proper product quality during the various stages of production. Consideration of customer satisfaction, then, results in at least a four-way interaction affecting inventory management: the sales group desires an overabundance of inventory to prevent the loss of a single sale due to stock-outs; the financial group wishes to minimize inventory levels; the production group is interested in an economical level of factory operations and cost reduction of the product; and the customers often want unrealistic delivery dates, product quality, and service.

Another basic objective of inventory management is reduction or control of costs of operations throughout the company. The ramifications of this objective are multitudinous; a few examples will illustrate the point. First, what is the most economical quantity of a specific raw material to order? Larger, but less frequent, purchase orders will decrease cost per unit for the paper work involved in ordering the materials, inspecting it upon arrival, and subsequent bookkeeping for recording the purchase and payment of the bill. In addition, larger purchase orders may reduce raw material costs due to decreased transportation costs resulting from carload lot rates and quantity discounts on larger orders from vendors. Against such decreased costs must be matched the increased carrying costs. Second, and more complicated, what is the most economical quantity of a product to process through the various stages of manufacturing in one run? In addition to the differing effects caused by those production costs which vary somewhat directly with the volume of production (e.g., power and direct labor) and those production costs which are relatively fixed in total amount (e.g., depreciation and property taxes on the plant building), many additional factors must be considered. Production planning must evaluate the availability of the facilities at the given time for the given volume of this product against other demands for the use of the same facilities. A steady, prolonged, production period—as opposed to seasonal demands—for products must be evaluated; temporary excess inventory may increase carrying costs. Similarly, indirect personnel costs, as unemployment compensation resulting from a fluctuating size of work force, hiring and training expenses, severance pay, overtime premium pay, and the image of the company as seen by its employees and community, must not be overlooked. These and other tangible and intangible factors must be weighed in the determination of the most economical lot-size of a product to manufacture. Third, and likewise complicated for a large organization, is the determination in which warehouses, in what quantities, and for how many products shall inventories of finished goods be maintained. Factors like location and size of customers, differentials in warehousing costs, and differing transportation costs must be considered. These examples illustrate the scope of inventory management in the area of effective cost control.

In summary, effective inventory management requires that the functions of purchasing, production (for a manufacturing business), and marketing be executed as efficiently as possible in relation to the costs of carrying the inventories of raw materials, work in process, and finished goods.

Inventory Management—How?

Effective inventory management has been studied by almost all medium- to large-sized businesses, and the object of many books and articles. Only a few of the considerations involved and the approaches taken will be mentioned here; detailed studies are available for the person desiring information in depth.

One of the primary factors in effective management is a proper evaluation of the composition of the inventory. Different portions of the total inventory may require different control procedures; for example, one study of inventories maintained by manufacturing companies revealed:

An analysis of an inventory generally will show:

    A. 70% of the dollar inventory value in 10% of the quantity of items
    B. 25% of the dollar inventory value in 25% of the quantity of items
    C. 5% of the dollar inventory value in 65% of the quantity of items[12]

---

[12] John E. Martin, "Production Control," *The Arthur Andersen Chronicle,* Vol. 13 (July, 1953), 149.

Other studies based on this "ABC" plan show very close correlation to the above relationships. Class "A" items should be scheduled for very frequent receipt—daily, if feasible—to minimize investment in inventory. At the other extreme, Class "C" items should be scheduled for receipt perhaps only a few times a year to minimize all of the paper work costs which any acquisition entails. Similar principles are, of course, applicable to a retail business. The "how" for effective inventory management and control must be different for $500 diamond rings and $2 charm bracelets.

The business trend to cut inventories will continue; care must be taken regarding how and where to cut. Recently, top management of a medium-sized steel company ordered a total inventory cut of 10 percent during the year. After the anguished screams had subsided, a thorough analysis of the inventory composition was made; it was found that 30 percent of the total inventory had not moved in four years. A planned inventory control program caused a reduction of total inventory considerably in excess of 10 percent when the "how" factor of inventory management was applied to specific items or groups rather than to total inventory.

In recent years, the "how" of effective inventory management has become increasingly scientific in approach. Practical applications of statistical techniques and advanced mathematical formulae by operations-research procedures, coupled with the use of electronic data processing equipment, have contributed greatly to inventory management.

Analytical methods using mathematical formulae are employed increasingly to aid the solution of the three problems mentioned in the section on "Basic Objectives of Inventory Management." To balance the carrying cost of inventory against cost savings resulting from less frequent but larger purchases of goods, the most economical order quantity (called the E. O. Q.) may be determined by a formula, as discussed and illustrated in Chapter 19. As a management aid in production planning, the most economical lot-size or quantity to manufacture (called the E. M. Q.) may be computed by mathematical techniques. And, by linear programming, the warehousing question of what quantities of which goods to store for minimum transportation costs (called the transportation-line theory) may be tackled.

A terse summary of one large company's present management of finished goods inventory is indicative of the trend. This particular well-diversified manufacturing company has plants and warehouses at many locations throughout the United States as well as some foreign operations. All domestic operations are linked by a private leased electronic communication system to the company's computer center, located near corporate headquarters. All sales orders, regardless of their point of origin, are transmitted to the computer center. Within thirty minutes, it is possible to determine which warehouses have the particular inventory item and from which warehouse it will be shipped to the customer, notify the salesman's office of the origin point of shipment, get the shipment started, adjust the perpetual inventory records, and process the paper to bill the customer.

Inventory Management—By Whom?

Historically, management of inventory appears to have been the responsibility of the purchasing function of a company; this is probably its focal point yet today. One large manufacturing company presently has its inventory management distributed by delegating responsibility for control of raw material inventories to a central purchasing office, work in process inventories to each plant manager, and finished goods inventories to the marketing manager of each product line. For all companies except the smallest, such management methods appear doomed.

The need for more science in business management will require a new approach to management control systems, and inventory management is a portion of any management control system. The use and application of financial, accounting, and economic data by analytical methods employing statistical techniques and mathematical formulae and models, aided by high-speed computers, will require a new approach to inventory control and management. It appears that the purchasing department approach to inventory management will soon be replaced by a new concept that will require a control group which is versed in financial-accounting-behavioral-economic concepts, which possesses a thorough knowledge of mathematics, and which is able to speak the language of the computer.

Inventory Management—By What?

Many companies have extensive inventory control systems, yet these systems do not always work. Why? Usually a deficiency in the system is blamed; the problem is often a misunderstanding of "what" controls inventories.

A company's inventory control system may contain all the paper work, formulae, and electronic data processing equipment necessary to its needs ranging from the perpetual inventory stock cards illustrated early in this chapter to the newest in computers. Yet, do these *control* inventory? Consider two illustrative cases which are quite typical.

The first case concerns a large oil company with extensive overseas operations. Commissary stocks for their Near East location usually required a lead time of six months from the date requisitioned to the date of delivery by refrigerated ship. Basic control was by the typical perpetual inventory cards, accompanied by minimum-maximum quantity points, for each food item. The cards were maintained by a bright young accounting graduate a few months out of school. When quantities reached the designated minimum level, he reordered. Orders were approved after review by his immediate supervisor; at first, the orders were carefully examined; later, in only a perfunctory manner, because the young man had "caught on." Unknown to the young man, during his third month on the job, his immediate supervisor and the mess chef embarked on a campaign to serve brussels sprouts twice a day before the excess inventory spoiled. The young man watching the perpetual inventory cards reordered brussels sprouts when they hit the minimum level. Then he remembered the six months lead time for refrigerated items and doubled the order. Suddenly he remembered a point he had learned in college—watch the monthly consumption pattern. "My gosh, how these fellows like brussels sprouts," he said as he again doubled the order! The company ended up with double the quantity that had been on hand prior to the commencement of the "eating campaign." Was the inventory control system inadequate?

The second case concerns a large manufacturing company which employed a computer to control inventories. One division had a large inventory of a certain type of small motor which it had manufactured that had become obsolete. In a desperate effort to unload the small motors, selling price was reduced to a point considerably below cost. The motors were sold, and this fact dutifully recorded by the computer. But, being a marvellous machine, the computer then proceeded to reorder more such motors. Someone had failed to push a button. At the originating division, the production line was set up for the manufacture of more obsolete small motors. Only very persistent questioning by one of the workmen on the production line halted the operation before it had gone very far. Was the inventory control system inadequate?

The obvious point of both cases is that paper and machines do not control; they only aid control. In the final analysis, real control must be by human beings. And, due to the increasing complexities in business, the humans must acquire much additional knowledge if inventory management, in the broadest sense, is to be effective. While giant mathematical computers cannot grind out orders to businessmen because human judgments are necessary for the consideration of many factors affecting our complex society, the expanding scientific method of inventory management should be used to aid, not to replace, human judgment.

QUESTIONS AND PROBLEMS

8-1. The Mason-Dixon Company purchases and sells a single commodity. Records of the company disclose the following activity with respect to this one item of inventory during January:

Inventory balance, January 1	1000 units at $15 unit cost ..	$15,000
Weekly purchases, in order of acquisition	500 units at $16 unit cost	$ 8,000
	500 units at $17 unit cost	$ 8,500
	500 units at $18 unit cost	$ 9,000
	1000 units at $21 unit cost ..	$21,000
Total January purchases	2500	$46,500
Daily January sales totaled	2000 units at $30 unit price .	$60,000
Inventory balance, January 31	1500 units	

Required

Complete the statement of income, as far as gross margin on sales, assuming that the company is on:
a. FIFO
b. LIFO
c. Weighted Average

	FIFO	LIFO	Weighted Average
Net Sales	$60,000	$60,000	$60,000
Cost of Goods Sold:			
Inventory, January 1	$15,000	$15,000	$15,000
Purchases			
Cost of Goods Available for Sale	$	$	$
Inventory, January 31			
Cost of Goods Sold	$	$	$
Gross Margin on Sales	$	$	$

8-2. For each of the following statements, choose the best answer to each and indicate your choice on an answer sheet with the number 1, 2, 3, or 4.

The Jeb Stuart Company purchases and sells a single commodity. Records of the company disclose the following activity with respect to this one item of inventory during January:

Inventory balance, January 1	1000 units at $25 unit cost	$25,000
Weekly purchases, in order of acquisition	500 units at $25 unit cost	$12,500
	500 units at $27 unit cost	$13,500
	500 units at $28 unit cost	$14,000
	500 units at $32 unit cost	$16,000
Total January purchases .	2000	$56,000
Total January sales	2000 units at $35 unit price ..	$70,000
Inventory balance, January 31	1000 units	

a. If inventory costs are accounted for on a FIFO basis, the cost of the January 31 inventory is:
 1. $27,500
 2. $30,000
 3. $26,000
 4. None of the above
b. If on FIFO, the January cost of goods sold is:
 1. $56,000
 2. $43,500
 3. $51,000
 4. None of the above

[CH. 8]   INVENTORIES AND INVENTORY MANAGEMENT   257

    c. If on FIFO, the gross margin on the statement of income would be:
       1. $19,000
       2. $14,000
       3. $16,500
       4. None of the above
    d. If inventory costs are accounted for on a LIFO basis (non-perpetual), the cost of the January 31 inventory is:
       1. $25,000
       2. $30,000
       3. $26,000
       4. None of the above
    e. If on LIFO, the January cost of goods sold is:
       1. $40,000
       2. $65,000
       3. $56,000
       4. None of the above
    f. If on LIFO, the gross margin on the statement of income would be:
       1. $ 5,000
       2. $14,000
       3. $20,000
       4. None of the above
    g. If inventory costs are accounted for on a weighted average basis, the cost of the January 31 inventory is:
       1. $25,000
       2. $29,000
       3. $27,000
       4. None of the above
    h. And, if on weighted average, the January cost of goods sold is:
       1. $58,000
       2. $54,000
       3. $50,000
       4. None of the above
    i. And, if on weighted average, the gross margin on the statement of income would be:
       1. $16,000
       2. $20,000
       3. $12,000
       4. None of the above

8-3. A few years ago, at one of a company's divisions, an EDP system was installed (by a management consulting firm). The system worked well, so the management consulting firm departed. Sometime thereafter it was discovered that the inventory on the company's records exceeded the actual physical inventory by $300,000. This was due to the failure to record some of the issuances of goods from inventory. Therefore, the shortage, item by item, was tabulated for the $300,000 of missing goods and fed into the computer to reduce the records for inventory by $300,000 and bring it into agreement with the actual physical inventory on hand. What do you think happened then? (Remember the case of the small motors mentioned near the end of this chapter.)

8-4. The same oil company that had the trouble with the brussels sprouts mentioned near the end of this chapter also had trouble with inaccurate typists at their Near East location. The order went out to write, not type, all future orders. An order was handwritten very distinctly for "8 tuns of cheese" and sent to headquarters in New York. Note: a *tun* of cheese is a round wheel of cheese. What do you think happened?

8-5. Select the one best answer to each of the following statements.
   a. If a company values its inventory at the lower of cost or market, and cost (determined by one of the acceptable cost determination methods) is $10, replacement cost $9, and selling price $23, the inventory will be shown on the published balance sheet at (assuming no other factors):
      1. $9.00
      2. $9.50
      3. $10.00
      4. $23.00
   b. The industry (according to Accounting Trends and Techniques) which shows most companies on LIFO is:
      1. bakery
      2. nonferrous metals (metals other than iron)
   c. For a heavy manufacturing company, annual carrying cost for inventory, as a percentage of the dollar amount of the inventory, approximates:
      1. 5 percent
      2. 20 percent
      3. 40 percent
   d. The "LIFO reserve" for Westinghouse Electric Corporation (principally on LIFO since January 1, 1956) and for Caterpillar Tractor Company (principally on LIFO since January 1, 1950) is probably:
      1. negligible in amount
      2. significant in amount
   e. From a theory point of view (and also practice by many companies), an inventory item purchased at $50 (invoice amount) plus $2 for shipping charges less $1 cash discount for paying the invoice promptly, should result in the inventory being shown at a cost of:
      1. $49
      2. $50
      3. $51
      4. $52
   f. The purchase price of a certain inventory item changes frequently. The cost of the inventory of this item at year end will be the same if perpetual records are kept as it would be under a periodic inventory method only if the cost is computed under the:
      1. weighted average method
      2. first-in, first-out method
      3. last-in, first-out method

   (Adapted from Uniform CPA Examination)

8-6. Manson Company sells over 100 different products; the facts presented pertain to only one of these products. The January 1, 1972, inventory contained

400 units, each of which had been purchased at a cost of $6. During 1972, cost prices rose steadily, but competitive conditions forced the company to keep its selling price at $15 per unit throughout the year. During 1972, Manson Company made the following purchases and sales of this product:

January 27	Purchased	300 units @ $ 7
April 15	Sold	400 units @ 15
August 13	Purchased	500 units @ 8
November 28	Sold	400 units @ 15

A physical inventory count on December 31, 1972, revealed 400 units on hand.

Required

a. Compute the cost of the December 31, 1972, inventory balance.

b. Prepare a statement of income for the year 1972 through the point of gross margin on sales. Indicate clearly the determination of the cost of goods sold amount.

For comparison, requirements a and b are to be prepared under each of the following six assumptions:

Perpetual inventory system maintained for both quantities and amounts	Periodic inventory system
1. First-in, first-out basis	2. First-in, first-out basis
3. Last-in, first-out basis	4. Last-in, first-out basis
5. Moving average basis	6. Weighted average basis

Carry unit cost calculations to the nearest cent.

8-7. Manson Company, which had been subject to rising cost levels in 1972 (see problem 8-6), experienced stable costs for goods acquired in 1973. And, throughout 1973, the company maintained a selling price of $15 per unit. During 1973, Manson Company made the following purchases and sales:

February 16	Purchased	300 units @ $ 8
June 18	Sold	500 units @ 15
October 23	Purchased	500 units @ 8
December 11	Sold	200 units @ 15

A physical inventory count on December 31, 1973, revealed 500 units on hand.

Required

For 1973, solve requirements a and b as stated for problem 8-6, except, for comparison, assume only the periodic inventory system throughout. This will limit the comparison to assumptions 2, 4, and 6 as listed in the preceding problem. Remember that the ending inventory under each of the three assumptions in the preceding problem will be the opening inventory for this problem.

8-8. Manson Company, which had, at first, been subject to rising cost levels and then, to stable costs (see problems 8-6 and 8-7), experienced declining costs for goods acquired in 1974. Despite falling costs, the company was able to maintain a selling price of $15 per unit throughout the year. During 1974, Manson Company made the following purchases and sales:

March 18	Purchased	500 units @ $ 6
May 5	Sold	400 units @ 15
July 31	Purchased	300 units @ 5
November 16	Sold	500 units @ 15

A physical inventory count on December 31, 1974, revealed 400 units on hand.

Required

For 1974, solve requirements stated for 1973 in the preceding problem.

8-9. Manson Company, which had experienced rising, stable, and declining acquisition costs (see problems 8-6, 8-7, and 8-8) on the product in question, believed that this product would soon become obsolete because of a recent technological break-through which would revolutionize the product. Therefore, in January of 1975, they quickly sold the 400 units in their opening inventory for $10 each and discontinued the product.

Required

a. Compute the gross margin on the 1975 sale of the 400 units by matching the revenue received ($4,000) with the January 1 inventory carrying cost. (See the three December 31 inventory amounts arrived at in problem 8-8.)

b. Summarize the results of Manson Company's experience over the period 1972–1975 by preparing and completing the following table:

Year	First-in, First-out			Last-in, First-out			Weighted Average		
	Sales	Cost of Sales	Gross Margin	Sales	Cost of Sales	Gross Margin	Sales	Cost of Sales	Gross Margin
1972									
1973									
1974									
1975									
Totals									

c. The management of Manson Company is considering a change in its inventory pricing method for all of its products. For years, the weighted average method has been used, but the management believes that this method is a compromise between FIFO and LIFO, which makes both the balance sheet and the statement of income somewhat unrealistic. Furthermore, it believes that it is at a tax disadvantage, because it does not use LIFO. The short-lived experience and resultant profit pattern encountered with the product in question over the years 1972–1975 is true for about 50 percent of the company's volume. The other 50 percent of volume is characterized by rising costs and rising selling prices. On the whole, you believe management favors a 100 percent switch to LIFO. Prepare a statement giving your recommendations and the reasons behind your recommendations.

8-10. Henderson Company is wholly dependent upon ABC Company for its source of supply of a raw material which it uses in large quantities. Any interruption in the operations of ABC Company would force Henderson Company to suspend its own operations. The status of current union negotiations between ABC Company and its employees indicates that the company is faced with either a prolonged strike six weeks hence or a substantial wage increase. In the event of a prolonged strike, Henderson Company will lose its source of supply, as none other will be available domestically and transportation costs from foreign sources are prohibitive. In the event of a wage increase, cost prices to Henderson Company probably will be increased substantially for this raw material. As the person in the management of Henderson Company charged with the responsibility for inventory management of raw materials, what analyses would you prepare to aid the determination of what quantity, if any, of this raw material should be stockpiled within the next six weeks?

8-11. Big Steel Company, like many large steel companies, has carried its inventories on a LIFO basis for many years. As a result, the inventory dollar amount is considerably below current replacement cost. Also, like most steel companies, Big Steel Company has a fiscal year that coincides with the calendar year. In mid-July, after prolonged labor negotiations, an industry-wide strike closes Big Steel Company. In late October, not knowing when the strike will end (it actually ended in mid-November after 116 days), you, as a consultant to the company, are presented with the following problem:

> Our inventories are severely depleted below our January 1 level. Considerable inroads will be made into our LIFO basis, assuming that we cannot build inventory quantities back up to their past January 1 level by this December 31. Assuming no inventory build-up will be possible by December 31, we lose two ways. First, any build-up after December 31 must go into inventory at the then current prices. Second, the partial liquidation of our LIFO base this year will have an abnormal effect on income because of the sale of that equivalent quantity of goods at current selling prices contrasted with their exceedingly low cost basis. What can we do?

Assuming that no inventory build-up is possible by December 31, what possible courses of action would you present to Big Steel Company?

8-12. Select the one best answer to each of the following statements.
   a. When inventories are valued at the lower of cost or market, "market" refers to:
   1. the price that the market will bear
   2. present selling price
   3. current replacement cost
   b. Due to automation, high-speed computers, and electronic data processing, inventory quantities can now be controlled by:
   1. machines
   2. people pushing buttons on machines
   3. machines as an aid to intelligent people

c. The industry (according to *Accounting Trends and Techniques*) which shows most companies on LIFO is:
   1. bakery
   2. non-ferrous metal
   3. chemicals
d. LIFO, coupled with C or M, the lower, is:
   1. a reversion to FIFO, when costs decline, and therefore not legal for tax purposes
   2. never used for external reporting purposes
e. Utility companies are not greatly concerned with the problems of whether or not to shift to LIFO.
   1. True.
   2. False.
f. NIFO, rather than LIFO, could present a more realistic picture of economic income.
   1. True.
   2. False.
g. The LIFO "cushion" is:
   1. the amount inventories are below current replacement cost
   2. shown by most balance sheets, because of its materiality
   3. a provision for a possible decline in prices
h. A company can switch *to* LIFO any year it wishes (assuming Internal Revenue Service approval of the technical mechanics of the Company's LIFO system).
   1. True
   2. False

8-13. The timing of certain events over which management *does* have control can have an impact on certain short-run financial results. Consider the following case concerning the timing of the company's year-end purchase of 10,000 units of Product A.

BOULDER CORPORATION
Balance Sheet
December 31, 1971

ASSETS		LIABILITIES	
Current Assets:		Current Liabilities:	
Various	$200,000	Various	$150,000
Inventory of Merchandise	100,000		
Total Current Assets	$300,000		

The January 1, 1972, inventory of merchandise of $100,000 consisted of 20,000 units of Product A at $5 each. During 1972, Boulder Corporation sold 80,000 units at $12 each and purchased 70,000 units at $7 each. Because the year-end inventory quantity is only one-half its level of a year ago, the company plans to purchase 10,000 units in early January of 1973;

current replacement cost is still $7 per unit. Following are the resultant 1972 financial statements; they assume; first, that the company is on FIFO; second, that the company is on LIFO.

Statement of Income
For the Year Ended December 31, 1972

	FIFO Basis	LIFO Basis
Net Sales	$960,000	$960,000
Cost of Goods Sold	520,000	540,000
Gross Margin	$440,000	$420,000
Operating Expenses	220,000	220,000
Net Income before Income Tax	$220,000	$200,000
Federal and State Income Taxes @ 50%	110,000	100,000
Net Income for Year	$110,000	$100,000

Balance Sheet
December 31, 1972

	FIFO Basis	LIFO Basis
Current Assets:		
Various	$330,000	$330,000
Inventory of Merchandise	70,000	50,000
Total Current Assets	$400,000	$380,000
Current Liabilities:		
Various	160,000	150,000
Working Capital	$240,000	$230,000
Current Ratio	2.50 to 1	2.53 to 1

Required

Assume that, instead of replacing inventory in early January of 1973, Boulder Corporation replaces the liquidated inventory in late December of 1972 by purchasing (and paying for) 10,000 units at $7 each to restore the inventory quantity to its January 1, 1972, level. Assuming first FIFO, then LIFO, prepare:

a. Revised statements of income for 1972.

b. Revised partial balance sheets as of December 31, 1972.

c. Revised calculations of working capital and current ratio.

d. Short statement concerning the differing effect upon the flow of funds.

e. Short statement giving your recommendations to Boulder Corporation about the timing of year-end purchases of merchandise.

8-14. Montebello Company sells three products. Inventories at December 31 for two successive years are as follows:

	December 31, 1971			December 31, 1972		
Product	Cost (FIFO)	Market	C or M, the lower	Cost (FIFO)	Market	C or M, the lower
A	$10,000	$10,000	$?	$10,000	$12,000	$?
B	9,000	9,200	?	16,000	17,000	?
C	11,000	8,000	?	7,000	7,000	?
Total	$30,000	$27,200	$?	$33,000	$36,000	$?

Condensed statements of income for the two successive years are as follows:

	1971	1972
Net Sales	$220,000	$300,000
Cost of Goods Sold:		
Inventory, January 1	$ 25,000	$?
Purchases	122,000	$162,000
	$147,000	$?
Inventory, December 31	?	?
Cost of Goods Sold	?	?
Gross Margin on Sales	$?	$?
Selling & Administrative Expenses	50,000	60,000
Net Income before Income Taxes	$?	$?

Required

a. Complete the above comparative statements of income assuming that Montebello Company values inventories on the basis of cost (FIFO).

b. Complete the above comparative statements of income assuming that Montebello Company values inventories on the basis of the lower of cost (FIFO) or market, with the cost or market determination based on each individual product in inventory. Inventory is reflected in the cost of goods sold section at the lower of cost or market, not necessarily cost.

c. Prepare a report analyzing the effect of the two valuation bases upon reported profits. Include in the report your recommendations to Montebello Company concerning the choice of a valuation basis for inventories.

8-15. The statements of income for Stonewall Company for the past four years reveal the following facts:

	1968	1969	1970	1971
Net Sales	$100,000	$100,000	$100,000	$120,000
Cost of Goods Sold	70,000	72,000	68,000	84,000
Gross Margin	$ 30,000	$ 28,000	$ 32,000	$ 36,000
Operating Expenses	24,000	29,000	23,000	23,000
Net Income or (Loss)	$ 6,000	$ (1,000)	$ 9,000	$ 13,000

On September 6, 1972, a fire completely destroyed the store and merchandise. The inventory of merchandise on hand at the start of the year was $15,000; purchases to the date of the fire totaled $35,000; sales up to September 6, 1972, amounted to $60,000. What was the approximate cost of the inventory destroyed in the fire? No perpetual inventory records have been maintained by Stonewall Company. Thus, Stonewall Company is having difficulty with the fire insurance company concerning the amount of loss sustained. Support your answer with all necessary computations.

Note: The rate of gross margin (gross margin divided by net sales) has been fairly constant for the past several years.

8-16. Proprietor Kent purchased 5,000 units of Product X for $32,000. He expects to sell all of them this year while incurring operating expenses of $3,600. He desires a net profit for the year equal to 20 percent (before tax) of net sales. What unit selling price will be necessary to accomplish this objective?

8-17. Stonewall Jackson Company purchases and sells a single commodity, "Champ." Records of the company disclose the following activity for "Champ" during January of 1972:

	Units	Unit Cost
Inventory balance, January 1	500	$10
Purchases during month:		
January 10	1,000	$11
January 20	2,000	12
Total purchases	3,000	
Sales during month:		
January 5	200	
January 15	800	
January 25	2,100	
Total sales	3,100	
Inventory balance, January 31	400	

Indicate the inventory cost at January 31 and the cost of goods sold for the month of January under six different possible methods by choosing from among the following possible answers:

1.	$ 4,200	8.	4,400	15.	35,800
2.	4,000	9.	4,100	16.	4,701
3.	4,571	10.	35,200	17.	35,429
4.	4,800	11.	35,900	18.	36,167
5.	4,667	12.	34,100	19.	35,299
6.	35,600	13.	31,000		
7.	36,000	14.	37,200		

a. Method: FIFO. Perpetual inventory is maintained and units sold are costed out of inventory currently.
   Inventory, January 31: Answer .... ( )
   Cost of goods sold: Answer .... ( )

b. Method: FIFO. No perpetual inventory record is operated.
   Inventory, January 31: Answer .... ( )
   Cost of goods sold: Answer .... ( )

c. Method: LIFO. Perpetual inventory is maintained and units sold are costed out of inventory currently.
   Inventory, January 31: Answer .... ( )
   Cost of goods sold: Answer .... ( )

d. Method: LIFO. No perpetual inventory record is operated.
   Inventory, January 31: Answer .... ( )
   Cost of goods sold: Answer .... ( )

e. Method: Moving average. Perpetual inventory is maintained and units are costed out of inventory currently.
   Inventory, January 31: Answer .... ( )
   Cost of goods sold: Answer .... ( )

f. Method: Weighted average.
   Inventory, January 31: Answer .... ( )
   Cost of goods sold: Answer .... ( )

8-18. This problem contains several statements designed to test your knowledge of the effects upon financial statements caused by differing methods of pricing inventories and costing goods issued or sold. Indicate your answer to each statement by choosing from among the following three possibilities:
1. FIFO
2. LIFO
3. Moving average

a. During a period of constantly rising prices for goods purchased:
   Ending inventory will be highest using .... ( )
   Cost of goods sold will be lowest using .... ( )
   Net profit for the period will be lowest using .... ( )

b. During a period of constantly falling prices for goods purchased:
   Ending inventory will be lowest using .... ( )
   Cost of goods sold will be lowest using .... ( )
   Net profit for the period will be highest using .... ( )

c. The pricing method that most nearly matches current costs with current revenue is .... ( )

d. In a period of rising prices, the inventory on the balance sheet is valued nearest to current cost when the inventory method used is . ( )

e. An inventory method which may be used for federal income taxes only if it is used for general accounting is .... ( )

f. In situations where there is a rapid inventory turnover, an inventory method which produces almost the same results as FIFO is .. ( )

8-19. Assume the following facts for the first month of business of Elterich Company. (The March 1 inventory of 400 units constitutes a portion of the original investment in the business.)

[CH. 8] INVENTORIES AND INVENTORY MANAGEMENT 267

			Units	Unit Cost
March	1	Inventory of Merchandise balance	400	$6.00
	5	Units purchased	200	7.00
	12	Units sold	300	
	20	Units purchased	500	8.00
	31	Units sold	600	

There were 200 units in the inventory of merchandise at March 31. The company does not use a perpetual inventory method.

a. *Weighted Average Method of Cost Determination:*
   Cost is determined by multiplying the number of units on hand at the end of the period by the weighted average unit cost. The weighted average unit cost is determined by dividing the total cost of units available for sale by the total number of units available for sale during a particular period. Compute the cost of merchandise inventory as of March 31.

b. *First-in, First-out Method of Cost Determination:*
   1. Cost is determined by assuming for pricing purposes that the first units purchased will be the first units sold. Thus, the final inventory will be priced at the latest unit costs incurred to acquire the number of units on hand. Compute the cost of merchandise inventory as of March 31.
   2. If the final inventory of merchandise had consisted of 600 units instead of 200 units, what would have been the cost of the inventory?

c. *Last-in, First-out Method of Cost Determination:*
   1. Cost is determined by assuming for pricing purposes that the last units purchased will be the first units sold. Thus, the final inventory will be priced at the earliest unit costs incurred to acquire the number of units on hand. Compute the cost of merchandise inventory as of March 31.
   2. If the final inventory of merchandise had consisted of 600 units instead of 200 units, what would have been the cost of the inventory?

d. *Comparative Results of Various Methods of Inventory Pricing:*
   In addition to the facts assumed initially, use net sales of $9,000 (900 units @ $10 selling price) to complete the comparative table provided on page 268.
   The table shows that, due to price fluctuations, inventory values at the end of the accounting period—and reported profits for the period—will differ under various methods of inventory pricing. Observe that changes in the amount of the gross margin on sales during the first month of business correspond exactly with the increase or decrease in the ending inventory. This occurs because the cost of goods sold is affected inversely by variations in the cost of the ending inventory. It should be recognized that the inventory method used initially must be consistently followed in subsequent months.
   1. During a period of rising cost prices, what method of inventory pricing tends to reduce the amount of reported profit?
   2. During a period of falling cost prices, what method of inventory pricing tends to maximize the inventory shown on the balance sheet?

Comparative Table Showing Effect of Various Methods of Inventory Pricing

	Weighted Average	First-in, First-out	Last-in, First-out
Net Sales	$9,000	$9,000	$9,000
Cost of Goods Sold:			
Inventory of Merchandise, March 1	$2,400	$2,400	$2,400
Purchases			
Cost of Merchandise Available for Sale	$	$	$
Less: Inventory of Merchandise, March 31			
Cost of Goods Sold	$	$	$
Gross Margin on Sales	$	$	$

8-20.* Gay Manufacturing Company uses steel in the production of its finished product. At any given time, its three inventories (raw materials, work in process, finished goods) all contain steel: raw steel, steel in goods in process, steel in finished goods. While the levels of the inventories may fluctuate during the year, assume an overall total inventory of steel (in all categories) of 18,000 tons at the end of each year, 1956 through 1960, the same quantity as there was at the end of 1955. Steel wage increases per hour over the five years are: 1956—17¢; 1957—12¢; 1958—12¢; 1959—12¢ and 1960—12¢. Assume a price increase in steel (thus, an increase in cost of steel, a raw material, to Gay Manufacturing Company) of 60¢ per ton for each 1¢ per hour wage increase granted to steelworkers.

a. If Gay Manufacturing Company adopts LIFO for the steel portion of its inventory, what will be the estimated tax reductions for the years 1956 through 1960? Use a tax rate of 54% (federal plus state).

b. How could further tax reductions be attained by expanding the scope of the LIFO election in these years? Federal Income Tax Regulations of the Treasury Department state, "a manufacturer or processor who has adopted LIFO can elect to have such methods confined to raw materials only (including those included in goods in process and in finished goods)."

c. Do you believe that the LIFO method of costing inventories and goods sold is a sound accounting procedure or merely a tax savings device? Explain.

---

*This problem has been adapted from "Should LIFO Be Adopted in 1956?" by R. A. Hoffman, *The Price Waterhouse Review,* September, 1956; with permission of Price Waterhouse & Company.

9

Long-Term Debt, Stockholders' Equity

The typical business entity has two principal sources of capital: creditors' equity (debt) and owners' equity (investment). The illustrative summary balance sheet shown below indicates that the sources of the $50,000,000 capital (total assets) of ABC Company are $15,000,000 of debt equity and $35,000,000

ABC COMPANY
Balance Sheet
December 31, 1972

ASSETS		EQUITIES	
Current Assets	$12,000,000	Current Liabilities	$ 5,000,000
Property, Plant and		Long-term Debt	10,000,000
Equipment (net)	38,000,000	Total Liabilities	$15,000,000
		Owners' Equity	35,000,000
Total Assets	$50,000,000	Total Equities	$50,000,000

of ownership equity. The typical business will always have some amount of current liabilities representing debts like accounts payable, taxes payable, and accrued salaries and wages. In addition to exercising proper administration of current or short-term debt, the management of the company (particularly the treasurer and the finance committee) must be aware of the effects of decisions concerning ways of raising and managing the more permanent capital of the company; namely, the long-term debt and the investment of the owners. This chapter will be concerned with the salient factors of these long-term equities of a business entity.

LONG-TERM DEBT

Long-term debt refers to liabilities which will not become due within a short period of time, usually a year. Such debt may be evidenced by long-term promissory notes, bonds, mortgages, or some other form of instrument. The balance sheet usually indicates the maturity date of such long-term debts; any portion of the debt that will become due within the coming year should be shown as a current liability.

Forms of Long-term Debt

The three principal forms of long-term debt are promissory notes, bonds, and mortgages. Illustrations from the consolidated balance sheets of General Dynamics Corporation, Dresser Industries, Inc., Procter & Gamble Company, and Season-All Industries, Inc. are presented as examples of these forms of long-term debt.

The balance sheet of General Dynamics Corporation shows long-term indebtedness in the form of notes owed to an insurance company, banks, and others. Those amounts, totaling $7,498,000, which are due within the coming

**GENERAL DYNAMICS CORPORATION
AND SUBSIDIARIES
December 31, 1969**

Long-term debt at December 31, 1969, was as follows:	
Notes Payable to an insurance company, 5%-5.2%	$ 66,470,000
Notes Payable to banks under Credit Agreement, at prime rate until December 31, 1970, plus ¼% above prime thereafter	60,000,000
Other	8,408,000
	134,878,000
Less—Amounts due within one year (included in current liabilities on balance sheet)	7,498,000
	$127,380,000

year, 1970, are shown under current liabilities. Reference to Note B to the balance sheet of Dresser Industries discloses the installment payment dates of the debt, the covenant regarding the maintenance of a stipulated amount of working capital, and the restriction on dividends until the debt is liquidated.

DRESSER INDUSTRIES INC.
October 31, 1968

Long-term Debt—Note B
  Note payable $85,807,000
  Subordinated debentures 977,000

Note B: Long-term debt and dividend restrictions—Notes payable (4⅞%
  to 7½%), including $4,911,000 equipment trust notes, require
  annual or semi-annual prepayments, and mature from 1973 to
  1983. The subordinated debentures require annual prepayments
  and are due in 1977.
    Annual maturities and payments required on long-term debt
  amount to $6,304,000 during the 1969 fiscal year, and $9,784,000,
  $9,752,000, $9,720,000 and $29,688,000 during the succeeding
  four years.
    The loan agreements and the indenture contain requirements
  as to the maintenance of working capital and certain restrictions
  as to the payment of dividends. Under the most restrictive of these
  provisions, $59,600,000 of consolidated retained income was free
  of dividend restrictions as of October 31, 1968.

The balance sheet of Procter & Gamble Company discloses that a portion of its long-term debt is in the form of bonds. Debentures are a form of bonded indebtedness secured only by the general credit of the company.

THE PROCTER & GAMBLE COMPANY AND SUBSIDIARY COMPANIES
June 30, 1970

Long-term Debt
  Debentures, 3⅞% .... $ 36,613,000
  Other, principally debt of subsidiaries 95,389,000
                                                       $132,002,000

The majority of the long-term debt of Season-All Industries is in the form of a mortgage on real estate owned by the company.

SEASON-ALL INDUSTRIES, INC.
December 31, 1970

Long-term Debt—less portion due within one year
  Mortgages payable $619,233
  Equipment note 124,167
                                                        $743,400

In addition to the three principal forms of long-term debt illustrated above, there are other forms of such indebtedness like long-term loans payable, accounts payable, and contracts payable. Long-term leases, as discussed on page 208 in Chapter 7, also may give rise to a long-term debt for the property involved. As was explained in Chapter 7, leases are classified into two types, operating and financing. The operating lease gives rise to a commitment by the lessee to make a series of periodic payments during the term of the lease to the owner of the property in return for its use during the period of the lease. The obligation under such a lease is shown in the footnotes to the balance sheet. Typical of the form in which operating leases are disclosed is the following excerpt from the 1969 annual report of the F. W. Woolworth Co.:

Notes to Financial Statements

Note I: Long-Term Leases—Minimum annual rentals under more than 4,000 property leases in effect at December 31, 1969 amounted to $96,045,108 which summarized according to lease expiration periods: 1970–74, $17,222,987; 1975–79, $24,260,045; 1980–89, $45,404,080; 1990–99, $7,057,800; and subsequently $2,100,196.

The financing lease is essentially an installment purchase despite the leasing form in which the agreement is cast. A.P.B. No. 5 (see Chapter 7) requires that in the case of financing leases the substance of the transaction rather than the legal form be disclosed. Thus, in the case of a financing lease the payments required by the lease are discounted to the date the lease begins at the interest rate the Company pays on its long-term debt. This amount is shown as a non-current liability on the balance sheet. The Century Electric Company disclosed its obligation under various financing leases in its 1969 annual report in the following manner:

Long-Term Debt—Less portion classified as current liability:
    Capitalized Lease Obligations—Note B $4,334,833

Note B: *Capitalization of Leases*—The capitalized lease obligations relate to land, buildings, machinery and equipment leased from municipalities. Capitalized lease obligations on December 31, 1969 are as follows:

Leased from—	Lexington, Tenn.	Alcorn Co., Miss.	Total
Capitalized lease obligation	$1,479,333	$3,035,000	$4,514,333
Less portion classified as a current liability	59,500	120,000	179,500
	$1,419,833	$2,915,000	$4,334,833

The annual payments made under a financing lease are treated as if they were payments on a debt, e.g., a mortgage or installment purchase. One part is considered a payment of interest on the obligation disclosed on the balance sheet. The balance of the payment is applied to payment on the principal of the debt.

Types of Bonds

Bonds are usually classified by the type of lien, if any, which they have upon the assets of the issuing company and by any special privileges which the bonds confer upon their holder. An exhaustive treatment of the various types of bonds is beyond the scope of this book, yet an understanding of the more common types of bonds is necessary for a person involved with financial matters.

Debenture bonds are backed only by the general credit of the issuer. No specific assets are pledged as security for the debt represented by such borrowing. In the preceding section, it was shown that The Proctor and Gamble Company incurred long-term debt by issuing this type of bonds, which mature over 11 years.

Subordinated debentures represent long-term debt which ranks below debt owed to certain other creditors. For example, the October 31, 1969 balance sheet of International Harvester Company showed:

Long-Term Debt
3½% loan, repayable $5,000,000 annually to 1982	$ 60,000,000
Subordinated debentures—4⅝% due 1988	58,642,000
Subordinated debentures—4.80% due 1991	57,827,800
Sinking fund debentures—6¼% due 1998	50,000,000
Other (page 25)	86,213,252
Total long-term debt	$312,683,052

With respect to payment of principal and interest, the 4⅝ percent and 4.80 percent debentures, backed by the general credit of the company, are subordinated to certain other debts of International Harvester Company such as the 6¼ percent debentures and any current notes payable to banks.

Mortgage bonds are secured by a lien on property of the issuing corporation. For example, at December 31, 1970, Iowa-Illinois Gas and Electric Company had $119,805,000 of its debt in First Mortgage Bonds. Such bonds are a lien on substantially all of the properties of the company.

Sinking fund bonds require the issuer of the bonds periodically to set aside or remit a specific sum of money, usually to a trustee under the bond indenture, toward the retirement of the bonds. For example, as of January 3, 1971, approximately one-half of the long-term debt of Arvin Industries, Inc., consisted of:

5.1% Sinking Fund Debentures, due 1990 ($750,000 to be retired annually 1972 to 1989)—note B	18,000,000

Frequently, contributions to a sinking fund are used by the fund's trustee to purchase outstanding bonds in the open market or call the appropriate amount by lot, whichever course requires the least funds. In such a case, the sinking fund is in reality a "purchase fund."

Serial bonds are issued on a single date, but mature at different dates. The Schuylkill County (Pennsylvania) Municipal Authority, for example, had an issue of serial bonds dated July 1, 1962, to mature in installments on July 1 of the years indicated in the following schedule:

Par Amount	Coupon Interest Rate	Year of Maturity	Par Amount	Coupon Interest Rate	Year of Maturity
$100,000	2.75%	1965	$ 130,000	3.70%	1974
100,000	2.90%	1966	140,000	3.75%	1975
105,000	3.00%	1967	145,000	3.80%	1976
110,000	3.10%	1968	150,000	3.85%	1977
110,000	3.20%	1969	160,000	3.85%	1978
115,000	3.30%	1970	165,000	3.90%	1979
120,000	3.40%	1971	175,000	3.90%	1980
125,000	3.50%	1972	1,453,000	4.00%	1987
130,000	3.60%	1973	4,767,000	4.25%	2002

Convertible bonds may be exchanged at the option of the bondholder for a stipulated amount of stock of the same corporation. The exchange usually must be made within a certain time period and may require an additional cash payment by the bondholder. In effect, the bondholder—a creditor—becomes a stockholder—an "owner"—upon such a conversion. An example of convertible bonds is contained in the 1970 annual report of Virginia Electric and Power Company as follows:

> Convertible Debentures
> 20 Year 3⅝% due May 1, 1986
> Authorized and outstanding $50,000,000
> Convertible: Into Common Stock at $36.75 per share

Income bonds represent debt on which the interest is paid in a given year only if the net earnings of the issuing corporation are sufficient to cover the amount of the interest. Whether any unpaid interest accumulates depends upon the bond indenture. Often, these bonds arise from a reorganization of the company. For example, the October 31, 1970, balance sheet of the Pittsburgh Brewing Company showed:

> Long Term Debt—5% Sinking Fund Income Subordinated Debentures due October 31, 1992 (less reacquired debentures in treasury) (Note 1) $2,646,750

Note 1 to the balance sheet disclosed that the income bonds were issued pursuant to a plan of reorganization adopted by the board of directors on November 27, 1957. Frequently, the trust indenture of income bonds requires that the board of directors decide whether the periodic interest will be paid. Thus, these interest payments are formalized in a manner very similar to that of dividend

[CH. 9] LONG-TERM DEBT, STOCKHOLDERS' EQUITY 275

declarations on preferred stock. If interest is in arrears on income bonds, this does not mean that the bonds themselves are in default.

Refunding bonds are issued by a corporation in exchange for, or to raise funds to redeem, a currently outstanding bond issue.

Callable bonds are those which the issuing corporation may, if it wishes, redeem prior to the maturity date by giving proper notice to the bondholders. An example of a mortgage bond issue that is both refunding and callable is shown in the 1969 annual report of Virginia Electric and Power Company, as follows:

First and Refunding Mortgage Bonds

		Outstanding
Series E	2¾%, due March 1, 1975	$ 61,200,000*
Series F	3%, due March 1, 1978	10,000,000
Series G	2⅞%, due June 1, 1979	20,000,000
Series H	2¾%, due Sept. 1, 1980	20,000,000
Series I	3⅜%, due Dec. 1, 1981	20,000,000
Series J	3¼%, due Oct. 1, 1982	20,000,000
Series K	3⅛%, due May 1, 1984	25,000,000
Series L	3¼%, due June 1, 1985	25,000,000
Series M	4⅛%, due Oct. 1, 1986	20,000,000
Series N	4½%, due Dec. 1, 1987	20,000,000
Series O	3⅞%, due June 1, 1988	25,000,000
Series P	4⅝%, due Sept. 1, 1990	25,000,000
Series Q	4⅞%, due June 1, 1991	30,000,000
Series R	4⅜%, due May 1, 1993	30,000,000
Series S	4½%, due Dec. 1, 1993	30,000,000
Series T	4½%, due May 1, 1995	60,000,000
Series U	5⅛%, due Feb. 1, 1997	50,000,000
Series V	6⅞%, due Dec. 1, 1997	50,000,000
Series W	7⅛%, due Jan. 1, 1999	85,000,000
Series X	7¾%, due June 1, 1999	75,000,000
	Total Outstanding	$701,200,000

*Excludes $2,800,000 in treasury.
Interest: Semiannually.
Callable: As a whole or in part on at least 30 days' notice, at specified percentages of principal amount, plus accrued interest.

Often callable bonds, if called before maturity, require the issuing corporation to pay the bondholder a specific premium above the par of the bond.

Although additional types of bonds could be enumerated and described, these types and combinations of these provide an adequate insight into the bonds which are commonly encountered.

Interest Cost of a Bond Issue

The usual bond issue requires the issuing corporation to make periodic interest payments at a fixed rate on the face (or par) amount of the bonds. Typically, such interest payments are made semi-annually; for example, a $10,000,000 face (par amount), ten-year bond issue, bearing an interest rate of 6 percent payable semi-annually on June 30 and December 31, would require interest payments of $300,000 on each of these two dates.

The individual bonds constituting a given issue bear a face (or par) value of a designated amount, such as $1,000, $500, or $100. Thus, if the $10,000,000 bond issue consisted of $1,000 par value bonds, 10,000 bonds would be issued; if the face of each bond was only $500, then 20,000 such bonds would be sold.[1]

If the $10,000,000 bond issue is sold at par (or face), the annual interest cost is 6 percent of that amount, or $600,000. However, it is rarely possible to predetermine the exact interest rate required to sell a bond issue at precisely the par amount. Typically, bonds are issued at a price above or below par. This premium or discount at issuance is a modification of the contractual interest rate of the bond issue to determine an adjusted interest rate based upon factors such as the current conditions of the money market, the credit rating of the company, and present interest rates.

Assume that the previously mentioned $10,000,000, ten-year, 6 percent bond issue is sold at a premium; namely, at 110, i.e., 110 percent of par. Basically, the bonds are sold at a premium because the contractual interest rate of 6 percent is greater than necessary under the circumstances prevailing at the time the bond issue is sold. The premium received of $1,000,000, 10 percent of the par of the issue, is not income to the corporation. In effect, it is an amount collected at the issuance of the bonds that will result in an adjustment to the interest expense of the corporation as interest is paid during the ten-year life of the debt. Therefore, the adjusted interest rate to the corporation is not 6 percent, but only 5 percent, determined as follows:

Cash received by corporation:	
Face (par) plus premium upon issuance of bonds	$11,000,000
Cash to be disbursed by corporation:	
Annual interest payments of (6% of $10,000,000)	
$600,000 for 10 years	$ 6,000,000
Face (par) of bonds to be paid at maturity	10,000,000
	$16,000,000
Excess of total disbursements over receipts	$ 5,000,000
Average net cost per year for 10 years	$ 500,000
Adjusted annual interest rate $\left(\dfrac{\$500,000}{\$10,000,000}\right)$	5%

Though the contractual interest of 6 percent on $10,000,000 ($600,000) is paid to the bondholders each year, this amount represents a net interest cost

---

[1] Care should be exercised in reading stock and bond quotations. For example, a stock quoted at 105 on the New York Stock Exchange indicates a price of $105 per share. But a bond quoted at 105 on the same exchange indicates a price of 105 percent of the par or face value of the bond; the actual dollar price of a bond cannot be determined without a knowledge of its par value.

of only $500,000. The $1,000,000 premium received at issuance is amortized over the ten-year life of the bonds as a reduction of the interest expense actually paid. On a straight-line basis, this amortization is $100,000 per year. In effect, each year's interest payments totaling $600,000 represent $500,000 of expense and $100,000 of return to the bondholders of the premium received by the company at issuance of the bonds.

When bonds bear a contractual interest rate which is less than the rate required by prevailing market conditions for the risk involved, they are sold at a discount. Such discount is similar to interest paid in advance to the purchasers of bonds. Assume that a $10,000,000, ten-year, 6 percent bond issue is sold at a discount; namely, at 90, or 90 percent of par. In effect, the discount of $1,000,000 is interest paid in advance and will result in an adjustment to the interest expense of the corporation as interest is paid during the ten-year life of the debt. Therefore, the adjusted interest rate to the corporation is not 6 percent, but 7 percent, determined as follows:

Cash received by corporation:	
Face (par) less discount upon issuance of bonds	$ 9,000,000
Cash to be disbursed by corporation:	
Annual interest payments of (6% of $10,000,000)	
$600,000 for 10 years	$ 6,000,000
Face (par) of bonds to be paid at maturity	10,000,000
	$16,000,000
Excess of total disbursements over receipts	$ 7,000,000
Average net cost per year for 10 years	$ 700,000
Adjusted annual interest rate $\left(\dfrac{\$700,000}{\$10,000,000}\right)$	7%

The $1,000,000 discount incurred at issuance of the bonds is amortized over the ten-year life of the bonds as an addition to the interest actually paid. On a straight-line basis, this amortization of $100,000 per year increases the annual interest cost from the $600,000 of interest actually paid to an adjusted cost (disregarding the time differential) to the company of $700,000.

Statement Presentation of Bonded Indebtedness Factors

Bonds payable, at face or par, represent long-term debt. Any portion of this debt that will come due within the coming year should be shown as a current liability with a corresponding reduction in long-term indebtedness.

There are two possible presentations of the balance of the unamortized bond premium or discount as of a given date. One adds the amount of premium not yet written off to the face amount of the long-term debt or subtracts the unamortized discount from this face amount. As the premium or discount is amortized, the net balance of the debt will be decreased or increased so that it will equal the face amount at maturity. Illustrative of this presentation is the data, condensed from the 1970 annual report of Sacramento Municipal Utility District, shown below. Such a presentation of premium (or discount) shows the net liability as of a given date.

Description of various outstanding bonds at December 31, 1970, totaling	$210,847,000
Less—Amount due within one year (shown as current liability)	5,898,000
	$204,949,000
Plus—Premium on Power Bonds of 1938, on Series D ..	533,762
	$205,482,762
Purchase Agreement, 3¾%, 1971 to 2000	1,424,989
	$206,907,751

The second possibility shows any unamortized bond premium as a deferred credit or liability separate from all other liability classifications and any unamortized bond discount as a deferred charge or asset near the end of the asset classifications. For example, the December 31, 1970, Consolidated Balance Sheet of Gulf States Utilities Company lists the unamortized bond premium as a liability following the current and long-term liability classifications, as follows:

Unamortized premium on debt $1,290,985

Typical of the presentation of unamortized bond discount as an asset (deferred charge) is the following from the December 31, 1970, Balance Sheet of Gulf States Utilities Company:

Unamortized debt discount and expense $600,559

The words "and expense" in the caption refer to the costs involved in the issuance of the bonds for items such as printing, legal and accounting fees, and underwriting commissions. Typically these costs are added to the discount upon issuance or subtracted from the premium, and then amortized as a component of the discount or premium.

On the statement of income for the period, the item Interest Expense on Long-term Debt, shown as a non-operating expense, is usually an amount adjusted for the period's amortization of any applicable premium or discount. Occasionally, the details are separately stated, as in the 1970 Statement of Net Revenue of the Sacramento Municipal Utility District, which shows:

Interest on long-term debt	$7,985,181
Amortization of bond redemption premium, discount and expense	218,696
Less—	
Amortization of bond premium	115,554
Interest charged to construction	3,346,839
Total income deductions	$4,741,484

This presentation also indicates that portion of interest which has been capitalized as a part of the cost of property and plant whose construction is financed in part with the proceeds of certain bond issues.

Often, the terms of a bond issue, as contained in the bond indenture, require the issuing corporation to accumulate a sinking fund by installment contributions so that the assets necessary to retire the debt will definitely be available in liquid form at the maturity date. The segregated asset, Sinking Fund, should not be shown as a current asset, because the amount is not available as working capital for business operations; instead, this fund should be shown in a non-current classification of assets. Reference to the December 31, 1970 Balance Sheet of Sacramento Municipal Utility District discloses the following special asset section:

SEGREGATED FUNDS, consisting of cash and
    securities, at cost:
        For construction purposes $30,037,371
        In reserve funds for Revenue
          Bonds 5,804,519
                                                  $35,841,890

Often the annual sinking fund requirements for a bond issue may be fulfilled by purchasing or calling certain of the outstanding bonds and delivering them to the trustee of the fund in satisfaction of the current installment due to the fund.

A bond indenture may require a restriction on the retained earnings of a corporation until the bonds are retired. Any such restriction on retained earnings may be in conjunction with, or independent of, any sinking fund requirements. The usual purpose of such a restriction on retained earnings is to limit dividend declarations, thus keeping an equivalent amount of assets in the business until the debt is liquidated. Presented below are two illustrations of such restrictions.

SMITH-CORONA MARCHANT INC.
Consolidated Balance Sheet
June 30, 1961

Liabilities (partial only):

    Long-term debt (Note 4) $28,746,740

Stockholders' Equity (partial only):

    Retained earnings (Note 4) 15,321,397

Portion of Note 4:
    The indenture relating to the convertible subordinated debentures and the loan agreements relating to the various notes include certain restrictions on the payment of cash dividends. As a result of these restrictions, none of the retained earnings at June 30, 1961, were available for dividends.

LIGGETT & MYERS TOBACCO COMPANY
Consolidated Balance Sheet
December 31, 1963

Liabilities (partial only):

≈≈≈

Debentures .... $ 61,250,000

≈≈≈

Stockholders' Equity (partial only):

≈≈≈

Retained earnings (Note 3) 170,145,567

Note 3:
Under the terms of the indenture covering the 2⅝% sinking fund debentures, $65,746,318 of retained earnings is restricted as to payment of cash dividends on common stock. This limitation does not apply to stock dividends on common stock, nor does it restrict payment of dividends on preferred stock.

The first illustration shows a situation in which the restriction on retained earnings was so complete that no dividends could be declared by Smith-Corona Marchant Inc. (now the SCM Corporation) at June 30, 1961. The second illustration presents a situation where the restriction on the retained earnings of Liggett & Myers Tobacco Company (now Liggett & Myers Incorporated) was unimportant. Cash dividends of Liggett & Myers, each year for the preceding four years, had been $7 per share on the preferred stock (about $1,200,000 each year) and $5 per share on the common stock (about $19,750,000 each year). With net earnings exceeding $24,000,000 each year for the preceding nine years and unrestricted retained earnings of $104,399,249 ($170,145,567 minus $65,746,318) at December 31, 1963 (and a current ratio of almost 13 to 1), the restriction on retained earnings was of little consequence. It is interesting to note that as of June 30, 1969, with respect to SCM Corporation, $15,000,000 of its total retained earnings of $76,513,000 *were* available for dividends; and that as of December 31, 1969, with respect to Liggett & Myers Incorporated, $31,867,567 of its total retained earnings of $192,908,804, *were* available for dividends.

A corporation may purchase its own bonds on the market and hold them as treasury bonds. These treasury bonds may then be cancelled, resold, or used to meet a sinking fund requirement. Treasury bonds are not an asset but are shown as a reduction of the long-term indebtedness of the corporation, as shown in the following illustration taken from the December 31, 1970, Balance Sheet of General Motors Corporation.

3¼% Debentures Due 1979 (less reacquired debentures
in treasury of $122,528,000 .... $35,522,000

A discussion of the factors influencing decisions on whether to raise needed additional capital by the incurrence of long-term debt or by the issuance of capital stock will be presented after the basic factors constituting stockholders' equity have been discussed.

STOCKHOLDERS' EQUITY

Stockholders' equity, often referred to as shareholders' equity, capital, or net worth, represents the excess of the company's assets over its liabilities. Basically, stockholders' equity is derived from two sources—capital contributions by the stockholders (and possibly others) and net earnings reinvested in the business.

Capital Stock and Its Terminology

One of the two sources of stockholders' equity is capital contributions. On the typical balance sheet, the amount of capital contributions is subdivided into two categories. The first of these two categories is "capital contributed for, or assigned to, shares, to the extent of the par or stated value of each class of shares presently outstanding."[2] The second category is "capital in excess of par or stated value." The first category of contributed capital is discussed in this section, and the second, in the following section.

Various terms commonly encountered in relation to shares of capital stock will be discussed and illustrated prior to any detailed analysis of an entire stockholders' equity section.

One such category of terms concerns the present status of the total number of shares of capital stock authorized in the charter granted to the corporation by the state in which the company is incorporated. For example, Hershey Foods Corporation, as of December 31, 1970, had 20,000,000 shares of common stock authorized, 12,228,710 shares issued, and 430,805 shares of treasury stock. Using these amounts, it is possible to illustrate certain capital stock terminology as follows:

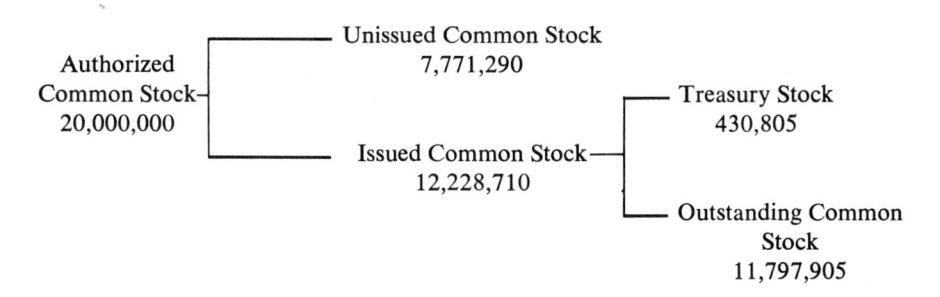

```
                         ┌── Unissued Common Stock
  Authorized             │      7,771,290
  Common Stock ──┤                              ┌── Treasury Stock
  20,000,000             │                      │      430,805
                         └── Issued Common Stock ┤
                              12,228,710        │
                                                └── Outstanding Common
                                                     Stock
                                                     11,797,905
```

---

[2] *Accounting Terminology Bulletin Number 1,* "Review and Résumé," p. 30. Copyright American Institute of Certified Public Accountants, Inc.

Of the 20,000,000 authorized shares, 7,771,290 shares are *unissued,* since they have never been sold, whereas 12,228,710 have been *issued.* But, of the 12,228,710 shares which have been issued and for which the corporation has received consideration, 430,805 have been reacquired by the company and not cancelled but held in *treasury;* the remaining 11,797,905 shares of the issued shares remain *outstanding* in the hands of the public.

A second category of terms relates to the predetermined dollar amount, if any, assigned to each share and printed on the face of the stock certificates. If a predetermined fixed dollar amount is assigned to each share of capital stock, the stock is known as *par value* stock. It is unfortunate that the word *value* is coupled with the word *par* because the dollar amount designated as par is an arbitrary amount and rarely reflects the value of the stock. For example, few would know offhand, or be interested in knowing, the present par value of the shares of common stock of the following corporations:

	Par
United States Steel Corporation	$30
Bethlehem Steel Corporation	8
General Motors Corporation	1⅔
Aluminum Company of America	1
Sterling Precision Corporation	.10
Carrier Corporation	2.50

Starting with New York in 1912, state corporation codes have been amended so that today all states permit the issuance of *no-par value* stock. No-par value stock has no specific or predetermined fixed dollar amount assigned to each share. However, some state corporation codes require the assignment of a *stated value* per share to no-par stock, and certain states permit the board of directors to assign a stated value. Any stated value assigned to no-par shares removes them from the category of "true" no-par stock and makes them very similar to par stock. Typical examples of no-par stock issues are the following:

>Caterpillar Tractor Co., common stock, no-par value
>Minnesota Mining and Manufacturing Company, common stock, without par value
>Beatrice Foods Co., common stock, without par value, stated value per share of $3.65
>Standard Brands Incorporated, common, without par value, stated value per share—$2

A third category of terms describing capital stock relates to the different classes of stock. If a corporation has only one class of stock, like Standard Oil Company of New Jersey and Gulf Oil Corporation, the stock may be referred to only as *capital* stock. But, if a corporation has more than one class of stock, one class may be called *preferred* stock, and the other, *common* stock.[3] Pre-

---

[3] It is not unusual to find a company with just one class of stock designating it as common, rather than capital, stock.

ferred stock has certain designated rights which supersede those belonging to common stock. The two preferences most frequently associated with preferred stock are the right to dividends before common stock and a prior claim on assets in event the company is liquidated. In exchange for such preferences, all other rights are usually reserved to the common stock, whose principal reserved right is often the right to vote for the directors of the corporation. To explain the different rights attached to different classes of stock, two illustrations are presented. First, Scott Paper Company has stock outstanding of the following classes:

> Cumulative preferred shares without par value:
> $3.40 series
> $4.00 series
> Common shares without par value

Both series of preferred stock have equal preference for assets and dividends and are entitled to $100 per share if the company is involuntarily liquidated. Since both series of preferred are *cumulative,* any dividends not declared when due accumulate and should any such dividend arrearages ever occur, they must be paid before any dividends can be declared on the common stock. Neither series of preferred stock has any voting rights except on default of dividends for one year. Other than this possible restriction, the common stock has the sole voting power. Second, United States Steel Corporation had, until 1966, the following two classes of outstanding stock:

> Preferred stock, 7% cumulative, par value $100
> Common stock, par value $16⅔ per share

In any liquidation, the preferred stock was entitled to preference over the common to the par amount of $100 per share. The preferred also had preference over the common to cumulative dividends of 7 percent per annum. During the depression of the 1930's, the dividends on the preferred fell in arrears. Since the stock was cumulative, such arrearages had to be paid (and were in 1936 and 1937) before any dividends could be paid on the common stock. Should preferred stock of a company be *non-cumulative* in nature, any dividends not declared will lapse. Note that when the preferred stock is par stock, as in the case of United States Steel Corporation, the annual dividend rate is expressed as a percent of par, in this instance 7 percent of $100 or $7 annually (actually $1.75 per quarter) per share. But, when the preferred stock is no-par stock, as in the case of Scott Paper Company, the annual dividend rate is expressed as so many dollars per share. Unlike the owners of preferred stock of Scott Paper Company, the preferred stockholders of United States Steel Corporation were entitled to vote; in fact, each share of preferred had six votes. (Note: On January 1, 1966, United States Steel Corporation exchanged its preferred stock for debentures.) Occasionally preferred stock is *participating* preferred stock. Then, the preferred stock is entitled to participate with the common stock and receive additional dividends over and above the stipulated preferred dividend rate once the common stockholders have received a certain dividend. However, most preferred stock is *non-participating;* preferred stockholders normally are entitled to only the fixed dividend rate regardless of the amount of dividends declared to the common stockholders.

Capital in Excess of Par or Stated Value

The term Capital in Excess of Par or Stated Value refers to the second category of the contributed capital portion of the stockholders' equity.

There are several terms widely used as alternates for Capital in Excess of Par or Stated Value. Capital Surplus, which has been objected to by accounting authorities for many years because of possible misinterpretation, is still widely used to denote this portion of the stockholders' equity.[4] A survey of 600 annual reports issued in 1968 discloses the following frequencies of use for the various terms which describe this portion of contributed capital.[5]

Capital surplus	141	
Paid-in surplus	38	
Other terms containing term "surplus"	3	
Total retaining term "surplus"		182
Capital in excess of par or stated values	137	
Additional paid-in capital	112	
Paid-in capital, or other paid-in capital	15	
Additional capital, or other capital	38	
Other captions using the term "capital"	18	
Captions avoiding use of term "capital"	10	
Total replacing term "surplus"		330
		512
No such items presented on balance sheets		88
		600

Some of the usual sources of contributed capital in excess of the amount assigned to the par or stated value of outstanding shares are as follows:

1. Capital contributed for shares as a result of the original issuance of par-value shares at amounts exceeding their par value. Usually this excess is referred to as "premium on capital (or common or preferred) stock."
2. Capital contributed for shares as a result of the original issuance of no-par value shares at amounts exceeding their stated value.

---

[4] For a comprehensive analysis of the objections to the term "capital surplus," see *Accounting Terminology Bulletin Number 1,* "Review and Résumé," pp. 28–32. Copyright American Institute of Certified Public Accountants, Inc.

[5] Condensed from American Institute of Certified Public Accountants, *Accounting Trends and Techniques in Published Corporate Annual Reports,* 23rd. ed., p. 127. Copyright (1968) American Institute of Certified Public Accountants, Inc. This reference also clearly indicates the trend in past years away from either capital surplus or paid-in surplus and toward alternate titles.

3. From treasury stock transactions.
4. From the issuance of additional shares of the corporation's own stock as the result of a stock dividend.
5. Capital contributed other than for shares of stock. Occasionally such a source of contributed capital results from assets donated to a corporation.

Four illustrations are presented to clarify the first four sources of contributed capital. The December 31, 1969, Balance Sheet of Gulf States Utilities Company illustrates the first source; namely, premium on par value capital stock (on their preferred stock, $100 par value).

Capital Stock (details not reproduced) and Retained Earnings:	
Preferred stock, cumulative, $100 par value	$ 82,500,000
Common stock, without par value	119,082,725
Premium on preferred stocks	600,251
Retained earnings	103,366,168
Total capital stock and retained earnings	$305,549,144

The Balance Sheet amount of Capital Surplus at December 31, 1970, shown by The Goodyear Tire & Rubber Company is clarified by an attached Capital Surplus Statement indicating the sources of the increase in Capital

Capital Surplus at Beginning of Period	$233,551,000
Proceeds in excess of stated value, from issuance of common stock of the Company	6,383,000
Capital Surplus at End of Period, per balance sheet	$239,934,000

Surplus during the year. In this case, the increase comes from source two enumerated above; namely, the issuance of no-par value shares at an amount exceeding the stated value.

The notes to the financial statements contained in the annual report of the Coca-Cola Company include the following schedule to support the December 31, 1969 amount of $25,101,233 shown by the Balance Sheet as Capital Surplus:

	Capital Surplus
Balance December 31, 1968	$21,771,490
Previously unissued shares sold to employees exercising stock options	2,533,198
Proceeds in excess of cost of 14,084 shares of treasury stock sold to employees exercising stock options	43,858
Excess of market price over cost of 13,250 shares of treasury stock issued for capital stock of Belmont Springs Water Co., Inc.	752,687
Other	0
Balance December 31, 1969	$25,101,233

This contains two illustrations of the third source enumerated; namely, additional capital resulting from the disposal of treasury stock at an amount exceeding its acquisition cost.

The 1969 annual report of Litton Industries, Inc., discloses, on the Statement of Additional Paid-in Capital, the item of:

> Excess of market value over par value of
> common stock issued for stock dividend $41,966,000

This is illustrative of the fourth source enumerated above; namely, a stock dividend when market value exceeds par or stated value. The theory underlying a stock dividend is discussed later in this chapter.

Summary—total contributed capital. Contributed capital represents the *total* amount contributed to the corporation by the stockholders (and possibly by others if there are donated assets) in the form of assets and services. This total amount typically is subdivided into two categories: *capital stock*—that portion of the contributed capital assigned to shares in the amount of the par or stated value of the various classes of shares of outstanding stock, and *capital in excess of par or stated value*—that portion of the contributed capital in excess of the amount assigned to the par or stated value of the various classes of stock.[6]

Retained Earnings

The second principal source of stockholders' equity is retained earnings. Retained earnings, often still called "earned surplus," represents that portion of the company's total net earnings over the years of its existence which has *not* been distributed to the stockholders as dividends, but reinvested in the business. The term "undivided profits" could be used to explain the meaning of retained earnings if there were no possibility that the word "undivided" might imply that such an amount was actually to be divided among the stockholders at some stated time in the future. Of course, the amount of retained earnings or undivided profits, though legally available for dividend declaration, normally could not be paid out as dividends, because it merely represents the amount already plowed back into the business in various forms as additional working capital, plant and equipment, investments in subsidiaries; i.e., an overall increase in the net assets of the company.

Despite the previously mentioned opposition to the term *surplus,* its usage, though declining, is still encountered. The survey of 600 annual reports discloses the following:[7]

---

[6] Rarely is stock issued at a discount (i.e., for less than par value) because of the possible individual stockholder liability to creditors of the corporation to the extent of the discount in the event of the corporation's failure. Basically, there is no reason to issue shares at a discount when the opportunity exists to authorize no-par shares or when par may be predetermined at almost any given amount at the time the application is filed for a corporate charter.

[7] Condensed from American Institute of Certified Public Accountants, *Accounting Trends and Techniques in Published Corporate Annual Reports,* 23rd ed., p. 131. Copyright (1968) American Institute of Certified Public Accountants, Inc.

Number of Companies
Replacing the term "earned surplus" 555
Retaining the term "earned surplus" 45

                                              600

The phrase most frequently used in lieu of *earned surplus* is *retained earnings.* Such usage follows the recommendation of the Committee on Terminology of the American Institute of Certified Public Accountants, that:[8]

> The term earned surplus be replaced by terms which will indicate source, such as retained income, retained earnings, accumulated earnings, or earnings retained for use in the business. In the case of a deficit, the amount should be shown as a deduction from contributed capital with appropriate description.

The term *deficit* should be used as the opposite to *retained earnings,* as illustrated by the 1970 Balance Sheet of Hygrade Food Products Corporation.

Retained Earnings (deficit) .... (3,737,125)

Possible restrictions upon retained earnings, as mentioned earlier in connection with long-term debt, will be more fully discussed in a subsequent section of this chapter.

Illustrative Presentation of Stockholders' Equity

To summarize the pertinent factors presented to this point regarding stockholders' equity, it is worthwhile to explain an illustrative set of facts for a fictitious company, the McCandless Corporation.

> FACTS: On January 2, 1972, the McCandless Corporation received its charter with an authorized capital of 3,000 shares of preferred stock, 7 percent non-cumulative, non-participating, par value $100; and 6,000 shares of no-par common stock. The following transactions affecting stockholders' equity occurred during 1972:
>
> January 3 Issued 1,000 shares of preferred stock for cash at par.
>
> January 4 Issued 2,000 shares of common stock for cash at $55 per share. The McCandless Corporation is incorporated in a state which permits the company to allocate a portion of the proceeds from the issuance of no-par stock to a capital in excess of stated value category. The directors of the McCandless Corporation established a stated value of $50 per share on all common no-par stock.
>
> January 15 Issued 100 shares of common no-par stock in payment of attorney's costs of $5,500 incurred in the organization of the corporation.

---

[8] *Accounting Terminology Bulletin Number 1,* "Review and Résumé," p. 31. Copyright American Institute of Certified Public Accountants, Inc.

February 9   In consideration for the corporation's locating a large plant in its vicinity, the City of Erewhon unconditionally donated land with a fair market value of $20,000. The donation was legal under the state law.

February 12 Issued 100 shares of preferred stock to Mr. Doe in payment for an adjacent plot of land which the directors valued at $10,000.

March 12   Issued 500 shares of preferred stock for cash at $103 per share.

April 14   Issued 1,000 shares of common no-par stock at $56 per share.

December 31 The net income for the year was $40,000.

December 31 The directors declared a 7 percent dividend on the preferred stock and a $2 per share dividend on the common stock.

Each of the foregoing transactions is analyzed for its effect upon stockholders' equity in the following summary:

SUMMARY ANALYSIS

Date	Preferred Stock Issued Number of Shares	Preferred Stock Issued Amount @ $100 share	Common Stock Issued Number of Shares	Common Stock Issued Amount @ $50 share	Capital in Excess of Par or Stated Value	Retained Earnings
Jan. 3	1,000	$100,000			$ –0–	
4			2,000	$100,000	10,000 (1)	
15			100	5,000	500 (1)	
Feb. 9	—	—	—	—	20,000 (2)	
12	100	10,000			–0–	
Mar. 12	500	50,000			1,500 (3)	
Apr. 14			1,000	50,000	6,000 (1)	
Totals	1,600	$160,000	3,100	$155,000		

(1) Capital in Excess of Stated Value of No-Par Stock	$16,500
(2) Capital from Donated Land	20,000
(3) Premium on Preferred Stock	1,500
Total Capital in Excess of Par or Stated Value	$38,000

Dec. 31	Net income for the year increases retained earnings	$ 40,000
31	Dividend declarations reduce retained earnings:	
	On preferred: 7 percent of $160,000 or $7 times 1,600 shares	(11,200)
	On common: $2 times 3,100 shares	(6,200)
	Retained earnings reinvested in the business at December 31	$ 22,600

The summary analysis of the facts may be presented in the following format as a portion of the balance sheet:

SOLUTION
STOCKHOLDERS' EQUITY

Contributed Capital:
7 percent, Non-cumulative, Non-participating
  Preferred Stock, Par $100
    Authorized .... 3,000 shares
    Less: Unissued .... 1,400 shares
    Issued and Outstanding .... 1,600 shares .. $160,000

Common Stock, No-Par Value,
  $50 Stated Value
    Authorized .... 6,000 shares
    Less: Unissued .... 2,900 shares
    Issued and Outstanding .... 3,100 shares .. 155,000

Capital in Excess of Par or Stated Value:
    Premium on Preferred Stock .... $ 1,500
    Capital in Excess of Stated Value 16,500
    Capital from Donated Land 20,000   38,000
        Total Contributed Capital $353,000
Retained Earnings 22,600
Total Stockholders' Equity $375,600

Dividends

The usual corporate notice of a dividend declaration will read similarly to the following:

> At a meeting held October 1, your Board of Directors declared a cash dividend of $1 per share to shareholders of record at the close of business on November 1 and payable on December 1.

It is on the first date, the date that the dividend is declared (October 1), that the dividend becomes a liability of the corporation; retained earnings are decreased and current liabilities are increased by the total amount of the dividend declaration. It is on the third date, the date that the dividend is paid (December 1), that the liability for the dividend is liquidated; current liabilities and current assets are decreased by the total amount of the dividend. The intermediate date, the date of record (November 1), is the last day on which anyone who has recently purchased shares can have them transferred to his name to receive the dividend already declared. On the New York Stock Exchange, usually a stock sells "ex-dividend" on the third business day before the record date.

Asset dividends. The typical profit distribution is a cash dividend to the stockholders, as discussed in the preceding paragraph. However, though not too common a practice, a dividend which distributes corporate profits may be paid with assets other than cash. For example, in addition to quarterly cash dividends, Standard Oil Company (Indiana) had a special year-end dividend, during the years 1948–1963, payable in shares it owned of Standard Oil Company (New Jersey).

Stock dividends. A stock dividend is an issuance of additional shares of the corporation's own stock to its shareholders, not a distribution of cash or any other assets. In effect, a stock dividend is a permanent capitalization of earnings; it causes a decrease in retained earnings and an increase in contributed capital but does not change the total amount of stockholders' equity. Technically, a stock dividend is not a distribution of corporate earnings, but a capitalization of such earnings: such a dividend does not change any stockholder's proportionate equity in the company.

The effect of a stock dividend upon the stockholders' equity section of the balance sheet is (1) to decrease retained earnings by the "fair value" of the shares issued, (2) to increase capital stock by the par or stated value amount of the shares, and (3) to increase capital in excess of par or stated value by the amount of the excess of "fair value" over par or stated value. On the date a stock dividend is declared, retained earnings are decreased. But no current liability for "dividends payable" is created, as for an asset dividend. Since a stock dividend is only a shift from retained earnings to contributed capital without any effect upon the total dollar amount of stockholders' equity, the "stock dividend payable" amount remains within the stockholders' equity section between the declaration and payment dates. A typical presentation of this situation is the following from the December 31, 1966, statement of Consolidated Financial Position of Radio Corporation of America:

Shareholders' Equity

Capital stock, no par, at stated value	
$3.50 cumulative first preferred stock, shares authorized 920,300, outstanding 183,639 (preference on liquidation $100 per share, $18,363,900)	$ 2,971,000
Common stock, authorized 80,000,000 shares; issued 59,458,337 shares	39,639,000
2 percent stock dividend payable, 1,184,597 shares	790,000
Capital surplus	411,835,000
Reinvested earnings	237,702,000
Total Shareholders' Equity	$692,937,000

"Fair value" per share, as determined by the directors of a company, typically has a reasonable relationship to market value.[9] For example, the closing market price per share on the day preceding the stock dividend declaration was used by Sears, Roebuck and Co. to determine fair value per share for its 1 percent stock dividend declared on November 13, 1956. The approximate market price per share on the stock dividend record date was used by Ashland Oil, Inc., to determine fair value per share for its 2 percent stock dividend in 1960.

The Committee on Accounting Procedure of the AICPA recommended that an amount equal to the fair value of shares to be issued by a stock dividend should be capitalized by a transfer from Retained Earnings to Common Stock and Capital in Excess of Par when the shares issued as a dividend are less than approximately 20 percent to 25 percent of the shares previously outstanding.[10] For example, the Board of Directors of PPG Industries, on October 10, 1962, declared a stock dividend of 2 percent (that is, at the rate of one share for each 50 shares held), payable on January 21, 1963. The Company's "earnings retained for use in the business" was reduced $46.26 for each share of the common stock issued as a result of this stock dividend. Of that sum, the par value of $10.00 per share was transferred to capital stock, and $36.26 per share was transferred to "capital contributed for stock in excess of par value."

A stock dividend is a formal recognition by the company that such an amount is to be permanently retained in the business. Notices to shareholders concerning stock dividend declarations typically contain statements as: "The stock dividend was declared with the objective of broadening the base for future earnings by conserving cash for the continuing growth of the Corporation's business" (Radio Corporation of America, January 29, 1962); and "The purpose of this stock dividend is to effect a capitalization of earnings which will conserve working capital in the interests of the Company's business" (Ashland Oil, Inc., August 1, 1960). Because, theoretically, a stock dividend "gives" a stockholder "nothing" (merely more shares of stock but with each share representing a proportionately smaller equity in the corporation), the typical stock dividend is not taxable income to the recipient for federal income tax purposes.

Illustration of Effect of Dividends upon Stockholders' Equity

The corporate codes of the 50 states differ with respect to possible dividend declarations (both cash and stock dividends) from "capital in excess of par or

---

[9] An exception to the procedure of capitalizing the fair value per share for a stock dividend could occur when the fair value per share is less than the legal minimum required to be capitalized according to the law of the state of incorporation. In this case, the higher amount—legal minimum per share—would be capitalized. Such a situation might occur if fair value per share is less than par value.

[10] *Accounting Research Bulletin No. 43,* "Restatement and Revision of Accounting Research Bulletins," Chapter 7. Copyright (1952) American Institute of Certified Public Accountants, Inc.

stated value" (paid-in surplus or capital surplus) and, though rarely encountered because an appraisal write-up of assets is not generally accepted accounting, any "recorded appreciation of assets" (appraisal or revaluation surplus). This is beyond the scope of the present discussion. Therefore, assume in the two cases below that dividend declarations are from retained earnings (earned surplus).

The following stockholders' equity section was taken from the balance sheet of the Skoner Corporation, a fictitious company, as of December 31, 1971:

Stockholders' Equity

Capital Contributions
Common Stock—Par $100:
Authorized	80,000 shares		
Less: Unissued	50,000 shares		
Issued and Outstanding	30,000 shares	$3,000,000	

Capital in Excess of Par:
Premium on Common Stock	$70,000		
Capital from Donated Land	50,000	120,000	

Retained Earnings 1,380,000

Total Stockholders' Equity $4,500,000

Case one. The board of directors met and declared a 5 percent cash dividend ($150,000) on January 2, 1972, payable February 1, to stockholders of record on January 15. Assuming no changes in stockholders' equity other than those caused by the declaration and payment of the dividend:

1. The summary form on the next page presents the revised amounts constituting the stockholders' equity section of the balance sheet;
2. Shows the revised book value per share; and
3. Shows the change in equity of a stockholder owning 20 shares of stock.

Case two. Revert to the original stockholders' equity section as of December 31, 1971, and assume that the directors had declared, on January 2, a stock, instead of a cash, dividend payable on February 1 to stockholders of record on January 15. The dividend was equal to one share for every 20 shares outstanding (5 percent). The board of directors placed a "fair value" of $160 per share on the shares issued as a result of the 5 percent stock dividend. The cash dividend decreases stockholders' equity (specifically, retained earnings) by the total amount of the dividend and the book value per share by the amount of the per share dividend because of the asset distribution. The stock dividend capitalizes the fair value ($160) of the shares issued (1,500) without affecting total stockholders' equity; retained earnings is decreased $240,000 ($160 × 1,500 shares), but contributed capital is increased the same amount—common stock by $150,000 ($100 par × 1,500 shares) and capital in excess of par by $90,000 ($60 × 1,500 shares). Furthermore, the proportionate equity of the stockholder is unchanged; 21 shares represent the same equity as the 20 previous shares.

SUMMARY

	Before Dividend	After Cash Dividend	After Stock Dividend
Outstanding Common Stock	$3,000,000	$3,000,000	$3,150,000
Capital in Excess of Par	120,000	120,000	210,000
Retained Earnings	1,380,000	1,230,000	1,140,000
Total Stockholders' Equity	$4,500,000	$4,350,000	$4,500,000
Number of shares outstanding	30,000	30,000	31,500
Book value per share	$150.00	$145.00	$142.86
Equity per corporate books of assumed stockholder	$ 150.00 × 20	$ 145.00 × 20	$142.86 × 21
	$ 3,000	$ 2,900	$ 3,000
Cash received by stockholder	—	$ 100	$ -0-

Stock Split

A stock split involves the issuance of additional shares to present stockholders without changing the total dollar amount of any of the items constituting the stockholders' equity section of the balance sheet. To illustrate this point, analyze case three for Skoner Corporation.

Case three. Revert to the original stockholders' equity section as of December 31, 1971, and assume that the directors had recommended (and the stockholders approved) a two for one stock split effective on February 1, with par value of each share to be reduced from $100 to $50. Only the number of shares changed, having doubled because of the two for one split. But par per share has been halved; if the stock had been no-par stock without a stated value, even

	Before Split	After Split
Outstanding Common Stock	$3,000,000	$3,000,000
Capital in Excess of Par	120,000	120,000
Retained Earnings	1,380,000	1,380,000
Total Stockholders' Equity	$4,500,000	$4,500,000
Number of shares outstanding	30,000	60,000
Book value per share	$150	$ 75
Equity per corporate books of assumed stockholder	$ 150 × 20	$ 75 × 40
	$3,000	$3,000

this formality would not have been necessary. Note that the individual stockholder, who now has twice as many shares, still has identical equity in the company. The only possible gain to an individual stockholder would be if the market value per share on the stock exchange does not drop to exactly one-half of its former price; this is a distinct possibility because stock splits are viewed as "bullish" by the market.

The typical reason for a stock split is "to increase the number of outstanding shares for the purpose of effecting a reduction in their unit market price and, thereby, of obtaining wider distribution and improved marketability of the shares."[11] In a similar vein, a letter dated November 30, 1959, to its common stockholders concerning a proposed two for one split by Westinghouse Electric Corporation stated, "Your directors took this action because they believe that these changes are likely to create a broader market for the Common Stock, which should in turn increase public interest in the business and products of the Corporation."

There are two basic differences between a stock dividend and a stock split. The former results in a permanent capitalization of earnings by the transfer of a given dollar amount from retained earnings to contributed capital, while the latter need not involve any transfer. The second basic difference is the number of shares involved. There is no doubt that a 3 percent distribution of shares is a stock *dividend,* while a 300 percent distribution is a stock *split.* But where is the line to be drawn to distinguish between the two? On this point, the following recommendation of the Committee on Accounting Procedure of the AICPA's is as reasonable an answer as any:

> The committee believes that the corporation's representations to its shareholders as to the nature of the issuance is one of the principal considerations in determining whether it should be recorded as a stock dividend or a split-up. Nevertheless, it believes that the issuance of new shares in ratios of less than, say, 20% or 25% of the previously outstanding shares, or the frequent recurrence of issuances of shares, would destroy the presumption that transactions represented to be split-ups should be recorded as split-ups.[12]

Rarely is a split encountered in which shares are distributed in a ratio of less than an additional one-half share for each full share currently outstanding.

Treasury Stock

Treasury stock is the corporation's own stock which was fully paid for when issued and has later been reacquired but not cancelled. Because its acquisition results in a reduction of the number of shares of stock outstanding in the hands

---

[11] *Ibid.,* p. 49.
[12] *Ibid.,* p. 53.

of the public, such an acquisition is usually reflected as a reduction in stockholders' equity to the extent of the cost of such shares. An example of the usual presentation of treasury stock is shown by the following, taken from the December 31, 1970, Consolidated Balance Sheet of Continental Can Company:

Stockholders' Equity
(in thousands of dollars)

Capital Stock	
$4.25 Cumulative Preferred (stated value $100)	$ 5,525
Common (par value $1)	28,997
Paid in Surplus	219,095
Retained Earnings	504,187
	$757,804
Less—Common Stock in Treasury, at Cost (314,745 shares)	8,525
	$749,279

Slightly more than two-thirds of the 600 survey companies covered in the analysis of 1968 annual reports by the 1969 edition of *Accounting Trends and Techniques* published by the AICPA referred to treasury stock in their reports.

To illustrate the effect of the acquisition and subsequent disposal of treasury stock, assume the following stockholders' equity section of a balance sheet:

Stockholders' Equity
(before purchase of treasury stock)

Capital Contributions:	
Capital Stock, par $100; 600,000 shares authorized; 400,000 shares issued and outstanding	$40,000,000
Capital in Excess of Par:	
Premium on Capital Stock	2,000,000
Retained Earnings	25,000,000
Total Stockholders' Equity	$67,000,000

If the corporation now purchases 1,000 shares of its own outstanding capital stock at $102 per share, total assets (specifically, cash) is decreased $102,000 and total stockholders' equity is decreased the same amount. Within the stockholders' equity section shown below (which now totals $66,898,000), the wording opposite the capital stock amount is altered to indicate that, though 400,000 shares are still issued, 1,000 of these are no longer outstanding in the hands of the public. The cost of the 1,000 shares of treasury stock is usually subtracted, as shown, to arrive at the decreased total of stockholders' equity. Now, assume that the 1,000 shares of treasury stock are sold for $104 per share at a later date. The "gain" of $2 per share is not income within the usual meaning of the term and thus should not affect retained earnings.[13] Rather,

---

[13] Nor is it taxable income by the provisions of the Internal Revenue Code.

Stockholders' Equity
(after purchase of treasury stock)

Capital Contributions:	
Capital Stock, par $100; 600,000 shares authorized; 400,000 shares issued (of which 1,000 are in the treasury)	$40,000,000
Capital in Excess of Par:	
Premium on Capital Stock	2,000,000
Retained Earnings	25,000,000
	$67,000,000
Less: Cost of Treasury Stock (1,000 shares)	102,000
Total Stockholders' Equity	$66,898,000

the entire proceeds, including the so-called "gain," constitute contributed capital. As shown by the stockholders' equity below, the $104,000 increases stockholders' equity that same amount by an increase in capital in excess of par by $2,000 (the $2 per share excess of selling price over cost) and by the

Stockholders' Equity
(after sale of treasury stock)

Capital Contributions:		
Capital Stock, par $100; 600,000 shares authorized; 400,000 shares issued and outstanding		$40,000,000
Capital in Excess of Par:		
Premium on Capital Stock	$2,000,000	
From Disposition of Treasury Stock	2,000	2,002,000
Retained Earnings		25,000,000
Total Stockholders' Equity		$67,002,000

removal of the $102,000 deduction for the cost of the treasury stock. Because all of the issued stock is again outstanding, the wording opposite the capital stock amount of $40,000,000 is identical to that prior to the purchase of the treasury stock. Retained earnings has remained unchanged during the treasury stock transactions; normally, it would be affected only by net income for the intervening period and by any dividend declarations.

The reasons for acquiring treasury shares are varied. Sometimes, management desires to remove excess capital no longer needed in the business; then, the treasury shares actually might be retired rather than remain as treasury shares. Often, shares are purchased on the market; then, these treasury shares, rather than some of the unissued shares, are sold to fulfill employee stock purchase and stock option plans for executives and key employees. Preferred shares are often reacquired and temporarily held as treasury stock under a plan calling for the periodic redemption and retirement of a specified amount of preferred stock. In certain instances, common shares are reacquired and held as treasury stock so that they may be used when the company's convertible preferred stock is tendered for conversion into common shares. Occasionally, treasury stock is used to make payments to the company's employees under an incentive compensation plan.

The possibility of a restriction on the retained earnings of the company because of its acquisition of treasury shares is included in the discussion of restrictions on retained earnings in the next section of this chapter.

Restrictions on Retained Earnings

The amount of retained earnings is not represented by any specific asset, nor is there any relationship between the amount of cash and the amount of retained earnings. Retained earnings (earned surplus) represents that portion of the total amount of the company's net earnings over the years of its existence which has not been distributed to the stockholders as dividends, but which has been reinvested in the business. Thus, retained earnings represents a source of assets, but not any specific asset. Theoretically, it represents the amount legally available for dividend declarations. Of course, it would be rare for a board of directors to consider the total amount of retained earnings as actually available for dividend declarations, because retained earnings are usually plowed back into the business as added working capital, for new plant and equipment, and in various other forms.

In addition to the practical limitation of considering total retained earnings as legally available for dividend declarations, there are often formal *restrictions* on retained earnings limiting dividend declarations. These formal restrictions on retained earnings are of two general types: voluntary restrictions based upon management policies and legal or contractual restrictions.

As an illustration of the effect of a voluntary restriction upon retained earnings, refer to the stockholders' equity section of the balance sheet of the McCandless Corporation on page 289. This statement shows $22,600 of retained earnings legally available for dividend declarations. However, assume that it is the desire of management formally to restrict dividend declarations to permit the retention of assets in the business for future plant expansion. In accordance with this plan, three-fourths of retained earnings are to be restricted until the contemplated future expansion has been accomplished. Disclosure of this restriction, at December 31, 1972, may be presented by revising the retained earnings portion of the previously presented stockholders' equity section on page 289 as follows:

Retained Earnings:
    Unrestricted .... $ 5,650
    Restricted:
        For Future Plant Expansion 16,950
    Total Retained Earnings $22,600

The total amount of retained earnings ($22,600) is unchanged; the total amount has merely been subdivided, by vote of the board of directors, to indicate that $16,950 is retained for a specific purpose. No cash or any other assets have been segregated or set aside by the establishment of this restriction; segregation would require the establishment of a special fund as one of the assets of the corporation.

Sometimes, the unrestricted amount of retained earnings ($5,650 in the illustration) is referred to as the "free" retained earnings. Such a caption on this item may be definitely misleading to the user of financial data, since he might believe that this amount is definitely earmarked and available for dividends. Actually, it (as well as the $16,950) has already been reinvested in the business and is distributed among the various assets of the company.

Occasionally, the restricted amount of retained earnings ($16,950 in the illustration) is referred to as either the "appropriated" or "reserved" retained earnings. These captions may be similarly misleading to those using financial data. Nothing of a tangible nature has been segregated, appropriated, reserved, or set aside to expand the plant; the restriction only indicates the intention of management to use assets in the manner indicated someday.

To avoid these possible misinterpretations, a marked trend toward a revised presentation which indicates restrictions by a footnote to the financial statements has occurred in recent years. Such a presentation would appear as follows:

> Retained Earnings (Note 1) $22,600
> Notes to Financial Statements:
> Note 1: By resolution of the Board of Directors, $16,950 of retained earnings is restricted for plant expansion purposes and thus decreases possible dividend declarations by that amount; only $5,650 of retained earnings is unrestricted.

Additional illustrations of this presentation will be shown in subsequent examples.

Some of the additional voluntary restrictions upon retained earnings occasionally encountered are those:

> For Working Capital
> For Contingencies
> For Sudden Obsolescence of Fixed Assets
> For Higher Costs of Replacing Fixed Assets
> For Possible Casualty Losses

All restrictions on retained earnings are established by reducing the amount of the unrestricted (free) retained earnings to indicate the intention of the directors to limit dividend declarations and thereby keep an equivalent amount of assets in the business for the use indicated by the title of the restriction established on retained earnings. Any voluntary restriction may be removed in the same manner by which it was established; namely, by vote of the board of directors.

The second basic type of formal restrictions on retained earnings consists of those required for legal purposes and/or contractual arrangements. Typical of this category are those restrictions required:

> By Long-term Indebtedness
> By Credit and Loan Agreements
> For Redemption of Preferred Stock
> By Purchases of Treasury Stock

Restrictions such as these are not voluntary; they are mandatory and are required to fulfill stipulated agreements.

Two examples of restrictions occasioned by the incurrence of long-term debt through notes and bond issues have already been presented on pages 279–280. Both Smith-Corona Marchant Inc. (now SCM Corporation) and Liggett & Myers Tobacco Company (now Liggett & Myers Incorporated) disclosed restrictions by notes to the financial statements. In the case of the former company, the restriction completely eliminated the possibility of cash dividends on June 30, 1961; while, for the latter company, the restriction will have little, if any, effect upon dividend declarations.

Similarly, retained earnings are often restricted when debt is incurred by the issuance of notes rather than by a bond issue. For example, the notes to the financial statements contained in the 1969 annual report of General Dynamics Corporation show such a restriction with respect to its long-term debt, principally notes payable (reproduced on page 270). A portion, "Note 4," to the statements reads as follows:

> The notes payable to an insurance company are payable as follows: $5,529,000 in 1970 through 1977, $16,239,000 in 1978, $4,000,000 in 1979 and the balance of $2,000,000 in 1980. The notes payable to banks under the Credit Agreement of February, 1969, are payable in twenty equal quarterly installments commencing March 31, 1971 ($12,000,000 annually).
>
> Under the most restrictive provisions of the long-term debt agreements, $13,237,000 of the Corporation's retained earnings of $265,793,000 were unrestricted as to the payment of dividends as of December 31, 1969. In addition, the Corporation is required to maintain $125,000,000 of working capital and $300,000,000 of net worth.

Similar to the manner by which retained earnings may be restricted because of the raising of additional capital through the incurrence of debt, so restrictions may also be imposed when equity capital is raised through the issuance of preferred stock. Often, a corporation's charter of incorporation will place limitations on dividend declarations as long as any preferred stock is outstanding. An example of such a limitation is the following from the December 31, 1965, Consolidated Balance Sheet of Owens-Illinois, Inc.:

> Retained Earnings (Note 3) $304,364,834
>
> Portion of Note 3: The articles of incorporation and certain long-term debt agreements include covenants restricting the payment of dividends. At December 31, 1965, $250,363,310 of consolidated retained earnings was not available for the payment of dividends under the covenants in the debt agreements. The provisions in the articles of incorporation, appli-

cable while any of the 4 percent preferred shares are outstanding, are presently less restrictive.

To protect creditors, many state corporate codes require that corporations maintain a stipulated amount of *legal* or *stated* capital. The legal provisions of these state codes are varied and highly technical, and thus beyond the scope of this discussion. However, it should be apparent to the reader that the creditors of a company could be left in an untenable position should the company's management use corporate resources to acquire considerable treasury stock while continuing with a liberal dividend policy on the remaining outstanding shares. To prevent such a possibility, many states require that retained earnings be restricted by the cost of the treasury stock to limit dividend declarations. This restriction on retained earnings limits the *total* of all distributions to stockholders through returns *of* capital investment (corporate acquisitions of treasury stock) and by returns *on* capital investment (corporate dividend declarations) to the amount of retained earnings. Thus, the required legal capital cannot be impaired by any attempt to do two things with the resources provided by retained earnings. . . . .return capital and pay dividends; dividends can be declared only to the extent that resources provided by retained earnings have not been used for treasury stock acquisitions. Illustrative of this type of restriction is the following from the annual report (financial review section) of Scott Paper Company, with respect to its Reinvested Earnings at December 31, 1969 in the amount of $305,539,000:

> *Reinvested earnings,* under Pennsylvania law, were restricted and not available for dividends or other payments to the extent of $18,546,000, the cost of common shares in treasury at December 31, 1969. There were no other restrictions on reinvested earnings at year end.

Unlike voluntary restrictions on retained earnings, legal and/or contractual restrictions cannot be removed until the commitment which required the restriction has been fulfilled.

FACTORS IN PLANNING THE FINANCIAL STRUCTURE

Planning the financial structure of the company is a top management function. In so doing, two basic sources of funds are available to management. These sources are debt and ownership equity—the two segments of the right-hand side of the balance sheet which provide the resources or assets shown by the left-hand side of the statement. Like any plan, that for the financial structure of the company should be reviewed and revised as required by changing conditions. Initially, as the business is formed, and continually, as the business requires additional funds, balance should be maintained in the financial structure. The company must have an adequate ownership equity as the base upon which to incur debt, as an individual buying a home should have an adequate ownership equity (the down payment) upon which to incur debt (the mortgage payable).

General Factors Which Influence the Determination of a Proper Balance

The balance maintained between debt and ownership equity will vary in accordance with many factors, one of which is the philosophy of the top management of the company. At one extreme is the idea that debt, other than the bare minimum of current liabilities, is to be abhorred, that all risk should be avoided whenever possible. At the other extreme is the "thin" corporation whose small ownership equity and heavy debt ratio creates financial leverage so great that, at times, the soundness of the financial structure is questionable. In between is the philosophy that all current factors must be considered in determining a balance which assures financial soundness while providing an equitable return on the investment of the owners.

A second factor to consider in determining the proper distribution between debt and ownership equity is the type of industry. The utility industry, for example, with its basic profit stability, steady growth in most cases, and heavy investment in long-lived plant and equipment, usually has a higher total debt to total assets ratio than that of many other industry groups. In Exhibit 9–1, note that the percentage of total debt to total assets is 52 percent for utilities, while the same ratio is 42 percent for manufacturing corporations. However, these statistics may be misleading, because they consider only industry groups; for example, in Exhibit 9–2, note the wide variation within the manufacturing group. Not only is there a wide variation in the total debt to total assets ratio, but also within the composition of total debt itself; i.e., the proportion of both current liabilities and non-current liabilities to total assets.

Regardless of the philosophy of the top management of the company and the industry group or subdivision thereof of which the company is a part, a third factor, the conditions within the given company itself, may greatly negate the influence of the first two. For the individual company, its growth rate of sales, trend of profit margins, competitive position within the industry, vulnerability to cyclical fluctuations, and present ratio of debt to assets, are all considerations which exert considerable influence on the availability of particular sources of funds.

In addition to these variables which influence the balance between debt and ownership equity, management must consider the effect of various specific factors, presented next, in its determination of the best source of funds.

Effect of Specific Factors

Many specific factors, considered in planning the financial structure of the company for their long-run effect, must be weighed when choosing the proper sources of capital to be utilized in any given instance. Several of these factors will be mentioned as guidelines to be employed for shaping this kind of decision.

EXHIBIT 9-1

Percentages of Debt and Stockholders' Equity to Assets

	In percent	
Major Industrial Groups	Total Debt to Total Assets	Total Stockholders' Equity to Total Assets
Agriculture, Forestry, and Fisheries ...	55	45
Mining	41	59
Manufacturing	42	58
Transportation, Communication, Electric, Gas, and Sanitary Service	52	48
Wholesale Trade	56	44
Retail Trade	55	45
Finance, Insurance, and Real Estate ...	85	15
Services	67	33

Source: United States Treasury Department, Internal Revenue Service, *Statistics of Income, 1966, Corporation Income Tax Returns,* December 30, 1969.

EXHIBIT 9-2

Sources of Capital (Total Assets),
as of December 31, 1969

INDUSTRY	PERCENT OF TOTAL ASSETS			
	Current Liabilities	Non-Current Liabilities[2]	Total Liabilities[3]	Stockholders' Equity[3]
All manufacturing corporations	24.9	20.4	45.4	54.6
Durable goods	27.8	19.5	47.3	52.7
Transportation equipment	36.6	14.6	51.1	48.9
Motor vehicles and equipment[1]	28.2	11.8	40.0	60.0
Aircraft and parts[1]	50.0	17.7	67.7	32.2
Electrical machinery, equipment and supplies	31.9	19.5	51.4	48.6
Other machinery	27.0	17.3	44.3	55.7
Metalworking machinery and equipment[1]	26.8	18.6	45.5	54.5
Other fabricated metal products	28.1	19.4	47.5	52.5
Primary metal industries	18.0	27.7	45.7	54.3
Primary iron and steel[1]	18.6	26.0	44.6	55.4
Primary nonferrous metals[1] ..	17.1	30.1	47.2	52.8
Stone, clay, and glass products .	18.4	21.7	40.1	59.8
Furniture and fixtures	28.2	12.5	40.7	59.3

EXHIBIT 9-2
(*Continued*)

INDUSTRY	Current Liabilities	Non-Current Liabilities[2]	Total Liabilities[3]	Stockholders' Equity[3]
Lumber and wood products, except furniture	21.1	27.8	48.9	51.1
Instruments and related products	25.0	14.8	39.8	60.2
Miscellaneous manufacturing and ordnance	31.6	17.0	48.6	51.4
Nondurable goods	21.7	21.6	43.1	56.9
Food and kindred products	28.0	20.2	48.3	51.8
Dairy products[1]	26.1	18.0	44.1	55.9
Bakery products[1]	23.1	23.6	46.7	53.2
Alcoholic beverages[1]	24.4	18.5	43.0	57.0
Tobacco manufacturers	22.0	27.4	49.4	50.6
Textile mill products	24.9	19.2	44.1	55.9
Apparel and other finished products	41.1	14.6	55.6	44.4
Paper and allied products	18.5	27.1	45.7	54.3
Printing and publishing	23.5	21.0	44.6	55.4
Chemicals and allied products	19.8	22.2	42.0	58.0
Basic chemicals[1]	17.6	27.4	45.0	55.0
Drugs[1]	22.7	12.0	34.7	65.3
Petroleum refining and related industries	15.4	21.2	36.7	63.3
Petroleum refining[1]	15.4	21.3	36.6	63.4
Rubber and miscellaneous plastic products	28.2	22.7	50.8	49.2
Leather and leather products	30.3	16.0	46.2	53.8

PERCENT OF TOTAL ASSETS

[1] Included in major industry above
[2] Principally long-term debt
[3] Figures are rounded and may not add to total
Source: Federal Trade Commission—Securities and Exchange Commission, *Quarterly Financial Report for Manufacturing Corporations.*

One prime factor is that of control. Normally, creditors do not vote, while stockholders do. If additional capital is raised by a large stock issue, control is unaffected in most large companies where it is rare to find any single stockholder owning as much as 1 percent of the outstanding voting stock. But, in the small to medium-sized company, such a stock issue, if purchased by other than present stockholders, might lead to a shift in control and management of the company. Thus, other things being equal, management of a smaller company might be inclined to maintain control by raising additional capital through borrowing (debt) or the issuance of some class of non-voting stock (ownership equity).

A second factor is income taxes. Interest paid on debt is a deductible business expense. Dividends declared on stock are not a business expense; dividends are the distribution of a portion of the after-tax net income to the owners of the corporation. If $10,000,000 of additional capital is raised at an annual gross cost of 4 percent when the tax rate is 50 percent, the full cost of $400,000 annually is out-of-pocket to the company if it represents dividends because the capital was procured through a stock issue; but if the capital was obtained by borrowing, the out-of-pocket cost is only $200,000 ($400,000 of of interest paid less a $200,000 reduction in taxes to be paid). Any calculation such as this is subject to many refinements; only the basic point of this second factor has been presented.

Third, debt matures at some specific future date and must be repaid. But stockholders are owners of the company, and their investment does not carry a maturity date. Creditors may take legal action against the company and perhaps force its liquidation if the debt is not repaid when due. Ownership equity carries with it no such possibility; the claims of creditors have preference over the claims of owners on the assets of the company. Debt requires payment at specific dates; occasionally, these dates may find the company in a strained financial position.

The rigidity of the claim on the income of the company is a fourth factor to consider. Debt requires paying a predetermined, fixed, interest rate regardless of the profit or loss situation of the company at a particular time. (An exception, of course, is an issue of income bonds when it is not required to accumulate the interest if it is not earned in some year.) Dividends are not a fixed claim upon earnings of the company; the frequency and the rate of dividends on stock are at the discretion of the board of directors of the company. In poor years, dividends may be omitted; in prosperous years, extra dividends may be declared. Normally, the only recourse of an unhappy stockholder is to vote against the present directors or sell his stock. (An exception, of course, is an issue of preferred stock which is cumulative in regard to dividends.)

A fifth factor in the determination of a proper debt-ownership ratio is financial leverage. As discussed in Chapter 5, trading on the equity is profitable and favorable to the common stockholders when funds procured through debt or preferred stock issues are employed in the business profitably enough to earn a greater return than the fixed cost (of interest or preferred dividends) incurred for the use of the funds.

Closely related to the leverage factor is that of earnings per share of common stock. Regardless of management's feeling concerning the importance of earnings per share, it is a key factor in the appraisal of a company's performance by financial analysts as well as prospective and present stockholders. Thus, this sixth factor must be considered in planning the financial structure of the company; the proceeds from any additional common stock issue should be employed profitably enough in the business to avoid any dilution of earnings per share.

Last, and not very specific, is the factor of gazing into the crystal ball and coming up with the right answers for future economic and environmental conditions. For example, consider those who raised additional capital by a 20-year bond issue in 1916 as opposed to those who did likewise in 1939. Many who borrowed in 1916 found it difficult or impossible to meet the interest charges on the debt during the depression of the 1930s and were forced into bankruptcy. But most of those who borrowed funds for 20 years in 1939 experienced no difficulty in meeting the interest charges in the ensuing years. To the contrary, at maturity in 1959, they found that, owing to the changed value of the dollar, they were paying off debt with cheap dollars although good dollars had been borrowed. Many other facets, like changing tax rates, wars, inventions, and laws, preclude any perfect weighing of all the specific factors involved in planning the financial structure of a company.

Because any company is only a minute segment of a dynamic economic system subject to changing political, legal, economic, and ethical considerations, it is impossible to prepare any static and complete list of specific factors and their effect upon management's decisions in the determination of the most feasible sources of capital to employ. Thus, these considerations should be viewed only in regard to present conditions. What sources of capital are companies currently employing? The statistics in Exhibit 9–3 are indicative of the present situation.

EXHIBIT 9-3

Sources Utilized for Expansion of U.S. Corporations[1]

Year	1959	1961	1963	1965	1967	1969
Amount of expansion in billions of dollars[2]	$38.5	$40.0	$46.7	$66.6	$84.8	$97.8

Sources of financing of above expansion:
   Internal sources ....
     Retained earnings (net income less dividends) plus depreciation expense
   External sources ....
     Principally new stock and new long-term borrowing
		In the range of 72% to 81%
		
		 In the range of 28% to 19%

Composition of external sources:
   New stock issues
   New bond issues and other long-term borrowing
		Varied widely with an approximate range between 2 to 1 and 6 to 1 in favor of new bond issues and other long-term borrowing

[1] All U.S. corporations excluding banks, savings and loan associations, insurance companies, and investment companies.

[2] Expansion consists of: increase in net working capital, investment in additional plant and equipment in the U.S., and investment in other assets including fixed assets of foreign subsidiary companies—principally the second of the three items.

Source: Securities and Exchange Commission, *Statistical Bulletin: Working Capital of U.S. Corporations.*

The patterns of these statistics, which have varied little in the past several years, indicate that approximately three-fourths of business expansion is financed from funds provided by current profitable operations (net income for the period less dividends and plus the depreciation expense, since this expense does not require the use of funds). The use of external financing sources accounts for approximately one-fourth of business expansion. And the predominate method of utilizing the external sources is through the incurrence of long-term debt, not by stock issues.

QUESTIONS AND PROBLEMS

9-1. The following stockholders' equity section was taken from the balance sheet of Nanty-Glo Corporation as of December 31, 1972:

Capital Stock, Par $100; 1,000,000 shares authorized; issued and outstanding 200,000 shares	$20,000,000
Additional Paid-in Capital	5,000,000
Retained Earnings	15,000,000
Total Stockholders' Equity	$40,000,000

For the succeeding year, 1973, the corporation had a net income for the year of $4,000,000. Quarterly dividends paid during the year (on March 15, June 15, September 15, and December 15) *totaled* $4 per share for the year. No shares were sold or reacquired during the year. At December 31, 1973, market value per share was $300.

Required

Complete the below stockholders' equity sections at December 31, 1973, assuming:
a. Only the information above.
b. The above information plus a year-end 5 percent stock dividend.
c. The above information, exclusive of the year-end stock dividend (i.e., ignore requirement b), plus a four for one stock split on December 31. Assume a proportionate change in the par of each share.

	Requirement a	Requirement b	Requirement c
Capital Stock; 1,000,000 shares authorized; issued and outstanding are ...	Par $100 200,000 shares	Par $ _____ _____ shares	Par $ _____ _____ shares
Capital Stock at par	$20,000,000	$	$
Additional Paid-in Capital	$ 5,000,000	$	$
Retained Earnings	$	$	$
Total Stockholders' Equity	$	$	$

9-2. On January 1, 1972, the Severna Park Manufacturing Company sells 1,000 ten-year, 6 percent, sinking fund bonds. Face (par) value for each bond is $1,000. Interest is to be paid semi-annually on June 30 and December 31. Annually, according to the provisions of the bond indenture, $100,000 (less the earnings in the fund each year) is to be deposited with a trustee to provide the amount needed to retire the bonds at maturity. Also, the company is required to restrict retained earnings in an amount equal to the balance of the fund.

Required

a. Complete the form below under the three assumptions for the original issue price of the bonds.

	Bonds sold at		
Description of facts	Face (100%)	95 (95%)	105 (105%)

January 1, 1972
 (1) Face of total issue ..
 (2) Upon issuance, total amount of:
   Bond discount ....
   Bond premium ...
	$	$
		
		 $
			$
			
			 $

June 30, 1972 (1) Semi-annual interest payment	$	$	$

December 31, 1972
 (1) Semi-annual interest payment ....
 (2) Amount of annual straight-line amortization of:
   Bond discount ....
   Bond premium ...
 (3) Interest Expense on Bonds (net) shown by annual statement of income
	$
	
	 $
		$
		
		 $
		
		 $
			$
			
			 $
			
			 $

b. Complete the form below for the sinking fund and restriction on retained earnings requirements.

Description of facts	Amount
December 31, 1972 (1) First annual contribution to sinking fund .... (2) Restriction on retained earnings	$ $
December 31, 1973 (1) Second annual contribution to sinking fund (during 1973 the fund increased $5,000 because of income earned on the first contribution) .... (2) Additional restriction on retained earnings, equal to total increase in fund during 1973	 $ $

December 31, 1981 (1) Tenth annual contribution to sinking fund (during 1981 the fund increased $45,000 because of income earned on the $900,000 balance in the fund as of December 31, 1980) ..... (2) Additional restriction on retained earnings, equal to total increase in fund during 1981	$ $
January 1, 1982 (1) Retirement of bond issue (no bonds had been redeemed during ten years) will require the use of the sinking fund to the extent of .... (2) This retirement of the bonds will permit the removal of the restriction on retained earnings in the amount of	$ $

9-3. For each of the following statements, choose the one best answer to each and indicate your choice on an answer sheet with a number.

a. The establishment of a fund (e.g., sinking fund for bond redemption) out of cash:
1. decreases the amount of current assets
2. decreases the amount of total assets
3. increases the amount of current assets
4. increases the amount of total assets
5. changes the amount of total retained earnings
6. none of the above

b. The incurrence of long-term debt as a method of securing funds for a capital expansion program is indicative of:
1. a venturesome "gambling" management
2. the manner in which a majority of new capital has been raised from external sources by companies since World War II
3. ultra-conservatism in management
4. none of the above

c. A company sells $1,000,000 face (par) of 8 percent bonds at a premium, viz., 105 (105 percent of par). They mature in 20 years. The annual interest expense (after amortization of premium on a straight-line basis) shown on the income statement for any of the twenty years is:
1. $77,500
2. $80,000
3. $82,500
4. none of the above

d. A company sells 200 5 percent bonds at a discount, viz., 90 (90 percent of par). The face amount of each bond is $500, and they mature in ten years. The annual interest expense (after amortization of discount on a straight-line basis) shown on the income statement for any of the ten years is:
1. $5,000
2. $6,000

[CH. 9] LONG-TERM DEBT, STOCKHOLDERS' EQUITY 309

       3. $7,000
       4. none of the above
    e. Assume you purchase a $1,000 face (par) bond from a corporation the day it is issued (April 1) for 105. The bond bears an annual interest rate of 8 percent, payable April 1 and October 1. Then you sell the bond on July 1 for 104½ plus accrued interest. You will have:
       1. $5 capital loss and $20 of interest income
       2. $15 capital gain and no interest income
       3. $5 capital loss and $40 of interest income
    f. Income bonds pay interest:
       1. only once every year
       2. when the company receives revenues
       3. when the company earns enough to have first met its preferred dividend requirements
       4. when net earnings of the year cover interest requirements
       5. if company wishes to pay interest

9-4. For each of the following statements, choose the one best answer to each and indicate your choice on an answer sheet with a number.
    a. When United States Steel Corporation, in 1966, exchanged $175 principal amount of 4⅝ percent subordinated debentures for each outstanding $100 par value 7 percent cumulative preferred share, the effect upon earnings per share of common stock (assume no other changes in the capital structure) was:
       1. to increase earnings per share
       2. none
       3. to decrease earnings per share
    b. In the average manufacturing company, if assets equal 100 (percent), then, approximately:
       1. liabilities will be 40 and stockholders' equity 60
       2. liabilities will be 60 and stockholders' equity 40
       3. liabilities will be 50 and stockholders' equity 50
    c. In the average utility company (transportation, gas, electric, communication, sanitary service), if assets equal 100 (percent), then approximately:
       1. liabilities will be 30 and stockholders' equity 70
       2. liabilities will be 50 and stockholders' equity 50
       3. liabilities will be 70 and stockholders' equity 30
    d. Since World War II, most corporate expansion has been financed by:
       1. profits not distributed in dividends (plus add-back of depreciation expense)
       2. incurring long-term debt
       3. new stock issues
    e. If a corporation had total assets of 100 (percent), it would be a "thin" incorporation if:
       1. liabilities are 50 and stockholders' equity 50
       2. liabilities are 10 and stockholders' equity 90
       3. liabilities are 90 and stockholders' equity 10

9-5. Old Beulah Corporation was incorporated in 1946. The balance sheet disclosed the following stockholders' equity section at December 31, 1972.

6 percent Cumulative, Non-Participating, Non-Convertible, Preferred Stock, Par $100; 400,000 shares authorized; 100,000 shares issued and outstanding	$ 10,000,000
Common Stock, Par $50; 1,000,000 shares authorized; 600,000 shares issued, of which 100,000 are in the treasury	30,000,000
Capital in Excess of Par	15,000,000
Retained Earnings (total)	55,000,000
	$110,000,000
Less: Treasury Stock, Common (100,000 shares @ $70 cost)	7,000,000
Total Stockholders' Equity	$103,000,000

During 1972 no shares of either class of stock were sold or purchased. The treasury stock was purchased in 1967. There are no dividends in arrears on the preferred stock.

The Statement of Retained Earnings for 1972, disclosed the following:

Retained Earnings, January 1, 1972				$52,600,000
Net Income for the Year 1972		$5,000,000		
Dividends during 1972:				
On preferred Stock ($6 per share)	$ 600,000			
On Common Stock ($4 per share)	2,000,000	2,600,000		2,400,000
Retained Earnings, December 31, 1972				$55,000,000

Required

Compute the 1972 Earnings per common share.

9-6. Refer to the facts in the preceding problem. Then on January 1, 1973, Old Beulah Corporation sold one-half of its treasury stock at $90 per share. Assuming no other facts, prepare below the stockholders' equity section of the balance sheet on January 1, 1973, immediately after the sale of the treasury stock.

6 percent Cumulative Preferred Stock (unchanged)	$ 10,000,000
Common Stock, Par 50; 1,000,000 shares authorized;	

(complete the description for common stock)	
Capital in Excess of Par	$
Retained Earnings (total)	$
	$
Less: Treasury Stock, Common ( )	
Total Stockholders' Equity	$

9-7. Approximately eight years from December 31, 1972, management plans to add to plant capacity by an estimated expenditure of $160,000. It is decided that, annually, beginning with December 31, 1972, $20,000 shall be set aside in a Plant Extension Fund. The amount of the annual contribution to the fund will be reduced by whatever amount the fund increases during the current year due to its earnings. It is also decided that a portion of retained earnings will be restricted (formally titled Retained Earnings Restricted for Plant Extension), the amount of which restriction is to be kept equal to the related fund. Each December 31, a restriction of retained earnings will be made for the total increase in the amount of the fund that year.

At December 31, 1979, the balance of the Plant Extension Fund is $144,200, including $4,200 of interest earned by the fund during 1979 and already recorded, but excluding the last annual contribution to be made on December 31, 1979. No additional provision has been made to restrict retained earnings since December 31, 1978.

The following table shows the actual accumulation of the fund:

Year Ended	Income Earned by Fund	Annual December 31 Contribution	Total Fund
December 31, 1972	$ —	$20,000	$ 20,000
December 31, 1973	800	19,200	40,000
December 31, 1974	1,600	18,400	60,000
December 31, 1975	3,000	17,000	80,000
December 31, 1976	3,400	16,600	100,000
December 31, 1977	5,000	15,000	120,000
December 31, 1978	3,600	16,400	140,000
December 31, 1979	4,200	?	160,000

Required

a. Determine the amount of the contribution to the Plant Extension Fund on December 31, 1979.

b. Determine the amount of the additional restriction made to retained earnings on December 31, 1979.

c. If an additional plant building is purchased on January 8, 1980, for $157,000, what will happen to:

  1. the balance remaining in the Plant Extension Fund?
  2. the restriction on retained earnings?

  Note: Assume no further plant extension is contemplated.

9-8. **Required**

a. Where would a fund (e.g., Sinking Fund for Bond Redemption, Plant Extension Fund) be shown in the balance sheet?

b. How would a restriction on retained earnings (e.g., Retained Earnings Restricted for Bond Redemption, Retained Earnings Restricted for Plant Extension) appear in the balance sheet?

312   FINANCIAL ACCOUNTING CONCEPTS   [CH. 9]

    c. Where would the income earned by a fund (e.g., Income Earned by Sinking Fund, Income Earned by Plant Extension Fund) during a given year be reflected on the annual statement of income?

    d. What is the purpose of a fund?

    e. What is the purpose of a restriction on retained earnings?

    f. Why have *both* a fund and a restriction on retained earnings?

    g. Discuss this statement: "Once the bonds have been retired (or the plant expansion program completed) and the restriction on retained earnings removed (causing a sudden increase in unrestricted retained earnings), the corporation is in an excellent position to pay a large dividend."

    Note: This problem may be used independently or as an additional requirement to either of problems 9-2 or 9-7.

9-9. a. Compute the selling price of a face (par) $1,000 bond if the market quotation is:

        93   94½   95¼
        111   100½   102⅜

    b. Compute the selling of a face $500 bond if the market quotation is 97⅞.

    c. On May 1, 1972, West Lafayette Manufacturing Company issued $100,000 of 6 percent first mortgage bonds at 98½. Face of each bond is $1,000. The bonds are payable in ten years, with interest payable semi-annually on May 1 and November 1.

        One of the bonds was purchased by Brown, an individual investor, on May 1, 1972. On August 13, 1972, Brown sold the bond to Smith at 99 plus accrued interest. Smith held the bond until December 13, 1972, when he sold it to Green at 98 plus accrued interest.

        Determine the following:

    1. Cost of bond to Brown
    2. Gain or loss on sale of bond by Brown
    3. Interest earned on the bond by Brown
    4. Cost of bond to Smith (exclusive of accrued interest)
    5. Gain or loss on sale of bond by Smith
    6. Interest earned on the bond by Smith

9-10. R & F Corporation has issued $1,000,000 of 5 percent debenture bonds at par to mature in 20 years. The bond indenture requires the corporation to accumulate a sinking fund and to restrict retained earnings for dividend declarations.

Required

Select the best answer to the following three statements:

    a. On the balance sheet, the Sinking Fund would be shown as:
       1. an investment asset
       2. a current asset
       3. a restriction on retained earnings
       4. a fixed asset

    b. On the same balance sheet, the amount of the restriction on retained earnings would be shown as:

[CH. 9] LONG-TERM DEBT, STOCKHOLDERS' EQUITY 313

      1. an investment asset
      2. a current asset
      3. a portion of the stockholders' equity section
      4. a reduction of bonds payable

   c. On the statement of income for the year, the annual $50,000 of interest expense on the bonds would be shown as:
      1. an administrative expense
      2. a financial management expense (Other Expenses and Losses section) to be deducted after the determination of net operating income
      3. a portion of cost of goods sold, because the proceeds from the bond were used to build a new manufacturing plant
      4. not shown at all, but treated as are dividends on capital stock (i.e., as a distribution of the net income for the year and, thus, a direct charge against retained earnings)

9-11. For each of the following statements, choose the one best answer to each and indicate your choice on an answer sheet with a number.

   a. The establishment of a restriction on retained earnings (e.g., restriction for contingencies):
      1. changes the amount of total assets
      2. changes the amount of total liabilities
      3. changes the amount of *total* retained earnings
      4. changes the amount of *total* stockholders' equity
      5. none of the above

   b. When an issue of preferred stock is purchased and permanently retired (cancelled) by the issuing corporation for less than its original issue price, proper accounting for the retirement:
      1. increases the amount of dividends available to common shareholders
      2. increases the contributed capital of the common shareholders
      3. increases reported net income for the period
      4. increases the treasury stock held by the corporation
   (Adapted from Uniform CPA Examination)

   c. The sale for $15,000 of 1,000 shares of treasury stock (par $20) which had cost $18,000 results in a *decrease* in stockholders' equity *at the time it is sold of:*
      1. $2,000
      2. $3,000
      3. $5,000
      4. $15,000
      5. none of the above

   d. If you own 100 shares of a stock and subsequently receive a 5 percent stock dividend, followed a year later by a two for one stock split, you then own:
      1. 205 shares
      2. 210 shares
      3. 195 shares
      4. none of the above

   e. A cash dividend distributes earnings, a stock dividend capitalizes earnings, a stock split normally does not affect retained earnings.

1. True
2. False

9-12. For each of the following statements, choose the best answer to each and indicate your choice on an answer sheet with a number.

a. The incurrence of long-term debt as a method of securing funds for a capital expansion program is indicative of:
1. a venturesome "gambling" management
2. the manner in which a majority of new capital has been raised from external sources by companies since World War II
3. ultra-conservatism in management
4. none of the above

b. Treasury stock is *usually* shown on a company's balance sheet as:
1. an investment
2. a reduction in stockholders' equity
3. unissued stock
4. a reduction of liabilities
5. outstanding stock

c. Restrictions on retained earnings *normally:*
1. freeze cash
2. freeze earnings
3. freeze dividends
4. guide management planning
5. reduce corporate taxes
6. reduce profits
7. none of the above

d. The maximum amount of treasury stock which a company can purchase is:
1. unlimited
2. limited only by its cash position
3. limited only by its net income for the year
4. limited by certain provisions in many state corporation codes, for the protection of creditors
5. limited only by the Securities and Exchange Commission

9-13. For each of the following statements, choose the best answer to each and indicate your choice on an answer sheet with a number.

a. The declaration of a cash dividend to be paid at a later date has the following effect on the company's financial statements at the time of *declaration:*
1. reduces cash and retained earnings
2. reduces retained earnings and increases current liabilities
3. no effect
4. reduces net income for the period

b. When a previously declared cash dividend is paid, it has the following effect on the company's financial statements at the time of *payment:*
1. reduces cash and current liabilities

[CH. 9] LONG-TERM DEBT, STOCKHOLDERS' EQUITY 315

    2. reduces cash and retained earnings
    3. no effect
    4. reduces net income for the period

  c. The declaration of a stock dividend to be "paid" at a later date (by the issuance of unissued shares) has no effect on either *total* liabilities or *total* stockholders' equity at the time of *declaration*.
    1. True
    2. False

  d. A stock split has no effect on either *total* assets, *total* liabilities, or *total* stockholders' equity.
    1. True
    2. False

  e. A cash dividend distributes earnings, a stock dividend capitalizes earnings, a stock split does not affect retained earnings.
    1. True
    2. False

  f. Retained earnings are permanently capitalized by:
    1. a stock split
    2. a stock dividend
    3. a cash (asset) dividend
    4. cancellation of Treasury stock

  g. An "Irish" dividend is a:
    1. distribution of inventory instead of cash
    2. reverse stock split
    3. dividend declared on March 17
    4. dividend from excess profits resulting from lucky ventures

9-14. From the following information selected from the balance sheets of three different corporations as of December 31, 1972, determine the missing facts:

	De Sota Corporation	Hall Corporation	Ellsworth Corporation
Total Assets	$500,000	$700,000	$?
Total Liabilities	?	300,000	100,000
Issued and Outstanding Capital Stock	250,000	300,000	600,000
Retained Earnings	?	?	(200,000)*
Total Stockholders' Equity	300,000	?	?

* Indicates Deficit

9-15. For the year ended December 31, 1972, the Statement of Income of Lunga Corporation disclosed a net income for the year of $90,000. The only changes in Retained Earnings during 1972 were attributable to dividends declared and the net income for the year. Comparative balance sheets were as follows:

LUNGA CORPORATION
Comparative (Condensed) Balance Sheets

	December 31, 1971	December 31, 1972
Total Assets	$800,000	$810,000
Total Liabilities	$350,000	$290,000
Issued and Outstanding		
Capital Stock	$300,000	$300,000
Retained Earnings	150,000	220,000
Total Stockholders' Equity	450,000	520,000
Total Equities	$800,000	$810,000

Required

a. Calculate the amount of cash dividends declared during 1972.

b. Prepare a Statement of Retained Earnings for the year ended December 31, 1972.

9-16. In answering this problem, insert a plus sign, a minus sign, or a zero in each of the twelve squares to indicate the effect of dividends and stock splits.
Insert a plus if the total dollar amount of the item increases.
Insert a minus if the total dollar amount of the item decreases.
Insert a zero if the total dollar amount of the item is unchanged.

Item	Cash Dividend	Stock Dividend	Stock Split
Capital Stock Outstanding (Par)			
Capital in Excess of Par			
Retained Earnings			
Total Stockholders' Equity			

Note: Fair value per share exceeds par value per share.

9-17. Pavuvu Corporation was organized in 1921 and has operated continuously since that date. The authorized capital stock of the corporation is 10,000 shares with a $50 par value per share. The information that follows is taken from the balance sheets on the dates indicated.

	December 31, 1971	December 31, 1972
Capital Stock Outstanding ..	$350,000	$400,000
Premium on Capital Stock ..	50,000	52,000
Retained Earnings	220,000	250,000

On December 1, 1972, one thousand shares of previously unissued stock were sold for cash.

A 4 percent dividend ($2 per share) was declared on September 15, 1972, to stockholders of record on October 10, 1972, payable October 31, 1972.

[CH. 9] LONG-TERM DEBT, STOCKHOLDERS' EQUITY 317

Required

Determine the following:

a. Total amount of dividend declared and paid in 1972.

b. Per share price of stock issued December 1, 1972.

c. Since a Statement of Income has not been provided, calculate the net income or net loss for the year 1972. Indicate clearly your method in arriving at the amount of the profit or loss.

9-18. As of December 31, 1972, the following amounts are shown on the balance sheet of the Banika Corporation:

Cash	$ 200,000	
Accounts Receivable	300,000	
Estimated Doubtful Accounts		$ 3,100
Inventories	250,000	
Machinery and Equipment	400,000	
Accumulated Depreciation—Machinery and Equipment		120,000
Notes Payable		60,000
Accounts Payable		150,000
Capital Stock Issued		600,000
Premium on Capital Stock		12,000
Retained Earnings		210,000
Treasury Stock (100 shares at cost)	5,100	
	$1,155,100	$1,155,100

The authorized capital stock of the corporation is 30,000 shares of $50 par value stock.

Banika Corporation was organized in July, 1942.

The balance sheet as of December 31, 1971, showed Retained Earnings of $175,000.

Cash dividends of $30,000 were declared (and paid) in 1972.

Required

a. Prepare, in proper form, the stockholders' equity section of the balance sheet as of December 31, 1972.

b. Calculate the book value per share as of December 31, 1972.

c. Inasmuch as a Statement of Income has not been provided, calculate the net income or net loss for the year 1972. Indicate clearly your method in arriving at the amount of the net income or loss.

9-19. The following facts were selected from various sections of the balance sheet of the Keim Corporation as of December 31, 1972:

Capital Stock, $100 par value; 14,000 shares authorized; 8,800 shares issued, of which 800 shares are in the treasury	$880,000
Treasury Stock (800 shares)	80,000
Premium on Capital Stock	27,500
Retained Earnings (unrestricted)	226,000
Retained Earnings Restricted by Treasury Stock Purchases	80,000
Accumulated Depreciation to Date	22,500
Retained Earnings Restricted for Bond Redemption	24,000
Capital in Excess of Par from Donated Assets	6,500
Sinking Fund for Bond Redemption	24,000

Required

a. Using the above information:
  1. prepare the stockholders' equity section of the balance sheet as of December 31, 1972.
  2. compute the book value per share of outstanding stock as of December 31, 1972.
b. A cash dividend of $40,000 was declared and paid during the first week of January, 1973. Compute the book value per share immediately after the payment of the cash dividend. (Assume no other changes in the stockholders' equity section.)
c. In addition to the cash dividend in requirement b. above, the company declared and paid a stock dividend of one share for every forty shares outstanding and valued the dividend shares at $120. The dividend was declared and paid during the second week of January, 1973. Compute the book value per share immediately after the payment of the stock dividend. (Assume no other changes in the stockholders' equity section other than that noted in requirement b. above.)

9-20. The stockholders' equity section of the consolidated balance sheet of United States Steel Corporation at December 31, 1937, appeared as follows:

Capital Stock and Surplus	
United States Steel Corporation	
Preferred 7% Cumulative Stock—	
Par Value $100	$ 360,281,100.00
(Authorized 4,000,000 shares; issued 3,602,811 shares)	
Common Stock—Par Value $100	870,325,200.00
(Authorized 12,500,000 shares; issued 8,703,252 shares)	
Capital Surplus	81,250,021.42
Earned Surplus of U.S. Steel Corporation and Subsidiary Companies	280,356,143.55
Total Capital Stock and Surplus	$1,592,212,464.97

On this same balance sheet, the property category was subdivided into tangible and intangible amounts. The intangible assets were shown at $260,368,521.53.

During the 36 years following the formation of U.S. Steel in 1901, a total of $508,302,500 of intangible assets was written off. Following a change in the capital structure of U.S. Steel in April of 1938, the board of directors authorized a further write-off of the intangibles, from $260,368,521.53 to the nominal amount of $1.00.

Amendments to the certificate of incorporation of U.S. Steel, proposed by the board of directors, were adopted by the stockholders at the annual meeting in April of 1938. These amendments effected the following changes in the corporate capital structure:

a. Common stock changed from $100 par value shares to no-par value shares.

b. Authorized common shares were increased from 12,500,000 shares to 15,000,000 shares.

A stated capital amount of $75 per share was set on the 8,703,252 outstanding common no-par shares. The decrease of $25 per share in capital stock resulted in a transfer of this amount to capital surplus. Capital surplus then consisted of:

Premium on par value common stock	$ 81,250,021.42
Transfer from common capital stock	217,581,300.00
Total capital surplus	$298,831,321.42

It was against this total capital surplus that the intangible assets were written down to $1.00.

For the year 1938, the corporation had a net loss of $7,717,453.69. No dividends were declared on the common stock, but regular dividends totaling $7 per share were declared on the preferred stock.

Required

a. Prepare the stockholders' equity section of the consolidated balance sheet of the United States Steel Corporation at December 31, 1938.

b. To what degree was the real value of the intangible assets affected by the book reduction to $1?

c. Why were the intangible assets not written off against earned surplus (retained earnings)?

9-21. The stockholders' equity section of the Consolidated Balance Sheet of Texaco Inc. appeared as follows as of December 31, 1960:

Stockholders' Equity (Note 3):
Capital stock—par value $25:
Shares authorized—75,000,000
Shares issued—62,440,298 including

treasury stock	$1,561,007,450
Paid-in capital in excess of par value (Note 4)	118,748,636
Retained earnings used in the business	1,078,033,813
	$2,757,789,899

Less—Capital stock held in treasury—
691,024 shares, at cost 21,074,871
Total stockholders' equity $2,736,715,028

(Notes not reproduced)

At a special stockholders' meeting in July, 1961, the stockholders approved an increase in Texaco's authorized capital stock from 75,000,000 shares with a par value of $25 each, to 150,000,000 shares with a par value of $12.50 each. In August of 1961, Texaco distributed one new share of stock for each share held by the stockholders of record on July 19, 1961 (in effect, a 2 for 1 split). As a result, the number of issued shares was exactly doubled. Other transactions affecting stockholders' equity in 1961 were:

a. Net income for the year was $430,116,577.

b. Cash dividends paid during the year totaled $191,510,329.

c. Treasury shares sold to stock option holders during the year resulted in an increase to paid-in capital in excess of par value in the amount of $1,196,575, and left 1,303,567 treasury shares at a cost of $20,853,893 as of December 31, 1961.

Required

a. Prepare the stockholders' equity section of the consolidated balance sheet as of December 31, 1961.

b. Compute the book value per share of outstanding stock as of December 31, 1961, and compare it to market value on that same date.

9-22. Tenaru River Corporation was incorporated on August 9, 1942, with an authorized capital consisting of 4,000 shares of 5 percent cumulative, nonparticipating preferred stock of $100 par value and 5,000 shares of no-par common stock. The corporation was incorporated in a state whose corporate code (law) permits the crediting of a capital in excess of stated value account with a portion of the proceeds from the sale of no-par shares. The directors of the corporation passed a resolution stipulating that $40 per share should be credited to the Common Stock—No-Par account.

The following information was taken from the stockholders' equity section of the balance sheet of Tenaru River Corporation as of December 31, 1972:

Preferred Stock Outstanding—5 percent Cumulative	$300,000
Common Stock Issued—No Par	188,000
Treasury Stock—Common No Par (200 shares at cost) ..	8,500
Retained Earnings (free)	120,000
Retained Earnings Restricted for Contingencies	20,000
Premium on Preferred Stock	15,000
Retained Earnings Restricted for Plant Extension	30,000
*Appreciation of Fixed Assets	10,000
Capital in Excess of Stated Value	7,000
Capital from Donated Assets	12,000
Retained Earnings Restricted by Treasury Stock Purchases	8,500

* Land purchased in 1942 was written up $10,000 during 1972.

[CH. 9] LONG-TERM DEBT, STOCKHOLDERS' EQUITY 321

Required

In proper form prepare the detailed stockholders' equity section of the corporation's balance sheet as of December 31, 1972.

9-23. For each of the following statements, choose the one best answer to each and indicate your choice on an answer sheet with a number.

a. When a given company, as a very few have done, increases a given fixed asset, as land, on its balance sheet from historical cost to current cost, it:
   1. increases total assets
   2. increases total stockholders' equity
   3. increases liabilities
   4. is not conforming to generally accepted accounting principles
   5. 1 and 2
   6. 1, 2, and 3
   7. 1 and 3
   8. 1, 2, 3, and 4
   9. 1, 3, and 4
   10. 1, 2, and 4
   11. none of the above

b. A plant site (land) donated by a township to a company that plans to open a new factory should be shown on the company's statement of financial position at:
   1. the nominal cost of taking title to it
   2. its market value
   3. one dollar (since the land cost nothing but should be included in the balance sheet)
   4. the value assigned to it by the company's directors

(Adapted from Uniform CPA Examination)

c. When Indiana Telephone Corporation increased its Telephone Plant (fixed assets) from historical cost to current cost, it also resulted in an increase in:
   1. liabilities
   2. retained earnings
   3. stockholders' equity (total)
   4. depreciation expense for the year
   5. 2 and 4
   6. 3 and 4

9-24. Shaffer Corporation, incorporated in 1923, would be characterized by many as a growth company. The last ten years have been especially profitable, but the past decade has also been marked by a tight financial situation. Rapid expansion has been financed solely from internal sources. It became apparent, in mid-1972, that, if the company is to continue its expansion and growth, additional capital of $40,000,000 must be raised from external sources in early 1973. Following are Shaffer Corporation's financial statements, in condensed form, for 1972:

Balance Sheet
December 31, 1972

Current Assets	$ 80,000,000
Current Liabilities	50,000,000
Working Capital	$ 30,000,000
Property, Plant and Equipment (net)	200,000,000
Stockholders' Equity	$230,000,000

Details of Stockholders' Equity:

5% Cumulative, Non-Participating, Non-Convertible Preferred Stock, Par $100; 500,000 shares authorized; none issued	$ –0–
Common Stock, Par $100; 2,000,000 shares authorized; 1,000,000 shares issued and outstanding	100,000,000
Capital in Excess of Par	10,000,000
Earnings Reinvested in the Business	120,000,000
	$230,000,000

Statement of Income and Earnings Reinvested
in the Business
For the Year 1972

Net Sales	$300,000,000
Cost of Goods Sold	180,000,000
Gross Margin (40 percent)	$120,000,000
Marketing and Administrative Expenses	75,000,000
Net Operating Income (15 percent)	$ 45,000,000
Income Taxes (50 percent rate)	22,500,000
Net Income for the Year	$ 22,500,000
Earnings Reinvested in the Business, January 1	105,500,000
	$128,000,000
Dividends in 1972; $8 per share	8,000,000
Earnings Reinvested in the Business, December 31	$120,000,000

Assume that:

a. The new financing to raise an additional $40,000,000 is accomplished successfully as of January 1, 1973. The cost of capital is 5 percent regardless of the external source utilized.

b. The funds are immediately employed in the business to produce an increased volume of production and sales at costs and prices the same as those of the preceding year; i.e., no change in rates of gross margin, net operating income, and income taxes.

c. The sales volume for 1973 is $345,000,000.

[CH. 9] LONG-TERM DEBT, STOCKHOLDERS' EQUITY 323

d. The dividend rate of 8 percent on the $100 par value common stock is to be maintained.

e. Only the common stock is voting stock.

Required

a. Compute earnings per share of common stock for 1972.

b. A statement of income (include calculation of earnings per share of common stock) and earnings reinvested in the business for the year 1973 if the $40,000,000 of capital is raised by:
   1. Issuing 400,000 shares of 5 percent preferred stock at par
   2. Issuing 5 percent bonds at par
   3. Issuing 250,000 shares of common stock at $160 per share (An $8 dividend per share on $160 raised per share equals 5 percent cost of capital.)

c. State your choice of the three methods of raising the additional $40,000,000 of capital and the reasons for your decision.

9-25. On January 1, 1972, four men formed a corporation to manufacture and sell astro-powered cigarette lighters. The certificate of incorporation authorized 40 shares of no-par value capital stock. The only issuance of stock was to the incorporators, as follows:

Mr. A—10 shares @ $100	$1,000
Mr. B—10 shares @ $100	1,000
Mr. C—10 shares @ $100	1,000
Mr. D—10 shares @ $100	1,000
Total contributed capital	$4,000

$300,000 of additional capital was raised by the issuance of "Fifteen-year 2 percent Debenture Bonds" in registered form and one-year 9 percent notes, as follows:

Mr. A—Bonds and notes	$ 50,000
Mr. B—Bonds and notes	50,000
Mr. C—Bonds and notes	50,000
Mr. D—Bonds and notes	50,000
	$200,000
Investors other than stockholders—Bonds	100,000
Total debt	$300,000

This capital structure is known as a "thin incorporation," because the primary initial source of capital is from loans, not stock investment.

Required

a. What is the purpose of such an obviously excessive debt structure?

b. Give all possible arguments to prove that interest expense on debt is, in reality, the payment of dividends.

9-26. The following stockholders' equity section was taken from the balance sheet of Tulagi Corporation as of December 31, 1971:

Stockholders' Equity

Capital Stock, Par $100:		
Authorized	200,000 shares	
Less: Unissued	150,000 shares	
Outstanding	50,000 shares	$ 5,000,000
Capital in Excess of Par		500,000
Retained Earnings		6,000,000
Total Stockholders' Equity		$11,500,000

For the succeeding year, 1972, the corporation had a net income (after taxes) of $1,000,000. Below are six different stockholders' equity sections of the balance sheet as of December 31, 1972. Each indicates that corporate net worth has been affected by some type or types of capital transactions during 1972. If additional shares of stock were issued, assume that fair market value per share at the date of issuance was $200. Indicate the capital transaction(s) which occurred by choosing from among the following six possibilities:

a. A quarterly cash dividend of $1 per share

b. A quarterly cash dividend of $1 per share and the sale (issuance) of 2,000 additional shares for cash early in the third quarter

c. A 10 percent stock dividend

d. A two for one stock split

e. A two for one stock split in January and a 4% stock dividend in December

f. A quarterly cash dividend of $1 per share and a year-end 4% stock dividend

Required

From the above choices, select the one best answer to each of the following six resultant stockholders' equity sections.

a. Capital Stock, Par $50
    (100,000 shares outstanding) .... $ 5,000,000
  Capital in Excess of Par 500,000
  Retained Earnings 7,000,000
    Total Stockholders' Equity $12,500,000

b. Capital Stock, Par $100
    (50,000 shares outstanding) .... $ 5,000,000
  Capital in Excess of Par 500,000
  Retained Earnings 6,800,000
    Total Stockholders' Equity $12,300,000

[CH. 9]　　　LONG-TERM DEBT, STOCKHOLDERS' EQUITY　　　325

    c. Capital Stock, Par $100
        (52,000 shares outstanding) .... $ 5,200,000
        Capital in Excess of Par 700,000
        Retained Earnings 6,400,000
           Total Stockholders' Equity $12,300,000

    d. Capital Stock, Par $100
        (52,000 shares outstanding) .... $ 5,200,000
        Capital in Excess of Par 700,000
        Retained Earnings 6,796,000
           Total Stockholders' Equity $12,696,000

    e. Capital Stock, Par $100
        (55,000 shares outstanding) .... $ 5,500,000
        Capital in Excess of Par 1,000,000
        Retained Earnings 6,000,000
           Total Stockholders' Equity $12,500,000

    f. Capital Stock, Par $50
        (104,000 shares outstanding) .... $ 5,200,000
        Capital in Excess of Par 1,100,000
        Retained Earnings 6,200,000
           Total Stockholders' Equity $12,500,000

9-27. This problem concerns consolidated financial statements. Select the one best answer to each of the following three statements.
    a. Consolidated statements are used to present the result of operations and the financial position of:
       1. a company and its branches
       2. a company and its subcontractors
       3. a company and its subsidiaries
       4. any group of companies with related interests
    b. Consolidated statements are intended primarily for the benefit of:
       1. stockholders of the parent company
       2. taxing authorities
       3. creditors of the subsidiary companies
       4. management of the subsidiary companies
    c. H is the parent company and would probably treat K as an investment, not a consolidated subsidiary, in the proposed consolidated statement of H, J, and K if:
       1. H and J manufacture electronic equipment; K manufactures ball bearings
       2. H and J manufacture ball-point pens; K is a bank
       3. all three companies manufacture steel products; H owns 100 percent of J but only 98 percent of K

9-28. This problem concerns corporate capital transactions. Select the one best answer to each of the following:

a. The purchase of treasury stock will:
   1. reduce the number of authorized shares
   2. increase total assets
   3. reduce total stockholders' equity
   4. reduce total liabilities

b. One hundred shares of treasury stock originally repurchased and carried at $101 per share (par is $100) are sold for cash at $104 per share. The sale of the treasury stock will:
   1. increase outstanding capital stock by $10,400
   2. increase retained earnings by $300 and capital contributions by $10,100
   3. increase total stockholders' equity by $10,400, of which $300 will increase "capital in excess of par"
   4. have no effect on total stockholders' equity

c. Because of the possibility of litigation against the company, the board of directors voted to create a "surplus reserve" for contingencies in the amount of $100,000. This restriction on retained earnings will:
   1. set aside cash in a fund
   2. increase liabilities
   3. decrease total stockholders' equity
   4. have no effect on total retained earnings.

d. One year later, the board of directors voted to remove the unnecessary restriction on retained earnings (see part "c"); litigation against the company no longer appeared probable. This "closing" of the surplus reserve for contingencies of $100,000 will:
   1. free "frozen" assets, thus permitting larger dividend payments
   2. increase the year's net profit by $100,000
   3. increase total stockholders' equity
   4. have no effect on total retained earnings

e. When the board of directors authorized the write-up of certain fixed assets to values established by a reliable appraisal, it increased fixed assets on the balance sheet and also increased:
   1. appreciation of fixed assets (revaluation or appraisal surplus)
   2. retained earnings
   3. net profit for the year
   4. working capital

f. A calendar year corporation declared a cash dividend on December 15, to stockholders of record on December 29, payable on January 15. The December 31 balance sheet showed the dividend as a current liability. When the dividend is paid on January 15, it will:
   1. decrease retained earnings and current liabilities
   2. decrease cash and current liabilities
   3. have no effect on the balance sheet
   4. reduce net profit by the amount of the dividend

9-29. Savo Island Corporation was incorporated on January 2, 1971. The information below pertains to the first two years of its business, as reflected by the following stockholders' equity section of the statements of financial position at the end of each year.

	December 31, 1971	December 31, 1972
Capital Contributions:		
Common Stock—par $100; 2,000 shares authorized; 1,500 and 1,600 shares issued respectively at the end of each year, of which 100 shares are in the treasury	$150,000	$160,000
Capital in Excess of Par: Premium on Common Stock	5,000	10,000
Retained Earnings	51,500	95,500
Total	206,500	265,500
Deduct Cost of Treasury Stock—Common (100 shares)	10,500	10,500
Total Stockholders' Equity	$196,000	$255,000

Additional information:

The 100 shares of treasury stock were purchased on August 1, 1971.

There were no issuances of capital stock in December of either year. The 100 shares issued in 1972 were sold on February 8, 1972.

As yet, the company has no regular quarterly dividend policy. To date, each December 1 the company has declared a year-end dividend as follows:

December 1, 1971—3 percent ($3 per share)
December 1, 1972—4 percent ($4 per share)

Each dividend was payable on December 29 to stockholders of record on December 15.

Required

Indicate your answer to each of the six statements below by choosing from among the following seventeen possible answers:

1. $ 4,500
2. 4,200
3. 4,185
4. 55,700
5. 51,500
6. 47,300
7. $56,000
8. 6,000
9. 6,400
10. 3,820
11. 140.00
12. 150.00
13. $170.00
14. 95,500
15. 44,000
16. 50,000
17. Some other amount not given

a. The total amount of the dividend declared and paid in 1971 was .... ( )
b. The net income for 1971, the first year of business was .... ( )

328   FINANCIAL ACCOUNTING CONCEPTS   [CH. 9]

c. Book value per share of stock at December 31, 1971, was ..... ( )
d. The per share price received for the stock issued on February 8, 1972, was .... ( )
e. The total amount of the dividend declared and paid in 1972 was .... ( )
f. The net income for 1972 was .... ( )

Part 2

Cost Accounting Concepts, Controls, and Decision Aids

10

Framework of Manufacturing Costs

Earlier chapters have explained how the periodic gross margin of a business is obtained by matching the cost of goods sold during a period with the revenues realized from their sale. These chapters have also explained that the cost of saleable goods, which should be associated with revenues of future periods, is retained in the periodic inventory. In trading concerns (such as wholesalers and retailers), the costs ordinarily associated with the items in the inventory are the acquisition costs (that is, the prices paid when they were purchased). Similarly, acquisition costs also represent the costs of the items which a trading concern sells during a period.

In a manufacturing enterprise, the determination of the cost of the items sold and the cost of the items retained is more involved; complication is created by the production process of the manufacturing concern. Unlike a trading company, which ordinarily inventories and sells the same items it originally bought, a manufacturer purchases raw materials and, through a production process, transforms their physical nature into new items which are to be sold. As explained in Chapter 3, the manufacturer arrives at the cost of goods sold by first adding the acquisition costs of the raw materials used and, perhaps, transportation and handling charges to the cost of labor and any other costs incurred to determine the cost of producing the finished goods. Then, when finished goods are sold, their calculated cost represents cost of goods sold during a period. The raw materials, plus the labor and other costs incurred in converting these materials into finished goods which are not included in the cost of goods sold during a period, represent costs which should be associated with future revenues. Until this association becomes possible by future sales, these costs should be properly identified and, according to their characteristics, classified under one of the following three inventories:

1. Raw Materials Inventory—the acquisition cost of raw materials not yet placed in the manufacturing process.
2. Work in Process Inventory—the cost of raw materials and related conversion costs of goods still in the production process.
3. Finished Goods Inventory—the cost of raw materials and related conversion costs of completely processed goods which are on hand and available for sale.

A comparison of the costs of the items sold and the items retained by a trading company with those of a manufacturing concern can be made by studying the abbreviated financial statements presented below:

Statement of Income

Trading Company			Manufacturing Company		
Sales		$90,000	Sales		$90,000
Cost of Goods Sold:			Cost of Goods Sold:		
Inventory of Merchandise 1/1	$ 60,000		Inventory of Finished Goods 1/1	$ 60,000	
Net Cost of Purchases	45,000		Cost of (Finished) Goods Manufactured	45,000	
Available for Sale	$105,000		Available for Sale	$105,000	
Inventory of Merchandise 1/31	55,000		Inventory of Finished Goods 1/31	55,000	
Cost of Goods Sold		50,000	Cost of Goods Sold		50,000
Gross Margin on Sales		$40,000	Gross Margin on Sales		$40,000

Balance Sheet

Trading Company		Manufacturing Company	
Current Assets:		Current Assets:	
Inventory of Merchandise	$55,000	Inventory of Raw Material	$38,000
		Inventory of Work in Process	5,500
		Inventory of Finished Goods	55,000

Notice that the cost of items sold in a trading company is determined by the net cost of purchases adjusted for changes in the inventory of merchandise, while the cost of items sold by a manufacturing concern is determined by the cost of (finished) goods manufactured adjusted by changes in the inventory of finished goods. For the manufacturing concern to know the cost of the finished goods manufactured, it must adjust the cost of raw material purchased by changes in the inventory of raw material, and it must adjust the cost of material used, labor consumed, and other production charges by changes in the inventory of work in process. These adjustments force a manufacturing concern to keep three separate categories of costs for items retained and to reflect these categories on its balance sheet, while a trading company needs only a single inventory.

The initial step taken by a trading concern to ascertain the basic cost of the items in its inventory may also be used to obtain the basic cost of the items in the raw materials inventory of a manufacturing concern. Under either situation, the acquisition cost of an inventory item may be obtained from the invoice of a vendor. While the pricing methods employed—FIFO, LIFO, average, etc.—may complicate the valuation process to a degree, the unit acquisition costs are readily identifiable. Beyond this point the manufacturer must employ different cost identification procedures. No longer are unit costs given; they must be determined. In addition to the pricing methods employed, the valuations placed on the work in process inventory, finished goods inventory, and the cost of goods sold in a manufacturing concern depend upon, and are determined by, the calculation of the unit cost of an item at each stage. It is this need for unit cost accumulation, identification, determination, and reporting that requires a kind of accounting known as manufacturing accounting, or, by its all-inclusive term, cost (or industrial) accounting.

In instances where the problem can be satisfactorily solved through using totals, the information needed can be obtained directly by financial accounting which records, accumulates, presents, and reports events of a financial character. However, in most instances, totals provide inadequate answers, because they do not give management as much useful information as it should obtain from the accounting records. For example, they do not show the amount of material, labor, and other manufacturing cost which is applicable to each item produced. Cost accounting furnishes this information and arranges the detailed cost figures in ways which aid managerial control and certain policy decisions. But, rather than a different kind of accounting, cost accounting is an extension of financial accounting. Both systems gather and report data in accordance with generally recognized accounting principles. Cost accounting, however, concentrates upon the material, labor, and related costs which are required to make and sell each product.

The costs of making and selling products represent the total costs which are deducted from sales revenue to obtain period profit. Total costs, in a manufacturing activity, include the costs of two distinctly different functions which should be classified as manufacturing cost and commercial expenses. The commercial expenses of a manufacturer, like those of a trading concern, should be divided into three groups: distribution (selling or marketing) expenses, administration expenses, and financial expenses. Distribution expenses consist of the costs of selling and delivering products after they have been produced and are ready for sale. Administration expenses cover the overall costs of directing and controlling the enterprise. Financial expenses include items like interest and other costs relating to borrowed capital. Manufacturing cost, often called production cost or factory cost, is the sum of the material, labor, and manufacturing overhead which enter into the cost of production. It is this latter phase of total cost which constitutes the primary consideration of cost accounting.

Initially, the primary purpose of cost accounting was to determine the valuation of inventories and the period cost of goods sold to obtain the period gross profit of a manufacturing concern. Although this initial purpose of manufacturing or cost accounting is as valid today as it was originally, the scope of cost accounting has broadened to include objectives like cost reduction, appraising individual performance, budgetary control, profit planning, aiding the determination of pricing policies, and assisting those responsible for making managerial decisions. However, unless the cost of goods produced and the cost of goods sold can be established accurately, it is impossible to periodically prepare reliable statements of income and balance sheets for most manufacturing concerns.

The basic problem which must be solved to achieve the fundamental objective of cost accounting is the accurate determination of the cost of the items produced. Such determination requires recognition of the three elements of factory cost: direct material, direct labor, and manufacturing overhead.

THE ELEMENTS OF MANUFACTURING COST

Direct materials (sometimes called raw materials) refers to all materials that become an intrinsic part of, and can be readily and practically associated with, the finished product. That material which is consumed in the productive process or becomes an integral, nonassociative part of the finished product is classified as *indirect* material; rivets, tacks, glue, thread, and grease are examples of this latter category.

Direct labor (sometimes called productive labor) is the labor effort applied by the worker, either by physical contact or through the medium of a machine, upon materials to transform them into finished products. That labor which cannot feasibly be associated with the finished products or is not performed directly upon the material being converted into finished products is classified as *indirect* labor. Inspectors, general helpers, foremen, cleaners, and other such labor costs belong in this category.

Manufacturing overhead (sometimes called factory burden, manufacturing expense, indirect cost, or simply *overhead*) consists of all factory costs, except direct material and direct labor, which are connected with the production of a product. The distinguishing feature of this heterogeneous mixture of manufacturing costs is their inability to be traced to individual units of product. They are either incurred jointly to benefit a group of products or in such insignificant individual units that the expense of tracing them to finished products is prohibitive. Unlike direct materials and direct labor, which can be readily and directly associated with a finished product, manufacturing overhead costs must be indirectly related to finished products through some equitable assignment. Some of the many types of manufacturing costs which are included in manufacturing overhead are indirect material, indirect labor, property taxes—factory, fire insurance—factory, light, heat and power—factory, repairs and maintenance—factory, depreciation of factory equipment and machinery, and depreciation of factory building.

Cost Per Unit

The proper segregation of total factory costs into the three basic elements of manufacturing costs defined above will not ordinarily provide unit costs for the items produced. In addition, to obtain a unit cost for each element, the total dollars of each cost element should be divided by the number of units of activity which created that cost. The sum of the unit costs for the three elements represents the total cost of manufacturing a unit. For example, assume that 10,000 identical chairs were produced through incurring the following costs:

	Total	Unit
Direct material	$20,000	$2.00
Direct labor	15,000	1.50
Manufacturing overhead	7,500	.75
Total	$42,500	$4.25

From this example, it may be seen that it cost $42,500, or $4.25 per unit, to produce 10,000 chairs. The $4.25 total unit cost may be obtained by dividing the total costs by the total units produced or by the addition of the unit costs for each of the three cost elements which result from dividing the total element cost by the number of units completed or the equivalent number of units produced. The former method is expedient and may be used if the total cost for each element represents costs required to commence and completely finish the same number of identical units. Since this example shows the total costs incurred in producing 10,000 identical chairs, the former method can be used. But the problem is not always solved so easily. If the costs shown above represent costs which originated in this period to finish chairs that had been partly completed in the last period, then the latter method should be followed to obtain the equivalent number of finished units which the activity would have processed completely in this period. Or, if the $42,500 should represent costs which originated in this period to totally complete 10,000 chairs and partly complete 2,000 chairs, the latter method would provide more realistic unit costs for the chairs completed. Moreover, if the total direct material required to complete 3,000 of the 12,000 chairs considered had been partly processed during the preceding period, the use of the unit element cost method is mandatory. Finally, consider the complications that would arise if the 12,000 chairs involved three chair styles requiring different material and labor specifications. Apart from other numerous and vital reasons, the technical aspects just covered illustrate that the unit element cost method is the only method acceptable under many circumstances.

The preceding explanation of the calculation of total unit cost emphasizes the need for recognizing the costs of partly completed products in determining the costs of products which are totally finished. This is done, for any period under consideration, by placing the costs of partly completed products in an ending work in process inventory. Obviously, the ending work in process inventory of one period becomes the beginning work in process inventory of the subsequent period. In most instances, the calculation of the unit cost of production requires that both beginning and ending work in process inventories be considered.

Financial Statements of a Manufacturer

It is customary for a manufacturing enterprise to summarize its production activities by preparing a separate statement or schedule showing the components of the cost of goods manufactured, as revealed by the statement shown below.

Three major components in this statement are the elements of manufac-

THE MALLOY MANUFACTURING COMPANY
Statement of Cost of Goods Manufactured
For the Month Ended January 31, 1972

Direct material:			
Raw material inventory, January 1, 1972		$30,000	
Purchases	$31,000		
Less: Purchases returns and allowances	3,000	28,000	
Material available for use		$58,000	
Less: Raw material inventory, January 31, 1972 ..		38,000	
Direct material used			$20,000
Direct labor			15,000
Manufacturing overhead:			
Indirect labor		$ 1,900	
Property taxes—factory		600	
Fire insurance—factory		800	
Light, heat and power—factory		1,100	
Repairs and maintenance—factory		500	
Depreciation of factory equipment and machinery .		1,400	
Depreciation of factory building		1,200	
Total manufacturing overhead			7,500
Total manufacturing costs originating this period			$42,500
Add: Work in process inventory, January 1, 1972 ..			7,000
Total manufacturing costs			$49,500
Less: Work in process inventory, January 31, 1972 ..			4,500
Cost of goods manufactured			$45,000

turing cost which provide total charges into production of $42,500 during January. A fourth is the cost of (finished) goods manufactured, a cost which is obtained by adjusting the total manufacturing costs originating this period for the difference between the beginning and ending work in process inventories. This adjustment is necessary, because a decrease in the work in process inventory means that the cost of finished goods produced exceeds the cost of the charges placed into production during a period, while an increase in the work in process inventory means that the cost of the finished goods completed is less than the charges entered into production. The $45,000 cost of goods manufactured is in turn reflected on the statement of income of a manufacturing company as a replacement for "net purchases" that would appear on the income statement of a trading concern. A statement of cost of goods manufactured, frequently called a statement of production, can be converted into a statement of cost of goods sold simply by adjusting the cost of goods manufactured for the difference between the beginning and ending finished goods inventories. Using the cost of goods manufactured computed in the preceding statement, this determination would be made by the method shown in the following schedule:

Cost of goods manufactured	$ 45,000
Add: Finished goods inventory, January 1, 1972	60,000
Cost of goods available for sale	$105,000
Less: Finished goods inventory, January 31, 1972	55,000
Cost of goods sold	$ 50,000

If the additional lines of this schedule had been added to the preceding statement, the title of that statement would have changed to statement of cost of goods manufactured and cost of goods sold. With this statement, the amount for cost of goods sold can be shown on the statement of income as a single item. There should be no difference between the statement of income of a manufacturer and that of a trading concern when the cost of goods sold is shown as a single amount. In fact, under this condition, the only significant difference between the financial statements of a manufacturing business and those of a trading concern would appear on the balance sheet under "Current Assets," because three inventory items would replace a single item: the manufacturer's statement would show raw materials inventory, work in process inventory, and finished goods inventory, while the trader's statement would show only merchandise inventory.

The cost of goods sold cannot be ascertained unless the costs of producing finished units is first determined, and knowledge of the costs of manufacturing finished units in turn requires recognition of the costs which should be associated with partly completed units. Approximations of this information can, under certain conditions, be obtained through a deductive process. For example, if the ending inventory of raw materials is subtracted from the sum of the beginning raw material inventory plus period net purchases, the remainder may be presumed to represent the material issued during the period. Then, if the material issued plus the labor and manufacturing overhead incurred during the period is reduced by the estimated material, labor, and manufacturing overhead associated with partly completed products, the remainder may be considered the cost of the products completed during the period. Finally, the estimated cost of products completed plus the beginning finished goods inventory less the ending finished goods inventory, may be accepted as the cost of goods sold during the period. This procedure is unsatisfactory for three major reasons:

1. The dollar amount of each inventory should be determined on the basis of a physical or perpetual inventory at the end of each period.
2. Waste, spoilage, and theft are either overlooked or inadequately recognized.
3. The problem of assigning realistic values to partly completed products is extremely difficult. This difficulty intensifies as the variety of different products increases.

All three of these objections can be overcome by the correct use of a proper system of cost accounting. In fact, the third and most perplexing objection constitutes what many believe to be the basic problem of cost accounting. This problem is: How can the proper amounts of material, labor, and manufacturing overhead be determined for one or a variety of partly completed products? If only one product is involved, a reasonable and usable answer could be obtained through following the approximation procedures previously explained. But, if more than one kind of product is manufactured, no simple calculation would provide answers which would make due allowances for one product's using more material, labor, or manufacturing overhead than another. Instead, some means must be used which will give proper consideration to these differences. This requires a recognition of the nature of the productive process and the selection of a method or system which fits the facts of the situation involved. Cost accounting does this by using two basic methods of assigning manufacturing costs to individual products: process costing and job order costing.

PROCESS COSTING AND JOB ORDER COSTING

Essentially, under process costing, costs are collected by the department, and the time period is an integral factor in the calculation of product unit cost; under job order costing, costs are collected by the physically identifiable job, and the time period is not directly involved in the calculation of product unit cost.

Process costing assigns manufacturing costs to individual units when the productive output is continuous and routine. This method is used by manufacturing concerns which mass-produce standardized products for warehouse stock to be sold to customers whose identity is usually unknown; it is suitable whenever the identity of a single product unit is lost. Process costing is usually found in industries like cement, flour, coal, sugar, paper, rubber, tobacco, dairy, automobile, textile, steel, chemical, electrical appliances, and oil refining. Also, certain public utilities like electric power, gas, water, and steam heat cost their products by process costing. Since many of the industries listed do have some special job production, it should not be presumed that they depend exclusively on process costing.

In continuous process production, a product ordinarily moves from raw material to finished form through a designated sequence of departments or cost centers. A department or cost center is one operation or a cluster of homogeneous operations wherein a specific step is performed in the completion of a product. The department or cost center provides the basis for process costing. Costs are accumulated by the department for a time period, like a month, without any attempt to associate costs with individual units. At the end of the period, the total costs collected for the department are divided by the physical output of the department to obtain an average unit cost. The average unit cost of the completed units times the number of units transferred becomes, in effect, the cost of the material entering succeeding departments, or the cost of the products placed into finished goods, if all productive operations have been completed.

A process costing system requires that a record of manufacturing costs and physical output be maintained by the department for each period of time. Not only will such a record provide the basis for the calculation of average unit costs, but, if the proper organizational structure is present, it will permit the measuring of performance within each area of responsibility. This record, known as a cost of production report, shows the cost of the direct material, direct labor, and manufacturing overhead used to process a unit through each department and the cost of each unit of finished product. To explain the cost flow as it appears on a cost of production report, it is assumed that Baldrige Manufacturing Company produces a single product which is processed through three departments, incurring the following department costs:

	Cutting	Assembling	Painting
Direct Material	$16,000	$2,000	—
Direct Labor	8,000	4,000	$12,000
Manufacturing Overhead	4,000	2,000	6,000

The cost of production report, which assumes that 8,000 units are started and completed in each department and that there are no beginning or ending inventories, is shown on page 340. This example has been highly simplified to emphasize the essentials of the flow of product costs in process costing. It ignores problems like lost units, multiple products, increase in units, and departmental opening and closing inventories. There is no need now to go into the extensive and detailed study required to cover the numerous and sometimes complex variations which might be encountered. The problem of inventories, however, arises regularly and therefore requires explanation at this point.

In the example, 8,000 units were started and completed during the period in each department. More frequently than not, the situation is complicated by: first, units that were started by a department in prior periods and completed in the current period; and second, units that were started by a department in the

BALDRIGE MANUFACTURING COMPANY
Cost of Production Report
For the Month of January, 1972

	Cutting		Assembling		Painting	
Quantity schedule (units):						
Started in process	8,000					
Received in department			8,000		8,000	
Transferred to next department	8,000		8,000			
Transferred to finished goods					8,000	
	Total Cost	Unit Cost	Total Cost	Unit Cost	Total Cost	Unit Cost
Departmental costs:						
Direct material	$16,000	$2.00	$ 2,000	$ .25	–0–	–0–
Direct labor	8,000	1.00	4,000	.50	$12,000	$1.50
Manufacturing overhead ...	4,000	.50	2,000	.25	6,000	.75
Total Departmental costs	$28,000	$3.50	$ 8,000	$1.00	$18,000	$2.25
Cost transferred into department			28,000	3.50	36,000	4.50
Total cost accumulated	$28,000	$3.50	$36,000	$4.50	$54,000	$6.75
Cost transferred to next department	$28,000	$3.50	$36,000	$4.50		
Cost transferred to finished goods					$54,000	$6.75

current period but not completed. Since all of the costs of units both started and completed were incurred in the current period and since only a part of the cost of the other two types of units belongs to the current period, the three types of units cannot be added together. Instead, they must be converted to a common denominator, termed *equivalent unit,* which is equal to one unit which is 100 percent completed. Sometimes the assumption is made that all units in the beginning and ending inventories are 50 percent completed. Consequently, it would take two such units to equal a unit that was both started and completed during the period. In other instances, all units in the work in process inventories are ignored, or the beginning and ending inventory units are assumed to be equal. Although expedient, none of these methods should be used when departmental inventories are significant and substantial differences exist between the beginning and ending inventories. Instead, a more exact procedure should be employed.

A more precise determination of the equivalent units of production can be obtained through a valid estimate of the actual stages of completion. For example, if 10,000 units were completed during the period, 4,000 additional units were 75 percent completed at the end of the period, and 2,000 units were only 50 percent completed at the beginning of the period, the number of equivalent units completed would be 12,000, determined as follows:

Units finished during month	10,000
Plus: 75% × 4,000 units at end of month	3,000
	13,000
Less: 50% × 2,000 units at start of month	1,000
Equivalent units produced during month	12,000

If total costs incurred during the period were $24,000, the cost of an equivalent unit would be $2.00. The 4,000 units in the ending inventory would be costed at $1.50 apiece. The 10,000 units completed would be costed at $2.00 for the 8,000 units both started and completed and at $1.00 plus whatever costs had already been accumulated on the 2,000 units which comprised the beginning inventory. Obviously, such a calculation applies only when the three elements of cost have equal stages of completion. Otherwise, equivalent units of production must be computed separately for material, labor, and manufacturing overhead. This condition frequently exists when material is not added beyond the initial department.

Job order costing assigns manufacturing costs to individual units when the productive output is neither continuous nor stereotyped. This method is used by manufacturing concerns that produce in accordance with special designs or specifications which are supplied by the customer. Repeat orders may be infrequent and rarely is productive output scheduled for warehouse stock. Instead, production ordinarily lags behind the receipts of customers' orders. This method should be used whenever it is possible physically to distinguish each unit or each group of units from all other units throughout the productive process. For example, it is the only method adaptable to the construction industry. It is ideally suited to account for the costs of any single unit like a turbine locomotive or aircraft. Also, it is applicable to factories and workshops where identical or similar products are covered by a single production order (e.g., printing, foundry or furniture).

In job order production, a product or group of products moves from raw material to finished form through one or more departments. The department, however, is not the primary determinant in calculating product unit cost. Nor is dominant importance attached to the time period. The all-important factor is the job, or order, for which costs are accumulated, regardless of the number of time periods involved, until the job is finished. Upon completion, the total costs accumulated for the job divided by the number of units produced is the product unit cost.

Throughout the productive process, material, labor, and manufacturing overhead costs are collected on a separate form reserved for each job. This form, or summary sheet, is called a job order cost sheet or job cost sheet, and it contains spaces to record the material, labor, and manufacturing overhead costs that are identified with each job by a job order number. (Individual job order numbers provide correct identification when several jobs are moving through the factory at the same time.) In addition, the job cost sheet usually shows other pertinent information like date ordered, number of items to be produced, date completed, specifications, and a description of the job. An example of a job cost sheet is shown on page 343.

Job order cost sheets should be designed to provide a manufacturing concern with the information it needs. Consequently, their content, arrangement, and form differ among various users. Although the example provided has been highly simplified to show the basic cost requirements, it does contain information concerning the profitability of the job. This knowledge can be used as a guide for future price quotations on similar jobs. In addition to aiding pricing decisions, job cost information helps management to appraise manufacturing efficiency by providing current product costs for comparison with past product costs or estimated product costs.

ACCOUNTING FOR COST ELEMENTS

The two preceding sections have explained how given amounts of direct material, direct labor, and manufacturing overhead are combined to obtain unit product costs under both process costing and job order costing. But neither section explained how the proper amounts of these cost elements are ascertained. The purpose of this section is to describe how such amounts are obtained.

Direct material costs are obtained from material requisitions which show the type, quantity, unit cost, and total cost of materials used in production. If the material is issued to a job, the job order number is shown on the requisition. The total cost of all requisitions bearing a specific job number represents the cost of direct material for a particular job. In process costing, departmental costs are identified by substituting the name or number of the department for the job order number on the material requisitions.

Direct labor costs are computed by using work or time tickets which show, among other things, the time worked, rate of pay, total earnings, description of work, and employee's name. If the work was performed on a job, the job order number is shown so that all time tickets bearing a given job number will, when totaled, provide the direct labor cost on that job. In process costing, the department identification is used, not the job order number. If an employee works in only one department, time tickets are not required under process costing, since the departmental direct labor costs can be obtained from the payroll or clock cards which show the amount of time worked each day.

Manufacturing overhead costs are not as readily traced to product units as the prime costs of direct material and direct labor. Since these costs are not associated directly with the products produced, it is impossible to measure

Job Order Cost Sheet
WILDWOOD MANUFACTURING COMPANY

Customer	Allison Brothers and Company	Job Order Number	9474
Specifications	Attached	Date Ordered	10/18/---
Blueprint	Attached	Date Commenced	12/1/---
Description	Generator No. 226A4	Date Completed	12/13/---
Quantity	10	Date Shipped	12/15/---

Direct Materials

Date	Department	Requisition	Amount
12/1	71	4128	$3,000
12/1	72	4129	2,000
12/1	73	4210	1,000
		Total	$6,000

Direct Labor

Date	Department	Operation	Amount
12/1-6	71	112	$2,400
12/6-10	72	231	1,600
12/10-13	73	317	1,000
		Total	$5,000

Manufacturing Overhead

Date	Department	Basis	Amount
12/6	71	D. L. hrs.	$2,880
12/13	72	Machine hrs.	960
12/13	73	200% of D. L.	2,000
		Total	$5,840

Summary

Direct Materials	$ 6,000
Direct Labor	5,000
Manufacturing Overhead	5,840
Total Manufacturing Cost	$16,840
Units Produced	10
Unit Cost	$ 1,684
Selling Price	$28,000
Manufacturing Cost	16,840
Gross Margin	$11,160
Commercial Expenses (30% of Sales)	8,400
Net Profit	$ 2,760

exactly how much manufacturing overhead cost should belong to a given product. Total manufacturing overhead, however, is incurred because of production and is a proper part of the cost of manufacturing products. Consequently, some feasible method must be devised to charge an equitable amount of manufacturing overhead to each product unit.

Although manufacturing overhead costs cannot be traced directly to a unit of product, they can be traced directly to a unit of activity. These units are producing departments in which operations are performed directly upon the product being manufactured and service departments in which particular benefits are provided for producing departments or producing and other service departments. The expenses incurred in operating both types of departments represent the total manufacturing overhead costs which belong to the products manufactured. Individual expenses may be traced directly to producing departments and indirectly to product units; they may be traced directly to service departments, indirectly to producing departments, and then again indirectly to product units. An illustration of this tracing procedure is provided by the Manufacturing Overhead Distribution Sheet shown on page 345.

In the following simplified illustration, each manufacturing overhead expense was assigned directly to the three producing and the two service departments by the most equitable basis obtainable for this company. That is, departmental time tickets were used to ascertain how much of the total indirect labor expense belonged to each department; department material requisitions were used to establish the amount of the indirect material that had been issued to each department; the total expenses for taxes and insurance were prorated according to the cubic space occupied by each department; departmental square footage was used to prorate other expense; meters measured each department's share of light, heat, and power; and the dollar amount of equipment located in each department was used to prorate the total expense from depreciation of equipment.

After each manufacturing overhead expense was directly assigned to the appropriate department, the total cost for the general service department was distributed to the storeroom and the three producing departments according to the number of man hours associated with each department. Storeroom had 1,000; finishing, 5,000; assembling, 6,000; and cutting, 8,000. The $23,600 cost in the general department came to $1.18 per man hour for the 20,000 total man hours. The $1.18 hourly rate times the number of man hours in each department was the share of the general service department's cost which was distributed to each department. A similar procedure was used to distribute the $8,880 total cost of the storeroom to the three producing departments. In this instance, however, costs were distributed according to the dollar value of material requisitions which had been issued to each department. Finishing received $8,000 of material requisitions; assembling, $2,000; and cutting, $30,000.

After all manufacturing overhead costs had been distributed and accumulated in the three producing departments, an equitable basis was selected for apportioning the total department costs to the products that were worked on in each department: that factor which correlated most closely with the generation

Manufacturing Overhead Distribution Sheet

Departmental Overhead	Total	Producing Departments			Service Departments	
		Cutting	Assembling	Finishing	Storeroom	General
Indirect labor	$32,900	$12,200	$ 8,700	$ -0-	$ -0-	$ 12,000
Indirect material	36,200	14,000	9,000	6,200	2,400	4,600
Property taxes—factory	11,400	4,400	3,000	2,000	1,000	1,000
Fire insurance—factory	8,300	3,200	2,000	1,100	800	1,200
Light, heat, & power—factory	25,100	13,800	4,600	3,700	1,200	1,800
Depreciation of equipment	28,500	13,500	6,000	5,500	1,700	1,800
Other	16,600	7,300	4,100	3,400	600	1,200
Total	$159,000	$68,400	$37,400	$21,900	$ 7,700	$ 23,600
General		9,440	7,080	5,900	1,180	$(23,600)
Storeroom		6,660	444	1,776	$(8,880)	
	$159,000	$84,500	$44,924	$29,576		
Machine hrs.		5,000				
Direct labor hrs.			10,000			
Direct labor cost				$20,000		
Rate per machine hr.		$16.90				
Rate per labor hr.			$4.4924			
Rate per labor dollar				147.88%		

of manufacturing overhead in each department was chosen. Analyses revealed that causal relationship existed between manufacturing overhead and machine hours in the cutting department and between manufacturing overhead and direct labor hours in the assembling department. In the finishing department, direct labor hours and direct labor cost were about equally desirable; direct labor cost was selected, because it was more readily obtainable. The unit of production method was considered and rejected, since the variety of the multiple products being produced made that method inequitable; no common unit could be equitably associated with all products. Material cost was considered for the cutting department, but no logical relationship could be established between the material costs of the products and the manufacturing overhead used in their production. For example, one product requiring a small amount of processing but made with high-priced material would have been charged with far more than its fair share of manufacturing overhead.

As shown in the lower part of the preceding Manufacturing Overhead Distribution Sheet, the basis selected to apportion departmental manufacturing overhead costs caused departmental manufacturing overhead rates to be established as follows:

Cutting Department	$16.90 per machine hour
Assembling Department	$4.4924 per labor hour
Finishing Department	147.88% per labor dollar

Using these departmental cost rates, manufacturing overhead costs may be traced to a given unit of product by ascertaining and employing relevant product data. For example, if a product required twelve minutes in the cutting department, twenty minutes in the assembling department, and one dollar of labor cost in the finishing department, its manufacturing overhead cost would be $6.3563, computed as follows:

Cutting Department:	Twelve minutes × $16.90 per machine hour =	$3.38
Assembling Department:	Twenty minutes × $4.4924 per labor hour =	1.4975
Finishing Department:	One dollar labor cost × 147.88% =	1.4788
Total manufacturing overhead cost		$6.3563

The use of a manufacturing overhead distribution procedure provides a convenient arrangement for apportioning manufacturing overhead to the various products worked on in each department. Such a distribution sheet, however, cannot be prepared until the end of the period, after the total cost of each manufacturing overhead expense item has been ascertained. This means that the manufacturing overhead applicable to each unit of product manufactured during a period cannot be determined until the end of the period. Under process costing, when production is for warehouse stock, this timing presents little difficulty. Under job order costing, when production is for customer order and a job may be completed and shipped in the early part of a period, it is impractical to wait until the end of the period to find out what the job costs. Proper control of cost is impossible if management has to wait long after a job is completed to learn the cost of a job. Instead, it is advantageous to charge a finished job at the time it is completed with a reasonable share of manufacturing overhead so that the total cost of the job becomes available immediately. How can this be done when the actual amount of these expenses is often not known until the end of the period?

Jobs can be charged with manufacturing overhead at any time by predetermined applicable manufacturing overhead rates for each department. This requires that an estimate of departmental expenses and related activity be made before a period begins. Then, the estimated departmental expenses divided by the estimated activity measure will provide a predetermined manufacturing overhead rate. A problem arises, however, as to how to make reliable estimates. One approach is to determine the individual expense-activity relationship which has existed in the past, and then to project this relationship for the level of activity expected in the future. If events which invalidate the historical relationship have occurred, adjustments should be made to correct those expenses that are involved. After the total amount of each manufacturing overhead expense has been estimated for a period, all manufacturing overhead expenses should be assigned and distributed to service and producing departments and then apportioned to estimated activity measures as they previously were on the manufacturing overhead distribution sheet. Since this action is taken before a period commences, not at the end of a period, a manufacturing overhead budget, rather than a manufacturing overhead distribution sheet, is prepared.

Through predetermined rates, manufacturing overhead can be charged whenever the machine hours, direct labor hours, direct labor cost, or other applicable activity measure is known. Practicality, however, usually demands that such charges be made either weekly or monthly and when the job is completed. In this manner, manufacturing overhead charges can be made in a convenient and orderly fashion and still enable the manufacturing overhead applicable to a job to be known when the job is finished.

In any accounting period, the predetermined manufacturing overhead charged to production will equal the actual manufacturing overhead only if the estimated activity and manufacturing expenses were predicted with absolute accuracy, an unlikely occurrence. The difference between the manufacturing overhead charged and that which is actually incurred is considered to be *underapplied* if the actual manufacturing overhead is larger, *overapplied* if the actual manufacturing overhead is smaller. The disposition, as well as the usefulness of such information, will be explained in the next chapter.

QUESTIONS AND PROBLEMS

10-1. Identify *four* methods or bases used in applying or allocating manufacuring overhead costs. What are the advantages *and* disadvantages of each method?

(Adapted from Uniform CPA Examination)

10-2. Michigan Manufacturing Company manufactures and sells product "A". The following facts were taken from their books and records as of December 31, 1972:

Cash	$ 36,000
Accounts Receivable	72,000
Inventory of Raw Materials, 1/1/72	12,000
Inventory of Work in Process, 1/1/72	14,000
Inventory of Finished Goods, 1/1/72	10,000
Inventory of Raw Materials, 12/31/72	16,000
Inventory of Work in Process, 12/31/72	8,000
Inventory of Finished Goods, 12/31/72	18,000
Plant and Machinery	360,000
Accumulated Depreciation on Plant and Machinery	46,000
Accounts Payable	15,700
Accrued Taxes Payable	300
Capital Stock	400,000
Retained Earnings, 1/1/72	67,200
Sales	440,000
Sales Returns and Allowances	4,000
Purchases of Raw Materials	242,000
Transportation In	6,000
Purchase Returns and Allowances	2,000
Direct Labor	100,000
Indirect Labor	10,000
Property Taxes—Factory	2,000
Depreciation on Plant and Machinery	18,000
Light, Heat, and Power	10,000
Repairs to Machinery	1,000
Payroll Taxes—Factory	6,000
Factory Supplies Used	4,000
Advertising	1,200
Transportation Out	2,000
Salesmen's Salaries	34,000
Payroll Taxes (Selling 2,000; Office 1,400)	3,400
Office Salaries	20,000
Office Expenses	4,000
Loss on Sale of Machinery	400
Gain on Sale of Equipment	800

Note: Apportion Light, Heat, and Power as follows:
  60% to manufacturing
  20% to selling
  20% to office

Required

Prepare the following:

a. Statement of Cost of Goods Manufactured for the year ended December 31, 1972.

[CH. 10] FRAMEWORK OF MANUFACTURING COSTS 349

b. Statement of Income and Retained Earnings for the year ended December 31, 1972.
c. Balance Sheet as of December 31, 1972.

10-3. The following facts were taken from the books and records of the Denver Rug Company as of December 31, 1972:

Cash	$ 10,000
Accounts Receivable	15,000
Inventory, Raw Materials, 1/1/72	3,000
Inventory, Work in Process, 1/1/72	2,000
Inventory, Finished Goods, 1/1/72	4,000
Inventory, Raw Materials, 12/31/72	6,000
Inventory, Work in Process, 12/31/72	1,000
Inventory, Finished Goods, 12/31/72	2,000
Depreciation of Plant and Equipment	5,000
Direct Labor	25,000
Indirect Labor	3,000
Factory Supplies Used	3,000
Light, Heat, and Power—Factory	4,000
Repairs to Machinery	600
Sales Salaries	9,000
Capital Stock	106,000
Retained Earnings, 1/1/72	15,800
Sales	120,000
Sales Returns and Allowances	1,700
Sales Discounts	500
Purchases, Raw Materials	60,000
Purchase Discounts	1,200
Transportation In	1,500
Retained Earnings, 12/31/72	?
Plant and Equipment	100,000
Accumulated Depreciation of Plant and Equipment	15,000
Shipping Expenses	1,200
Advertising	500
Administrative Salaries	8,000
Office Expenses	1,000
Dividends Declared	–0–

Required

Prepare the following:

a. Statement of Cost of Goods Manufactured for the year ended December 31, 1972.
b. Statement of Income for the year ended December 31, 1972. Show clearly the determination of the cost of goods sold either in the body of the statement or by an attached schedule.
c. Statement of Retained Earnings for the year ended December 31, 1972.
d. Balance Sheet as of December 31, 1972.

350 COST ACCOUNTING CONCEPTS [CH. 10]

10-4. Ratliff Manufacturing Corporation prepared the following statement of income (with the cost of production data incorporated therein instead of being shown as a separate statement) at the end of its first year in business:

RATLIFF MANUFACTURING CORPORATION
Statement of Income
For the Year Ended December 31, 1972

Sales		$900,000
Less: Cost of Goods Sold:		
Cost of Goods Manufactured:		
Purchases, Raw Materials	$300,000	
Inventory, Raw Materials, December 31	60,000	
Cost of Raw Materials Used	$240,000	
Direct Labor	200,000	
Manufacturing Overhead Cost	160,000	
Charges to Production	$600,000	
Inventory, Work in Process, December 31	40,000	
Cost of Goods Manufactured	$560,000	
Inventory, Finished Goods, December 31	60,000	
Cost of Goods Sold		500,000
Gross Margin on Sales		$400,000
Marketing and Administrative Expenses		150,000
Net Operating Income		$250,000
Other Income:		
Purchase Discounts on Raw Materials Purchased		6,000
Net Income for Year Before Income Taxes		$256,000

The analysis of the cost elements contained in the December 31 inventories is as follows:

	Raw Materials	Work in Process	Finished Goods
Raw Materials	$60,000	$20,000	$25,000
Direct Labor	—	12,000	20,000
Manufacturing Overhead	—	8,000	15,000
	$60,000	$40,000	$60,000

All raw materials purchased during the year were charged into inventory at *gross* cost, $300,000. All such purchases were subject to a 2 percent discount. In every instance, the invoices for the purchased materials were paid within the discount period. The discounts were treated as a source of miscellaneous income.

Required

Assume that the company suddenly decides at year end that such cash discounts are *not* income but, in reality, a savings. As a savings, such discounts

[CH. 10] FRAMEWORK OF MANUFACTURING COSTS 351

are in effect a reduction in the cost of the purchase of raw materials. Prepare a revised statement of income for the year. Charge all raw materials purchased into inventory at *net* cost and revise all subsequently affected items on the statement.

10-5. Bryan Manufacturing Company manufactures and sells a small electric motor. From the company's books and other records, the following data were taken on December 31, 1972:

	Jan. 1, 1972	Dec. 31, 1972
Inventory of Raw Materials	$16,000	$18,500
Inventory of Goods in Process	12,500	18,500
Inventory of Finished Goods	24,000	?
Sales @ $30 each		$533,250
Sales Returns		4,500
Cost of Goods Sold		370,125
Direct Labor		140,000
Factory Expenses, Miscellaneous		7,000
Indirect Labor		42,000
Purchases, Raw Materials		162,400
Purchase Returns and Allowances		1,400
Freight In, Raw Materials		1,500
Depreciation of Plant and Equipment		19,000
Heat, Light and Power—Factory		21,000
Indirect Materials		16,000

Note: The unit cost of production in 1971 was $20. On December 31, 1972, the inventory of finished goods included 200 units produced in 1971 and 12½ percent of the units produced in 1972.

Required

a. Statement of Cost of Production (Cost of Goods Manufactured) for the year 1972.

b. Statement of Income as far as gross margin on sales. State the method of costing used for the inventory of finished goods (FIFO, LIFO, or specific identification).

10-6. Estes Company manufactures and sells a large electric toy. From the company's books and other records, the following data are taken on December 31, 1972:

Inventory of Finished Goods, January 1, 1972	$ 72,000
Royalties Paid	18,000
Sales Allowances	2,000
Sales Returns	12,000
Sales	660,000
Inventory of Finished Goods, December 31, 1972	?
Cost of Production	468,000

The inventory of finished goods on hand January 1, 1972, totaled 6,000 units, of which 600 still remain on hand at the end of 1972. A royalty of $.50 is paid the holder of the basic patent for every toy manufactured. The selling price of each electric toy is $20, and all sales returns are at the same price.

Required

a. Determine the cost of the inventory of finished goods as of December 31, 1972. Show all computations. (Assume specific identification method.)
b. Prepare a statement of income through gross profit on sales.

10-7. The Howe Manufacturing Company is engaged in manufacturing items to fill specific orders received from its customers. While at any given time it may have substantial inventories of work in process and finished goods, all such amounts are assignable to firm sales orders which it has received.

The company's operations, including the administrative and sales functions, are completely departmentalized. Its cost system is on a job order basis. Direct materials and direct labor are identified with jobs by the use of material issue tickets and daily time cards. Overhead costs are accumulated for each factory service, administrative and selling department. These overhead costs, including administrative and selling expense, are then allocated to productive departments and an overhead rate computed for each productive department. This rate is used to apply overhead to jobs on the basis of direct labor hours. The result is that all costs and expenses incurred during any month are charged to work-in-process accounts for the jobs.

Required

a. Compare this system, as it affects inventory valuation, with the usual system for manufacturing businesses.
b. Criticize the system as it affects inventory valuation and income determination.
c. State any justification which you see for the use of the Howe Company's system.

(Adapted from Uniform CPA Examination)

10-8. The Baker Manufacturing Company maintains a job order cost system. On January 1, 1972, the only work in process was job 1270 on which the following costs had been accumulated:

Direct material	$15,000
Direct labor	25,000
Manufacturing overhead	10,000
Total	$50,000

On the same date, the company's books showed a raw materials inventory of $380,000 and job 1269 which had been completed at a cost of $74,000. During the month of January the manufacturing data are:

(1)

Job No.	Direct Material	Direct Labor
1270	$ 60,000	$200,000
1271	100,000	300,000
1272	110,000	220,000
	$270,000	$720,000

(2) In addition $25,000 of raw materials are issued as indirect material, indirect laborers earn $75,000, and the factory superintendent earns $5,000.

(3) Manufacturing overhead incurred exclusive of material issues and factory payroll costs:

Power	$30,000
Depreciation on plant and equipment	95,000
Maintenance	25,000
Insurance	15,000
Taxes	10,000
Miscellaneous	5,000

(4) Manufacturing overhead is applied to jobs by use of a predetermined rate of 40 percent of direct labor costs. Overapplied or underapplied manufacturing overhead is closed to cost of goods sold.

(5) Jobs 1270 and 1271 are completed during the month. Jobs 1269 and 1270 are shipped and billed to customers during January at 200 percent of the cost of production.

Required

a. Determine, in itemized form, the individual total costs of each of the jobs as of the end of January.

b. Calculate the dollar amount for each of the three inventories on January 31, 1972.

c. Prepare the Statement of Cost of Goods Manufactured for the period ending January 31, 1972.

d. Prepare the Statement of Income through the gross margin on sales for the month of January.

10-9. The Incredible Gadget Corp. manufactures a single product. Its operations are a continuing process carried on in two departments—the Machining department and the Assembly and finishing department. *Materials are added to the product in each department without increasing the number of units produced.*

In the month of May 1972, the records showed that 75,000 units were put in production in the machining department. Of these units, 60,000 were completed and transferred to assembly and finishing, and 15,000 were left in process with all materials applied but with only one-third of the required labor and manufacturing overhead.

In the assembly and finishing department 50,000 units were completed and transferred to the finished stock room during the month. Nine thousand units were in process on May 31, 1,000 units having been destroyed in production with no scrap value. All required materials had been applied to the 9,000 units and two-thirds of the labor and manufacturing overhead, but only one-half of the prescribed material and labor had been applied to the 1,000 units lost in process.

There was no work-in-process in either department at the first of the month.

354 COST ACCOUNTING CONCEPTS [CH. 10]

The cost of units lost in production should be treated as additional manufacturing overhead in the assembly and finishing department.

Cost records showed the following charges during the month:

	Materials	Labor	Manufacturing Overhead
Machining department	$120,000	$ 87,100	$39,000
Assembly and finishing department	41,650	101,700	56,810*

* Does not include the cost of spoiled units

Required

a. Prepare in good form a statement showing the unit cost for the month.

b. Prepare a schedule showing the details of the work-in-process inventory in each department.

(Adapted from Uniform CPA Examination)

10-10. You are engaged in an audit of the ABC Manufacturing Company's financial statements as of December 31, 1972, and are verifying the pricing of the company's inventory of work-in-process and finished goods which is recorded on the company's books as follows:

Finished goods inventory, 110,000 units $504,900
Work-in-process inventory, 90,000 units, 50% completed 330,480

The company follows the practice of pricing the above inventories at the lower of cost or market on a first-in, first-out method. You learn that materials are added to the production line at the start of the process, and that manufacturing overhead is applied to the product at the rate of 75 percent based on direct labor dollars. You also learn that the market value of the finished goods inventory and the work-in-process inventory is greater than the amounts shown above, with the exception of the defective units in the ending inventory of finished goods, the market value of which amounts to $1.00 per unit.

A review of the company's cost records shows the following information:

		Amounts	
	Units	Materials	Labor
Beginning inventory, January 1, 1972, 80% completed	100,000	$100,000	$160,000
Additional units started in 1972	500,000		
Material costs incurred		550,000	
Labor costs incurred			997,500
Units completed in 1972—			
Good units	500,000		
Defective units	10,000		
Finished goods inventory at December 31, 1972, includes 10,000 defective units			

[CH. 10]   FRAMEWORK OF MANUFACTURING COSTS   355

You also learn that the defective units occur at the end of the process, i.e., units are found to be defective at the point of final inspection.

Required

Prepare schedules indicating:

a. Effective or equivalent production.
b. Unit costs of production of materials, labor and manufacturing overhead.
c. Pricing of inventories of finished goods, defective units, and work-in-process; indicate apparent amounts by which inventories are overvalued.

(Adapted from Uniform CPA Examination)

10-11. Crews Company produces a chemical agent for commercial use. The Company accounts for production in two cost centers: (1) Cooking and (2) Mix-Pack. In the first cost center liquid substances are combined in large cookers and boiled; the boiling causes a normal decrease in volume from evaporation. After the "batch" is cooked, it is transferred to Mix-Pack, the second cost center. The "batch" then has a quantity of alcohol added equal to the liquid measure of the "batch," is mixed, and bottled in one-gallon containers.

Material is added at the beginning of production in each cost center and labor is added equally during production in each cost center. Manufacturing overhead is applied on the basis of 80 percent of labor cost. The method of neglect is used in accounting for lost units (that is, all costs are allocated only to equivalent good units); the process is "in control" so long as the yield ratio for the first department is not less than 78 percent.

The FIFO method is used to cost work-in-process inventories, and transfers are at an average unit cost, i.e., the total cost transferred divided by the total number of units transferred.

The following information is available for the month of October 1972:

Cost Information	Cooking	Mix-Pack
Work in process, October 1, 1972		
Materials	$ 990	$ 120
Labor	100	60
Prior department cost		426
Month of October		
Materials	39,600	15,276
Labor	10,050	16,000

Inventory and production records show that Cooking had 1,000 gallons 40 percent processed on October 1 and 800 gallons 50 percent processed on October 31; Mix-Pack had 600 gallons 50 percent processed on October 1 and 1,000 gallons 30 percent processed on October 31.

Production reports for October show that Cooking started 50,000 gallons into production and completed and transferred 40,200 gallons to Mix-Pack, and Mix-Pack completed and transferred 80,000 one-gallon containers of the finished product to the distribution warehouse.

Required

a. Prepare in good form a quantity report for the Cooking cost center and for the Mix-Pack cost center which accounts for both actual units and equivalent unit production.

b. Prepare in good form a Production Cost Report for each of the two cost centers which computes total cost and cost per unit for each element of cost in inventories and October production. Total cost and cost per unit for transfers should also be computed.

c. Compute the yield ratio for Cooking and state whether or not the process was "in control" during October.

(Adapted from Uniform CPA Examination)

10-12. The Roberts Manufacturing Company has three producing departments—A, B, C—and two service departments—maintenance and factory office. The company has been using a single manufacturing overhead cost rate. The management has been aware of the deficiencies of using such a rate and is now interested in developing departmental manufacturing overhead rates.

Manufacturing overhead costs direct to departments for the period ending December 31, 1972 are:

		Producing Departments			Service Departments	
Direct Costs	Total	Dept. A	Dept. B	Dept. C	Maintenance	Factory Office
Indirect labor	$54,000	$5,000	$11,000	$10,000	$15,400	$12,600
Foremen salaries	25,000	2,700	6,000	5,000	5,500	5,800
Depreciation—equipment	6,000	2,000	1,000	2,000	800	200
Indirect material	3,000	1,100	900	500	200	300
Compensation insurance	1,000	100	200	200	300	200
Telephone	300					300

Manufacturing overhead costs that require allocation are:

Superintendent's salary	$12,000
Rent	15,000
Power	12,000
Light	1,000
Fire Insurance—equipment	2,000

The following data are available:

		Producing Departments			Service Departments	
Factor	Amount	Dept. A	Dept. B	Dept. C	Maintenance	Factory Office
Square footage	30,000	6,000	10,000	9,000	2,000	3,000
No. of employees	120	20	50	30	10	10
Equipment cost	$50,000	$20,000	$5,000	$22,500	$1,000	$1,500
Horsepower hours	60,000	25,000	10,000	20,000	5,000	none
Maintenance hours	5,460	2,400	460	2,600		
Kilowatt hours	5,000	2,000	500	2,000	300	200
Direct labor hours	240,000	50,000	100,000	90,000		

Most of the efforts of the Factory Office Department are devoted to records concerning employees. The Maintenance Department does not serve the Factory Office Department.

Required

a. Prepare a manufacturing overhead distribution sheet distributing, where applicable, service departments to appropriate service and/or producing departments.
b. Calculate the departmental manufacturing overhead costing rates per direct labor hour.
c. Compare the use of departmental manufacturing overhead rates with the practice of using a single manufacturing overhead rate for the Roberts Manufacturing Company.

(Adapted from Uniform CPA Examination)

11

Behavior, Flow, and Classification of Production Costs

Management needs manufacturing cost data for planning and controlling current operations. For cost information to be available when needed, a means of communicating it must be established. One of the most effective vehicles for conveying cost information to management is an informative financial report or statement. Financial reports, however, must be designed for maximum clarity and use by management, or they will fail to accomplish their purpose. On the other hand, management must be aware of the influences, concepts, and classifications underlying the costs contained on financial reports if it is to appraise plans effectively or establish and maintain policies to control operations. It is the purpose of this chapter to examine some of the factors influencing manufacturing costs; to show how financial statements reflect different types of cost flows; and to analyze certain fundamental cost classifications.

COST BEHAVIOR

Certain costs tend to remain unchanged in amount regardless of the volume of activity or production, while others tend to vary in proportion to changes in activity. Unless this distinction is recognized and given due consideration, cost accumulations and analyses may inadequately inform those in management who use such data. Knowledge of this distinction depends upon an understanding of *activity variations* and the *variability of costs*.

When the volume of production is homogeneous, activity can be measured by quantities of physical output. For instance, the activity or volume of a single product plant can be measured by the number of units produced. But, if production is so heterogeneous that output in units is not a suitable measure, it is necessary to select some common denominator by which all types of physical output can be reduced to comparable measurement. Commonly used measurement bases are direct labor hours, machine hours, and direct labor cost.

A most significant characteristic of cost variability is that *total* manufacturing costs do not tend to vary in direct proportion to changes in aggregate activity, while direct material and direct labor costs do. This fact, combined with the knowledge that direct material and direct labor costs also tend to vary in proportion to productive output, suggests that changes in all or a part of the remaining element of manufacturing cost (manufacturing overhead costs) correlate more closely with some factor other than production volume. This suggestion implies that additional factors must be used to establish the degree of variability existing among those costs comprising manufacturing overhead.

In a typical manufacturing enterprise, manufacturing overhead costs can be divided into at least two principal categories of variability:

1. Costs which tend to fluctuate in proportion to the total volume of production, but are not ordinarily identified as being generated by any specific unit of output. Such costs tend to be a function of productive activity; they display characteristics of variability similar to those associated with direct material and direct labor costs. Consequently, these costs may be classified as variable manufacturing overhead costs.
2. Costs which tend to be constant in total amount within a specified range of productive volume. Since this range ordinarily covers a period of time within which management expects production to be handled by existing facilities and organization, these costs may be considered a function of time instead of productive activity. Some such costs are fixed because of their inherent nature; others are fixed by the action of management. Regardless of whether their fixity results from inherent qualities or is a matter of managerial decision, these costs may be classified as fixed or non-variable manufacturing overhead costs.

Some costs do not fall precisely into either category, because they possess both fixed and variable characteristics. Consequently, the fixed component of this type of cost may be included in the fixed category, while the variable component may be combined with other costs comprising the variable category. These costs are described as semi-variable manufacturing costs.

An understanding of the role played by both variable and fixed manufacturing overhead costs is a vital prerequisite to proper interpretations of cost data. The total amount of a variable cost like indirect materials tends to change with the volume of production, but the cost per unit tends to remain constant. Fixed costs like depreciation, property taxes, and fire insurance react in an opposite manner; though the total amount is constant, the cost per unit tends to vary inversely with the volume of production. Total manufacturing overhead cost is a composite of variable, fixed, and semi-variable components, and consequently, it possesses an overall semi-variable character.

COST FLOW

Exhibits 11–1, 11–2, and 11–3 emphasize the significance of the cost-volume relationship under each of three different types of cost flows. Through holding all other cost determinants constant during two months of operations, the influence of a change in volume is isolated in each instance. The two months of activity illustrated by each model are based upon the following assumptions:

1. A single product is manufactured.
2. 10,000 units of product represent the normal monthly volume of production.
3. Production is continuous mass production.
4. Unit selling price is a constant $5.00 amount throughout the two-month period.
5. No inventory is on hand as of January 1.
6. During January, 10,000 units are produced, and 8,000 units are sold. Production costs are:

Direct material	$10,000
Direct labor	10,000
Variable manufacturing overhead costs	6,000
Fixed manufacturing overhead costs	4,000

7. During February, 5,000 units are produced, and 4,000 units are sold. Production costs are:
    a. All variable costs are "perfect" variables and equal 50 percent of the amount of total variable costs in January, since production volume has been reduced by one-half.
    b. Total fixed costs of $4,000 remain unchanged from the amount incurred in January.

Exhibit 11–1 traces the cost flow and shows the effect upon financial statements of manufacturing costs which are generated by the operation of an actual cost system. In January, the $30,000 cost of production divided by the 10,000 units produced provides a $3.00 average unit cost of production. Since there was no beginning inventory, the $3.00 unit cost of production becomes the unit cost of goods sold on the January statement of income. The $16,000 gross margin in January results from selling 8,000 units which cost $3.00 apiece ($24,000) for $5.00 per unit ($40,000). The 2,000 unsold units times their

$3.00 unit cost become the $6,000 inventory shown on the balance sheet as of January 31.

In February, the 50 percent reduction in productive activity reduces the cost of production to $17,000. This amount divided by the 5,000 units produced provides an average unit cost of production of $3.40, which is $.40 greater than the unit cost of production in January. This increase occurs because the $4,000 of fixed manufacturing overhead was apportioned to 10,000 units in January, while it is apportioned to only 5,000 units in February. None of this increase is attributable to the variable costs, because the unit cost of direct material, direct labor, and variable manufacturing overhead is identical in both months. When the 5,000 units costing $3.40 apiece are combined with the 2,000 units in the beginning inventory which cost $3.00 apiece, 7,000 units, costing a total of $23,000, are available for sale during February. The company uses a weighted average unit cost of $3.286 to cost both the 3,000 units on hand on February 28 and the 4,000 units which are sold during the month.[1]

A comparison of the two income statements reveals that the rate of gross margin has decreased from 40 percent in January to 34 percent in February. How could this unfavorable development occur when, in both months, exactly 80 percent of the units produced are sold, the selling price remains constant, the variable unit costs are identical, and the total fixed costs remain unchanged? The answer to this question is found in the only factor which does change, and this is volume. Volume is solely responsible for the variance in the gross profit rate.

Furthermore, a comparison of the two balance sheets reveals that the cost assigned to the inventory in February has increased disproportionately to the increased number of units in the inventory. The $6,000 inventory has increased 64 percent to $9,858, while the number of units in the inventory has increased from 2,000 to 3,000, or only 50 percent. How should a plant manager interpret this phenomenon? Should he assume that the units in inventory are worth more because of the relative scarcity of units due to February's decreased production, that the value assigned to the inventory is unduly inflated, or that idle plant costs have been included in the valuation of an asset on the balance sheet?

Exhibit 11–1 and this discussion indicate that while all other factors remain constant a change in volume of productive activity may cause certain financial statements to hinder, rather than aid, management's appraisal of operating conditions. This confusing situation may be alleviated by using alternative costing methods which will isolate the effect of volume changes. Such alternative methods include:

1. A historical (actual) cost system which utilizes a normal manufacturing overhead rate.

---

[1] Weighted average unit cost $= \dfrac{\$23{,}000 \text{ (Cost of goods available for sale)}}{7{,}000 \text{ (No. of units available for sale)}} = \$3.286$

EXHIBIT 11-1

Flow of Costs
Actual Cost System

MONTH OF JANUARY

Cost of Production

Direct Material	$10,000
Direct Labor	10,000
Manufacturing Overhead:	
Variable	6,000
Fixed	4,000
Cost of Production	$30,000

Unit Cost of Production:
$30,000 ÷ 10,000 units = $3.00

Statement of Income

Sales (8,000 units × $5.00)		$40,000
Cost of Goods Sold:		
Cost of Production (10,000 × $3.00)	$30,000	
Less: Inventory,		
January 31 (2,000 × 3.00)	6,000	
Cost of Goods Sold (8,000 × 3.00)		24,000
Gross Margin on Sales		$16,000
Less: Operating Expenses:		
Marketing Expenses	$ 4,000	
Administrative Expenses	1,000	5,000
Net Operating Income		$11,000

Rate of Gross Margin:
$16,000 ÷ $40,000 = 40%

Balance Sheet
As of January 31

ASSETS
Current Assets:
  Inventory $6,000

Exhibit 11-1 (Continued)

MONTH OF FEBRUARY

Cost of Production

Direct Material	$ 5,000
Direct Labor	5,000
Manufacturing Overhead:	
Variable	3,000
Fixed	4,000
	$17,000

Unit Cost of Production:
$17,000 ÷ 5,000 units = $3.40

Statement of Income

Sales (4,000 units × $5.00)			$20,000
Cost of Goods Sold:			
Inventory, Feb. 1	(2,000 × $3.00)	$ 6,000	
Cost of Production	(5,000 × 3.40)	17,000	
Cost of Goods			
Available for Sale	(7,000 × 3.286)	$23,000	
Inventory, Feb. 28	(3,000 × 3.286)	9,858	
Cost of Goods Sold	(4,000 × 3.286)		13,142
Gross Margin on Sales			$ 6,858
Less: Operating Expenses:			
Marketing Expenses		$4,000	
Administrative Expenses		1,000	5,000
Net Operating Income			$ 1,858

Rate of Gross Margin:
$6,858 ÷ $20,000 = 34%

Balance Sheet
As of February 28

ASSETS
Current Assets:
Inventory $9,858

2. A historical (actual) cost system which utilizes the theory of direct costing.
3. A predetermined (standard) cost system which may, or may not, utilize direct costing theory.

Alternative 1. will be presented by Exhibit 11–2 and the accompanying discussion. Exhibit 11–3, accompanied by a related explanation, will present alternative 2. A discussion of the third alternative, however, has been reserved for Chapter 14.

To prevent widely fluctuating unit costs due to volume changes from affecting the usefulness of cost data contained on financial statements and other reports, the effect of volume upon unit costs must be isolated. Variable costs, which tend to change in proportion to production volume, present little difficulty. Fixed costs, which tend to be constant in total amount regardless of volume, are the crux of the problem. For example, if fixed manufacturing overhead costs amount to $10,000 and one unit of product is produced, the fixed manufacturing overhead applicable to this unit is $10,000; if 5,000 units are produced, the unit manufacturing overhead cost would be only $2.00. Consequently, when activity fluctuates from period to period, changes in unit costs will occur unless fixed costs are stabilized per unit regardless of the volume of activity. Constant fixed manufacturing overhead costs per unit can be obtained by dividing the estimated annual total amount of such costs by the estimated annual volume of production, and then using the derived unit fixed manufacturing overhead cost to cost each unit produced throughout the year. This calculation provides an estimated or normal fixed manufacturing overhead unit rate and will accomplish two important objectives: first, the elimination of changes in unit cost which are due solely to changes in the volume of production; and second, the provision of a predetermined fixed manufacturing overhead rate which, when combined with a predetermined variable manufacturing overhead rate, may be used for costing at any time during a period. In our illustration, the fixed manufacturing overhead amounts to $4,000 a month ($48,000 a year), while the normal volume of activity is 10,000 units a month (120,000 units per year). A normal fixed manufacturing overhead rate would be calculated as follows:

$$\text{Normal fixed manufacturing overhead rate} = \frac{\$48,000}{120,000 \text{ units}} = \$.40 \text{ per unit}$$

Exhibit 11–2 traces the flow of manufacturing costs through the pertinent financial statements when a normal fixed manufacturing overhead rate is used in conjunction with an otherwise actual cost system. It discloses, for the month of January, results identical to those shown in Exhibit 11–1, because January is a month of normal productive volume. Thus, in Exhibit 11–2, the fixed manufacturing overhead charged to production by the normal fixed manufacturing overhead rate ($.40 × 10,000 = $4,000) is identical to the actual amount of fixed manufacturing overhead charged to production in Exhibit 11–1.

In February, however, the two exhibits show different financial "results." Exhibit 11–1 shows fixed manufacturing overhead of $4,000 and a unit cost of $3.40, while Exhibit 11–2 shows fixed manufacturing overhead of only $2,000 and a unit cost of $3.00. Exhibit 11–2 has the same unit cost of production in each month, because a normal fixed manufacturing overhead rate per unit is employed. The statements of income in Exhibit 11–2 show the same rate of gross margin for both months; while the amount of February's gross margin is exactly one-half of January's, when twice as many units were produced and sold. Furthermore, none of the fixed manufacturing overhead costs in excess of $.40 per unit are placed into February's ending inventory amount as they were in Exhibit 11–1 when a normal manufacturing overhead rate was not employed. Thus, the use of a normal fixed manufacturing overhead rate eliminates the unit cost deviations which are caused by a change in volume when actual fixed manufacturing overhead costs are used,[2] and the rate of gross margin and the unit cost for inventory are the same in each period regardless of the level of activity.

Although the use of a normal fixed manufacturing overhead rate resolves unit cost difficulties which result from fluctuating activity, it creates another complexity when the actual and estimated volume of production are not identical. For example, in Exhibit 11–2, the fixed manufacturing overhead rate of $.40 is predicated on a production volume of 10,000 units. Since 10,000 units are produced in January, the fixed manufacturing overhead applied to production is equal to the actual fixed manufacturing overhead. But, when 5,000 units are produced in February, only $2,000 (5,000 units × $.40) of fixed manufacturing overhead is applied to production. This means $2,000 of the actual fixed manufacturing overhead of $4,000 has not been absorbed as a production cost. Obviously, this condition would exist any time that actual and estimated activity differ. If actual exceeds estimated activity, then normal manufacturing overhead costs are overapplied; if estimated exceeds actual activity, then normal manufacturing overhead costs are underapplied. In Exhibit 11–2, the underapplied fixed manufacturing overhead represents a monetary measure of the extent to which estimated capacity was not used (e.g., the $2,000 of underapplied fixed manufacturing overhead divided by the $.40 normal fixed manufacturing overhead unit rate provides the number of units of normal production which were not produced).

In Exhibit 11–2, the $2,000 of underapplied manufacturing overhead for February is deducted from the gross margin on sales to obtain an adjusted gross margin. (A variation of this method would provide an adjusted cost of goods sold through adding the underapplied manufacturing overhead to the initial cost of goods sold.) As a result, the net income for the month of Febru-

---

[2] In Exhibit 11–2 a normal rate is used for fixed manufacturing overhead costs, while the actual amount is used for variable manufacturing overhead costs. Variable costs are not normalized, because they tend to vary in proportion to activity. They could, however, be completely normalized by the use of an overall normal manufacturing overhead rate. For example, if normal variable manufacturing overhead costs are $6,000, then $.60 per unit could be used as a normal rate for variable manufacturing overhead costs as $.40 is used for fixed costs. Moreover, the separate variable and fixed manufacturing overhead rates could be combined into one overall normal rate which would also avoid unit cost deviations caused by a change in operating activity.

EXHIBIT 11-2
Flow of Costs
Actual Cost System with Normal Fixed Manufacturing Overhead Rate

Cost of Production

Direct Material	$10,000
Direct Labor	10,000
Manufacturing Overhead:	
Variable	6,000
Fixed	4,000
Cost of Production	$30,000

Unit Cost of Production
$30,000 ÷ 10,000 units = $3.00

MONTH OF JANUARY
Statement of Income

Sales (8,000 units × $5.00)			$40,000
Cost of Goods Sold:			
Cost of Production (10,000 × $3.00)	$30,000		
Less: Inventory, January 31 (2,000 × 3.00)	6,000		
Cost of Goods Sold (8,000 × 3.00)			24,000
Gross Margin on Sales			$16,000
Less: Operating Expenses:			
Marketing Expenses		$4,000	
Administrative Expenses		1,000	5,000
Net Operating Income			$11,000

Rate of Gross Margin:
$16,000 ÷ $40,000 = 40%

Balance Sheet
As of January 31

ASSETS
Current Assets:
  Inventory $6,000

Exhibit 11–2 (Continued)

MONTH OF FEBRUARY

Cost of Production

Direct Material		$ 5,000
Direct Labor		5,000
Manufacturing Overhead:		
Variable	3,000	
Fixed	2,000	
Cost of Production		$15,000

Unit Cost of Production:
$15,000 ÷ 5,000 units = $3.00

Statement of Income

Sales (4,000 units × $5.00)			$20,000
Cost of Goods Sold:			
Inventory, Feb. 1	(2,000 × $3.00)	$ 6,000	
Cost of Production	(5,000 × 3.00)	15,000	
Cost of Goods			
Available for Sale	(7,000 × 3.00)	$21,000	
Inventory, Feb. 28	(3,000 × 3.00)	9,000	
Cost of Goods Sold	(4,000 × 3.00)		12,000
Gross Margin on Sales			$ 8,000
Underapplied Fixed Manufacturing Overhead			2,000
Gross Margin on Sales (adjusted)			$ 6,000
Less: Operating Expenses:			
Marketing Expenses		$ 4,000	
Administrative Expenses		1,000	5,000
Net Operating Income			$ 1,000

Rate of Gross Margin:
$8,000 ÷ $20,000 = 40%

Rate of Gross Margin (adjusted):
$6,000 ÷ $20,000 = 30%

Balance Sheet
As of February 28

ASSETS
Current Assets:
  Inventory $9,000

ary is reduced by the total amount of the underapplied (idle capacity) cost. An alternative treatment would be to divide it between the finished goods inventory and the cost of goods sold in the proportion of the costs which originated in the current period that each contained. Another alternative would be to eliminate it from the statement of income and to defer it on the balance sheet in expectation that it would be offset by an overapplied amount in some succeeding month of the year. This latter alternative is not a generally accepted accounting procedure for annual financial statements, but it could be used for interim internal statements. Among these possibilities, the one actually used in Exhibit 11–2 and the one which converts an initial into an adjusted cost of goods sold are the procedures having the most widespread popularity.

The second alternative method proposed on page 364 for counteracting the effect of volume changes on unit costs is a historical (actual) cost system which utilizes direct costing. Exhibit 11–3 traces the flow of manufacturing costs when the theory of direct costing is employed, and shows the effect of direct costing upon both manufacturing costs and financial statements. But, before discussing Exhibit 11–3, a brief explanation of direct costing is necessary to introduce the theory, objectives, and methodology of this costing method.[3]

"Direct costing is a plan for providing management with information about cost-volume-profit relationships and for presenting this information in a form more readily understandable by management at all levels."[4] Under direct costing, only the direct, incremental, or out-of-pocket costs needed to produce an item comprise the manufacturing cost of production. As a result, the total cost of a manufactured item placed into inventory or transferred to cost of sales is an amount equal to the sum of the direct material, direct labor, and *variable* manufacturing overhead cost which is incurred in producing the item; it is the sum of those costs which would not have been incurred if an item had not been produced. Under direct costing, the cost of production is equal to the variable manufacturing costs incurred; the cost of production excludes all fixed manufacturing overhead costs. Direct costing is based upon the premise that fixed manufacturing overhead costs should be given the same treatment as that given to other fixed expenses. The question of whether fixed expenses belong to administration, distribution, or manufacturing is irrelevant, since they are all a function of time, and, as such, should be charged to operations during the period in which they are incurred. Following this line of thinking, fixed manufacturing overhead costs are removed from cost of production, inventory, and cost of sales. They are deducted currently on the income statement in a manner like the deduction for the fixed administrative and marketing expenses. The diagram on page 371 contrasts absorption costing with direct costing by showing the composition, calculation, and flow of cost of the same unit under both costing methods.

---

[3] See Chapter 14 for a more comprehensive discussion of direct costing.
[4] National Association of Cost Accountants, Research Series No. 23, *Direct Costing* (New York, 1953) p. 2.

EXHIBIT 11-3

Flow of Costs

Actual Cost System Utilizing Theory of "Direct Costing"

Cost of Production

Direct Material	$10,000
Direct Labor	10,000
Manufacturing Overhead:	
Variable	6,000
Cost of Production	$26,000

Unit Cost of Production:
$26,000 ÷ 10,000 units = $2.60

MONTH OF JANUARY
Statement of Income

Sales (8,000 units × $5.00)			$40,000
Cost of Goods Sold:			
Cost of Production	(10,000 × $2.60)	$26,000	
Less: Inventory, January 31	(2,000 × 2.60)	5,200	
Costs of Goods Sold	(8,000 × 2.60)		20,800
Manufacturing Margin			$19,200
Less: Variable Operating Expenses			—
Marginal Income			$19,200
Less: Fixed Expenses:			
Fixed Manufacturing Overhead		$ 4,000	
Fixed Operating Expenses		5,000	9,000
Net Operating Income			$10,200

Balance Sheet
As of January 31

ASSETS

Current Assets:

Inventory $5,200

Exhibit 11–3 (Continued)

MONTH OF FEBRUARY

Cost of Production

Direct Material	$ 5,000
Direct Labor	5,000
Manufacturing Overhead:	
Variable	3,000
Cost of Production	$13,000

Unit Cost of Production:
$13,000 ÷ 5,000 units = $2.60

Statement of Income

Sales (4,000 units × $5.00)			$20,000
Cost of Goods Sold:			
Inventory, Feb. 1	(2,000 × $2.60)	$ 5,200	
Cost of Production	(5,000 × 2.60)	13,000	
Cost of Goods			
Available for Sale	(7,000 × 2.60)	$18,200	
Inventory, Feb. 28	(3,000 × 2.60)	7,800	
Cost of Goods Sold	(4,000 × 2.60)		10,400
Manufacturing Margin			$ 9,600
Less: Variable Operating Expenses			—
Marginal Income			$ 9,600
Less: Fixed Expenses:			
Fixed Manufacturing Overhead		$ 4,000	
Fixed Operating Expenses		5,000	9,000
Net Operating Income			$ 600

Balance Sheet
As of February 28

ASSETS
Current Assets:
Inventory $7,800

	Absorption Costing	Direct Costing	
*Direct material	$1.00	$1.00	
*Direct labor	1.00	1.00	
Manufacturing overhead:			
*Variable	.60	.60	
**Fixed	.40	X ⟶	To statement of income in current period
	$3.00	$2.60	

*Function of Production

**Function of time

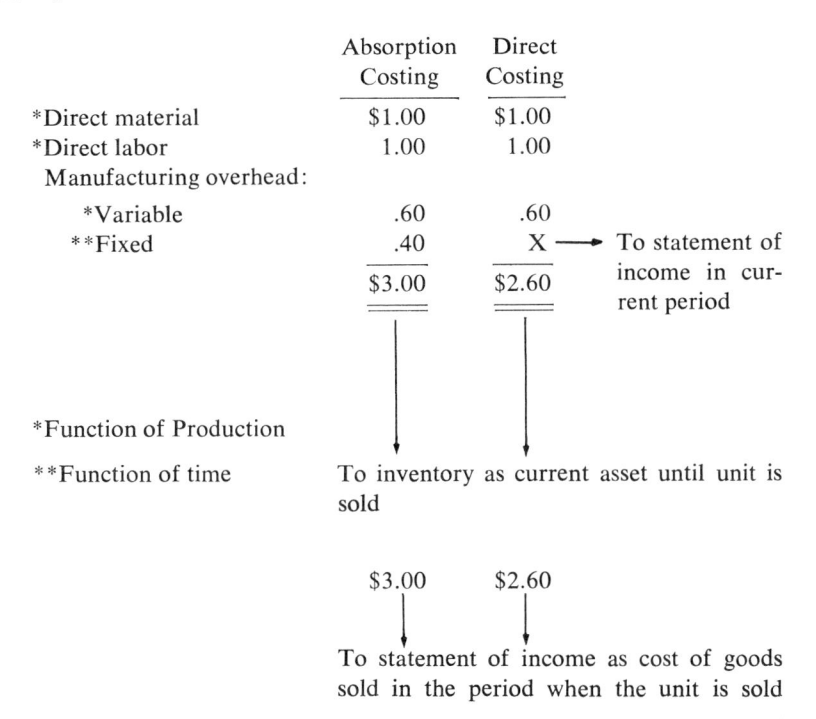

To inventory as current asset until unit is sold

$3.00 $2.60

To statement of income as cost of goods sold in the period when the unit is sold

Exhibit 11–3 shows how direct costing affects the flow of costs and related financial statements. Notice that none of the fixed manufacturing overhead costs are included in the cost of production, cost of sales, or inventory in either January or February. Instead, the $4,000 of fixed manufacturing overhead cost is deducted each month from marginal income on the statement of income. Marginal income is the difference between the revenue from sales and the variable costs of producing and selling the item sold. The relationship between marginal income and sales income cannot be changed by volume; it can only be changed by different variable costs or selling prices. For example, it is 48 percent in January when 10,000 units are sold, and it is 48 percent in February when only 5,000 units are sold. Contrast this stability in the percentage of marginal income with the percentages of gross margin in Exhibit 11–1, which were vulnerable to distortion by volume fluctuations. Observe that the amount of marginal income varies in direct proportion to sales volume, while the amount of gross margin is affected by both sales volume and production volume. Notice also that unit costs remain constant regardless of the volume of activity. Consequently, no idle plant costs can be included in the inventory on the balance sheet. Clearly, the inclusion of direct costing in an actual cost system rectifies the confusion created by a changing volume of activity. It is necessary to emphasize that, although direct costing solves the fluctuating volume problem satisfactorily, it creates certain other difficulties. A discussion of these points is included in the more comprehensive treatment afforded direct costing in Chapter 14.

COST CLASSIFICATION

In this and the preceding chapter, there have been introduced many terms, concepts, and classifications which are important to management's understanding and use of manufacturing cost data. Distinctions have been made between fixed and variable costs, producing and service department costs, job and process costs, product and period costs, and historical and predetermined costs. Illustrations and explanations have described various types of cost flows. The discussion has dealt with direct material cost, direct labor cost, manufacturing overhead cost, unit cost, average cost, incremental cost, and other cost terms. There are a number of other terms and classifications used to describe manufacturing and other costs which are expressed in monetary terms and which are ordinarily derived from an accounting information system for the use of management as an aid to control, planning, and making decisions. Those terms which need clarification at this point are described in the remaining part of this chapter.

Prime Cost is the sum of the material and labor elements which comprise direct material and direct labor cost. These can be specifically traced to the products produced. This term originated when these two elements were the major factors of product cost. Today, due to the increasing impact of manufacturing overhead costs, the term has lost much of its former significance.

Conversion Cost is the sum of direct labor and manufacturing overhead costs. It represents the total cost of converting direct materials into finished products.

Direct and Indirect Costs are easily confused. Perhaps this difficulty arises because a specific cost, from different points of view, can be concurrently and correctly identified as both direct and indirect. The inherent characteristics of a cost do not necessarily make it direct or indirect; the determining factor is the traceability of a cost to a specific unit under the conditions considered. For example, direct material and direct labor are direct product costs. Certain manufacturing overhead costs which can be directly charged to producing departments are indirect product costs when multiple products are produced. Manufacturing overhead costs which can be directly traced to a service department become indirect costs of producing departments and indirect product costs. Whenever a cost must be prorated or allocated, it becomes indirect for that purpose, though it may be considered direct when traced to the original costing unit. Direct costs may be called "traceable" costs, and indirect costs identified as "common" costs.

Controllable and Non-controllable Costs are sometimes called "direct" and "indirect" department costs. The inference in such reference is that any cost which must be allocated or distributed to a department is uncontrollable. But this is not always correct. Any cost is controllable to a certain degree by someone at some time; though a cost is not controllable at one level, it may be controllable at another. Therefore, controllability must be related to a period of time and to a specific unit of activity. Ordinarily, the period of time used is the accounting period, and the activity unit is the department or cost center, which may be termed a responsibility center when costs are collected for such a unit. Controllable costs are those costs within a responsibility center which can be controlled by the responsible head, foreman, or executive. Usually, these costs comprise variable costs which originate from one of the following two sources:

1. Within the center for items like direct material, direct labor, indirect material, and indirect labor.
2. Outside the center for items like power and certain types of maintenance which have a unit cost that originates outside of the department of use. It is not the unit cost of such items, but the extent of their use which is the responsibility of the consuming department.

Uncontrollable costs are those which cannot be changed by the head of the responsibility center within a given period of time. The unit amount of allocated costs should be so classified, because the amount is determined by the allocating method used, not by the action of the head of the responsibility center. Usually, fixed costs are uncontrollable costs for a given responsibility center, because they are a function of time.

Out-of-Pocket and Sunk Costs may be segregated by their requirements on current resources. Out-of-pocket costs require current resources which may be saved if the cost is not incurred. The incurrence of this cost is subject to a decision to incur the cost, not to incur the cost, or to revise a decision which has already been made. If incurred, such costs are usually chargeable directly to production and, consequently, largely constitute variable costs. In contrast, sunk costs do not require the use of current resources. They are past costs which cannot be revised by current decisions. Ordinarily, they have been incurred for specific facilities which are not readily adaptable for new purposes. As such, they usually result in fixed costs.

Avoidable and Unavoidable Costs can usually be segregated by the degree of their fixity. All unavoidable costs are fixed; all variable costs are avoidable. It would seem to follow that unavoidable costs are sunk costs, and avoidable costs are out-of-pocket costs. To a large extent, such logic is correct. However, there are exceptions, like the general manager's salary which is usually unavoidable, but is not a sunk cost. It is more accurate to say that an avoidable cost is one which can be eliminated if an activity is discontinued, but will continue if an activity remains unchanged. An unavoidable cost will remain unchanged regardless of whether an activity is discontinued.

Opportunity Costs are an important consideration in decision making. An opportunity cost is the profit lost by an opportunity foregone. Since it is not a measure of a completed transaction, it is not recorded for accounting. Nevertheless, it is extremely useful in comparing alternative opportunities. For example, if an auditorium having a daily operating cost of $200 can be rented today at $500 or for the next three days at $1800 (provided it is unused today so that workmen may install necessary lighting fixtures), the $300 profit forsaken to obtain the $1800 rental is actually a cost, assuming the auditorium may be rented regularly on a day by day basis. Or, assume that the auditorium may be rented to either A or B. If it can be rented to A for $500 with an operating cost of $200, the opportunity cost of not renting to A is $300. The concept applies equally well when one considers replacing an old product with a new product, further processing a product or selling it in its current form, and in various other instances where alternative courses of action exist.

QUESTIONS AND PROBLEMS

11-1. Some manufacturing businesses identify or allocate all manufacturing overhead to productive departments. A manufacturing overhead rate then may be established for each productive department based on direct labor cost. Using this rate, manufacturing overhead is then applied to jobs or products.

Discuss the possible advantages and disadvantages of the direct labor cost basis for applying manufacturing overhead to jobs or products as opposed to other commonly used bases for manufacturing overhead distribution, such as machine hours or cost of material used.

(Adapted from Uniform CPA Examination)

11-2. The Dopern Company employs departmental budgets and performance reports in planning and controlling its process costing operations. Department A's budget for January was for the production of 1,000 units of equivalent production, a normal month's volume.

The following performance report was prepared for January by the Company's accountant:

Variable costs	Budget	Actual
Direct material	$20,000	$23,100
Direct labor	10,000	10,500
Indirect labor	1,650	1,790
Power	210	220
Supplies	320	330
Total	$32,180	$35,940
Fixed costs		
Rent	$ 400	$ 400
Supervision	1,000	1,000
Depreciation	500	500
Other	100	100
Total	$ 2,000	$ 2,000
Grand total	$34,180	$37,940

Direct material is introduced at various stages of the process. All conversion costs are incurred uniformly throughout the process. Because production fluctuates from month to month, the fixed manufacturing overhead is applied at the rate of $2 per equivalent unit of direct labor.

Variable costs are applied monthly as incurred.

There was no opening inventory at January 1. Of the 1,100 new units started during January, 900 were completed and shipped. There was no finished goods inventory. The units in process at January 31 were estimated to be 75 percent complete as to direct materials and 80 percent complete as to conversion costs. There is no shrinkage, spoilage, or waste of materials.

Required

a. Prepare a schedule of equivalent production for January.

b. Prepare a schedule computing the amount of under- or overapplied manufacturing overhead at January 31.

c. Prepare a schedule computing the cost of goods shipped and the cost of the work-in-process inventory at January 31 at actual cost.

d. Comment on the performance report in 150 words or less. What specific conclusions, if any, can be drawn from the report?

(Adapted from Uniform CPA Examination)

11-3. Match each of the ten (a through j) items with the *one* term listed below (1 through 18) which *most specifically* identifies the cost concept indicated parenthetically.

(*Caution:* An item of cost may be classified in several ways, depending on the purpose of the classification. For example, the commissions on sales of a proposed new product line might be classified as *direct, variable,* and *marginal,* among others. However, if such costs are being considered specifically as to the amount of *cash outlay* required in making a decision concerning adoption of the new line, the commissions are *out-of-pocket costs.* That would be the most *appropriate* answer in the context.)

On your answer sheet list the letters a through j. Indicate your choice of answer for each item by *printing* beside the item letter the number which identifies the term you select.

Term	Term	Term
1. By-product costs	7. Historical cost	13. Out-of-pocket costs
2. Common or joint costs	8. Imputed costs	14. Prime costs
3. Controllable costs	9. Differential cost	15. Replacement costs
4. Direct costs	10. Indirect costs	16. Standard costs
5. Estimated costs	11. Opportunity costs	17. Sunk costs
6. Fixed costs	12. Original cost	18. Variable costs

a. The management of a corporation is considering replacing a machine which is operating satisfactorily with a more efficient new model. *Depreciation* on the cost of the existing machine is omitted from the data used in judging the proposal, because it has little or no significance with respect to such decision. (The omitted cost.)

b. In *public utility accounting,* regulatory bodies require that assets be carried at the cost to those owners who *first devoted the assets to public use.* (The cost described.)

c. One of the problems encountered by a bank in attempting to establish the cost of a *commercial-deposit* account is the fact that many facilities and services are shared by many revenue-producing activities. (Costs of the shared facilities and services.)

d. A company declined an offer received to rent one of its warehouses and elected to use the warehouse for storage of extra raw materials to insure uninterrupted production. Storage cost has been charged with *the monthly amount of the rental offered*. (This cost is known as ?)

e. A manufacturing company excludes all "fixed" costs from its valuation of inventories, assigning to inventory only *applicable portions of costs which vary with changes in volume of product*. (The term employed for the *variable* costs in this context by advocates of this costing procedure.)

f. The sales department urges an increase in production of a product and, as part of the data presented in support of its proposal, indicates the *total additional cost involved for the volume-level it proposes*. (The increase in total cost.)

g. A CPA takes exception to his client's inclusion in the cost of a fixed asset of an "interest" charge based on *the client's own funds* invested in the asset. The client states the charge was intended to obtain a cost comparable to that which would have been the case if funds had been borrowed to finance the acquisition. (The term which describes such *interest* charges.)

h. The "direct" production cost of a unit includes those portions of manufacturing overhead, *labor and materials* which are obviously traceable directly to the unit. (The term used to specify the last *two* of the named components.)

i. Calling upon the special facilities of the production, planning, personnel, and other departments, a firm estimated its future unit cost of production and used this cost (analyzed by cost elements) in its accounts. (The term used to specify this scientifically predetermined estimate.)

j. A chemical manufacturing company produces three products originating in a common initial material mix. Each product gains a separate identity part way through processing and requires additional processing after the "split." Each contributes a significant share of revenue. The company plans to spread the costs up to the "split" among the three products by the use of relative market values. (The term used to specify the costs accumulated up to the point of the *split*.)

(Adapted from Uniform CPA Examination)

11-4. American Manufacturing Company commenced business January 1, 1972, with a paid-in cash capital equal to the sales for the year 1972.

The net profit for the year 1972 was $26,100.

Of the total charges to manufacturing during the year, 40 percent was for materials, 30 percent for productive labor, and 30 percent for manufacturing overhead expenses (including 5 percent depreciation on the cost of plant and machinery, amounting to $3,000).

The value of the materials used was 80 percent of the amount purchased, and 90 percent of the amount purchased was paid during the year.

The inventory value of finished goods on hand at December 31, 1972, was 10 percent of the cost of finished units delivered to the warehouse, and the work in process at that date was equal to 50 percent of the cost of units delivered to the warehouse.

The selling and administrative expenses were equal to 20 percent of the sales and to 40 percent of the cost of goods sold. 90 percent of these selling and administrative expenses were paid during the year 1972.

Plant and machinery purchased during the year were paid for in cash.

All labor and manufacturing expenses (exclusive of depreciation) were paid in full up to and including December 31, 1972.

Of the total sales for the year, 80 percent was collected and 1 percent charged off as worthless. The 1 percent charge for worthless accounts was not included in the amount previously given for total selling and administrative expenses. (Disregard income taxes in fulfilling the requirements set forth below.)

Required

a. Prepare the Statement of Income for the year ended December 31, 1972, showing the cost of goods manufactured, the cost of goods sold, and the net profit for the year.

b. Prepare the Balance Sheet at December 31, 1972.

c. Support all amounts determined on the statements by proper schedules and supporting computations.

(Adapted from Uniform CPA Examination)

11-5. E. Scaries Manufacturing Company started business January 1, 1972. The financial statements, books, and other records disclosed the following information at December 31, 1972:

Cost of Goods Manufactured	$300,000
Net Income for the Year	$ 40,000
Number of finished units produced in 1972	20,000 units
Number of units in the December 31, 1972 inventory of finished goods, all of which were produced in 1972	1,500 units

There was no inventory of work in process at December 31, 1972.

Upon audit of the books, you discover that $2,000 of Depreciation on Sales Equipment was included in manufacturing overhead as a cost of production. This $2,000 item appeared only in the statement of Cost of Goods Manufactured. No other errors were made by the Company.

Required

Compute the correct net income for the year 1972.

11-6. The Wabash Manufacturing Company has decided to develop appropriate departmental rates that may be used to apportion manufacturing overhead to its products, all of which are manufactured on special orders. The company's records show that manufacturing overhead for the six months ended June 30, 1972 consists of the following:

Indirect labor		$ 41,740
Factory rent		2,400
Insurance—machinery and equipment		4,216
Compensation insurance		2,486
Superintendence		6,000
Factory clerical salaries		4,950
Machine maintenance and repairs		31,010
Depreciation of machinery and equipment		42,800
Fuel		3,172
Electricity		2,178
Manufacturing supplies used		3,617
Social security taxes		9,210
Factory office supplies		879
Miscellaneous factory expense		1,212
Total		$155,870

Additional data: The manufacturing operations are carried on in three production departments, A, B, and C, with the aid of two service departments, numbered 1 and 2, respectively. Other data are as follows:

		Departments				
	Total	A	B	C	1	2
Plant floor space, sq. ft.	30,000	10,000	5,000	2,000	7,500	5,500
Number of employees	109	50	20	4	25	10
Number of labor hours	113,360	52,000	20,800	4,160	26,000	10,400
Number of machine hours	47,952	31,912	9,640	560	5,840	–0–
Salaries and wages	$161,307	$76,180	$28,472	$9,975	$37,230	$9,450
Cost of machinery and equipment	$1,019,047	$623,225	$250,960	$20,210	$112,862	$11,790
Annual depreciation rates		8%	8%	10%	10%	20%

In developing department rates, manufacturing overhead expenses shall be allocated to departments as follows:

On the basis of floor space:
    Factory rent
    Fuel
    One-fourth electricity

On the basis of salaries and wages:
    Compensation insurance
    Superintendence
    Manufacturing supplies used
    Social security taxes
    Factory office supplies
    Miscellaneous factory expense

On the basis of investment in machinery and equipment:
    Insurance—machinery and equipment
    Machinery maintenance and repairs
    Three-fourths of electricity

Departmental depreciation on machinery and equipment is to be determined by applying the annual depreciation rates to the cost of machinery and equipment shown under the above additional data. Factory clerical salaries should be charged to Department No. 1, $4,500 of indirect labor is to be allocated to Department No. 2, the balance of indirect labor is allocated to Department No. 1.

Department No. 1 is to be distributed, one-tenth to Department No. 2, the balance to all other departments on the basis of machine hours.

Department No. 2 is to be distributed to Departments A, B, and C on the basis of machine hours.

Required

a. Prepare a distribution sheet showing the total amount of manufacturing overhead to be associated with each producing department.

b. Develop appropriate departmental manufacturing overhead rates per machine hour in Departments A and B and per labor hour in Department C.

c. Illustrate their use in determining the cost of Job 771 by applying the rates developed. Data applicable to Job 771 are as follows:

Material, $487.92; direct labor, $465.00.
Machine hours: Department A, 50 hours
                Department B, 12 hours
Labor hours: Department C, 20 hours

(Adapted from Uniform CPA Examination)

11-7. Capatch Production Corporation prepared the following statement of income (with the cost of production data incorporated therein instead of being shown as a separate statement) at the end of its first year in business:

CAPATCH PRODUCTION CORPORATION
Statement of Income
For the Year Ended December 31, 1972

Sales (47,000 units at $10 each)		$470,000
Less—Cost of Goods Sold:		
Cost of Production		
Direct Material	$120,000	
Direct Labor	100,000	
Manufacturing Overhead Expenses	80,000	
Charges to Production	$300,000	
Inventory, Work in Process, December 31	25,000	
Cost of Production	$275,000	
Inventory, Finished Goods, December 31	16,500	
Cost of Goods Sold		258,500
Gross Margin on Sales		$211,500
Marketing Expenses	$ 60,000	
Administrative Expenses	40,000	100,000
Net Income for the Year before Income Taxes		$111,500

The inventory of work in process at December 31 consists of $7,000 of direct materials, $10,000 of direct labor, and $8,000 of manufacturing overhead expenses. The amount of manufacturing overhead expenses applicable to the work in process inventory has been determined by the direct labor dollar method of apportionment.

Required

a. 50,000 units of finished goods were produced in 1972, of which 3,000 remain in inventory at December 31. Show how the $16,500 inventory amount was computed.
b. Show how the $8,000 amount of manufacturing overhead expenses applicable to the work-in-process inventory was determined.
c. As a step toward "direct costing," the corporation decides to remove the depreciation of plant and equipment ($20,000) from manufacturing overhead expenses and to charge it off in its entirety in the same manner as all marketing and administrative expenses. Prepare a revised statement of income for 1972.
d. Obviously, a portion of the $40,000 of administrative expenses is the result of administrative supervision of the manufacturing division of the business. Explain why many companies often make no attempt to prorate some allocable share of such expenses back to the manufacturing division as additional "manufacturing overhead expense."

11-8. W. T. Dohr Company manufactures and sells an electric fan. From the company's books and other records, the following data are taken on December 31, 1972:

	Jan. 1, 1972	Dec. 31, 1972
Inventory of Raw Materials	$35,600	$25,600
Inventory of Work in Process	18,000	25,300
Inventory of Finished Goods	66,000	?

Sales Returns	$ 22,000
Office Supplies Used	2,500
Plant and Machinery	712,000
Sales	1,584,000
Direct Labor	350,000
Power and Light—Factory	20,000
Insurance—Factory	3,000
Purchase Returns and Allowances	6,200
Salesmen's Traveling Expense	15,000
Depreciation of Office Equipment	1,800
Donations	1,200
Factory Superintendent's Salary	10,000
Small Tools Expense	2,500
Factory Supplies Used	14,700
Interest on Plant Mortgage	14,000
Advertising	16,000
Machine Royalty Rentals	35,000

[CH. 11] BEHAVIOR AND FLOW OF PRODUCTION COSTS 381

Telephone and Telegraph	500
Miscellaneous Manufacturing Overhead	8,500
Indirect Labor	41,000
Salesmen's Commissions	72,000
Purchases of Raw Materials	402,200
Depreciation of Plant and Machinery	30,000
Repairs to Plant and Machinery	11,100
Office Equipment	20,000
Office Salaries	43,000
Sales Allowances	2,200
Transportation In	7,000
Depreciation of Sales Equipment	1,500
Property Taxes—Factory	21,000
Factory Workmen's Compensation Insurance	12,000
Factory Superintendent's Bonus	5,000

Notes: (a) Unless otherwise stated, a distributable expense should be charged entirely to that function which normally would receive the greatest benefit from the expenditure.

(b) Machinery royalties are paid each year on a flat basis regardless of the number of items produced or sold.

(c) The inventory of finished goods is priced on a first-in, first-out basis.

(d) The inventory of finished goods on January 1, 1972, totaled 6,000 units.

(e) All sales were at the same price per unit during the year, and all sales returns were at this same price.

(f) The factory superintendent is to receive a bonus of $.50 (fifty cents) on each fan produced over 60,000 during the year.

(g) The salesmen are paid a commission based on gross sales at the rate of $1.00 for each fan sold.

(h) When taking the physical inventory of finished goods on December 31, 1972, it was discovered that among the stock on hand were 100 fans that had been produced in 1971.

Required

a. Prepare a Statement of Cost of Goods Manufactured for the year 1972.

b. Submit figures to find the cost of the inventory of finished goods December 31, 1972.

c. Prepare a schedule of the Cost of Goods Sold for the year 1972.

11-9. The MacKay Company manufactures a single product, a mechanical device known as "Klebo." The company maintains a process cost type of accounting system.

The manufacturing operation is as follows:

Material K, a metal, is stamped to form a part which is assembled with one of the purchased parts "X." The unit is then machined and cleaned, after which it is assembled with two units of part "Y" to form the finished device known as a "Klebo." Spray priming and enameling is the final operation.

Time and motion studies indicate that of the total time required for the manufacture of a unit the first operation required 25 percent of the labor cost, the first assembly an additional 25 percent, machining and cleaning 12.5 percent, the second assembly 25 percent, and painting 12.5 percent. Manufacturing overhead expense is considered to follow the same pattern by operations as does labor.

The following data are presented to you as of October 31, 1972, the end of the first month of operation:

Material K purchased—100,000 lbs.	$25,000
Part X purchased—80,000 units	16,000
Part Y purchased—150,000 units	15,000
Primer and enamel used	1,072
Direct labor—cost	45,415
Manufacturing expenses	24,905

	Unit Quantity
Units finished and sent to finished goods warehouse	67,000
Units assembled but not painted	5,000
Units ready for the second assembly	3,000
Inventories at the end of the month:	
Finished units	7,500
Material K (lbs.)	5,800
Part X (units of part X)	5,000
Part Y (units of part Y)	6,000
Klebos in process (units)	8,000

Required

Prepare the following:

a. A schedule of equivalent labor production.

b. A schedule of total and unit costs incurred in production for:
   (1) Each kind of material   (3) Manufacturing overhead expense
   (2) Labor cost   (4) Total cost of production

c. A schedule of detailed material, labor, and manufacturing costs assigned to the units left in process.

(Adapted from Uniform CPA Examination)

11-10. XYZ Corporation is a small manufacturing company producing a highly flammable cleaning fluid. On May 31, 1972, the company had a fire which completely destroyed the in-process inventory.

After the fire a physical inventory was taken. The raw materials were valued at $30,000, the finished goods at $60,000, and supplies at $5,000.

The inventories on January 1, 1972, consisted of:

Raw materials	$ 15,000
Work in process	50,000
Finished goods	70,000
Supplies	2,000
	$137,000

A review of the accounts showed that the sales and gross profit for the last five years were:

	Sales	Gross Profit
1967	$300,000	$ 86,200
1968	320,000	102,400
1969	330,000	108,900
1970	250,000	62,500
1971	280,000	84,000

The sales for the first five months of 1972 were $150,000. Raw material purchases were $50,000. Freight on purchases was $5,000. Direct labor for the five months was $40,000; for the past five years manufacturing overhead was 50 percent of direct labor.

Required

Compute the value of inventory lost.

(Adapted from Uniform CPA Examination)

12

Flexible Budgeting

The determination and utilization of predetermined manufacturing overhead rates were illustrated in the preceding chapter. It was demonstrated how the use of an estimated or normal manufacturing overhead rate permits the determination of the cost of a job or product immediately upon its completion and thus eliminates any need for waiting until the end of a fiscal period when all of the actual costs are accumulated. Moreover, it was shown how the use of this rate stabilizes a unit cost even when different levels of production are encountered. Of course, the use of a predetermined manufacturing overhead rate usually causes either overapplied or underapplied manufacturing overhead at the end of a period. Although the treatment accorded such manufacturing overhead variances creates an additional accounting consideration, the added effort is insignificant compared to the benefits received; in addition to the advantages already described, the variance itself can provide some very useful information. For example, the magnitude of the variance is a rough measure of the ability to predict future operational cost and activity accurately. Furthermore, a closer analysis of the variance can identify separate causes which are responsible for its existence.

To illustrate identification of different factors in the manufacturing overhead variance, let us assume that a company is confronted with the following situation at the end of a period:

Estimated Direct Labor Hours	10,000	
Actual Direct Labor Hours	9,000	
Estimated Manufacturing Overhead:	Total	Per D.L.H.
Fixed	$27,000	$2.70
Variable	20,000	2.00
Total	$47,000	$4.70
Actual Manufacturing Overhead	$44,000	

The predetermined manufacturing overhead rate of $4.70 per direct labor hour times the actual hours worked would have applied $42,300 of manufacturing overhead, not the $44,000 actually incurred. Therefore, $1,700 of underapplied manufacturing overhead exists. An analysis of this $1,700 will provide management with meaningful information about the operating efficiency of the past period. The $4.70 rate used during the period, although only 9,000 actual direct labor hours were worked, is one reason that manufacturing overhead was underapplied. Included in the $4.70 rate is $2.70 of fixed manufacturing overhead; the $2.70 amount applies total fixed manufacturing overhead when a production level of 10,000 direct labor hours is reached. With only 9,000 actual direct labor hours, the fixed rate required to apply total fixed manufacturing overhead is $27,000 ÷ 9,000, or $3.00. The difference between the normal fixed rate of $2.70 and the $3.00 rate that applies to the production level reached is $.30. This difference multiplied by the 9,000 actual hours equals $2,700, which is a measure of the fixed costs unapplied because the company operated at less than estimated capacity. This amount, sometimes called a volume variance, can also be computed by multiplying the 1,000 idle hours by the $2.70 fixed manufacturing overhead rate. Since the company operated at less than estimated activity, the volume variance is unfavorable. In instances where actual exceeds estimated activity, the volume variance is considered to be favorable.

After that portion of the variance which is attributable to volume has been isolated, the original $1,700 variance has been converted into a favorable $1,000 balance. An analyst should not accept this $1,000 as a measure of the control provided variable costs until additional proof is available. Support can be found by subtracting the fixed costs from the total actual manufacturing overhead and comparing the remainder with what the variable costs should have been at the level of production obtained. ($44,000 − $27,000 = $17,000 variable costs in total actual manufacturing overhead). The estimated variable cost rate of $2.00 multiplied by actual hours of 9,000 equals $18,000 variable costs, a figure which should have existed, in contrast to the $17,000 actually incurred. Therefore, the variable costs were $1,000 below expectations. This difference, sometimes termed expense variance, controllable variance, or budget variance, is favorable, because estimated variable costs exceeded actual variable costs.

This discussion explains how overapplied or underapplied manufacturing overhead can be analyzed to provide volume indicators which are either favorable or unfavorable and expense variances which may be either favorable or unfavorable. Little can be learned from breaking down the volume variance into individual fixed manufacturing overhead expense items. But much can be gained by a breakdown of the total variable cost variance and comparing each actual variable expense with the related estimated expense; some might be found to be more, others less, than the estimated amounts. Since these are variable expenses, they should be the responsibility of a designated individual and should be controlled by him.

At least two major criticisms can be brought against this analysis. The first is that the predetermined rate was based upon estimated manufacturing overhead costs and an estimated level of operating activity. Therefore, the predetermined rate can be no more accurate than the estimates from which it was derived. Further, overapplied or underapplied manufacturing overhead which results from an inaccurate predetermined rate is subject to any error contained in that rate. Consequently, as long as the rate is predicated upon estimates, the rate, the manufacturing overhead variance, and related conclusions must be given less than unquestioned acceptance. The second criticism concerns how the causes underlying the manufacturing overhead variance were identified. The volume variance was calculated by comparing what the fixed costs per unit should have been at the level of operations attained with the predetermined fixed manufacturing overhead rate. The difference was then multiplied by the activity units in the production level actually attained. Subsequently, an alternate method which avoided recalculating a fixed manufacturing overhead rate was described. But, for the variable cost variance, there was no alternative to determining what the variable costs should have been at the actual level of operating activity. Consequently, guide lines for control by an estimated predetermined rate require that, at the end of a period, new calculations be made to determine what the variable costs should be for the level of activity attained.

In summary, the two major objections to an estimated predetermined rate are:

1. The questionable reliability of an estimated rate for costing.
2. The after the fact calculation of what the costs should be for control.

An arrangement cannot be devised which will completely eliminate the objectionable features of an estimated rate and permit its advantages to be retained. The timing and calculating aspects of the second objection could be readily eliminated by predetermining what the costs should be for any level of anticipated activity. But that aspect of the second objection which involves "what the costs should be" presents a problem like the one contained in the first objection; neither can be perfectly solved unless the estimates are predicted with absolute accuracy. Nevertheless, much of the questionable reliability can be removed by replacing the estimates with more precise predictive techniques.

Sophisticated forecasting techniques, to the extent considered feasible by management, can be used to predetermine the amount of manufacturing overhead required at the anticipated level of operating activity, the amount required to achieve each of several specified volumes of activity, or the amount required for any volume of activity within a significant range of operations. Such predeterminations actually constitute a budget of manufacturing overhead costs. If the costs are predetermined for only the anticipated level of operating activity, they comprise a fixed or static budget. If the costs are predetermined for several specified levels of activity or for any level of activity within a meaningful range of operations, the budget is considered to be flexible.

FLEXIBLE BUDGETS

The preparation of a flexible, sometimes termed a semi-variable or variable, manufacturing overhead expense budget usually follows a pattern which conforms to one of two major categories of construction. The first category contains those flexible budgets which are prepared by developing a series of fixed budgets. The second contains those flexible budgets which are ascertained by formula. The first category describes those budgets which set forth the manufacturing overhead cost allowable for each of several specified volumes of activity, while the second contains those budgets which provide for an allowed manufacturing overhead at any level of activity within a given operating range.

For control, both types of flexible budgets have certain minor disadvantages. A series of fixed budgets requires interpolation when the actual level of activity or volume falls between any two of the preselected, fixed activity levels in the series. A formula type of budget contains a rigidity that is not equally justifiable for each level of production volume. In spite of those slight disadvantages, the underlying principle of a flexible manufacturing overhead budget is that there is a norm of costs for each level of operating volume and that this norm should be predetermined so that management can plan, guide, measure, and control the operating performance of a manufacturing enterprise. It has been shown that managerial control over manufacturing activities is best accomplished when operations are segregated by departments or cost centers. Consequently, a flexible budget should be prepared for each such area of production. Then, the various departmental or cost center budgets should be combined into a composite flexible budget covering the total manufacturing activity of a plant.

To illustrate the two major categories of flexible budgets, assume that a producing department is confronted with the following manufacturing overhead costs:

(1) Variable costs equal $0.30 per direct labor hour worked.
(2) Semi-variable costs are $2,000 at 5,000 direct labor hours and, thereafter, increase $150 per 1,000 direct labor hours.
(3) Fixed or non-variable costs amount to $6,300.

Using these condensed manufacturing overhead cost data to prepare a budget constructed as a series of fixed budgets, the abbreviated flexible budget would appear as in Exhibit 12–1.

If the same basic data is incorporated into the formula form of a flexible budget, some decision must be made on how semi-variable costs are to be handled.

EXHIBIT 12-1

Departmental Flexible Manufacturing Overhead Budget

Direct Labor Hours	5,000	6,000	7,000	8,000	9,000	10,000	11,000
Manufacturing Overhead:							
Variable ...	$1,500	$1,800	$2,100	$2,400	$2,700	$3,000	$3,300
Semi-variable .	2,000	2,150	2,300	2,450	2,600	2,750	2,900
Fixed	6,300	6,300	6,300	6,300	6,300	6,300	6,300
Total Budgeted Costs	$9,800	$10,250	$10,700	$11,150	$11,600	$12,050	$12,500

Assuming that they are divided into $1,335 of fixed costs and $0.133 per direct labor hour of variable costs, the total fixed costs would now amount to $7,635, and the combined variable costs would become $0.433 per direct labor hour.

The revised cost data would appear in the formula form of a flexible budget as follows:

$$\text{Budgeted Cost} = \$7,635 + (\$0.433 \times \text{No. of direct labor hours})$$

Substituting into the formula the activity levels used in the preceding example, budgeted costs of $9,800, $10,233, $10,666, $11,100, $11,532, $11,965, and $12,398 would be obtained at the 5,000, 6,000, 7,000, 8,000, 9,000, 10,000, and 11,000 direct labor hour levels.

The slightly different amounts obtained in the two examples at the same level of activity were caused by the treatment provided semi-variable costs. As will be shown later in this chapter, these costs can be handled in a much more precise manner. The arbitrary division made above was employed to expedite the comparison between the two major categories of flexible budgets; both examples were greatly simplified so that their underlying concepts might be compared easily.

As shown in these examples, a flexible budget sets forth the amount of cost considered necessary for each level of activity. This enables the flexible budget to help management accomplish different purposes. Before a period commences, it may be used as a planning guide to show what the manufacturing overhead costs should be for the anticipated level of activity and to establish a predetermined manufacturing overhead rate. At the end of a period, it may be used as a control mechanism to show management what the costs should have been for the productive volume actually achieved. Maximum benefits from a flexible budget are dependent upon proper answers furnished for the following three important questions:

1. What unit should be used to measure productive volume or activity?
2. How is capacity established for flexible budgeting purposes?

3. What is the proper amount of manufacturing overhead expense applicable to each level of productive output?

Activity Measure

The first of these three questions received considerable attention in the two preceding chapters. It was explained that activity may be measured by physical units, labor hours, labor dollars, machine hours, or other homogeneous units. The discussion identified and associated certain disadvantages with various activity measures. Further, it was emphasized that the primary requisite of a proper measuring unit is that it possess the closest possible correlation with the manufacturing overhead cost generated by manufacturing activity. Finally, it was pointed out that care must be exercised to insure that a measuring unit reflects minimum response to changes in variables other than volume. This brief review of the more pertinent factors surrounding the selection of a measuring unit for activity is adequate at this point; a more comprehensive coverage may be gained through reviewing the explanations provided in previous chapters.

Capacity Considerations

The starting point for preparing a flexible budget is the determination of normal capacity. Normal capacity (sometimes called normal activity, normal volume, or standard capacity) is that point in productive activity which minimizes the range of variations between normal and actual activity; the normal capacity point provides the basis for the determination of a normal manufacturing overhead rate. Although the two preceding ideas describe what normal capacity is, neither explains how normal capacity is established. To understand how normal capacity is established, certain interpretations of the term capacity must be understood.

In usage, the word "capacity" has various meanings and connotations to different persons. From a physical point of view, capacity consists of that amount of plant, machinery, and equipment with which management expects to operate a business. From an operating point of view, it also includes the personnel employed to conduct the business. The basic concept of capacity is ordinarily classified into various categories which identify significant graduations of volume, the highest of which is termed theoretical capacity.

Theoretical Capacity. The theoretical, sometimes called *theoretical maximum,* capacity of a plant is a measure of its ability to operate at full speed without interruptions. This theoretical maximum, frequently no more than a paper calculation, is largely a mirage for practical purposes. It is physically impossible for a plant to operate at full capacity 100 percent of the time because of various interruptions like unexpected machine breakdowns, pattern and model changes, setup time, repairs, defective material, shortage of material, inefficiencies, and time lost by employee absenteeism, vacations, Sundays, and holidays. Some of these interruptions are considered to be humanly preventable; others are not. Regardless of the causes behind their existence, they all originate within a business and they all prevent sustained operation at a theoretical capacity level. When the level of theoretical capacity has been reduced by an allowance for internal interruptions, the level remaining is frequently termed practical capacity.

Practical Capacity. The practical, sometimes called *maximum potential,* capacity of a plant is that level of production that will be maintained if external influences do not interfere: no internal interruption is expected to cause a plant to operate below its practical capacity. It might appear, then, that this is the level at which a typical plant operates. Unfortunately, this is not correct in the majority of instances. All too frequently, external influences prevent a plant from being operated at its practical capacity. The chief external cause recognized as a barrier to achieving practical capacity is an inadequate amount of customers' orders. This interference, however, is an extremely important consideration. For example, if a company cannot sell 2,000 of the 10,000 units which its plant can produce each month, the significance attached to practical capacity is reduced considerably. Instead of practical capacity, this company needs a different capacity measure to identify that productive level which it can normally expect. This level of activity is often called normal capacity.

Normal Capacity. When practical capacity has been reduced by an allowance for plant idleness due to external influences, the level of capacity which remains is called normal capacity. Normal, sometimes called *average,* capacity is the level of operation that will produce the products needed to meet the average sales demand over a time period of sufficient length to balance the fluctuations from seasonal and cyclical causes. For short periods of time, a plant may produce below-normal capacity because of a lack of orders, while, at other times, business conditions may justify production at a level in excess of normal capacity. The lower and upper limits of the operating levels just described constitute the normal range. The normal capacity level is located within the normal range. Ideally, in the long run, the normal capacity should equal the volume of production both produced and sold.

In a given period, the excess of normal capacity over actual activity represents idle capacity. Facilities made temporarily idle by a cutback in production, however, are restored to use as soon as conditions warrant their operation. In fact, if production above normal capacity is needed temporarily, a fuller utilization of the facilities required for normal capacity must be employed. The facilities used to produce above normal capacity are the same facilities used at any other point within the normal range of activity. As such, they are the same facilities upon which the normal manufacturing overhead rate is based at the normal capacity level. None of these facilities comprises excess capacity; only that part of practical capacity which is greater than the facilities needed at the upper limit of the normal range represents excess capacity. Facilities comprising excess capacity should not be included in the base for a normal manufacturing overhead rate; ordinarily, they should be eliminated. If retained, expenses arising from such facilities should be excluded from the calculation of the normal manufacturing overhead rate and be given separate identification on the statement of income.

Illustration of Capacity Relationships

Using the direct labor hour as an activity measure, gradations of capacity are represented by the following data:

Measure of Capacity	Direct Labor Hours
Theoretical capacity	16,000
Practical Capacity	13,000
Upper limit of normal range	12,000
Lower limit of normal range	8,000
Normal capacity	10,000
Actual (capacity) volume	9,200
Excess capacity	1,000
Idle capacity	800

To illustrate their relationship to each other, these data are arranged graphically in Exhibit 12–2.

As shown by Exhibit 12–2, excess capacity is the difference between the upper limit of the normal range and practical capacity, while idle capacity is the

EXHIBIT 12–2

Capacity Relationships

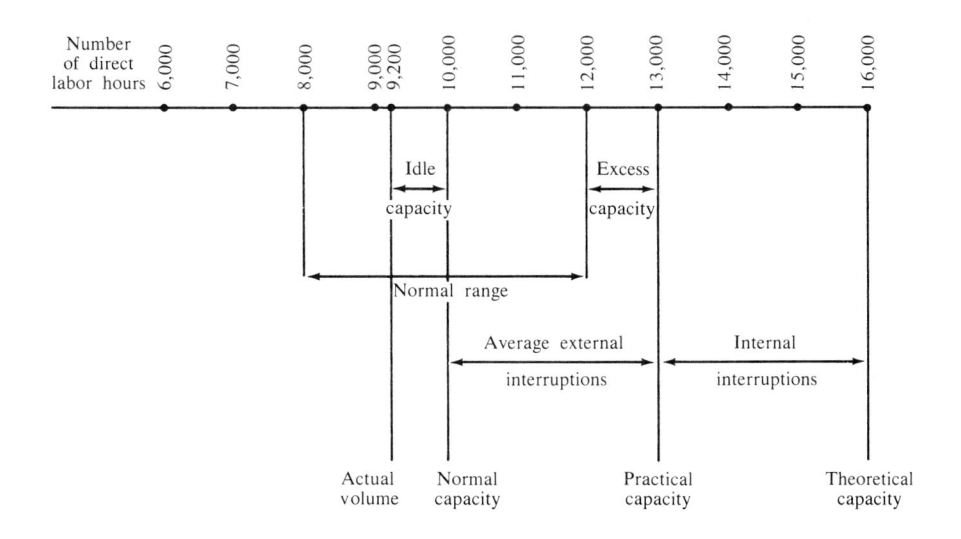

difference between actual and normal capacity. Elimination of these two depends upon different types of managerial action. Idle capacity can be utilized by raising productive activity to the normal capacity level through correcting a temporary shortage in customers' orders. On the other hand, the elimination of excess capacity depends upon the disposal of heretofore unnecessary facilities or upon management's initiating action which will provide a relatively permanent upward revision in the operational levels of the business.

Some of the relationships shown by Exhibit 12–2, although realistic, may appear far-fetched. For example, the reduction from theoretical capacity to practical capacity of approximately 20 percent causes a practical capacity level of about 80 percent of theoretical capacity, an amount which may seem low but which falls well within the range of 75 percent to 85 percent that is usually encountered. Similarly, the normal capacity of approximately 77 percent of practical capacity and about 63 percent of theoretical capacity is not unduly distorted when one realizes that normal capacity is often as low as 50 percent of theoretical capacity. Nevertheless, the criticism that normal capacity is an inadequate percentage of practical capacity has merit. As is true in many companies, this percentage can be improved substantially by the elimination of excess capacity through one of the methods suggested in the preceding paragraph.

Normal capacity should be established for the entire plant, and then used as a basis for determining departmental normal capacity levels. The normal capacity for the plant may cause one department to have excess capacity when another has insufficient capacity. Inequality in departmental capacities is not unusual, and managerial action is required to bring these inequalities into balance. This action might be purchasing additional equipment, scheduling overtime, or sub-contracting to overcome the problem of inadequate capacity, while the problem of excess capacity might be solved through disposal of excess facilities or the location of special orders which would utilize the facilities of a specific department.

Scheduling overtime as a remedial measure for insufficient facilities is unlikely unless the normal capacity is established on less than a three-shift operation. This may raise a question regarding how many shifts should be included in establishing normal capacity. Normal capacity may be based on a one-, two-, or three-shift operation and for whatever length of working week the plant is expected to operate.

Manufacturing Overhead Allowances

Of the three major problems underlying the preparation and maximum utilization of a flexible budget, attention has been given to the selection of an activity measure and to the determination of a normal capacity. The third major problem is the determination of the amount of manufacturing overhead deemed applicable for each level of operating volume in the flexible budget. Because of the importance and scope of this third problem, the remainder of this chapter will be devoted to establishing and including manufacturing overhead allowances in flexible budgets.

To determine the amount of manufacturing overhead which is applicable to each level of operating activity, an examination of the nature and behavior of each item of manufacturing overhead expense must be made. Although the behavior of each expense can be studied in relation to different variables, the most important one here is the volume of activity. The cost-volume relationship problem was discussed briefly in the preceding chapter. No longer, however, can the problem be handled by showing that costs are classified as fixed, variable, or semi-variable according to how they respond to changes in the volume of activity. Instead, the extent to which each manufacturing expense reacts to a change in the volume of activity must be ascertained with whatever degree of accuracy is considered feasible in each situation. In doing so, it should be recognized that most expenses conform rather closely to one of four patterns of variability. Graphically portrayed, their behavior presents the rather generalized picture shown by Exhibit 12–3.

In Exhibit 12–3, Figure 1 portrays variable expenses, which tend to change directly and proportionally with activity. Maintenance of machinery, supplies, and perishable tools often are examples of variable expenses. Of course, direct material and direct labor are classic examples, but they are not included in a manufacturing overhead budget.

Figure 2, Exhibit 12–3, illustrates fixed expenses, which do not vary with volume. Straight-line depreciation, salaries of factory executives, foremen, watchmen, property insurance, and property taxes are often classified as fixed expenses. This classification does not mean that these expenses are unalterable or permanently fixed. They are fixed only for the period of time during which management decisions do not alter the circumstances under which they were classified.

If all manufacturing expenses were either completely variable or fixed, the preparation of a flexible budget would be greatly simplified. But this is not the case. Coal, fuel oil, telephone, clerks, supervisors, purchased gas, water, and power often fall into a semi-variable category; that is, they display both fixed and variable characteristics. Furthermore, the variable components of semi-variable expenses tend to vary according to one of two patterns. In Exhibit 12–3, Figure 3 illustrates, by a broken line, a fixed portion of a semi-variable expense that remains constant regardless of the activity involved. It also shows, by an unbroken line, a variable portion that increases proportionately to increases in activity. A different behavior is portrayed for the semi-variable expense illustrated by Figure 4. Here, the expense varies by discrete steps similar to those which would occur when a new storeroom clerk is added for every additional 25 percent increase in activity. The broken line, in this figure, represents the fixed portion that remains unchanged regardless of the activity involved. The unbroken line does not show a linear relationship, since it increases by successive static stages. Under most conditions, however, the effect of this

EXHIBIT 12-3

Expense—Activity Patterns

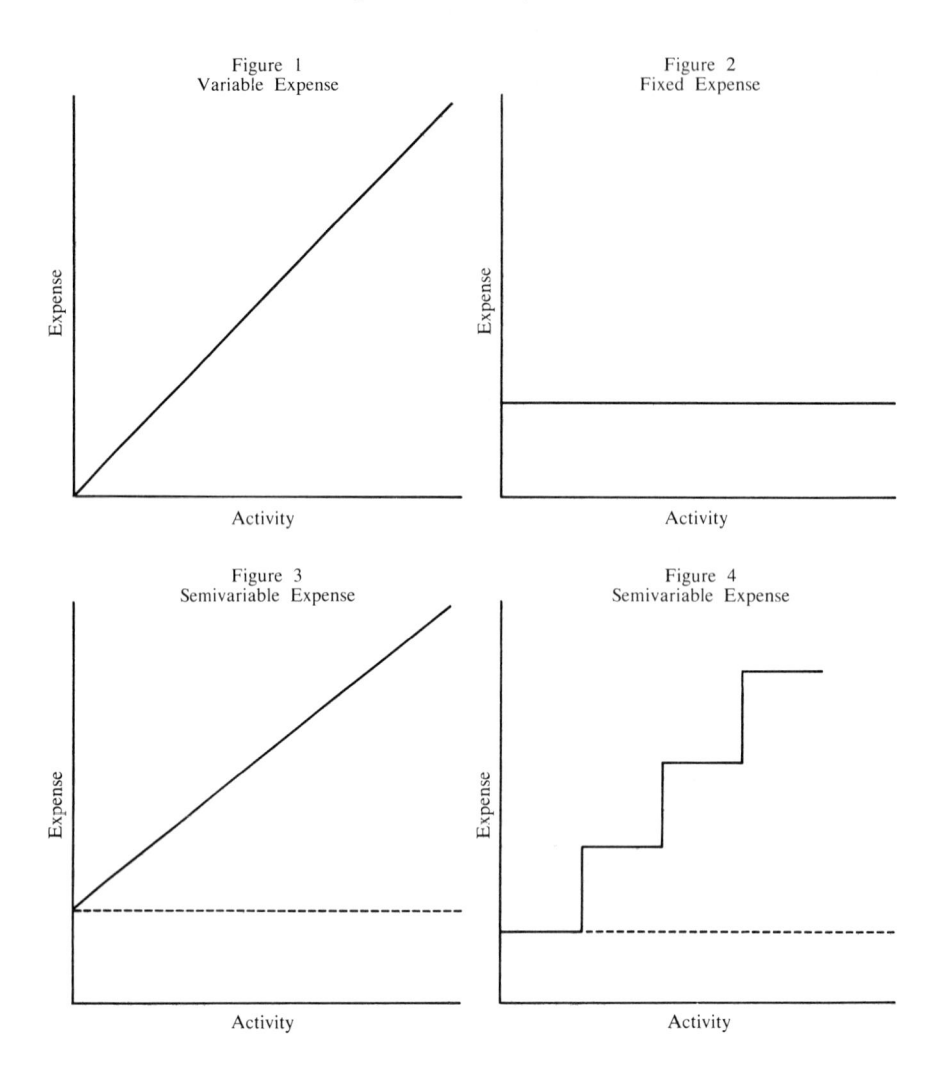

Figure 1
Variable Expense

Figure 2
Fixed Expense

Figure 3
Semivariable Expense

Figure 4
Semivariable Expense

nonlinear relationship is relatively unimportant to the total budget allowance, and techniques may be used to provide step expenses with an approximated linear function.

Recognizing that individual expenses vary differently with changes in activity and that their behavior closely resembles one of the four patterns illustrated above, the problem becomes one of selecting a method which will provide an acceptable determination of the variability of each expense. The methods for determining how expenses vary with activity fall generally into the following three categories:

1. Judgmental identification
2. Statistical analysis of the relationship between historical expense and activity
3. Analytical studies of how expenses should vary with activity

Judgmental identification is the simplest of the three methods. It may be used to save time by one who has considerable knowledge of the conditions under which each manufacturing overhead expense is incurred. Based upon such knowledge, certain expenses are identified as variable or non-variable. Regardless of the amount of knowledge behind such decisions, there is always a considerable number of expenses which cannot be classified satisfactorily by judgment only. At best, this method reduces the number of expenses which must be analyzed by one of the other two methods suggested above. At the same time, such judgmental decisions are suspect, either because of inadequate confidence in the knowledge behind the identifications or because of the recognition that minor classification errors have been accepted as a matter of expediency.

Statistical analysis of the relationship between historical expenses and activity is dependent upon the availability of suitable data from previous periods. The data should cover a range of time that does not encompass abnormal conditions like strikes, wars, or rapidly changing price levels. In addition, this data should be collected monthly, because the objective is to prepare a monthly flexible budget. The number of expense items for which data must be assembled depends upon the reason for the use of the statistical method. If judgmental identification has already identified those expenses which are either variable or fixed, statistical analysis is required only for the remaining items. On the other hand, if all expenses are to be subjected to statistical analysis, which is usually the wisest course, a greater number of items are involved. In either event, the statistical analysis employed may be by any one of several methods, typical of which are the following three:[1]

1. Visual inspection
2. High-low, and
3. Least squares.

Regardless of whether the fixed and variable components of a given expense are determined by the visual inspection, high-low, or least squares method, the data employed in each method is historical. Consequently, the answers obtained should be viewed as preliminary amounts for flexible budgeting purposes; they should be analyzed and adjusted for any events which justify changes in the original data. Only after necessary adjustments have been completed should the final budget be prepared.

Analytical studies. To a certain extent, an analytical study is combined with any one of the statistical techniques already identified. An after-the-fact study ordinarily is used to review critically and, wherever necessary, to justify revisions in the preliminary budget allowances that have been established by statis-

---

[1] For a detailed discussion and various illustrations concerning the calculation and use of these methods, see the "Regression Analysis" section in Chapter 19.

tics. For example, if wages have risen by 5 percent since last year, preliminary budget allowances for indirect labor costs which have been statistically established upon the data of the past year should be increased 5 percent for the final budget. Under such circumstances, the analytical study is limited to reviewing, appraising, and revising historical costs, while the true analytical approach goes beyond the evaluation of historical costs in attempting to determine the future.

The development of flexible budget allowances through analytical studies usually is accomplished by an industrial engineering approach. Engineering studies are made of facts like supply requirements and manpower needs at different volume levels. The operations in each department are analyzed to ascertain how many employees should be added or removed when activity increases or decreases.

Power, fuel, and other requirements are measured by their physical relationships to productive output, not by historical observations. In certain instances, statistical analysis may be used as a guide whenever the available data is inadequate to support a valid conclusion. The statistical analysis utilized in analytical studies, however, ordinarily deals with current or future data, not with historical information. Although the analytical approach consists primarily of engineering studies, the final budget is the product of the combined effort of industrial engineers and accountants belonging to the budget department's or controller's staff.

Flexible budget allowances determined by judgmental decision, statistical analysis of past experience, or analytical studies may be used with any type of accounting system. But, since the analytical studies method makes extensive use of physical observations in determining what expenses should be, it is ordinarily a rather expensive method to use. Consequently, it is rarely used with historical cost systems that employ either actual or predetermined manufacturing overhead rates. Its widest use is found in the operation of standard cost systems which, by their nature, demand the determination of the most precise allowances feasible. Additional attention will be directed toward this point in the next chapter.

Preparing the Flexible Budget

Considerable attention has been given to the basic procedures which underlie the development of the details which enter into the preparation of a flexible budget. The format of the budget itself has been largely ignored. The direction of the discussion, however, is justified, because the flexible budget is practically prepared once the details have been completed. When the details have been worked out, acceptable solutions have been provided for the capacity and the expense variability problems. Fixed expenses have been identified, and the fixed elements in semi-variable expenses have been isolated. With the total amount of fixed expense ascertained and a variable rate of expense established, the manufacturing overhead allowance for any level of activity is relatively simple to compute. The selection of the form of the budget and the mechanical summary of the appropriate budget allowances constitute the final step in the preparation of the budget.

To illustrate a flexible budget, it is assumed that the manufacturing overhead expenses in a producing department have been subjected to analytical studies which have developed data contained in Exhibit 12–4.

EXHIBIT 12–4

MIXING DEPARTMENT—NORMAL CAPACITY OF 5,000 DIRECT LABOR HOURS PER MONTH		
Manufacturing Overhead Expense	Fixed Expense Total	Variable Rate per D.L.H.
Controllable:		
Indirect materials		$ .02
Indirect labor	$ 720	.04
Repairs to machinery and equipment	200	.01
Light, power and heat	110	.06
Water	20	.02
Uncontrollable:		
Taxes, property	140	
Insurance, fire	90	
Supervision	800	
Depreciation	600	
Distributed from:		
Engineering Department	700	.06
Stores Department	430	.03
Maintenance Department	390	.12
Total	$4,200	$ .36

In Exhibit 12–4, the manufacturing overhead expenses have been divided into their fixed and variable elements. Also, they have been classified as controllable or uncontrollable according to the degree of control possible by the department head. The expenses classified as distributed are the result of a distribution of expenses from the service departments, which render services to the mixing department. The fixed element of each service department expense represents that portion of the service department's readiness-to-serve expense which equitably belongs to the mixing department. The variable rate for each service department expense is obtained by subtracting the total fixed expenses from the total expenses at normal capacity and dividing the remainder by the total direct labor hours of all departments. The department head cannot be held fully accountable for the distributed expense from service departments, because he is only responsible for the quantity of service consumed by his department.

A tabular flexible budget of the information contained in Exhibit 12–4 is presented in Exhibit 12–5.

EXHIBIT 12–5

Monthly Flexible Manufacturing Overhead Budget—Mixing Department

Direct labor hours allowed	3,000	3,500	4,000	4,500	5,000	5,500	6,000
Percentage of normal capacity	60%	70%	80%	90%	100%	110%	120%
Indirect materials	$ 60	$ 70	$ 80	$ 90	$ 100	$ 110	$ 120
Indirect labor	840	860	880	900	920	940	960
Repairs to machinery and equipment	230	235	240	245	250	255	260
Light, power and heat	290	320	350	380	410	440	470
Water	80	90	100	110	120	130	140
Overtime						500	1,000
Taxes, property	140	140	140	140	140	140	140
Insurance, fire	90	90	90	90	90	90	90
Supervision	800	800	800	800	800	800	800
Depreciation	600	600	600	600	600	600	600
Engineering Department	880	910	940	970	1,000	1,030	1,060
Stores Department	520	535	550	565	580	595	610
Maintenance Department	750	810	870	930	990	1,050	1,110
Total Expenses	$5,280	$5,460	$5,640	$5,820	$6,000	$6,680	$7,360
Rate per direct labor hour at normal capacity					$1.20		

The 10 percent capacity interval shown in Exhibit 12–5 is an arbitrary selection. The interval could be 1 percent, 5 percent, 15 percent, or any other percentage which might be deemed more appropriate. The range of 60 percent to 120 percent of normal capacity is related to those levels of operating capacity below or above which the company does not expect to produce. With the same given information, the range could be expanded from 0 percent to 120 percent. Additional information, however, might be needed to provide budget allowances above 120 percent of normal capacity.

A study of Exhibit 12–5 will reveal certain advantages of flexible budgeting. First, a $1.20 predetermined rate of manufacturing overhead expense has been established. Second, regardless of the actual level of production in a given month, the manufacturing overhead expense which is "allowable" may be compared with the expenses actually incurred. Any difference between these two amounts represents a variance which can be analyzed for control. In fact, the analysis can reveal what part of the variance is attributable to deviations in efficiency, expense, and volume factors as well as controllable and uncontrollable factors. This analysis is presented in the next chapter on standard costs. Furthermore, the segregation of fixed and variable expenses for flexible budgeting is also necessary, or at least useful, in determining break-even point, selling prices, product profitability, and other vital considerations which will be discussed in subsequent chapters.

[CH. 12] FLEXIBLE BUDGETING 399

QUESTIONS AND PROBLEMS

12-1. What are some of the relative advantages to be gained by using a flexible budget instead of a static budget?

12-2. How would you determine the amount of a manufacturing overhead variance that resulted from operating at below-normal capacity?

12-3. What causes manufacturing overhead control procedures to differ from those used to control prime costs?

12-4. If a company expects to operate at only 60 percent of normal capacity during the following period, should it cost production with manufacturing overhead budgeted at that level of capacity? Explain.

12-5. What is the objective underlying the use of flexible budgets?

12-6. A tabular flexible budget shows the following total budget allowances:

70%	$6,590
80%	$7,400
90%	$8,290
100%	$9,000

If the actual activity for a month equals 85 percent of normal capacity, what is the amount of the budget allowance?

12-7. On a lined sheet of paper alphabetize the first ten lines from a through j. Select the graph which matches the alphabetized factory cost or expense data and write the number identifying the graph on the appropriate alphabetized line.

The vertical axes of the graphs below represent *total* dollars of expense and the horizontal axes represent volume of production. In each case the zero point is at the intersection of the two axes. The graphs may be used more than once.

Required

a. Depreciation of equipment, where the amount of depreciation charged is computed by the machine hours method.

b. Electricity bill—a flat fixed charge, plus a variable cost after a certain number of kilowatt hours are used.

c. City water bill, which is computed as follows:

First 1,000,000 gallons or less	$1,000 flat fee
Next 10,000 gallons	.003 per gallon used
Next 10,000 gallons	.006 per gallon used
Next 10,000 gallons	.009 per gallon used
etc., etc., etc.	

400 COST ACCOUNTING CONCEPTS [CH. 12]

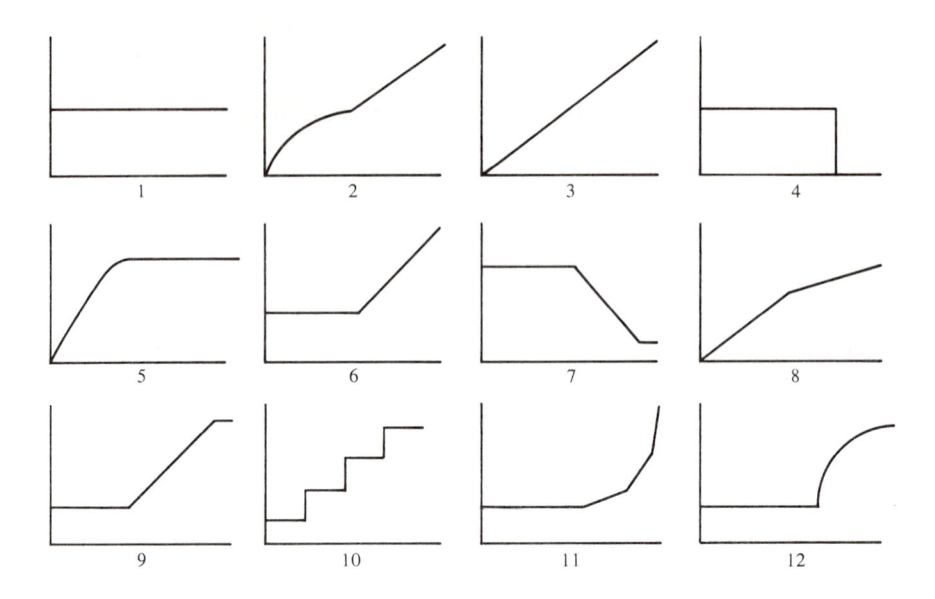

[Graphs numbered 1 through 12]

d. Cost of lubricant for machines, where cost per unit decreases with each pound of lubricant used (for example, if one pound is used, the cost is $10.00; if two pounds are used, the cost is $19.98; if three pounds are used, the cost is $29.94; with a minimum cost per pound of $9.25).

e. Depreciation of equipment, where the amount is computed by the straight-line method. When the depreciation rate was established it was anticipated that the obsolescence factor would be greater than the wear and tear factor.

f. Rent on a factory building donated by the city, where the agreement calls for a fixed fee payment unless 200,000 man-hours are worked, in which case no rent need be paid.

g. Salaries of repairmen, where one repairman is needed for every 1,000 hours of machine hours or less (i.e., 0 to 1,000 hours requires one repairman, 1,001 to 2,000 hours requires two repairmen, etc.).

h. Federal unemployment compensation taxes for the year, where labor force is constant in number throughout year (average annual salary is $6,000 per worker).

i. Cost of raw material used.

j. Rent on a factory building donated by county, where agreement calls for rent of $100,000 less $1 for each direct labor hour worked in excess of 200,000 hours, but minimum rental payment of $20,000 must be paid.

(Adapted from Uniform CPA Examination)

12-8. Match each of the eight capacity measures with the appropriate direct labor hours listed below (A through H).

[CH. 12]	FLEXIBLE BUDGETING	401

Measure of Capacity	Direct Labor Hours
(1) Theoretical capacity	A. 1,600
(2) Practical capacity	B. 32,000
(3) Upper limit of normal range	C. 24,000
(4) Lower limit of normal range	D. 2,000
(5) Normal capacity	E. 20,000
(6) Actual volume	F. 26,000
(7) Excess capacity	G. 18,400
(8) Idle capacity	H. 16,000

12-9. If a department produced 12,000 tons during a month when practical capacity equaled 24,000 tons and normal capacity was set at 15,000 tons, the department operated at 50 percent of normal for the month. Do you agree? Why?

12-10. If "a" equals $7.50 and "b" equals $.055 and normal capacity has been set at 10,000 direct labor hours, the preliminary monthly manufacturing overhead expense amount for the manufacturing overhead item in question (solved by the least squares method) is $_____?

12-11. A formula form of a flexible budget shows the following:

MONTHLY FLEXIBLE BUDGET—DEPARTMENT 94

Manufacturing Overhead Expense	SV and V Unit Expense Computation	Expense Classification			Total Normal Manufacturing OH Expense
		Total NV	Unit SV	Unit V	
			Based on Department Operating Hours	Based on Normal Capacity	
Direct:					
Heat	$400 ÷ 20,000	$ 50		$.02	$ 450
Foremen	350 ÷ 175	750	$2.00		1,100
Depreciation Buildings		250			250
Indirect:					
Stores	800 ÷ 20,000			.04	800
Total Direct and Indirect		$6,000	$4.00	$.80	?

Normal capacity is 20,000 direct labor hours in Department 94. Departmental operating hours amount to 175 hours at normal capacity.

Required

a. What is the amount of the total normal manufacturing overhead expense?

b. What is the normal manufacturing overhead rate?

12-12. In Question 12-11, the distributed amount of the service department expenses has been included as a variable item in Department 94. If the total of the service department expenses distributed to Department 94 amounts to $4,000.00, compute:

a. The direct normal manufacturing overhead rate.

b. The indirect normal manufacturing overhead rate.

12-13. Based on the data contained in question 12-11 for Department 94, assume that production during the month of March amounted to 16,000 allowed direct labor hours, that 150 departmental operating hours were incurred, that actual manufacturing overhead was $19,048 and compute:

a. the total normal manufacturing overhead charge into production

b. the total budget allowance for the level of activity achieved

c. the total variance

d. two components of the total variance.

12-14. The budget department of Wildwood Country Club is currently engaged in preparing a non-variable and variable expense analysis for its flexible budget. The following is the sales income and the cost of electricity for each of the last twelve months:

	Sales Income	Cost of Electricity
January	$ 51,000	$ 980
February	48,000	960
March	51,000	930
April	46,500	795
May	58,500	835
June	63,000	750
July	60,000	720
August	47,000	690
September	50,000	710
October	50,500	820
November	64,500	870
December	72,000	1,040
Total	$662,000	$10,100

Required

a. Determine the non-variable cost and the degree of variability of the variable element for electricity using:
  1. The high and low points method
  2. The method of least squares
  3. Scatter diagram with a trend line fitted by inspection

b. Discuss the validity and usefulness of the above answers.

12-15. Your company desires to establish flexible budgets for the production departments. You have been appointed chairman of the budget committee. To explain to the members of your committee how the preliminary amounts for the expenses should be ascertained, you have selected four expenses and determined their preliminary amounts and have prepared a written presentation with appropriate explanatory remarks. Show a copy of your presentation to the comptroller for his review and appraisal.

12-16. In establishing a predetermined burden rate, the following flexible budget was prepared:

Percent Capacity	Estimated Burden
100 (or normal)	$500,000
90	465,000
80	440,000
70	425,000

During a month 9,000 units of product (90 percent of capacity) were produced. Actual burden incurred was $505,000. Compare (X) the dollar amount of budget variance with (Y) the dollar amount of volume variance.

Required

With respect to the relationship of X and Y, state whether:

a. X equals Y.
b. X is greater than Y.
c. X is less than Y.
d. X is equal to or greater than Y.
e. X is equal to or less than Y.

(Adapted from Uniform CPA Examination)

12-17. A Company, engaged in production of heavy equipment, has applied manufacturing overhead to its product on the basis of an average rate of 115 percent of direct labor cost. This rate, at the time it was established, was based on the following information as to expected operations:

Direct labor hours		136,000
Direct labor cost		$163,200.00
Average rate per hour		1.20
Fixed manufacturing overhead	$ 57,936.00	
Variable manufacturing overhead	129,744.00	
Total manufacturing overhead		$187,680.00

At December 31, 1972, the end of the first accounting period, the records disclosed the following information:

Direct labor hours	130,000
Direct labor cost	$183,040.00
Average rate per hour	1.408
Fixed manufacturing overhead	$ 75,400.00
Variable manufacturing overhead	145,600.00
Total manufacturing overhead (actual expense)	$221,000.00
Underabsorbed manufacturing overhead	10,504.00

The management is concerned with the fact that it failed to absorb manufacturing overhead of $10,504.00 in the year's operations.

Required:

a. You are to discuss and criticize the system currently being used to absorb manufacturing overhead.

b. You are to prepare an explanation for management showing why the $10,504.00 underabsorption existed. You are to compute and show the effect of variation in direct labor rates and direct labor hours on the absorption of both fixed and variable manufacturing overhead. Support your conclusions with computations and explanatory comments setting forth the significance of each item in the analysis. (Computations should be corrected to the nearest dollar.)

(Adapted from Uniform CPA Examination)

12-18. Given below are the details pertaining to the Power Service Department.

Schedule of Horsepower-Hours

	Producing Departments		Service Departments	
	A	B	X	Y
Needed at capacity production	10,000	20,000	12,000	8,000
Used during the month of April	8,000	13,000	7,000	6,000

During the month of April the expenses of operating the Power Service Department amounted to $9,300; of this amount, $2,500 was considered to be fixed costs.

Required

a. What dollar amounts of the Power Service Department expense should be allocated to each producing and service department?

b. What are the reasons for allocating the costs of one service department to other service departments as well as to producing departments?

(Adapted from Uniform CPA Examination)

12-19. You have been engaged to install a cost system for Martin Company. Your investigation of the manufacturing operations of the business discloses these facts:

[CH. 12] FLEXIBLE BUDGETING 405

a. The company makes a line of lighting fixtures and lamps. The material cost of any particular item ranges from 15 percent to 60 percent of total factory cost, depending on the kind of metal and fabric used in making it.

b. The business is subject to wide cyclical fluctuations since the sales volume follows new housing construction.

c. About 60 percent of the manufacturing is normally done in the first quarter of the year.

d. For the whole plant the wage rates range from $1.75 to $3.75 an hour. However, within each of the eight individual departments, the spread between the high and low wage rate is less than 5 percent.

e. Each of the products made uses all eight of the manufacturing departments but not proportionately.

f. Within the individual manufacturing departments, manufacturing overhead ranges from 30 percent to 80 percent of conversion cost.

Required

Based on the above information, you are to prepare a statement for the president of the company explaining whether in its cost system Martin Company should use:

a. a normal manufacturing overhead rate or an actual manufacturing overhead rate?

b. an overall manufacturing overhead rate or a departmental manufacturing overhead rate?

c. a method of manufacturing overhead distribution based on direct labor hours, direct labor cost or prime cost?

Include the *reasons* supporting *each* of your *three recommendations*.

(Adapted from Uniform CPA Examination)

12-20. Select the *one* answer which *best* states a logical conclusion based on the facts stated.

If a company uses a predetermined rate for application of manufacturing overhead, the volume variance is the:

a. underapplied or overapplied fixed cost element of manufacturing overhead

b. underapplied or overapplied variable cost element of manufacturing overhead

c. difference in budgeted costs and actual costs of fixed manufacturing overhead items

d. difference in budgeted costs and actual costs of variable manufacturing overhead items

e. none of the above

(Adapted from Uniform CPA Examination)

12-21. The Cox Company, the manufacturer of a single product, operated at 80 percent of normal capacity in 1972. Since Cox bases its manufacturing overhead rate on normal capacity, the Company had a substantial amount of underapplied manufacturing overhead for the period.

Early in 1973 Cox receives an order for a substantial number of units at 30 percent off the regular $7.00 sales price. The controller wants to accept the order because $.80 of the total manufacturing cost of $5.00 per unit is fixed manufacturing overhead and because the additional units can be produced within the Company's practical capacity.

The president of Cox Company wants to know if you agree with the controller.

Required:

a. Differentiate among
   1. theoretical capacity
   2. practical capacity
   3. normal capacity
b. Discuss the financial considerations that the president should review before accepting or rejecting the order.
c. The financial statements of Cox Company as of December 31, 1973 are likely to show overapplied manufacturing overhead.
   1. What is overapplied manufacturing overhead?
   2. What are likely to be the major causes of overapplied manufacturing overhead in 1973?
   3. How, if at all, should overapplied manufacturing overhead be treated in the financial statements as of December 31, 1973?

(Adapted from Uniform CPA Examination)

13

Manufacturing Cost Control Through Standard Costs

The evolution of cost accounting has been a history of new concepts and methods devised to enable management to exercise greater control over the costs of an enterprise. At first, managerial control through cost accounting was largely a matter of comparing current costs with historical costs. Then, the development of predetermined manufacturing overhead rates enabled management to compare estimated with actual manufacturing overhead costs, calculate differences between the two, and use the differences as rough guides to identify areas requiring further analysis and possible remedial action. The advantages gained by estimating manufacturing overhead costs prompted management to extend estimating techniques to material and labor costs. Although these steps provided improved control, dependence upon a given difference was limited by the validity of the estimate employed. Poor estimates frequently caused differences between actual and estimated costs to be used to revise the estimates, not to identify areas needing remedial action. It soon became apparent that there was a great need for a measure which would not only estimate what the cost would be but also reveal what it should be. This need gave rise to the development of standard costs.

A standard is that which is established by authority as a ruler, or that which is set up as a gauge to measure weight, quality, quantity and value, or that which is an example, test, criterion or model. Accountants informally define a cost standard as "a par," "an index," "a benchmark," "a gauge," or "a yardstick." All of these definitions describe the cost accounting use of the term. A standard cost is a monetary measure against which an actual cost is compared so that the quantity, excellence, or correctness represented by the actual cost may be ascertained. When the actual cost is found to differ from the standard cost, the actual cost is presumed to be wrong, and remedial action is taken so that a future actual cost will more closely agree with the standard cost. Unlike an estimated cost, which may be corrected when it differs from an actual cost, a standard cost is not changed unless there is conclusive evidence that it was incorrectly established.

Since standard costs are measures of what costs should be, careful analysis and accuracy must enter into their determination. They are not mere averages of past costs. They are developed with painstaking care and are set as accurately as possible. Much of their reliability comes from their being based on studies which provide quantitative physical standards. Material standards are established by determining what raw materials are needed to obtain the desired quality of a product and what quantities of these materials are required to make a unit of product. Labor standards are established by ascertaining the best operating methods and by using time and motion studies to set the standard time required for each labor operation which enters into a manufacturing process. Industrial engineering studies establish the extent to which a manufacturing process must use manufacturing facilities and services. When these quantitative standard amounts of material, labor, and manufacturing facilities and services are converted into monetary measures, standard costs are obtained.

Once standard costs have been set, their use may conform to one of two basic concepts. If a standard cost is to be used as an index number against which all future costs for an indeterminable period of time are to be measured, it is termed a basic or static standard. If a standard is to be used only for a certain period of time and under certain circumstances, it is termed a current standard.

A static standard is not changed so long as the manufacturing process remains unchanged. Consequently, considerable differences are likely to develop between static standard costs and actual costs during periods of sustained trends in price changes. On the other hand, a static standard adjusted for price changes readily provides information concerning cost trends. Static standards are frequently maintained as statistical guides which are not an integral part of the accounting records.

A current standard is changed whenever a change in method or price justifies its revision. It substitutes for actual cost in the accounting records and financial statements. Since it is set in accordance with current conditions, any difference between a current standard cost and an actual cost is considered to result from an unanticipated development.

Regardless of whether a static or a current standard concept is used, standards may be set at any one of the following three levels:

1. *Ideal standards* are set at the level of maximum efficiency. Instead of representing a practical norm, these standards act as a goal which can seldom be

achieved. Because they are relatively unobtainable, ideal standards frequently create a demoralizing effect upon operating personnel.

2. *Normal standards* reflect the conditions which are expected to prevail over a period of time of sufficient length to level the effects of seasonal and cyclical fluctuations. This level is particularly applicable for establishing a standard for manufacturing overhead expense.

3. *Expected actual standards* are set as closely as possible to that level which represents anticipated conditions. These standards are particularly useful in setting price standards for materials and labor. Of course, this level can be used for manufacturing overhead expenses, provided an expected actual, rather than a normal, manufacturing overhead rate is desired.

There is no rule that one type of standard must be used exclusively in a standard cost system; all three types may be used in the same system. In fact, more than one type of standard may be used to set the standard cost of a single cost element. For example, to set a material standard, the quality standard may be ideal, the quantity standard may be normal, and the price standard may be expected actual. The type of standard used is determined by managerial policy. It is important that both management and the operating personnel thoroughly understand the type of standard which underlies each cost factor.

Many assume that standard costs replace actual costs. This is an incorrect impression. Standard costs are not an alternative to actual costs; they complement actual costs. An accounting system which incorporates standard costs must continue to accumulate actual costs. Although standard costs may be used to cost the work-in-process inventory, finished goods inventory, and the cost of goods sold, the difference between actual and standard costs must be considered in determining the actual net profit for the period. Both types of costs are useful for different purposes. A comparison of both types of costs is more useful to management than either type of cost alone.

When a standard cost does not equal its corresponding actual cost, the difference is termed a variance. If the actual cost exceeds the standard cost, the variance is considered to be unfavorable; when the standard cost exceeds the actual cost, the variance is termed favorable. Through observation of these variances, management, at all levels, keeps informed about the effectiveness of manufacturing operations and enhances its ability to control them.

Management uses variances to appraise individual performances and to identify specific conditions which require remedial action. In making the evaluation, management often employs the principle of exceptions. That is, the analyst dismisses variances which indicate insignificant deviations and concentrates upon those which merit detailed investigation and corrective action. In doing this, the analyst must recognize that the total variance from standard is an inadequate indication of performance. A particular variance may be a composite of several factors which are all favorable, all unfavorable, or a combination of the two. Therefore, before meaningful interpretation can be made, a variance must be resolved into its intrinsic components, which must also be identified as favorable or unfavorable.

The detailed variances comprising a "total" material, labor, or manufacturing overhead expense variance are ascertained by different procedures. Although the cost accountant or analyst must understand and utilize these procedures, a familiarity with them will help management to recognize the proper significance of each detailed variance. Therefore, considerable attention will be given next to the identification and determination of the detailed variances which comprise the "total" variance associated with each element of manufacturing cost. Concurrently, consideration will be directed toward the composition of the standard cost which is established for each of the three cost elements.

DIRECT MATERIAL STANDARDS

To establish direct material cost standards, standards must be set for direct material quantities and for direct material prices. The quantity of raw material items needed to manufacture a unit of product is the direct material quantity standard for one unit. The direct material quantity standard for one unit of product times the number of products actually produced equals the standard direct material quantity for the production attained. The direct material needed for one unit of product is obtained from material specifications prepared by the product engineering department or by others who are responsible for determining such requirements. Whether the material specifications set forth requirements classified as bare minimum, bare minimum plus unavoidable waste, or bare minimum plus unavoidable waste and certain avoidable allowances depends upon the policy of the company. In any event, the nature of the material specifications must be considered when the direct material quantity variances are interpreted.

Although material price standards may be normal or ideal, expected actual standards are considered advantageous in most instances. Since such standards frequently require predictions of the prices that may be expected to prevail for the forthcoming period, they are somewhat difficult to set, because, to a great extent, they depend on external factors beyond the control of management. Setting material price standards requires coordination between the cost and purchasing departments. If large stocks of raw materials are carried, the price actually paid is available as the standard direct material cost; if materials are contracted for well before their use, the contract price becomes the standard direct material cost. Otherwise, the purchasing department utilizes whatever assistance is available in forecasting the prices anticipated for the coming period. Of course, if no important change is anticipated in prices, the prices used are those in effect as of the date the standard is set. Direct material price standards are reviewed and revised periodically unless some major price change justifies an immediate revision.

Direct Material Variances

Price and quantity standards are used to compute the standard direct material cost which, when compared with the actual direct material cost for a period (day, week, or month), results in the total direct material variance. To illustrate this procedure, assume that predetermined material standards for the processing of one unit of product "X" in Department 61 require one unit of store item number R–156, which is priced at $10.00 per unit. During the month of January, 1,000 units of product "X" are completely processed by the department through the use of 1,010 actual units of store item R–156, which actually cost $9.00 apiece. The direct material involved in the production of product "X" for the period could be summarized and compared as follows:

	Quantity	Unit Price	Amount
Actual direct material cost	1,010	$ 9.00	$ 9,090
Standard direct material cost	1,000	10.00	10,000
Total direct material variance			$ 910 F

The "F" shown to the right of the $910 indicates that the total direct material variance is favorable, because actual cost is less than standard direct material cost. But the $910 favorable variance alone does not explain whether it is attributable to price, quantity, a combination of both, or other factors. Further information can be obtained through such additional computations as the following:

$$\text{Direct material price variance} = \text{Difference in price} \times \text{Actual quantity used}$$

Direct material price variance = $1 F × 1,010
Direct material price variance = $1,010 F

$$\text{Direct material quantity variance} = \text{Difference in quantity} \times \text{Standard unit price}$$

Direct material quantity variance = 10 U × $10
Direct material quantity variance = $100 U

This may be summarized as follows:

Direct material price variance	$1,010 F
Direct material quantity variance	100 U
Total direct material variance	$ 910 F

These variances are marked favorable whenever the standard cost exceeds actual cost and unfavorable whenever the reverse is true. Management must not be satisfied with a variance identified as simply favorable or unfavorable; this identification is merely a signal which indicates direction. The extent of the direction is expressed by a dollar amount. This information results from the dollar's use as a common denominator to provide monetary yardsticks. But neither knowledge of the direction nor the extent of the direction provides control over a given condition. Genuine and effective control is accomplished by investigating and determining what caused these dollar "signals" and by instituting whatever remedial action may be required.

Investigations frequently reveal causative factors other than those which appear on the surface. For instance, the $1,010 favorable price variance appears to indicate that the purchasing department has operated efficiently, buying material below its standard price, while this condition actually may be the result of purchase and use of material which is inferior to the standard quality. Similarly, the unfavorable material quantity (sometimes termed usage) variance may be the result of a favorable price variance which sacrificed quality, and not of defective workmanship, as it might first appear. The specific causes which create variances must be ascertained if maximum value is to be derived from a standard cost system.

Peculiar to the material price variance is the time at which such a variance is recognized. For example, the difference between the actual and standard cost of raw materials may be recognized when material is purchased. This timing measures the performance of the purchasing department in a given period regardless of when the purchased material is actually used in production. This method has the possible disadvantage of showing, on the statement of income at the end of a period, price variances which do not apply to the material actually used in production. This disadvantage can be overcome by not accounting for the price variance until the material is used in production, as was done for the $1,010 price variance obtained in the foregoing illustration. But this method also has disadvantages. For instance, it measures the performance of the purchasing department when the material is used, a time which may not represent the period in which the material was bought. Moreover, it requires painstaking recordkeeping to insure that proper price variances are correctly associated with the material used in production. Since both methods have advantages as well as disadvantages, the decision to use either method depends upon company policy.

Under certain conditions, there is some question concerning the acceptability of the procedure used to separate price and quantity variances in the preceding example. To illustrate, assume the following data regarding direct material costs for one unit of product:

	Standard	Actual
Number of raw material units	6	5
Price per unit of raw material	$ 3	$ 4
Cost per unit of complete product	$18	$20

Using this information, the procedure shown for computing material variances would result in the following data:

Direct material price variance	$5 U
Direct material usage variance	3 F
Total direct material variance	$2 U

The costs and variances in this situation are portrayed in Exhibit 13–1. In the exhibit, the rectangle formed by solid lines represents the standard cost, while the rectangle formed by dotted lines represents the actual cost. The usage and price variances are indicated by the two areas where the two rectangles fail to coincide. Thus far, the variances are readily reconciled and no question is likely to arise concerning the technique by which they were computed. But, when

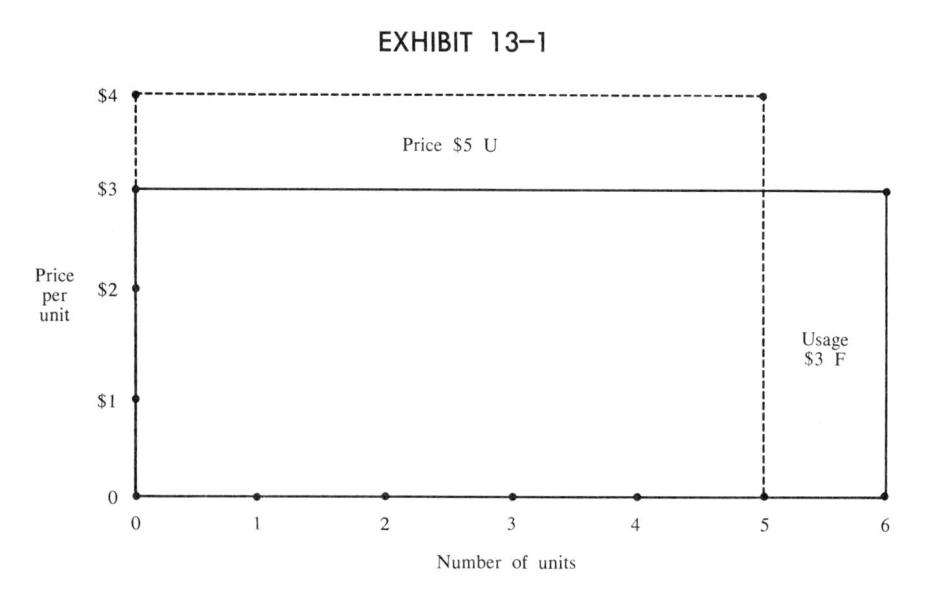

EXHIBIT 13–1

both variances are either favorable or unfavorable, the use of the suggested technique results in variances which contain, and readily reveal, a slight error. The problem can be illustrated by using the direct material costs shown by the following situation:

	Standard	Actual
Number of raw material units	6	7
Price per unit of raw material	$ 3	$ 4
Cost per unit of completed product	$18	$28

Using the suggested technique, the following direct material variances would be computed:

Direct material price variance	$ 7U
Direct material usage variance	3 U
Total direct material variance	$10 U

Exhibit 13–2 shows a diagram of the material costs and variances. With the standard cost portrayed by the solid rectangle and the actual costs portrayed by the larger broken rectangle, the area between the two represents the total direct material variance. Clearly, of the area portraying total material variance, $3 of

the space depicts a usage variance and $6 of the space shows a price variance. This leaves $1 of the space (shown by the smaller broken rectangle) to represent both excess usage and excess price. The suggested procedure has the effect of assigning all of the $1 to price variance. Other techniques could be used

EXHIBIT 13-2

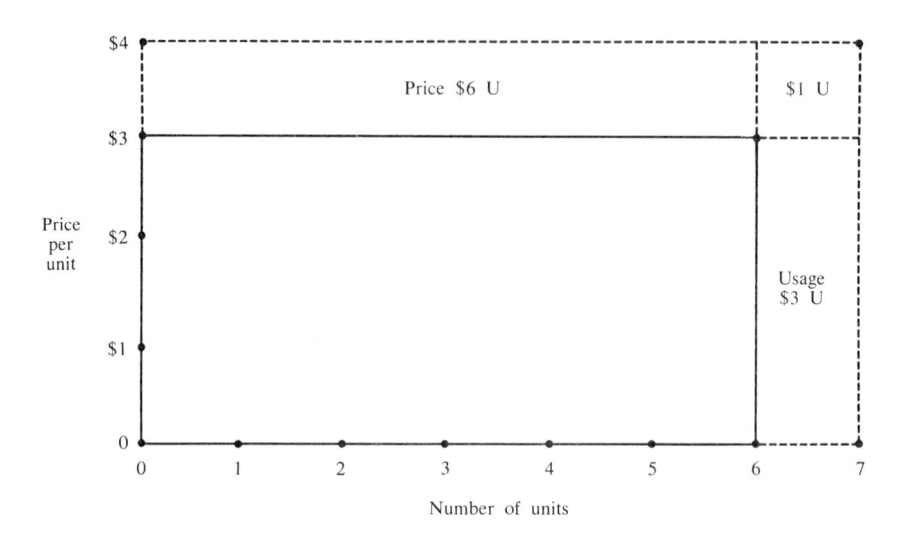

which would identify this usage-price variance separately, but the benefit provided is ordinarily not considered sufficient to justify their use. Consequently, the suggested technique is used to calculate direct material variances even though it presents a slight distortion. A similar problem is encountered in the calculation of the labor variances.

DIRECT LABOR STANDARDS

A direct labor cost standard consists of two separate and distinct factors similar to those that comprise a direct material cost standard. The quantity or usage standard for direct material becomes a time, quantity, usage, or efficiency standard for direct labor. The price standard for direct material is termed a wage, rate, or price standard for direct labor. Usually, the two standards comprising a direct labor cost standard are identified as time and rate standards.

The standard time multiplied by the standard rate equals the standard direct labor cost of a unit of product. The standard direct labor cost of a unit of product times the number of products produced equals the standard direct labor cost for the period under consideration.

The standard time required to produce a product is ordinarily established by determining the standard time needed to perform each labor operation that enters into its production. This is accomplished by first selecting the best operating method available and then identifying all of the labor operations comprising the method which are required to process a product. Standard operating time allowances are next established for the various labor operations through time and motion studies. These studies analyze the operations into distinct elementary motions and carefully measure the time required to perform each motion under allowed conditions.

If a company desires tight labor performance standards, it uses the minimum time observed for each labor operation. On the other hand, if company policy favors labor performance standards which represent reasonably attainable performance, then the labor time standards combine the minimum time with a normal time allowance for fatigue and other personal delays. Non-personal delays like time for setups, change-overs, and machinery breakdowns are usually included in the manufacturing overhead standard instead of the direct labor standard.

Normal or ideal standards are rarely used to set direct labor rate standards; labor rates are ordinarily set as expected actual standards, since most companies change labor rate standards whenever labor rates change.

The setting of labor rate standards demands careful attention to the method of wage payment in use. If straight piece rates are in effect, they automatically become the labor rate standards. However, if piece rates become labor rate standards where a day rate minimum is in effect, some method must be devised to charge manufacturing overhead with the premiums paid to operators whose piece rate earnings fall below the daily guaranteed pay. Often, standard labor rates are established by collective bargaining agreements and union contracts. In other instances, hourly wages and various bonus plans require different methods of setting labor rates for each operation. Sometimes, it is expedient to set a single average standard labor rate for a specific operation, though the rate paid individual workers may vary slightly owing to seniority considerations. Because of the variety of wage payment methods, it is imperative that special attention be devoted to each situation.

Regardless of the method of payment, if direct labor rate standards are changed when actual labor rate changes occur, the labor rate variances should be relatively slight if the usual "labor-mix" is maintained. These variances are the responsibility of the department head or foreman. If labor rate standards are not kept current, actual labor rate changes must be eliminated from labor rate variances to establish the responsibility of a department head or foreman.

Direct Labor Variances

The calculation of the standard direct labor cost requires the multiplication of the standard direct labor time by the standard direct labor rate. Any difference which exists between the standard direct labor cost and the actual direct labor cost represents the total amount of the direct labor variance. To illustrate how the total direct labor variance is obtained, assume that the direct labor time standard for the processing of one unit of product "X" is five hours at a standard direct labor rate of $1.90 per hour in Department 61. During the month of January, the department uses 5,100 actual direct labor hours at $2.00 per hour to process 1,000 units of product "X." The direct labor costs relating to the production of product "X" are compared below:

	Hours	Hourly Rate	Amount
Actual direct labor cost	5,100	$2.00	$10,200
Standard direct labor cost	5,000	1.90	9,500
Total direct labor variance			$ 700 U

The $700 total direct labor variance is unfavorable, because the actual direct labor cost exceeds the standard direct labor cost. But the total variance does not indicate whether it was unfavorable because of undue time, excessive labor rates, or a combination of various factors. It is apparent from a review of the data that 100 hours of labor in excess of the allowed hours were required, and that each hour of actual labor costs ten cents more than the predetermined standard hourly rate. This information is converted into a direct labor time variance and a direct labor rate variance in the following manner:

Direct labor time variance = Difference in hours × Standard hourly rate
Direct labor time variance = 100 U × $1.90
Direct labor time variance = $190 U
Direct labor rate variance = Difference in rates × Actual hours worked
Direct labor rate variance = $0.10 × 5,100
Direct labor rate variance = $510 U

These variances may be summarized as follows:

Direct labor time variance	$190 U
Direct labor rate variance	510 U
Total direct labor variance	$700 U

Direct labor variances, like direct material variances, are provided for managerial guidance and control. The variances themselves do not provide control; effective control is obtained through the action which results from an analysis of the variances. Action which identifies the causes underlying the variances enables management to institute measures designed to correct unsatisfactory conditions. Sometimes there is a question about who should interpret the variances and make the necessary investigations. One study reveals:

> Experience of the companies interviewed seems to show that the explanation and interpretation of variances is best developed through indepen-

[CH. 13]   COST CONTROL THROUGH STANDARD COSTS   417

dent analysis made by the cost accountant working in close collaboration with operating supervisors. While interpretation of events in terms of variance causes is primarily a function of the operation supervisor or executive, the cost department collects and organizes statistical information relating to variance causes.[1]

Investigations of direct labor variances are likely to uncover numerous causes. The following few examples of causes compiled jointly by accounting and top factory operating management were selected from a study by the National Association of Accountants.[2]

EXHIBIT 13-3

Department Manufacturing Efficiency on Completed Operations

DEPARTMENT NO. _____   MONTH OF _____

Reason for Variance (C means controllable; N non-controllable)		Actual Hours	Variance Hours	Cost
No reason, variance less than 10 percent	C			
Estimated running time too high. Reported to Standards Department	N			
Men's effort and/or ability above average	C			
New machine, standard has not been changed	N			
Total Gains				
Standard too low. Reported to Standards Department	N			
First time job was made	C			
Operation not performed correctly. Added time required	C			
Parts spoiled. Had to make more parts	C			
Oversized material used	N			
Total Loses				
Total				

In Exhibit 13-3, the first example illustrates a variance for which no reason is required. The explanation given for not requiring a reason is that the variance is "less than 10 percent." This example was not included to suggest that

---

[1] National Association of (Cost) Accountants, Research Series No. 22, "The Analysis of Manufacturing Cost Variances" (August, 1952), p. 1556.
[2] Ibid., p. 1561.

variances under 10 percent are never analyzed nor investigated; it was listed to illustrate the practice followed by a firm included in the study. But it does raise the question of what percentage of variation merits analysis and action. No precise answer can be made to this question, since no single percentage would apply equally to all situations.

In each company, management decides when a specific percentage of variance justifies action. Certain factors may cause different decisions by the management of various companies. If a company's policy limits the amount of effort which can be expended on analyzing and correcting non-standard performance in a given period, attention should be directed toward those variances which constitute the most serious exceptions. Consequently, the point below which a variance would not be investigated would vary in accordance with the number and significance of the variances established in a given period.[3] The nature of the standard is another factor which affects decisions. For example, a 10 percent variation might be more acceptable to a company using tight standards than a 5 percent variation would be to a company employing loose standards.

Some of the other selected reasons shown in Exhibit 13–3 might also be considered questionable in certain situations, but the examples listed do demonstrate how detailed analyses and investigations of variances can provide a means of control, how the principle of exceptions can be applied to a standard cost system, and how the responsibility of a supervising official may be identified.

MANUFACTURING OVERHEAD STANDARDS

Manufacturing overhead standards are developed and converted into standard manufacturing overhead rates for the various functional units, cost centers, or departments into which a manufacturing activity is divided for costing and control. Ordinarily, these divisions are established on a departmental basis.

Before a departmental standard manufacturing overhead rate can be set properly, the following questions must be answered:

1. What is the unit used to measure volume of productive activity?
2. What is the standard volume of productive activity?
3. What is the total dollar amount of manufacturing overhead expense at standard volume?

The procedures to be followed in answering these questions are similar to those contained in Chapters 10, 11, and 12 concerning the determination of a measure of activity, the establishment of normal volume, and the determination of manufacturing overhead expenses applicable to a normal volume of operating activity. After these answers have been provided, a departmental standard manufacturing overhead rate can be ascertained by dividing the total standard

---

[3] For a detailed discussion and illustration of statistical testing for significant variances, see the section on "Control Charts for Variances" in Chapter 19.

[CH. 13] COST CONTROL THROUGH STANDARD COSTS 419

manufacturing overhead expense by the number of units at standard volume of productive activity.

In answering the questions, recall that the manufacturing overhead expense applicable to a *normal volume* of activity can be ascertained through a fixed or a flexible budget. Similarly, both types of budgets may be used with a standard cost system to determine the total standard manufacturing overhead expense applicable to the *standard volume* of productive activity. It must be recognized, though, that the total standard manufacturing overhead includes both variable and fixed expenses. Consequently, when the standard manufacturing overhead is converted into a standard costing rate, that rate consists of both fixed and variable components.

The fixed component of the standard costing rate will charge production with the total amount of fixed expenses contained in the total standard manufacturing overhead expense only when the volume of operations equals the volume on which the rate was based. At that point, the fixed costs charged to production will equal the fixed costs contained in the budget at the standard volume of productive activity. At any other point of productive volume, the amount of the fixed costs charged to production by the standard costing rate will be more or less than the amount contained in the budget. This difference, called a variance, becomes management's monetary measure of the utilization of standard capacity. Either a flexible or a fixed budget may be employed to measure this utilization.

A fixed budget is not readily adaptable under all conditions to the measurement and control of variable manufacturing overhead expenses. It is true that a fixed budget contains the total amount of variable expenses applicable to the standard volume of productive activity. It is also true that the variable component of a standard costing rate properly represents the variable expenses associated with each standard unit used to measure the standard volume of productive activity. Therefore, when the volume of operations equals the standard volume of productive activity, the variable expenses charged to production through the standard costing rate will equal those contained in the fixed budget at the standard volume of productive activity.

Whenever the volume of operations deviates from the standard volume of productive activity, the standard costing rate will charge to production an amount of variable expenses which differs from the variable expenses contained in the fixed budget at the standard volume of productive activity. This difference measures whether the variable expenses charged to production were greater or less than the variable expenses contained in the fixed budget; it does not measure whether the variable expenses were greater or less than they should have been for the volume of operations attained. This vital information, however, can be supplied by a flexible budget. Since either budget can be used to measure fixed expenses, but only a flexible budget can readily provide measurements to guide the control of variable expenses, it is more advantageous to use a flexible budget with a standard cost system. It must be recognized, however, that, even when a flexible budget is used, the standard and budget cost figures will be identical only at the standard volume of productive activity due to the treatment afforded fixed expenses. At other levels of productive activity, differences between the standard costs and budget allowances are variances which represent monetary measures of capacity utilization, and differences between actual manufacturing overhead expenses and applicable flexible budget allowances are variances which represent monetary measures of the control obtained over manufacturing overhead expenses.

Standard Manufacturing Overhead Rate

To provide a basis for the calculation of a standard manufacturing overhead rate, Exhibit 13–4 summarizes, by variability classification and total amount for each 20 percent increment in productive volume from point of shutdown to 120 percent of standard capacity, the monthly flexible manufacturing overhead expense budget for Department 61. (Although Exhibit 13–4 illustrates 20 percent increments from point of shutdown, it will be recalled from Chapter 12 that flexible budgets may contain intervals of any percentage within any range of operating activity that may be considered useful to management.)

EXHIBIT 13–4

Monthly Flexible Manufacturing Overhead Expense Budget
Department 61

Units of production	0	250	500	750	1,000	1,250	1,500
Direct labor hours allowed	0	1,250	2,500	3,750	5,000	6,250	7,500
Percentage of standard capacity	0%	20%	40%	60%	80%	100%	120%
Variable expenses	$ 0	$ 850	$1,700	$2,550	$3,400	$4,250	$5,100
Non-variable expenses	4,500	4,500	4,500	4,500	4,500	4,500	4,500
Total departmental expenses	$4,500	$5,350	$6,200	$7,050	$7,900	$8,750	$9,600

Exhibit 13–4 shows that the total manufacturing overhead expenses at 100 percent of standard capacity are $8,750. This amount divided by the standard unit used to measure volume of productive activity will provide the standard manufacturing overhead rate. For example, if units of production are used to measure productive activity, the following standard manufacturing overhead rate would be computed:

$$\frac{\$8,750}{1,250 \text{ units}} = \$7.00 \text{ per unit of production}$$

If direct labor hours are used to measure productive activity, the standard manufacturing overhead rate would be computed as follows:

$$\frac{\$8,750}{6,250 \text{ hours}} = \$1.40 \text{ per direct labor hour}$$

Another way to obtain a standard manufacturing overhead rate would be by computing and then adding together separate variable and non-variable expense rates for the standard volume of productive activity. This procedure is illustrated below using direct labor hours as the activity measure for the flexible budget developed in Exhibit 13–4.

			Per D.L.H.
Variable expense rate	=	$\dfrac{\$4,250}{6,250 \text{ D.L.H.}}$ =	$ .68
Non-variable expense rate	=	$\dfrac{\$4,500}{6,250 \text{ D.L.H.}}$ =	.72
Standard manufacturing overhead rate			$1.40

Since Exhibit 13–4 shows that one unit of production requires five direct labor hours, a standard manufacturing overhead rate calculated for one of these measures could readily be converted into a standard manufacturing overhead rate for the other measure. This procedure is acceptable as long as a single product or products which could be equated to an equivalent physical unit of product is produced. But, when multiple products which cannot be converted into equivalent physical units are produced, a standard manufacturing overhead rate must be computed for a measure which will equitably relate manufacturing overhead to different products like the measures used to apportion actual manufacturing overhead expenses in Chapter 10. In this respect, a standard manufacturing overhead rate is similar to a normal manufacturing overhead rate used in an actual cost system.

Predetermination is another similarity which exists between standard manufacturing overhead rates and normal manufacturing overhead rates. There is, however, a distinct difference between the two that involves how the cost of production is charged with manufacturing overhead expenses. For example, if the $1.40 per hour direct labor rate calculated from Exhibit 13–4 is used with an actual cost system where eleven direct labor hours have been incurred, the normal manufacturing overhead expense would be $15.40 regardless of the number of units completed. But, if the same situation exists in a standard cost system which requires five direct labor hours for each unit of product produced and two units are made, the standard manufacturing overhead expense would be $14.00 regardless of the number of actual labor hours incurred. To summarize, the normal manufacturing overhead expense is based upon the actual inputs of the activity measure, while the standard manufacturing overhead expense is based upon the number of standard activity measurement inputs allowed for the actual productive output achieved.

Manufacturing Overhead Variances

The determination of the amount of the standard manufacturing overhead expense included in the cost of production for a given period is the result of multiplying the number of allowed units at the given production level by the standard manufacturing overhead expense rate. The standard manufacturing overhead thus computed is compared with the actual manufacturing overhead expense for the same period. Any difference which exists between the two represents a total manufacturing overhead variance. This variance may be ascertained by the day, week, month, or any period desired by management.

To illustrate the total manufacturing overhead variance, the data used on page 416 to explain direct labor variances for Product "X" in Department 61 will be employed with the flexible budget developed in Exhibit 13–4. The standard direct labor time established for the processing of one unit of Product "X" in Department 61 is five hours. During the month of January, 5,100 actual direct labor hours are used to process 1,000 units of Product "X," while standard (or allowed) direct labor hours total 5,000 (1,000 units × five hours). Assume that the actual manufacturing overhead for Department 61 in January amounts to $7,400. Based upon this information, the total manufacturing overhead variance is computed as follows:

	Allowed Direct Labor Hours	Standard Rate per Hour	Amount
Standard manufacturing overhead expense ...	5,000	$1.40	$7,000
Actual manufacturing overhead expense			7,400
Total manufacturing overhead variance			$ 400 U

The $400 total, or net manufacturing overhead variance, is unfavorable, because the actual manufacturing overhead expense exceeds the standard manufacturing overhead expense. But the total variance does not indicate whether it is unfavorable because of inadequate volume, inefficient use of time, excessive incurrence of manufacturing expenses, or some combination of these factors. Consequently, further analysis of the total variance is needed to identify specific indicators for managerial action.

Various companies use alternate procedures to analyze total manufacturing overhead variance. Consequently, the analyses described in this chapter should not be considered the only possibilities. As will be seen from subsequent examples, various methods may identify the same variances, different variances, or some combination of both types. This situation does not negate the usefulness of the various methods as long as their underlying concepts are understood; the objective of an analysis is not to provide a precise measure in every instance, but to isolate variances which guide investigations, force identification of the specific causes, and spur remedial action.

All the methods agree on the amount of the total manufacturing overhead variance. Disagreements arise, however, regarding the proper amount of the budget allowance used to analyze the total variance. Should the allowance be based on standard capacity hours, standard hours allowed for the production achieved, or hours actually worked? Should budget allowances for both stan-

[CH. 13] COST CONTROL THROUGH STANDARD COSTS 423

dard allowed and actual hours be used to analyze the total variance? These questions are asking whether budget allowances used to analyze variances should be based on budgeted output, actual output, actual input, or both actual output and actual input. The answer depends upon the information desired by management; different allowances will provide different kinds of information.

When a company uses standard capacity hours to determine a budget allowance, it is actually employing a fixed or static budget. This practice assumes slight deviations between actual production and the volume of production upon which standard capacity has been established. If large deviations occur, a completely meaningful analysis of the total overhead variance is impossible; even a slight volume deviation produces an analysis which provides less than proper control information for expenses. Consequently, a static budget allowance provides an invalid analysis of a total manufacturing overhead variance unless actual operating activity equals the activity established at standard capacity. Since such a condition rarely exists, the use of a static budget allowance will not be illustrated here. Instead, flexible budget allowances will be used to illustrate various analyses of the $400 total manufacturing overhead variance under discussion.

Budget Allowance Based on Actual Hours. A budget allowance based on the actual hours worked overcomes the principal defect in a budget allowance based on standard capacity: it establishes the amount of the manufacturing overhead expenses that should be incurred for the hours actually worked, and it permits the calculation of a budget variance which represents a meaningful guide for control. As a result, efficiency, budget, and capacity variances are computed as indicated below:

	Total Variance	Efficiency Variance	Budget Variance	Capacity Variance
Standard manufacturing overhead (Standard hours allowed × standard manufacturing overhead rate) (5,000 × $1.40)	$7,000	$7,000		
Actual manufacturing overhead	7,400		$7,400	
Actual hours × standard manufacturing overhead rate (5,100 × $1.40)		7,140		$7,140
Budget allowance for actual hours worked				
Variable expenses (5,100 hours × $.68 variable rate) = $3,468				
Non-variable expenses 4,500			7,968	7,968
Total Variance—Unfavorable	$ 400			
Efficiency Variance—Unfavorable		$ 140		
Budget Variance—Favorable			$ 568	
Capacity Variance—Unfavorable				$ 828

The preceding efficiency variance is identical to the efficiency variance which would be computed by using a static budget. It represents the difference between the actual hours worked and the allowed hours earned by the output achieved multiplied by the standard manufacturing overhead rate. (5,100 − 5,000 × $1.40 = $140).

The $828 capacity variance measures the extent to which the standard capacity was utilized during the period. It represents the difference between the standard capacity hours and the hours actually worked multipled by the standard non-variable manufacturing overhead rate. (6,250 − 5,100 × $.72 = $828). Moreover, the $828 capacity variance may be divided by the $.72 standard non-variable manufacturing overhead rate to obtain the number of standard capacity hours which were unused during the period. ($828 ÷ $.72 = 1,150).

Unlike the budget variance which would be computed by using a static budget, this budget variance is realistic since it is related to the 5,100 hours actually worked. The $568 budget variance actually measures the amount that the manufacturing overhead incurred was below what was expected for the actual hours worked. It does not, however, measure the difference between the actual manufacturing overhead incurred and the amount of the manufacturing overhead allowed for the effective level of production achieved. To accomplish this, another method of analysis must be followed.

Budget Allowance Based on Allowed Hours. This allowance is ascertained by adding the non-variable expenses to the variable expenses allowed for the actual production completed. The variable expenses allowed are computed by multiplying the standard (allowed) hours by the variable manufacturing overhead expense rate. This allowance represents the manufacturing overhead expense "cleared into cost" for the output achieved. It ignores actual hours worked and standard capacity hours, and it permits the combination of efficiency and expense deviations into a single controllable variance. It also isolates a volume variance, as shown in the analysis on page 425.

A volume variance thus isolated measures the difference between the standard capacity output and the allowed output obtained. In the following analysis, the $900 unfavorable volume variance divided by the $.72 non-variable expense rate per hour shows that 1,250 of the standard capacity hours were not required by the output attained. These 1,250 hours combine the 1,150 idle capacity hours (6,250 standard capacity hours—5,100 actual hours worked) with the 100 excessive hours (in standard allowed hours) used (5,100 actual hours worked—5,000 allowed hours) to measure the amount of additional output which could have been produced if standard capacity had been utilized efficiently.

The $568 favorable budget variance and the $68 variable portion of the $140 unfavorable efficiency variance (isolated by the budget allowance based on actual input) are combined in the $500 favorable controllable variance

	Total Variance	Volume Variance	Controllable Variance
Standard manufacturing overhead (Standard hours allowed × standard manufacturing overhead rate) (5,000 × $1.40)	$7,000	$7,000	
Actual manufacturing overhead	7,400		$7,400
Budget allowance for allowed hours Variable expenses (5,000 hours × $.68 variable rate) = $3,400 Non-variable expenses 4,500		7,900	7,900
Total Variance—Unfavorable	$ 400		
Volume Variance—Unfavorable		$ 900	
Controllable Variance—Favorable			$ 500

shown in the analysis. This allows controllable efficiency and expense factors, which are the responsibility of a department head or foreman, to be shown as a single amount. Although this procedure identifies the total or net amount of controllable variations for responsibility, it can be misleading when an unfavorable component is offset by a favorable component. As a result, some companies favor an analysis which isolates controllable factors into separate efficiency and expense variances.

Budget Allowances Based on Actual Hours and Allowed Hours. An analysis of a total manufacturing overhead variance which utilizes budget allowances for both actual hours and allowed hours separates controllable factors into spending variance and efficiency variance. In this respect, it is very similar to an analysis made with a budget allowance based on actual input. The two analyses differ, however, in their treatment of the non-variable expenses which are related to the "unproductive" hours worked. Recall that an analysis based on actual input includes such non-variable expenses in an efficiency variance. An analysis based on both actual and allowed budget allowances places these expenses in the volume variance computed with a budget allowance based on actual output. It should now be recognized that an analysis involving both input and output budget allowances resembles an input analysis for controllable elements and an output analysis for the volume element. Thus, three variances are isolated, as illustrated on page 426.

In this analysis, the $900 unfavorable volume variance identifies that portion of the total non-variable expense which measures the combined idle capacity and ineffective productive activity. The $568 favorable spending variance measures the amount that actual manufacturing overhead expenses were less than the amount expected for the actual hours worked. The $68 unfavorable efficiency variance measures the amount of variable expenses provided for the 100 actual hours worked in excess of the allowed time.

	Total Variance	Volume Variance	Spending Variance	Efficiency Variance
Standard manufacturing overhead (Standard hours allowed × standard manufacturing overhead rate) (5,000 × $1.40)	$7,000	$7,000		
Actual manufacturing overhead	7,400		$7,400	
Budget allowance for allowed hours Variable expenses (5,000 hours × $.68 variable rate) = $3,400 Non-variable expenses 4,500		7,900		$7,900
Budget allowance for actual hours Variable expenses (5,100 hours × $.68 variable rate) = $3,468 Non-variable expenses 4,500			7,968	7,968
Total Variance—Unfavorable	$ 400			
Volume Variance—Unfavorable		$ 900		
Spending Variance—Favorable			$ 568	
Efficiency Variance—Unfavorable				$ 68

Summary of Manufacturing Overhead Analyses

Four different analyses of the total manufacturing overhead variance have been discussed. They are:

1. Three variances based on a budgeted capacity allowance
2. Three variances based on an actual input budget allowance
3. Two variances based on an actual output budget allowance
4. Three variances based on both actual input and actual output budget allowances

It would be quite natural to ask which analysis is best. It has already been indicated that an analysis based on a budgeted capacity allowance contains a rigidity which causes inadequate information in the majority of instances. The three analyses which are based on flexible budget allowances provide meaningful, but slightly different, kinds of information. The type of analysis to be used depends upon the needs of a company, and the selection is really determined by the need of the management concerned. All three of the analyses are commonly used in actual practice; the two-variance analysis based on an allowed budget seems to be the most popular.

PRODUCT STANDARD COST

It is customary for a company to maintain a separate record of the standard cost of each product produced. This record contains the standard direct material, direct labor, manufacturing overhead, and total cost required to produce one unit of product. Based upon the data contained in this chapter, a record of the standard product cost for one unit of product "X" would include the information shown in Exhibit 13–5.

EXHIBIT 13–5

Standard Product Cost Record

PRODUCT "X"							
			\multicolumn{4}{c}{Department}
			61	62	63	Total
Direct Material						
Quantity	Description	Price				
1	Store item #R-156	$10.00	$10.00			$10.00
Direct Labor						
Operation Number	Standard Hours	Standard Rate per hour				
61–24–8	5	$ 1.90	$ 9.50			$ 9.50
Manufacturing Overhead						
	Standard Hours	Standard Rate per hour				
	5	$ 1.40	$ 7.00			$ 7.00
Total Standard Product Cost per Unit						$26.50

SUMMARY OF STANDARD COSTS

Throughout this chapter, standard costs have been analyzed and illustrated through the development of direct material, direct labor, and manufacturing overhead standards for product "X" in Department 61. A summary of the standards established for one unit of product "X" was provided in the section immediately preceding this discussion. Although standard costs aid management by simplifying production costing procedures and establishing guides for proposed selling prices, their greatest value lies in their ability to measure actual operations, aid in the control and reduction of costs, and in their contribution to the promotion of efficiencies. In summary, primary indicators in the form of monetary variances are obtained by comparing actual with standard costs. These primary variances are then subjected to detailed analyses which identify the direction and significance of specific deviations. By using these specific variances as guides, management can investigate the identified areas to establish the reason or reasons underlying the variances and to initiate the necessary remedial actions. The comparison of actual with standard costs to obtain total variances which are analyzed as specific variances is a primary contribution of a standard cost system. Based on the data developed and illustrated in this chapter, Exhibit 13-6 summarizes the January production costs for product "X" in Department 61. Detailed manufacturing overhead variances are derived from a budget allowance based on allowed hours for the output attained.

EXHIBIT 13-6

Summary of Production Costs

Department 61	PRODUCT "X"		Month of January	
Cost Element	Standard Cost	Actual Cost	Total Variance	Detailed Variances
Direct Material	$10,000	$9,090	$910 F	
Price Variance				$1,010 F
Quantity Variance				100 U
Direct Labor	9,500	10,200	700 U	
Rate Variance				190 U
Time Variance				510 U
Manufacturing Overhead Expense	7,000	7,400	400 U	
Controllable Variance				500 F
Volume Variance				900 U
TOTALS	$26,500	$26,690	$190 U	$190 U

QUESTIONS AND PROBLEMS

13-1. In a standard cost system, the ending work in process inventory must be computed before the standard cost of production can be ascertained. Do you agree? Why?

13-2. At any point of productive output above standard, will the amount of the manufacturing overhead expense budget be more or less than the amount of the standard manufacturing overhead charged to production? Why?

13-3. Standard costing procedures are widely used in manufacturing operations and, more recently, have become common in many nonmanufacturing operations.

Required

a. Define standard costs. Distinguish between basic and current standards.

b. What are the advantages of a standard cost system?

[CH. 13] COST CONTROL THROUGH STANDARD COSTS 429

    c. Present arguments in support of each of the following three methods of treating standard cost variances for purposes of financial reporting:
       1. They may be carried as deferred charges or credits on the balance sheet.
       2. They may appear as charges or credits on the income statement.
       3. They may be allocated between inventories and cost of goods sold.

   (Adapted from Uniform CPA Examination)

13-4. During the month of April, 20,000 pieces of store item number 1208 and 10,000 pieces of store item 1209 were purchased for the production of product "X" in cost center 92.

Store's Item Number	Actual Cost	Standard Cost
1208	$1.02	$1.00
1209	.85	.92

No pieces of these store items were on hand on April 1. None of these store items were issued to production during the month of April.

Required

a. If the company recognizes a material price variance upon acquisition, what would be the material price variance for the month of April?

b. If the company uses a material price variance at the time of issue, what would be the material price variance for the month of April?

c. Discuss the advantages and disadvantages of the two practices described in a and b.

13-5. Assume that the company discussed in the preceding question records a material price variance when materials are issued and that, during the month of April, 3,020 pieces of store item number 1208 and 9,100 pieces of store item number 1209 were issued for the production of 3,000 units of product "X." There was no work in process in cost center 92 on either April 1 or April 30. The standard bill of materials for one unit of product "X" in cost center 92 calls for one piece of store item number 1208 and three pieces of store item number 1209.

Required

Calculate the following variances and indicate whether they are favorable or unfavorable.

a. total direct material variance

b. direct material usage variance

c. direct material price variance

13-6. The standard allowed time for the production of one unit of product "X" in cost center 92 is 2⅔ hours. As stated in question 13-5, 3,000 units of product "X" were produced during April. The standard hourly direct labor rate in cost center 92 is $2.50. During April, the payroll showed 8,100 actual hours worked at an hourly rate of $2.53.

Required

Calculate the following variances and indicate whether they are favorable or unfavorable.

a. total direct labor variance

b. direct labor time variance

c. direct labor rate variance

13-7. The flexible manufacturing overhead budget for cost center 92 discloses the following:

Total non-variable expense	$ 3,500.00
Variable expense rate per direct labor hour	$ 1.15
Standard capacity in direct labor hours	10,000

Required

Compute

a. the total standard manufacturing overhead expense

b. the standard manufacturing overhead rate

13-8. If, during April, the productive output in cost center 92 amounted to 8,000 standard allowed direct labor hours, compute:

a. the standard manufacturing overhead expense for the production achieved during the month

b. the budget allowance for April's production (Use allowed hours to calculate the budget allowance)

13-9. Actual manufacturing overhead expenses totaled $12,000.00 during April in cost center 92. Combine the information contained in questions 13-7 and 13-8 with this question and calculate the following variances. (Indicate whether the variances are favorable or unfavorable.)

a. total manufacturing overhead variance

b. controllable variance

c. volume variance

13-10. Compute the standard unit product cost of product "X" in cost center 92. Use the data contained in the six preceding questions to answer this question as shown below:

a. standard unit direct material cost

b. standard unit direct labor cost

c. standard unit manufacturing overhead cost

d. standard unit product cost

13-11. Calculate the total standard cost of production for product "X" for April in cost center 92. You should arrive at the same standard cost of production by each of the methods below.

[CH. 13]   COST CONTROL THROUGH STANDARD COSTS   431

Method one

a. Total standard direct material cost (question 13-5) .... $_____
b. Total standard direct labor cost (question 13-6) .... $_____
c. Total standard manufacturing overhead cost (question 13-8) $_____
d. Total standard cost of production .... $_____

Method two

Number of units produced (3,000) times standard unit cost of production (question 13-10) .... $_____

13-12. Assume that a flexible manufacturing overhead budget was used for cost center 92 and that both input and output budget allowances were calculated for the production activity in April. Use the data contained in the preceding questions regarding cost center 92 to calculate the following variances and indicate whether they are favorable or unfavorable.

a. volume variance
b. spending variance
c. efficiency variance

13-13. Assume that a flexible manufacturing overhead budget was used for cost center 92 and that the budget allowance for the production attained in April was based on the actual direct labor hours worked. Use the data contained in the preceding questions concerning cost center 92 to calculate the following variances and indicate whether they are favorable or unfavorable.

a. efficiency variance
b. budget variance
c. capacity variance

13-14. The Koh Company is a process manufacturer of gidgets. The cost system is of the standard-absorption type. Standard cost of production of one gidget is:

Direct Material	5 lbs. of metal @ $1.00 per lb. .	$ 5.00
Direct Labor	3 hours @ $2.00 per hour	6.00
Manufacturing Overhead	3 hours @ $3.00 per DLH	9.00
Standard unit cost of production		$20.00

Following, in summary form, is the monthly flexible manufacturing overhead expense budget:

Direct Labor Hours	0	24,000	27,000	30,000	33,000
Percentage of Standard Capacity	0%	80%	90%	100%	110%
Variable Expenses: Factory Supplies Power etc.					
Total	$ 0	$48,000	$54,000	$60,000	$66,000

Non-Variable Expenses: Depreciation Insurance etc.					
Total	$30,000	$30,000	$30,000	$30,000	$30,000
Total	$30,000	$78,000	$84,000	$90,000	$96,000

Data for April:
    Finished Goods:
        Inventory, April 1 .... 3,000 units at $20
        April production .... 9,000 units
        April sales .... 11,000 units at $35
        Inventory, April 30 .... 1,000 units at $20
    Work in Process:
        None at beginning or end of month.
    Direct Materials:
        Koh Company recognizes a material price variance at the time the materials are purchased.
        Inventory, April 1 .... 40,000 lbs. @ $1.00
        Purchases .... 60,000 lbs. @ $1.02
        Issues to production .... 45,400 lbs.
        Inventory, April 30 .... 54,600 lbs.
    Direct Labor Payroll:
        26,800 hours at $2.05 .... $54,940
    Actual Manufacturing Overhead Expense:
        Variable $53,500
        Non-Variable $30,000
                                                               $83,500

Required

    a. Compute the following variances and indicate whether they are favorable or unfavorable:
        1. direct materials purchase price variance
        2. direct materials usage variance
        3. total direct labor variance
        4. direct labor time variance
        5. direct labor rate variance
        6. total manufacturing overhead variance
        7. controllable variance
        8. volume variance

    b. Split the controllable variance ascertained for requirement a-7 into an efficiency variance and a spending variance.

[CH. 13] COST CONTROL THROUGH STANDARD COSTS 433

c. Prepare a partial statement of income through gross margin on sales for the Koh Company for the month of April showing all variances as an adjustment to the standard cost of goods sold.

13-15. Ross Shirts, Inc. manufactures short- and long-sleeve men's shirts for large stores. Ross produces a single quality shirt in lots to each customer's order and attaches the store's label to each. The standard costs for a dozen long-sleeve shirts are:

Direct materials	24 yards @ $ .55	$13.20
Direct labor	3 hours @ $2.45	7.35
Manufacturing overhead	3 hours @ $2.00	6.00
Standard cost per dozen		$26.55

During October 1972 Ross worked on three orders for long-sleeve shirts. Job cost records for the month disclose the following:

Lot	Units in Lot	Material Used	Hours Worked
30	1,000 dozen	24,100 yards	2,980
31	1,700 dozen	40,440 yards	5,130
32	1,200 dozen	28,825 yards	2,890

The following information is also available:
1. Ross purchased 95,000 yards of material during the month at a cost of $53,200. The materials price variance is recorded when goods are purchased and all inventories are carried at standard cost.
2. Direct labor incurred amounted to $27,500 during October. According to payroll records, production employees were paid $2.50 per hour.
3. Manufacturing overhead is applied on the basis of direct labor hours. Manufacturing overhead totaling $22,800 was incurred during October.
4. A total of $288,000 was budgeted for manufacturing overhead for the year 1972 based on estimated production at the plant's normal capacity of 48,000 dozen shirts per year. Manufacturing overhead is 40 percent fixed and 60 percent variable at this level of production.
5. There was no work in process at October 1. During October lots 30 and 31 were completed and all material was issued for lot 32, and it was 80 percent completed as to labor and manufacturing overhead.

Required

a. Prepare a schedule computing the standard cost for October 1972 of lots 30, 31 and 32.
b. Prepare a schedule computing the materials price variance for October 1972 and indicate whether the variance is favorable or unfavorable.
c. Prepare schedules computing (and indicating whether the variances are favorable or unfavorable) for each lot produced during October 1972 the:
   1. materials quantity variance in yards
   2. labor efficiency variance in hours
   3. labor rate variance in dollars

d. Prepare a schedule computing the total controllable and noncontrollable (capacity) manufacturing overhead variances for October 1972 and indicate whether the variances are favorable or unfavorable.

(Adapted from Uniform CPA Examination)

13-16. The Johnson Company began operations on January 1, 1972. It manufactures a single product. The company installed a standard cost system, but *will adjust all inventories to actual cost for financial statement purposes at the end of the year.*

Under its cost system, raw material inventory is maintained at actual cost. Charges made to work-in-process are all made at standard prices. Variance accounts are used into which all variances are entered as they are identified.

One-half of the cost of raw material for each unit is put into production at the beginning of the process and the balance when the processing is about one-third completed.

Standard cost was based on 256,000 direct labor hours with a production of 1,600 units. The standard was as follows:

Materials (100 lbs. @ $2.00)	$200
Direct labor (160 hrs. @ $1.25)	200
Manufacturing overhead (based on direct labor hours) (160 @ $0.25)	40
Total standard cost per unit	$440

A summary of the transactions for the year ended December 31, 1972, shows the following:

Material purchased (180,000 lbs. @ $2.20)	$396,000.00
Direct labor (247,925 hrs. @ $1.30)	322,302.50
Manufacturing overhead	49,585.00
Material issued to production	177,600 lbs.
Units processed:	
Units completed	1,500
Units one-half complete	150
Units one-fourth complete	30

Required

Determine the following variances:

a. materials—price variance
b. materials—quantity variance
c. labor—rate variance
d. labor—hours variance
e. manufacturing overhead—efficiency variance
f. manufacturing overhead—capacity variance
g. manufacturing overhead—budget variance

(Adapted from Uniform CPA Examination)

13-17. Conti Pharmaceutical Company processes a single compound-product known as NULAX and uses a standard cost accounting system. The process requires preparation and blending of three materials in large batches with a variation from the standard mixture sometimes necessary to maintain quality. Conti's cost accountant became ill at the end of October 1972, and you were engaged to determine standard costs of October production and explain any differences between actual and standard costs for the month.

The following information is available for the Blending Department:

1. The standard cost card for a 500-pound batch shows the following standard costs:

	Quantity	Price	Total Cost	
Materials:				
Mucilloid	250 pounds	$.14	$35	
Dextrose	200 pounds	.09	18	
Ingredients	50 pounds	.08	4	
Total per batch	500 pounds		$ 57	
Labor:				
Preparation and blending	10 hours	$3.00		30
Overhead:				
Variable	10 hours	$1.00	10	
Fixed	10 hours	.30	3	13
Total standard cost per 500-pound batch				$100

2. During October 410 batches of 500 pounds each of the finished compound were completed and transferred to the Packaging Department.

3. Blending Department inventories totaled 6,000 pounds at the beginning of the month and 9,000 pounds at the end of the month (assume both inventories were completely processed but not transferred and consisted of materials in their standard proportions).

Inventories are carried on the company's books at standard cost prices.

4. During the month of October the following materials were purchased and put into production:

	Pounds	Price	Total Cost
Mucilloid	114,400	$.17	$19,448
Dextrose	85,800	.11	9,438
Ingredients	19,800	.07	1,386
Totals	220,000		$30,272

5. Wages paid for 4,212 hours of direct labor at $3.25 per hour amounted to $13,689.

6. Actual manufacturing overhead costs for the month totaled $5,519.

7. The standards were established for a normal production volume of 200,000 pounds (400 batches) of NULAX per month. At this level of production variable manufacturing overhead was budgeted at $4,000 and fixed manufacturing overhead was budgeted at $1,200.

Required

a. Prepare a schedule presenting the computation for the Blending Department of:
   1. October production in both pounds and batches
   2. the standard cost of October production itemized by components of materials, labor and manufacturing overhead

b. Prepare schedules computing the differences between actual and standard costs and analyzing the differences as:
   1. materials variances (for each material) caused by
      (a) price differences
      (b) usage differences
   2. labor variances caused by
      (a) rate difference
      (b) efficiency difference
   3. manufacturing overhead variances caused by
      (a) controllable factors
      (b) volume factors

(Adapted from Uniform CPA Examination)

13-18. The Jones Furniture Company uses a standard cost system in accounting for its production costs.

The standard cost of a unit of furniture follows:

Lumber, 100 feet @ $150 per 1,000 feet		$15.00
Direct labor, 4 hours @ $2.50 per hour		10.00
Manufacturing overhead:		
Fixed (30 percent of direct labor)	$3.00	
Variable (60 percent of direct labor)	6.00	9.00
Total unit cost		$34.00

The following flexible monthly manufacturing overhead budget is in effect:

Direct Labor Hours	Manufacturing Overhead
5,200	$10,800
4,800	10,200
4,400	9,600
4,000 (normal capacity)	9,000
3,600	8,400

The actual unit costs for the month of December were as follows:

Lumber used (110 feet @ $120 per 1,000 feet)	$13.20
Direct labor (4¼ hours @ $2.60 per hour)	11.05
Manufacturing overhead ($10,560 ÷ 1,200 units)	8.80
Total actual unit cost	$33.05

Required

Prepare a schedule which shows an analysis of each element of the total variance from standard cost for the month of December.

(Adapted from Uniform CPA Examination)

13-19. The H. G. Company uses a standard cost system in accounting for the cost of one of its products.

The standard is based on budgeted monthly production of 100 units per day for the usual 22 work days per month. Standard cost per unit for direct labor is 16 hours at $1.50 per hour. Standard cost for manufacturing overhead was set as follows:

Fixed manufacturing overhead per month	$29,040
Variable manufacturing overhead per month	39,600
Total budgeted manufacturing overhead	$68,640
Expected direct labor cost	$52,800
Manufacturing overhead rate per dollar of labor	$ 1.30
Standard manufacturing overhead per unit	$ 31.20

During the month of September, the plant operated only 20 days. Cost for the 2,080 units produced were:

Direct labor, 32,860 hours @ $1.52 = $49,947.20
Fixed manufacturing overhead 29,300.00
Variable manufacturing overhead .. 39,065.00

Required

a. Compute the variance from standard in September for
　1. direct labor cost
　2. manufacturing overhead
b. Analyze the variances from standard into identifiable causes for
　1. direct labor
　2. fixed and variable manufacturing overhead

(Adapted from Uniform CPA Examination)

13-20. Following is the previously computed standard cost of Product X, manufactured by the XYZ Manufacturing Company:

	Prime Cost	Manufacturing Overhead—50%	Total
Material A	$10		$10.00
Material B	5		5.00
Material C	2		2.00
Direct Labor—Cutting	8	$4.00	12.00
Direct Labor—Shaping	4	2.00	6.00
Direct Labor—Assembling	2	1.00	3.00
Direct Labor—Boxing	1	.50	1.50
Total	$32	$7.50	$39.50

The budget called for the manufacture of 10,000 of Product X at a total cost of $395,000 for the period under review.

438 COST ACCOUNTING CONCEPTS [CH. 13]

The following variance accounts relating to Product X appear on the books for the period:

	Unfavorable	Favorable
Material price variance		
Due to a favorable purchase of total requirements of Material A		$19,500
Material usage variance		
Excessive waste during period	$ 3,000	
Labor rate variance		
5 percent wage increase to direct workers	7,500	
Labor productivity variance		
Due to shut-down caused by strike	15,000	
Volume variance—fixed manufacturing overhead		
Due to shut-down caused by strike	6,000	
Controllable variance—variable manufacturing overhead		
Due to permanent savings in costs of certain services		12,000
Totals	$31,500	$31,500

The inventory at the end of the period is as follows:

100 units Material A	@ $10.00	$ 1,000
100 units Material B	@ 5.00	500
100 units Material C	@ 2.00	200
200 units Product X in process—cut	@ 29.00	5,800
200 units Product X in process—shaped	@ 35.00	7,000
200 units Product X in process—assembled ...	@ 38.00	7,600
200 units Product X finished and boxed	@ 39.50	7,900
Total		$30,000

Required

a. Prepare a schedule of revised standard cost which will clearly indicate the cumulative standard for each successive operation.

b. Prepare a schedule applying the revised standard to the ending inventory.

(Adapted from Uniform CPA Examination)

14

Direct Costing

Product unit costs are meant to help managers take proper action and make correct decisions; under certain circumstances, however, they may inadequately inform or mislead managers. This can happen when product unit costs fluctuate in an actual cost system because of changes in the volume of production. Such fluctuations are caused by unit fixed costs which vary inversely with production volume and are unaffected by operating performance. These fluctuations can be prevented through the use of costing procedures which, regardless of the actual volume of production, stabilize the amount of fixed cost related to each unit produced.

Costing procedures which nullify the effect of changes in the volume of production upon the fixed manufacturing overhead costs allocated to each unit of product use predetermined rates to allocate these costs. One such method was illustrated in Chapter 11, in which a predetermined unit fixed cost rate was obtained by dividing the estimated annual total amount of fixed manufacturing overhead costs by the estimated annual volume of production. Another method was discussed in Chapter 12, where a predetermined normal manufacturing overhead rate was obtained by dividing the total manufacturing overhead expenses for a period by the normal volume of production. Yet another method was shown in Chapter 13, in which a predetermined standard manufacturing overhead expense rate was computed and used to illustrate the operation of a standard cost system.

Any of the methods described may be used to avoid confusing those in management who may be misled by product unit cost fluctuations which are caused by changes in the volume of production. Another problem, however, is created when the actual and predetermined volume of production are not the same. Under such conditions, a problem arises, because production is charged with an amount of fixed expenses which does not equal the amount upon which the predetermined rate was based. Depending on the type of predetermined rate used, this difference may be considered to be overapplied or underapplied fixed manufacturing overhead, or to be a favorable or unfavorable capacity or volume variance. Regardless of how it is described, this difference poses a problem concerning its disposition at the end of a period.

Various solutions may be used to dispose of the problem created by the overapplied or underapplied manufacturing overhead at the end of a period. Some of these were advanced in Chapter 11, in which it was pointed out that, among other methods, this balance could be used as an adjustment to the gross margin on sales, as an adjustment to the cost of sales, or distributed among the ending inventories and cost of goods sold in proportion to the manufacturing overhead costs which originated during the period that each contains.

The disposal method selected may violate the costing theory which underlies the existence of such balances. These balances originate because predetermined rates are used to charge production with fixed costs in accordance with a method of absorption costing. Under absorption costing, all manufacturing costs should be charged to the products manufactured and thus become a part of the product cost inventoried until the products are sold. When sales occur, the costs associated with the products sold are matched with the sales revenue recognized to determine gross margin. Consequently, those methods which do not relate overapplied or underapplied manufacturing overhead balances to inventories and cost of goods sold are inconsistent with absorption costing. In fact, they are disposing of the balance as a period cost.

Annual statements frequently show the annual overapplied or underapplied balance or variance as a period cost. Often, this practice causes statements which reflect a disposal of a relatively immaterial balance, because the predetermined rate is based on an annual or long-range volume of production and because a year is frequently enough time to cancel out many of the overages and underages which occur. Although management usually accepts such immaterial balances readily, larger balances appearing on monthly or quarterly statements frequently are neither accepted readily nor explained easily. Since management is ordinarily more interested in short-range than long-range reports, the difficulties involved in explaining overapplied or underapplied balances may be encountered frequently. Thus, a paradox exists when product cost information which may mislead management is eliminated through the use of predetermined rates which produce overapplied or underapplied manufacturing overhead balances whose disposition may create misunderstanding.

Absorption costing, as discussed above, may mislead management by providing historical product unit costs which fluctuate inversely with the volume of production. Or it may confuse management through generating and disposing of overapplied or underapplied balances or volume variances which result from eliminating the effect of volume changes on product unit costs. It may cause more misunderstanding by the way it determines profit on the income statement, because absorption costing assigns all manufacturing time costs incurred in a period (excluding those contained in volume variances) to either inventory or cost of goods sold. Consequently, the manufacturing time costs matched with the sales revenue of a period to determine gross margin are those assigned to cost of goods sold; on the other hand, all non-manufacturing costs incurred in a period are subtracted from gross margin and thereby matched with the sales revenue of a period. This situation may mislead management when sales and production volumes are different.

Although the usefulness of cost information for management has improved greatly from developments like predetermined rates, flexible budgets, standard costs, and variance analyses, absorption costing methods may mislead those in management who interpret cost data. Management is always seeking more understandable answers which can be obtained in a quick and simple manner. Cost information which reflects the advantages and minimizes the disadvantages of developments connected with absorption costing is the kind of cost data that management needs. The same information can be derived from statistical studies carried on apart from those accounting processes which follow absorption costing theory, but this is time consuming and expensive. This raises the question of whether some costing method might be used which would integrate the techniques of statistical studies into the cost accounting process. For this reason, and throughout the past several years, cost accountants have departed from absorption costing to investigate and develop a method of cost accounting which conforms more closely to the demands of management. This costing method is known as direct costing.

DIRECT COSTING

Direct costing was introduced in Chapter 11 as a costing method which could be used to provide uniform product unit costs. As illustrated, this was accomplished through segregating the fixed and variable components of manufacturing overhead costs. The non-variable manufacturing overhead costs were deducted on the statement of income in the month in which they were incurred. The sum of the variable manufacturing overhead, direct material, and direct labor costs determined the costs of the products produced. The costs of direct material and direct labor were treated exactly as they would have been under absorption costing; only manufacturing overhead costs were treated differently.

Although uniform product unit costs are an incidental feature of direct costing, their derivation from direct costing procedures illustrates and emphasizes a primary premise upon which direct costing is based: variability with volume determines whether a manufacturing cost should be treated as a period cost (deducted from revenue immediately) or a product cost (assigned to units produced). Variability with volume does not necessarily mean that manufacturing costs must be traced directly to a specific product unit. In fact, it would be misleading to imply that only direct costs are used in direct costing to determine product costs. Manufacturing overhead costs, which cannot be identified with any specific product unit, are also included in product costs when they vary with the volume of productive activity. This position is clearly indicated in the definition of direct costing which follows:

> Direct costing should be defined as segregation of manufacturing costs between those which are fixed and those which vary directly with volume. Only the prime costs plus variable factory costs are used to value inventory and cost of sales. The remaining factory expenses are charged off currently to profit and loss.[1]

The definition emphasizes cost variability. The unit cost of direct material and direct labor tends to be constant for each unit produced. Total variable manufacturing overhead costs tend to be proportional to volume and thereby tend to be constant per unit within limited ranges of activity. Unit costs which tend to be constant in amount tend to vary directly wih volume of production. Therefore, variable production costs are direct material costs, direct labor costs, and variable manufacturing overhead costs. These variable production costs are the costs which increase as production increases. Or, in other words, these costs would not be charged to production if products were not produced.

The emphasis in this definition and the preceding discussion is on the variability of the costs contained in inventory and costs of sales. Variable manufacturing costs have the same effect on the cost determination of inventory and costs of sales by either absorption costing or direct costing; the basic difference between the two costing methods lies in the handling of fixed manufacturing overhead costs. Absorption costing includes these costs as a part of product cost; direct costing excludes them from product cost and classifies them as period costs. The difference between these two methods is a matter of timing. Under absorption costing, fixed manufacturing costs are matched with sales when the finished units in inventory are sold; under direct costing, fixed manufacturing costs are expensed immediately in the period when they are incurred. Direct costing treats fixed manufacturing costs as period costs on the premise that they arise from providing and maintaining capacity for a relevant range of production volume and that they tend to remain constant regardless of the extent to which that range is utilized. Further, it considers that the costs of having capacity for production available expire with time and that the opportunity to use this capacity expires with time regardless of the extent to which that capacity is used.

Up to this point, the discussion of direct or variable costing has defined variable and fixed costs in terms of manufacturing costs. Non-manufacturing costs are also variable or fixed. But, since non-manufacturing costs are excluded from product cost, fixed non-manufacturing costs are considered period costs by both absorption costing and direct costing. Nevertheless, the segregation of variable and fixed non-manufacturing costs plays an important role in direct costing considerations.

---

[1] National Association of Accountants, Research Series No. 23, *N.A.(C.)A. Bulletin*, "Direct Costing" (April, 1953), p. 2.

Illustration of Absorption Costing and Direct Costing—Statements of Income

The differences between statements of income resulting from absorption costing and those resulting from direct costing are illustrated in Exhibit 14–1. Assuming that the actual and budgeted variable expenses are identical, the comparative statements of income for four consecutive months of operations shown in this exhibit are prepared from the following physical production and unit cost data.

	May	June	July	August	Four Months Combined
Opening inventory	—	—	20,000	5,000	—
Production	50,000	60,000	40,000	50,000	200,000
Sales	50,000	40,000	55,000	55,000	200,000
Closing inventory	—	20,000	5,000	—	—

	Per Unit
Manufacturing costs:	
Direct materials	$ 2.00
Direct labor	1.00
Variable manufacturing overhead	.50
Fixed manufacturing overhead	
($75,000 ÷ 50,000 units in normal volume equals $1.50)	1.50
Manufacturing unit cost	$5.00
Non-Manufacturing costs:	
Variable selling expenses	$ 1.00
Fixed selling and administrative expenses	
($100,000 ÷ 50,000 units in normal volume equals $2.00)	2.00
Non-Manufacturing cost per unit	$ 3.00
Total cost to make and sell	$ 8.00
Sales price	$10.00

EXHIBIT 14–1

Absorption Costing Statements of Income

	May	June	July	August	Four Months Combined
Sales	$500,000	$400,000	$550,000	$550,000	$2,000,000
Direct materials	$100,000	$120,000	$ 80,000	$100,000	$ 400,000
Direct labor	50,000	60,000	40,000	50,000	200,000
Variable manufacturing overhead	25,000	30,000	20,000	25,000	100,000
Fixed manufacturing overhead	75,000	90,000	60,000	75,000	300,000

Cost of goods manufactured	$250,000	$300,000	$200,000	$250,000	$1,000,000
Add opening inventory	—	—	100,000	25,000	
Cost of goods available for sale	$250,000	$300,000	$300,000	$275,000	
Less ending inventory	—	100,000	25,000	—	
Cost of goods sold	$250,000	$200,000	$275,000	$275,000	$1,000,000
Under or (over) applied manufacturing overhead	—	(15,000)	15,000	—	
Adjusted cost of goods sold	$250,000	$185,000	$290,000	$275,000	$1,000,000
Gross margin	$250,000	$215,000	$260,000	$275,000	$1,000,000
Selling and administrative expenses	150,000	140,000	155,000	155,000	600,000
Net operating income	$100,000	$ 75,000	$105,000	$120,000	$ 400,000

Direct Costing Statements of Income

	May	June	July	August	Four Months Combined
Sales	$500,000	$400,000	$550,000	$550,000	$2,000,000
Direct materials	$100,000	$120,000	$ 80,000	$100,000	$ 400,000
Direct labor	50,000	60,000	40,000	50,000	200,000
Variable manufacturing overhead	25,000	30,000	20,000	25,000	100,000
Cost of goods manufactured	$175,000	$210,000	$140,000	$175,000	$ 700,000
Add opening inventory	—	—	70,000	17,500	
Cost of goods available for sale	$175,000	$210,000	$210,000	$192,500	
Less ending inventory	—	70,000	17,500	—	
Cost of goods sold	$175,000	$140,000	$192,500	$192,500	$ 700,000
Manufacturing margin	$325,000	$260,000	$357,500	$357,500	$1,300,000
Less variable selling expenses	50,000	40,000	55,000	55,000	200,000
Marginal income	$275,000	$220,000	$302,500	$302,500	$1,100,000
Less fixed expenses:					
Manufacturing overhead	$ 75,000	$ 75,000	$ 75,000	$ 75,000	$ 300,000
Selling and administrative expenses	100,000	100,000	100,000	100,000	400,000
Total fixed expenses	$175,000	$175,000	$175,000	$175,000	$ 700,000
Net operating income	$100,000	$ 45,000	$127,500	$127,500	400,000

Comparison of the Effects of Absorption Costing and Direct Costing on Statements of Income

A comparison of the two types of statements of income illustrated in Exhibit 14–1 reveals the following four specific differences:

1. The direct costing statements do not show the overapplied or underapplied manufacturing overhead balances contained on the absorption costing statements.
2. The direct costing statements do not contain the gross margin figures shown on the absorption costing statements. They do show manufacturing margins and marginal income figures which are not revealed on the other statements.
3. The inventory amounts shown on the direct costing statements are consistently lower than those on the absorption costing statements.
4. The two types of statements reflect different net operating income calculations in three of the four months shown.

The first difference is readily reconciled. Since direct costing considers fixed manufacturing costs as period costs, the direct costing statements would be unaffected by the difference between applied and budgeted fixed costs. The three differences remaining are not reconciled so readily. The second and third differences will be discussed after attention has been given to the fourth, which is the most complex. The discussion sequence should also facilitate an understanding of the specific differences involved.

Net Income Differences. The comparative results of absorption costing and direct costing on the net incomes shown in Exhibit 14–1 lead to the following generalizations:[2]

1. When sales and production are in balance at standard (normal) volume, direct and absorption costing methods yield the same profit. Under both methods, the amount of fixed manufacturing overhead cost incurred during the period is charged against the revenue of the period. (See month of May in Exhibit 14–1.)
2. When production exceeds sales (i.e., when in-process and finished inventories are increasing), the net income reported under absorption costing is higher than that reported under direct costing. By absorption costing, a portion of the fixed manufacturing overhead costs is deferred to future periods in the ending inventories, while under direct costing, the total manufacturing overhead costs are charged to the statement of income. (See month of June in Exhibit 14–1.)
3. When sales exceed production (i.e., when in process and finished inventories are decreasing), direct costing shows a higher net income than does absorption costing. By absorption costing, fixed manufacturing overhead costs previously deferred in inventory and those incurred in a given period are charged against revenue in the period in which the goods are sold. Total fixed manufacturing overhead costs charged against revenue therefore exceed those incurred during the period. Under direct costing, the total manufacturing overhead costs charged against revenue are limited to the amount incurred for the period. (See month of July in Exhibit 14–1.)

---

[2] *Ibid.* p. 42. (Adapted.)

4. When sales volume is constant but production volume fluctuates, direct costing yields a constant net income figure, because net income is not affected by inventory changes. Under the same circumstances, absorption costing yields an erratic net income figure which will be directly affected by the direction and amount of inventory changes. (See months of July and August in Exhibit 14–1.)
5. If production volume is constant, changes in net income are directly proportional to changes in sales volume in either direct or absorption costing. The net income will move in the same direction, but will move by a greater amount under direct costing than it does under absorption costing. (See months of May and August in Exhibit 14–1.)
6. The differences between periodic net income figures computed by direct costing and absorption costing methods tend to be smaller for long periods than for short periods, because variations between production and sales volume tend to approach equality over a long period. Consequently, in the long run, the two methods should give substantially the same result, because sales cannot continuously exceed production, nor can production continuously exceed sales. (See four months combined in Exhibit 14–1.)

These generalizations describe the comparative effects of absorption and direct costing on net income when various relationships exist between sales and production volumes. The differences in the net income amounts reported by income statements which reflect these different costing concepts were shown in Exhibit 14–1. These differences may be reconciled easily, because all factors other than production and sales volume were held constant (that is, the income statements, under both concepts, were prepared on the assumptions that selling prices remained constant, that no changes occurred in either the actual fixed costs of manufacturing or the selling and administrative expenses, and that no changes developed in either the actual variable unit cost of manufacturing or the selling and administrative expenses). It was also assumed that manufacturing overhead was applied at predetermined rates based on normal capacity and that the overapplied and underapplied manufacturing overhead represented an adjustment to cost of goods sold. Under these conditions, changes between the monthly net incomes reported by either absorption or direct costing are the result of changes in volume, while any difference between the net income reported by the two concepts in a given month is the result of the costing method.

Differences between the net operating incomes determined by absorption costing and by direct costing in Exhibit 14–1 are summarized below:

Differences in Net Operating Incomes

	May	June	July	August	Four Months Combined
Net operating income:					
Absorption costing	$100,000	$75,000	$105,000	$120,000	$400,000
Direct costing	100,000	45,000	127,500	127,500	400,000
Difference	–0–	$30,000	$(22,500)	$ (7,500)	–0–

The differences between the net incomes shown are equal to the changes in the ending inventory dollar amounts as determined by absorption costing and direct costing. Ending inventories calculated from the data provided for Exhibit 14–1 are as follows:

	Ending Inventories			
	May	June	July	August
Absorption costing				
–0– units	—			
20,000 units @ $5.00*		$100,000		
5,000 units @ $5.00			$25,000	
–0– units				—
Direct costing				
–0– units	—			
20,000 units @ $3.50**		70,000		
5,000 units @ $3.50			17,500	
–0– units				—

* unit cost by absorption costing
** unit cost by direct costing

The differences in the changes of the ending inventories illustrated above can also be summarized:

	Differences in Changes of Ending Inventories			
	May	June	July	August
Inventory increase (decrease):				
Absorption costing	—	$100,000	$(75,000)	$(25,000)
Direct costing	—	70,000	(52,500)	(17,500)
Difference in Inventory Changes	—	$ 30,000	$(22,500)	$ (7,500)
Fixed Manufacturing Overhead in Inventory changes:				
Change in number of inventory units	—	20,000	(15,000)	(5,000)
Unit fixed manufacturing overhead cost	—	$1.50	$1.50	$1.50
Change in fixed manufacturing overhead in inventory	—	$ 30,000	$(22,500)	$ (7,500)

A comparison of the differences in the net operating incomes calculated above with the differences in the changes of the ending inventories calculated in the preceding illustration shows that the two represent identical amounts. Therefore, the difference in the net operating income determined by absorption costing and by direct costing can be reconciled to the difference in the change of the ending inventories determined by each concept. This reconciliation, however, does not explain why the two methods produce different inventory changes.

Inventory Differences. Differences between inventories determined under absorption costing and direct costing are attributable to the procedure of accounting for fixed manufacturing overhead costs. Inventories computed by absorption costing *include fixed and variable* manufacturing overhead costs, while inventories calculated by direct costing *exclude fixed* manufacturing overhead cost. Accordingly, inventories under direct costing are always smaller in dollar amounts than inventories under absorption costing. Since the difference between the inventory amounts computed by the two methods consists of fixed manufacturing overhead costs, the difference between the change in the ending inventories computed by the two concepts must result from the same source. This may be proved by the following formula:

$$\text{Difference in change of ending inventories} = \text{Fixed manufacturing overhead—per unit} \times \text{Change in number of inventory units}$$

Application of this formula to the information contained in Exhibit 14–1 was demonstrated in the preceding illustration, which shows that the difference in the change of the ending inventories is equal to the change of the fixed manufacturing overhead contained in the ending inventories. Therefore, it may be concluded that the difference between the net income reported by both costing methods equals the change in the fixed manufacturing overhead contained in the ending inventories.

Difference in Gross Margin, Manufacturing Margin and Marginal Income. At this point in the discussion, it should be apparent that the difference between gross margin and manufacturing margin is caused by the manner in which fixed manufacturing overhead costs are treated. If they are included in inventories and costs of goods sold, the difference between sales revenue and costs of goods sold is identified as gross margin or gross profit. If they are excluded from inventories and costs of goods sold, the difference between sales revenue and costs of goods sold is called manufacturing margin. Fixed and variable non-manufacturing costs are deducted directly from the gross margin to obtain net operating profit. Variable non-manufacturing costs are deducted directly from manufacturing margin to obtain marginal income, from which fixed manufacturing and non-manufacturing costs are deducted to obtain net operating income.

ADVANTAGES OF MARGINAL INCOME TO MANAGEMENT

The difference between sales revenue and its related variable costs is usually called marginal income. Marginal income emphasizes and measures that portion of total sales revenue, individual product revenue, individual territory revenue, or any other segment of total revenue which represents a contribution toward fixed costs and/or net income. As a result, it is frequently called "contribution margin." Other terms for marginal income include "profit contribution," "variable gross margin," "marginal balance," "marginal profit," and "contribution to fixed costs."

Marginal income information is often considered the principal advantage of the direct costing method of presenting operating results. Management finds it particularly useful in profit planning, since it permits measurement of the relationship between profit and the major factors affecting profit. It does this by combining the major factors of selling price, sales mix, sales volume, and variable manufacturing and non-manufacturing costs into a single index of profitability. This index, expressed as a positive amount or as a ratio, facilitates the analysis of cost-volume-profit relationships, the impact of two or more contemplated courses of action, and aids in answering many questions which arise in profit planning. The advantages of the information provided by the marginal income concept may be related to the product income statement illustrated in Exhibit 14–2.

EXHIBIT 14–2

Statement of Income by Products
(in thousands of dollars)

	Total Amount	Pct.	A Amount	Pct.	B Amount	Pct.	C Amount	Pct.
Net sales	$1,000	100.0	$500	100.0	$300	100.0	$200	100.0
Variable manufacturing cost of sales	520	52.0	200	40.0	180	60.0	140	70.0
Manufacturing margin	$ 480	48.0	$300	60.0	$120	40.0	$ 60	30.0
Variable non-manufacturing costs	80	8.0	40	8.0	30	10.0	10	5.0
Marginal income	$ 400	40.0	$260	52.0	$ 90	30.0	$ 50	25.0
Traceable fixed costs:								
Manufacturing	$ 132	13.2	$ 90	18.0	$ 36	12.0	$ 6	3.0
Non-manufacturing	48	4.8	20	4.0	24	8.0	4	2.0
Total traceable fixed costs	$ 180	18.0	$110	22.0	$ 60	20.0	$ 10	5.0
Contribution to common fixed costs	$ 220	22.0	$150	30.0	$ 30	10.0	$ 40	20.0
Common fixed costs:*								
Manufacturing	$ 80	8.0	$ 40	8.0	$ 24	8.0	$ 16	8.0
Non-manufacturing	40	4.0	20	4.0	12	4.0	8	4.0
Total common fixed costs	$ 120	12.0	$ 60	12.0	$ 36	12.0	$ 24	12.0
Net income	$ 100	10.0	$ 90	18.0	$ (6)	(2.0)	$ 16	8.0

* Common fixed costs are allocated in the ratio of sales dollars

1. Marginal incomes help management to decide whether a product line should be discontinued. As indicated in Exhibit 14–2, Product B appears to be a profit "detractor" when measured by its net income. Further analysis, however, reveals that Product B has a marginal income of $90,000, an amount

which covers its variable costs and traceable fixed costs and still contributes $30,000 toward the joint fixed costs. This information would lead management to realize that dropping of Product B represents a potential $30,000 reduction in the overall net income.

2. Marginal incomes allow management to ascertain how many units must be sold to realize desired net incomes from products. This is accomplished by dividing the marginal income ratio for a specific product into the sum of the fixed costs and profit desired for a product to obtain the product sales dollar objective. Then, the sales dollar objective is divided by the product unit sales price to derive the number of units required. For example, if a $12,000 income (instead of a $6,000 loss) is desired for Product B in Exhibit 14-2, $12,000 would be added to the $60,000 of traceable costs and to the $36,000 of allocated costs to obtain $108,000, an amount which would be divided by the 30 percent marginal income ratio to obtain sales dollar objective. This calculation would produce a $360,000 sales dollar objective, an amount which would be divided by the unit sales price to determine the number of units required. If the unit sales price is $20, 18,000 units must be sold to provide a $12,000 net income.

3. The marginal income ratio may be used to determine the amount of additional sales volume required to justify extra expenditures for sales promotion. Under such circumstances, the marginal income ratio would be divided into the sum of the proposed expenditures, existing fixed costs, and net income to determine the new sales dollar objective. The new sales dollar objective minus the current sales volume would provide the amount of sales dollars needed to justify the proposed expenditures.

4. The question of which products should be emphasized to improve the sales mix ordinarily can be answered quickly by comparing the product marginal incomes. In instances where a multi-product plant having limited capacity is being operated, pushing the product with the largest marginal income may not maximize total profits. Actually, the product having the largest marginal income per hour of production becomes the most attractive.[3]

5. Decisions as to whether profits can be improved by a price decrease, which may expand volume, or by a price increase, which may reduce volume, can be guided by adjusting the marginal income of a product for the estimated changes. If, for example, it is proposed that a 5 percent decrease in the price of Product C in Exhibit 14-2 will increase the sales volume by 20 percent, the profitability of this action could be measured as follows. A price reduction of 5 percent would decrease the marginal income to $40,000, an amount which would then be increased by 20 percent to equal $48,000. Since $48,000 is $2,000 less than the $50,000 marginal income already being realized, the proposal appears to be unattractive.

---

[3] For a detailed discussion and illustration of statistical allocation of scarce resources among competing products to maximize profits, see the section on "Linear Programming" in Chapter 19.

6. When selling prices are established by the interplay of market forces, marginal income information helps management to decide whether it should compete on a short-run or long-run basis. When prices can be influenced by the producer, the desired marginal income helps guide management in establishing the most advantageous price.

CONSIDERATIONS UNDERLYING THE POSITION OF DIRECT COSTING

Described in the preceding section are various advantages which marginal income figures or ratios possess for appraising the relative profitability of products. Most of these advantages also apply when marginal income information is used to evaluate territories or other segments of a business.

In addition to the marginal income advantages, advocates of direct costing claim that it has a number of other advantages over absorption costing including:

1. Direct costing emphasizes the impact of fixed costs on net income by showing the total amount of such costs separately in financial reports to management.

2. Cost data needed to aid profit planning and decision-making are readily available from the regular accounting records and statements. Thus, management does not need auxiliary and time-consuming analyses to determine cost-volume-profit relationships.

3. Management understands data presented in a direct costing format more readily. Many persons maintain that this is because direct costing reports closely conform to how most business managers think. They expect net incomes to rise or fall as sales volume increases or decreases. Under absorption costing, inventory or production variations may prevent such correlations.

4. Out-of-pocket expenditures required to manufacture products conform closely with the valuation of inventory when direct costing is used.

In view of the advantages claimed by supporters of direct costing it might be expected that direct costing would be used in all manufacturing concerns. Such is not the case. Although all accountants recognize that direct costing may have some advantages for certain managerial decisions, many reject it for either internal or external financial reporting or for both types of reporting. Among the disadvantages cited by those who reject direct costing are the following:

1. Direct costing fails to provide full product cost figures which can be used for long-range policy decisions. Therefore, supplementary allocation of fixed manufacturing overhead must be made to determine total product costs needed for long-range pricing and other purposes.

2. Management may be misled by improper product cost variability obtained through separating semi-variable manufacturing costs into fixed and variable components by methods that cannot be completely precise.
3. Direct costing is not necessary, because the same information can be derived from absorption cost records through supplementary analyses without making any change in the existing accounting procedures.
4. The use of direct costing may cause income tax problems which are not encountered under absorption costing. It also may cause controversy over "cost" figures for production completed under government contracts.
5. Stockholders, creditors, employees, investment analysts, and others are misled by financial statements which are prepared on a direct costing basis.

In the preceding discussion, the advantages and most of the disadvantages accredited to direct costing concern managerial use. Management uses different costs for different purposes; whether the information is derived through absorption or direct costing procedures is determined by managerial prerogative. Consequently, a company may use whatever accounting method it finds useful for internal statements and reports. On the other hand, external reporting must be accomplished by those accounting methods which conform with generally accepted accounting principles. Whether direct costing qualifies under such standards revolves around the question of what constitutes product cost. If product cost must include all manufacturing overhead costs, then direct costing understates inventories on the balance sheet and fails to match costs and revenue on the statement of income correctly. On the other hand, if fixed manufacturing overhead cost is a period cost, then direct costing is acceptable for external reporting. Although direct costing has not been recognized as an "accepted accounting principle" for external financial reporting or for income taxes, no conclusive answer has yet been provided to the question of what constitutes product cost. Without this answer, there cannot be complete agreement on whether direct costing violates recognized accounting standards.

The standards of the major accounting associations are often broad and leave considerable range for individual interpretation. Nevertheless, the Committee on Concepts and Standards Underlying Financial Statements of the American Accounting Association provided definite opinion against direct costing in its 1957 report:

> . . . the cost of a manufactured product is the sum of the acquisition costs reasonably traceable to that product and should include both direct and indirect factors. The omission of any element of manufacturing cost is not acceptable.[4]

---

[4] "Accounting and Reporting Standards for Corporate Financial Statements: 1957 Revision," *The Accounting Review,* Vol. XXXII (October, 1957), 539. (Two members of the Committee dissented from this portion of the statement.)

In contrast to the firm position of the American Accounting Association, the American Institute of Certified Public Accountants took a less positive, but a seemingly unfavorable, position in Accounting Research Bulletin No. 43:

> . . . Although principles for the determination of inventory costs may be easily stated, their application, particularly to such inventory items as work in process and finished goods, is difficult because of the variety of problems encountered in the allocation of costs and charges. For example, under some circumstances, such items as idle facility expenses, excessive spoilage, double freight, and rehandling costs may be so abnormal as to require treatment as current period charges rather than as a portion of the inventory cost. . . . It should be recognized that the exclusion of all overheads from inventory costs does not constitute an accepted accounting procedure. . . .[5]

Many proponents of direct costing maintain that this statement does not make direct costing an unacceptable practice in external reporting. They feel that the statement prohibits the exclusion of all manufacturing overhead from inventory but does not specifically indicate what manufacturing overhead must be included in inventory.

Various publications of the National Association of Accountants seem to indicate that their attitude toward the use of direct costing in both internal and external reports may be favorable. However, this appraisal is a matter of opinion, since the N.A.A. does not issue official judgments concerning accounting practices.

Outside of the major accounting associations, the Securities and Exchange Commission and the Internal Revenue Service are also interested in financial statements used for external reporting and income taxes. The Securities and Exchange Commission objects to direct costing because, first, it is not a "generally accepted accounting procedure"; and second, the commission favors consistency among reporting companies. The position of the Internal Revenue Service against direct costing is guided by the Internal Revenue Code, which states:

> . . . . inventories shall be taken . . . on such basis as the Secretary or his delegate may prescribe as conforming as nearly as may be to the best accounting practice in the trade or business and as most clearly reflecting the income.[6]

Along with the income tax regulations stating that consistency in inventory practice is more important than any specific method of inventory costing, the "best accounting practice" contained in Section 471 of the Code indicates that

---

[5] Committee on Accounting Procedure, *Accounting Research Bulletin No. 43*, pp. 28–29. Copyright 1952 by the American Institute of Certified Public Accountants, Inc.

[6] Internal Revenue Code of 1954, Section 471.

the Internal Revenue Service wants tax accounting to follow "generally accepted accounting principles." Consequently, unless the A.I.C.P.A. considers direct costing to be a "generally accepted accounting practice," it appears that the Internal Revenue Service will continue to oppose direct costing.

QUESTIONS AND PROBLEMS

14-1. "Direct costing is an accounting concept, not an accounting system." Explain.

14-2. What are the basic differences between absorption costing and direct costing?

14-3. Distinguish between common fixed costs and traceable fixed costs.

14-4. A proponent of direct costing states: "Although direct costing places stress on cost variability, our control of fixed cost is more effective than it was with absorption costing." State why you agree or disagree.

14-5. A university rents a large arena for its home basketball games. It offers half-price admission to high school groups under the condition that tickets be purchased in quantity at the university at least one day preceding the game. What factors influence this policy?

14-6. Distinguish among:
a. gross margin
b. manufacturing margin
c. marginal income

14-7. An author states: "One of the principal advantages of direct costing is that it provides the basis for accounting for past costs consistent with accounting for present costs and future costs." What is meant by this statement?

14-8. "Direct costing reports present information in cost-volume-profit relationships." Explain. Compare with absorption costing reports.

14-9. The controller of a firm using direct costing commented recently: "We like direct costing because of its relevant, instant information characteristics, which are invaluable to us in making quick decisions, especially at times of special promotions." What did he mean?

14-10. "Timing as to when fixed manufacturing overhead costs are charged against sales revenue is the essential difference between absorption costing and direct costing." In what way?

14-11. "Reported profits and losses are likely to fluctuate more extensively if determined by direct costing rather than absorption costing." Do you agree? Why?

14-12. What characteristics distinguish product cost from period costs? Are these precisely and readily determinable? Where distinction is not clear, what factors may influence decision?

14-13. "In support of absorption costing, it is contended that, for long-range price considerations, the full cost of a product must be known, since more than the cost must be recovered in the long run if the product is to be determined profitable or unprofitable." Does direct costing fail to provide relevant information for long-range planning? Are fixed costs assignable to a product constant and immutable in the long run?

14-14. Why is direct costing not recognized as an "accepted accounting principle"?

14-15. In what way might each of the parties listed below be misled by a financial statement prepared on a direct costing basis?
a. creditors
b. investors

14-16. What is the marginal income ratio? How does it differ from the gross margin ratio?

14-17. "Costing rates prepared by absorption costing methods hold only for the specific volume used in computing the costs." What disadvantages are inherent in such rates?

14-18. The Kindal Company is facing a severe financial crisis. An examination of the operating results of its twenty regional stores has been made. You are asked to review the statement of income for the Houston store which appears below.

KINDAL COMPANY
(Houston store)
Statement of Income
For the Year Ended December 31, 1972

Sales		$1,000,000
Less: Variable Cost of Sales		800,000
Gross Margin on Sales		$ 200,000
Less: Selling and Administrative Expenses:		
Variable Selling Expense	$100,000	
Houston Fixed Expense (1)	60,000	
Corporate Administrative Expense (2)	80,000	240,000
Net Loss		($ 40,000)

(1) Consists of store manager's salary of $30,000; clerical help of $10,000; and store rent of $20,000.
(2) One-twentieth of Corporate Headquarters expense.

Required

a. Estimate the impact on overall corporate profits which would result from closing the Houston store.

b. Identify and support any assumptions you employed in arriving at your answer for requirement a.

14-19. The trimming department of the Colesar Whistle Manufacturing Company uses a standard cost system. The department operates eight hours per day, 25 days per month and employs twelve men who are paid $4.00 per hour. Each man trims 40 whistles per hour. Depreciation amounts to $378 per month, and a maintenance charge of $122 per month is made against the department. Raw materials cost 10¢ per whistle. Miscellaneous manufacturing overhead consists of fixed manufacturing overhead of $76 per month and variable manufacturing overhead of 8¢ per direct labor hour.

Required

Compute the standard cost per unit of production, assuming:
a. absorption costing
b. direct costing

14-20. You have a client engaged in a manufacturing business with relatively heavy fixed costs and large inventories of finished goods. These inventories constitute a very material item on the balance sheet. The company has a departmental cost accounting system that assigns all manufacturing costs to the product each period.

The controller of the company has informed you that the management is giving serious consideration to the adoption of direct costing as a method of accounting for plant operations and inventory valuation. The management wishes to have your opinion of the effect, if any, that such a change would have on:

1. the year-end statement of financial position
2. the statement of net income for the year
3. the audit certificate on the year-end statements

State your reply to the request and the reasons for your conclusions.

(Adapted from Uniform CPA Examination)

14-21. Select the *one* answer which *best* states a logical conclusion based on the facts stated.

If companies A and B manufacture similar products that require negligible distribution costs, and if their assets, operations, and accounting are similar in all respects except that A uses direct costing and B uses absorption costing,

a. A would report a higher inventory value than B for the years in which production exceeds sales

b. A would report a higher inventory value than B for the years in which production exceeds the normal or practical capacity

c. B would report a higher inventory value than A for the years in which production exceeds sales

d. B would report a higher net income than A for the years in which production equals sales

e. none of the above.

(Adapted from Uniform CPA Examination)

14-22. Coverly Manufacturing Company has operated its production facility on an eleven-month basis. In the month of December, the manufacturing employees take vacations of one month. The sales and administrative employees work as usual during December.

Sales during the current year were approximately 10 percent off expectations and, early in October, the condition was reviewed because of the rapid inventory accumulation. A decision was made to terminate manufacturing operations for the year at the end of October. It was believed that the inventory would be adequate for expected sales of November, December, and one-half of January.

On October 31, inventory amounted to 50,000 units. During November, 30,000 units were sold at an average price of $6.50.

Unit cost data pertaining to the inventory were as follows:

	Cost per unit
Material and direct labor	$3.00
Manufacturing overhead—Variable	.50
Manufacturing overhead—Fixed	1.00
	$4.50

In the past, operations have been scheduled uniformly over the first eleven months of the year, and the fixed manufacturing overhead of $220,000 annually has been absorbed in inventory at the rate of $20,000 per month.

Variable selling and administrative expenses amount to 50 cents per unit. Fixed selling and administrative expenses of $185,000 annually are divided evenly over twelve months.

Required

a. Prepare a statement of income for November assuming the company uses:
   1. absorption costing
   2. direct costing
b. How do you account for the difference?
c. What is the cost of idle capacity for November?
d. Can there be an idle-capacity loss under direct costing?

14-23. Whittle Company manufactures three sizes of drills. Bid D is sold to producers of basic metals, Med D is sold to metal fabricators, and Small D is sold to distributors for the "do-it-yourself" market. The demand for all three sizes has been brisk, and the plant has been operating at near practical capacity. The salesmen of each market report sales at the established prices are limited only by availability of product.

The budget committee reviews the matter and concludes the favorable market conditions are likely to continue for a few months. Therefore, a decision is made to utilize the remaining capacity. The available equipment is equally suitable for any of the three products. Which product would provide maximum profit? Information pertinent to the decision is presented below.

Per unit data

	Big D	Med D	Small D
Sales price	$50.00	$40.00	$30.00
Variable manufacturing and non-manufacturing costs	30.00	28.00	21.00
Marginal income	$20.00	$12.00	$ 9.00
Machine time—minutes	60	30	20

Required

a. Show calculations determining which product provides the greatest profit in utilizing the remaining capacity.

b. Under the conditions, should revision of scheduling be further studied? Why?

14-24. Darlok Company makes locks of superb quality. A standard cost accounting system is employed at the lock division. Operations are relatively uniform throughout the year. Data relating to a month's operations is presented below.

Standard Unit Cost

Normal volume 20,000 locks

Direct materials	$4.00
Direct labor	2.00
Manufacturing overhead—Variable	1.00
Manufacturing overhead—Fixed	2.00
Total	$9.00

Budgeted selling and administrative expenses amount to $3.00 per unit, of which one-third is variable. No standards have been established for non-manufacturing costs.

Sales price	$15.00
Operating and cost data:	
Beginning inventory	2,000 units
Production	22,000 units
Sales	18,000 units
Direct materials used	$90,000
Direct labor	42,000
Manufacturing overhead—Variable	23,000
Manufacturing overhead—Fixed	40,000
Selling and administrative—Variable	18,000
Selling and administrative—Fixed	40,000

All variances are considered adjustments of standard gross margin or standard marginal income.

Required

a. Prepare statements of income comparing absorption cost determinations with direct costing results.
b. Account for the differences.
c. Comment on the effect of variances on marginal income.
d. The management is disappointed in this month's sales results and is considering increasing advertising and other sales promotion at an additional cost of $10,000 per month. If this action were taken, determine sales volumes that must be achieved to earn:
   1. the budgeted profit of $60,000
   2. increased profits of 10 percent

Round percentages to two places and amounts to nearest thousands.

14-25. Kronen-Wetter Company began operations on January 1, 1971, producing electronic components. Mr. A. W. Kronen, president and organizer of the company, had previously served as sales manager of a large electronic firm. In fact, all the officers of the new firm had previously been employed in executive capacities by firms producing electronic components.

The controller had substantial experience in standard cost accounting, and he installed a workable system so expeditiously that the reports for 1971 were presented on a standard cost basis. In the beginning, it was necessary for the controller to explain the significance of the data presented in reports. However, the net income for the first year was so surprisingly good that the president was not concerned with his failure to understand thoroughly the annual report.

Sales in the second year were approximately 14 percent greater than in the first, but the president was stunned to find the net income and gross margin had decreased. Explanations were offered, but, being sales oriented, he could not reconcile increased sales with decreased profits.

After much deliberation, the controller concluded that conversion of the income statements to a direct costing basis would provide information in a more understandable form.

Income statements for 1971 and 1972, as reported on absorption costing basis, appear below.

THE KRONEN-WETTER COMPANY
Income Statement
Years 1971 and 1972

	1971	1972
Net Sales	$700,000	$800,000
Cost of goods sold—standard		
Beginning—inventory	—	$180,000
Cost of goods manufactured	600,000	420,000
Goods available for sale	$600,000	$600,000
Ending inventory	180,000	120,000
Cost of goods sold	$420,000	$480,000

Variances:
Material variances	$ 1,000	$ (1,000)
Labor variances	2,000	3,000
Manufacturing overhead—controllable	—	(1,000)
Manufacturing overhead—volume	—	45,000
	$ 3,000	$ 46,000
Adjusted cost of goods sold	$423,000	$526,000
Gross Margin	$277,000	$274,000
Selling and administrative expenses	200,000	205,000
Net income	$ 77,000	$ 69,000

Other data:

Standard unit cost:
Materials	$2.50
Labor	1.50
Manufacturing overhead	2.00
Total	$6.00

Standard volume is 100,000 units.

	1971	1972
Beginning inventory	0	30,000
Production	100,000	70,000
Sales	70,000	80,000
Ending inventory	30,000	20,000

There were no inventories in process at the end of either year.

The selling and administrative expenses in 1971 were 17½ percent variable and 82½ percent fixed. In 1972, the variable expenses per unit were the same as in 1971. The fixed expenses remained constant in total.

Required

a. Convert the absorption costing statement to a direct costing statement.

b. Account for the differences in net income.

c. In what manner would the direct costing statement be more understandable and useful to the president?

d. Assuming no variances and that all fixed costs remained at the same level, what volume of sales would yield a net income of $100,000?

14-26. Darygard Company manufactures toys, home products, and industrial supplies. The management has recently begun a program of plant decentralization according to product lines. For some time, the monthly statements have caused bitter differences of opinion on operating results. With manufacturing decentralization almost completed, the controller suggests that the accounting of one of the divisions be converted to a direct costing basis. It was agreed that direct costing would be employed at one of the plants producing a completely new line of products.

[CH. 14] DIRECT COSTING 461

To strike at the heart of the matter quickly, the controller decided that, for the first three months of operation, he would show the difference in inventory values resulting from absorption costing and direct costing. Differences of opinion on inventory values had frequently been points of controversy.

Operating and accounting data for the first three months of operation of the Bracy division of the firm are presented below.

		September	October	November
Beginning inventory	(cases)	—	1,000	2,000
Production	(cases)	10,000	12,000	9,000
Ending inventory	(cases)	1,000	2,000	500
Direct materials used		$70,000	$84,000	$63,000
Direct labor		30,000	36,000	27,000
Manufacturing overhead—Variable		10,000	12,000	9,000
Manufacturing overhead—Fixed		30,000	30,000	30,000

Volume for calculation of the predetermined manufacturing overhead rate is 10,000 cases.

Required

a. Determine inventory cost at the end of each month by:
   1. absorption costing
   2. direct costing
b. Determine the difference in operating income by absorption costing and direct costing.
c. To which class of manufacturing costs is the operating income difference attributable?
d. Which basis provides the fairer inventory value? Defend your answers on the basis of
   1. principle of asset valuation
   2. principle of matching revenue and expense
   3. materiality of effect

14-27. Metal Industries, Inc. operates its production department only when orders are received for one or both of its two products, two sizes of metal discs. The manufacturing process begins with the cutting of doughnut-shaped rings from rectangular strips of sheet metal; these rings are then pressed into discs. The sheets of metal, each 4 feet long and weighing 32 ounces, are purchased at $1.36 per running foot. The department has been operating at a loss for the past year as shown below.

Sales for the year	$172,000
Expenses	177,200
Net loss for the department	$ 5,200

The following information is available:
1. Ten thousand 4-foot pieces of metal yielded 40,000 large discs, each weighing 4 ounces and selling for $2.90, and 40,000 small discs, each weighing 2.4 ounces and selling for $1.40.

2. The Corporation has been producing at less than "normal capacity" and has had no spoilage in the cutting step of the process. The skeletons remaining after the rings have been cut are sold for scrap at $.80 per pound.
3. The variable conversion cost of each large disc is 80 percent of the disc's direct material cost and variable conversion cost of each small disc is 75 percent of the disc's direct material cost. Variable conversion costs are the sum of direct labor and variable manufacturing overhead.
4. Fixed costs were $86,000.

Required

a. For each of the parts manufactured, prepare a schedule computing:
   1. unit material cost after deducting the value of salvage
   2. unit variable conversion cost
   3. unit contribution margin
   4. total contribution margin for all units sold
b. Assuming you computed the material cost for large discs at $.85 each and for small discs at $.51 each, compute the number of units the Corporation must sell to break even based on a normal production capacity of 50,000 units. Assume no spoiled units and a product mix of one large disc to each small disc.

(Adapted from Uniform CPA Examination)

14-28. Calper Plastell Company manufactures one product in a single process. Pertinent data relating to costs and operations are presented below.

Budgeted costs per unit
Normal volume 100,000 units

Direct materials	$3.00
Direct labor	2.00
Manufacturing overhead	1.00
Manufacturing unit cost	$6.00
Non-manufacturing costs:	
Variable selling expenses	$ .50
Fixed selling expenses	.70
Fixed administrative expenses	.50
Non-manufacturing cost per unit	$1.70
Total cost to make and sell	$7.70

(Fixed costs represent 60 percent of the budgeted manufacturing overhead at normal.)

(Normal volume represents 80 percent of practical capacity. No additional fixed costs would be incurred to practical capacity.)
Sales price is $9.00 per unit.
Other operating data:

[CH. 14] DIRECT COSTING 463

Sales	1971	90,000 units
Sales	1972	104,000 units
Production	1971	85,000 units
Production	1972	110,000 units

The inventory on January 1, 1971, consisted of 15,000 units at budgeted unit cost. There was no work in process inventory at the end of any period.

Required

Assume that all variable costs were incurred as budgeted and fixed cost remained constant.

a. Prepare income statements for years 1971 and 1972 on "absorption costing basis" and with direct costing basis. Overabsorbed or underabsorbed manufacturing overhead is to be considered an adjustment of cost of goods sold.

b. Prepare a schedule reconciling the differences in net income with the differences in the changes in inventory.

15

Cost-Volume-Profit Relationships

In planning for the future, management is vitally concerned with the short-run relationship between total cost and total revenue. This concern resolves itself into a search for that combination of costs, revenue, and volume which will be most profitable. Changes in production and marketing facilities, production and marketing methods, or prices paid for these cost factors are reflected in production and marketing costs. Changes in selling prices and in sales mixture are reflected in sales revenue. Moreover, whether the preceding determinants of cost and revenue are changed or remain static, fluctuations in volume also cause variations in profit. These changing circumstances confront management with the problem of selecting among alternative courses of action when each alternative has its own different combination of costs, revenue and volume.

For the most satisfactory solution to this problem, those in management must have knowledge of the estimated costs, revenue, and volume which should be associated with each alternative. This knowledge may be obtained by an analysis of the cost-volume-profit relationships which exist under different combinations of assumed conditions. Various approaches and techniques are used to study, prepare, and summarize the analyses of such relationships. Break-even, profit-volume, differential, and direct costing analyses, charts and statements are widely used for this purpose. Chapter 14 pointed out how management may use the marginal income concept of direct costing to provide such information. The remaining three suggested approaches will be discussed in this chapter.

BREAK-EVEN ANALYSIS

The sales volume at which sales revenue equals the cost to make and sell the products or services sold is of prime interest to management. The sales activity which equates total revenue with related costs and results in neither profit nor loss is called the break-even volume or break-even point. If all costs varied with volume, profits would vary proportionately with sales, and the break-even point would be located at zero activity (shut-down point). If all costs were non-variable, profits would vary disproportionately higher with sales, and the break-even point would be located where the sales activity equated total revenue with non-variable costs. Consequently, the location of a break-even point is predicated in part on the cost structure and cannot be ascertained unless costs have been separated into their variable and non-variable components.

Previous discussions of cost behavior have pointed out that the separation of costs into those which are constant for a period of time and those which vary with the volume of activity is an extremely complex endeavor which, at best, provides only reasonably accurate approximations. But the identification of those costs which are presumed to vary with volume is basic to the calculation of a break-even point; the reliability of the calculation depends upon the accuracy and the inherent limitations of the data from which it is computed.

The logic underlying the determination of a break-even point is easy to understand. It can be comprehended quickly by answering the following question. "How many articles, have a unit cost of six dollars and a selling price of ten dollars, must I sell to recover a $400 fee paid for exclusive right to a sales territory?" The answer can be determined by dividing the four-dollar difference between the unit cost and selling price into the $400 fee. The solution could be shown as follows:

$$\frac{\text{Fee}}{\text{Unit Sales Price} - \text{Unit Cost}} = \frac{\$400}{\$10 - \$6} = \frac{\$400}{\$4} = 100 \text{ units}$$

To obtain the answer, the four-dollar difference between the unit cost, which comprised the unit variable cost, and the sales price was ascertained. This difference was significant, since it represented the limit of the unit contribution to the amount of the fee which represented the non-variable cost. In break-even analysis, this difference is called the contribution margin or marginal income. Once determined, it can be used to calculate the number of break-even units as follows:

$$\text{Number of Break-Even Units} = \frac{\text{Non-Variable Costs}}{\text{Unit Contribution Margin}}$$

The unit contribution margin is the amount of the sales price of each unit which is available to cover the non-variable costs. When the contribution margin of four dollars is divided by the ten-dollar sales price, a quotient of 40 percent is obtained. The calculation reveals that 40 percent of each sales dollar is available for the coverage of non-variable costs; this 40 percent is known as the marginal contribution percentage or ratio. It may also be computed by subtracting the variable cost percentage of 60 percent from 100 percent of the sales dollars. When the marginal contribution ratio is divided into the amount of the non-variable costs in the above illustration, the amount of the sales dollars required to break even is obtained as follows:

$$\frac{\text{Non-Variable Costs}}{\text{Marginal Contribution Ratio}} = \frac{\$400}{.40} = \$1,000$$

This computation differs from the previous calculations because it expresses all data either in dollars or as a ratio and does not reveal the number of units involved. Of course, the number of break-even units in the example can be obtained by dividing the unit selling price into the amount of break-even dollars. This determination is made possible by the fact that the example is concerned with the sale of one particular product.

If multiple products are sold at different prices, the number of break-even units could not be determined by this procedure, and the previously calculated unit contribution margin method could not be used to compute a break-even point. The marginal contribution ratio could be used to calculate the break-even point, however, because it shows what percentage of the dollars used to measure sales volume is available for coverage of non-variable costs. Since most firms sell different products, the overall break-even point is widely expressed in sales dollars, as is illustrated by the data shown for Company A in the following example.

COMPANY A
Marginal Income Statement

Sales	$200,000	100%
Variable Costs	120,000	60%
Marginal Contribution	$ 80,000	40%
Non-Variable Costs	60,000	30%
Net Income	$ 20,000	10%

$$\text{Break-Even point} = \frac{\text{Non-Variable Costs}}{\text{Marginal Contribution Ratio}} = \frac{\$60,000}{40\%} = \$150,000$$

That the break-even point equals $150,000 can be proved as follows:

Break-Even Sales	150,000	100%
Variable Costs	90,000	60%
Marginal Contribution	$ 60,000	40%
Non-Variable Costs	60,000	40%
Net Income	$ -0-	0%

In this example and proof, the marginal contribution ratio equals the difference between 100 percent of sales and their related variable cost percentage of 60 percent. The data contained in the last example is employed to illustrate that this relationship is the basis for the following widely used break-even formula:

$$\text{Break-Even} = \frac{\text{Non-Variable Costs}}{1 - \dfrac{\text{Variable Costs}}{\text{Sales}}}$$

$$\text{Break-Even} = \frac{\$60{,}000}{1 - \dfrac{\$120{,}000}{\$200{,}000}}$$

$$\text{Break-Even} = \frac{\$60{,}000}{1 - .60}$$

$$\text{Break-Even} = \frac{\$60{,}000}{.40} \leftarrow (\text{marginal contribution ratio})$$

$$\text{Break-Even} = \$150{,}000$$

The actual sales of Company A amount to $200,000. The $50,000 of sales above break-even point equal the sum of their related variable costs and the net income: $50,000 = $30,000 + $20,000. This indicates that, when the net income is divided by the marginal contribution ratio, the amount of sales in excess of the break-even point is obtained: $20,000 ÷ .40 = $50,000. Consequently, when the marginal contribution ratio is divided into the sum of non-variable costs and net income, total sales are obtained: ($60,000 + $20,000) ÷ .40 = $200,000. This last calculation is obvious when it is remembered that any income statement can be expressed by the following equation:

Sales = Variable Costs + Non-Variable Costs + Net Income or Minus Loss

This equation may be adapted to provide another technique for calculating the break-even point for Company A as follows:

Let S = Break-even sales in dollars
S = Variable costs + Non-variable costs

$$S = \frac{\text{Variable costs}}{\text{Sales}} \text{ Sales} + \text{Non-variable costs}$$

$$S = \frac{\$120{,}000}{\$200{,}000} S + \$60{,}000$$

$$S = .60S + \$60{,}000$$
$$.40\,S = \$60{,}000$$
$$S = \$150{,}000$$

Whether the equation or the formula technique is used to ascertain the break-even point is unimportant; the technique employed is a matter of personal preference. It is important, however, that the user recognizes that the significant element in either method is the marginal income concept.

Margin of Safety

The excess of the actual sales over the break-even sales volume for Company A amounts to $50,000. Obviously, this is the amount by which the sales could be reduced before Company A suffers a loss. This excess is known as the margin of safety. When the margin-of-safety dollars are divided by the actual sales dollars, a margin-of-safety ratio is obtained as follows:

$$\text{Margin-of-Safety Ratio} = \frac{\text{Margin of Safety Sales}}{\text{Actual Sales}} = \frac{\$50,000}{\$200,000} = 25\%$$

The margin-of-safety ratio indicates the percentage by which the actual sales may be reduced before they fall below the break-even volume of sales; the higher the margin-of-safety ratio, the better the position of the company. Of course, the validity of this ratio depends upon the accuracy of the data utilized.

Break-Even Charts

The break-even point can be portrayed on a break-even chart, which also presents a graphic view of the relationship between costs, sales, and net income at varying levels of activity. Break-even charts may be constructed in a simple or elaborate manner. Exhibit 15–1 is an example of a simple and traditional form of break-even chart. In the exhibit, the volume of sales is measured along the horizontal axis; costs and sales revenue related to any volume of sales are measured along the vertical axis. The vertical distance between the sales revenue and total cost line measures the estimated net income or loss at the related volume. The non-variable cost line runs parallel to the horizontal axis. The variable cost line is superimposed on the non-variable cost line and moves upward uniformly with volume at the rate of 60 percent of sales. The sales revenue line begins at the point of origin and moves upward uniformly with volume. The intersection of the sales revenue line with the total cost line is the break-even point.

Many analysts prefer a break-even chart which shows non-variable costs superimposed on variable costs; they maintain that this arrangement conforms more closely to marginal income thinking, since it emphasizes the recovery of non-variable costs at various levels of volume. Using the data shown in Exhibit 15–1 for Company A, such a break-even chart is illustrated in Exhibit 15–2.

Assumptions Underlying Break-Even Analysis

Break-even analysis is based upon many assumptions, some of which are more valid than others. Variance of fact from theory in any one of the assumptions will have some effect on the validity of the break-even point. Among the more important assumptions are the following six:

1. All costs can be reliably separated into their variable and non-variable components.
2. Non-variable costs will remain constant in total amount throughout the contemplated volume range.
3. Variable costs will not change per unit and will fluctuate in direct proportion to volume.
4. Selling prices will remain unchanged at any volume.
5. There will be no change in sales mix.
6. Production and sales volume will be equated.

EXHIBIT 15-1

Break-Even Chart
(Variable Costs Superimposed on Non-Variable Costs)

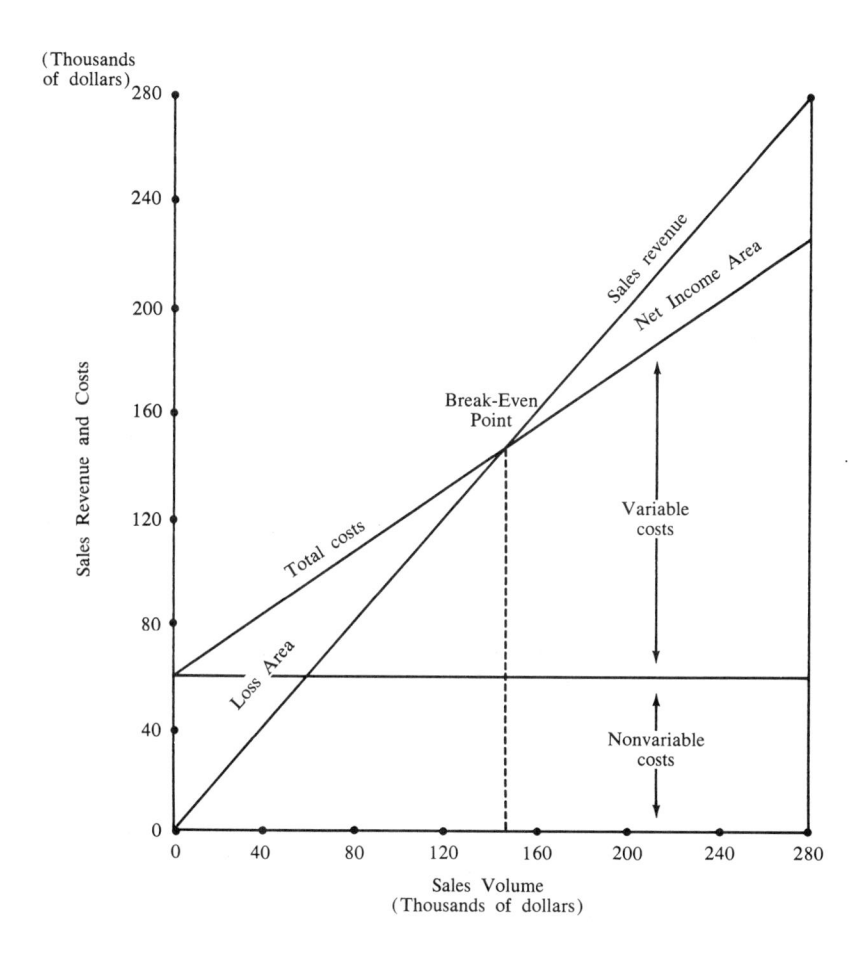

It is important that anyone who prepares or interprets a break-even analysis recognizes its limitations due to the given assumptions. The greater the variance of actual fact from the given assumptions, the more invalid the break-even calculation. And, since at least one variance from theory is almost inevitable in a typical situation, undue reliance upon a particular break-even point may be delusive. Different sets of assumptions may be illustrated by the preparation of a series of break-even analyses and charts; a limited number of different assumptions may be shown on the same break-even chart. A break-even chart best portrays the effect of volume changes, while other changes are more appropriately illustrated by profit-volume charts, which will be considered in the next section of this chapter.

EXHIBIT 15-2

Break-Even Chart
(Non-Variable Costs Superimposed on Variable Costs)

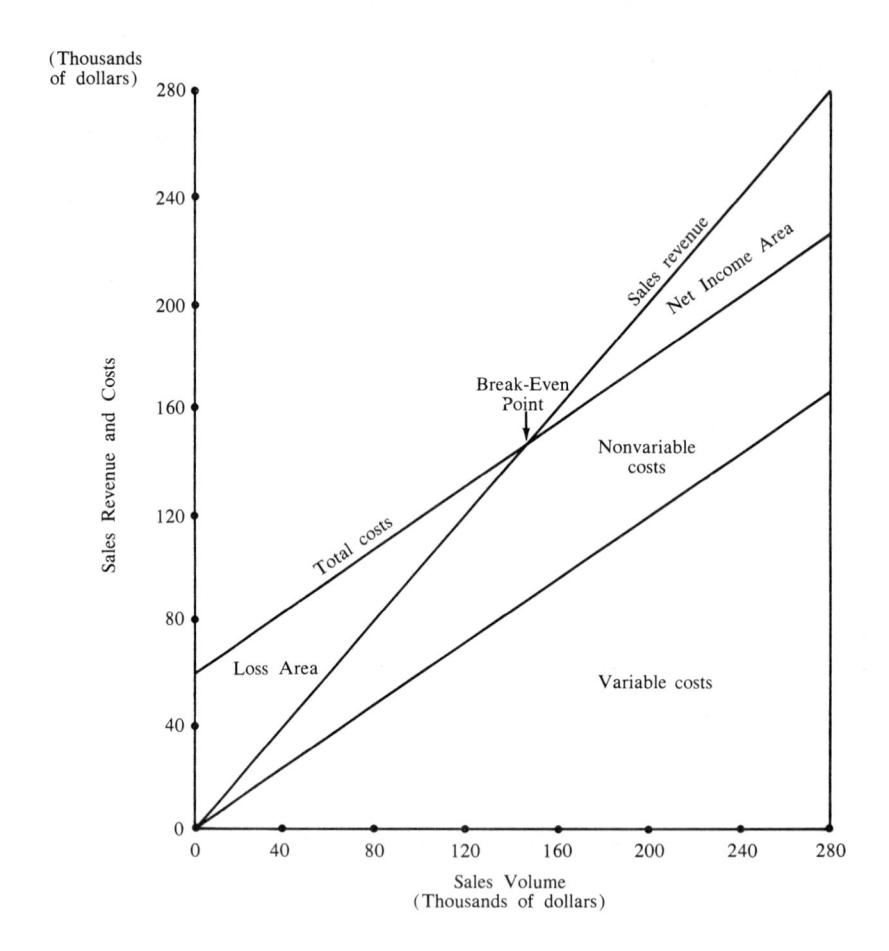

PROFIT-VOLUME ANALYSIS

A single break-even chart represents a set of conditions in which all factors other than volume remain constant. It indicates the amount of costs, sales revenue, and net income which should result when volume is increased or decreased. In doing so, however, it assumes that the behavior of all factors will remain unchanged at any level of volume. At best, the position of the lines on the chart are reliable only within a limited range of volume fluctuations; a conventional chart is not likely to show much useful information for volume levels which fall outside the relevant range. It would be more realistic, in most instances, if the lines on the chart were not carried back to the vertical axis.

[CH. 15] COST-VOLUME-PROFIT RELATIONSHIPS 471

Nevertheless, the basic data contained on a break-even chart represent a starting point from which to project further study of the profit pattern. This study should indicate how profits may be expected to vary when changes occur in the behavior of costs and revenue whether volume changes or not.

The results of such studies can be presented best by the use of profit-volume charts. These charts, sometimes called P/V charts or P/V graphs, supplement break-even charts. Separate lines for costs and revenues are eliminated from a P/V chart, because the plotting is limited to profit differences. As a result, break-even charts and P/V charts are often used together to obtain the advantages peculiar to each.

Profit-Volume Chart

A profit-volume chart is prepared by scaling the sales volume on the horizontal axis as it is on a break-even chart. Above and parallel to the horizontal axis another line is drawn, called the break-even line. (This line may also be used to measure sales revenue.) This line is perpendicular to the profit or loss vertical line at the point of zero profits. Dollars of profit are measured by the vertical scale above the break-even line; dollars of losses are measured by the vertical scale below the break-even line.

Data for Company A, which was used in the earlier illustrations of break-even charts, are used in the P/V chart in Exhibit 15–3. The chart makes it easy to visualize what changes will take place in the profit-and-loss pattern as conditions are altered. Since only the net effect of revenue or cost changes is reflected in the profit line, the profit lines showing the estimated results of various proposed changes can be visualized and compared easily from the same profit-volume chart.

Profit-Volume Ratio

Along with profit-volume charts or graphs, most analysts use the P/V ratio to describe the marginal contribution ratio. The use of this term sometimes conveys the mistaken impression that it represents the relationship between net income and sales revenue. Actually, it represents this relationship only after the break-even point has been reached and non-variable costs have been recovered. Nor is the P/V ratio determined by dividing sales revenue into net income. Instead, it is ascertained as a marginal contribution ratio is calculated. Since both terms have the same meaning and identical uses, the more common *P/V ratio* will replace *marginal contribution ratio* throughout the remainder of this chapter.

Revenue and Cost Changes

The estimated effect of changes in sales volume can be readily visualized by the set of conditions portrayed on a single break-even chart or profit-volume

EXHIBIT 15-3
Profit-Volume Chart

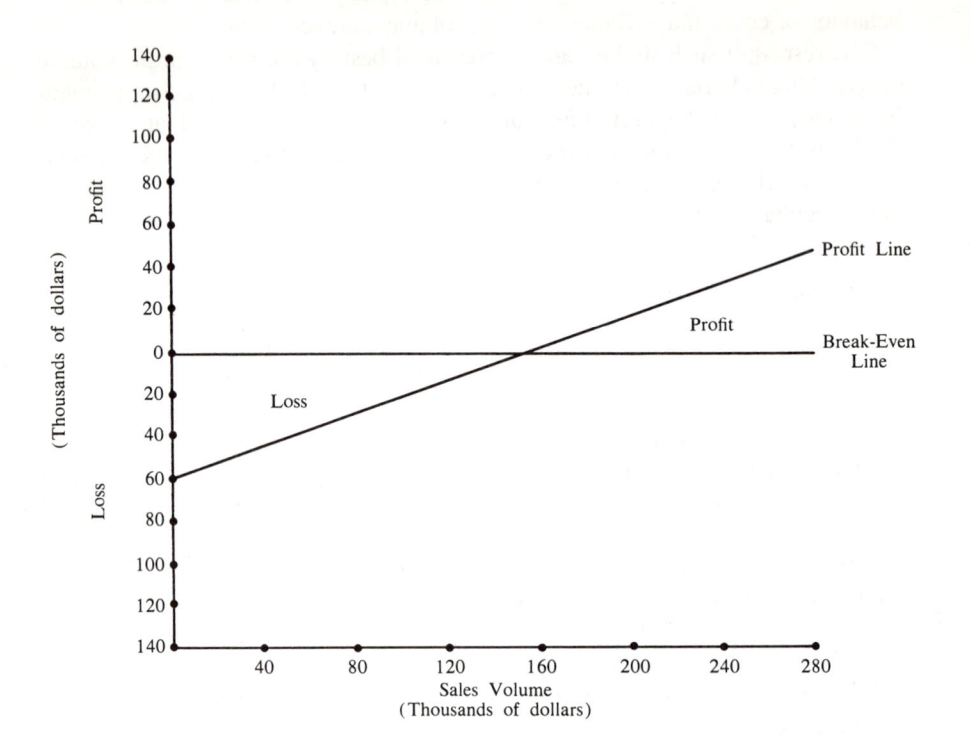

graph. But changes in factors other than volume create different conditions from those revealed by a single chart. The estimated effect of such changes usually requires a new analysis and a revised chart presentation. A knowledge of the effect on profits of changes other than volume is a prerequisite to the proper understanding of profit-volume relationships.

Effect of Price Changes. A change in selling prices alters the P/V ratio, the break-even point, and the profits above and the losses below the break-even point. A price change may cause a change in sales volume. But since a price change alone does not change sales volume, the cost pattern remains the same as before the price change was made. To illustrate how well a profit-volume chart lends itself to portraying different profit lines, those data for Company A used in previous illustrations are revised for a single product and expanded according to the following schedule:

[CH. 15] COST-VOLUME-PROFIT RELATIONSHIPS 473

	Price Increase		At Present	Price Decrease	
	20%	10%		10%	20%
Number of units	10,000	10,000	10,000	10,000	10,000
Unit selling price	$24	$22	$20	$18	$16
Sales revenue	$240,000	$220,000	$200,000	$180,000	$160,000
Variable costs	120,000	120,000	120,000	120,000	120,000
Marginal income	$120,000	$100,000	$ 80,000	$ 60,000	$ 40,000
Non-variable costs	60,000	60,000	60,000	60,000	60,000
Net income	$ 60,000	$ 40,000	$ 20,000	$ –0–	($ 20,000)
P/V ratio	50%	45½%	40%	33⅓%	25%
B/E point	$120,000	$132,000	$150,000	$180,000	$240,000

EXHIBIT 15-4

Profit-Volume Chart
Effect of Changes in Selling Prices on Profits
and Break-Even Points

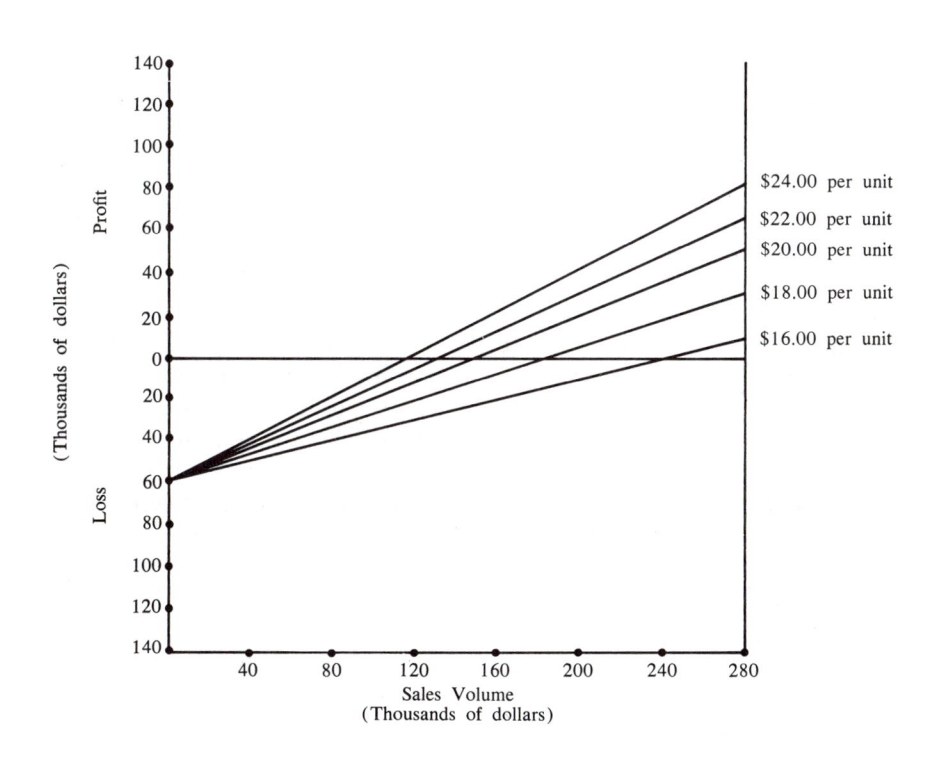

The data from the schedule have been used in Exhibit 15–4, which illustrates how many different proposals may be combined into a single chart which permits the viewer to measure, and compare with ease, the distinct advantage of a profit-volume chart.

Changes in Non-Variable Costs. Proposed changes in non-variable costs alter the break-even point, but they do not change the profit-volume ratio. An increase in the amount of non-variable costs decreases profits above and increases losses below the break-even point by the amount of the increase; a decrease in the amount of non-variable costs increases profits above and decreases losses below the break-even point by the amount of the decrease. When changes are made in the original amount of the non-variable costs included in the data for Company A, the effects are as indicated below.

	Non-Variable Costs		
	$10,000 Increase	Original Amount	$10,000 Decrease
Non-variable costs	$ 70,000	$ 60,000	$ 50,000
P/V ratio	40%	40%	40%
Break-even point	$175,000	$150,000	$125,000
Break-even point change	+$ 25,000	–0–	–$ 25,000
Variable cost change to B/E	+ 15,000*	–0–	– 15,000*
Change in net income	–$ 10,000	–0–	+$ 10,000

* Equals 60% of the change in sales needed to break even

If this information were portrayed on a profit-volume chart, the slope of the profit lines would remain the same; the profit lines would originate at different points on the vertical axis but would always be parallel.

Changes in Variable Costs. A change in variable costs per unit changes the P/V ratio, the break-even point, and the profit or loss at any sales volume. These are the same factors which are altered by a change in selling price. Changes in selling prices, however, have effects opposite from those caused by changes in variable costs. This may be illustrated by assuming that the unit price increases or decreases, previously used to show the effect of price changes, are instead changes in the unit variable costs shown by the schedule on page 475. Compare the figures with those used to show the effect of price changes and observe that whether unit variable costs are decreased or unit selling prices increased by the same amount, the same marginal income figures are obtained, and the net income amounts agree. Break-even points, however, differ when opposite changes of like amounts are made in the unit variable costs or selling prices. Break-even points react more violently to changes in variable costs than they do to the same changes in selling prices.

Shifts in Sales Mix. A change in the mixture of products sold usually affects the break-even point and the average profit-volume ratio. In most situations, a number of products are made and sold in different models and styles. Some

	Variable Costs				
	Unit Increase		At	Unit Decrease	
	$4.00	$2.00	Present	$2.00	$4.00
Number of units	10,000	10,000	10,000	10,000	10,000
Unit selling price	$20	$20	$20	$20	$20
Sales revenue	$200,000	$200,000	$200,000	$200,000	$200,000
Variable costs	160,000	140,000	120,000	100,000	80,000
Marginal income	$ 40,000	$ 60,000	$ 80,000	$100,000	$120,000
Non-variable costs	60,000	60,000	60,000	60,000	60,000
Net income	($ 20,000)	–0–	$ 20,000	$ 40,000	$ 60,000
P/V ratio	20%	30%	40%	50%	60%
B/E point	$300,000	$200,000	$150,000	$120,000	$100,000

products cost more to make and sell than others, and different products are likely to have different mark-ups. As a result, changes in the mixture of products sold affect profits and the break-even point. For illustration, assume that a company has developed data concerning the three products it markets, as follows.

	Product			
	A	B	C	Total
Sales	$500,000	$300,000	$200,000	$1,000,000
Variable costs	400,000	210,000	120,000	730,000
Marginal income	$100,000	$ 90,000	$ 80,000	$ 270,000
Non-variable costs				135,000
Net income				$ 135,000
P/V ratio	20%	30%	40%	27%
Break-even sales				$ 500,000

If $200,000 of the sales shown for Product A, the low P/V product, in the above analysis could be switched equally to Product B and Product C, the total sales would remain the same, but the profit and the break-even point would be changed as follows.

	Product			
	A	B	C	Total
Sales	$300,000	$400,000	$300,000	$1,000,000
Variable costs	240,000	280,000	180,000	700,000
Marginal income	$ 60,000	$120,000	$120,000	$ 300,000
Non-variable costs				135,000
Net income				$ 165,000
P/V ratio	20%	30%	40%	30%
Break-even sales				$ 450,000

The illustration indicates how profit-volume analysis can aid management by forecasting the probable effect on profit which would result from emphasizing certain products at the expense of others. This kind of presentation, however, fails to reflect the costs that might be necessary to accomplish the change. The missing cost data may be supplied through differential analysis, which is discussed in the next section of this chapter.

DIFFERENTIAL ANALYSIS

A differential analysis deals with the cost and revenue elements that apply to a specific situation. Differential costs and revenues, sometimes called marginal costs and revenues or incremental costs and revenues, are those that are expected to change from one alternative to another. Costs and revenues that are not changed by a choice are not relevant in making a decision. When differential revenues exceed differential costs, other things being equal, a favorable opportunity exists. Likewise, when differential cost reductions exceed related revenue reductions, other things being equal, a favorable situation exists.

Earlier illustrations have suggested that the effect on profit of changes in product mix, variable costs, non-variable costs, prices, and volume could be estimated by profit-volume or break-even analysis. Each of these estimates provides information which can aid management in making certain decisions. But managers constantly are faced with choices; some choices require more or different information from that which is provided by the typical profit-volume analysis. When such a situation arises, a differential analysis may be used to reflect some of the effects of the alternate choices available.

Differential analyses may involve problems of alternative choice such as:

1. Volume (increase, decrease, or shut down)
2. Price (volume-price relationships, business at special prices, etc.)
3. Products (new additions, territories or marketing channels)
4. Dispositions (sell or process products further)
5. Acquisitions (make or buy component parts, facilities, etc.)

Previous illustrations have indicated some basic approaches toward analyzing the volume and price type of problem. These two problems, however, are dealt with more comprehensively by the differential analysis presented in the next chapter. Make or buy decisions, like expansion of present facilities and new product decisions, often require application of capital budgeting techniques. These are illustrated in Chapter 18, which discusses capital expenditure decisions. To illustrate the differential analysis technique, an example involving a sell or further processing problem will be used.

Assume that a refiner has on hand 100,000 gallons of fuel oil. The company must choose between selling the fuel oil at 10¢ per gallon or cracking it into gasoline and residual fuel oil. The current price of gasoline is 15¢ a gallon. Yields from cracking a gallon of fuel oil are 80 percent gasoline, 15 percent residual fuel oil, and 5 percent loss. It costs 5¢ to crack a gallon of fuel oil.

These data would be analyzed as follows:

Potential revenue from cracking:	
Gasoline (80,000 gallons @ 15¢)	$12,000
Residual fuel oil (15,000 gallons @ 10¢)	1,500
Total potential revenue from cracking	$13,500
Less potential revenue from fuel oil:	
Fuel oil (100,000 @ 10¢)	10,000
Differential revenue	$ 3,500
Less differential costs:	
Cracking fuel oil (100,000 gallons @ 5¢)	5,000
Potential loss from cracking fuel oil	$ 1,500

Of course, the $1,500 is not an accounting loss. But, since the refiner would end up with $1,500 less profit by cracking the fuel oil, this choice would be tantamount to losing $1,500.

SUMMARY

Analyses of cost-volume-profit relationships provide guidance for those in management who are planning and selecting among alternative courses of business action. Various techniques may be used to help solve this complex cost-volume-profit relationship problem; break-even, profit-volume, and differential analyses are widely used for this purpose. This chapter has discussed and illustrated how these three methods provide information which may be used in this area to arrive at satisfactory decisions.

Break-even and profit-volume studies have distinct disadvantages and severe constraints. Their underlying assumptions may easily trap the novice into making dangerous conclusions. Charts portraying such studies provide useful pictorial summaries but are too inflexible to be used directly in many decision-making situations. Marginal contribution ratios or profit-volume ratios are significant indicators but frequently fail to provide a complete measurement of potential profit. Nevertheless, qualified people do prepare meaningful break-even and profit-volume analyses to measure and forecast the effect of alternative choices.

Differential costs are costs relevant for making decisions. Differential analysis substantially or completely overcomes the major disadvantages attributed to break-even and profit-volume techniques. However, the typical differential analysis also has shortcomings which must not be ignored when certain types of long-range decisions are considered. Despite these limitations, differential analyses, when supplemented by break-even and profit-volume techniques, are extremely valuable tools which help management to make short-range decisions.

QUESTIONS AND PROBLEMS

15-1. Why must the conventional income statement be restated prior to the calculation of a break-even point? List the types of items which must be restated or rearranged. What type of income statement is needed?

15-2. How would a desired profit objective be included in the determination of a break-even point?

15-3. What is the difference between the contribution marginal ratio and the ratio of net income?

15-4. What effect do uneven sales and production volumes have in break-even analysis?

15-5. What effect, if any, would each of the following have on the break-even point?
   a. decrease in selling prices
   b. increase in the physical volume of sales
   c. decrease in total fixed costs
   d. increase in variable unit cost
   e. decrease in the marginal contribution ratio

15-6. "Break-even points for multi-product firms are likely to be less reliable than for single product firms." Do you agree or disagree? Why?

15-7. How does a profit-volume chart differ from a break-even chart? What are the advantages and disadvantages of each type of chart?

15-8. "When Congress passes a reduction in the corporate income tax rates, our break-even point will be lower." Do you agree or disagree? Why?

15-9. The Viewcrest Company presents the following data:

Present sales volume	$200,000
Total non-variable cost	100,000
Unit selling price	$2.00
Unit variable cost	.80

The sales manager maintains that a 10 percent reduction in the unit sales price will generate a 15 percent increase in the physical volume of sales. If his assumption is correct, should the company decrease the unit selling price to $1.80?

15-10. The production manager of a company argues that whether comparable reductions are made in variable or non-variable costs is unimportant. He believes that a cost reduction accomplishes the same result wherever it is made. Is he right or wrong? Why?

[CH. 15] COST-VOLUME-PROFIT RELATIONSHIPS 479

15-11. The statistician for a company finds that the sum of the break-even points for his company's products is different from the single break-even point calculated for all products. Has he made a mistake? Why?

15-12. Are "relevant costs" the same as "differential costs"? Explain.

15-13. Is there a difference between the accountant's "differential cost" and the economist's "marginal cost"? Explain your position.

15-14. Why is the distinction between sunk costs and out-of-pocket costs important in decision making?

15-15. Why might those in management prefer to operate at a loss rather than close down a factory until business recovers?

15-16. If a company changes from a one- to a two-shift operation, would total unit costs be likely to increase or decrease? If one company made this change and obtained a reduction in total unit costs, what would you conclude? If another company found that a change to two shifts increased their total unit cost, what would you conclude?

15-17. Differential costs are ordinarily considered to be increment costs that are related to increased business. What role, if any, would differential costs play in studies dealing with decreased business?

15-18. The Metal Products Co. manufactures three different models of a single product. From the following data you are to prepare a schedule, supported by computations, showing the sales quantity and sales dollar figure for each model necessary to enable the company to cover its non-variable costs.

Model Number	Annual Sales Budget (Units)	Budgeted Unit Sales Price	Budgeted Sales Allowances for a Year
100	30,000	$15.00	$1,260
200	16,000	18.00	480
300	10,000	25.00	410

1973 ESTIMATES

Model Number	Quantity Budgeted For Production	Total	Variable Cost	Non-Variable Cost
100	30,500	$15.072	$ 9.871	$5.201
200	15,000	17.335	10.250	7.085
300	10,000	23.756	15.436	8.320

(Adapted from Uniform CPA Examination)

15-19. Whereon Company manufactures a single product called "Eron." The accountant for the company prepared the following statement at the end of the fiscal year:

WHEREON COMPANY
Income Statement
Year Ended December 31, 1972

Sales revenue		$800,000
Cost of sales:		
Variable	$500,000	
Non-Variable	50,000	550,000
Gross margin		$250,000
Selling and administrative expenses:		
Variable	$ 25,000	
Non-Variable	45,000	70,000
Net income		$180,000

Required

a. Determine the company's break-even point.

b. Prepare a break-even chart with non-variable costs parallel to the "X" axis.

c. During 1973, the company expects to operate at 90 percent of the level shown for 1972. Prepare an estimate of the net income that may be expected for 1973.

d. Prepare a break-even chart for 1973 with non-variable costs plotted parallel to the variable costs.

15-20. The following is a statement of a company for a month in which its two products provided equal amounts of sales revenue:

	Total	Product X	Product Y
Sales revenue	$100,000	$50,000	$50,000
Variable costs	60,000	35,000	25,000
Marginal income	$ 40,000	$15,000	$25,000
Non-Variable costs	30,000		
Net income	$ 10,000		

Required

a. Compute the P/V ratio for each product; and then compute the P/V ratio, break-even point, and net profit for the company under each of the following assumptions:
  1. sales revenue divided 70 percent to Product X and 30 percent to Product Y.
  2. sales revenue divided 30 percent to Product X and 70 percent to Product Y.

b. Prepare a profit-volume chart showing the profits estimated on sales up to $150,000 per month for each of the sales mixes provided in a.

[CH. 15] COST-VOLUME-PROFIT RELATIONSHIPS 481

15-21. Flear Company has a maximum productive capacity of 210,000 units per year. Normal capacity is regarded as 180,000 units per year. Standard variable manufacturing costs are $11 per unit. Fixed manufacturing overhead is $360,000 per year. Variable selling expenses are $3 per unit and fixed selling expenses are $252,000 per year. The unit sales price is $20.

The operating results for 1972 are: sales, 150,000 units; production, 160,000 units; beginning inventory, 10,000 units; and net unfavorable variance for standard variable manufacturing costs, $40,000. All variances are written off as additions to (or deductions from) standard costs of sales.

Required

Solve the following questions. (For items a, b and c assume no variances from standards for manufacturing costs.)

a. What is the break-even point expressed in dollar sales?
b. How many units must be sold to earn a net income of $60,000 per year?
c. How many units must be sold to earn a net income of 10 percent on sales?
d. Prepare formal income statements for 1972 under:
   1. conventional costing
   2. "direct" costing
e. Briefly account for the difference in net income between the two income statements.

(Adapted from Uniform CPA Examination)

15-22. A client has recently leased manufacturing facilities for production of a new product. Based on studies made by his staff, the following data have been made available to you:

Estimated annual sales	24,000 units	
Estimated costs:	Amount	Per Unit
Material	$ 96,000	$4.00
Direct labor	14,400	.60
Manufacturing overhead	24,000	1.00
Administrative expense	28,800	1.20
Total	$163,200	$6.80

Selling expenses are expected to be 15 percent of sales and profit is to amount to $1.02 per unit.

Required

a. Compute the selling price per unit.
b. Project a profit and loss statement for the year.
c. Compute a break-even point expressed in dollars and in units assuming that manufacturing overhead and administrative expenses are fixed but that other costs are fully variable.

(Adapted from Uniform CPA Examination)

15-23. Springfield Manufacturing Company produces number learning games for children. Pertinent budget data for the coming year are as follows:

Sales	100,000 units
Selling price	$1.00 per unit
Variable costs	$ .40 per unit
Non-variable costs	$54,000

In anticipation of the various questions which might be raised at the next meeting of the financial committee, the budget director has computed the profit or loss that should be realized under different conditions.

Required

What form of presentation should the budget director use to reveal his findings? What estimated profit would the budget director have associated with each of the following changes (consider each change separately):

a. 20 percent increase in physical sales volume
b. 20 percent decrease in physical sales volume
c. 5 cents increase in unit variable costs
d. 5 cents decrease in unit variable costs
e. 10 percent increase in non-variable costs
f. 10 percent decrease in non-variable costs
g. 10 percent decrease in unit selling price and a 20 percent increase in physical sales volume
h. 10 percent increase in unit selling price and a 20 percent decrease in physical sales volume
i. $10,000 variable cost decrease accomplished by a $16,000 non-variable cost increase

15-24. One of the products which Relifo Company manufactures is called "Foreil." It has $20,000 of non-variable cost per month. The normal capacity is 20,000 units per month. Sales are averaging 8,000 units per month at $1.25 per unit. Unit variable costs are $.50 each. Losses on the income statements are approximately $14,000 per month. The company believes it can sell 10,000 units per month in a foreign market at $.80 per unit. However, to do so will require the payment of shipping costs amounting to $.10 per unit.

Required

a. Should the company attempt to acquire the foreign business? If the foreign business would materialize as predicted, what change would it make in the monthly profit or loss?
b. The sales manager maintains that a price reduction of $.25 per unit will permit the current 8,000 units and an additional 10,000 units to be sold in the domestic market. He believes this action to be more profitable than the potential entrance into the foreign market. Is he correct? What profit change could the sales manager's proposition bring?

15-25. Flexite Company makes different products in two production departments. One of its products can be sold after department one processing in a semi-finished condition for $100.00 per unit; or it can be processed through the second department and sold for $125.00 per unit. Unused capacity is available in both departments. Unit costs for this product are as follows:

	Department 1	Department 2	Total
Direct material	$30.00	$10.00	$40.00
Direct labor	20.00	5.00	25.00
Variable cost	10.00	5.00	15.00
Non-variable cost	10.00	5.00	15.00
Total unit cost	$70.00	$25.00	$95.00

Required

a. Should the product be disposed of at the end of the first department or processed through both departments?

b. Assuming that 2,000 units are involved, compute the profit resulting from:
1. sale of the units after the first department
2. sale of the units after the second department

c. Would a shortage of capacity in the first department have any effect upon your answer?

15-26. Saturn Company manufacturers one product, sold exclusively in the domestic market. The firm is currently operating at 60 percent of normal volume with little hope for improvement in the near future. Accounting for costs conforms to the absorption costing principle. Unit cost of product is direct material, $8.00; direct labor, $4.00; manufacturing overhead, $8.00. Selling and administrative expenses amount to $5.00 per unit. The selling price is relatively stable at $40.00.

The president receives an offer from an exporter to buy enough units at $22.00 per unit to increase volume to 80 percent of normal. The exporter will sell the product under his brand. The president presents the facts to the controller with the comment that he cannot accept the order, since it will result in a loss of $3.00 per unit.

a. On the basis of the facts given, what should the controller recommend?

b. Would knowledge of the following additional facts alter the decision:
1. The manufacturing overhead unit cost is 70 percent fixed and 30 percent variable.
2. The selling and administrative unit cost is 80 percent fixed and 20 percent variable.

15-27. When you had completed your audit of The Sooner Company, management asked for your assistance in arriving at a decision whether to continue manufacturing a part or to buy it from an outside supplier. The part, which is named Faktron, is a component used in some of the finished products of the Company.

From your audit working papers and from further investigation you develop the following data as being typical of the Company's operations:

484   COST ACCOUNTING CONCEPTS   [CH. 15]

1. The annual requirement for Faktrons is 5,000 units. The lowest quotation from a supplier was $8.00 per unit.
2. Faktrons have been manufactured in the Precision Machinery Department. If Faktrons are purchased from an outside supplier, certain machinery will be sold and would realize its book value.
3. Following are the total costs of the Precision Machinery Department during the year under audit when 5,000 Faktrons were made:

Materials	$67,500
Direct labor	50,000
Indirect labor	20,000
Light and heat	5,500
Power	3,000
Depreciation	10,000
Property taxes and insurance	8,000
Payroll taxes and other benefits	9,800
Other	5,000

4. The following Precision Machinery Department costs apply to the manufacture of Faktrons: material, $17,500; direct labor, $28,000; indirect labor, $6,000; power, $300; other, $500. The sale of the equipment used for Faktrons would reduce the following costs by the amounts indicated: depreciation, $2,000; property taxes and insurance, $1,000.
5. The following additional Precision Machinery Department costs would be incurred if Faktrons were purchased from an outside supplier: freight, $.50 per unit; indirect labor for receiving, materials handling, inspection, etc., $5,000. The cost of the purchased Faktrons would be considered a Precision Machinery Department cost.

Required

(The following requirements are of approximately equal weight.)

a. Prepare a schedule showing a comparison of the total costs of the Precision Machinery Department
   1. when Faktrons are made
   2. when Faktrons are bought from an outside supplier
b. Discuss the considerations in addition to the cost factors that you would bring to the attention of management in assisting them to arrive at a decision whether to make or buy Faktrons. Include in your discussion the considerations that might be applied to the evaluation of the outside supplier.

(Adapted from Uniform CPA Examination)

15-28. The management of the Southern Cottonseed Company has engaged you to assist in the development of information to be used for managerial decisions.

The Company has the capacity to process 20,000 tons of cottonseed per year. The yield of a ton of cottonseed is as follows:

Product	Average Yield Per Ton of Cottonseed	Average Selling Price Per Trade Unit
Oil	300 lbs.	$ .15 per lb.
Meal	600 lbs.	50.00 per ton
Hulls	800 lbs.	20.00 per ton
Lint	100 lbs.	3.00 per cwt.
Waste	200 lbs.	

A special marketing study revealed that the Company can expect to sell its entire output for the coming year at the listed average selling prices.

You have determined the Company's costs to be as follows:

1. Processing costs
   Variable: $9 per ton of cottonseed put into process
   Fixed: $108,000 per year
2. Marketing costs
   All variable: $20 per ton sold
3. Administrative costs
   All fixed: $90,000 per year

From this information you prepared and submitted to management a detailed report on the Company's break-even point. In view of conditions in the cottonseed market, management told you that they would also like to know the average maximum amount that the Company can afford to pay for a ton of cottonseed.

Management has defined the average maximum amount that the Company can afford to pay for a ton of cottonseed as the amount that would result in the Company's having losses no greater when operating than when closed down under the existing cost and revenue structure. Management states that you are to assume that the fixed costs shown in your break-even point report will continue unchanged even when the operations are shut down.

Required

a. Compute the average maximum amount that the Company can afford to pay for a ton of cottonseed.

b. You also plan to mention to management the factors, other than the costs that entered into your computation, that they should consider in deciding whether to shut down the plant. Discuss these additional factors.

c. The stockholders consider the minimum satisfactory return on their investment in the business to be 25 percent before corporate income taxes. The stockholders' equity in the Company is $968,000. Compute the maximum average amount that the Company can pay for a ton of cottonseed to realize the minimum satisfactory return of the stockholders' investment in the business.

(Adapted from Uniform CPA Examination)

16

Cost Accounting Guides for Pricing Decisions

Although the recognition and use of proper selling prices have an important effect upon a manufacturer's success, pricing, in practice, is often treated in an inadequate and haphazard manner; in many otherwise well-managed firms, pricing does not become a problem of top management until a crisis arises. But pricing is a profit planning problem which faces management constantly. The variety, scope, and complexity of pricing problems demand exacting analysis and research into the alternatives available for their successful solution. Accounting can help management make proper pricing decisions by providing anticipated costs to make and sell products and the estimated profits which may be obtained from proposed selling prices.

The ideal solution to a pricing problem requires the selection of that price which offers the greatest promise of realizing the objective which management desires. Since no price can logically achieve different objectives with equal success, management should determine the objective desired before attempting to establish a price. This determination requires that, for each pricing problem, management must decide whether the objective is a matter of profit maximization, company growth, steady employment, national welfare, share of the market, compliance with government regulation, a combination of such factors, or some other consideration.

Management's primary objective is usually said to be profit maximization or cost minimization. Under many circumstances, this statement is correct but to assume that it is true for all situations is unjustified. Baumol says that not only may some other objective be the dominant consideration in a given instance, but, under certain conditions, multiple goals may displace profit maximization.[1]

Whenever an objective other than profit maximization is desired, cost analysis can help management determine whether the goal is worthwhile by showing the profit penalty to be paid for its attainment. This may be accomplished through calculating the estimated profits realizable at alternative prices; the difference between the estimated maximum profit and the estimated profit obtainable at a lower price represents the penalty projected by selecting that price. A comparison of the non-profit benefits with the estimated penalties associated with a specific price reduction may be used by management as a basis to accept or reject a given objective. Here is an excellent example of the way in which cost accounting can help management make decisions.

If the primary objective is one of profit maximization, cost analysis can help select that price which will yield the greatest profit. Under this condition, cost accounting aids management by furnishing estimated costs to make and sell a given volume of product and, also, the estimated profits which may be obtained at different prices. But, if a flexible volume of goods can be produced and sold, the estimated maximum profit is a questionable approximation, since techniques for forecasting the volume of goods that can be sold at different prices are inadequate. Regardless of the stability or flexibility of the volume to be produced and sold, the selection of the ideal price should not be based solely on the calculations of anticipated costs; it should evolve from the information contributed by the statistician, economist, market analyst, cost accountant, and other specialists. Nevertheless, cost computations are an essential aid to the judgment exercised in price determination.

Throughout the analysis which follows in this chapter, the discussion will be predicated upon the notion that the behavior of management is motivated by the desire to maximize profits. To achieve this goal, management must discover precisely which price-volume-cost relationship will be most profitable. The problem is complicated, because these three unknown factors are variables which can react to change in each other. How does cost accounting help management to discover the best combination of price, volume, and cost? It analyzes how product costs vary with volume changes anticipated for various tentative prices. It also indicates which price and related volume would be most advantageous to the company. But it does not completely answer the question of the unknown price, because it cannot ascertain market price; an adequate understanding of this unknown factor requires a thorough knowledge of competition and customer demand.[2] Since cost analysis is concerned with the sell-

---

[1] For a discussion concerning the frequency of company growth and market share as ultimate aims, subject to a minimum-profit constraint, see William J. Baumol, "Marginalism and the Demand for Cash in Light of Operations Research Experience," *The Review of Economics and Statistics*, Vol. XL (Cambridge, Mass.: Harvard University Press, 1958), p. 213. (Reprinted by permission of the publishers.)

[2] For conditions suggested as significant in the consideration of potential competition, see Joel Dean, "Pricing Policies," in Fiske and Beckett (eds.), *Industrial Accountants' Handbook* (Englewood Cliffs, N.J.: Prentice-Hall, Inc., 1954), p. 608. For an explanation of the aspects involved in demand analysis, see John A. Howard, *Marketing Management, Analysis and Planning* (Homewood, Ill.: Richard D. Irwin, Inc., 1963), pp. 31–133.

er's own costs and their use as an aid for determining proposed selling prices, the ascertainment of market price, as well as pricing strategy and practices, is beyond the scope of this discussion.

The Influence of Costs as a Pricing Tool

The influence of costs in pricing varies with the circumstances encountered. In a liquidation sale, costs are relatively unimportant; in a cost-plus contract, they become the primary determinant of price. Ordinarily, the influence of costs in pricing falls somewhere between these two extremes. But within these limits, costs assume distinct gradations of importance in pricing decisions, since they play different roles in the determination of proposed prices. For example, costs may play a significant role in pricing a new product, a differential product, or products produced to customer order. On the other hand, whenever a standardized product competes in an established market with other products serving the same purpose, price is established by the competitive market and is relatively unaffected by the costs of the individual supplier. Instead of a pricing tool, costs, in the latter case, serve primarily to indicate the profitability with which a product might participate in an established market at the current or predicted future price. Or, if the costs of a product prohibit it from being sold in the competitive market at a satisfactory profit, they are used to inform management that it should discontinue the product or discover ways by which it may be produced and marketed less expensively.

Nature of Costs Used in Pricing

Proposed selling prices apply to sales which will be made at some future date. This raises a question concerning the nature of the costs on which these prices are based. Accounting theorists maintain that when accountants compare acquisition with disposition prices, their principal concern is the periodic matching of costs and revenues. The purpose of this matching is accurate income determination. However, different procedures, based upon the time elapsed between cost incurrence and cost disposition, are recommended for different costs.[3] The elapsed time factor becomes even more crucial when costs are used for pricing, since the major issue then becomes the cost of replacing the products being priced. This issue must be solved by projecting, as accurately as possible, what the costs will be when the products are sold. Future costs thus become relevant costs for pricing.

The greater the period of time between pricing and anticipated sales dates, the greater the chance that important changes will develop between current and replacement costs. Since the likelihood of current and historical costs being applicable decreases as the time interval lengthens, their principal contribution to pricing resides in their ability to guide the forecasting of future costs. Both current and historical costs represent an excellent starting point for forecasting

---

[3] American Institute of Certified Public Accountants, *Changing Concepts of Business Income* (New York: The Macmillan Company, 1952), p. 28.

anticipated costs, since future products will be produced with the facilities now being used. Under these conditions, current or historical costs, adjusted for forecasted changes in current price levels, will ordinarily provide usable costs to aid pricing decisions in many instances. Additional adjustments, however, for changes in material requirements, labor needs, and manufacturing overhead composition, may be necessary.

COST PRICING METHODS

In addition to non-cost considerations which influence its pricing decisions, management needs cost calculations for aid in determining the profitability of proposed prices or testing the desirability of established market prices. Questions arise concerning which cost data are useful and how they should be employed. The answers to these questions are complicated, because more than one type of cost may be needed for management to consider different aspects of a given problem.[4] The concepts of cost deemed appropriate for most pricing situations fall into recognizable categories. But the methods used to ascertain applicable cost figures within a category may differ among companies even when their pricing problems are similar.

To illustrate typical procedures employed to provide proposed prices, five different approaches appear worthy of examination: first, full costing; second, conversion costing; third, return-on-investment costing; fourth, differential costing; and fifth, direct costing. Although each of these is frequently considered a distinctly different approach, they all represent, to a certain degree, full cost pricing. For comparison, many of the examples presented will be based on the facts assumed for Product A by a company confronted with the following simplified situation.

PRODUCT A

		Total		Per Unit
Practical capacity		12,000 Direct labor hours		
Budgeted capacity		10,000 Direct labor hours		
Units produced per direct labor hour		2		
Estimated costs:				
Direct material		$140,000		$ 7.00
Direct labor ($4.00 per labor hour)		40,000		2.00
Manufacturing overhead:				
Fixed	$100,000		$5.00	
Variable	20,000	120,000	1.00	6.00
Selling and administrative:				
Fixed	$ 80,000		$4.00	
Variable	20,000	100,000	1.00	5.00
		$400,000		$20.00

---

[4] Howard C. Greer, in the 1952 Dickinson Lectures, stated: "The cost of a product is not some single precisely calculable figure . . . cost-finding for pricing purposes is necessarily the assemblage of a variety of cost facts, which can be combined in a variety of ways to produce a variety of answers." Howard C. Greer, "Cost Factors in Price-Making," *The Harvard Business Review* (July–August, 1952), p. 38.

Full Cost Pricing

A proposed selling price based on full costs requires determination of the unit cost of making and selling a product, plus a mark-on for the desired amount of profit. Therefore, if the company desires a profit, before taxes, of 50 percent on full costs, the calculation of the proposed price would be as follows:

	Per Unit
Direct material	$ 7.00
Direct labor	2.00
Manufacturing overhead	6.00
Selling and administrative	5.00
Cost to make and sell	$20.00
Mark-on (50 percent of cost to make and sell)	10.00
Proposed selling price	$30.00

The full cost approach to pricing tends to follow a modification of nineteenth century classical economic theory, which demanded the long-run recovery of costs by firms wishing to perpetuate their existence. Most present-day economists maintain that the full cost approach is a misapplication of long-run analysis to short-run problems. Nevertheless, "some economists would assign to full cost a definite role in economic doctrine."[5] Moreover, according to various investigations, "a majority of businessmen set prices on the basis of cost plus a fair profit percentage."[6] This position can be explained partly by the fact that some concerns, purporting to use the full cost method, actually calculate proposed prices which are subjected to adjustment for demand consideration, competition, and market conditions. Additional explanation may be found in such publicly controlled pricing as that computed under public utility regulations. Another contributing factor is the cost-plus pricing so prevalent in military contracts. For companies not categorized by any of the preceding explanations, full cost pricing is ordinarily most widely employed by those manufacturing and marketing clearly differentiated products or custom-made goods.

Despite its apparently widespread popularity, there are serious limitations to the full cost method of pricing. It ignores the vital economic considerations of demand and competition. It is prone to distortion by accounting misapplications like an undue reliance upon historical cost, an unjustifiable inclusion of manufacturing overhead based upon predetermined rates, and an ignorance of the effect of volume on unit costs and profits. Moreover, through applying a flat percentage to the total cost of each product without providing any recogni-

---

[5] Richard B. Heflebower, "Full Costs, Cost Changes and Prices," *Business Concentration and Price Policy* (National Bureau of Economic Research, 1955), p. 362.

[6] Joel Dean, *Managerial Economics* (Englewood Cliffs, N. J.: Prentice-Hall, Inc., 1951), p. 445.

[CH. 16] COST ACCOUNTING GUIDES FOR PRICING DECISIONS 491

tion of the various elements which comprise total cost, it presents an additional limitation under certain circumstances. For example, products having purchased materials as the largest percentage of their total cost would be priced equally with other products having the same total cost derived almost entirely from factory labor and manufacturing overhead. In an attempt to overcome this particular limitation, some companies employ a method known as conversion cost pricing.

Conversion Cost Pricing

Under full cost pricing, two different products would have the same selling price if their total cost of making and selling were equal. This condition would exist despite a wide disparity in labor and overhead costs, as illustrated below:

	Product A	Product B
Direct material	$ 7.00	$ 3.00
Direct labor	2.00	3.00
Manufacturing overhead	6.00	9.00
Cost to make	$15.00	$15.00
Selling and administrative	5.00	5.00
Cost to make and sell	$20.00	$20.00
Mark-on (50 percent of cost to make and sell)	10.00	10.00
Proposed selling price	$30.00	$30.00

Although the two products illustrated have the same proposed selling price and the same proposed profit per unit, Product B requires 50 percent more labor and manufacturing overhead than Product A. If the same facilities will produce either product, three units of Product A or two units of Product B can be produced at any given level of operating activity. If, as originally proposed, Product A can be sold at the same price as Product B, Product A has one and a half times the potential profit of Product B when facilities are devoted entirely to the production of Product A. Consequently, it would be highly advantageous for the company to promote the sale of A and discourage the sale of B. Because Product B requires 150 percent of the factory labor and manufacturing overhead needed to produce Product A, under conversion costing its production could be justified only by a commensurable adjustment in the mark-on used to calculate its proposed selling price. This could be accomplished through applying the profit margin to the conversion costs exclusively. As a result, profit would be based solely on the cost incurred by manufacturing, and purchased materials would earn no profit. On the basis of the data previously employed and assuming a desired mark-on of 100 percent of conversion cost, proposed selling prices would be computed as illustrated on following page.

	Product A	Product B
Direct labor	$ 2.00	$ 3.00
Manufacturing overhead	6.00	9.00
Conversion cost	$ 8.00	$12.00
Mark-on (100% of conversion cost)	8.00	12.00
Total	$16.00	$24.00
Direct material	7.00	3.00
Selling and administrative	5.00	5.00
Proposed selling price	$28.00	$32.00

As shown above, at a given level of operating activity, Product B must sell for $32.00 per unit to earn the same total profit that Product A will yield at $28.00 per unit. Or, if both products can be sold at the same price, the exclusive production and sale of Product A will maximize total profits. Whenever a shortage of labor or productive facilities exists, conversion costing can assist management in deciding what products to produce and how to determine those prices which will yield the highest potential profit. But whenever more normal conditions exist, it does not seem logical that a company should be satisfied with a pricing method which involves trading dollars on direct material costs. Nevertheless, this method can be readily adapted to normal situations by using a reduced profit margin on purchased materials. For example, if, in the illustration, a mark-on of 50 percent on purchased materials had been desired, the proposed prices for Products A and B would have been increased to $31.50 and $33.50.

Return on Investment Pricing

Neither of the two previously explained methods recognizes capital investment in determining proposed selling prices. Yet the return on capital required to produce, finance, and distribute products is widely recognized as a crucial index of managerial efficiency. Consequently, management can aid its performance by knowing what selling price will produce a given rate of return on capital. The failure of selling prices to reflect the effect of capital utilization could create an illogical price structure and mislead management to the extent that proper dividends and growth might not be maintained. This may be illustrated by considering the following data.

	Product A	Product B
Net Sales	$600,000	$500,000
Total Costs	400,000	420,000
Net Profit	$200,000	$ 80,000
Margin of Profit on Sales	33.3%	16%

From this analysis, it appears that A is the more profitable product. If our hypothetical company were determining proposed prices by the full cost method, it would presumably increase its effort toward promoting the sale of the product which appears most profitable. But if our hypothetical company determined prices through the return on investment method, it would need additional information concerning the average annual capital investment required for each product. Let us assume this additional information as it appears below.

	Product A	Product B
Cash	$ 40,000	$ 15,000
Receivables	60,000	25,000
Inventories	100,000	60,000
Fixed Capital	1,000,000	300,000
Total Capital	$1,200,000	$400,000
Net Profit (per above)	$ 200,000	$ 80,000
Return on Investment	16.7%	20.0%

Now our company would either emphasize the sale of Product B or increase the proposed selling price of Product A so that both products would yield a 20 percent return on investment. In either event, the action would differ from that which appeared to be advantageous when the return on investment consideration was ignored.

Proposed selling prices determined by procedures which provide for return on capital considerations are ordinarily derived by a percentage mark-on applied to product costs. A basic formula for this calculation follows.[7]

$$\frac{\text{Percentage mark-on}}{\text{on cost}} = \frac{\text{Capital}}{\text{Total annual cost}} \times \frac{\text{Desired rate of}}{\text{return on capital}}$$

When a 20 percent desired rate of return on $1,200,000 of capital and the $400,000 of total costs previously associated with Product A are substituted in the formula, it would appear as:

$$60\% = \frac{\$1,200,000}{\$400,000} \times 20\%$$

The application of the 60 percent mark-on to $400,000 of costs would provide total sales of $640,000 and a profit of $240,000, which would equal the 20 percent desired rate of return on $1,200,000 of capital. However, the basic formula presupposes the existence of a somewhat unrealistic relationship between total capital and total costs. A movement in total costs is likely to change total capital, but this movement would correlate much more closely with that portion of capital which is variable. Formulas have been designed which recognize that a variable volume of activity should correlate with variable capital instead of total capital; an example of such a formula appears on page 494.

---

[7] National Association of Accountants, Research Report No. 35, *Return on Capital as a Guide to Managerial Decisions* (New York, 1959), p. 43.

$$\text{Price} = \frac{\text{Cost} + (\%\ \text{return} \times \text{fixed capital})}{\text{Volume}} \Big/ \left[1 - (\%\ \text{return} \times \%\ \text{current assets to sales})\right]$$

Using the figures for Product B on pages 492 and 493 and an assumed volume of production and sales of 10,000 units, this formula may be applied as below:

$$\text{Price} = \frac{\dfrac{\$420{,}000 + (.2 \times \$300{,}000)}{10{,}000}}{1 - (.2 \times .2)}$$

$$\text{Price} = \frac{\dfrac{\$480{,}000}{10{,}000}}{.96}$$

$$\text{Price} = \$50.00$$

This computation indicates a unit selling price of $50.00. That a unit price of $50.00 will provide a return on capital of 20 percent is evident from the product profitability and annual investment figures previously provided for Product B.

Since the formula relates variable capital to variable activity as measured by sales, a slight distortion could arise, because a change in selling price would have little or no relationship to the investment in inventory and to the other assets which are stated at cost. This difficulty can be overcome by establishing separate ratios for sales-related assets to sales and for cost-related assets to cost of sales, by multiplying both ratios by the rate of return desired, adding the ratio of non-manufacturing expenses to sales on to the adjusted ratio of sales related assets to sales, and by dividing one plus the cost ratio by one minus the sales ratio. The result will be the mark-on to cost required to obtain the desired selling price.[8]

Other questions arise from the use of return on investment to determine selling prices. Chief among these would be: first, what capital assets should be included; second, how such assets should be valued; and third, how the assets should be allocated to products. For a discussion of these and related questions, refer to Chapter 5.

In spite of the problems surrounding the use of rate of return on capital, this method is an excellent analytical tool for appraising alternative selling prices. Not only does it guide management in determining what selling price will provide a given rate of return, but it may be used to show what rate of return a given price will bring.

Differential Cost Pricing

Full cost pricing establishes one proposed price for all units produced at any given level of activity. It is designed to recover total costs (whether fixed or

---

[8] For an illustration of such an application, see Peter M. Chiuminatto, "Satisfying Your Company's Need for Capital and Employing It Effectively," *N.A.A. Bulletin* (September, 1957), pp. 75–88.

variable) in a proposed product price. When fixed costs are recoverable at the price proposed for an initial level of production, full cost pricing ignores the fact that the only costs attributable to the production of additional units are the variable costs of those units plus whatever new fixed costs may be incurred. As a result, the proposed price calculated for additional units may be unnecessarily inflated and may thereby cause potential business to be lost. Thus, strict adherence to full cost pricing may not always be consistent with the objective of profit maximization.

The recognition of differential (i.e., marginal or incremental) costs makes it possible to overcome certain limitations of full cost pricing. Although the terms "differential costs" and "marginal costs" are, to some degree, used interchangeably, they do not mean precisely the same thing. To the economist, the marginal cost is that resulting from the production of one additional unit. To the accountant, the differential cost is that resulting from the production of an additional block of units. The accountant uses differential costs, because the marginal cost of an additional unit is not ordinarily readily available in the accounting records and because the expense involved in accumulating such information is frequently prohibitive. Both marginal costs and differential costs can be specifically associated with a particular decision to produce; they are costs which will not occur unless additional production is undertaken. Since differential costs are equal to the variable costs per unit times the number of units of additional production plus any new fixed costs which may be incurred, differential cost analysis requires a careful delineation between variable and fixed costs.

The basic data presented on page 489 are used to illustrate differential cost analysis as shown on the following page. In this illustration, fixed costs were assumed to be unchanged within the range of 90 to 120 percent of budgeted activity. Consequently, only the variable costs accounted for the difference in total costs between any two levels of activity. The average unit differential cost, in each instance, was computed by dividing the increase in variable costs by the number of additional units produced. It is apparent that, although the average unit cost ranges from $21.00 to $18.50, the average unit differential cost is $11.00 wherever additional units are produced. It follows that if 18,000 units can be profitably disposed of at a unit price which exceeds $21.00, the sale of additional units at any unit price in excess of $11.00 will increase profits if overall marketing conditions are not disturbed. The problem then becomes one of holding the original market intact and discovering a second outlet for the additional production. The solution may be found through differentiating products, institutional selling, or "dumping" into some existing market which demands greatly reduced prices. Perhaps the solution may be found by using differential cost analysis to guide the decision on the desirability of "bidding" for additional business.

The basic differential cost analysis provides useful information for pricing and profit planning when the entire productive output is disposed of in a single market. To support this point, one need only observe that the average unit cost change, in the illustration provided, indicates the amount by which unit price may be reduced to obtain increased sales volume and still permit the earning of

Differential Cost Analysis

Percentage of Budgeted Capacity	90	10	100	10	110	10	120
Level of Activity in units	18,000	2,000	20,000	2,000	22,000	2,000	24,000
Fully Variable Costs	$198,000	$22,000	$220,000	$22,000	$242,000	$22,000	$264,000
Non-Variable Costs	180,000		180,000		180,000		180,000
Total Costs	$378,000	$22,000	$400,000	$22,000	$422,000	$22,000	$444,000
Average Unit Differential Cost		$11.00		$11.00		$11.00	
Average Unit Cost	$21.00		$20.00		$19.18		$18.50
Average Unit Cost Change		$1.00		$0.82		$0.68	

the same profit margin on each unit sold. Under such conditions, profits will increase by an amount equal to the unit profit margin multiplied by the additional units to be sold. For example, if 18,000 units can be sold at $32.00 apiece, and if the indicated $1.00 price reduction will permit 20,000 units to be sold at $31.00 each, total profits will increase $22,000 (constant unit profit margin of $11.00 × 2,000 additional units).

Differential cost analysis provides another advantage which is closely related to economic marginal analysis. The economist maintains that, to maximize its income, a firm should produce at the point where marginal cost equals marginal revenue. As explained on page 495, the accountant uses "differential" as the economist uses "marginal"; therefore, the accountant reasons that a firm should produce at the point where differential cost equals differential revenue. Or, because the accountant ordinarily theorizes in blocks or groups of units instead of a single unit, he reasons that a firm should produce those blocks of units which will realize differential revenues in excess of differential costs. In illustrating this point, the basic data used will be taken from the previous differential cost analysis, with the additional assumptions that selling price is $30.00 a unit at 100 percent of budgeted capacity and that price varies $2.00 per unit with each 10 percent change in capacity.

Percentage of Capacity	No. of Units	Average Unit Price	Average Unit Cost	Total Revenue	Total Cost	Differential Revenue	Differential Cost	Net Income
20	4,000	$46.00	$56.00	$184,000	$224,000			($ 40,000)
30	6,000	44.00	41.00	264,000	246,000	$80,000	$22,000	18,000
40	8,000	42.00	33.50	336,000	268,000	72,000	22,000	68,000
50	10,000	40.00	29.00	400,000	290,000	64,000	22,000	110,000
60	12,000	38.00	26.00	456,000	312,000	56,000	22,000	144,000
70	14,000	36.00	23.85	504,000	334,000	48,000	22,000	170,000
80	16,000	34.00	22.25	544,000	356,000	40,000	22,000	188,000
90	18,000	32.00	21.00	576,000	378,000	32,000	22,000	198,000
100	20,000	30.00	20.00	600,000	400,000	24,000	22,000	200,000
110	22,000	28.00	19.18	616,000	422,000	16,000	22,000	194,000
120	24,000	26.00	18.50	624,000	444,000	8,000	22,000	180,000

This illustration shows that net income will be maximized at 100 percent of budgeted capacity, because, at this point, the differential revenue still exceeds the differential cost. Beyond this point, net income will be reduced by the excess of differential cost over differential revenue for each incremental block of units. This is true, even though the excess of the average unit price over the average unit cost at 110 or 120 percent of capacity appears to indicate that either of these levels of operation might be more profitable.

This analysis departs from economic marginal theory. It shows a constantly decreasing average unit cost, because perfect variability is assumed for variable costs and fixed costs are held constant in total amount throughout the entire range of operating capacity.[9] While this condition is somewhat unrealistic, its use does not invalidate the point being illustrated.

Although important benefits may be obtained from using differential costs to guide pricing, indiscriminate reliance upon this method can be extremely dangerous. For example, it may cause pricing decisions which tend to disregard the necessity of recovering total costs in the long run. Or special order business accepted below normal prices on a temporary basis may tend to cause a shift of sales from regular production into differentially costed products. Moreover, special price reductions may have unfavorable repercussions on regular customers or impel competitors to take similar action. Above all, there must be no violation of the Robinson-Patman Act of 1936, an act of Congress which provides

> That it shall be unlawful for any person engaged in commerce, in the course of such commerce, either directly or indirectly, to discriminate in price between different purchasers of commodities of like grade and quality

unless the price variations

> make only due allowance for differences in the cost of manufacture, sale or delivery resulting from the differing methods or quantities in which commodities are to such purchasers sold or delivered. Provided, however, that the Federal Trade Commission may . . . fix and establish quantity limits . . . where it finds that available purchasers of greater quantities are so few as to render differentials on account thereof . . . promotive of monopoly in any line of commerce.

In interpreting this exception provision, the Federal Trade Commission and the Courts have uniformly rejected defenses which have been based on "due allowances" derived by differential production cost calculations. When price discrimination complaints are made under this act, the burden of rebutting the *prima-facie* case falls upon the seller; the act provides, however, "That nothing herein contained shall prevent a seller rebutting the *prima-facie* case thus made by showing his lower price . . . was made in good faith to meet an equally low price of a competitor . . ." In summary, differential cost accounting can help management make pricing decisions, but it does not replace judgment.

Pricing Based on Direct Costing

There is considerable similarity in how differential costs and direct costing are used to calculate product cost. In fact, under both methods, the unit product cost of producing additional units would be identical if incremental units could

---

[9] For a discussion concerning short range cost-volume differentials, see National Association of Cost Accountants, Research Series No. 24, *Product Costs for Pricing Purposes* (New York, 1953), Chapter 6.

be produced without increasing non-variable costs. This is true, because, under such conditions, both methods would calculate a unit product cost equal to the unit increase in variable costs. The two methods differ, however, when additional production increases non-variable manufacturing costs; such increases become a part of unit differential cost but are not included in the unit cost calculated by direct costing. Another difference arises from how each method treats varying levels of activity: differential costs are concerned with the costs associated with units produced beyond a given volume of activity, while direct costing applies equally to all units produced regardless of whether such units belong to initial or incremental production activity.

It is this last point which causes what is, perhaps, the greatest distinction between the two methods. Differential production costs are, essentially, costs calculated by absorption costing procedures wherein both variable and non-variable manufacturing costs are assigned to products for matching with revenues in the period when the products are sold. But the total differential costs method, which includes both manufacturing and non-manufacturing cost increases, departs from the absorption costing method, which discriminates between costs incurred for a manufacturing or for a non-manufacturing function. Consequently, all cost increases, whether they be variable, non-variable, manufacturing, or non-manufacturing, are included in the total differential cost for matching with revenues in the period when these revenues are recognized.

On the other hand, direct costing makes a distinction between variable and non-variable cost in determining when costs are to be matched with revenue. Under direct costing at any level of operating activity, costs of manufacturing and selling products are matched with revenues recognized when those products are sold, while period or time costs are charged against revenue in the period when these costs are incurred. The difference between the variable cost and revenue related to any given quantity of products is called *marginal income* or *contribution margin,* terms which measure the contribution those products make toward meeting period costs and desired profit. Thus, the unit contribution margin is the total profit change that results from a unit change in volume. Below break-even volume, the unit marginal income represents a contribution toward period costs; above break-even volume, it represents an increase in total profit.

Using a budgeted sales price of $30.00 per unit and the budgeted costs previously shown on page 489, a cost analysis prepared by the direct costing approach appears on the following page.

The usefulness of direct costing in decisions concerning possible price changes may be illustrated by assuming that our hypothetical company is actually operating as budgeted (i.e., 20,000 units at $30.00).[10] The sales department desires to know how certain price revisions would change the number of units which must be sold for the budgeted profit to be earned. Under direct costing, the answers would be provided as noted on page 500:

---

[10] For a list of pricing problems to which direct costing has been applied, see National Association of Accountants Research Report No. 37, *Current Application of Direct Costing* (New York, 1961), p. 45.

	Total	Per Unit
Net revenue (20,000 units)	$600,000	$30.00
Variable costs:		
Direct material	$140,000	$ 7.00
Direct labor	40,000	2.00
Direct manufacturing overhead	20,000	1.00
Direct selling	20,000	1.00
Total direct costs	$220,000	$11.00
Marginal income	$380,000	$19.00
Non-variable costs:		
Manufacturing overhead	$100,000	$ 5.00
Selling and administrative	80,000	4.00
Total period costs	$180,000	$ 9.00
Net Profit	$200,000	$10.00

The last line shows the number of units which must be sold at each price level for the $200,000 budgeted profit to be realized. It should be apparent from this analysis that as long as activity remains within the volume range for which total period cost remains unchanged, total profits will exceed budgeted profits by an amount equal to the number of units sold in excess of the units ascertained for each price level multiplied by the appropriate unit marginal income. For example, if a 10 percent price reduction were to enable 24,000 units, instead of 23,750 units, to be sold, total profit would exceed budgeted profit by $4,000.00 (250 units × $16.00 unit marginal income). Or, if a 10 percent price increase reduced the number of units sold from 20,000 to 17,500 instead of to 17,273, total profits would exceed budgeted profit by $4,994 (227 units × $22.00 unit marginal income). Conversely, unit sales below those indicated

Basic Data	Price Decrease 10%	Price Decrease 5%	Current Price	Price Increase 5%	Price Increase 10%
Unit Price	$27.00	$28.50	$30.00	$31.50	$33.00
Variable Costs	11.00	11.00	11.00	11.00	11.00
Marginal Income	$16.00	$17.50	$19.00	$20.50	$22.00
Period Costs	$180,000	$180,000	$180,000	$180,000	$180,000
Budgeted Profit	200,000	200,000	200,000	200,000	200,000
Total Period Costs and Budgeted Profit	$380,000	$380,000	$380,000	$380,000	$380,000
Sales Units (Total Period Costs and Budgeted Profit ÷ Unit Marginal Income)	23,750	21,714	20,000	18,537	17,273

for each price level would reduce total profit by the appropriate unit marginal income times the number of units not sold.

Direct costing does not imply any specific pricing policy. Nevertheless, a company rarely continues selling a product at a price below variable cost unless this action aids the sales of other products which are profitable. Therefore, variable costs establish a lower limit for proposed selling prices. They also guide decisions for dropping or adding a product. For example, if a given product shares the same period costs with other products, the sale of the given product at any price above its variable cost provides a positive contribution to period cost and produces more overall total profit for the company than would have been the case had the given product been abandoned because it could not absorb its full share of non-variable costs.

In each of the preceding instances, proposed selling prices were related to the recovery of variable costs. In contrast, the recovery of both period and variable costs in proposed selling prices presents a more involved situation because of two complicating factors—first, the determination of that portion of period cost which should be identified with individual products, and second, the determination of the number of units that can be sold in a given period. Assuming that these two unknowns were resolved satisfactorily in the budgeted figures provided on page 489, the procedure of using costs to aid in determining a proposed price by direct costing would be:

$$\frac{\$180,000 \text{ (Period Costs)}}{20,000 \text{ (Units to be sold per period)}} = \$9.00 \text{ Marginal income required per unit}$$

Variable cost	$11.00
Marginal income	9.00
Break-even selling price	$20.00

The $20.00 selling price calculated above would recover both direct and period costs but would not provide any profit. If a rate of return of 20 percent was desired on the $1,200,000.00 investment required to make and sell our hypothetical product, the calculation would become:

$$\frac{\$180,000 \text{ (Period Costs)} + \$240,000 \text{ (Profit)}}{20,000 \text{ (Number of units)}} = \$21 \text{ Marginal income required per unit}$$

Variable cost	$11.00
Marginal income	21.00
Proposed selling price	$32.00

If the number of units to be sold cannot be forecasted, similar calculations should be made at several alternative volumes to enable management to test proposed prices and to select that volume over which it intends to unitize period cost. If the period costs comprise both traceable and joint costs, the latter can be assigned only by allocation. A lower reliability should be placed on that part of the product cost which has been allocated, for the basis of the allocation is necessarily subjective. Since the percentage of joint period costs which can be reliably related to a product line is usually greater than the percentage which can be related to individual products within a line, the assignment of period costs may be limited to a product line. The marginal income ratio for the line is then used to propose prices for individual products by dividing the direct cost of a product by the complement of the marginal income ratio for the entire line.

SUMMARY

Pricing products is an extremely complicated procedure. Before attempting to establish price, it is vital that management determine whether its primary objective is profit maximization. If it is, maximum profits are achieved through ascertaining the best combination of price, volume, mix, and cost. Although cost is frequently considered the starting point in pricing, selling prices rarely have a rigid relationship to cost. Competition, elasticity of customer demand, and nature of the product also enter into pricing decisions.

When selling prices are established in the market, the alternatives of an individual company are to sell or not to sell at the prevailing prices. Under such conditions, knowledge of product costs is used by a company to measure the profitability of the established prices and as a guide to the product decision, not as a guide for determining proposed prices. On the other hand, when the market position of a company permits independent pricing, product costs are used to measure the profitability of proposed prices and as a guide to setting selling prices. In the majority of instances, using product costs as a guide for determining proposed selling prices lies somewhere between these extremes.

Effective use of cost data for pricing requires the recognition that more than one type of cost may be needed for different aspects of a given situation. Uppermost in the consideration is the knowledge that future costs become relevant costs for pricing. Within this framework of understanding, various procedures may be employed to determine proposed prices. Although five of these procedures have been examined as somewhat different approaches, they all represent, to a certain extent, full cost pricing. In the final analysis, effective pricing requires the selection of the most appropriate cost information which accounting can provide for the circumstances. Although costs alone rarely supply the answer for any pricing problem, they do aid management in making a pricing decision.

QUESTIONS AND PROBLEMS

16-1. List five costing approaches which might be used to calculate proposed selling prices.

16-2. How are costs used in a pricing decision when the price of the product involved is determined by a competitive market?

16-3. What are the major influences on a pricing decision?

16-4. "Variable cost provides a pricing floor." Do you agree? Why?

16-5. Under what conditions would the accounting measurement of variable cost closely approximate the economist's measurement of marginal cost?

16-6. Describe the circumstances under which it would be profitable to sell a product at a price below the average unit cost amount.

16-7. Many companies use a fixed mark-on percentage to convert full costs into selling price quotations. How do they determine the fixed mark-on percentage?

16-8. What rationale would you use to defend proposed selling prices which had been established by each of the following cost-pricing methods?

    a. Full costing

    b. Conversion costing

    c. Direct costing

    d. Differential costing

    e. Rate of return costing

16-9. Mabphad Company produces two products in a plant where production is limited to 5,000 direct labor hours per month. Although the production facilities may be used to produce either product, 2,500 direct labor hours of each product are produced each month. The company has never been able to produce enough units of either product to satisfy the demand. The selling price of each product is determined by adding a 100 percent mark-on to the unit cost of production. The sales manager argues that only product "A" should be produced because it has lower unit material costs. The production manager maintains that product "A" should be eliminated and that all facilities should be used to produce product "B." Production data for the two products are shown below.

Data	Product "A"	Product "B"
Units produced per hour	2	4
Unit direct material cost	$5.50	$7.75
Direct labor cost per hour	$3.00	$3.00
Variable non-labor cost per hour	$4.00	$4.00
Non-variable cost per hour	$2.00	$2.00

Required

    a. What is the unit and total net income for each product under current conditions?

    b. Using existing selling prices for 5,000 direct labor hours of production, would it be more profitable to adopt the plan of the sales manager or of the production manager?

    c. If selling prices are determined by a 400 percent mark-on to conversion costs, compute

1. the unit selling price and net profit for each product
2. the total potential profit of each plan

d. Comment on the relationship between the potential profits of both plans.

16-10. The president of Bonncris Corporation, which manufactures tape decks and sells them to producers of sound reproduction systems, anticipates a 10 percent wage increase on January 1 of next year to the manufacturing employees (variable labor). He expects no other changes in costs. Manufacturing overhead will not change as a result of the wage increase. The president has asked you to assist him in developing the information he needs to formulate a reasonable product strategy for next year.

You are satisfied by regression analysis that volume is the primary factor affecting costs and have separated the semi-variable costs into their fixed and variable segments by means of the least-squares criterion. You also observe that the beginning and ending inventories are never materially different.

Below are the current year data assembled for your analysis.

Current selling price per unit	$80.00
Variable cost per unit:	
Material	$30.00
Labor	12.00
Manufacturing overhead	6.00
Total	$48.00
Annual volume of sales	5,000 units
Fixed costs	$51,000

Required

Provide the following information for the president:

a. What increase in the selling price is necessary to cover the 10 percent wage increase and still maintain the current profit-volume-cost ratio?

b. How many tape decks must be sold to maintain the current net income if the sales price remains at $80.00 and the 10 percent wage increase goes into effect?

c. The president believes that an additional $190,000 of machinery (to be depreciated at 10 percent annually) will increase present capacity (5,300 units) by 30 percent. If all tape decks produced can be sold at the present price and the wage increase goes into effect, how would the estimated income before capacity is increased compare with the estimated income after capacity is increased?

(Adapted from Uniform CPA Examination)

16-11. In June, 1972, the Hot & Cold Co. sold 50 air conditioning units for $200 each. Costs included material costs of $50 a unit and direct labor costs of $30 a unit. Manufacturing overhead was computed at 100 percent of direct labor cost. Interest expense on a 6 percent bank loan was equivalent to $1.00 a unit. Income tax was equivalent to $15 a unit.

Effective July 1, 1972, material costs decreased 5 percent and direct labor costs increased 20 percent. Also, effective July 1, 1972, the interest increase on the bank loan was equivalent to $.25 per unit.

a. Assuming no change in the rate of manufacturing overhead in relation to direct labor costs, compute the sales price per unit that will produce the same ratio of gross profit.

b. Assuming that $10 of the manufacturing overhead consists of fixed costs, compute the sales price per unit that will produce the same ratio of gross profit.

(Adapted from Uniform CPA Examination)

16-12. The D. P. Manufacturing Company produces one principal product. The income from sales of this product for the year 1972 is expected to be $200,000. Cost of goods sold will be as follows:

Materials used	$40,000
Direct labor	60,000
Fixed manufacturing overhead	20,000
Variable manufacturing overhead	30,000

The company realizes that it is facing rising costs and in December is attempting to plan its operations for the year 1973. It is believed that if the product is not redesigned the following results will be obtained:

Material prices will average 5 percent higher and rates for direct labor will average 10 percent higher. Variable manufacturing overhead will vary in proportion to direct labor costs. If sale price is increased to produce the same rate of gross profit as the 1972 rate, there will be a 10 percent decrease in the number of units sold in 1973.

If the product is redesigned according to suggestions offered by the sales manager, it is expected that a 10 percent increase can be obtained in the number of units sold with a 15 percent increase in sale price per unit. However, change in the product would involve several changes in cost.

A different grade of material would be used but 10 percent more of it would be required for each unit. The price of this proposed grade of material has averaged 5 percent below the price of the material now being used and that 5 percent difference in price is expected to continue for the year 1973. Redesign would permit a change in processing method enabling the company to use less-skilled workmen. It is believed that the average pay rate for 1973 would be 10 percent below the average for 1972 due to that change. However, about 20 percent more labor per unit would be required than was needed in 1972. Variable manufacturing overhead is incurred directly in relation to production. It is expected to increase 10 percent because of price changes and to increase an additional amount in proportion to the change in labor hours.

Assuming the accuracy of these estimates, you are to prepare statements showing the prospective gross profit if:

a. the same product is continued for 1973

b. the product is redesigned for 1973

(Adapted from Uniform CPA Examination)

16-13. Bedrock Company has prepared the following income statement for its estimated operations during the coming period:

Sales (15,000 units)			$300,000
Cost of sales:			
Materials		$90,000	
Labor		60,000	
Manufacturing overhead:			
Non-variable	$40,000		
Variable	30,000	70,000	220,000
Gross margin on sales			$ 80,000
Non-manufacturing expenses			30,000
Net income			$ 50,000

Cutrate Company has offered to purchase 5,000 units at a unit price of $15.00. This offer would not affect the present sales. Present plant capacity is 22,000 units. If the offer is accepted, non-variable manufacturing overhead is estimated to increase by $3,000.

Underbid Company has asked Bedrock Company to quote a unit price on 7,000 units. Since Underbid Company plans to dispose of the 7,000 units through a foreign subsidiary, Bedrock's domestic market would not be affected by this sale.

Required

a. Assuming no change in the non-manufacturing costs, compute the gain that would be realized by accepting the offer of Cutrate Company.

b. If Bedrock Company could increase production to the limit of capacity without increasing non-variable manufacturing costs beyond those required for the production of 20,000 units, what unit price could it quote to Underbid Company that would increase, by 10 percent, the potential profit to be gained from accepting the offer of Cutrate Company?

16-14. The Carson Company manufactures a line of dolls and a doll dress sewing kit. The president has requested your assistance in determining an economical sales and production mix for the coming year. The company's marketing division provides the following data:

Name of Product	Estimated Demand for Next Year (Units)	Estimated Net Price (Units)
Dawn	50,000	$5.20
Susan	42,000	2.40
Valerie	35,000	8.50
Barbara	40,000	4.00
Sewing Kit	325,000	3.00

To promote sales of the sewing kit there is a 15 percent reduction in the established net price for a kit purchased at the same time that a Carson Company doll is purchased.

[CH. 16] COST ACCOUNTING GUIDES FOR PRICING DECISIONS 507

From the cost accounting records you develop the following data:
1. The production standards per unit are:

Name of Product	Direct Material	Direct Labor
Dawn	$1.40	$ .80
Susan	.70	.50
Valerie	2.69	1.40
Barbara	1.00	1.00
Sewing Kit	.60	.40

2. The labor rate of $2.00 per hour is expected to continue without change in the next year. The plant has an effective capacity of 130,000 direct labor hours per year on a single shift basis. Present equipment can produce all of the products.

3. Next year's total non-variable costs will be $100,000. Variable costs will be equivalent to 50 percent of direct labor cost.

4. The company's small inventory of its products should be ignored.

Required

a. Prepare a schedule showing the marginal contribution of a unit of each product.

b. Prepare a schedule showing the marginal contribution of a unit of each product per direct labor dollar expended on the product.

c. Prepare a schedule showing the total direct labor hours required to produce the estimated sales units for next year. Indicate the product and number of units that you would recommend be increased (or decreased) in production to attain the company's effective productive capacity.

d. Without regard to your answer in c, assume that the estimated sales units for next year would require 12,000 direct labor hours in excess of the company's effective productive capacity. Discuss the possible methods of providing the missing capacity.

(Adapted from Uniform CPA Examination)

16-15. The Bonito Manufacturing Company makes and sells a single product, TOSVEX, through normal marketing channels. You have been asked by its president to assist in determining the proper bid to submit for a special manufacturing job for the Catez Sales Company. Below is the information you have collected.

1. The special job is for ACFOM, a product unlike TOSVEX, even though the manufacturing processes are similar.

2. Additional sales of ACFOM to the Catez Sales Company are not expected.

3. The bid is for 20,000 pounds of ACFOM. Each 1,000 pounds of ACFOM requires 500 pounds of material A, 250 pounds of material B, and 250 pounds of material C.

4. Bonito's materials inventory data follow:

Material	Pounds in inventory	Acquisition cost per lb	Current replacement cost per lb
A	24,000	$.40	$.48
B	4,000	.25	.27
C	17,500	.90	.97
X	7,000	.80	.85

Material X may be substituted for material A in ACFOM. Material X, made especially for Bonito under a patent owned by Bonito, is left over from the manufacture of a discontinued product, is not usable in TOSVEX, and has a current salvage value of $180.

5. Each 1,000 pounds of ACFOM requires 180 direct labor hours at $3.00 per hour (overtime is charged at time and a half). However, Bonito is working near its two-shift capacity and has only 1,600 hours of regular time available. The production manager indicates that he can keep the special job on regular time by shifting the production of TOSVEX to overtime if necessary.

6. Bonito's cost clerk informs you that the hourly burden rate at normal production is as follows:

Fixed element	$ .20 per direct labor hour
Variable element	.80 per direct labor hour
Total hourly burden rate	$1.00 per direct labor hour

7. The bid invitation states that a performance bond must be submitted with the bid. A local agent will bond Bonito's performance for 1 percent of the total bid.

Required

a. Prepare a schedule to compute the minimum bid (i.e., the bid that would neither increase nor decrease total profits) that Bonito Manufacturing Company may submit.

b. Bonito's president also wants to know what his new competitor, Harper Manufacturing Company, probably will bid. You assume that Harper's materials inventory has been acquired very recently and that Harper's cost behavior is similar to Bonito's. You know that Harper has ample productive capacity to handle the special job on regular time. Prepare a schedule to compute the minimum bid (i.e., the bid that would neither increase nor decrease total profits) that Harper Manufacturing Company might submit.

(Adapted from Uniform CPA Examination)

16-16. The management of Goodspeed Manufacturing Corporation provides you with the following information:

Factory cost	$100,000
Administration expense	20,000
Selling expense	10,000
	$130,000
Fixed capital	$100,000
Volume of production and sales	10,000 units
Ratio of current assets to sales	30%

You are requested to use the above information to calculate the unit sales price that would enable the company to earn a 20 percent return before income taxes on the necessary investment. What price would you propose? Prepare a statement to prove the validity of your proposed price.

(Adapted from N.A.A. Research Report No. 35, pp. 44–45)

16-17. You have been engaged to assist the management of the Roland Corporation in arriving at certain decisions. The Roland Corporation has its home office in Chicago and leases factory buildings in Vermont, Indiana, and Alabama. The same single product is manufactured in all three factories. The following information is available regarding 1972 operations:

	Total	Vermont	Indiana	Alabama
Sales	$900,000	$200,000	$400,000	$300,000
Fixed costs:				
Factory	$180,000	$ 50,000	$ 55,000	$ 75,000
Administration	59,000	16,000	21,000	22,000
Variable costs	500,000	100,000	220,000	180,000
Allocated home office expense	63,000	14,000	28,000	21,000
Total	$802,000	$180,000	$324,000	$298,000
Net profit from operations	$ 98,000	$ 20,000	$ 76,000	$ 2,000

Home office expense is allocated on the basis of units sold. The sales price per unit is $10.

Management is undecided whether to renew the lease of the Alabama factory, which expires on December 31, 1973 and will require an increase in rent of $15,000 per year if renewed. If the Alabama factory is shut down, the amount expected to be realized from the sale of the equipment is greater than its book value and would cover all termination expenses.

If the Alabama factory is shut down, the Company can continue to serve customers of the Alabama factory by one of the following methods:
1. Expanding the Vermont factory, which would increase fixed costs by 15 percent. Additional shipping expense of $2 per unit will be incurred on the increased production.
2. Entering into a long-term contract with a competitor who will serve the Alabama factory customers and who will pay the Roland Corporation a commission of $1.60 per unit.

The Roland Corporation is also planning to establish a subsidiary corporation in Mexico to produce the same product. Based on estimated annual Mexican sales of 40,000 units, cost studies produced the following estimates for the Mexican subsidiary:

	Total Annual Costs	Percentage of Total Annual Cost That is Variable
Material	$193,600	100%
Labor	90,000	70
Manufacturing overhead	80,000	64
Administration	30,000	30

The Mexican production will be sold by manufacturer's representatives who will receive a commission of 8 percent of the sales price. No portion of the United States home office expense will be allocated to the Mexican subsidiary.

Required

a. Prepare a schedule computing the Roland Corporation's estimated net profit from United States operations under each of the following procedures:
   1. expansion of the Vermont factory
   2. negotiation of long-term contract on a commission basis
b. Management wants to price its Mexican product to realize a 10 percent profit on the sales price. Compute the sales price per unit that would result in an estimated 10 percent profit on sales.
c. Assume that your answer to part b is a sales price of $11 per unit. Compute the break-even point in sales dollars for the Mexican subsidiary.

(Adapted from Uniform CPA Examination)

17

The Master Budget

The budget in any organization is a basic tool for good management. Through the budget process, planning and control of the organization's activities are facilitated. On the planning side budgeting affords management the opportunity to preview or anticipate the effects of a given set of events on the organization and its resources. In regard to control, the budget can become a benchmark against which events can be measured as they occur.

Budgeting is defined as a systematic plan for the utilization of resources. Thus, budgets can take a variety of forms, depending upon the portion of the operating unit covered, the detail contained in the formal plans (usually called schedules), and the classes of resources covered. Many firms perform only fragments of the full budget process, developing only that portion of the schedules their management considers appropriate for the problem at hand. Others find it necessary to develop elaborate firm-wide plans for virtually all of the organization's resources.

The budgeting procedure illustrated in this chapter is a *fully coordinated* and *comprehensive* master budget. A *fully coordinated* master budget is one in which the plans of the various subunits in the firm all begin from a common set of assumptions. A firm might begin with a typical set such as the assumptions that sales would be $1,000,000, product mix would be 60 percent product A and 40 percent product B, and the firm's usual policies concerning production, quality control, etc., would continue to apply. The resulting plans of the various subunits are reviewed by the Budget Committee to insure internal consistency. A *comprehensive* budget is one that covers all facets of the firm's resources—from cash flows to operating costs. The degree of comprehensiveness needed by any company depends upon the needs of management at the various levels. For certain functions, particularly long-range planning, very general estimates of variables such as sales volume and profit are adequate, especially for top management at the outset of the budgeting process. In other cases, a very detailed analysis of a particular facet of the firm's existence may be needed. For example, a management expecting a cash squeeze may need a detailed schedule of forecasted cash flow. The decision as to how extensive a budgeting process the firm undertakes must rest ultimately on a cost-benefits analysis.

The mechanics of a company's master budgeting process are a function of the company's organizational structure and operating characteristics, for the budgeting process usually follows lines of organization. However, all comprehensive budgeting processes include certain programs and procedures, and it is these that will be discussed in this chapter. Generally, any budget program requires a coordinated flow of information so that all parties begin from a common base. Information contained in the schedules must be accurate and timely so that budgets can be available before the start of the period but represent the best estimate of the future. The more sophisticated the information handling techniques and estimation techniques, the more potentially reliable the firm's budget becomes.

LIMITATIONS ON COMPREHENSIVE BUDGETS

It should be clear at the outset that the complexity of so many businesses today presents a significant barrier to developing accurate and detailed master budgets. This is particularly true where the budget involved is either for a complex multi-product firm or involves a long time period. In such instances the desire for completeness and accuracy may be compromised by the equally important considerations of cost, timeliness, and the physical size of the resulting document. It is up to top management to evaluate the company's needs and the cost it is capable of accepting to meet them.

STEPS IN THE PROCESS

The budgeting process usually has its origin in the decisions of top management concerning broad policy goals for the period under study. Depending upon the nature of the organization, these policies may also reflect the feelings of subordinates. In some firms the estimates and opinions of lower level managers, aggregated by their superiors into a coherent picture, can constitute a pre-budget that aids in setting goals. In others, the goals will be transmitted from upper levels to lower levels of management, taking more specific form as they travel down through the organization. Under either circumstance, *the setting of profit and/or sales goals for the firm by its top managers is the initial step in the budgeting process.*

The Budget Committee

Responsibility for the budget process normally rests with a Budget Committee which, in turn, is directed by a Budget Officer. While there is no blueprint for the composition of the Committee, upper management, the accounting department, and other major line and staff functions are usually represented. The budget officer quite frequently comes from the accounting or financial area. This Committee, along with upper management, is primarily responsible for the establishment of the procedures, the timely gathering and coordination of all data, and the preparation of the final master budget. Policy decisions relevant to matters of planning and resource allocation are of central concern to the Committee, for one of the budget's objectives is to stipulate levels of activity and state obligations of funds. With experience and time, a firm's management can develop a set of standardized operating procedures for the budgeting process. It is to this end that a formalized Budget Manual is ordinarily prepared and used as a positive guide and policy tool to aid all those involved in the creation of the budget.

Static and Flexible Master Budgets

In general, master budgets can be either fixed or flexible. This classification parallels the dichotomy found in manufacturing overhead budgets. (See Chapter 12.) The arguments favoring one or the other type of budget are not markedly different from those presented in discussing manufacturing overhead budgeting. However, the relationships present in master budgets are more complex than those discussed earlier for manufacturing overhead. Thus, despite the obvious theoretical advantages of flexible budgets, most firms utilize static master budgets. To compensate for the likelihood that its master plan may be outdated by changes in levels of economic activity from those forecast in the master budget, most firms revise their static budgets periodicly as actual activity experienced during the period gives signs of departing significantly from planned levels.

A limited number of firms have attempted to develop the equivalent of flexible master budgets for all or a portion of their operations by using computers along with simulation models. These models are discussed in greater detail at the end of this chapter.

The Budget Period

A firm may budget for any time period. Budget forecasts are internal documents; their sole function is to assist management. The most common budget period for which detailed master budgets are developed is one year. This undoubtedly reflects the influence of financial accounting and the annual cycle on management's thinking.

As part of the process of developing its one year master budgets, many firms prepare forecasts of selected variables, such as sales, for much longer periods ranging, from five to twenty years. Management is selective in determining which variables to examine for long periods because it is difficult to develop accurate multi-period estimates for such variables as personnel needs and detailed cash flows.

For specific decisions and planning situations, budgets for periods less than one year may be needed. A canner who pays his suppliers cash for raw materials (raw fruits and vegetables) may have to wait several months before his production and sales cycle converts his finished goods into cash. While this operation is profitable on an annual basis and yields a positive net cash inflow, the firm may need bank loans at the outset of the period to pay its suppliers. These loans are repaid as the goods are sold and receivables collected. To forecast the extent of bank credit needed, management must prepare a detailed cash flow schedule to cover the time period when there will be a cash shortage.

BUDGETING MECHANICS—AN OVERVIEW

Before studying the details of the mechanics of preparing a comprehensive master budget, the budgets and schedules which are usually a part of the process should be listed and each discussed briefly. The schedules and budgets listed below are typical of those usually included in the creation of a comprehensive master budget. The decision to subdivide them into "Operating Budgets" and "Financial Budgets" is an arbitrary one. However, this division does indicate which budgets are needed for profits forecasts and which are needed for ascertaining estimates of financial condition.

Operating Budgets
- Forecasted sales budget
- Production requirements schedule
- Direct materials purchases budget
- Direct labor budget
- Manufacturing overhead budget
- Selling expense budget
- Administrative expense budget
- Other revenues and expenses budget
- Forecasted income statement

Financial Budgets
- Direct materials inventory schedule
- Finished goods inventory schedule
- Accounts receivable budget
- Accounts payable budget
- Capital expenditures budget
- Cash budget
- Forecasted balance sheet

The Operating Budgets

The budgeting process usually begins with an estimate of sales volume, projected by the sales or marketing department. The basis for the estimate will vary from firm to firm. Any given firm may use some mix of past experience, economic analysis, market surveys, and personal opinion. Sales is usually the starting point for the budget process because it represents the figure in the budget that is closest to an exogenous variable, i.e., a factor over which management has no control.

The *forecasted sales budget* summarizes the sales volume estimates that will be the firm's target during the coming budget period. Like all budgets and schedules it will be structured in the fashion most useful to management. Thus, sales may be arranged by product, product groups, sales territory, or operating division. The final sales budget included in the master budget will be the aggregate of several budgets produced at different levels or in different divisions of the organization and summarized by the budget committee.

Having projected sales and product mix for the budget period, these data are used in preparing several other budgets and schedules. Among these is the production requirements schedule. This schedule summarizes, by time periods, the production of finished goods needed to meet the forecasted level of sales. The schedule must allow for any policy decisions concerning finished goods inventory levels, rates of production, overtime, and smoothened versus seasonal production patterns. Once completed, the production schedule is used in preparing the direct materials, direct labor, and manufacturing overhead budgets.

The *direct materials purchases budget* summarizes the direct material needs for the period. Given the time required from the date an order is placed until it arrives and is ready for use, the direct materials purchases budget provides the basis for setting approximate re-order dates. Unlike many other budgets, it requires the joint participation of two functions—purchasing and production—that usually are separate departments. Their potentially conflicting goals can lead to friction in the budget process. Many firms have minimized at least this one source of friction by utilizing inventory models to ascertain order points. (See Chapter 19.)

The *direct labor budget* in the master budget process is primarily an input to the cost of production in profit planning and serves only as a very crude tool for planning and control. During the operating period, short-term schedules of direct labor staffing requirements based on the labor budget and other data will be developed by management. These schedules guide the allocation of the available supply of labor.

The *manufacturing overhead budget* is intended to indicate the expected amount of manufacturing overhead cost at the level of activity projected in the production requirements schedule. Many supporting schedules reflecting the behavior of a wide range of costs must be aggregated and summarized in this schedule. As is shown in Schedule F, page 524, it is the most detailed of the various schedules and budgets. In examining the manufacturing overhead budget, it is important to bear in mind the discussion of manufacturing overhead budgets presented in Chapter 12.

The only budget for which the level of sales is not an exogenous variable is the *marketing expense budget*. Advertising expenditures can affect sales volume. However, many other items are discretionary. Unfortunately, marketing managers frequently have an inadequate understanding of the interrelationships needed to prepare the marketing expense budget.

Like the comparable item on the income statement, the budget for other incomes and expenses is the equivalent of a miscellaneous category for nonoperating items. It is an attempt by management to forecast the level of nonrecurring items and financial income and expense. Of all the budgets, it is the most difficult to prepare accurately because of the unplanned nature of many of its components. Normal cost-volume analysis does not permit this kind of forecasting. In those cases where detailed cash budgeting is expected to show either the need for temporary loans or excess cash balances for investment, the other items budget will be the last budget prepared in final form (except for the forecasted balance sheet and income statement).

All of these schedules must be used to arrive at a projected or *pro forma* income statement, which is an attempt by management to ascertain before events occur the profits resulting from plans for the coming period. If the initial projected profit level is not satisfactory, management will attempt to improve it by changing one or more of the assumptions. For example, alternatives that would raise sales volume, such as a price cut or an increase in advertising could be considered. In other instances, the budget committee may feel that profits can only be increased by decreasing the level of costs. A directive might then go out to the various units to recheck their cost estimates in those areas where some discretion exists. Marketing and administrative overhead are likely to be examined carefully for waste. Alternatively, the budget committee in some firms may make specific recommendations concerning particular items. When the projected income statement is put in its final form by the budget committee, it should yield a profit (or rate of return) as close as possible to the standards initially set for the firm by top management.

Financial Budgets

The financial budgets are used to evaluate the effect of forecasted operations on the financial position of the firm. The schedules, supplemented with additional data about non-operating events, provide the data necessary to project a balance sheet for the end of the budget period. The projected balance sheet and the necessary detailed data for the cash budget are the primary needs fulfilled by the preparation of the various financial budgets.

The interrelationships among the financial budgets do not force the budget committee to proceed in a progression from one budget to another. Several financial budgets draw upon data contained in various operating budgets rather than other financial budgets. Thus, the sequence of events described below is flexible. Only the cash budget and the forecast balance sheet occupy fixed positions in the illustrated sequence.

The *accounts receivable budget* analyzes the changes occurring in the firm's receivables during the budget period. Using the sales forecasts of the sales budget, company policy on credit terms (for example, net 30 days after billing date) and past experience with collections, the periodic increases (sales) and decreases (payments, bad debts) are analyzed systematically in this budget. The accounts receivable budget is important to management for two reasons.

First, it depicts in detail the transition from a sale to cash receipts. Second, the budget is the standard against which management will evaluate how the individuals responsible for the credit and collection function are performing their job. Fewer bad debts and a more rapid rate of payment are strong indications that the job is being well done. Conversely, deterioration in the performance in these areas may be a bad sign.

The *accounts payable budget* performs a similar function for payables by depicting the changes in the firm's accounts payable during the period. The liabilities incurred are increases and the payments, decreases. The accounts payable budget draws upon all of the operating budgets that involve cash outflows. These are all operating budgets except the sales forecast and the projected income statement. The firm's policy on payment of its accounts determines the timing of the firm's cash outflows. The accounts payable budget is primarily a planning tool, for its purpose is to serve as an input to the detailed cash budget and projected balance sheet. It has little value in control except to indicate trends that differ from the forecast. (However, an explanation of the causes of these trends will lie elsewhere.)

The *capital expenditures budget* must be distinguished from the capital budgeting process. The latter authorizes capital projects to begin during the forthcoming period. The capital *expenditures* budget is related to that budget, for it indicates when the authorized expenditures actually take place. This distinction is important to any management interested in projecting its financial condition. Authorization may be granted in one period for a project that will require expenditures in several budget periods. Indeed, the period of greatest expenditure on the project may not be the initial period after authorization. The items included in the capital budget are used for the expansion, modernization, or betterment of the firm's productive resources. Because of the sums of money involved, most firms distinguish between acquisitions treated as revenue expenditures and those included in the capital budgeting process by setting an arbitrary dollar limit of, for example, $500 or $1000. Those projects requiring less expenditure than the limit are included in the normal budget process as revenue expenditures. Any project requiring more than that amount is submitted to capital budgeting procedures.

The *cash budget* is a chronology of the changes which are projected in the cash account. As such, its importance to management will vary. In some firms its purpose is to minimize interest costs when a high degree of seasonality is present in its cash inflows and outflows. The cash budget summarizes all the cash transactions found in the other budgets. It is directly or indirectly dependent upon nearly all of the previous budgets and schedules. Since the cash flows from operations are summarized in the accounts receivable and payable budgets, the preparation of these budgets is much of the preliminary work needed for the cash budget. However, there may still be a need to refer to other operating budgets for individual items such as cash sales or those cash expenditures that were not included in the payables budget.

Typically, increases in the cash account that are added to the period's opening balance include the cash inflows from receivables, cash sales and other income budgets, and any added equity (loans, capital stock) that actually is paid in during the period. Outflows will include those summarized in the accounts payable, capital expenditures, and other expense budgets as well as repayment of loans and payment of dividends.

Upon completion of the cash budget the budget committee may find it necessary to revise some of the assumptions under which the financial budgets were prepared. For example, the net cash flows for the period may be inadequate. To compensate for this situation, the assumed level of capital expenditures may be reduced or added loans considered. Similarly, the timing of the cash inflows may lead to temporary cash shortages during part of the period. This could cause management to alter its assumptions about the timing of certain large capital expenditures, to attempt to accelerate collection of receivables, to defer its own payments, or to incur the added cost of short-term financing.

After completing all of the operating and financial budgets and schedules, management will have calculated many of the figures that would appear on a projected balance sheet for the end of the period. These account balances (cash, receivables, inventory, payables, and certain types of debt) are among the most important figures included on any balance sheet. In many situations the budget committee will feel these data are adequate for their needs. When this is true, the comprehensive budget process ends with the preparation of a satisfactory cash budget. If the committee feels a complete projected balance sheet is needed, various transactions must be analyzed so that their full effect on the accounts is included. Many of these entries will affect non-current assets and liabilities whose balances were not updated during the regular budget process.

A projected balance sheet is useful when management is concerned not only with the level of the various accounts, but also with the relative balance between types of assets, between types of equities, or between assets and equities. For example, management may need to know not only its current cash balance, but the ratio of its liquid assets to its current liabilities. In such a situation a projected balance sheet may be prepared.

THE BUDGETING PROCESS: AN ILLUSTRATION

In this section the various steps of a comprehensive budgeting process will be illustrated. The example is the master budget for a manufacturing firm, R. M. S. Company, which makes and sells three products: A, B, and C. The budget for R. M. S. Company is to cover the year 1973. Quarterly data will be used when intraperiod data are necessary. (The choice of quarterly data was made solely for ease in presentation. In an actual budget monthly data or even weekly data might be required in some forecasts.) The financial position of R. M. S. at the beginning of the period is shown in a balance sheet.

To facilitate the calculation of product costs a standard cost system is assumed to exist in this illustration. If no such standard cost system existed, per-

R. M. S. COMPANY
Balance Sheet
As of December 31, 1972

ASSETS			LIABILITIES		
Current Assets:			Current Liabilities:		
Cash		$ 135,000	Accounts Payable		$ 21,400
Accounts Receivable		80,000	Accrued Payables		10,000
Inventories:			Income Taxes Payable		55,000
Raw Materials		9,550	Total Current Liabilities		$ 86,400
Finished Goods		121,100			
Prepaid Expense—			Long Term Debt:		
Insurance		16,000	6%, 10 Year		
Total Current Assets		$ 361,650	Debentures		$500,000
			Total Liabilities		$586,400
Property, Plant and Equipment:					
Land		$ 30,000			
Buildings		360,000	STOCKHOLDERS' EQUITY		
Equipment		650,000	Capital Stock		$ 400,000
Total		$1,040,000	Retained Earnings		165,250
Less: Accumulated			Total Stockholders'		
Depreciation		250,000	Equity		$ 565,250
Net Property, Plant			Total Liabilities		
and Equipment		$ 790,000	and Stockholders'		
Total Assets		$1,151,650	Equity		$1,151,650

sonnel from production, accounting, and purchasing would assist in estimating the appropriate unit costs. The standard costs for products A, B, and C are shown on Schedule A.

Unit Standard Costs
For Products A, B, and C

SCHEDULE A

		Product A		Product B		Product C	
Direct Material							
Item	Price	Quantity	Amount	Quantity	Amount	Quantity	Amount
101	$3.00	2	$ 6.00	4	$12.00	4	$ 12.00
102	2.50	2	5.00	3	7.50	3	7.50
103	3.50	1	3.50	1	3.50		
104	5.50					2	11.00
105	6.50					1	6.50
Total Direct Material			$14.50		$23.00		$ 37.00

	Hours		Hours		Hours	
Direct Labor ($4.00 Hourly Rate)	5.5	22.00	8.5	34.00	16.5	66.00
Manufacturing Overhead ($2.00 Hourly Rate)	5.5	11.00	8.5	17.00	16.5	33.00
Standard Unit Manufacturing Cost		$47.50		$74.00		$136.00

Operating Budgets and Schedules

Forecasted Sales Budget (Schedules B-1, B-2, B-3) The sales department of R. M. S. Company is responsible for providing the budget committee with the initial sales forecasts for all three products. These figures are reviewed by the budget committee for reasonableness. Estimated unit sales for the year 1973 are shown in Schedule B-1.

The forecast in B-1 is the basis for deriving several of the following schedules. The first of these is the sales forecast in dollars, Schedule B-2. Each of the numbers in this schedule is the result of the forecast volume of a given product for a given period multiplied by the standard price for that product as shown in Schedule B-2. For example, the sales revenue for product A in the first quarter is 1,000 units at $70 per unit, or $70,000. All other entries are calculated in a similar fashion.

The *net* sales schedule, Schedule B-3, adjusts the figures in Schedule B-2 for the estimated discounts and allowances of 2 percent of gross sales. For exam-

R. M. S. COMPANY
Forecasted Sales Budget
For Year Ending Dec., 31, 1973

SCHEDULE B-1

Sales in Units:

Product	Qtr. 1	Qtr. 2	Qtr. 3	Qtr. 4	Annual
A	1,000	1,500	2,000	3,000	7,500
B	1,500	2,000	3,000	4,000	10,500
C	600	800	800	1,000	3,200

SCHEDULE B-2

Sales in Dollars:

Product	Qtr. 1	Qtr. 2	Qtr. 3	Qtr. 4	Annual
A at $70	$ 70,000	$105,000	$140,000	$210,000	$ 525,000
B at $110	165,000	220,000	330,000	440,000	1,155,000
C at $180	108,000	144,000	144,000	180,000	576,000
Totals	$343,000	$469,000	$614,000	$830,000	$2,256,000

SCHEDULE B-3

Net Sales Schedule:

	Qtr. 1	Qtr. 2	Qtr. 3	Qtr. 4	Annual
Gross Sales	$343,000	$469,000	$614,000	$830,000	$2,256,000
Less: Discounts and Allowances; 2 percent of gross	6,860	9,380	12,280	16,600	45,120
Net Sales	$336,140	$459,620	$601,720	$813,400	$2,210,880

ple, the estimate for the first period was 2 percent of $343,000 or $6,860. (Schedules B-2 and B-3 could be combined into a single schedule by expanding Schedule B-2 to include the estimated discounts and allowances.)

Production Requirements Schedule (Schedule C) The sales forecast in units (Schedule B-1) is the starting point for calculating the production in any given period. The sales figures plus the desired ending inventory reflect the amount of goods that must be made available during the quarter. Opening inventory for the quarter will supply a portion of these needs. The remainder must be met through the production of the period.

The desired closing inventory shown in Schedule C is set by management. In some cases, a rule of thumb, for example, 80 percent of the *next* quarter's sales, is used. In other cases a detailed quarter-by-quarter analysis is made. R. M. S. made such an analysis and decided to have on hand an inventory of 1,000 units of A at the end of the first quarter. Adding this to the sales forecast of 1,000 units of A contained in Schedule B-1, a requirement of 2,000 units available was calculated. Of that amount 600 units were already on hand at the start of the period and 1,400 were to be produced during the period. Note the (B-1) after "forecasted sales" indicating the source of that figure, Schedule B-1.

R. M. S. COMPANY
Production Requirements Schedule
For Year Ending Dec. 31, 1973
(in units)

SCHEDULE C

Product A	Qtr. 1	Qtr. 2	Qtr. 3	Qtr. 4	Annual
Desired closing Inventory	1,000	1,300	1,600	500	
Plus: Forecasted Sales (B-1)	1,000	1,500	2,000	3,000	7,500
Total Unit Requirement	2,000	2,800	3,600	3,500	
Less: Opening Inventory	600	1,000	1,300	1,600	
Production Requirement	1,400	1,800	2,300	1,900	7,400

Product B	Qtr. 1	Qtr. 2	Qtr. 3	Qtr. 4	Annual
Desired Closing Inventory	900	1,100	2,100	600	
Plus: Forecasted Sales (B-1)	1,500	2,000	3,000	4,000	10,500
Total Unit Requirement	2,400	3,100	5,100	4,600	
Less: Opening Inventory	700	900	1,100	2,100	
Production Requirement	1,700	2,200	4,000	2,500	10,400

Product C	Qtr. 1	Qtr. 2	Qtr. 3	Qtr. 4	Annual
Desired Closing Inventory	400	400	600	300	
Plus: Forecasted Sales (B-1)	600	800	800	1,000	3,200
Total Unit Requirement	1,000	1,200	1,400	1,300	
Less: Opening Inventory	300	400	400	600	
Production Requirement	700	800	1,000	700	3,200

Direct Materials Purchases Budget (Schedules D-1, D-2) Schedule D-1 shows the purchase requirements for material 101, one of the raw materials used in the manufacture of A, B, and C. It consists of those units needed for production plus or minus any change in raw material inventory. The quarterly production requirements are calculated by taking expected production requirements (in units) of each product from Schedule C and multiplying that by the standard amount for material 101 shown in Schedule A. Thus, the 12,400 units of 101 required for production in the first quarter was calculated as follows:

Product	Standard 101	Volume	Total 101
A	2	1,400	2,800
B	4	1,700	6,800
C	4	700	2,800
			12,400

The forecast level of purchases for the period is 12,800 units. This reflects production of 12,400 units and an increase in inventory of 400 units. The dollar cost is calculated by multiplying the purchase requirement of 12,800 units by the standard price of $3 shown in Schedule A.

Schedule D-2 shows the dollar purchase requirements for materials 101, 102, 103, 104, and 105. (Each of the dollar amounts shown for materials 102, 103, 104, and 105 were calculated in the same manner as that illustrated for material 101.) Because we are using one quarter as the shortest time period, it is reasonable to assume that the materials are ordered and received within the same period. If we used a shorter time period and one of the products had a long time between order and receipt, the purchase requirements schedule and a schedule showing order dates would be more complicated. For example, assume that material 102 must be ordered four months ahead of delivery. If this were the case, then the purchase requirements of material 102 needed on hand in the second quarter would be ordered during the first period.

Purchase Requirements for Material 101

SCHEDULE D-1

Material 101 ($3.00 per unit)	Qtr. 1	Qtr. 2	Qtr. 3	Qtr. 4	Annual
Desired Closing Inventory	1,600	2,500	1,700	1,400	
Current Qtr. Requirement	12,400	15,600	24,600	16,600	69,200
Total Requirement	14,000	18,100	26,300	18,000	
Less: Opening Inventory	1,200	1,600	2,500	1,700	
Unit Purchase Requirement	12,800	16,500	23,800	16,300	69,400
Dollar Purchase Requirement	$38,400	$49,500	$71,400	$48,900	$208,200

R. M. S. COMPANY
Direct Materials Purchase Budget
For Year Ending Dec. 31, 1973

SCHEDULE D-2

Material	Qtr. 1	Qtr. 2	Qtr. 3	Qtr. 4	Annual
101	$38,400	$ 49,500	$ 71,400	$ 48,900	$208,200
102	25,750	33,250	47,250	33,000	139,250
103	11,200	14,700	21,350	15,400	62,650
104	7,700	9,350	10,450	8,250	35,750
105	4,550	5,850	5,525	4,550	20,475
Totals	$87,600	$112,650	$155,975	$110,100	$466,325

Direct Labor Budget (Schedule E) The direct labor budget is arrived at in the same fashion as the production requirements of Schedule D-1. Each product's volume of production for the quarter (Schedule C) is multiplied by the required standard labor hours per unit shown in Schedule A. Thus, the 7,700 direct labor hours shown for product A in the first quarter is the result of multiplying its expected production for that quarter, 1,400 units, by the standard labor hours for product A, 5.5 hours per unit.

R. M. S. COMPANY
Direct Labor Budget
For Year Ending Dec. 31, 1973

SCHEDULE E

Direct Labor Hours (DLH)

Product	Qtr. 1	Qtr. 2	Qtr. 3	Qtr. 4	Annual
A	7,700	9,900	12,650	10,450	40,700
B	14,450	18,700	34,000	21,250	88,400
C	11,550	13,200	16,500	11,550	52,800
Total Hours	33,700	41,800	63,150	43,250	181,900
Total Dollars ($4/DLH)	$134,800	$167,200	$252,600	$173,000	$727,600

Manufacturing Overhead Budget (Schedule F) The manufacturing overhead budget is determined by summarizing all of the projected amounts required for the individual manufacturing overhead accounts at the predicted level of activity. (The process of ascertaining the amounts required for individual accounts was discussed in Chapter 12.) Note that while in Schedule F there may be an over- or underapplication of overhead estimated in any given quarter, management is forecasting a zero variance for the year.

R. M. S. COMPANY
Manufacturing Overhead Budget
For Year Ending Dec. 31, 1973

SCHEDULE F

At Actual	Qtr. 1	Qtr. 2	Qtr. 3	Qtr. 4	Annual
Supervision Salaries	$24,000	$26,000	$ 29,000	$26,000	$105,000
Indirect Labor	12,500	15,600	23,800	16,100	68,000
Social Security Taxes	8,100	10,200	14,900	9,800	43,000
Compensation Insurance	3,800	4,900	7,300	5,000	21,000
Factory Supplies	3,100	3,900	5,900	4,100	17,000
Utilities	3,300	4,100	5,500	3,900	16,800
Maintenance & Repair	2,900	4,000	4,500	3,600	15,000
Equipment Rental	7,000	7,000	9,000	9,000	32,000
Property Tax	3,000	3,000	3,000	3,000	12,000
Depreciation	6,000	6,000	7,000	7,000	26,000
Property Insurance	2,000	2,000	2,000	2,000	8,000
Totals	$75,700	$86,700	$111,900	$89,500	$363,800

At Standard							
Period	No. DLH	Manufacturing Overhead Rate					
Qtr. 1	33,700	$2.00	67,400				
Qtr. 2	41,800	$2.00		83,600			
Qtr. 3	63,150	$2.00			126,300		
Qtr. 4	43,250	$2.00				86,500	
Annual	181,900	$2.00					363,800
(Under)—overapplied Mfg. OH.			($ 8,300)	($ 3,100)	$ 14,400	($ 3,000)	$ –0–

Selling and Administrative Expense Budgets (Schedules G and H) Based upon the projected level of operation and management's understanding of expense-volume behavior, the selling and administrative expense budgets are drafted. The quantities for some items, such as depreciation, are fixed independent of volume. Others, such as sales commissions, are responsive to changes in the level of sales. All such cause and effect relationships must be considered in making up these budgets.

R. M. S. COMPANY
Selling Expense Budget
For Year Ending Dec. 31, 1973

SCHEDULE G

	Qtr. 1	Qtr. 2	Qtr. 3	Qtr. 4	Annual
Salaries and Commissions	$23,000	$24,500	$29,000	$23,500	$100,000
Social Security Taxes	1,600	1,750	1,950	1,700	7,000
Compensation Insurance	1,100	1,300	1,400	1,200	5,000
Office Expenses	4,000	5,000	7,000	6,000	22,000
Advertising	9,300	20,000	25,000	12,700	67,000
Utilities and Phone	1,800	2,100	2,700	2,400	9,000
Traveling Expense	3,500	6,000	9,000	8,000	26,500
Employee Pensions	2,000	2,200	2,700	2,100	9,000
Property Tax	2,500	2,500	2,500	2,500	10,000
Depreciation	3,750	3,750	3,750	3,750	15,000
Property Insurance	1,000	1,000	1,000	1,000	4,000
Totals	$53,550	$70,100	$86,000	$64,850	$274,500

R. M. S. COMPANY
Administrative Expense Budget
For Year Ending Dec. 31, 1973

SCHEDULE H

	Qtr. 1	Qtr. 2	Qtr. 3	Qtr. 4	Annual
Salaries	$16,400	$16,800	$17,200	$17,600	$ 68,000
Social Security Taxes	1,000	1,500	1,600	1,300	5,400
Compensation Insurance	1,000	1,000	1,000	1,000	4,000
Office Supplies	3,100	3,200	4,200	4,100	14,600
Utilities & Phone	1,500	1,500	2,000	2,000	7,000
Legal Expenses	1,200	1,400	1,100	1,300	5,000
Credit and Collection	1,100	800	700	1,400	4,000
Employee Pensions	1,400	1,500	1,500	2,600	7,000
Property Tax	1,750	1,750	1,750	1,750	7,000
Depreciation	2,000	2,000	2,000	2,000	8,000
Property Insurance	1,000	1,000	1,000	1,000	4,000
Totals	$31,450	$32,450	$34,050	$36,050	$134,000

Other Revenues and Expenses Budget (*Schedule I*) For the sake of simplicity no "other revenues" have been included in the budget. Only an interest expense on debenture bonds is included below.

R. M. S. COMPANY
Other Expenses Budget
For Year Ending Dec. 31, 1973

SCHEDULE I

	Qtr. 1	Qtr. 2	Qtr. 3	Qtr. 4	Annual
Interest Expense	$7,500	$7,500	$7,500	$7,500	$30,000

Interest expense on 6 percent, 10-year debentures. (See balance sheet, page 519.) Total Debt is $500,000. The interest is paid semi-annually on June 30 and December 31.

Forecasted Income Statement The data from the various operating schedules and budgets can be collected to produce the projected income statement. The

R. M. S. COMPANY
Cost of Goods Sold Budget
For Year Ending Dec. 31, 1973

SCHEDULE J

Product	Qtr. 1	Qtr. 2	Qtr. 3	Qtr. 4	Annual
A	$ 47,500	$ 71,250	$ 95,000	$142,500	$ 356,250
B	111,000	148,000	222,000	296,000	777,000
C	81,600	108,800	108,800	136,000	435,200
Totals	$240,100	$328,050	$425,800	$574,500	$1,568,450

R. M. S. COMPANY
Forecasted Income Statement
By Quarters for the Year 1973

		Qtr. 1	Qtr. 2	Qtr. 3	Qtr. 4	Annual
Net Sales	*(B-3)	$336,140	$459,620	$601,720	$813,400	$2,210,880
Less: Cost of Goods Sold	(J)	240,100	328,050	425,800	574,500	1,568,450
Gross Margin, Unadjusted		$ 96,040	$131,570	$175,920	$238,900	$ 642,430
(Under)-overapplied Manu-facturing Overhead**	(F)	(8,300)	(3,100)	14,400	(3,000)	–0–
Gross Margin, Adjusted		$ 87,740	$128,470	$190,320	$235,900	$ 642,430
Selling Expenses	(G)	53,550	70,100	86,000	64,850	274,500
Administrative Expenses	(H)	31,450	32,450	34,050	36,050	134,000
Net Operating Profit		$ 2,740	$ 25,920	$ 70,270	$135,000	$ 233,930
Interest Expense	(I)	7,500	7,500	7,500	7,500	30,000
Net Income Before Income Taxes		$ (4,760)	$ 18,420	$ 62,770	$127,500	$ 203,930
Income Taxes***		(2,380)	9,210	31,385	63,750	101,965
Net Income for the Period		$ (2,380)	$ 9,210	$ 31,385	$ 63,750	$ 101,965

   * Identifies supporting schedule.

  ** Difference between standard manufacturing overhead charge and manufacturing overhead budget forecasted for the operating level in each quarter and for the year.

*** Assume 50 percent tax rate.

only figure not already calculated is the standard cost of goods sold. This data, derived by multiplying projected sales volumes of Schedule B-1 by the standard unit costs of Schedule A, is shown in Schedule J.

Financial Budgets and Schedules

Accounts Receivable Budget (Schedule K) Based upon the net sales budget, Schedule B-3, and the firm's customers' past history of payment, the periodic change in the accounts receivable balance is calculated in the accounts receivable budget, Schedule K. In this illustration, it is assumed that all of R. M. S. Company's sales are credit sales, that bills are sent with the merchandise and that, historically, 90 percent of net sales are collected in the period during which they are billed and the remaining 10 percent are collected during the period following. Thus 90 percent of the first quarter's net sales of $336,140 (or $302,526) is collected during that quarter. The remaining 10 percent (or $33,614) will be collected in the second quarter. Note that *net* sales are used in these calculations. This eliminates the need to consider in this schedule the proportion of accounts receivable which will not be collected.

R. M. S. COMPANY
Accounts Receivable Budget
For Year Ending Dec. 31, 1973

SCHEDULE K

	Qtr. 1	Qtr. 2	Qtr. 3	Qtr. 4
Opening Balance	$ 80,000	$ 33,614	$ 45,962	$ 60,172
Charge Sales (B-3)	336,140	459,620	601,720	813,400
Total	$416,140	$493,234	$647,682	$873,572
Less Collections From:				
Previous Quarter	80,000	33,614	45,962	60,172
Current Quarter	302,526	413,658	541,548	732,060
Total Collections	$382,526	$447,272	$587,510	$792,232
Closing Balance	$ 33,614	$ 45,962	$ 60,172	$ 81,340

Capital Expenditures Budget (Schedule L) Based upon the capital budget, the capital expenditures budget is developed. This schedule shows the timing of the various expenditures which have been established by the firm's plans for capital expansion and improvement. For simplicity the illustrative capital expenditures budget is assumed to include only one item; the purchase of new machinery on open account during the third quarter.

Accounts Payable Budgets (Schedule M) Schedule M shows the opening balance, additions, payments, and closing balance of accounts payable for each quarter of the annual budget period. The increases in accounts payable from direct material purchases are readily obtainable from the materials purchase budget. The quarterly charges for depreciation, property taxes and insurance

R. M. S. COMPANY
Capital Expenditures Budget
For Year Ending Dec. 31, 1973

SCHEDULE L

	Qtr. 1	Qtr. 2	Qtr. 3	Qtr. 4	Annual
New Machinery	—	—	$50,000	—	$50,000
Total	—	—	$50,000	—	$50,000

must be subtracted from the total quarterly budgeted amounts for manufacturing overhead, selling expenses, and administrative expenses in order to determine the increases in accounts payable that result from these budgets. (Depreciation represents an allocation of unrecovered costs, property taxes are accrued in a separate liability account, and insurance charges represent an amortization of the amount of the prepaid insurance carried on the December 31, 1972 balance sheet.)

Past experience has shown that 90 percent of the costs and expenses incurred are paid in the quarter recognized with the remaining 10 percent paid in the following quarter. To arrive at the figure for cash payments on accounts payable for the first quarter, the opening balance of $21,400 is added to 90 percent of $225,300 current charges to determine the $224,170 forecasted figure. The amount of accounts payable carried forward to the second quarter is then 10 percent of current charges, or $22,530.

Similar adjustments for depreciation, insurance, and property taxes are necessary to reconcile the forecasted additions to and payments of accounts payable in the second, third, and fourth quarters. The capital expansion addition that occurs in the third quarter is also assumed to be on short-term credit.

R. M. S. COMPANY
Accounts Payable Budget
For Year Ending Dec. 31, 1973

SCHEDULE M

	Qtr. 1	Qtr. 2	Qtr. 3	Qtr. 4
Opening Balance	$ 21,400	$ 22,530	$ 27,890	$ 41,393
Current Additions:				
Direct Materials	$ 87,600	$112,650	$155,975	$110,100
Manufacturing Overhead	64,700	75,700	99,900	77,500
Selling Expenses	46,300	62,850	78,750	57,600
Administration Expenses	26,700	27,700	29,300	31,300
Machinery	—	—	50,000	—
Total Current Charges	$225,300	$278,900	$413,925	$276,500
Total	$246,700	$301,430	$441,815	$317,893
Cash Payments	224,170	273,540	400,422	290,243
Closing Balance	$ 22,530	$ 27,890	$ 41,393	$ 27,650

Cash Budget (Schedule N) The cash budget draws upon the cash receipts and disbursements data contained in the previous schedules, particularly the accounts receivable, accounts payable, and direct labor budgets. The cash inflows arising from payment of receivables and any other sources such as anticipated loans are added to the opening balance of the cash account to calculate the total cash available during the period. The disbursements occur for such various reasons as payment of accounts payable or wages payable and repayment of loans. These are then subtracted from the cash available to arrive at the period's ending cash balance.

A variety of disbursements have been included in Schedule N to illustrate the diversity of potential cash outflows. As the illustration reveals, each type of disbursement need not be present in every quarter. For example, the disbursements for accounts payable will occur in each period, while the interest on the 6 percent debentures is paid only semi-annually. Each of these outflows were taken directly from their respective schedules, as is indicated in Schedule N. The income taxes paid during the second quarter are the taxes owed on the previous year's income.

The accrued wages represent the portion of the wages earned by the workers during the period that will be paid them on the next pay day. Since the end of the quarter period and the end of a pay period are not likely to coincide, a portion of the period's wages will be unpaid at the end of each quarter. In this example, it is assumed that 90 percent of the wages earned are paid during the period and only 10 percent are carried over to a pay period in the next quarter. Thus, the $163,960 of wages to be paid during the second quarter include $13,480 of first quarter wages to be paid in the second period and 90 percent of the second quarter wages of $167,200. The portion of the wages unpaid at the end of the quarter is included in the accrued wages, taxes, and interest shown on the forecasted balance sheet.

R. M. S. COMPANY
Cash Budget
For Year Ending Dec. 31, 1973

SCHEDULE N

		Qtr. 1	Qtr. 2	Qtr. 3	Qtr. 4
Opening Balance		$135,000	$162,036	$101,808	$ 44,836
Receipts	(K)	382,526	447,272	587,510	792,232
Total Available		$517,526	$609,308	$689,318	$837,068
Disbursements:					
Accounts Payable	(M)	$224,170	$273,540	$400,422	$290,243
Accrued Wages	(E)	131,320	163,960	244,060	180,960
Accrued Interest	(I)	—	15,000	—	15,000
Income Taxes Payable		—	55,000	—	—
Accrued Property Taxes		—	—	—	29,000
Dividends Payable		—	—	—	25,000
Total Disbursements		$355,490	$507,500	$644,482	$540,203
Closing Balance		$162,036	$101,808	$ 44,836	$296,865

Forecasted Balance Sheet The budgets that were discussed in the previous sections update the December 31, 1972, balance sheet and provide new quarterly balances for cash, accounts receivable, and accounts payable. These balances can be ascertained directly from the financial budgeting process. The data in the capital budget expenditures schedule permits an updating of the fixed asset accounts shown in the December 31, 1972, balance sheet to reflect the acquisitions planned for 1973. It shows a $50,000 purchase of machinery during the third quarter. (See Schedule L.)

By examining the various operating budgets' periodic changes to the amounts shown on the opening quarterly balance sheets and the data in Schedules A through D-2, the closing quarterly balances for direct materials and finished goods can be calculated. (See Schedules O and P.)

R. M. S. COMPANY
Direct Materials Inventory Budget
For Year Ending Dec. 31, 1973

SCHEDULE O

	Qtr. 1	Qtr. 2	Qtr. 3	Qtr. 4
Opening Balance	$ 9,550	$ 11,850	$ 18,200	$ 11,825
Purchases	87,600	112,650	155,975	110,100
Total Available	$97,150	$124,500	$174,175	$121,925
Issues	85,300	106,300	162,350	110,950
Closing Balance	$11,850	$ 18,200	$ 11,825	$ 10,975

R. M. S. COMPANY
Finished Goods Inventory Budget
For Year Ending Dec. 31, 1973

SCHEDULE P

	Qtr. 1	Qtr. 2	Qtr. 3	Qtr. 4
Opening Balance	$121,100	$168,500	$197,550	$313,000
Cost of Production	287,500	357,100	541,250	370,450
Total Available	$408,600	$525,600	$738,800	$683,450
Cost of Sales	240,100	328,050	425,800	574,500
Closing Balance	$168,500	$197,550	$313,000	$108,950

Other operating schedules indicate the amortization of the balances found in various asset accounts. One such asset is prepaid property insurance. The manufacturing overhead budget, Schedule F, indicates property insurance is being amortized at the rate of $2,000 per quarter. Schedules G and H, selling expenses and administrative expenses, each indicate a property insurance expense

[CH. 17] THE MASTER BUDGET 531

item of $1,000 per quarter. In total the property insurance is being written off at a rate of $4,000 per quarter or $16,000 per year. Since the opening balance in the account was $16,000, the account will be zero unless a premium is to be paid during the period. However, the data in the illustration indicate that no prepayment of this type is anticipated.

The quarterly change in accumulated depreciation reflects the periodic allocation of asset cost to production costs and selling and administrative expenses. These last two items are $3,750 and $2,000 per quarter respectively. The amount of depreciation included in the manufacturing overhead budget is $6,000 in each of the first two quarters and $7,000 per quarter after the capital improvements program takes place in period three. Thus, the balance of the accumulated depreciation account will rise by $11,750 in each of the first two quarters ($3,750 + $2,000 + $6,000) and $12,750 in each of the final two quarters ($3,750 + $2,000 + $7,000).

The balance of the accrued wages, taxes, and interest account summarizes claims accumulating against the firm which will be paid in a forthcoming quarter. The balance consists of the unpaid portion of the current quarter's production payroll, the amount of property taxes accrued up to the end of the quarter, and (in the first and third period) the accrued interest charges. Thus, the balance of $28,230 in the accrued wages, taxes, and interest account for the first quarter consists of $13,480 of unpaid wages (10 percent of the entire payroll of $134,800), $7,500 of accrued interest (one half of the $15,000 semi-annual charge), and property taxes of $7,250 from the manufacturing overhead, selling, and administrative expenses budgets ($3,000 + $2,500 + $1,750). In the second quarter, the balance of $31,220 will reflect only $16,720 of accrued wages and $14,500 of accrued property taxes. This is because the semi-annual interest payment of $15,000 is made at the end of the second quarter. The accrued property tax is the sum of the first and second quarter's accrual of $7,250 per quarter. Note in the cash budget that the property taxes will be paid in the fourth quarter. At that time, the year-end balance in the accrued liability account will consist solely of accrued wages of $17,300.

The income tax liability consists of any taxes owed from the previous year, 1972, and management's estimate of this year's accrued taxes. Since a loss is budgeted for the first period, the balance at the end of the first quarter consists of the $55,000 of the 1972 income taxes, which will not be paid until the second quarter of 1973, less $2,380 forecast tax reduction because of the loss projected for the first quarter. The remaining quarterly balances are 50 percent of the estimated net earnings to that date. The estimated liability of $101,965 on December 31, 1973, is the amount of the tax liability if the activities go as planned. Should profits exceed the forecast of $203,930, the liability shown on the December 31, 1973, balance sheet will be greater than $101,965. Should profits fail to meet expectations, the liability at that time will be less.

The balance in the retained earnings account is the net amount of forecasted profit after taxes less the anticipated dividend shown in the cash budget (Schedule N). The forecast net change in the retained earnings account during the year is, therefore, $76,965 ($101,965 − $25,000).

R. M. S. COMPANY
Forcasted Balance Sheet
By Quarters for the Year 1973

ASSETS		Mar. 31	June 30	Sept. 30	Dec. 31
Current Assets:					
Cash	*(N)	$ 162,036	$ 101,808	$ 44,836	$ 296,865
Accounts Receivable	(K)	33,614	45,962	60,172	81,340
Inventories:					
Raw Materials	(O)	11,850	18,200	11,825	10,975
Finished Goods	(P)	168,500	197,550	313,000	108,950
Prepaid Insurance	(F,G,H)	12,000	8,000	4,000	–0–
Total Current Assets		$ 388,000	$ 371,520	$ 433,833	$ 498,130
Property, Plant & Equipment:					
Land		$ 30,000	$ 30,000	$ 30,000	$ 30,000
Buildings		360,000	360,000	360,000	360,000
Equipment	(L)	650,000	650,000	700,000	700,000
Total		$1,040,000	$1,040,000	$1,090,000	$1,090,000
Less: Accumulated					
Depreciation	(F,G,H)	261,750	273,500	286,250	299,000
Net Property, Plant & Equipment		$ 778,250	$ 766,500	$ 803,750	$ 791,000
Total Assets		$1,166,250	$1,138,020	$1,237,583	$1,289,130
LIABILITIES					
Current Liabilities:					
Accounts Payable	(M)	$ 22,530	$ 27,890	$ 41,393	$ 27,650
Accrued Wages, Taxes &					
Interest	(E,F,G,H)	28,230	31,220	54,510	17,300
Income Taxes Payable		52,620	6,830	38,215	101,965
Total Current Liabilities		$ 103,380	$ 65,940	$ 134,118	$ 146,915
Long-Term Debt:					
6 percent Debentures		$ 500,000	$ 500,000	$ 500,000	$ 500,000
Total Liabilities		$ 603,380	$ 565,940	$ 634,118	$ 646,915
STOCKHOLDERS' EQUITY					
Capital Stock		$ 400,000	$ 400,000	$ 400,000	$ 400,000
Retained Earnings		162,870	172,080	203,465	242,215
Total Stockholders' Equity		$ 562,870	$ 572,080	$ 603,465	$ 642,215
Total Liabilities and					
Stockholders' Equity		$1,166,250	$1,138,020	$1,237,583	$1,289,130

* Identifies supporting schedules.

NEW PLANNING TECHNIQUES

The procedure described in this chapter develops a static budget. This means that the procedure does not include any explicit set of formulas which permit the revision of various figures if the initial assumptions prove incorrect. This is in marked contrast with flexible manufacturing overhead budgets where such changes are readily accomplished. It is not difficult to realize why most comprehensive budgets have been static budgets. The time needed to implement a flexible comprehensive budget has made both time and cost prohibitive. Instead, management has, through periodic review, traditionally altered and updated the static budget as significant changes were detected.

Recently this practice has begun to change. Through the use of computers, deterministic simulation models have been used to calculate the equivalent of flexible comprehensive budgets. Some of these budget models are similar to a large flexible manufacturing overhead budget. Given a certain level of activity, they prepare the budget schedules and statements for the user. Other models have been designed that include the capacity to forecast sales and other variables within the program. This type of model would relieve management of the primary responsibility for many of the necessary forecasts.

The primary advantage of such a model, regardless of whether it prepares any estimates, is the extent to which it increases management's capacity to compare alternatives. For example, should the initial budget fail to reach the target profit, several alternatives can be considered simultaneously. Without the computer, the number has been limited. In essence, management's horizon is broadened and its vision sharpened by these models.

However, it must always be remembered that devices such as a computerized budget program have their costs. By far the largest is the cost of developing such a program and of keeping it up to date. A significant change in the corporate environment will necessitate a revision in the model. In addition, the individual manager loses some insight into how the various aspects of the corporate plan go together because everything is done for him by the computer. The cost of the manager's potential decreased knowledge of the firm's interactions must not be ignored.

In balance, computer programs such as the ones just discussed serve to ease management's work load and to broaden its horizon, but costs must be incurred to obtain these advantages. Moreover, the final decision to accept one of the many budgets that such a program may suggest must still be solely the responsibility of management, for computers aid but do not displace judgment.

QUESTIONS AND PROBLEMS

17-1. The management of Small State's Supplies is concerned that the time and effort involved in a comprehensive budget process may be more than they can afford. What aspects of the process would you particularly recommend to them and why?

17-2. A manager feels that his company is not capable of making very accurate estimates of its sales levels, material needs, etc. He wonders if under these conditions a budget process of any sort would be beneficial. Draft a reply to him indicating what you feel would be the benefits arising from the budgets.

17-3. Describe how a firm could relate the budget process as part of the evaluation process within the firm.

17-4. Many firms feel, justifiably, that a corporate simulation model is too expensive. For such firms, an alternative is one of the general programs offered by various consultants. These models are not tailored to the user's needs but instead intended to answer the typical questions that arise. What are the strengths and weaknesses of this alternative?

17-5. Many firms that do not use a comprehensive budget do follow cash budgeting procedures. Why the emphasis on this particular schedule?

17-6. How might the budget process for a large highly diversified firm differ from the example presented in the chapter in the *organization* of the budgeting process?

17-7. In some instances, the best laid plans of any management may go awry.
   a. How could management design its reports to facilitate the likelihood of detecting these deviations?
   b. How could the budget process be expanded so as to collect data potentially useful in enhancing control?

17-8. What quantitative techniques could be used in the budget process?

17-9. As part of the planning process for 1973, the Budget Committee of A Company has requested a budget of projected cash inflows from credit sales for for 1973. The marketing department has forecast sales on a monthly basis. These estimates are:

January	$25,000	May	$40,000	September	$62,000
February	30,000	June	50,000	October	60,000
March	32,000	July	55,000	November	45,000
April	35,000	August	60,000	December	35,000

During 1972 collections lagged behind the historic pattern of only 1 percent bad debts. During 1973, added efforts are to be directed at this problem. It is expected that bad debts can be held to 2 percent of sales. Collections are expected to be made 80 percent in the month following the sale and 18 percent, the balance, in the next month.

The balance in Accounts Receivable less the 2 percent allowance for doubtful accounts on December 31, 1972, was $30,000. December sales accounted for $24,500 of this amount.

Required

a. Prepare a Net Sales Budget by months for 1973.

b. Prepare a schedule of cash inflows from Accounts Receivable by months to be used in the preparation of the Cash Budget for 1973.

c. Calculate the balance in Accounts Receivable on December 31, 1973.

[CH. 17] THE MASTER BUDGET 535

17-10. Use the 1973 sales forecast given in problem 17-9 in working this problem. Assume that 50 percent of the sales are cash sales and that the credit sales are subject to the same characteristics as in problem 17-9. Those are 80 percent of the credit sales paid in the month following the sale, 18 percent in the second month following the sale, and 2 percent bad debts. On December 31, 1972, Accounts Receivable less the 2 percent allowance for doubtful accounts is $15,000. Of that amount $12,250 is from December sales. The remainder is from November.

Required

a. Prepare a schedule of cash inflows from Sales and Accounts Receivable by months for 1973.
b. Calculate the balance in Accounts Receivable on December 31, 1973.

17-11. The accounting department has received the direct labor budget, the raw materials purchases budget, and the manufacturing overhead budget from the various departments. As part of the comprehensive budget process, the accounting department summarizes the periodic cash outflows and submits it to the Budget Committee.

SAMPLE COMPANY
Direct Labor Budget
January thru April, 1973

Month	Labor Class	Rate	Hours	Total Cost
January	A	$2.50	10,000	$ 25,000
	B	4.00	12,000	48,000
February	A	2.50	16,000	40,000
	B	4.00	18,000	72,000
March	A	2.50	14,000	35,000
	B	4.00	18,000	72,000
April	A	3.00*	13,000	39,000
	B	5.00*	16,000	80,000
			117,000	$411,000

* On March 31, 1973 the labor contract expires. No strike is expected. The rates for April, 1973 are the industrial relations department's best estimate of the new rates.

All workers are paid on the 15th and final workdays of each month.

SAMPLE COMPANY
Materials Purchases Budget
January thru April, 1973

Item	Order Date	Date of Receipt	Quantity	Price	Total
Sheet Plastic	January 1	March 10	100,000 yd.	$.10/yd.	$10,000
Metal Filament	February 1	February 15	40,000 ft.	$.01/ft.	$ 400
Cement	February 28	March 20	1,000 cases	$5.00/case	$ 5,000
Framing Wire	March 15	April 15	20,000 ft.	$.10/ft.	$ 2,000

All purchases are on credit except the framing wire for which the company must pay cash when it places the order. All credit items are paid for in the month following delivery.

SAMPLE COMPANY
Manufacturing Overhead Budget
January thru April, 1973

	January	February	March	April	Total
Indirect Labor	$ 4,000	$ 4,000	$ 4,000	$ 4,000	$16,000
Various Materials	500	100	100	100	800
Power	6,500	9,500	9,000	8,250	33,250
Heat and Light	1,500	1,400	1,200	1,000	5,100
Rent	1,000	1,000	1,000	1,000	4,000
Insurance, Taxes	400	400	400	400	1,600
	$13,900	$16,400	$15,700	$14,750	$60,750

Notes: Indirect Labor: Primarily maintenance workers and some semi-skilled repair crews for equipment.

All are paid semi-monthly on the 15th and the final work day of the month.

Various Materials: Cleaning supplies, lubricants, etc. These are purchased irregularly and considered an expense at time of purchase. They are usually shipped C.O.D.

Power and Heat and Light: The amounts shown for these items reflect the expected actual usage. Electricity is used for power and lighting. Gas is used for heat. Sample Company pays for its gas on a pro-rated basis of $175 per month. In December the gas company balances the account. The electric company reads the Sample Company's meter on the first business day of each month. The bill is mailed about three days later and due approximately the 20th day of the month. The separation of costs between gas and electricity for heat and light is:

	January	February	March	April	Total
Gas	$ 300	$ 280	$ 250	$ 200	$1,030
Electricity	1,200	1,120	950	800	4,070
Total	$1,500	$1,400	$1,200	$1,000	$5,100

The December 31, balance sheet contained an accrual for electricity of $7,000.

Rent: Sample Company pays its rent in two installments of $6,000 each. One is due in January, the other in July. The cost is pro-rated over the year.

Insurance and Taxes: The insurance is $1,200 annually. It is paid in two installments in December and June and the cost allocated over the year. The taxes for 1973 will be known in July and paid in August. The amount in the budget is an estimate.

[CH. 17] THE MASTER BUDGET 537

Required

a. Prepare a Statement of Cash Disbursements in good form from the above data. Show the cash outflows by month for January through April.

b. Prepare a schedule of items which will be Accounts Payable or Accrued Payables on April 30, 1973.

17-12. As chief budget officer for Smith, Inc., you are given the responsibility for preparing the final forecasted reports, the projected balance sheet and income statement. Smith, Inc., buys unfinished widgets and finishes them. You have been provided with the firm's balance sheet as of December 31, 1972 and the various budget schedules. Reproduced below are the balance sheet and the quarterly figures for the various budgets.

Required

Prepare in good form the forecasted income statement for January-March 1973 and balance sheet for March 31, 1973.

Balance Sheet
December 31, 1972

ASSETS			LIABILITIES	
Current Assets:			Current Liabilities:	
Cash		$ 10,000	Accounts Payable	$ 18,000
Accounts Receivable		15,000	Accrued Salaries Payable	1,000
Inventory*:			Total Current Liabilities	$ 19,000
Raw Materials		10,000		
Finished Goods		20,000		
Prepaid Rent		1,000		
Total Current Assets		$ 56,000	STOCKHOLDER'S EQUITY	
Fixed Assets:			Capital Stock	$ 40,000
Equipment		$100,000	Retained Earnings	70,000
Less: Accumulated			Total Stockholder's Equity	$110,000
Depr.		27,000		
Net Equipment		$ 73,000	Total Liabilities and	
Total Assets		$129,000	Stockholder's Equity	$129,000

* All inventories are carried at their standard cost.

Forecasted Sales Budget
For Quarter Ending March 31, 1973

Product	Quantity	Selling Price	Gross Sales	Discounts and Allowances	Net Sales
Widget	10,000	$15	$150,000	$5,000	$145,000

Note: All sales are credit sales

Production and Purchase Requirements Schedule
For Quarter Ending March 31, 1973

	Finished Widgets	Unfinished Widgets
Desired Ending Inventory	2,000 units	3,500 units
Period Requirement	10,000 units	9,500 units
Total Requirement	12,000 units	13,000 units
Less: Opening Inventory	2,500 units	2,500 units
Unit Requirement for Quarter	9,500 units	10,500 units
Standard Cost per Unfinished Widget		× $4
Dollar Purchase Requirement for Raw Materials		$42,000

Manufacturing Overhead
For Quarter Ending March 31, 1973

Actual Costs	Amount
Various Wages, Salaries and Fringes	$ 9,000
Supplies	500
Utilities	500
Rent	6,000
Depreciation	3,000
Total	$19,000
Standard (9,500 Direct Labor Hours at $2 per hour)	19,000
Over (Under) Applied Overhead	$ –0–

Selling and Administrative Expense Budgets
For Quarter Ending March 31, 1973

	Amount
Various Selling Expenses	$25,000
Administrative Expenses	
Salaries	$13,000
Depreciation on Office Equipment	2,000
Total Administrative Expenses	$15,000

Standard Cost—Widget
For Quarter Ending March 31, 1973

Raw Material: Unfinished Widget (1 unit at $4 per unit)	$4.00
Direct Labor (1 hour at $2 per hour)	2.00
Manufacturing Overhead (1 hour at $2 per hour)	2.00
Standard Cost per Unit	$8.00

Cash Budget
For Quarter Ending March 31, 1973

Opening Balance	$ 10,000
Payment on Accounts Receivable	140,000
New 10 percent, 10-year debentures issued 3/31/73	20,000
Total Available	$170,000
Disbursements	
Accounts Payable—Raw Materials	$ 42,000
Labor	19,500
Overhead—Manufacturing	15,000
Selling and Administrative Expenses	38,000
Prepaid Rent	1,000
Equipment Additions	25,000
Cash Dividend	10,000
Total Disbursements	$150,500
Closing Balance	$ 19,500

Other Information: The income tax rate for 1973 is 40 percent. In 1972, Smith, Inc., had pre-paid its income taxes in full. In 1973, it plans to accrue its income taxes quarterly. Rent amounts to $6,000 per quarter and $1,000 is paid for in advance. Supplies and utilities expensed during the period are paid by the end of the quarter.

17-13. Alpha Products manufactures small lamps that are sold for gifts. Each lamp consists of a wooden box, a set of Christmas tree lights, a plastic cover and some screws. The standard materials required for each lamp and their standard costs are shown below:

3 feet of #1 Redwood @ $.04 per foot	$ .12
2 plastic covers @ $.25 each	.50
1 string of Christmas tree lights at $.75 each	.75
20 screws @ $.50 per 100.	.10
	$1.47

In manufacturing the lamp the company cuts the redwood to form a rectangle, fastens it with screws, and one of the plastic covers is screwed in place. The string of bulbs is taped to the inside of the box and the cord is run out through a small hole in the side. The other cover is attached and the lamp is completed. Waste of about 10 percent occurs in cutting the redwood because of defects in the wood but is not allowed for in the standard.

In November, 1972, management is considering its raw material needs for the first quarter of 1973. The following data were collected by the plant manager:

1. Expected production:
    January—18,550 lamps
    February—24,600 lamps
    March—20,200 lamps

2. Current inventories:
   Redwood—20,000 feet
   Covers—20,00 covers
   Light Sets—9,500 sets
   Screws—150,000 items
3. The inventory of redwood is considered depleted and the production manager wants to add 10,000 feet above the production needs in January. All other items are at their "normal" levels. Inventory should not be permitted to fall below these levels at the end of any month.
4. Shipping dates:
   a. All lamps needed for sale in a given month can be produced during that month.
   b. All materials needed in a given month should arrive early in that month.
   c. Redwood is usually secured in a matter of days in lots of 2,000 feet from the local lumber yard. Screws are similarly available from a local supplier in lots of 10,000 items.
   d. Covers must be purchased in lots of 1,000 from a large manufacturer. Approximately one month from the order date is required for delivery.
   e. The light sets are also purchased from a large supplier in quantities of at least 2,500 sets. For the next six months at least two months from the order date is required to have an order filled.

Required

a. Forecast the raw material needs for January, February, and March.

b. From the forecast in part a, indicate the order quantities and order dates for the orders that must be placed. Assume all orders are placed on or about the first of the month.

c. All invoices are paid during the month following receipt of the goods and all purchases are made at the standard price. Develop a cash budget reflecting the cash outflows resulting from any purchases in requirement b, above.

17-14. The Standard Mercantile Corporation is a wholesaler and ends its fiscal year on December 31. As the company's CPA you have been requested in early January, 1973, to assist in the preparation of a cash forecast. The following information is available regarding the company's operations.

1. Management believes the 1972 sales pattern is a reasonable estimate of 1973 sales. Sales in 1972 were as follows:

January	$ 360,000
February	420,000
March	600,000
April	540,000
May	480,000
June	400,000
July	350,000
August	550,000
September	500,000

[CH. 17] THE MASTER BUDGET 541

October	400,000
November	600,000
December	800,000
Total	$6,000,000

2. The accounts receivable at December 31 total $380,000. Sales collections are generally made as follows:

During month of sale	60%
In first subsequent month	30%
In second subsequent month	9%
Uncollectible	1%

3. The purchase cost of goods averages 60 percent of selling price. The cost of the inventory on hand at December 31 is $840,000, of which $30,000 is obsolete. Arrangements have been made to sell the obsolete inventory in January at half of the normal selling price on a C.O.D. basis.

The company wishes to maintain the inventory as of the 1st of each month at a level equal to three months sales as determined by the sales forecast for the next three months. In January the inventory will be based on the sales forecast for February, March, and April. All purchases are paid for on the 10th of the following month. Accounts payable for purchases at December 31 total $370,000.

4. Recurring fixed expenses amount to $120,000 per month including depreciation of $20,000. For accounting purposes the company apportions the recurring fixed expenses to the various months in the same proportion as that month's estimated sales bears to the estimated total annual sales. Variable expenses amount to 10 percent of sales. Payments for expenses are made as follows:

	During Month Incurred	Following Month
Fixed expenses	55%	45%
Variable expenses	70%	30%

5. Annual property taxes amount to $50,000 and are paid in equal installments on December 31 and March 31. The property taxes are in addition to the expenses in item 4, above.

6. It is anticipated that cash dividends of $20,000 will be paid each quarter on the 15th day of the third month of the quarter.

7. During the winter unusual advertising costs will be incurred which will require cash payments of $10,000 in February and $15,000 in March. The advertising costs are in addition to the expenses in item 4, above.

8. Equipment replacements are made and paid for at the rate of $3,000 per month. The equipment has an average estimated life of six years.

9. The company must pay $60,000 in March, 1973, to cover a portion of its obligation on its 1972 Federal Income Tax.

10. At December 31, 1972, the company had a bank loan with an unpaid balance of $280,000. The loan requires a principal payment of $20,000 on the last day of each month plus interest at ½ percent per month on

the unpaid balance at the first of the month. The entire balance is due on March 31, 1973.

11. The cash balance at December 31, 1972 is $100,000.

Required

Prepare a cash forecast statement by months for the first three months of 1973 for The Standard Mercantile Corporation. The statement should show the amount of cash on hand (or deficiency of cash) at the end of each month. All computations and supporting schedules should be included.

(Adapted from Uniform CPA Examination)

18

The Capital Expenditure Program

CAPITAL BUDGETING

Among the most critical decisions facing management are those that involve capital expenditures. Of course, these decisions are not equally vital to all companies; the relative significance of this essential function in the total range of managerial activities varies according to the size of the company, the industry in which it is operating, and the rate of growth with which it is progressing. As a business expands, mechanizes, and automates, problems concerning long-range investment proposals tend to become increasingly important. The expansion and rapid technological advancement of industry throughout the post-war period have caused management to pay increased attention to the problems of evaluating long-range investment proposals. This trend shows every indication of continuing in the future.

Problems concerning capital expenditures differ greatly from those which relate to revenue expenditures. Revenue expenditures represent current operating problems which management attempts to solve through short-term planning. Capital expenditures, however, are long-term propositions which require planning beyond the immediate future. They usually require large outlays that must be financed out of some combination of working capital, equity capital, or long-term indebtedness.[1] In considering capital acquisitions, management is faced with the problem of choosing between present liquidity and, possibly enhanced future liquidity. Moreover, if management chooses to freeze a certain amount of present liquidity into capital expenditures, its action will affect the

[1] See last section of Chapter 9.

future profitability of a concern and, at the same time, commit the company to a set of strategies which can be modified only through incurring additional expenses in time and money. The profit-making potential, the flexibility, and the goals of an organization therefore affect and, in turn, are affected by the decision-makers' choices between accepting or rejecting proposed capital expenditures.

Capital Expenditures

Capital expenditures are expected to provide benefits over a fairly extended period of time.[2] The anticipated benefits may be derived from projects which are classified as either non-income-producing or income-producing. Non-income-producing projects include those that deal with investments for safety factors, public and employee relations, general plant improvements like sewer lines, road and parking areas, prestige expenditures like office redecoration and landscaping of grounds, or compliance with legal requirements. Non-income projects normally do not increase the earning power of a company to a measurable degree; instead, they are considered necessary requirements and are either undertaken or are scheduled for completion on the basis of capital fund availability. Income-producing projects would include cost reduction from the replacement of like or more efficient equipment, additional capacity, quality improvement of existing products, or the addition of new products. Income-producing projects are expected to increase the earnings of a company and should be evaluated by relating their profit potential to the investment required. In this chapter, attention will be focused primarily on analyses and selection of income-producing projects for capital budgeting.

CAPITAL EXPENDITURES BUDGET

A capital expenditures budget allows management to evaluate each project in its own right and in comparison with all other investment proposals.

All proposed projects are likely to possess certain desirable characteristics. Management must appraise the relative merits of each proposal to insure that approval is provided to only those capital expenditures which agree with the long-range objectives of the company, which make the most profitable use of available funds, and which do not impair the financial structure of the company or interfere with its future opportunities.

Management makes such appraisals through a capital budgeting process which classifies and ranks proposed projects according to their profitability and uses the company's minimum desired rate of return as one of the tests of their acceptability. Project profitability is ascertained by a rigorous analysis of the pertinent data associated with each proposal. The minimum desired rate of

---

[2] See earlier part of Chapter 6 for discussion and illustrations of capital expenditures.

return may be established in different ways, as will be shown later in this chapter. This information, combined with the proper recognition of risk and uncertainty, aids managerial judgment in the selection of those investment proposals which will best achieve the organization's goals.

Project Analysis

Until a searching analysis has established its pertinent characteristics, a capital expenditure project cannot be evaluated properly; these characteristics may be described as either qualitative or quantitative. Qualitative characteristics are those factors which are difficult to measure precisely in monetary or numerical terms. Unless they can be quantified validly, their assessment depends upon managerial judgment. Quantitative characteristics are those which may be easily expressed in monetary or numerical terms.

As the proportion of the measurable characteristics increases and the number of qualitative characteristics decreases, the pertinent data becomes more explicit, and it becomes easier for management to exercise proper judgment. Management, however, must guard against placing undue reliance on quantitative characteristics. Numerically expressed characteristics appear to be precise, established facts when they are actually estimated or forecasted figures. Decisions based solely on quantified information are not infallible; in fact, ignorance of their uncertainty may make them incorrect. Nevertheless, the valuable aid provided by the quantitative characteristics of a proposed project must be recognized.

Variations exist in the literature on capital budgeting and in practice concerning what quantitative factors are pertinent in the evaluation of a proposed project. Moreover, in practice, the pertinent quantitative factors are not always defined and calculated in the same way. There is widespread agreement that the quantitative factors of investment, economic life, income taxes, and savings or earnings are of particular importance to project evaluation.

Investment. Practice varies regarding the determination of the amount of capital employed in a proposed investment. This lack of uniformity may be caused by different methods of evaluation and/or how costs are recognized. Certainly, the starting point should be the amount of cost capitalized in the accounting records. If the company practice to write off costs quickly has caused related expenditures in research, engineering, market-testing, sales promotion, or others to be ignored, then the investment base will be understated. Care must be exercised to insure that all planned outlays related to a proposal are included in the investment base. Accordingly, incremental working capital associated with a proposal should be taken into consideration. Since, excluding more efficient practices, increased working capital can be released only by reducing the volume of products sold or by eliminating the sales of a product, it is a more permanent investment than expenditures for plant and equipment.

In instances where assets already owned are to be transferred to a new project, they should be included in the investment base at their current market value or at the value they represent in their best alternative use. When old assets are being replaced by new assets, the net proceeds received from the old assets should be deducted from the gross cost of the new assets. The important point to remember is that the proper capital investment base is the one that equals the additional or incremental costs which can be related to a project.

Economic Life. For decision making, the economic life of a project equals the expected number of years over which it will yield incremental income. Estimated economic life, like human life expectancy, is always subject to error because of the uncertainty involved in prediction. The possibility of a considerable difference between the economic life of a project for evaluation and its useful life for tax and depreciation should not cause any concern. For project evaluation, the important element is the period of time during which incremental income can be obtained. The useful life for depreciation and income tax is significant only in the respect that it influences the evaluation of related cash flows.

Income Taxes. Since the same income tax rate is applied to the before tax profits of competing projects, it might appear that income taxes are unimportant in project evaluation; this impression could be the cause of some invalid and very unfortunate decisions. It is true that the inclusion or omission of the tax effect upon the before tax profits of competing projects will not change their relative ranking. But the total impact of income taxes may change the before tax profitability and relative ranking among alternatives. In fact, the tax effect may become the controlling factor in a given decision. The tax consequences of investment proposals may differ because of considerations like the proportion of the original outlays which are to be capitalized, the proportion of the initial outlays which comprise non-depreciable assets, the timing of depreciation deductions, and the timing of the resultant tax effect on gains or losses from disposals of assets.[3]

Savings or Earnings. The savings or earnings, sometimes called the proceeds, is the amount of the after-tax, incremental net income that is expected to result from an investment in a proposed capital expenditure. Whether the earnings of a project take the form of savings due to reduction in operating costs or additional profits due to increased sales is immaterial, since both types of earnings have the same effect on net income.

The incremental net income of a proposed project is determined by using estimated amounts of future sales and operating costs. The forecasting of these estimated figures usually is one of the most difficult, if not the most complex, aspect in the analysis of a project. Predicted figures are subject to the danger inherent in uncertainty. As Spencer and Siegelman state,

---

[3] For a detailed discussion and various illustrations concerning the impact of income taxes see: National Association of Accountants, Research Report 35, *Return on Capital as a Guide to Managerial Decisions* (December, 1959), pp. 68–71.

> Uncertainty is a subjective phenomenon; no two individuals will view an event and necessarily formulate the same quantitative opinion. . . . all predictions are subjective and within the framework of each manager's own anticipations of the future. At best, subjective probabilities can be assigned to these anticipated outcomes, but the distribution of expectations resulting therefrom cannot be established with objective certainty.[4]

Schlaifer[5] and others have used expected value tables to help solve the difficult problem of prediction. (Their approach, however, is beyond the scope of this book.) Regardless of the methodology used to cope with the problem of uncertainty, the estimates involved should be restricted to relevant items only. To be relevant, an item must make a difference to the future. Items common to alternative situations are not relevant; neither are historical items. Decisions are choices among future courses of action having different costs and incomes.

Measuring Project Profitability

Many different techniques have been developed to help management measure the profitability of capital expenditure proposals. Some of these techniques are easy to understand and apply; others, although simple, are neither grasped nor applied so readily. The measures provided by the various techniques range from those which represent rough approximations to those which are relatively precise. The two primary characteristics that distinguish one technique from another are: first, the attention paid to cash flows, and second, the recognition given to the time value of money. Various techniques utilize these factors differently, as will be shown by the methods to be reviewed. These are:

1. Approximate rate of return
2. Payback
3. Discounted rate of return
4. Present value

The four methods listed involve only three different treatments of the primary characteristics, since the third and fourth methods identify two different variations of the discounted cash flow procedure. All of these methods will be illustrated by using the data associated with the proposed project which follows:

Proposed Project Ajax

Additional investment	$180,000
Economic life	5 years
Additional annual depreciation (straight line)	$ 36,000
Additional average annual after-tax income	24,000

---

[4] Spencer and Siegelman, *Managerial Economics* (Homewood, Ill.: Richard D. Irwin, Inc. 1964), p. 9.
[5] Robert Schlaifer, *Probability and Statistics for Business Decisions* (New York: McGraw-Hill Book Company, 1959), p. 25.

This information may be used to construct a cash flow schedule as follows:

Year	Additional Income Before Taxes	Additional Income Taxes 52%	Additional Net Income After Taxes	Additional Depreciation Reducing Income	Cash Flow After Taxes
1	$30,000	$15,600	$14,400	$36,000	$50,400
2	50,000	26,000	24,000	36,000	60,000
3	70,000	36,400	33,600	36,000	69,600
4	60,000	31,200	28,800	36,000	64,800
5	40,000	20,800	19,200	36,000	55,200

Approximate Rate of Return. The approximate rate of return method is also known as the book value method, the unadjusted rate of return method, the financial statement method, the accounting method, and by other titles. This method ascertains the ratio (expressed as a percentage) of the annual earnings to the related investment by following recognized accounting procedures for estimating the figures used for the annual earnings and the required investment. Although these figures are predicted, the method attempts to duplicate the figures which would be found in the accounting records if the proposed project should be undertaken. On the basis of the data provided previously for "Project Ajax," the approximate rate of return may be calculated as follows:

$$\text{Rate of return} = \frac{\text{Additional average annual net income}}{\text{Additional investment}}$$

$$\text{Rate of return} = \frac{\$24,000}{\$180,000} = 13\frac{1}{3}\%$$

A variation of this calculation is frequently encountered. It is used by those who maintain that a capital expenditure does not require the initial funds to be invested throughout the life of a project; instead, these persons assume that the funds originally invested are recaptured through depreciation expense as the investment produces earnings. Those who hold this position advocate the use of an average investment which arithmetically equals one-half of the additional investment; i.e., $\frac{\$180,000 + 0}{2}$. They would calculate the approximate rate of return in the following manner:

$$\text{Rate of return} = \frac{\text{Additional average annual net income}}{\text{Average additional investment}}$$

$$\text{Rate of return} = \frac{\$24,000}{\$90,000} = 26\frac{2}{3}\%$$

Many users prefer the total additional investment, because it is not affected by different depreciation methods and lends itself readily to comparisons and follow-up procedures for control. Regardless of which investment base is used, the relative ranking of various projects is not likely to change when the approximate rate of return is used for project selection.

Of more importance to management is the recognition that the approximate rate of return method contains serious limitations. Its use of an average annual income ignores annual income deviations which normally occur over the life of a project. Moreover, it fails to consider the time value of money by treating each future dollar of income equivalent to the dollars invested or earned presently. Finally, it disregards or inadequately allows for the cash flows which may be associated with a project. Accordingly, approximate rate of return methods usually are not considered sound criteria for evaluating the profitability of a project.

Payback. The title payback is not used uniformly. It is also called the payoff method, the payout method, and the payback period method. It is an old and very elementary method that is still widely used to provide a measure of the length of time which will be required for operations to recoup the funds invested in a proposed project. The length of time required to return an investment outlay is calculated by the following formula:

$$\text{Payback period} = \frac{\text{Investment}}{\text{Annual cash inflow}}$$

If a proposed investment of $60,000 is expected to produce a cash flow from operations of $15,000 a year, this formula may be used to compute a payback period of four years. This four-year payback period could be compared with a maximum acceptable payback period to determine whether the proposed project is acceptable. When the rapid recapture of funds is not a vital requisite, many advocates of the payback method reject it as a measure of the acceptability of a project. Since it focuses on cash recoupment, users of the payback method consider it most useful where the maximum acceptable payback period is relatively short because of a weak working capital position of the company or an extremely risky investment.

The payback method is concerned with the "net cash earnings" from an investment and therefore ignores depreciation expense, a non-cash deduction, in determining net income. As a result, the net cash inflow for a period is ascertained by adding back the depreciation expense to the net income for the period. For example, the data for the first year of "Project Ajax" shows a $50,400 cash flow which was ascertained through adding $36,000 of depreciation to the $14,400 of net income after taxes. The cash flows shown for each of the remaining years in the economic life of "Project Ajax" were calculated in a similar manner. Since the annual cash flows of "Project Ajax" are uneven, the formula suggested for the calculation of a payback period should not be used; instead, the annual cash flows should be accumulated until they equal or exceed the investment outlay. In this case, the payback period would be three years, since the accumulated cash flows at the end of the third year are exactly equal to the $180,000 investment outlay. If the formula is used, the average annual cash flows of $60,000 ($300,000 total cash flows ÷ by the economic life of five years) would also return the $180,000 investment in three years. In this case, the payback period is the same by both methods of calculation; ordinarily, the two methods will provide different payback periods.

"Project Ajax" shows that $120,000 of cash flows and $48,000 of net income should be realized after the payback period has ended. This situation reveals one of the chief disadvantages of the payback method: it basically ignores estimated returns which occur beyond the payback period. It does provide a rough indication of profitability, since the shorter the payback period is in relation to the economic life, the greater the profitability of a project will be. But it does not measure profitability. The primary purpose of investment is profitability, not recovery of the investment. Less profitable projects may possess shorter payback periods than more profitable projects. Yet, the payback method does not properly measure this profitability relationship. Nor does the payback method provide any way of deciding how long the maximum payback period should be. Moreover, it penalizes investments that produce small cash flows in their early years and heavy cash flows in their later years. Finally, the basic approach ignores the time value of money. Most of these criticisms result from the emphasis that the payback method places on liquidity, not profitability; this characteristic is its primary weakness.

Discounted Rate of Return. This method is also frequently referred to by many other names, including time-adjusted rate of return method, the investor's method, the adjusted rate of return method, and, very often, the discounted cash flow method. It is designed to utilize the strong points and overcome the failings and weaknesses of the approximate rate of return and the payback approaches for evaluating proposed capital expenditures by concentrating on cash inflows and outflows and by recognizing the time value of money.

The discounted rate of return may be defined as "the maximum rate of interest that could be paid for the capital employed over the life of an investment without loss on the project."[6] The "capital employed" in the definition refers to that capital which is unrecovered at any point in the life of a project, not to the initial or average amount invested. "The maximum rate of interest" is determined by the maximum rate that can be charged on unrecovered capital each year and deducted from each year's cash inflow without causing the sum of the remaining cash inflows to be less than the amount invested.

The use of this rate is illustrated in Exhibit 18–1, which shows that the cash inflows will recover the original investment and permit the payment of 20 percent interest on unrecovered capital. A higher interest rate would prevent the investment's recovery in five years. A lower interest rate would recover the investment in less than five years. Twenty percent, therefore, is the maximum rate of interest which will return the investment in exactly five years. This exhibit is based on the assumption that cash inflows are received at the end of each year and that the unrecovered investment in each year earns interest throughout the entire year.

Exhibit 18–1 also proves that the investment illustrated would be profitable if the cost of the capital were less than 20 percent and that it would be un-

---

[6] National Association of Accountants, Research Report 35, *Return on Capital as a Guide to Managerial Decisions* (New York, 1959), p. 57.

EXHIBIT 18–1
Investment Income and Recovery

	Investment	$2,991
	Annual cash inflow ...	$1,000
	Economic life	5 years
	Rate of return	20%

Year	Investment Unrecovered (when year starts)	Annual Cash Inflow (per year)	Interest Return at 20% (per year)	Investment Recovered (per year)	Investment Unrecovered (end of year)
1	$2,991	$1,000	$ 598	$ 402	$2,589
2	2,589	1,000	518	482	2,107
3	2,107	1,000	421	579	1,528
4	1,528	1,000	305	695	833
5	833	1,000	167	833	0
		$5,000	$2,009	$2,991	

profitable if the cost of capital exceeds 20 percent. The procedure shown in Exhibit 18–1 could be used to test whether proposed projects could pay a given cost of capital. The procedure, however, is a slow process which could be shortened by using the rate of interest to discount future cash inflows from the investment down to their present values. A comparison would then be made to determine whether the sum of the present values of the cash inflows would equal or exceed the investment outlay.

This alternate procedure follows the present value concept, which recognizes that a dollar obtained in the future is worth less than a dollar received today. Today's dollars can generate earnings before future dollars are received. For example, if today's dollar is invested at 6 percent, it will be worth $1.06 at the end of a year. Accordingly, with a current interest rate of 6 percent, a dollar to be received in one year is not worth a dollar today; it is worth only that amount of money which would provide one dollar at the end of a year if it were invested at 6 percent today. The unknown amount can be determined by dividing $1.00 by $1.06 to get .9427 cents. If a greater number of years were involved, $.9427 would be divided by $1.06 for the second year, and the quotient of that calculation would be divided by $1.06 for the third year, etc. Of course, this information can be obtained more simply by consulting present value tables, which show the present worth of a future dollar for given time periods and specified interest rates. (See Appendix B, Table I.)[7]

---

[7] Present value tables in Appendix B are based on discrete time intervals of one year. All illustrations in this chapter which involve discounting are based on the assumption that annual cash inflows are received at the end of each year. Tables giving present values of $-1/12 received monthly appearing in Eugene L. Grant's *Principles of Engineering Economy,* 3rd ed. (New York: Ronald Press Co., 1950). Continuous discounting tables appear in the Appendix to N.A.A. Research Report 35.

Using the data contained in Exhibit 18–1, Exhibit 18–2 proves that the sum of the present values of the cash inflows is equal to the investment outlay.

Since the cash flow is $1,000 for each year, it is unnecessary to discount each amount. The sum of the present values of identical cash flows for consecutive years of a period is equal to the present value of an annuity of those cash flows; therefore, the desired answer can be obtained more quickly by reference to a

EXHIBIT 18–2
Present Value of Cash Inflows Equated to Investment
(Discounted Rate of Return)

	Investment	$2,991	
	Annual cash inflow ...	$1,000	
	Economic life	5 years	
	Rate of return	20%	

Year	Net Cash Inflow	Present Value of $1.00 Discounted at 20% †	Present Value of Net Cash Inflow
1	$1,000	.833	$ 833
2	1,000	.694	694
3	1,000	.579	579
4	1,000	.482	482
5	1,000	.402	402
	$5,000		$2,990*

* Off $1.00 because decimal is rounded.
† Based on receiving annual cash inflows at the end of each year.

present value of an annuity table. Table II in Appendix B shows that the present value of $1.00 received in each of 5 years at 20 percent is 2.991. The annual cash flow of $1,000 × 2.991 equals $2,991, the amount of the investment indicated in Exhibit 18–2.

Exhibit 18–1 and Exhibit 18–2 illustrate how an investment can be recovered when a given rate of return is earned on the unrecovered investment. Neither exhibit, however, indicates how the given rate of return is ascertained. The determination of this unknown rate is the prime objective of the discounted rate of return method. It is accomplished through applying different discounting rates to the cash inflows and outflows of an investment on a trial-and-error basis until a rate is established which will equate the positive and negative cash flows. Exhibit 18–3 illustrates this procedure by using the data previously associated with the $180,000 investment for "Project Ajax."

In Exhibit 18–3, the first trial uses the present values of $1.00 at an interest rate of 20 percent to obtain a total of the present values of the cash inflows over five years of $177,345. Since this amount is below the initial investment of $180,000, it indicates that use should be made of a lower interest rate which

[CH. 18] THE CAPITAL EXPENDITURE PROGRAM 553

would produce higher present values for the cash inflows. The second trial uses an interest rate of 18 percent to obtain a sum of the present values of the cash

EXHIBIT 18–3
Rate of Return for "Project Ajax"
By Trial and Error
(Discounted Rate of Return)

		First Trial		Second Trial	
Year	Net Cash Inflow*	Present Value of $1.00 Discounted at 20%	Present Value of Net Cash Inflows	Present Value of $1.00 Discounted at 18%	Present Value of Net Cash Inflows
1	$50,400	.833	$ 41,983	.847	$ 42,689
2	60,000	.694	41,640	.718	43,080
3	69,600	.579	40,298	.609	42,386
4	64,800	.482	31,234	.516	33,437
5	55,200	.402	22,190	.437	24,122
			$177,345		$185,714

Interpolating:
18% plus 5,714/8,369 × 2%
18% plus .683 × 2%
18% plus 1.366 or 19.366% rate of return

* Source: see page 548 for "Cash Flow After Taxes"

inflows which amounts to $185,714. Since this amount is above the initial investment of $180,000, it is concluded that the rate of return on this project is below 20 percent and above 18 percent.

Additional trials could be made until a rate of interest which exactly equates the initial investment with the present value of the cash inflows is ascertained; the effort required to obtain such precision is seldom justified. Besides, a more precise approximation may be obtained quickly through interpolation. In Exhibit 18–3, interpolation is used to obtain a 19.366 percent rate of return. This rate may be used to measure the profitability of the project and to provide its relative ranking with competing investments.

Present Value. The present value method of evaluating investment opportunities should not be confused with the present value concept. The present value concept underlies any technique which recognizes the time value of money, while the present value method, like the discounted rate of return method, is a discounted cash flow approach which utilizes the present value concept.

Instead of determining the rate of return, as the discounted rate of return method does, the present value method assumes a desired minimum rate of return. (Ideally this rate would be established by the average cost of capital.) If the sum of the present value of the cash inflows of a project exceeds the sum of the present values of the cash outflows of the project's outlays when both are discounted by the same assumed rate, the project is considered to be desirable. The project is considered to be undesirable when a reverse result is obtained.

An index of the profitability of a project may be computed by using the formula which follows:

$$\text{Project Present Value Index} = \frac{\text{Present Value of Net Cash Inflows}}{\text{Present Value of Project Outlays}}$$

Profitability indexes expedite the ranking of competing projects when other considerations are excluded, since the higher the profitability index, the more desirable the project. This is true, because profitability indexes provide a common measure for investments of different magnitude by revealing the present value of projects per dollar of investment.

Exhibit 18-4 illustrates the present value method by using the information previously provided for "Project Ajax" and an assumed minimum rate of return of 16 percent.

EXHIBIT 18-4
Present Value of "Project Ajax"

Year	Net Cash Inflows**	Present Value of $1.00 Discounted at 16%	Present Value of Net Cash Inflows*
1	$50,400	.862	$ 43,445
2	60,000	.743	44,580
3	69,600	.641	44,614
4	64,800	.552	35,770
5	55,200	.476	26,275

Present value of net cash inflows $194,684
Present value of investment outlay 1.000 180,000

Excess present value $ 14,684

Profitability index:
   $194,684 ÷ $180,000 = 108.16%

* Rounded to the nearest dollar.
** Source: see page 548 for "Cash Flow After Taxes"

Exhibit 18-4 shows that "Project Ajax" has an excess present value of $14,684 and a profitability index of 108.16 percent when 16 percent is used as the desired minimum rate of return. Given a desired rate of return, this method is easy to understand and apply. But a problem arises concerning the determination of the rate to be used. This difficulty will be discussed in the next section of this chapter.

Cost of Capital

The use of the term *cost of capital* is uniform neither in practice nor in the literature on capital budgeting. Perhaps these variations arise because the term is used to identify two different concepts.

If the cost of capital is used to identify the rate of return that can be earned in the best alternative use available, it is describing the lending rate. The lending rate is predicated upon an alternative opportunity cost concept: if it is used to discount cash flows in the present value method, there is an implication that it is the rate that can be earned on alternative projects of equal risk.

If, on the other hand, cost of capital is used to identify the rate that a company must pay for capital, it describes the borrowing rate. Ordinarily, a proposed project would be unacceptable if it did not promise a return which exceeded the borrowing rate. The borrowing rate, however, usually reflects the overall risk of the firm involved, not the risk of a proposed project. Accordingly, highly hazardous projects should promise a return which greatly exceeds the borrowing rate.

Two approaches are used to compute the borrowing rate of the cost of capital. The first is the short-run or marginal approach, which views the financing of each project as a separate problem. This approach is dangerous, since it tends to ignore the cost of equity capital and can cause projects to have inexpensive financing that ignores the alternative earnings which might be realized from the same funds. The second is the long-run or average cost of capital approach, which weighs the after-tax cost of the total funds available from all sources.

An integral part of the capital expenditure program is the determination of the source, cost, and amount of available funds. Management's decision to limit the total amount of investment to be made at any time may impose a constraint which will eliminate projects showing a potential return in excess of the average cost of capital. The cost of funds, by source, may be classified as follows.[8]

1. The cost of preferred stock is the dividend rate.
2. The cost of long-term debt is the after-tax rate of interest.
3. The cost of common stock is the estimated future after-tax average earnings per share divided by the present market price.
4. The cost of retained earnings is the estimated future after-tax average earnings per share × (1 − marginal tax brackets of the shareholders) and ÷ by the present market price.

If the after-tax cost and the relative proportion of the total capital structure to be derived from each source have been established by a company in accordance with the above classifications, the average cost of capital could be computed as follows:

---

[8] For further discussions of the cost of capital, see Franco Modigliani and Merten H. Miller, "The Cost of Capital, Corporation Finance and the Theory of Investment," *American Economic Review* (June, 1958) pp. 261–97.

Source of Funds	Proportion of Total Funds	After-Tax Cost	Weights
Preferred Stock	10%	8.0%	80.0
Bonds	30	3.0%	90.0
Common Stock	40	15.0%	600.0
Retained Earnings	20	9.0% *	180.0
	100%		950.0
Weighted average cost of capital			9.5%

* 15.0% (after-tax cost of common stock) multiplied by 60% (1 — arbitrary average marginal tax bracket of shareholders) = 9.0%

SUMMARY

The capital expenditure program is one of the most important areas in which management must do long-range planning. As in other areas where management must reach decisions and make choices among alternatives on the basis of imperfect knowledge, capital budgeting is also characterized by alternatives and uncertainty.

Various capital expenditure projects typically proposed include replacement investments, improvement investments, expansion of facility investments, and new product investments. All such proposals should be stated as potential cost reductions or income-producing possibilities. And, since it is probable that the demand for funds exceeds the supply of funds available for such projects, management must select the alternatives which best further the aims of the organization.

Capital budgeting is essentially a procedure which helps management to choose among alternatives by ranking investment proposals according to some criterion. The approximate rate of return is a method that will permit projects to be ranked according to their approximate profitability. Payback is a method which may be used to rank projects according to how quickly the investment can be recovered. Both of these methods are easy to understand and are used widely. Both methods also have distinct disadvantages. The chief disadvantage common to both methods is the failure to recognize the time value of money.

The time preference of money is taken into account by techniques which discount cash flows. There are two principal variations of the discounted cash flow method. The first, called the discounted rate of return method, determines the interest rate at which the present value of the cash inflows of a project equals the present value of the investment cash outflows of a project. The interest rate so determined is used as the ranking criterion. The second, called the present value method, uses the desired minimum rate of return to discount the cash inflows and outflows of a project to their present values. The extent to which the sum of the present values of the cash inflows differs from the sum of cash outflows for the investment outlays is converted into a profitability index which is used as the ranking criterion.

[CH. 18] THE CAPITAL EXPENDITURE PROGRAM 557

Other factors play an important role in the capital expenditure program. Among these are the analysis of the project data, the effect of depreciation methods, income tax considerations, uncertainty, risk, cost of capital, project expenditure control and post-audit procedures.[9]

At this point, it is important that the reader remembers that techniques are only an aid to intelligent thinking on the part of management.

QUESTIONS AND PROBLEMS

18-1. Willow Corporation is considering three proposals having identical ultimate yields, but different payment dates.
   a. Use a zero rate of interest to determine the present values of the following yields:
      1. $5,000 received five years hence
      2. $1,000 received at the end of each year for five years
      3. $500 received at the end of each year for ten years
   b. Use an interest rate of 8 percent to rank the three yields according to their present values.

18-2. At what rates of return are the following pairs of proposals equivalent?
   a. $10,000 now or $10,000 five years from now
   b. $7,470 now or $10,000 five years from now
   c. $1,000 annually for ten years or $14,600 in ten years

18-3. a. Rank these proposals in order of preference, at a zero rate of interest:
      1. $1,000 now
      2. $2,000 in five years
      3. $3,000 in ten years
      4. $100 annually for 40 years
   b. Re-evaluate the four proposals using an interest rate of 8 percent.
   c. Re-evaluate the four proposals using an interest rate of 20 percent.

18-4. Ignore possible residual values and compute the payback period and rate of return (discounted) for these four proposals:

	Investment in Land	Annual Cash Flow	Life
a.	$100,000	$25,000	4 years
b.	$100,000	$25,000	6 years
c.	$100,000	$10,000	30 years
d.	$100,000	$10,000	8 years

---

[9] For a discussion of project expenditure control and post-audit procedures, see National Association of Accountants, *Accounting Practice Report* No. 17, "The Capital Expenditure Control Program" (March, 1959), pp. 21–29.

558 COST ACCOUNTING CONCEPTS [CH. 18]

18-5. Find the before-tax and after-tax cash flows caused by these exact transactions (assume a 48 percent tax rate):
   a. investment of $80,000 in land
   b. allocation of $80,000 of Working Capital to support a specific new capital project
   c. investment of $80,000 in research (to be expensed, not capitalized)
   d. saving of $10,000 per year in production costs
   e. an increase in depreciation expense of $5,000
   f. a reduction in production costs of $10,000 accompanied by an increase of $5,000 in depreciation
   g. investment in new equipment of $50,000, including $10,000 in installation cost which will be charged immediately as expense. This equipment replaces older equipment with an unrecovered cost of $6,000, which is to be sold for $4,000, the loss charged against the current year's income

18-6. The management of ABC Company wishes to purchase and install an automatic handling system for its warehouse. The investment of $80,000 is composed of these elements:

Conveyor system	$50,000
Controls	$10,000
Installation	$20,000 (to be expensed)

The system should permit reduction in out-of-pocket labor and manufacturing overhead costs amounting to $14,000 per year and should permit more rapid completion of customer orders. A 15-year economic life is estimated, with a net salvage value of zero. Straight-line depreciation would be used. Taxes are 50 percent of net income.

Required

   a. If a 24 percent before-tax return is required, is the investment recommended?
   b. If a 12 percent return on investment, after taxes, is required, would you recommend the expenditure?

18-7. Your firm may either rent a warehouse for a 20-year period at an annual rental of $40,000 which covers the cost of maintenance, heat, taxes, and repairs; or it may construct its own warehouse. If it builds its own warehouse, the following conditions exist: The land required for the warehouse can be purchased for $10,000 and resold for a like amount 20 years hence. Estimated costs of construction amount to $240,000. The estimated economic life of the building is 20 years, with an estimated salvage value of $40,000. The building would be depreciated on a straight-line basis. Maintenance, heat, taxes, and repairs would be $10,000 annually. (Assume income taxes to be 50 percent of net income.)

Required

Evaluate the above alternatives according to each of the four methods identified on page 547. (Use an 8 percent after-tax cost of capital for the present value method.)

18-8. Lincoln Manufacturing Company has been concerned about the rising costs of direct materials. The Product Engineering Department believes that a redesign of the product, involving an investment of $100,000, would reduce the material content of the product without impairing its performance. Savings of $25,000 a year for ten years are predicted.

The Methods Engineering Department offers another proposal. Purchase of new equipment for production would permit a lower cost raw material to be used, resulting in savings of $25,000 per year over the 10-year life of the machinery. The equipment, whose purchase is recommended, would cost $80,000; be depreciated on a straight-line basis; and have no estimated salvage value.

Note: In both proposals, savings do not include depreciation.

a. Using a 20 percent rate of return, develop a before-tax Profitability Index for each of the two proposals.

b. Considering the influence of income taxes estimated at 50 percent of net income, develop new Profitability Indices using a 10 percent after-tax return. The costs of product redesign may be expensed immediately.

c. Why has the ranking of the two proposals changed?

18-9. If the firm's cost of capital is 10 percent, is purchasing or leasing indicated? (Assume a 50 percent tax rate and use a sum-of-the-years' digits depreciation method.)

Purchasing	Leasing
$21,000 cost	$5,000 per year for six years
Useful life = 6 years	$2,000 Annual Operating Costs
Annual Operating Costs $2,000	

18-10. Arthur Company, a manufacturer of plastic toys, is considering investing $18,000 in tooling and dies for a new toy. The toy would be sold to distributors at a price of $.60 to retail for $1.00. Four people with long experience in the industry have supplied their estimate of sales of this new toy:

Toy Designer	80,000 annually for four years
Sales Manager	75,000 annually for four years
Production Manager	65,000 annually for four years
Distributor	60,000 annually for four years

The president of the company called in a marketing consultant who interviewed the four men and then furnished his own estimate: 70,000 units per year.

Estimated costs are:
Production:
$4,000 per year non-variable out-of-pocket costs
$4,500 per year depreciation
$.30 per unit variable costs
Sales and Administrative:
$4,000 per year non-variable out-of-pocket costs
$.10 per unit variable (freight, commissions) costs

Required

a. Determine the before-tax rate of return on investment for each of the five sales estimates.

b. Explain the wide fluctuations in the answers to a.

18-11. The Shocker Corporation sells computer services to its clients. The Company completed a feasibility study and decided to obtain an additional computer on January 1, 1972. Information regarding the new computer follows.

1. The purchase price of the computer is $230,000. Maintenance, property taxes and insurance will be $20,000 per year. If the computer is rented, the annual rent will be $85,000 plus 5 percent of annual billings. The rental price includes maintenance.

2. Due to competitive conditions, the Company feels it will be necessary to replace the computer at the end of three years with one which is larger and more advanced. It is estimated that the computer will have a resale value of $110,000 at the end of the three years. The computer will be depreciated on a straight-line basis for both financial reporting and income tax purposes.

3. The income tax rate is 50 percent.

4. The estimated annual billing for the services of the new computer will be $220,000 during the first year and $260,000 during each of the second and third years. The estimated annual expense of operating the computer is $80,000 in addition to the expense mentioned above. An additional $10,000 of start-up expenses will be incurred during the first year.

5. If it decides to purchase the computer, the Company will pay cash. If the computer is rented, the $230,000 can be otherwise invested at a 15 percent rate of return.

6. If the computer is purchased, the amount of the investment recovered during each of the three years can be reinvested immediately at a 15 percent rate of return. Each year's recovery of investment in the computer will have been reinvested for an average of six months by the end of the year.

7. The present value of $1.00 due at a constant rate during each year and discounted at 15 percent is:

Year	Present value
0–1	$ .93
1–2	.80
2–3	.69

The present value of $1.00 due at the end of each year and discounted at 15 percent is:

End of year	Present value
1	$ .87
2	.76
3	.66

[CH. 18] THE CAPITAL EXPENDITURE PROGRAM 561

Required

a. Prepare a schedule comparing the estimated annual income from the new computer under the purchase plan and under the rental plan. The comparison should include a provision for the opportunity cost of the average investment in the computer during each year.

b. Prepare a schedule showing the annual cash flows under the purchase plan and under the rental plan.

c. Prepare a schedule comparing the net present values of the cash flows under the purchase plan and under the rental plan.

d. Comment on the results obtained in parts a and c. How should the computer be financed? Why?

(Adapted from Uniform CPA Examination)

18-12. Ramond Corporation designs and manufactures toys. Past experience indicates that the product life cycle of a toy is three years. Promotional advertising produces large sales in the early years, but there is a substantial sales decline in the final year of a toy's life.

Consumer demand for new toys placed on the market tends to fall into three classes. About 30 percent of the new toys sell well above expectations, 60 percent sell as anticipated and 10 percent have poor consumer acceptance.

A new toy has been developed. The following sales projections were made by carefully evaluating consumer demand for the new toy:

Consumer demand for new toy	Chance of occurring	Estimated sales in Year 1	Year 2	Year 3
Above average	30%	$1,200,000	$2,500,000	$600,000
Average	60	700,000	1,700,000	400,000
Below average	10	200,000	900,000	150,000

Variable costs are estimated at 30 percent of the selling price. Special machinery must be purchased at a cost of $860,000 and will be installed in an unused portion of the factory which Ramond has unsuccessfully been trying to rent to someone for several years at $50,000 per year and has no prospects for future utilization. Fixed expenses (excluding depreciation) of a cash-flow nature are estimated at $50,000 per year on the new toy. The new machinery will be depreciated by the sum-of-the-years' digits method with an estimated salvage value of $110,000 and will be sold at the beginning of the fourth year. Advertising and promotional expenses will be incurred uniformly and will total $100,000 the first year, $150,000 the second year, and $50,000 the third year. These expenses will be deducted as incurred for income tax reporting.

Ramond believes that state and federal income taxes will total 60 percent of income in the foreseeable future and may be assumed to be paid uniformly over the year income is earned.

Required

a. Prepare a schedule computing the probable sales of this new toy in each of the three years, taking into account the probability of above average, average and below average sales occurring.

b. Assume that the probable sales computed in a are $900,000 in the first year, $1,800,000 in the second year, and $410,000 in the third year. Prepare a schedule computing the probable net income for the new toy in each of the three years of its life.

c. Prepare a schedule of net cash flows from sales of the new toy for each of the years involved and from disposition of the machinery purchased. Use the sales data given in part b.

d. Assuming a minimum desired rate of return of 10 percent, prepare a schedule of the present value of the net cash flows calculated in c. The following data are relevant:

Year	Present value of $1.00 due at the end of each year discounted at 10 percent	Present value of $1.00 earned uniformly throughout the year discounted at 10 percent
1	.91	.95
2	.83	.86
3	.75	.78

(Adapted from Uniform CPA Examination)

18-13. In planning for an underground parking garage in downtown Pittsburgh, a real estate syndicate had the following analysis of investment and return prepared.

Number of Levels	2	3	4	5	6
Initial outlay	$500,000	$650,000	$800,000	$1,000,000	$1,300,000
Annual cash flow*	$ 60,000	$100,000	$140,000	$ 165,000	$ 185,000

* After income taxes.

The garage has a useful life of 10 years. The syndicate has a number of similar proposals for garages in other cities. A large amount of capital is available for the projects with the restriction that these funds earn an 8 percent return after taxes.

Required

Determine what is the largest size garage that meets management's objective (number of levels). Provide proof for your decision.

18-14. Procrustes Bed Company is considering producing and selling a new adjustable bed. The proposal, developed after $10,000 of preliminary study, would require an additional $30,000 of product development expense in the coming year, 19A1. The following year, 19A2, $80,000 would be invested in new tools and fixtures (to be depreciated over a four-year period), $40,000 would be spent on sales promotion, and inventories of $180,000 would be built up to handle the projected demand.

Sales would begin in 19A3. At the end of the sixth year, 19A6, the product would be discontinued and the working capital investment recovered. Using sales estimates and projected unit costs and prices, the accounting department developed these *pro-forma* income statements for the new product line.

[CH. 18] THE CAPITAL EXPENDITURE PROGRAM 563

	19A3	19A4	19A5	19A6
Price per bed	$ 200	$ 180	$ 170	$ 170
Cost per bed*	$ 120	$ 110	$ 100	$ 100
Sales (beds)	10,000	20,000	20,000	10,000
Revenues	$2,000,000	$3,600,000	$3,400,000	$1,700,000
Cost of Goods Sold	1,200,000	2,200,000	2,000,000	1,000,000
Gross Margin	$ 800,000	$1,400,000	$1,400,000	$ 700,000
Sales and Administrative Expenses†	760,000	1,300,000	1,300,000	700,000
Pre-tax profit	$ 40,000	$ 100,000	$ 100,000	—
After-tax profit	$ 20,000	$ 50,000	$ 50,000	—

* Includes $20,000 annual depreciation on tooling.
† Includes a $40,000 share of corporation fixed costs allocated to the proposal.

The engineer in charge of the project urges its acceptance on this basis:
a. The average profit, after taxes, is $30,000 per year.
b. The average investment is
$ 10,000 Preliminary study
30,000 Additional development expense
180,000 Inventory build-up
80,000 New tools and fixtures
40,000 Sales promotion
$340,000 ÷ 2 = $170,000

c. Thus, the after-tax return on investment is $\frac{\$ 30,000}{\$170,000}$ or 17.6%

Required

An analysis using discounted cash flow to evaluate this proposal. The company's minimum objective on new product investments is 10 percent return, after taxes.

18-15. In planning the facilities needed for a new product line, a manufacturer must choose between two methods for painting the product: automatic and semi-automatic. Investment, operating costs, and capacity for the two types of systems are shown below:

	Automatic	Semi-automatic
Investment	$80,000 per system	$5,000 per system
Useful life	6 years	6 years
Estimated salvage value	$17,000	$ 800 per system
Non-variable costs (excluding depreciation)	$ 3,000 per year	$ 200 per year per system
Variable costs per unit painted { paint	$.04	$.06
direct labor	$.04	$.14
indirect labor	$.04	$.04
Capacity	100 units per hour	20 units per hour per system

The sales department forecasts sales of this new product for the next six years:

1973	140,000 units
1974	180,000 units
1975	180,000 units
1976	180,000 units
1977	140,000 units
1978	100,000 units

The factory normally operates on a 40-hour week, 50 weeks per year. Production is stabilized as much as possible during the year, with only small inventories carried over from year to year.

Depreciation is figured on a sum-of-the-years' digits basis. Taxes on income are 50 percent.

The Board of Directors of the firm will approve the additional investment in an automatic painting line if the return on the additional investment, after taxes, is greater than 10 percent.

Required

a. Calculate the number of the smaller semi-automatic systems needed, the differences in investment and costs for the two alternatives, and provide a recommendation to the Board of Directors.

b. How would you evaluate the impact of these factors? (Note: calculations are not possible due to lack of data; simply suggest a general procedure for considering them in the analysis.)
   1. Actual sales prove to be 50 percent higher than estimated.
   2. Actual sales fall 30 percent below estimates.
   3. Wage rates advance 5 percent per year.
   4. Because of high costs of shipping the finished product, the firm contemplates shifting one-half its production to a new plant located in California. This decision will be made in 1974.

18-16. Niebuhr Corporation is beginning its first capital budgeting program and has retained you to assist the budget committee in the evaluation of a project to expand operations designated as Proposed Expansion Project #12 (PEP #12).

1. The following capital expenditures are under consideration:

$ 300,000	Fire sprinkler system
100,000	Landscaping
600,000	Replacement of old machines
800,000	Projects to expand operations (including PEP #12)
$1,800,000	Total

2. The Corporation requires no minimum return on the sprinkler system or the landscaping. However, it expects a minimum return of 6 percent on all investments to replace old machinery. It also expects investments in expansion projects to yield a return that will exceed the average cost of the capital required to finance the sprinkler system and the landscaping in addition to the expansion projects.

[CH. 18] THE CAPITAL EXPENDITURE PROGRAM 565

3. Under Proposed Expansion Project #12 (PEP #12) a cash investment of $75,000 will be made one year before operations begin. The investment will be depreciated by the sum-of-the-years' digits method over a three year period and is expected to have a salvage value of $15,000. Additional financial data for PEP #12 follow:

Time period	Revenue	Variable costs	Maintenance, property taxes, and insurance
0–1	$80,000	$35,000	$ 8,000
1–2	95,000	41,000	11,000
2–3	60,000	25,000	12,000

The amount of the investment recovered during each of the three years can be reinvested immediately at a rate of return approximating 15 percent. Each year's recovery of investment, then, will have been reinvested at 15 percent for an average of six months at the end of the year.

4. The capital structure of Niebuhr Corporation follows:

	Amount	Percentage
Short-term notes at 5 percent interest	$ 3,500,000	10%
4 percent cumulative preferred stock, $100 par	1,750,000	5
Common stock	12,250,000	35
Retained earnings	17,500,000	50
	$35,000,000	100%

5. Additional data available to you are summarized below:

	Current market price	Expected earnings per share	Expected dividends per share
Preferred stock, noncallable	$120	—	$4.00
Common stock	50	$3.20	1.60

The average marginal tax rate for Niebuhr stockholders is estimated to be 25 percent.

6. Assume that the corporate income tax rate is 50 percent.
7. The present value of $1.00 due at the end of each year and discounted at 15 percent is:

End of year	Present value
2 years before 0	$1.32
1 year before 0	1.15
0	1.00
1 year after 0	.87
2 years after 0	.76
3 years after 0	.66

8. The present values of $1.00 earned uniformly throughout the year and discounted at 15 percent follow:

Year	Present value
0–1	$ .93
1–2	.80
2–3	.69

Required

a. Assume that the cutoff rate for considering expansion projects is 15 percent. Prepare a schedule calculating the
   1. Annual cash flows from operations for PEP #12.
   2. Present value of the net cash flows for PEP #12.

b. The budget committee has asked you to check the reasonableness of the cutoff rate. You realize that one of the factors to be considered is an estimate of the average cost of capital to this firm.

   Prepare a schedule, supported by computations in good form, to compute the average cost of capital weighted by the percentage of the capital structure which each element represents.

c. 1. Assume that the average cost of capital computed in b is 9 percent. Prepare a schedule to compute the minimum return (in dollars) required on expansion projects to cover the average cost of capital for financing the sprinkler system and the landscaping in addition to expansion projects. Assume that it is necessary to replace the old machines.
   2. Assume that the minimum return computed in c. 1 is $150,000. Calculate the cutoff rate on expansion projects.

(Adapted from Uniform CPA Examination)

19

Mathematical and Statistical Techniques Applied to Accounting

The accounting function has been one of the most important sources of information to management.[1] This information has been used in the exercise of the basic management function: decision making with regard to the acquisition and allocation of scarce resources (the economist's *factors of production*) among competing activities or ends. The size, complexity, diversity, and geographical dispersion of the modern business enterprise have greatly increased management's needs for a variety of informational inputs to its decision-making process. Where formerly accounting information, both direct and derived, had been adequate for management's needs, it is now becoming apparent that information generated by, and peculiar to, other organizational functions is also required by today's decision makers. The recent development of workable models of some of the other primary and subsidiary systems of the organization to complement the existing financial, or accounting, models has contributed to this expansion of informational needs. These newer models, such as facilities location models, quality control models, production scheduling models, inventory control models, etc., have been developed by many investigators in many disciplines. Significant contributions have been made by statisticians and mathematicians and by those trained in the fields of operations research or management science. Many of these newer models specify certain kinds of accounting

---

[1] We will not be concerned here with the fine difference posited by some authorities between "data" and "information." See, for example, S. C. Blumenthal, *Management Information Systems* (Englewood Cliffs, N.J.: Prentice-Hall, Inc., 1969), p. 30.

information as inputs. In addition, improved accounting models have been developed, and the accounting profession has adopted and adapted many of the non-accounting models for its own use. Thus, the requirements for accounting information have increased apace with the requirements for nonaccounting information. Satisfaction of these expanded requirements will require that accountants become knowledgeable of these newer mathematical and statistical models. This does not imply that accountants should be mathematical or statistical sophisticates.[2] It does imply an awareness and a modicum of understanding of these symbolic models to the end that their utilization by accounting practitioners may be enhanced, whenever justified.

This chapter does not presume to present all of the newer mathematical and statistical techniques currently available to the accountant. Neither does it present an exhaustive and derivational account of the few techniques chosen for exposition. It does provide examples of five techniques which have been selected to indicate their variety and potential for application. The five techniques to be illustrated include:

1. Economic order quantity determination
2. Regression analysis
3. Sampling
4. Control charts for variables
5. Linear programming

The reading list at the end of the chapter contains references which demonstrate many more techniques and applications as well as more detail concerning the techniques illustrated here.

One note of caution: A mathematical or statistical model is not a substitute for mature and considered judgment. It is an adjunct to such judgment. If an answer given by a model does not accord with your judgment, you are well-advised to check the model.

ECONOMIC ORDER QUANTITY DETERMINATION

The importance of inventories as an asset has been referred to previously. The role of the accountant in achieving effective control of this major asset item has also been noted.[3] Inventories, whether they are raw materials, work in process, finished goods, or supplies, would thus appear to be of basic concern to management at all levels of the enterprise. Although many analytical techniques (models) have been developed to assist management in its planning and control of inventories, there are fundamentally only two questions to which these

---

[2] Mathematics and accounting are not incompatible. In fact, Paciolo, a celebrated Italian mathematician, is generally credited with being the pioneer of double-entry bookkeeping. For an interesting account of this man's life and his work in accounting see R. G. Brown and K. S. Johnston, *Paciolo on Accounting* (New York: McGraw-Hill Book Company, 1963).

[3] See Chapter 8 of this text, pp. 224–55, and especially pp. 250–55.

techniques address themselves. These are the questions of when to order and how many to order. In this section we will briefly set forth the essential features of one decision model—the classical deterministic model—for answering these two questions. It is classical since it represents the first significant inventory model, and deterministic since it does not take uncertainty into account.

The essence of the classical deterministic model is contained in two diagrams. The first diagram, Exhibit 19–1, which depicts the behavior of inventory over time for some specific item which is stocked in anticipation of a demand for it, is shown below:

EXHIBIT 19–1

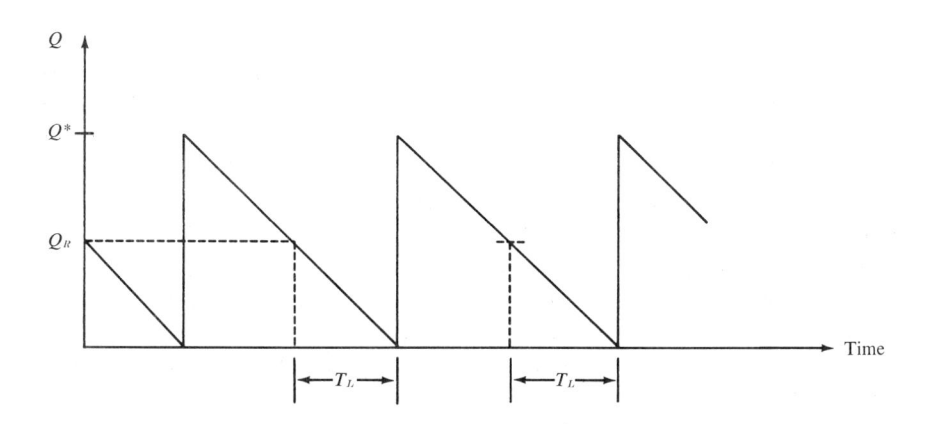

This diagram represents the following: the item is withdrawn from the storeroom at a constant, or nearly constant, rate until the inventory level, Q, reaches Q_R, the reorder point. At this moment in time a replenishment order is initiated for a quantity, Q^*. The time interval from the initiation of this replenishment order until the physical items ordered are received and available for disbursement from the storeroom is called the Lead Time, T_L. The Lead Time is assumed to be constant, or nearly so. Items are withdrawn from the storeroom at the same constant rate during the Lead Time. At the instant that the inventory reaches zero the replenishment order is received at the storeroom and the inventory level immediately increases to Q^*, the predetermined order quantity. This saw-tooth pattern is repeated. The adjective *deterministic* which is used to describe the model results from the assumed constancy of both the withdrawal rate and the Lead Time.

The order quantity, Q^*, is a specific value of the decision variable "how many to order" and is subject to management determination. It is assumed that in making this quantity determination, management is interested in minimizing over a specified time-period the sum of the variable costs associated with the resulting inventory. The specified time period is generally taken to be one year. The relevant variable costs can be included in one or the other of two variable cost categories: ordering costs or carrying costs.[4] The relationship of each of these variable cost categories to order quantity, Q, is depicted in the second diagram, Exhibit 19–2.

The ordering costs over some specified time period are a function of the demand or requirement in units for the item in question over the time period, S; the cost in dollars associated with placing an order, C_R, and the number of units of the item specified on the order, Q. The time period demand, S, divided by the number of units ordered each time an order is placed, Q, will give the number of orders placed during the time period. For example, if annual demand is 1000 units and the order quantity is specified to be 100 units then $1000 \div 100 = 10$ orders per year. Multiplication of the number of orders placed per time period by the cost of placing each order, C_R, will yield the time period ordering costs. Thus, to continue with the preceding example, if ordering costs are $5.00 per order, then the annual ordering costs will be 10 orders per year times $5.00 per order or $50.00. It will be seen from this very rudimentary analysis and from Exhibit 19–2 that the time period ordering costs, $SC_R \div Q$, decrease as the quantity ordered, Q, is increased. The ordering cost component of total variable costs operates to make Q as large as possible.

The carrying costs over some time period are a function of the number of units Q of the item specified on the order and the cost I in dollars associated with carrying one unit in inventory per time period. This cost, I, is the sum of a number of relevant cost sub-components: investment costs (interest or opportunity costs), warehousing costs, obsolescence costs, spoilage or shrinkage costs, pilferage costs, and taxes. These costs are generally determined on a percentage basis and then applied to the cost of the item per unit to give a dollar cost per unit per time period. Thus, if the total of the relevant cost sub-components is determined to be 25 percent per year, then for an item costing $4.00 per unit, the carrying cost per unit per year would be calculated as 0.25 times $4.00, or $1.00. Assuming that the carrying cost per unit per time period has been determined, there remains only the problem of determining the number of units of the item to which this unit carrying cost is applicable in order to calculate the total time period carrying costs. Exhibit 19–1, the behavior of inventory over time, shows that the number of units in inventory is constantly changing. Sometimes there will be Q^* units in inventory, the next instant there will only be $(Q^* - 1)$ units, and so forth until we reach the point at which there will be zero units in inventory and then the whole process repeats itself. How many units are in inventory, on the average, over the time period? It can be shown for the model depicted that if the order quantity is for Q^* units then

---

[4] The choice of variable costs as the relevant costs eliminates the necessity for considering the purchase price or the manufacturing cost of the item in question. Over any specified time period, say one year, the assumed constant withdrawal rate, say X pieces per day, uniquely determines a time period quantity, say $Y = 260X$ pieces per year, whose dollar value is constant regardless of how many pieces of the item are ordered at any one time. A constant, in this case one of dollar value, is not subject to management determination and need not enter into its decision-making model. The problem of "price breaks" is not considered in this elementary exposition.

EXHIBIT 19-2

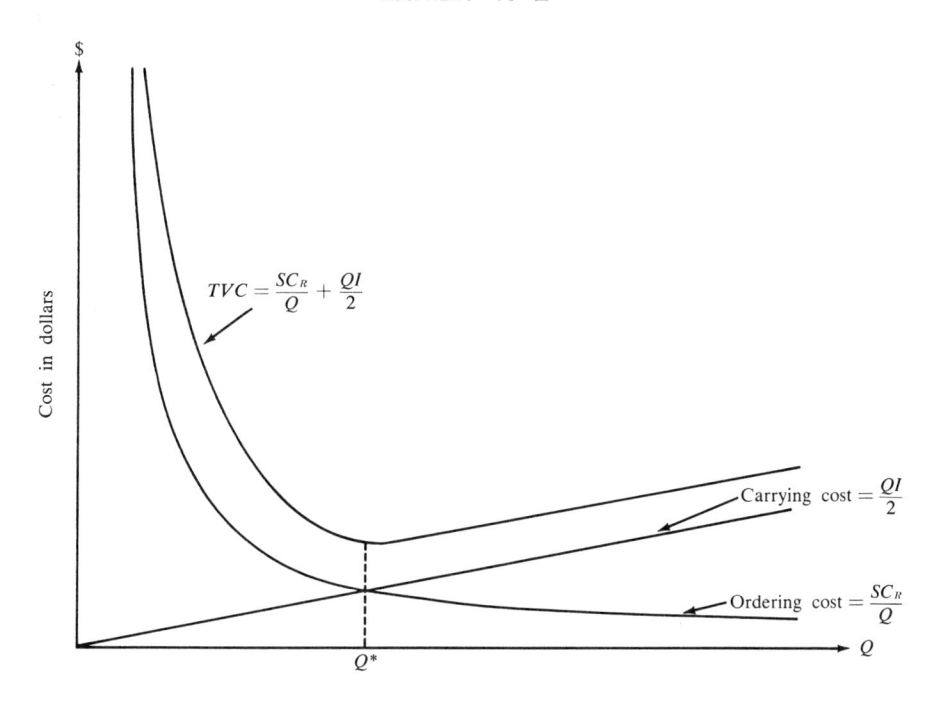

$$TVC = \frac{SC_R}{Q} + \frac{QI}{2}$$

Carrying cost $= \frac{QI}{2}$

Ordering cost $= \frac{SC_R}{Q}$

this is equivalent to having ($Q^* \div 2$) units in inventory over the entire time period. Thus, if the order quantity is for 1000 units and the withdrawal rate is constant, as shown in the exhibit, then this is no different from a carrying cost viewpoint than having $1000 \div 2 = 500$ units in inventory at all times. Based upon this reasoning the carrying costs are determined from the expression $(Q \div 2)I$, or $(QI \div 2)$. Exhibit 19-2 shows that carrying costs per time period increase as the quantity ordered, Q, increases. The carrying cost component of total variable costs operates to make Q as small as possible.

The characteristics of the two opposing cost components are summarized in the Total Variable Cost (TVC) curve which is defined as

$$TVC = \frac{SC_R}{Q} + \frac{QI}{2}$$

It is this total variable cost that management would like to minimize. The curve of TVC is seen to be high for small order quantities Q; to decrease as Q is increased until some minimum point is reached, Q^*; and thereafter to increase as Q continues to increase. Referring to the diagram it will be seen that the minimum point on the TVC curve appears to be where the two cost component curves intersect (have the same value). This is indeed the case and leads to a method for determining Q^*, that order quantity which minimizes TVC. Equating the expression for the two cost components, $\frac{SC_R}{Q}$ and $\frac{QI}{2}$, and solving the resulting equation for Q will yield

$$Q^* = \sqrt{\frac{2SC_R}{I}}$$

The value of Q that minimizes Total Variable Cost, a specific value of Q, is generally designated Q^* or $E.O.Q.$, The Economic Order Quantity. Assuming that values for S, C_R, and I are available, the formula provides a fairly simple mechanism for calculating Q^* and answers the question of how many to order.

The question of "when to order" may be approached in the following manner: If Q^* units are ordered each time an order is placed and S units are required per time period, then

$\frac{S}{Q^*} =$ number of orders that will be placed per time period.

$1 \div \frac{S}{Q^*} = \frac{Q^*}{S} =$ time interval between orders expressed as a fraction of the time period.

Example: Suppose that the following data are available for an item for which Q^* and the time interval between orders are required:

$S = 400$ units per year
$C_R = \$7.50$ per order
$I = \$0.60$ per unit per year

Then,

$$Q^* = \sqrt{\frac{2SC_R}{I}} = \sqrt{\frac{2(400)\,(\$7.50)}{\$0.60}}$$

$$Q^* = \sqrt{\frac{6000}{0.60}} = \sqrt{10000}$$

$$Q^* = 100 \text{ units}$$

Number of orders per year $= \frac{S}{Q^*} = \frac{400}{100} = 4$

Time interval between orders $= \frac{Q^*}{S} = \frac{100}{400} = \frac{1}{4}$ year, or order every 3 months

The basic inventory model presented here has many variations. Models which incorporate uncertainty, probabilistic models, have also been constructed. The supplementary readings contain references to these extensions; the interested reader is referred to these references for a more comprehensive treatment of inventory planning and control.

REGRESSION ANALYSIS

In many business problems, interest is centered not on the investigation of a single variable but on the simultaneous investigation of the behavior of several variables. In many of these problems we may be interested in predicting the value that one variable will take on, given that the other variable has some specified value. For example, assume that we have established (for some manufacturing unit of the enterprise) a relationship between Direct Labor Hours per time period and Power Expense in Dollars for a corresponding time period. We may be interested in predicting the Power Expense for some future time period, given that we know what the number of Direct Labor Hours will be for that same time period. The approach to this class of problems is called *regression analysis* and focuses on answering the question, "What is the kind of relationship between these variables?" There is a related concept in the study of relationships between variables called *correlation analysis*. In correlation studies, there may be one variable which is of interest to us and we study other variables which we believe might have some relationship to this variable in order to determine which one of these variables might show the "strongest" relationship to our variable of interest. For example, we may have reason to believe that both Direct Labor Hours and Machine Hours per time period bear some relationship to Power Expense for a corresponding time period. We would study the relationship between Power Expense and Direct Labor Hours and also the relationship between Power Expense and Machine Hours. We would select from these two relationships that one for further study and refinement which appeared to reflect, in some sense, the "strongest" relationship. The approach to this class of problems is called *correlation* and focuses on answering the questions, "Is there a relationship?" and "What is the measure (strength) of the relationship?" This section will address itself only to regression analysis and will leave the subject of correlation to be pursued by the interested reader in other texts. Furthermore, while this introductory presentation will be given in terms of only two variables, it is to be understood that the methods can be extended to deal with more than two.

A variety of methods exist for performing a regression analysis. Regardless of the particular method used, data in the form of past history is the *sine qua non*. This dependence upon past history imposes upon the investigator the responsibility not only for deciding how much data he needs, but also for determining its suitability in terms of representing what might be called "normal conditions." This means that data generated in periods of wars, strikes, acts of God, etc. will have to be culled from the historical data. In addition, the investigator will need to give some thought to the time dimension of the data since the data are frequently needed as rates—dollars per *week,* units per *month,* man-hours per *quarter,* etc. Knowledge of the required time dimension of the prediction, the result of the regression analysis, will assist the investigator in selecting the appropriate time dimension of the historical data.

The methods of regression analysis to be set forth here include *visual inspection, high-low,* and *least squares.* These methods progress from the purely subjective (visual inspection) to objective (the high-low and the least squares).[5] This objectivity, however, is not achieved without some cost: an increase in the time required for the analysis. These methodological and cost characteristics of the three methods are summarized in the following table:

---

[5] Objectivity is used here in the sense that if two or more investigators were given the task of performing a regression analysis using the same set of historical data, they would, as long as they used the same analytical technique, arrive at the same conclusions.

Regression method	Methodology	Relative amount of analysis time required	Does the technique provide for additional statistical analysis?
Visual inspection	Subjective	Least	No
High-low	Objective	Little	No
Least squares	Objective	Greatest	Yes

To illustrate the regression methods of this section, it will be assumed that a company has the following data concerning direct labor hours (activity or volume) and related power cost (overhead expense) for the preceding twelve month period:

Month	Direct Labor Hours	Power Expense
January	4,500	$ 335
February	4,300	315
March	3,700	280
April	3,300	285
May	3,000	250
June	2,800	245
July	2,700	230
August	2,500	220
September	2,800	240
October	3,100	260
November	3,800	300
December	3,500	275
Total	40,000	$3,235

Regardless of the regression method to be utilized, the construction of a scatter diagram is a necessary first step once the historical data is available in the required form. The scatter diagram is a simple statistical technique which calls for the plotting of the two variables in question on a graph. The plotting results in a pictorial representation indicating the kind of relationship which exists between the two variables. Prior to performing the plotting operation, the investigator must specify which of the variables is the independent variable (X-axis) and which is the dependent variable (Y-axis). The dependent variable is the variable whose value is to be predicted from knowledge of the value of the independent variable. No causal relationship is to be inferred from this specification of the independent variable—dependent variable relationship. The scatter diagram resulting from the plotting of the preceding 12-months data is shown in Exhibit 19–3. On this diagram, the X-axis represents activity or volume, which, in the example, is measured by direct labor hours. The Y-axis represents the related power expense. Both variables are expressed as rates per month.

EXHIBIT 19-3
Scatter Diagram Relating Power Expense
and Direct Labor Hours

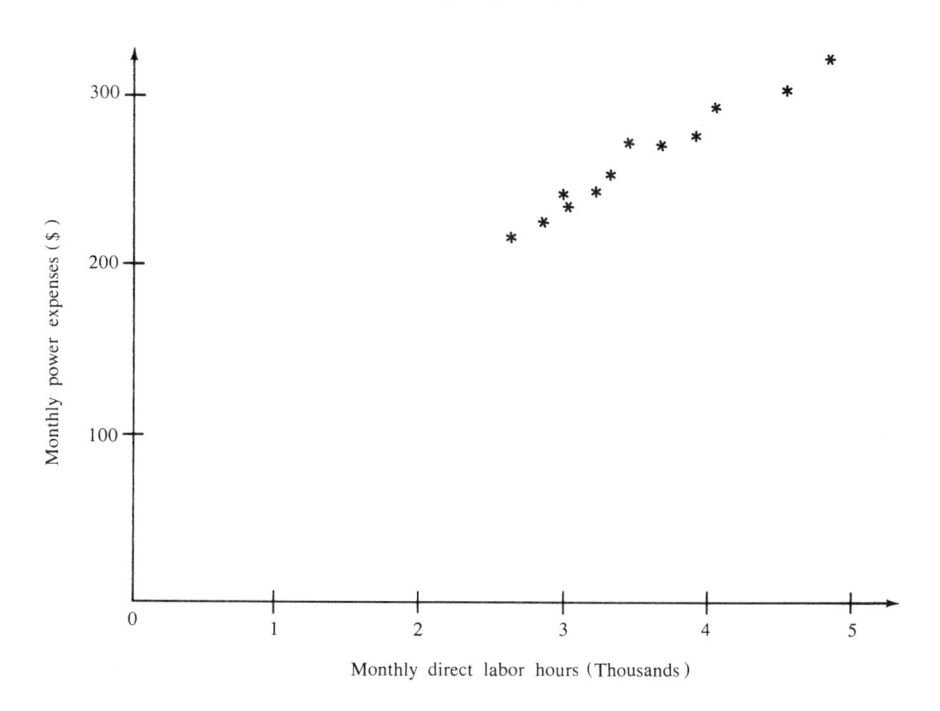

Examination of this scatter diagram would result in the tenable hypothesis that the relationship between direct labor hours per month and the corresponding power expense in dollars per month can be expressed by a straight line: a linear relationship. The problem now reduces itself to finding that straight line which best fits the plotted points.[6] As indicated previously, our discussion of regression analysis will touch upon three methods for fitting the line; and it is to the first of these methods, *visual inspection,* that we now turn.

Visual Inspection Method

Exhibit 19-4, page 576, shows a straight line which has been fitted to the scatter diagram of Exhibit 19-3, by a visual and mental process referred to as *visual inspection*. The investigator sees a straight line in his mind's eye and mentally adjusts its position until he achieves a good fit between points and

---

[6] If the relationship indicated by the scatter diagram appears to be a curvilinear rather than a linear one, then the fitting of a straight line represents an error of judgment. This judgmental error is generally more serious than an error introduced through investigator bias in fitting a straight line to a set of plotted points where a straight line is indicated. Statistical literature details various techniques to assist the investigator in determining the kind of line—straight or curved—to fit the plotted points.

EXHIBIT 19-4
Scatter Diagram and Line Fitted by Visual
Inspection Relating Power Expense and Direct
Labor Hours

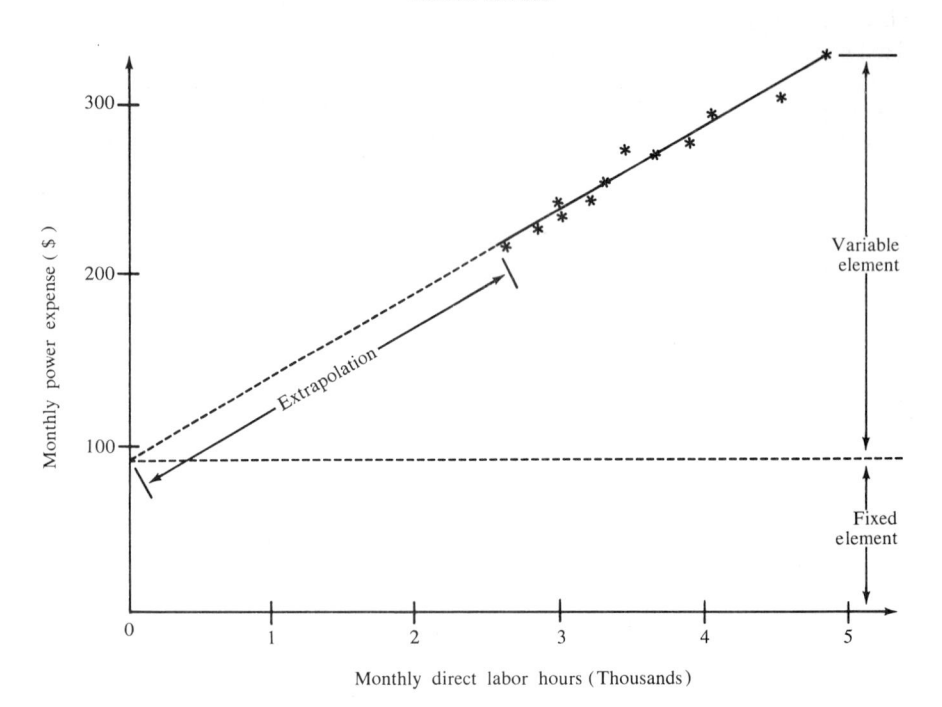

line. The process of fitting the line by this method is usually accomplished by positioning the line so that approximately one-half of the plotted points are above the line and the other half below, with compensation for the various distances of the points from the line. Admittedly, this technique is subjective and it is unlikely that different investigators confronted with the same scatter diagram would draw identical lines. The consequences of this subjective feature of the method can generally be evaluated in terms of the use to which the portrayed relationship is to be put. It is the investigator's responsibility to assess whether the position of his straight line is, or is not, accurate enough for the intended purpose.

The fitted line is the locus of all points which estimate (predict) the monthly power expense in dollars for any given value of monthly direct labor hours *within the range of hours covered by the historical data.* For example, if direct labor hours for a particular month are calculated to be 3,400, then the predicted power expense for that month will be seen to be approximately $275.

When the fitted line is projected to the left until it intersects the *Y*-axis, the point of intersection may be interpreted as representing the fixed element of monthly power expense. This extrapolation of the fitted line to include a range of values of monthly direct labor hours not included in the historical data should be performed only if the investigator has reason to believe that the assumed straight line relationship holds for the entire range, from 0 to 4500 hours per month. Extrapolation by projecting the fitted line to the right, to cover values of monthly direct labor hours greater than those included in the historical data, is subject to the same *caveat*. The approximate value of the fixed element of monthly power expense from Exhibit 19–4, page 576, is $90.

The variable element of monthly power expense is a function of the direct labor hours for the month and an expense rate. Specifically, the variable element is the product of the direct labor hours and the expense rate per hour. It is generally determined by making use of the fact that a straight line is strictly determined by two points. We might choose as one of the points on the fixed line the point (3,000, $255), that is, Direct Labor Hours of 3,000 and the associated Power Expense of approximately $255 which is as close as the curve can be read by most people. As the second point on the line, the point (4,000, $310) might be chosen. From these two points it can be determined that Power Expense increased from $255 to $310, an increase of $55, for a corresponding increase in Direct Labor Hours of $4,000 - 3,000 = 1,000$. The rate of increase is thereby calculated to be $55 \div 1,000 = \$0.055$ per Direct Labor Hour. Expressing this in conventional equation form will yield:

(1) $$\text{Monthly Power Expense in } \$ = 90 + 0.055 \text{ (Direct Labor Hours per Month)}$$

For example, if it were necessary to calculate the Power Expense for a month in which Direct Labor Hours were estimated to be 3200, then

$$\text{Monthly Power Expense in } \$ = 90 + 0.055 \, (3200)$$
$$= 90 + 176$$
$$= 266.00$$

The advantage of the visual inspection method lies in the speed with which a line can be fitted and drawn to the plotted points. The disadvantage of the method lies in its subjectivity, which may or may not be significant in any specific case. It is the responsibility of the investigator to assess the magnitude of whatever penalty may be incurred by reason of this subjectivity and to establish a clear need for an objective method of fitting the line. If such a need is indicated, then consideration should be given to the high-low method of fitting the line to the plotted points. This recommendation is made on the basis of the speed and objectivity which are characteristics of this method. It is to this second method that we now turn.

High-Low Method

The essence of the high-low method is to remove the necessity for judgment in fitting the straight line. This is achieved by disregarding all of the data except that represented by two points—the number of points needed to draw a straight line. The two points to be chosen are not left to the discretion of the investigator but are specified as the two points representing the highest and lowest activity contained in the historical data. For the historical data shown on page 574, these would be the points (4500, $335) and (2500, $220). A line is drawn connecting these two points and with extrapolation as required. The fixed and variable elements of total power expense are calculated directly from the data in the following manner:

	Power Expense							
Activity	Direct labor hours	Total expense		Variable expense				Fixed expense
High	4500	$335	minus	$258.75	(4500 × $.0575)	equals	$76.25
Low	2500	220	minus	143.75	(2500 × $.0575)	equals	76.25
Difference	2000	$115	minus	$115.00		equals	0
Variable rate = $115 ÷ 2000 hours = $.0575 per direct labor hour								

First, the variable expense per unit of activity is obtained by dividing the difference in the expense by the number of units representing the difference in volume. In the above calculation, this variable rate of $0.0575 per direct labor hour is multiplied by the number of direct labor hours at each of the two activities to provide $258.75 of variable expense at the high activity and $143.75 at the low activity. Subtraction of these variable expenses from the corresponding total power expense yields a fixed expense of $76.25 in each case. Expressing these results in conventional equation form will yield the following estimating equation:

(2) Monthly Power Expense in $ = 76.25 + 0.0575 (Direct Labor Hours per Month)

This method should be used with extreme caution because of its dependence on only two couplets of data from the entire set of historical data chosen for analysis. It is, however, a simple and objective method which, if properly understood and applied, can provide reasonable approximations of the fixed and variable elements of any given semi-variable expense category whose relationship to some activity indicator is adequately represented by a straight line. For a month in which Direct Labor Hours were estimated to be 3200, then

Monthly Power Expense in $ = 76.25 + 0.0575(3200) = 260.25

Least Squares Method

The extensive use of flexible budgets has triggered a spate of curve fitting in many enterprises. It is not surprising, therefore, that interest has centered on a curve-fitting method which is not only objective but which also utilizes all of the relevant historical data selected by the investigator. This method is called *least squares* and is a mathematically rigorous method which results in a line of best fit and provides a basis for an extended statistical analysis of the data if such an analysis is deemed desirable.[7]

The least squares method is based upon a mathematical formula for a straight line in which the sum of the squares of the vertical deviations from the computed line is minimized. In mathematical notation, this condition is expressed as

$$\text{Minimize} \sum_{i=1}^{n} (Y_i - Y'_i)^2$$

where $Y_i = i^{\text{th}}$ value of the dependent variable from the historical data, $i = 1, 2, 3, \ldots, n$

$Y'_i = i^{\text{th}}$ value of the dependent variable computed from the estimating equation $Y'_i = a + bX_i$

$X_i = i^{\text{th}}$ value of the independent variable from the historical data, $i = 1, 2, 3, \ldots, n$

$a =$ the intercept of the fitted line, i.e., the value of the dependent variable where the fitted line crosses, or intersects, the Y-axis,

$b =$ the slope of the fitted line, i.e., the amount by which the value of Y'_i increases per unit increase in the value of X_i

The minimizing expression may be rewritten as

$$\text{Minimize} \sum_{i=1}^{n} (Y_i - a - bX_i)^2$$

by substituting the right-hand side of the equation for Y'_i noted above. The minimization process is carried out by means of the calculus and results in the following normal equations which must be solved simultaneously to determine the values for a and b:

$$na + b \sum_{i=1}^{n} X_i = \sum_{i=1}^{n} Y_i$$

$$a \sum_{i=1}^{n} X_i + b \sum_{i=1}^{n} X_i^2 = \sum_{i=1}^{n} X_i Y_i$$

The values of a and b, so determined, become the parameters of the estimating equation

$$Y' = a + bX$$

The least squares method will be illustrated by the same data employed to illustrate the visual inspection and high-low methods. The detailed work is best performed by means of a table as shown in Exhibit 19–5.

---

[7] Reference is being made here to concepts such as "tests of significance of the regression coefficients," "confidence bands around the regression line," etc.

EXHIBIT 19-5

Calculations for the Least Squares Method

Month	X_i	Y_i	X^2_i	$X_i Y_i$
January	4,500	335	20,250,000	1,507,500
February	4,300	315	18,490,000	1,354,500
March	3,700	280	13,690,000	1,036,000
April	3,300	285	10,890,000	940,500
May	3,000	250	9,000,000	750,000
June	2,800	245	7,840,000	686,000
July	2,700	230	7,290,000	621,000
August	2,500	220	6,250,000	550,000
September	2,800	240	7,840,000	672,000
October	3,100	260	9,610,000	806,000
November	3,800	300	14,440,000	1,140,000
December	3,500	275	12,250,000	962,500
$n = 12$ $\sum$	= 40,000	= 3,235	= 137,840,000	= 11,026,000

The column sums from Exhibit 19–5, are substituted in the two normal equations to give

$$12a + 40,000b = 3,235$$
$$40,000a + 137,840,000b = 11,026,000$$

These two equations can be solved simultaneously to yield the values

$a = \$90.10$, the fixed element of power expense

$b = \$0.0538$, the power expense variable rate per hour

The estimating equation is, therefore,

(3)   Monthly Power Expense in $ =
90.10 + 0.0538 (Direct Labor Hours per Month)

For a month in which Direct Labor Hours were estimated to be 3200, then

Monthly Power Expense in $ = 90.10 + 0.0538(3200) = 262.26$

This brief exposition of regression analysis may be summarized by comparing the regression equations developed by each of the methods demonstrated and where MPE = Power Expense per Month and DLH = Direct Labor Hours per Month:

Visual Inspection	$MPE = \$90.00 + \$0.0550\ DLH$
High-Low	$MPE = \$76.25 + \$0.0575\ DLH$
Least Squares	$MPE = \$90.10 + \$0.0538\ DLH$

It will be seen for this particular example that the value of the fixed cost element shows good agreement between the visual inspection and least squares methods. On the other hand, the high-low method in this particular example yields a value of the fixed cost element which is approximately 15 percent below these values. The variable rate shows good agreement for all three of these methods varying only about 7 percent from the lowest rate of $0.0538 per Direct Labor Hour to the highest rate of $0.0575.

It is the responsibility of the investigator to select the appropriate method of analysis by considering such factors as (1) accuracy of the historical data, (2) any modifications made to the historical data to compensate for anticipated future changes, and (3) the ultimate use to be made of the results of the regression analysis. The old adage about "using a razor to cut down a tree" is particularly appropriate in this regard. It is also appropriate to conclude this section on regression analysis by reminding the reader that the exposition has been elementary, even cursory, in nature. The accountant who finds himself faced with the necessity of performing many multi-variate analyses, linear and/or curvilinear, would be well-advised to undertake an intensive study of the subject. A mastery of the subject combined with judgment rooted in the realties of practical operating conditions is the best insurance against the derivation of false or spurious relationships.

SAMPLING[8]

Individuals employed in the accounting profession, particularly those engaged in internal auditing or in the practice of public accounting, are frequently faced with the problem of either determining an amount for, or of attesting to the amount of, some asset or liability item. For example, a certified public accountant may be attesting to, among others, the fairness of the amount of the Accounts Receivable which will appear on the Balance Sheet as of a certain date. The company may have tens of thousands of customers' accounts, each with its own balance. To confirm the account balance of each customer in order to attest to the total dollar amount of Accounts Receivable would be both time consuming and costly. Instead, the accountant may select a specified number of accounts from the Accounts Receivable records and confirm this subset of the total number of accounts. This verification process helps the C.P.A. to draw conclusions about the dollar amount of the total Accounts Receivable. The process of inferring a characteristic of a set of objects (accounts receivable) from a subset of the objects is called *sampling,* or statistical inference. The subset of the objects selected for analysis is called a *sample* and the total set of objects is called a *population.*

The selection of the subset of the objects to be included in the sample may be made in a variety of ways. If, however, the elements of the sample are to be

---

[8] We will be concerned in this presentation only with "large" sample theory, i.e., samples in which the referent distribution is the normal distribution. We will not be concerned with "small" sample theory and its requirements for the *t*-distribution. In other words, we will be assuming that the sample size is large enough so that $\hat{\sigma}_x$ may be substituted for σ_x in problems concerning interval estimates without any appreciable error.

representative of the population in question and not biased in any manner, then the selection must result in a *random sample*. A random sample is a sample whose elements have been selected in a random manner, i.e., by a selection process in which each element of the population has the same chance (probability) of being selected as any other element.

As an illustration of the sampling process consider the problem of the internal auditor who wants to test the dollar amount of Accounts Payable represented by 1,000 invoices. Having determined from reliability considerations that a sample of 30 of the invoices will be sufficient, he prepares to randomly select the 30 invoices.[9] The random selection of the sample invoices may be accomplished in either of two ways. First, and in the manner of a lottery, the internal auditor could utilize a Table of Random Numbers. Such tables are prepared by a number of government and private institutions and most statisics texts contain at least one page of these numbers. For our purposes here a partial list of 3-Digit Random Numbers generated by an I.B.M. 7090 Computer is shown below. Three digit numbers can range from 000 to 999 and, hence, encompass 1000 such numbers. These random numbers are independent of one another and each number in the range has the same probability of

Table of Random Numbers					
075	086	622	133	592	755
416	969	823	938	714	916
990	394	450	628	223	045
595	034	798	551	128	864
879	347	554	022	937	427

appearing as any other number in the range. These two properties of random numbers permit them to be placed in a one-to-one correspondence with each element of the set of objects from which the sample is to be drawn. The result of the selection will be a random sample.

For example, if we start with the first column we would select the random number 075. This would tell us to select the 75th invoice for inclusion in the sample. The second random number chosen would be 416 which would tell us to select the 416th invoice. Continuing in this manner we would choose 427 as the thirtieth random number. This choice would tell us to select the 427th invoice to complete the selection of thirty invoices for the sample.

The second method of selecting the 30 invoices to be included in the sample is called *systematic sampling* and involves selecting every n^{th} invoice after a random start. For our illustration this would mean selecting every 33rd invoice

---

[9] It is beyond the scope of this elementary treatment of sampling methods to discuss the statistical concept of reliability and its relationship to sample size. Suffice it to state that the precision, or reliability, of an estimate increases as the sample size increases and vice versa. It is assumed in this example that the invoices are filed in ledger books or file drawers in such a manner as to make meaningful a natural ordering—1, 2, 3, . . . , 1000.

after the first invoice has been selected by a random start, i.e., by selecting a 2-digit random number less than or equal to 43.[10] Thus, and by using the Table of Random Numbers noted above, the first invoice to be selected for the sample would be the seventh since the first two digits of the first random number in the first column is 07.[11] The second invoice to be selected would be the $(7 + 33) = 40$th; the third would be the $(40 + 33) = 73$rd. The last invoice to be selected would be the $[7 + 29(33)] = 964$th.

Assuming that the auditor selects his sample of 30 invoices by the first method described above, he could abstract the relevant information from each invoice and display it as in the first four columns of Exhibit 19–6, page 584.

Having drawn the sample of 30 invoices it is possible to compute certain *sample statistics* which are descriptive of the sample of invoices. Among the more useful sample statistics are the sample mean, $\bar{X}$, which is a measure of central tendency of the sample data and the sample standard deviation, s, which is a measure of the variability of the sample data. The sample mean is defined as

$$\bar{X} = \frac{\sum_{i=1}^{n} X_i}{n}$$

where X_i is the value of the ith item in the sample, and n is the sample size.

For the invoice data,

$$\bar{X} = \frac{\sum_{i=1}^{30} X_i}{30} = \frac{\$2{,}095.55}{30} = \$69.85$$

The sample standard deviation is defined to be

$$s = \sqrt{\frac{\sum_{i=1}^{n} (X_i - \bar{X})^2}{n}}$$

which, for the invoice data, is computed as follows:[12]

---

[10] The interval between successive choices will be $1000 \div 30 = 33$, to the nearest integer. If we let $I =$ the number of the first invoice chosen, then $I + 29(33) \leq 1000$, so that $I \leq 43$.

[11] We will not be concerned here with the variety of ways in which a Table of Random Numbers can be read to yield a random sequence of numbers appropriate to a specific problem. The interested reader is referred to any elementary treatment on the subject of *Simulation* for such a discussion.

[12] We will be concerned here only with infinite populations or with finite populations in which the size of the sample is small relative to the size of the population, say $n \leq 0.05N$, where $n =$ sample size and $N =$ population size. This will make it unnecessary to discuss the *finite population correction factor*.

$$s = \sqrt{\frac{\sum_{i=1}^{30}(X_i - \bar{X})^2}{30}} = \sqrt{\frac{\$18{,}169.00}{30}}$$

$$s = \$24.61$$

EXHIBIT 19-6

Data Abstracted From a Random Sample of 30 Invoices of the Accounts Payable Records Enjay Company—January 19, 1972

Sample item number	Invoice selected	Invoice number	Invoice amount X_i	$X_i - \bar{X}$	$(X_i - \bar{X})^2$
1	75th	(Vendor's	$ 52.77	$-17.08	291.73
2	416th	name and	75.21	5.36	28.73
3	990th	Invoice	104.04	34.19	1168.96
4	595th	Number	61.29	− 8.56	73.27
5	879th	could be	10.41	−59.44	3533.11
6	86th	recorded	30.33	−39.52	1561.83
7	969th	here)	26.95	−42.90	1840.41
8	394th		80.95	11.10	123.21
9	34th		79.99	10.14	102.82
10	347th		101.13	31.28	978.44
11	622nd		90.00	20.15	406.02
12	823rd		77.17	7.32	53.58
13	450th		52.22	−17.63	310.82
14	798th		92.50	22.65	513.02
15	554th		100.50	30.65	939.42
16	133rd		99.00	29.15	849.72
17	938th		39.85	−30.00	900.00
18	628th		42.33	−27.52	757.35
19	551st		57.91	−11.94	142.56
20	22nd		41.30	−28.55	815.10
21	592nd		69.96	0.11	0.01
22	714th		70.91	1.06	1.12
23	223rd		90.81	20.96	439.32
24	128th		87.43	17.58	309.06
25	937th		84.53	14.68	215.50
26	755th		90.20	20.35	414.12
27	916th		89.33	19.48	379.47
28	45th		79.97	10.12	102.41
29	864th		76.31	6.46	41.73
30	427th		40.25	−29.60	876.16
			$2,095.55		18,169.00

[CH. 19] MATHEMATICAL AND STATISTICAL TECHNIQUES 585

Since our interest in these sample statistics arises only because of their usefulness in helping us to infer the values of the *population parameters* we must explore briefly the relationship between the chosen sample statistics and their counterparts in the population of invoices—the population mean and the population standard deviation.

It can be shown that the sample mean, $\overline{X}$, is an unbiased estimator of the population mean, μ. Thus, we can conclude that the average dollar amount of the 1000 invoices is $69.85. This is a point estimate and is the best single estimate that can be given for μ. It can also be shown that the sample standard deviation, s, is a biased estimator of σ, the population standard deviation. This bias can be removed, however, by multiplying the sample standard deviation by the factor

$$\sqrt{\frac{n}{n-1}}$$

Apply this bias correcting factor to our data leads to an unbiased estimate of σ given by[13]

$$\hat{\sigma}_X = s\sqrt{\frac{n}{n-1}} = \$24.61\sqrt{\frac{30}{30-1}}$$
$$\hat{\sigma}_X = \$24.61\,(1.017) = \$25.03$$

We can summarize our knowledge about the population of 1000 invoices at this point by stating that our best estimate of the average invoice dollar amount μ is $68.85 and an estimate of the variability of the invoice dollar values as measured by the standard deviation, $\hat{\sigma}_X$, is $25.03. Both of these estimates are unbiased. We do not have any knowledge *from the sample* of the shape of the distribution of invoice values. We do know, however, from the Central Limit Theorem of statistics that the distribution of sample means, $\overline{X}$'s, will approach a normal distribution as the sample size n increases regardless of the population distribution and will be exactly a normal distribution if the underlying population distribution happens to be normal. To understand this, it is necessary to reflect on the fact that our sample of 30 invoices represents only one out of a large number of possible samples, each of size 30, which could be drawn from the 1000 invoices.[14] We would not expect the sample means calculated for each one of these samples to be identical but would expect some variability. A fre-

---

[13] As the reader will have noticed, the magnitude of the correction factor decreases as the sample size n increases. It has become convention to disregard the correction factor for samples of size $n > 30$. The *carat* ^ is frequently used by statisticians to indicate "estimate" and the subscript, in this case X, is used to indicate the random variable to which the estimate applies.

[14] The total number of different samples that can be drawn is given by $_{1000}C_{30}$ which can be evaluated as 2.43×10^{57} samples. This number, if written out, would consist of the digits 243 followed by 55 zeros.

quency distribution of a large number of sample means, all with $n = 30$, would tend to appear as follows.

EXHIBIT 19–7

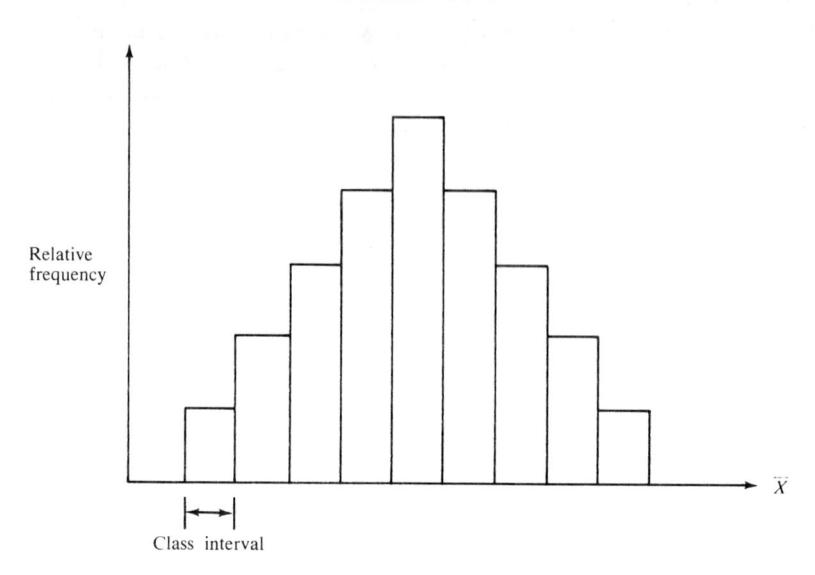

As we would increase the number of samples and decrease the size of the class intervals the frequency distribution would approach a continuous distribution called a normal distribution which would appear as follows and with the indicated parameters:

EXHIBIT 19–8

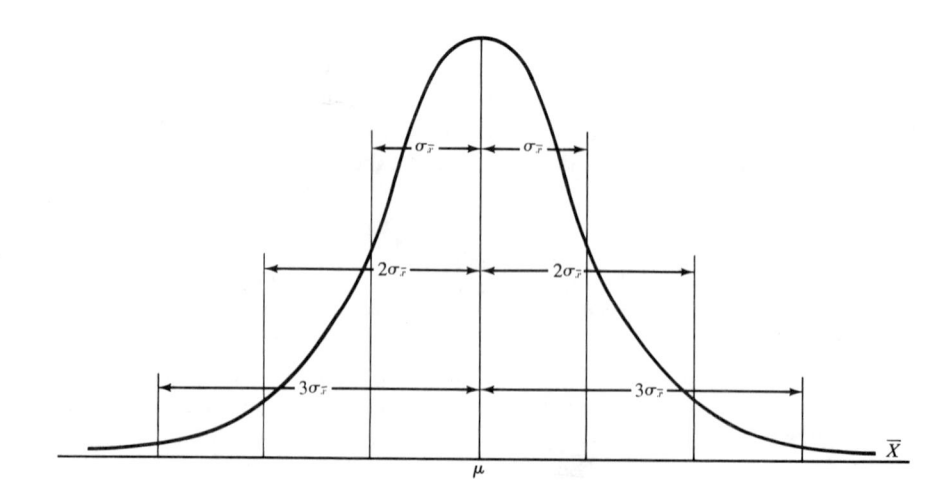

[CH. 19]   MATHEMATICAL AND STATISTICAL TECHNIQUES   587

The new parameter, $\sigma_{\bar{X}}$, is the standard deviation of the distribution of sample means. It is frequently referred to as the *standard error of the mean* and is related to the population standard deviation and the sample size by the expression

$$\sigma_{\bar{X}} = \frac{\sigma_X}{\sqrt{n}}$$

Since we have determined unbiased estimators of μ and σ_X from our single sample we can translate the general normal distribution given in Exhibit 19–8 into the specific normal distribution shown in Exhibit 19–9.

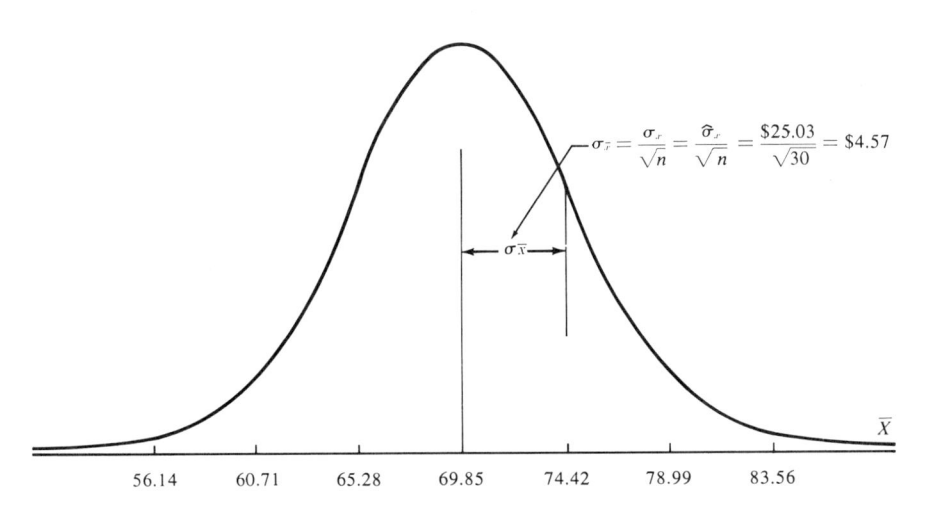

EXHIBIT 19–9

$$\sigma_{\bar{x}} = \frac{\sigma_x}{\sqrt{n}} = \frac{\hat{\sigma}_x}{\sqrt{n}} = \frac{\$25.03}{\sqrt{30}} = \$4.57$$

56.14   60.71   65.28   69.85   74.42   78.99   83.56

Now, statistical theory tells us that for a normally distributed random variable X

1. 68.27 percent of all of the values of the random variable are included in the interval between $\mu \pm \sigma_X$.
2. 95.45 percent of all of the values of the random variable are included in the interval between $\mu \pm 2\sigma_X$.
3. 99.73 percent of all of the values of the random variable are included in the interval between $\mu \pm 3\sigma_X$.

Thus, for example, we can state for our random variable $\bar{X}$ that 68.27 percent of all possible values for $\bar{X}$ will lie in the interval given by $\$69.85 \pm \$4.57$ or between $\$65.28$ and $\$74.42$. Since μ, the population mean, is a constant, we can restate this fact in the following manner: if 10,000 samples, each of size $n = 30$, are drawn from the population of 1000 invoices, then 6,827 of the intervals determined by $\bar{X} \pm \sigma_{\bar{X}}$ will include the population mean μ. In statistical terminology this fact is expressed by stating that the probability that μ is included in the interval $\bar{X} \pm \sigma_{\bar{X}}$ equals 0.6827, or

$$\Pr[\bar{X} - \sigma_{\bar{X}} \leqslant \mu \leqslant \bar{X} + \sigma_{\bar{X}}] = 0.6827$$
$$\Pr[\$65.28 \leqslant \mu \leqslant \$74.42] = 0.6827$$

The inclusive interval $65.28 to $74.42 is called a *confidence interval*. The end points of the confidence interval, $65.28 and $74.42, are called the 68.27 percent *confidence limits*. The probability, 0.6827, expressed as a percentage, 68.27%, is termed the *confidence level*. The coefficient of the standard deviation term in the expression of the confidence interval—$\bar{X} \pm \sigma_{\bar{X}}$, $\bar{X} \pm 2\sigma_{\bar{X}}$, $\bar{X} \pm 3\sigma_{\bar{X}}$—is called the *confidence coefficient*. Statisticians do not ordinarily employ integer confidence coefficients but, instead, use confidence coefficients which yield a 90 percent, 95 percent, or 99 percent confidence level. Thus, they have determined that:

$\pm 1.645 \sigma_{\bar{X}}$ yields a 90 percent confidence level
$\pm 1.96\ \sigma_{\bar{X}}$ yields a 95 percent confidence level
$\pm 2.58\ \sigma_{\bar{X}}$ yields a 99 percent confidence level

For our example, using a 95 percent confidence level, we would have

$$\Pr[\bar{X} - 1.96\ \sigma_{\bar{X}} \leqslant \mu \leqslant \bar{X} + 1.96\ \sigma_{\bar{X}}] = 0.95$$
$$\Pr[\$69.85 - 1.96\ (\$4.57) \leqslant \mu \leqslant \$69.85 + 1.96\ (\$4.57)] = 0.95$$
$$\Pr[\$69.85 - \$8.96 \leqslant \mu \leqslant \$69.85 + \$8.96] = 0.95$$
$$\Pr[\$60.89 \leqslant \mu \leqslant \$78.81] = 0.95$$

We are 95 percent confident that the mean value of our 1000 invoices lies between $60.89 and $78.81. If this interval is determined to be too large for the desired 95 percent confidence level then it may be reduced, but at the expense of increasing the sample size n. That this is so may be easily proven by recalling the definition of $\sigma_{\bar{X}}$:

$$\sigma_{\bar{X}} = \frac{\sigma_X}{\sqrt{n}}$$

For example, if it is desired that the 95 percent confidence interval be constrained to be the interval given by $\bar{X} \pm 0.05\bar{X}$, then

$$1.96\ \sigma_{\bar{X}} = 0.05\bar{X}$$
$$= 0.05\ (\$69.85)$$
$$= \$3.4925$$
$$\sigma_{\bar{X}} = \$3.4925 \div 1.96 = 1.782$$

but

$$\sigma_{\bar{X}} = \frac{\sigma_X}{\sqrt{n}} = \frac{\hat{\sigma}_X}{\sqrt{n}} = \frac{25.03}{\sqrt{n}}$$
$$1.782 = \frac{25.03}{\sqrt{n}}$$
$$\sqrt{n} = \frac{25.03}{1.782} = 14$$
$$n = 196 \text{ invoices}$$

An additional $(196 - 30) = 166$ invoices would have to be randomly selected from the population of 1000 invoices in order to satisfy the constraint on the size of the confidence interval.

The preceding analysis can be extended to provide a point estimate and a confidence interval for the total dollar amount of the 1000 invoices. For example, it would seem reasonable that the best estimate of the population total dollar amount would be given by

$$\hat{T} = N\bar{X}$$

where $\hat{T}$ = estimated population total dollar amount
N = the total number of invoices
$\bar{X}$ = sample mean dollar amount of an invoice so that

$$\hat{T} = 1000\,(\$69.85)$$
$$= \$69{,}850 \text{ for our example}$$

In a similar manner a confidence interval can be determined for this estimated population total dollar amount from the relationship

$$\hat{\sigma}_T = N\,\sigma_{\bar{x}}$$
$$= \frac{N\,\sigma_x}{\sqrt{n}}$$

where $\hat{\sigma}_T$ = estimated standard error, or standard deviation, of the estimated population total dollar amount

$\sigma_{\bar{x}}$ = standard error of the distribution of sample mean dollar amounts

$\hat{\sigma}_x$ = estimate of the standard deviation of the population of invoice dollar amounts

n = sample size, so that

$$\hat{\sigma}_T = \frac{1000\,(\$25.03)}{\sqrt{30}}$$
$$= 1000\,(\$4.57)$$
$$= \$4{,}570$$

For a 95 percent confidence interval of the population total we would have

Pr $[\hat{T} - 1.96\,\hat{\sigma}_T \leqslant T \leqslant \hat{T} + 1.96\,\hat{\sigma}_T] = 0.95$
Pr $[\$69{,}850 - 1.96\,(\$4{,}570) \leqslant T \leqslant \$69{,}850 + 1.96\,(\$4{,}570)] = 0.95$
Pr $[\$69{,}850 - \$8957.20 \leqslant T \leqslant \$69{,}850 + \$8957.20] = 0.95$
Pr $[\$60{,}893 \leqslant T \leqslant \$78{,}807] = 0.95$

It can be stated, once again, that if this interval is too large it can be reduced by increasing the sample size n. The investigator must balance the gain in precision against the increased costs of selecting and working with a larger sample size. Carried to its logical conclusion it would seem that we should include the population of invoices in our sample if we are to achieve the minimum, i.e., zero, confidence interval. This course of action is not only time consuming, hence costly, but is no guarantee of the true total dollar amount of the population of invoices. How many times has the reader added up a long list of numbers several times and gotten a different answer each time?

It must be emphasized that this description of statistical sampling is only intended to introduce the reader to the most basic concepts employed by the statistician. Statistics, generally, and sampling techniques in particular, are finding wide applicability in accounting and financial fields. Individuals contemplating a career in these professional fields are well advised to extend their understanding of statistics so as to enhance their professional development.

CONTROL CHART FOR VARIABLES

A logical extension of the sampling concepts presented in the preceding section and an excellent example of a technique developed for one functional field, quality control, having spin-off potential in the accounting–finance field is provided by the technique of Control Charts for Variables. Before proceeding with the discussion of control charts, however, it will be helpful to focus first on the concept and characteristics of a *system*.

A *system* may be defined as a set of interrelated components designed to accomplish some end. Most of the systems that we come into contact with in our culture are man-machine systems and vary in complexity from systems containing a very few components to those which consist of thousands of components. Basic systems become components of larger systems and these, in turn, become components of still larger systems, and so on without end. For example:

System	is a component of this	System
Cost Clerk	⟶	Cost Section
Cost Section	⟶	Accounting Department
Accounting Department	⟶	Plant No. 1, ABC Corp.
Plant No. 1, ABC Corp.	⟶	ABC Corporation
ABC Corporation	⟶	XYZ Industry
XYZ Industry	⟶	American Economy
and so on.		

Whether a set of related components is studied as a system in its own right or as one component of a larger system depends upon the objectives of the study. Furthermore, every system affects, and is affected by, the environment in which it functions. Every system transforms a mixture of inputs into outputs with the outputs of one system becoming the inputs to some other system. Our cost clerk system might input such factors as human time and skills, equipment consisting of desk, chair, calculator, files, electric power, etc., miscellaneous supplies of paper, pencils, forms and, of course, various production and related data. The outputs of this same system would be various cost reports and special studies. Now it is a feature of these systems that their output, as measured by certain measurable characteristics, is not constant but variable. For example, the number of source documents processed by the cost clerk (output) is not a constant per unit time but a variable. The value that this variable will take on is a func-

[CH. 19] MATHEMATICAL AND STATISTICAL TECHNIQUES 591

tion of the level and characteristics of the inputs to the system which exist at any particular time, e.g., motivation and quality of source documents. We tolerate certain variations in output characteristics because we recognize and accept as given certain variabilities in the inputs as reflecting constraints imposed by technology, economics, state of the art, etc. Such variation is termed *stable variation* and is considered to be the resultant of the operation of a stable system of chance causes. Identification of the stable variation in a system is desirable because it allows management to expend a minimal amount of attention on a system whose output characteristics fall within the bounds determined by stable variation. It may happen, however, that there will be a greater than expected variation in some output characteristic due to an assignable cause of variation which is foreign to the normal operation of the system, e.g., the cost clerk's calculator may fail; and if a replacement machine is not available, then the output characteristic "number of source documents processed per day" may show a significant decline until the calculator is repaired and operable again. These assignable causes of variation can generally be found and corrected. It is to such tasks that management must direct its attention if it is to adequately perform the control function of management. A simple example will help to make these concepts clear and will demonstrate the simplicity of the technique of constructing control charts.

Assume that a company wants to exercise greater control over the expense accounts of its salesmen. The company has determined that all ten of its salesmen operate in similar environments and under the same policy constraints and conditions. Accordingly, the ten salesmen can be treated as one system as far as expense accounts are concerned. Data have been gathered on expense accounts for the ten salesmen for a period of one week and is shown below.

Salesman number	Daily reported expenses					Total weekly expense	Mean daily expense	Range
	Mon.	Tues.	Weds.	Thurs.	Fri.			
1	$10.70	$11.33	$10.97	$ 8.56	$12.73	$54.29	$10.858	$4.17
2	9.63	10.42	13.23	12.57	9.91	55.76	11.152	3.60
3	13.80	11.27	9.38	10.69	11.73	56.87	11.374	4.42
4	11.45	12.21	9.27	8.13	9.25	50.31	10.062	4.08
5	8.72	10.31	9.98	10.32	8.69	48.02	9.604	1.63
6	12.35	11.71	11.75	10.53	9.75	56.09	11.218	2.60
7	10.98	11.16	10.77	10.93	9.98	53.82	10.764	1.18
8	16.15	14.37	17.21	10.18	16.23	74.14	14.828	7.03
9	14.42	12.10	11.73	10.19	11.21	59.65	11.930	4.23
10	15.90	10.13	14.75	9.18	8.17	58.13	11.626	7.73
					Totals	$567.08	$113.416	$40.67

A legitimate question to ask of this data would be "does it represent one of the measurable outputs of a stable system?" This question may be answered in the following manner.

If the assumption that the daily expense data is being generated by ten components of a single system is tenable then, certainly, the Mean Daily Expense for all salesmen is the best point estimate of daily expense. The mean daily expense for all salesmen may be calculated in either of two ways of which only one is demonstrated here, *viz:*

$$\bar{\bar{X}} = \frac{\sum_{i=1}^{m} \bar{X}_i}{m}$$

where $\bar{\bar{X}}$ = Grand Mean Daily Expense, i.e., mean daily expense for all salesmen

$\bar{X}_i$ = Mean Daily Expense of the ith Salesman, $i = 1, 2, 3, \ldots, m$, and

m = number of salesmen

$$\bar{\bar{X}} = \frac{\$113.416}{10} = \$11.342$$

Considering the Mean Daily Expense for each salesman as being a sample mean computed for a sample size of $n = 5$ days now allows us to introduce the Central Limit Theorem again. As the reader will recall, this theorem states that the distribution of sample means will approach a normal distribution as the sample size n increases, regardless of the shape of the underlying population distribution. The distribution of sample means has a mean which is equal to the population mean μ and a standard deviation, or standard error of the mean $\sigma_{\bar{x}}$ equal to the standard deviation σ_x of the population divided by the square root of the sample size n. Our best estimate of μ is $\bar{\bar{X}}$, the grand mean. At this point, therefore, our information about the distribution of sample means can be portrayed as in Exhibit 19–10.

EXHIBIT 19–10

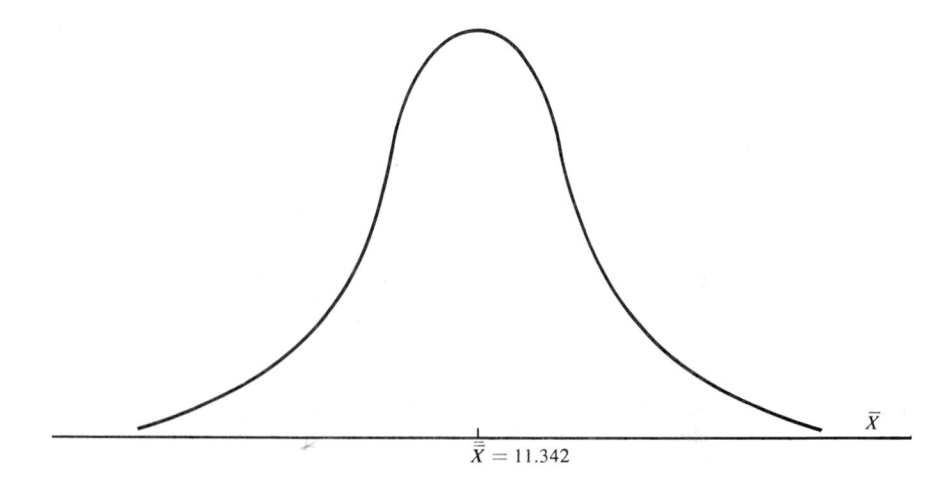

[CH. 19] MATHEMATICAL AND STATISTICAL TECHNIQUES 593

Can we calculate $\sigma_{\bar{x}}$ and complete our description of this normal distribution? The answer, of course, is yes, and a variety of methods exist for performing the calculation. The first method that might come to mind would be the following:[15]

$$\sigma_{\bar{x}} = \sqrt{\frac{\sum_{i=1}^{m}(\bar{X}_i - \bar{\bar{X}})^2}{m}}$$

where the notation is the same as defined previously.

Although this method would be correct, a much simpler method for calculating $\sigma_{\bar{x}}$ has been developed by the statistician which involves working with a new measure of variability, *the range*. The range is defined to be

$$R = X_{max} - X_{min}$$

so that, for the data for salesman number 1 of our example,

$$R_1 = \$12.73 - \$8.56$$
$$= \$4.17$$

Similarly for the other salesmen the ranges have been calculated and are shown in the last column of the table on page 591. It has been determined by advanced statistical methods that when samples of small size, $n \leq 25$, are drawn from a known, normal population that there exists a relationship between $\sigma_{\bar{x}}$ and $\bar{R}$ which can be expressed as

$$3\ \sigma_{\bar{x}} = A_2 \bar{R},$$

where $A_2 = $ a constant factor which depends on the sample size n

$$\bar{R} = \frac{\sum_{i=1}^{m} R_i}{m}$$

$R_i = $ the range of the ith sample (salesman)

The coefficient, 3, of $\sigma_{\bar{x}}$ in this expression is the confidence coefficient which is generally used in quality control applications in this country. A partial listing of A_2 values is shown in the table on page 594.

For the data of our example,

$$\bar{R} = \frac{\$40.67}{10} = \$4.067$$

For $n = 5$, $A_2 = 0.577$

$$3\ \sigma_{\bar{x}} = 0.577\ (\$4.067) = \$2.347$$

This result may now be used to complete our pictorial representation of the distribution of sample means of daily expenses, as shown by Exhibit 19–11, page 594.

---

[15] It would not be correct to calculate $\sigma_{\bar{x}}$ by first calculating σ_x using all of the 50 bits of expense data since this method would mask the between-sample variation which a control chart for variables is designed to disclose.

Factor A_2 for Calculating Control Limits
for Control Charts for Averages.[16]

Sample size n	A_2	Sample size n	A_2
2	1.880	12	0.266
3	1.023	13	0.249
4	0.729	14	0.235
5	0.577	15	0.223
6	0.483	16	0.212
7	0.419	17	0.203
8	0.373	18	0.194
9	0.337	19	0.187
10	0.308	20	0.180
11	0.285	21	0.173

EXHIBIT 19–11

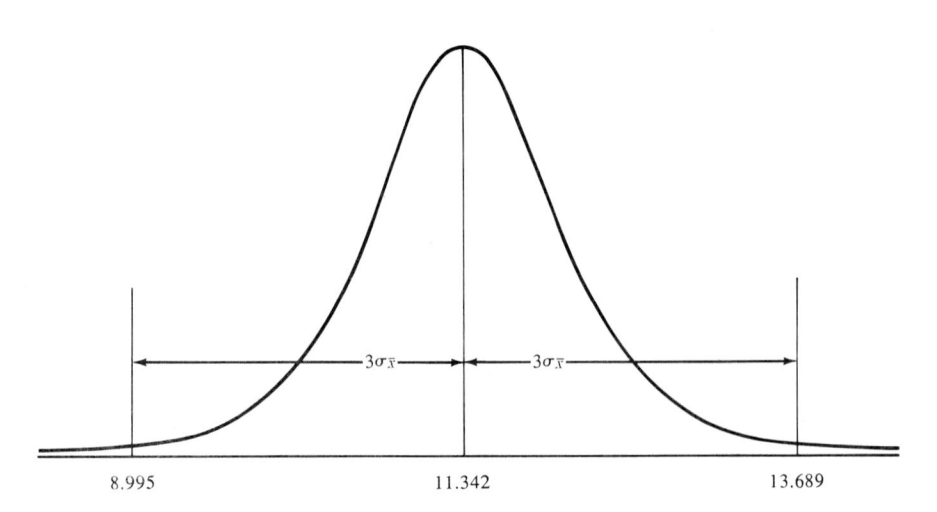

[Normal distribution curve with $3\sigma_{\bar{X}}$ marked on each side of center; x-axis values: 8.995, 11.342, 13.689]

A confidence coefficient of "3" means that 99.73 percent of the $\bar{X}$ values will fall within the confidence interval $8.995 to $13.689, inclusive, *provided that the system from which the samples are drawn remains stable*, i.e., maintains statistical stability.

A quality control chart for variables is easily constructed from the distribution of sample means by rotating the distribution 90° counter-clockwise and extending the marks indicating the confidence limits as shown in Exhibit 19–12.

---

[16] These values are reproduced with permission from Table B2 of the A.S.T.M. *Manual on Quality Control of Materials*, p. 115.

EXHIBIT 19-12

Control Chart for the Variable "Mean Daily Reported Expenses"

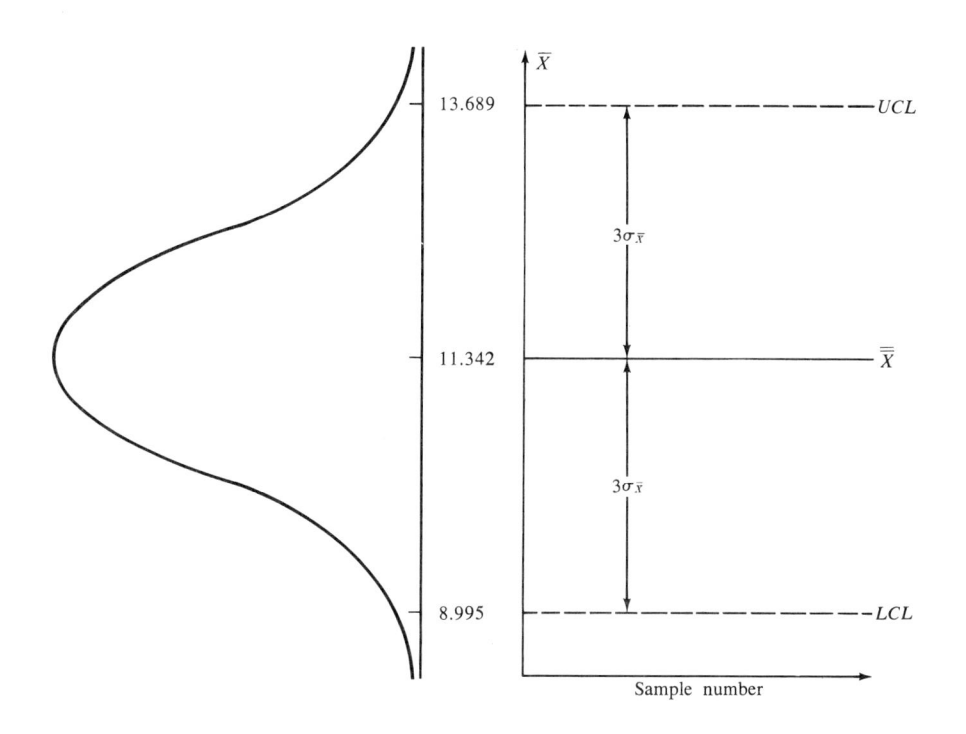

```
                          ↑ X̄
        13.689  |-------- · ----------- UCL
                          ↑
                          |
                         3σ_x̄
                          |
                          ↓
        11.342  |------------------------ X̿
                          ↑
                          |
                         3σ_x̄
                          |
                          ↓
         8.995  |-------- · ----------- LCL
                          └─────────────→
                              Sample number
```

The upper confidence limit, $13.689, is called the *Upper Control Limit, UCL,* in quality control applications. Similarly, the lower confidence limit, $8.995, is called the *Lower Control Limit, LCL.* The measure of central tendency, $\overline{\overline{X}}$, is in accord with statistical convention.

After constructing the control chart, the mean daily expense for each salesman would be plotted on the control chart to see if all of the plotted points fall within the control lines. If they do, the system is said to exhibit statistical stability and the chart can be used to control the daily expenses of the salesmen in future weeks. If all of the plotted points do not fall within the control lines then the system exhibits an out-of-control situation and a search must be initiated to find an assignable cause(s) for the out-of-control points. There is, however, a very slight chance that no assignable cause(s) will be found because the system is still stable and has not changed. This is due to the fact that the use of a 3 confidence coefficient allows $(100.00 - 99.73) = 0.27\%$ of the sample means to fall outside of the control limits even though nothing has happened to change the system. Reduction of this probability of searching for assignable causes of variation when none exists may be achieved by selecting a larger confidence coefficient, but this implies less control because of the resulting wider confidence interval.[17] Plotting the Mean Daily Expense for each salesman on the control chart of Exhibit 19–12 will yield the results shown in Exhibit 19–13, page 597.

It is readily seen from this exhibit that the system was not in a state of statistical control for the week in question. Sample (Salesman) Number 8 had a mean daily expense, $14.828, which fell outside the Upper Control Limit of $13.689. Some effort should be expended to ascertain if an assignable cause(s) for this out-of-control point can be discovered and corrective action initiated to prevent a reoccurrence. Regardless of whether or not an assignable cause(s) can be discovered, the control chart should be constructed with the data of sample number 8 eliminated from the calculations of $\bar{\bar{X}}$ and the control limits, *UCL* and *LCL*. The remaining nine sample points must then be plotted on this revised control chart. If all of the plotted points fall within the control limits, then it may be concluded that the reduced system exhibits the characteristics of a stable system; and the control chart may be used as a device for controlling the mean daily reported expenses of the salesmen. If all of the plotted points still do not fall within the control limits, then the process of looking for assignable causes of variation and recomputing limits must be repeated.[18] This iterative process for the illustrative example is left as an exercise for the reader (See problem 19–9).

Once the situation is reached in which all of the plotted points fall within the control limits the control chart is ready to be used as a control device for future reported expenses of the salesmen. As each week's expenses are reported, the Mean Daily Expense for each salesman is calculated and plotted on the control chart. Plotted points which fall within the control limits confirm the operation of a stable system. Plotted points which fall outside the control limits are indicators that the system may have changed and a search for assignable cause(s) should be initiated. Periodically, the values of $\bar{\bar{X}}$, *UCL,* and *LCL* should be recalculated to incorporate all of the data which has been plotted and found to be within control. This practice provides a better basis for estimating $\bar{\bar{X}}$ and $\bar{R}$ for samples of size $n = 5$ drawn from the underlying population.

It is proper to indicate at this point that control of a variable requires a minimum of two measures—a measure of central tendency and a measure of the variability. In our discussion of control charts we have been concerned with only the measure of central tendency, the so-called $\bar{X}$–chart. It is entirely possible for a Mean Daily Expense to fall within the control limits on the $\bar{X}$–chart but to exhibit such variability as to cast doubt on the conclusion that the system is stable. For example, consider the two cases shown on page 597.

---

[17] We will not discuss here the probability of plotted points falling within the control limits when the system has changed. The interested reader is referred to any standard Statistical Quality Control text.

[18] Too many iterations of the process with the resultant reduction in the number of sample points is an indication that the entire system is in need of study and standardization before any reasonable controls can be established. In the illustrative example two iterations would appear to represent the maximum amount of analysis warranted before such a conclusion is reached.

EXHIBIT 19–13
Control Chart for Mean Daily Reported Expenses

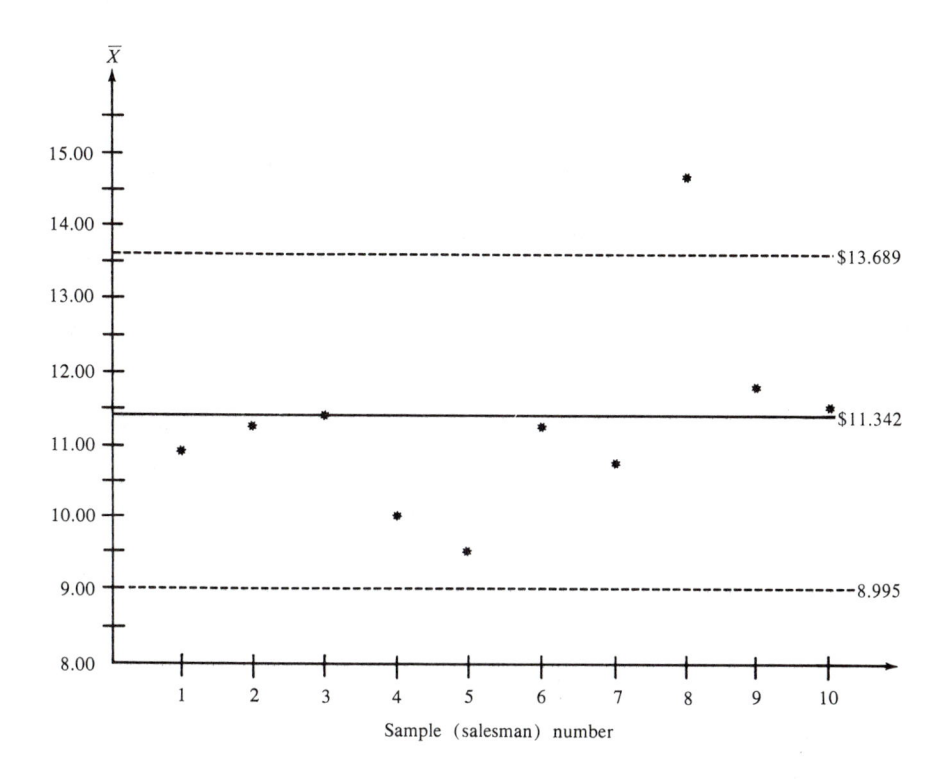

	Reported daily expenses	
Day	Salesman no. 1	Salesman no. 2
1	$11.15	$ 8.20
2	13.16	8.76
3	12.73	9.18
4	9.13	8.92
5	10.91	22.02
Total	$57.08	$57.08
$\bar{X}$	$11.416	$11.416
R	$ 4.03	$13.82

The mean $\bar{X}$ is identical for both salesmen but the range R for salesman number 2 is greater than three times the range for salesman number 1 and may be indicative of a change in the variability property of the system. Two control charts, an $\bar{X}$–chart and either a Range Chart or a Standard Deviation Chart, are required for adequate system control. The presentation of only the $\overline{X}$-chart in this section has been intended solely to illustrate the underlying philosophy of control charts, and the interested reader is referred to any standard text on statistical quality control for a complete exposition.

LINEAR PROGRAMMING[19]

It is characteristic of all organizations that they have limited resources which have to be allocated among a number of competing alternatives and in such a manner as to optimize, in some fashion, the objective of each organization. This is nothing more, in fact, than a restatement of the central problem of economics. The ubiquity of this allocation problem may be evidenced by reflecting upon the end points of a segment of the range of systems (organizations) faced with it. That is, the basic problem is the same for the individual—say, a student faced with the problem of allocating his available study time (resource) among the various courses in which he is enrolled (alternatives) so as to optimize his learning experience (objective)—and for the nation—whose government must allocate its revenue (resources) among a variety of domestic and foreign programs (alternatives) so as to optimize the general welfare (objective). The allocation problem is the same for the individual firm: allocate the existing scarce resources among the competing functions and product lines so as to maximize, say, long-run profits. In order to demonstrate the current solution technique which has been developed to solve this type of allocation problem we will use the following example:

The Ajax Manufacturing Company produces two products for the building industry, Product A and Product B. The accounting department has determined that each unit of Product A which is sold generates a profit of $3.00 and each unit of Product B a profit of $4.00. The manufacture of each unit of Product A requires five hours of machining time and five hours of painting time. Each unit of Product B requires eight hours of machining time and two hours of painting time. The company has available for total product production 40 hours of machining time and 20 hours of painting time per week. The allocation problem facing the company management is one of designing a feasible weekly production schedule which will maximize profits. That is, a weekly production schedule which can be realized within the limits of the hours available for production purposes. The essential facts of this example can be shown quite compactly in the following manner, where

---

[19] We will be concerned here only with graphical solutions to linear programming problems. This will restrict us to dealing with problems which have at most three unknowns, i.e., three-space, or-dimensions. It is the intent of this section to indicate only the kinds of problems which linear programming can help to solve and to illustrate a basic, though limited, solution technique. The more general algebraic solution technique, called the *Simplex*, will be found described in any elementary programming text.

[CH. 19]   MATHEMATICAL AND STATISTICAL TECHNIQUES   599

A = Number of units of Product A to be produced per week, and
B = Number of units of Product B to be produced per week.

Maximize: $\$3A + \$4B$ (Objective Function)

Subject to these constraints

$5A + 8B \leqslant 40$ (Machining Time Resource)
$5A + 2B \leqslant 20$ (Painting Time Resource)
$A, B \geqslant 0$ (Non-Negativity Restriction, the weekly production schedule cannot specify negative quantities of either product.)

The first constraint states that the total machining hours required for the weekly production schedule must not exceed the available machining capacity of 40 hours per week. Likewise, the second constraint states that the total painting hours required for the weekly production schedule must not exceed the available painting capacity of 20 hours per week. Both of these constraints must be satisfied simultaneously and in such a manner as to maximize the objective function, the weekly profit.

Since we are dealing with only two unknowns, A and B, in this problem, we can employ a graphical solution technique involving a two-dimensional coordinate system. In the cartesian coordinate system generally employed, this means that all solutions to this problem must lie in the plane of this page, as indicated in Exhibit 19–14. This total set of solutions is reduced by the third constraint, the non-negativity restriction noted above, which requires that both A and B have non-negative values. Accordingly, the feasible set of solutions is restricted to points in the first quadrant as shown in the exhibit.

EXHIBIT 19–14

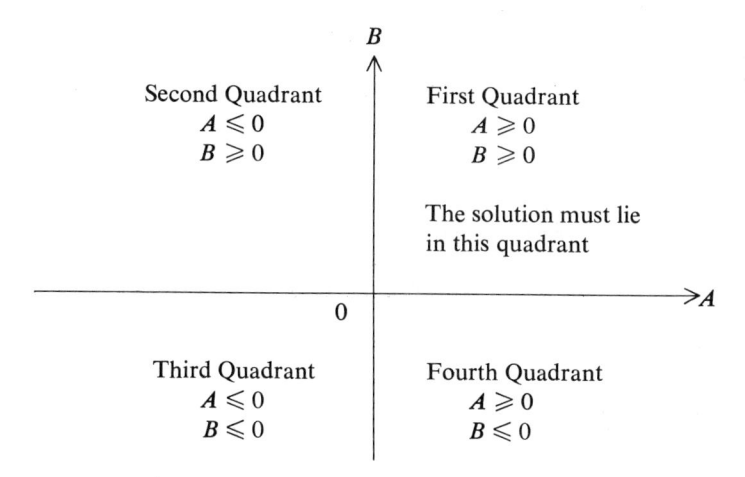

Second Quadrant $A \leqslant 0$ $B \geqslant 0$	First Quadrant $A \geqslant 0$ $B \geqslant 0$ The solution must lie in this quadrant
Third Quadrant $A \leqslant 0$ $B \leqslant 0$	Fourth Quadrant $A \geqslant 0$ $B \leqslant 0$

The first constraint, the Machining Time Constraint, can be plotted in the first quadrant by first considering it in its equation form, $5A + 8B = 40$. This is a linear equation, i.e., plots as a straight line, which requires only two points for its graph. Two easily determined points are obtained by letting each one of the unknowns, in turn, take on the value zero. That is, when $A = 0$, $B = 40 \div 8 = 5$; and when $B = 0$, $A = 40 \div 5 = 8$. Thus the two points are (0,5) and (8,0). These points and the line segment joining them are shown in Exhibit 19-15. All points on this line segment satisfy the equation $5A + 8B = 40$.

EXHIBIT 19-15
Graph of the Equation: $5A + 8B = 40$

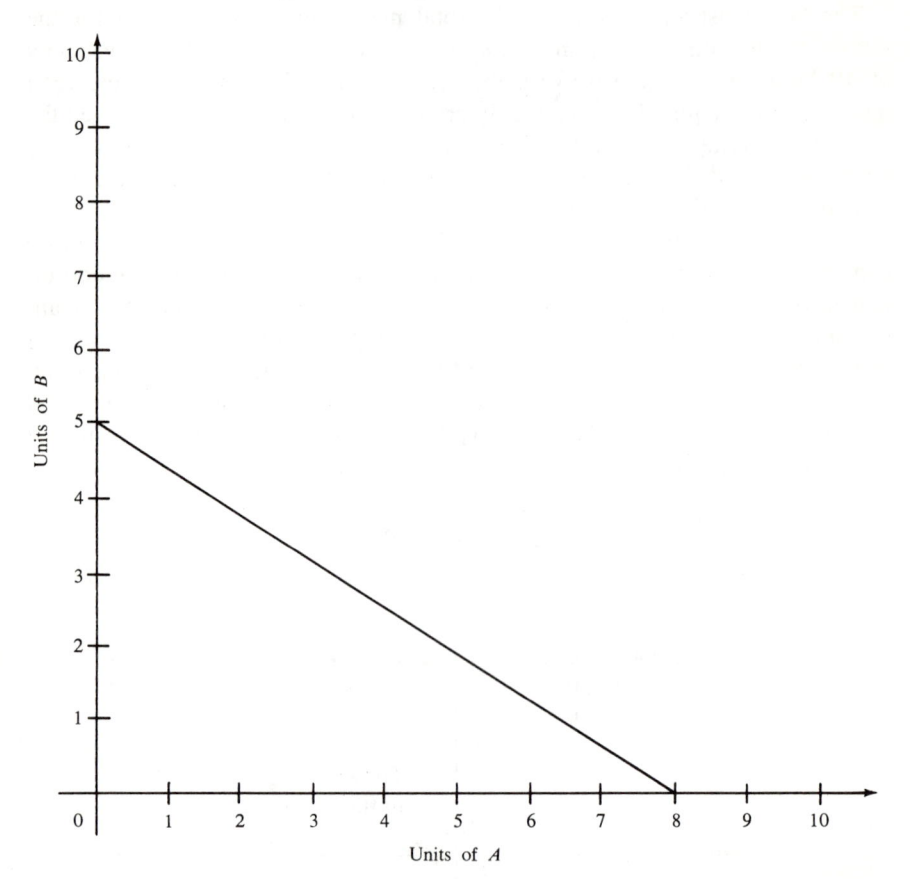

It must be remembered, however, that this first constraint is not strictly an equation but an inequality of the form $5A + 8B \leq 40$. We have considered only the equality condition of this inequality. How can we incorporate the "less than" condition of the inequality? The answer to this question is given by substituting the coordinates of several feasible points, i.e., points in the first quadrant and on each side of the line segment which satisfies the equation $5A + 8B = 40$. Consider, for example, the point with coordinates (0,0). If these coordi-

[CH. 19]   MATHEMATICAL AND STATISTICAL TECHNIQUES   601

nate values are substituted in the left-hand side of the inequality we will have

$$5(0) + 8(0) = 0$$

Since zero is less than 40 it appears that the point with coordinates (0,0) satisfies the inequality $5A + 8B \leq 40$ and must be included as a possible feasible solution to the inequality. Select another point, say the point given by the coordinates (4,2). Substitution of these coordinate values in the left-hand side of the inequality yields

$$5(4) + 8(2) = 20 + 16 = 36$$

Since 36 is less than 40 we conclude that this point (4,2) must also be included as a possible feasible solution to the inequality. What about the point with coordinates (8,4)? Substitution of these coordinate values yields

$$5(8) + 8(4) = 40 + 32 = 72$$

Since 72 is *not* less than 40 the point does not satisfy the inequality and cannot be included in the feasible set of solutions. A graphical portrayal of these trials is shown in Exhibit 19–16. Repeated trials with additional points will show that the only points which satisfy the inequality are those points which lie within the triangle XYZ or on its perimeter. The totality of all these points is called a *convex set*.

The convex set of feasible solutions which satisfies the second constraint, $5A + 2B \leq 20$, is determined in a similar manner. First, treating the inequality as an equation, $5A + 2B = 20$, and determining two points which satisfy this equation we learn that when $A = 0$, $B = 10$; and when $B = 0$, $A = 4$.

The line segment contained within the first quadrant and connecting these two points can now be drawn. The determination of the set of points which satisfies the constraint as a strict inequality is made as for Exhibit 19–16, below. The resulting convex set of feasible solutions is given by triangle KLM and its perimeter as shown in Exhibit 19–17.

The third constraint or restriction, $A, B \geq 0$, is, of course, satisfied by restricting the set of solutions to points contained in the first quadrant.

So far, we have treated the first two constraints as if they were separate problems. Actually, we must treat them simultaneously. That is, we must consider as possible solution points only those points which simultaneously satisfy both constraints. This will reduce the size of our convex region of feasible solutions to that shown in Exhibit 19–18, page 604.

There are an infinite number of feasible solution points in this convex set. Which one should we select? We should select that point in the convex set which will optimize our objective function, i.e., maximize the linear function $\$3A + \$4B$. This is accomplished in the following manner:

If the coordinates of any feasible solution point are substituted in the objective function, a specific value of profit, say P, will be determined. Therefore we may write in general terms $\$3A + \$4B = P$, a family of linear equations. Each member of this family of equations is strictly determined as soon as a value for

EXHIBIT 19–16

The Convex Set of Points Which Satsisfies the Inequality $5A + 8B \leqslant 40$

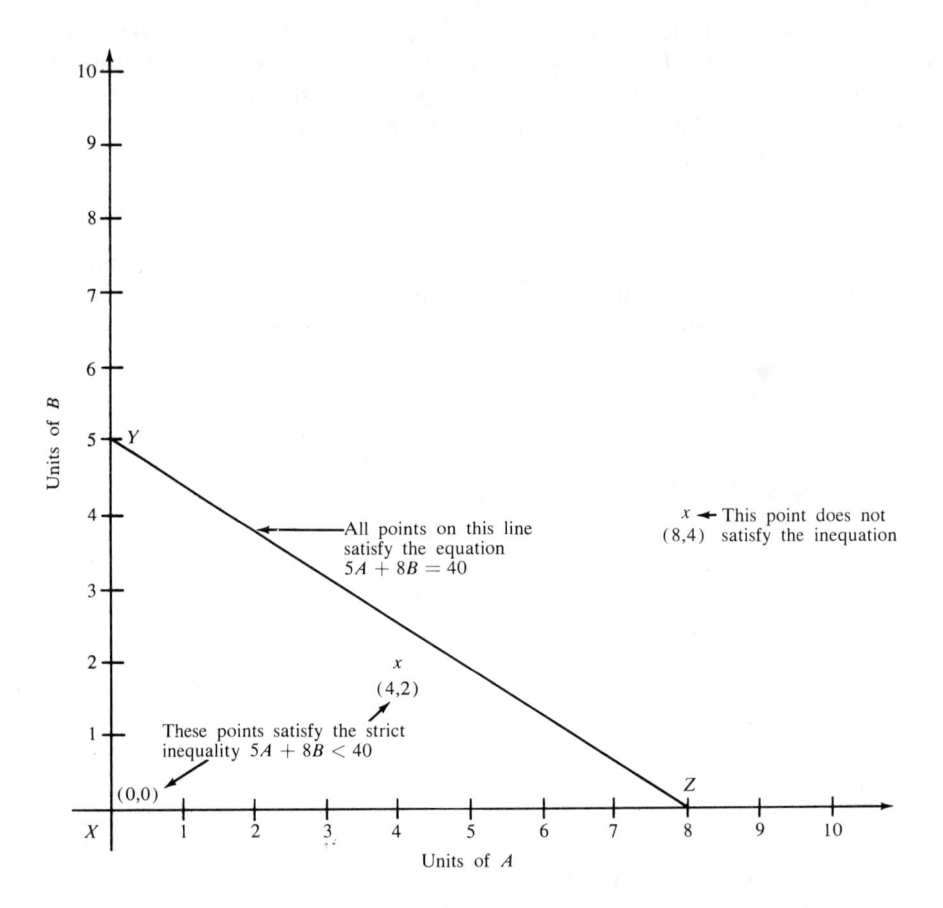

[Graph showing convex set with Units of B on y-axis (0-10) and Units of A on x-axis (0-10). Line from Y(0,5) to Z(8,0) representing $5A + 8B = 40$. Point (4,2) marked as satisfying strict inequality $5A + 8B < 40$. Point (8,4) marked as not satisfying the inequation. Origin labeled (0,0).]

Labels on graph:
- All points on this line satisfy the equation $5A + 8B = 40$
- $x \leftarrow$ This point does not (8,4) satisfy the inequation
- These points satisfy the strict inequality $5A + 8B < 40$

P is specified. We know that $P \geqslant 0$ since we have previously specified that both A and B must be non-negative. Let us specify a value for P of \$15 and see where the resulting line segment is positioned relative to the convex set of feasible solution points. The two points required to draw the line segment given by the equation $\$3A + \$4B = \$15$ are determined as previously: when $A = 0$, $B = 3\frac{3}{4}$; and when $B = 0$, $A = 5$. Any point on the portrayed line segment (see Exhibit 19–19), will yield values for A and B which will result in a profit of \$15. This constant value of \$15 for all points on this line segment is reflected in the name "isoprofit line." Furthermore, any point on the solid part of the portrayed line segment will lie within the convex set of feasible solutions and will satisfy the constraints. Since we are interested in maximizing profits, let us see what will happen to the position of the isoprofit line if we let P assume the value of \$30. The objective function will be expressed as $\$3A + \$4B = \$30$, and the line segment contained within the first quadrant can be determined by

[CH. 19] MATHEMATICAL AND STATISTICAL TECHNIQUES 603

EXHIBIT 19-17

The Convex Set of Points Which Satisfies the Inequality $5A + 2B \leqslant 20$

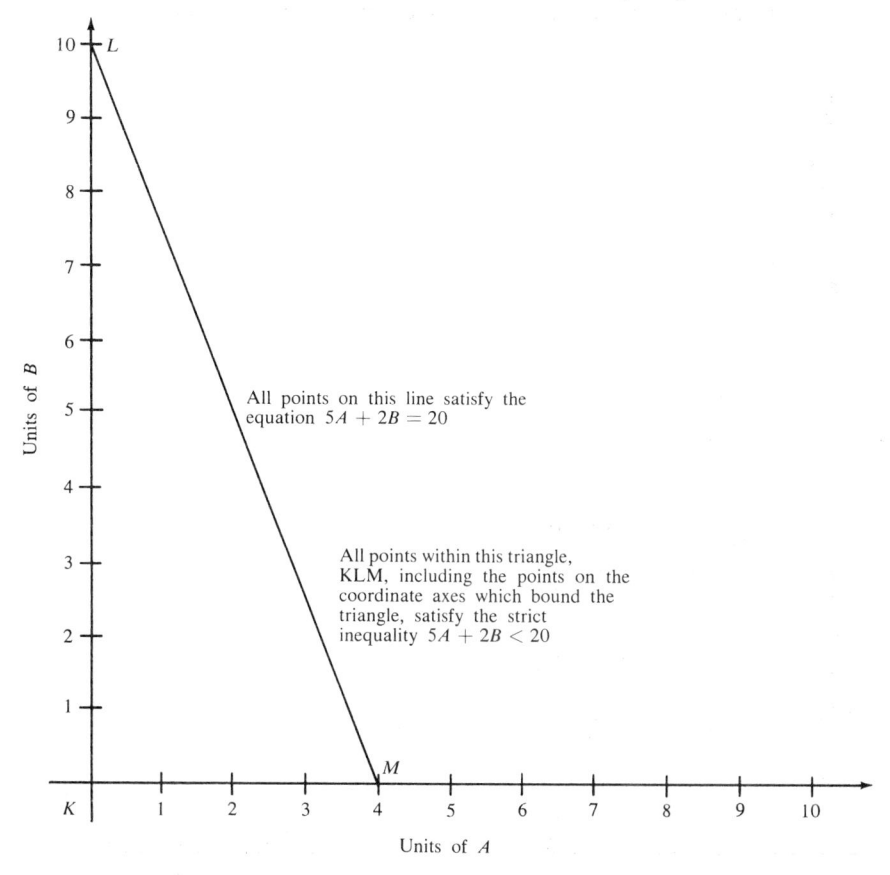

All points on this line satisfy the equation $5A + 2B = 20$

All points within this triangle, KLM, including the points on the coordinate axes which bound the triangle, satisfy the strict inequality $5A + 2B < 20$

two points as previously. For example, when $A = 0$, $B = 7\frac{1}{2}$; and when $B = 0$, $A = 10$.

Exhibit 19–20 shows that no segment of the isoprofit line for $P = \$30$ lies within or on the boundary line of the convex set of feasible solutions. Consequently, values for A and B which would yield a profit of $30 are not admissible. The isoprofit line for $P = \$30$ does yield two significant bits of information, however: first, for any two values of profit the isoprofit line segment for the larger profit is further removed from the origin of the coordinate axes than the isoprofit line segment corresponding to the smaller value of profit; second, for any given objective function the slopes of all possible isoprofit line segments are equal.[20] The first bit of information tells us that we will maximize profits

---

[20] The equality of slopes may be seen by writing the objective function in general slope-intercept form. Thus, $3A + 4B = P$, $4B = P - 3A$, $B = \frac{P}{4} - \frac{3}{4}A$. Regardless of the positive values assigned to P the resulting linear equations will all have a slope of $-3/4$. In other words, the objective function represents a family of parallel lines.

EXHIBIT 19-18

Convex Set of Feasible Solutions to the Ajax Manufacturing Company's Production Scheduling Problem

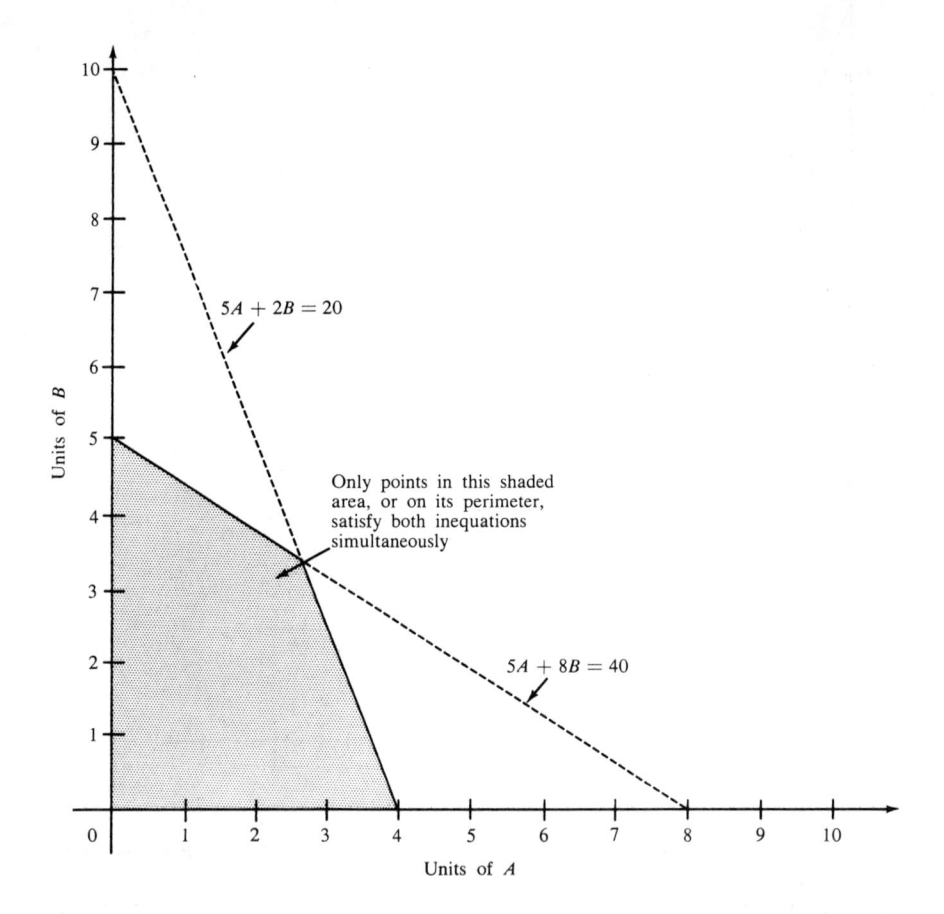

[Graph showing Units of B on y-axis (0-10) and Units of A on x-axis (0-10). Two dashed lines represent the constraints $5A + 2B = 20$ and $5A + 8B = 40$. The shaded feasible region is bounded by these lines and the axes. A note reads: "Only points in this shaded area, or on its perimeter, satisfy both inequations simultaneously"]

subject to the problem constraints if an isoprofit line is drawn as far from the origin as possible without leaving, or overshooting, the convex set of feasible solutions. The second bit of information tells us to draw this isoprofit line parallel to any convenient reference isoprofit line with the same slope. For our illustration the isoprofit line which maximizes the objective function is shown in Exhibit 19–21, on page 607. This graphical solution shows that the optimal value of the objective function is realized when $A = 2\frac{2}{3}$ units and $B = 3\frac{1}{3}$ units. For these weekly production figures the corresponding profit will be $\$3(2\frac{2}{3}) + \$4 (3\frac{1}{3}) = \$8.00 + \$13.33$, or $\$21.33$.

There is no other combination of weekly production rates which will yield as high a value for profit. If the Ajax management is dissatisfied with this rate of profit generation then it must take action to either relax the conditions rep-

EXHIBIT 19-19

Position of the Isoprofit Line for $P = \$15$ Relative to the Convex Set of Feasible Solutions

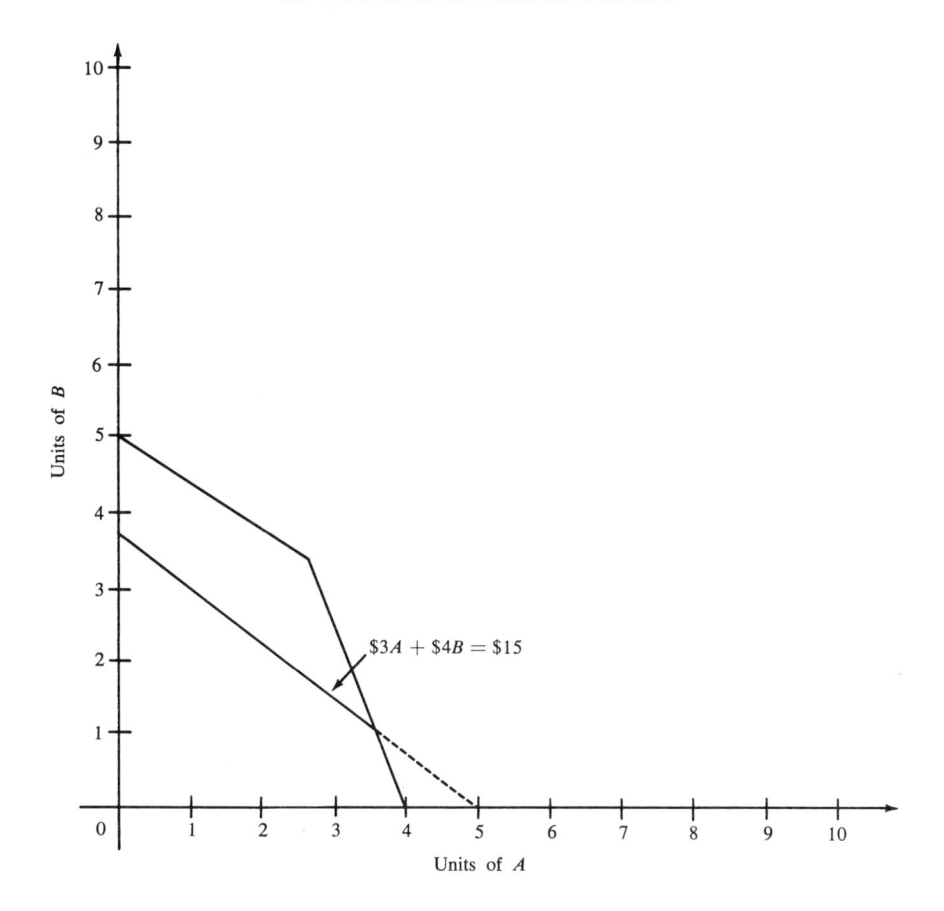

[Graph with Units of B on y-axis, Units of A on x-axis, showing line labeled $\$3A + \$4B = \$15$]

resented by the constraints, or change the parameters in the objective function, or both.[21]

With the illustration of Linear Programming (Exhibit 19–21) we end this exposition of some of the newer mathematical and statistical methods available to the accountant. The reader should be cautioned that these five examples have not exhibited all of the complexities involved in applying them to the typical problems faced in many organizations. In particular, they have (1) ignored the problems associated with data collection, (2) minimized the problems of establishing valid relationships between the variables of the model, and (3) de-

---

[21] The algebraic method for solving the generalized linear programming problem automatically provides information which is extremely valuable in the search for ways to modify the original model.

EXHIBIT 19-20

Position of the Isoprofit Lines
Relative to the Convex Set of Feasible Solutions

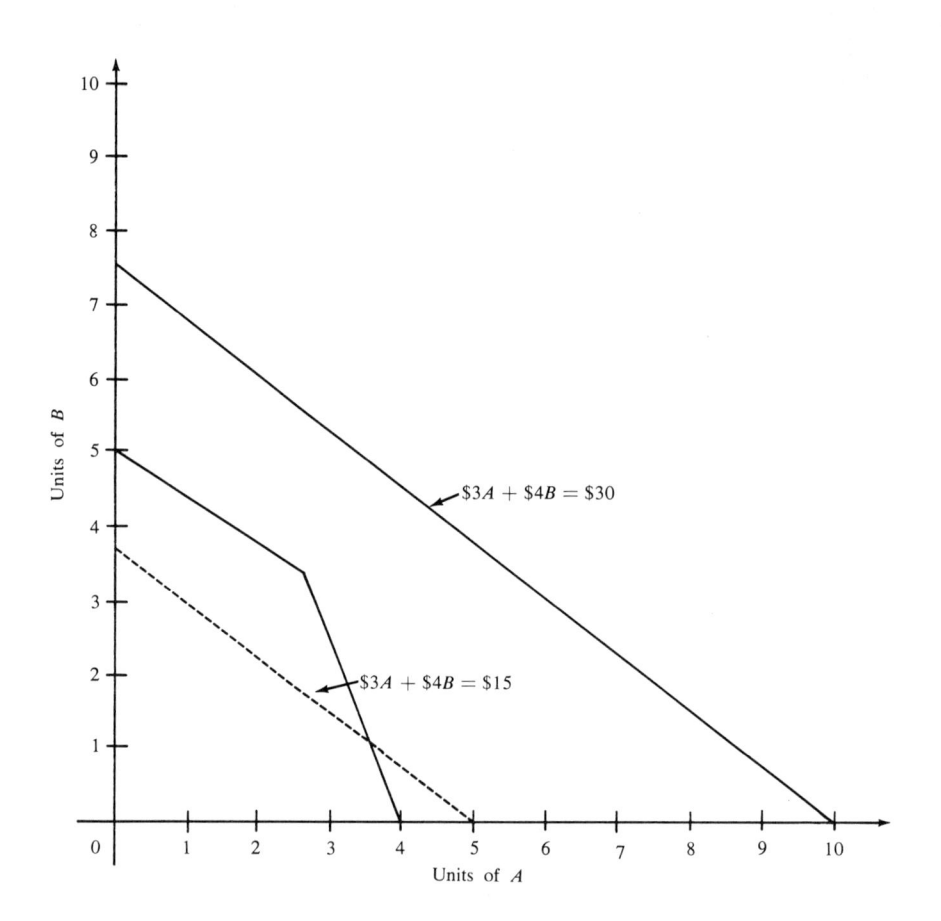

preciated the magnitude of the computational effort required to "solve the problem." Fortunately, the emphasis currently being given to computer-based management information systems and the computational speed of existing computer systems are operating to increase the tractability of (1) and (3), above. As for (2), modeling is still very much an art in which personal experience with the system to be modeled, an ability to reason from analogies, and a liberal sprinkling of sound judgment appear to be prime requisites for success.

EXHIBIT 19-21

Optimal Solution of the Ajax Manufacturing Company's Allocation Problem

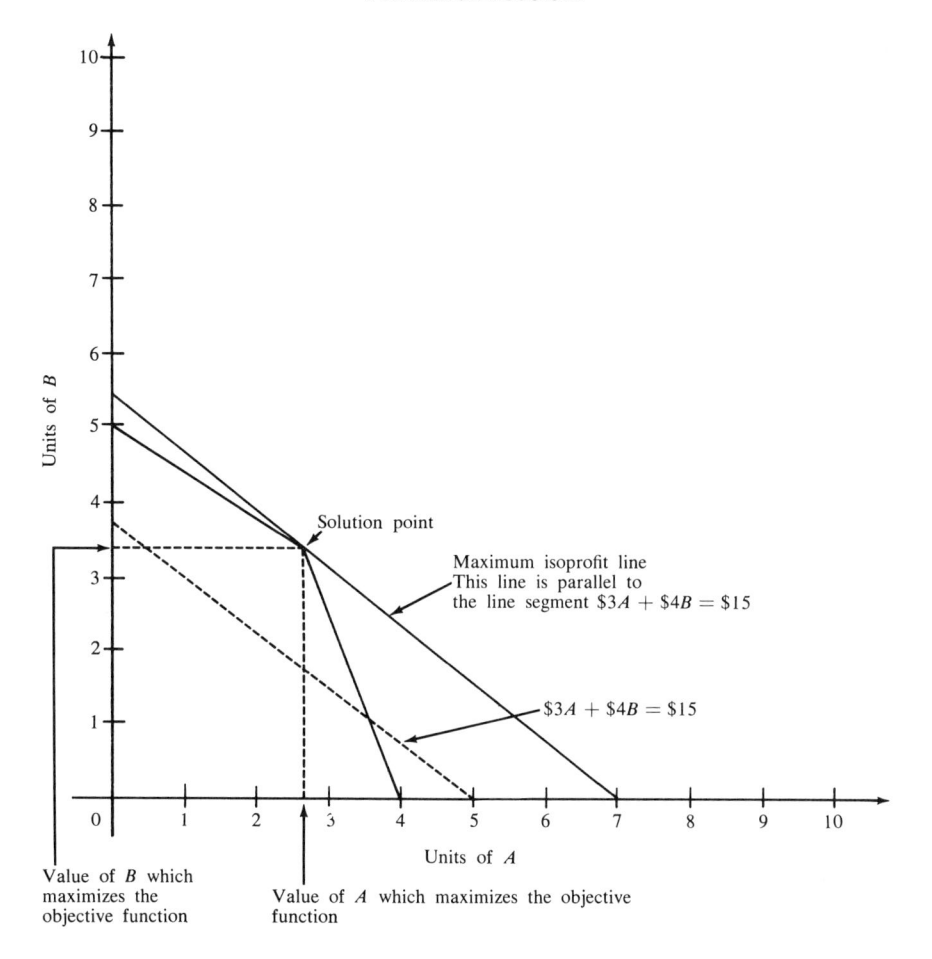

[Graph with Units of B on vertical axis and Units of A on horizontal axis. Labels: "Solution point", "Maximum isoprofit line — This line is parallel to the line segment $3A + $4B = $15", "$3A + $4B = $15", "Value of B which maximizes the objective function", "Value of A which maximizes the objective function"]

SUPPLEMENTARY READINGS

Arkin, H., "Computers and the Audit Test," *The Journal of Accountancy* (October, 1965), pp. 44–48.

Benston, G. J., "Multiple Regression Analysis of Cost Behavior," *The Accounting Review* (October, 1966), pp. 657–72.

Bierman, H., Jr., "Probability, Statistical Decision Theory, and Accounting," *The Accounting Review* (July, 1962), pp. 400–5.

———, L. F. Fouraker and R. K. Jaedicke, "A Use of Probability and Statistics in Performance Evaluation," *The Accounting Review* (July, 1961), pp. 409–17.

Cyert, R. M. and H. J. Davidson, *Statistical Sampling for Accounting Information* (Englewood Cliffs, N.J.: Prentice-Hall, Inc., 1962).

Dopuch, N., "Mathematical Programming and Accounting Approaches to Incremental Cost Analysis," *The Accounting Review* (October, 1963), pp. 745–53.

Fetter, R. B., *The Quality Control System* (Homewood, Ill.: Richard D. Irwin, Inc., 1967).

Knoblett, J. A., "The Applicability of Bayesian Statistics in Auditing," *Decision Sciences,* Vol. 1, No. 3 and 4 (July-October, 1970), pp. 423–40.

Oravec, R. J., "Statistical Inventory Management," *The Journal of Accountancy* (December, 1960), pp. 40–52.

Shao, Stephen P., *Statistics for Business and Economics,* 2nd. ed. (Columbus, Ohio: Charles E. Merrill Publishing Company, 1972).

Stockton, R. S., *Introduction to Linear Programming* (Homewood, Ill.: Richard D. Irwin, Inc., 1971).

Sweeney, R., "Business Use of Linear Programming," *Management Accounting* N.A.A. Bulletin (September, 1965), pp. 39–47.

Thompson, W. W., Jr., *Operations Research Techniques* (Columbus, Ohio: Charles E. Merrill Publishing Company, 1967).

QUESTIONS AND PROBLEMS

19-1. Compute the Economic Order Quantity EOQ for an article which has a yearly demand S of 7500 units, a cost per order C_R of $7.20, and a carrying cost per unit per year I of $1.20. What is the Total Variable Cost TVC for this EOQ?

19-2. Suppose that the order cost, $C_R = \$7.20$, of problem 19-1, is an estimate and that the "true" but unknown order cost is $6.55.

Required

a. What will be the actual TVC incurred annually?

b. Compute the actual annual TVC if the "true" but unknown order cost is $8.00.

c. What can you say about the sensitivity of TVC to errors in estimating the order cost? Does your answer have any implications for the value of determining "accurate," as opposed to "ballpark," estimates of order costs? Does this same reasoning apply to the other parameters of the model?

19-3. You have been engaged to install an accounting system for the Kaufman Corporation. Among the inventory control features Kaufman desires as a part of the system are indicators of "how much" to order "when." The fol-

[CH. 19] MATHEMATICAL AND STATISTICAL TECHNIQUES 609

lowing information is furnished for one item, called a komtronic, which is carried in inventory:

1. Komtronics are sold by the gross (12 dozen) at a list price of $800 per gross F. O. B. shipper. Kaufman receives a 40 percent trade discount off list price on purchases in gross lots.
2. Freight cost is $20 per gross from the shipping point to Kaufman's plant.
3. Kaufman uses about 5,000 komtronics during a 259-day production year and must purchase a total of 36 gross per year to allow for normal breakage. Minimum and maximum usages are 12 and 28 komtronics per day, respectively.
4. Normal delivery time to receive an order is 20 working days from the date a purchase request is initiated. A rush order in full gross lots can be received by air freight in five working days at an extra cost of $52 per gross. A stockout (complete exhaustion of the inventory) of komtronics would stop production, and Kaufman would purchase komtronics locally at list price rather than shut down.
5. The cost of placing an order is $10; the cost of receiving an order is $20.
6. Space storage cost is $12 per year per gross stored.
7. Insurance and taxes are approximately 12 percent of the net delivered cost of average inventory, and Kaufman expects a return of at least 8 percent on its average investment (ignore return on order and carrying cost for simplicity).

Required

a. Prepare a schedule computing the total annual cost of komtronics based on uniform order lot sizes of one, two, three, four, five, and six gross of komtronics. (The schedule should show the total annual cost according to each lot size.) Indicate the economic order quantity (economic lot size to order).

b. Prepare a schedule computing the minimum stock reorder point for komtronics. This is the point below which the komtronics inventory should not fall without reordering so as to guard against a stockout. Factors to be considered include average lead-period usage and safety stock requirements.

c. Prepare a schedule computing the cost of a stockout of komtronics. Factors to be considered include the excess costs for local purchases and for rush orders.

(Adapted from Uniform CPA Examination)

19-4. You are the budget analyst for the Ajax Rebuilt Machinery Company which specializes in repairing and rebuilding secondhand steel mill machinery, such as rolling mills, coilers, scrap chargers, etc. The operations include disassembly, general machining, welding, assembly and painting. You are undecided as to whether you should use man-hours or machine hours as the activity index for your proposed variable budget proposal. The relevant data is shown in the table below.

| | 1970 ||| 1971 |||
	Electrical power cost	Man-hours	Machine-hours	Electrical power cost	Man-hours	Machine-hours
Jan.	$250	7000.	3000.	$230	4600.	2200.
Feb.	243	6200.	2400.	231	4200.	1900.
Mar.	251	7200.	1800.	220	3800.	2000.
Apr.	245	7000.	2400.	224	3900.	3000.
May	247	6800.	2800.	224	4200.	1400.
June	236	6000.	2600.	239	5600.	1900.
July	242	5700.	2400.	230	5200.	1700.
Aug.	235	5200.	1800.	235	5500.	2400.
Sept.	236	5600.	2800.	249	6300.	2000.
Oct.	232	5600.	2000.	244	6600.	3000.
Nov.	240	5400.	3000.	244	6200.	1500.
Dec.	232	5200.	2400.	230	5400.	2800.

Required

a. Construct the appropriate scatter diagram for each one of the activity indices.

b. Which scatter diagram appears to reflect the best relationship?

c. Determine the linear equation for the variable which depicts the best relationship by the high-low method and by the method of least squares.

d. How do you account for the fact that the two linear equations which you have determined have different parameter estimates?

19-5. As budget analyst for the Quick Serv Company, suppliers of plumbing equipment to the building industry, you are interested in identifying and measuring the various items of expense which reduce the margin on all sales. One of your recent cost studies leads you to believe that most expenses of the paperwork variety are related directly to total number of invoice lines. That is, each line item means a separate posting on the stock ledger card; each line item is costed separately; each line item becomes a distinct invoice line, etc. These activities, of course, are required whether the line item is worth ten cents or ten dollars. The relevant information from the cost study is shown on page 611.

Required

a. Does a scatter diagram support your belief that there is a relationship between number of invoice lines and paperwork expense?

b. Calculate the regression line which indicates the nature of the relationship by the method of least squares.

19-6. A random sample of 50 delinquent charge accounts at the Bon Marche Department Store shows a sample mean of $62.00 and a sample standard

<table>
<tr><th colspan="3">Cost Study
Clerical Requirements, (Y) vs. Number of Invoice Lines, (X)</th></tr>
<tr><th>Order
number</th><th>Number of
invoice
lines</th><th>Total clerical
requirements
hours</th></tr>
<tr><td>A10568</td><td>3</td><td>.14</td></tr>
<tr><td>A27536</td><td>11</td><td>.42</td></tr>
<tr><td>A32065</td><td>17</td><td>.72</td></tr>
<tr><td>A37918</td><td>12</td><td>.49</td></tr>
<tr><td>A47623</td><td>1</td><td>.03</td></tr>
<tr><td>A59199</td><td>4</td><td>.16</td></tr>
<tr><td>A60273</td><td>18</td><td>.79</td></tr>
<tr><td>A74628</td><td>10</td><td>.35</td></tr>
<tr><td>A87321</td><td>9</td><td>.40</td></tr>
<tr><td>A90018</td><td>9</td><td>.35</td></tr>
<tr><td>B00502</td><td>12</td><td>.50</td></tr>
<tr><td>B11368</td><td>3</td><td>.11</td></tr>
<tr><td>B12007</td><td>18</td><td>.73</td></tr>
<tr><td>B28838</td><td>8</td><td>.35</td></tr>
<tr><td>B36518</td><td>4</td><td>.17</td></tr>
<tr><td>B48277</td><td>3</td><td>.10</td></tr>
<tr><td>B52680</td><td>2</td><td>.18</td></tr>
<tr><td>B64618</td><td>9</td><td>.33</td></tr>
<tr><td>B79568</td><td>12</td><td>.40</td></tr>
<tr><td>B84741</td><td>20</td><td>.80</td></tr>
</table>

deviation of $24.00. Construct a 95 percent confidence interval for the mean dollar amount of delinquent charge accounts at this store.

19-7. A random sample of 101 accounts receivable is selected from a population of 4,000 accounts. The mean of the sample is $150, and the sample standard deviation is $60. Calculate a 95 percent confidence interval for the population total dollar amount of the accounts receivable.

19-8. For the data of problem 19-7, determine how many more accounts receivable documents would have to be selected for the sample if the 95 percent confidence limits for the population mean are to be $\bar{X} \pm 0.05\bar{X}$.

19-9. Construct the control chart for the illustrative example in this chapter, pages 591–96, concerning Daily Reported Expenses of Salesmen with sample number 8 eliminated.

19-10. You are the assistant to the controller of the Nova Cereal Company. You have been charged with the responsibility for developing a procedure whereby the total weight of cereal packaged each day can be determined. This information is required by the controller as one piece of data for an independent perpetual inventory record of through-put. After investigation of the process by which each box is filled with cereal, you come to the conclusion that regardless of the fact that each filling machine is set to fill each box

612 COST ACCOUNTING CONCEPTS [CH. 19]

to the same weight, 8 oz, the actual weight placed in each box varies because of the many small but uncontrollable sources of variation in the filling process itself. This variation does not bother you because you know that as long as the process remains in control, statistically speaking, you will be able to estimate the total weight of cereal packaged per day per machine by multiplying the mean weight per box by the number of boxes packaged per day by each machine. In order to test your requirement for statistical control, you secure the sample evidence shown below from the operating records maintained for each machine.

Ounces of Cereal Per Box
Filling Machine F6

Sample number	Box number 1	2	3	4	5	Sum
1	7.52	7.90	8.00	8.29	7.48	39.19
2	8.38	7.48	8.69	7.68	8.41	40.64
3	7.70	8.21	7.64	8.17	7.97	39.69
4	8.23	8.03	7.81	7.94	7.81	39.82
5	7.93	8.07	8.33	8.21	8.23	40.77
6	8.05	8.50	8.16	7.58	7.90	40.19
7	7.55	7.67	8.05	7.67	7.98	38.92
8	7.74	7.57	7.95	8.02	8.14	39.42
9	8.07	7.31	7.76	7.93	7.75	38.82
10	8.31	7.66	8.15	8.09	7.92	40.13
11	8.41	8.21	8.16	7.67	7.81	40.26
12	8.31	7.74	8.21	7.81	7.90	39.97

Required

a. Is the filling process for the stated machine in control?

b. If Filling Machine F6 fills 110 boxes per minute and remains in a state of statistical control, what weight of cereal will be packaged per 8-hour day? Assume that 90 percent of the daily hours are available for production.

19-11. In an effort to control clerical expenses in the Quick Serv Company you decide to investigate whether or not the number of invoice lines per customer order (see problem 19-5) are random variables generated by a stable system of chance causes. If they are, you will be able to calculate the daily workload for the clerical force involved in processing the customer orders by multiplying the number of customer orders per day by the mean number of invoice lines per order. More importantly, you will be able to detect trends or unusual situations as they occur by sampling the number of invoice lines per customer order and plotting the mean of the sample on a control chart. You arrange to secure the data you need for your analysis for 25 days. The data are tabulated below.

MATHEMATICAL AND STATISTICAL TECHNIQUES

Number of Invoice Lines Per Customer Order

Day number	\multicolumn{5}{c}{Order number}	Sum	Day number	\multicolumn{5}{c}{Order number}	Sum
	1	2	3	4	5			1	2	3	4	5	
1	11	10	13	12	13	59	14	9	10	11	11	9	50
2	12	13	7	10	8	50	15	5	10	6	9	9	39
3	13	9	7	8	10	47	16	17	13	10	8	10	58
4	13	6	10	7	12	48	17	10	15	9	9	13	56
5	11	6	7	11	9	44	18	10	9	10	10	6	45
6	13	11	10	15	10	59	19	11	10	13	8	10	52
7	7	12	11	9	11	50	20	8	12	7	8	12	47
8	12	7	9	10	7	45	21	12	6	12	13	6	49
9	13	10	4	9	9	45	22	11	8	9	11	10	49
10	9	9	8	9	12	47	23	12	7	8	10	13	50
11	11	14	10	11	8	54	24	9	9	9	8	7	42
12	7	9	9	14	11	50	25	9	9	6	12	18	54
13	5	6	13	7	11	42							

Required

a. Test the hypothesis that the number of invoice lines per customer order are random variables generated by a stable system of chance causes.

b. What would you estimate the clerical requirements to be for a day on which 123 customer orders were received?

19-12. A company manufactures two different products, P1 and P2. The manufacturing process for each product consists of two operations. The unit time requirements, in machine hours, for each operation are as follows:

Part	Operation	Machine	Machine hours per unit
P1	1	M1	5
	2	M2	8
P2	1	M1	10
	2	M2	6

The number of machine hours available per week for each of the two machines are given below:

Machine	Machine hours available
M1	50
M2	48

It has been determined that the profit contribution for each of the products is $4.50 per unit for P1 and $5.00 per unit for P2. It is desired to maximize the total weekly profit contribution.

Required

a. Write a formal mathematical statement of this problem in terms of an objective function and inequality constraints.

b. Determine the optimal weekly production plan by graphical methods.

c. What is the value of the objective function for this optimal weekly production plan?

d. How does your feasible set of solutions change if management policy states that *at least* 2 units of P1 and *at least* 1 unit of P2 must be produced each week?

e. Does the optimal weekly production plan change as a result of adding these two constraints?

19-13. You are the chief financial officer of a government agency charged with the responsibility for developing a new feed mixture for cattle. The nutrition experts have narrowed the list of possible ingredients to two—ingredient X and ingredient Y. Their problem now is to determine the proportions of each ingredient to use in the feed mixture so that it will meet certain requirements relative to protein and vitamin content and bulk. Specifically, the protein value per pound of mixture must be at least six U.S.P. units; the vitamin value per pound of mixture must be at least eight U.S.P. units, and the bulk factor must be at least four units as measured by the appropriate methods. At the same time, fiscal limitations indicate a need for specifying a least-cost mixture. The characteristics of the ingredients under consideration are as shown in the table below. The nutrition experts are prepared to use a cut-and-try approach in the determination of the correct proportions of the two ingredients in the mixture. You recognize that this approach may be timely and costly and volunteer to solve their problem by a technique known as "linear programming."

Ingredients	Protein value U.S.P. units per pound	Vitamin value U.S.P. units per pound	Bulk factor per pound	Cost per pound cents
X	15	8	2	15
Y	4	10	10	18

Required

Assume that the ingredient characteristics combine in a linear fashion.

a. Write the formal mathematical statement of the problem in terms of an objective function and the appropriate constraints.

b. Determine by graphical methods the optimal amounts of each ingredient to be used in the mixture.

c. Determine the value of the objective function for this optimal feed mixture.

Appendices

Appendix A   Excerpts from annual reports

PPG Industries, Inc.
Armstrong Cork Company
Indiana Telephone Corporation

Appendix B   Tables

 I   *Present Value of $1.00*
 II   *Present Value of an Annuity of $1.00*

APPENDIX A–1

Financial Statements and Opinion of Independent Accountants

From the 1970 Annual Report of PPG Industries, Inc.*

STATEMENT OF CONSOLIDATED EARNINGS AND RETAINED EARNINGS

	Year Ended December 31,	
EARNINGS FOR THE YEAR	**1970**	**1969**
Net Sales	$1,093,791,000	$1,151,661,000
Equity In Net Earnings Of Jointly Owned Companies	2,227,000	801,000
Other Earnings	14,241,000	13,230,000
Total	1,110,259,000	1,165,692,000
Costs And Expenses:		
Cost of sales	746,267,000	773,533,000
Selling, general and administrative expenses	159,586,000	155,444,000
Depreciation and depletion	54,736,000	53,681,000
Research and development	33,526,000	30,947,000
Taxes—exclusive of taxes on income	31,066,000	29,971,000
Interest expense	21,306,000	16,387,000
Other charges—net	5,580,000	2,872,000
Total	1,052,067,000	1,062,835,000
Earnings Before Income Taxes, Minority Interest, And Extraordinary Items	58,192,000	102,857,000
Domestic And Foreign Taxes On Income	26,827,000	50,532,000
Minority Interest	273,000	1,797,000
Total	27,100,000	52,329,000
Earnings Before Extraordinary Items	31,092,000	50,528,000
Extraordinary Items, Net Of Income Taxes Of $554,000	126,000	—
Net Earnings	$ 31,218,000	$ 50,528,000
Earnings Per Common Share:		
Before Extraordinary Items	$1.51	$2.47
Net Earnings	$1.52	$2.47
RETAINED EARNINGS		
Balance At January 1, As Previously Reported		$ 462,972,000
Equity in Accumulated Losses of Subsidiaries Not Previously Consolidated		(4,620,000)
Balance At January 1, As Restated	$ 480,201,000	458,352,000
Net Earnings	31,218,000	50,528,000
Total	511,419,000	508,880,000
Cash Dividends (Per common share: $1.40)	28,695,000	28,679,000
Balance At December 31	$ 482,724,000	$ 480,201,000

The "Notes to Financial Statements" are an integral part of this statement.

NOTES TO FINANCIAL STATEMENTS

1. **Principles of Consolidation**—Effective January 1, 1970, the Corporation changed its principles of consolidation to include all significant subsidiaries, domestic and foreign, in the consolidated financial statements and to include investments in all jointly owned companies at equity.

Prior to 1970, only domestic, Canadian, and European subsidiaries and jointly owned companies, at equity, were included in the consolidated financial statements. The 1969 financial statements have been restated to reflect the current principles of consolidation and to that extent differ from those previously reported. Earnings for 1969 were reduced by $3,479,000 ($.17 per share) and earnings retained for use in the business at January 1, 1969, were reduced by $4,620,000, as a result of the change.

2. **Inventories**—Inventories are stated generally at the lower of cost or market. Cost excludes certain fixed expenses and is determined at either average or standard, which approximates actual cost. A comparison of inventories by major component at December 31, 1970 and 1969 is as follows:

	1970	1969
Finished Products	$119,875,000	$116,759,000
Work in Process	28,071,000	27,204,000
Raw Materials	51,280,000	45,431,000
Supplies	22,752,000	19,844,000
TOTAL	$221,978,000	$209,238,000

3. **Property**—A summary of total property, by major category, as of December 31, 1970 and 1969, is presented below:

	1970	1969
Land	$ 15,729,000	$ 16,074,000
Buildings	250,957,000	245,011,000
Machinery and Equipment	911,564,000	907,207,000
Other	35,133,000	49,765,000
Construction in Progress	133,111,000	63,943,000
TOTAL	$1,346,494,000	$1,282,000,000

4. **Long-term Debt**—At December 31, 1970, long-term debt consisted of the following:

$125,000,000, 9% debentures due in 1995 for which sinking fund payments of $8,000,000 will be made in each of the years 1980 to 1994. (In Jan. 1971, $16,900,000 of the $125,000,000, 9% debentures were received pursuant to Delayed Delivery Contracts and the remaining $3,500,000 will be received in March 1971.) ... $104,600,000

5⅝% debentures due in 1991 for which sinking fund payments of $6,250,000 will be made in each of the years 1972 to 1991 ... 125,000,000

4½% term bank loan payable in 1972 ... 5,833,000

Various other debts, primarily debt incurred by consolidated subsidiaries ... 42,171,000

TOTAL ... $277,604,000

Notes payable at December 31, 1970, includes commercial paper borrowings of $33,700,000.

5. **Pensions and Retirement Plans**—The Corporation has pension plans covering substantially all employees. The major portion of the various pension plan costs, as accrued, is paid to trust funds and insurance companies which administer these funds for payment to retired employees. Costs absorbed by the Corporation in 1970, amounting to $18,875,000, provide for current service and amortization of prior service costs over a 30-year period or less. The inventory value of the assets in

* Used by permission of PPG Industries, Inc.

APPENDIX A-1
(Continued)

STATEMENT OF CONSOLIDATED SOURCE AND USE OF FUNDS

	Year Ended December 31, 1970	1969
SOURCE OF FUNDS		
Net earnings	$ 31,218,000	$ 50,528,000
Depreciation and depletion	54,736,000	53,681,000
Amortization of intangible assets	3,537,000	3,916,000
Provision for future income taxes	6,854,000	8,493,000
Increase in accumulated provisions	12,669,000	4,407,000
Change in long-term debt	95,502,000	(4,013,000)
Property sold	22,272,000	4,779,000
Investments sold	2,852,000	436,000
Other sources—net	(1,796,000)	2,036,000
Total	227,844,000	124,263,000
USE OF FUNDS		
Expenditures for property	132,992,000	89,715,000
Increase in investments	20,215,000	20,991,000
Cash dividends paid	28,695,000	28,679,000
Increase in deferred charges	10,320,000	1,340,000
Decrease in minority interest in consolidated subsidiaries	8,705,000	(1,110,000)
Total	200,927,000	139,615,000
Change in Working Capital	26,917,000	(15,352,000)
Working Capital at Beginning of Year	196,948,000	212,300,000
Working Capital at End of Year	$223,865,000	$196,948,000
Working Capital Represented by:		
Current Assets	$445,446,000	$436,263,000
Current Liabilities	221,581,000	239,315,000
Total	$223,865,000	$196,948,000
Current Ratio	2.0 to 1	1.8 to 1

The "Notes to Financial Statements" are an integral part of this statement.

---

the various pension funds amounted to approximately $208,000,000 at December 31, 1970.

6. Capital Stock—Changes in Common Stock issued and Common Stock in Treasury for the year ended December 31, 1970, are as follows:

Common Stock Issued

	Shares	Amount
Balance January 1, 1970	21,730,607	$213,039,000
Shares issued under employee stock option plans	3,550	63,000
Balance December 31, 1970	21,734,157	$213,102,000

Common Stock in Treasury

	Shares	Amount
Balance January 1, 1970	1,241,280	$ 42,630,000
Shares issued under employee stock option plans	(2,950)	(102,000)
Shares delivered to retired employees under incentive compensation agreements	(2,253)	(77,000)
Balance December 31, 1970	1,236,077	$ 42,451,000

Amounts shown on the balance sheet for "Common Stock" represent the par value of shares issued plus capital contributed for stock in excess of par.

7. Stock Option and Incentive Compensation Plans—As of December 31, 1970, the Corporation had reserved 413,521 shares of its common stock for issuance upon exercise of employee stock options. Of these, 252,521 shares were under option at various prices ranging from $22.53 to $33.13 per share. Options on 6,500 shares were exercised in 1970 at prices ranging from $22.53 to $30.02 per share. Options on 185,771 shares were exercisable at December 31, 1970.

The Corporation had also reserved 46,722 shares of its common stock at year-end for future issuance under incentive compensation agreements with certain key employees. During 1970, the Corporation issued 2,253 shares from its Treasury to retired employees under these agreements.

8. Commitments and Contingencies—Lease commitments as of December 31, 1970, which are for periods in excess of two years, have aggregate annual rentals of approximately $13,700,000. The Corporation is contingently liable for approximately $21,400,000 as a guarantor of lines of credit in connection with the financing of the sale of Corporation products and bank loans. As explained on page 23 in the Financial Review section, the Corporation is contesting assessments for income tax deficiencies for the years 1960 through 1963. In the opinion of management, the final outcome of this and other pending litigation is not expected to have a material effect upon the earnings or balance sheet of the Corporation.

9. Reference is made to pages 22 and 23 of the Financial Review section for additional information regarding extraordinary items; amounts required to complete capital projects approved prior to December 31, 1970; details of the provisions for taxes on income; and description of depreciation method.

618

APPENDIX A-1
(*Continued*)

CONSOLIDATED BALANCE SHEET

ASSETS

		December 31, 1970	December 31, 1969
Current Assets:	Cash	$ 23,460,000	$ 32,743,000
	United States Government and other marketable securities—at lower of cost or market	242,000	4,312,000
	(Quoted market value: 1970, $258,000; 1969, $4,316,000)		
	Notes and accounts receivable (less estimated losses: 1970, $4,208,000; 1969, $4,606,000)	180,736,000	177,590,000
	Inventories	221,978,000	209,238,000
	Prepayments and other current assets	19,030,000	12,380,000
	Total Current Assets	445,446,000	436,263,000
Investments:	Investments in jointly owned companies—at equity	77,185,000	59,961,000
	Other—at cost or less	9,299,000	7,630,000
	Total Investments	86,484,000	67,591,000
Property—At Cost:	Land, buildings, machinery and equipment, etc.	1,346,494,000	1,282,000,000
	Less accumulated depreciation and depletion	639,995,000	629,971,000
	Property—Net	706,499,000	652,029,000
Other Assets:	Deferred charges	26,450,000	16,793,000
	Excess of cost of investments in consolidated subsidiaries over equities in net assets— unamortized balance	5,442,000	8,327,000
	Total Other Assets	31,892,000	25,120,000
	Total	$1,270,321,000	$1,181,003,000

The "Notes to Financial Statements" are an integral part of this statement.

ACCOUNTANTS' OPINION
PPG INDUSTRIES, INC.:

We have examined the financial statements of PPG Industries, Inc. and its consolidated subsidiaries for the year ended December 31, 1970. Our examination was made in accordance with generally accepted auditing standards, and accordingly included such tests of the accounting records and such other auditing procedures as we considered necessary in the circumstances. We did not examine the financial statements of certain Canadian subsidiaries consolidated and certain jointly owned foreign companies the investments in which are carried at equity, but we were furnished with reports of other accountants on their examinations of the financial statements of such companies for the year. Our opinion expressed below, insofar as it relates to the amounts included for such companies, is based solely upon such reports.

In our opinion, the accompanying consolidated balance sheet and statements of consolidated earnings, retained earnings, and source and use of funds present fairly the financial position of PPG Industries, Inc. and consolidated subsidiaries at December 31, 1970 and the results of their operations and sources and uses of their funds for the year then ended, in con-

APPENDIX A–1
(*Continued*)

LIABILITIES

		December 31, 1970	December 31, 1969
Current Liabilities:	Notes payable	$ 53,180,000	$ 58,648,000
	Current maturities of long-term debt	14,037,000	12,223,000
	Accounts payable and accrued expenses	126,804,000	124,829,000
	Domestic and foreign taxes on income	27,560,000	43,615,000
	Total Current Liabilities	221,581,000	239,315,000
Long-Term Debt		277,604,000	182,102,000
Deferred Credits And Accumulated Provisions:	Future income taxes	51,533,000	44,679,000
	Investment credit—unamortized balance	14,005,000	16,038,000
	Maintenance and repairs	12,946,000	10,086,000
	Foreign operations	9,411,000	1,865,000
	Insurance and unfunded and uninsured pensions	5,930,000	3,355,000
	Other	1,600,000	1,912,000
	Total Deferred Credits And Accumulated Provisions	95,425,000	77,935,000
Minority Interest:	Minority interest in consolidated subsidiaries	22,336,000	31,041,000
Shareholders' Equity:	Cumulative preferred stock—authorized but unissued 5,000,000 shares, without par value	—	—
	Common stock—authorized 50,000,000 shares, par value $2.50	213,102,000	213,039,000
	Retained earnings	482,724,000	480,201,000
	Common stock in treasury—at cost	(42,451,000)	(42,630,000)
	Shareholders' Equity	653,375,000	650,610,000
	Total	$1,270,321,000	$1,181,003,000

formity with generally accepted accounting principles applied on a basis consistent with that of the preceding year (after revision, which we approve, of the financial statements for that year as explained in note 1 to the financial statements).

HASKINS & SELLS

Pittsburgh, Pennsylvania
February 2, 1971

TRADEMARKS

These registered trademarks of PPG Industries, Inc., are used in this report: PPG Industries (monogram), *Color Dynamics, Duracron, Graylite, Herculite, Hercuvit, Manor Hall, Rigiduct, Selectrofoam, Solarban, Twindow, Spandrelite, Sun-Proof, Tri-Ethane, Vertiglas.*

Other trademarks of PPG Industries appearing in this report are: *Hycor, Solarcool, Trianti.*

APPENDIX A-2

Financial Statements and Independent Accountants' Report

From the 1970 Annual Report of Armstrong Cork Company*

Armstrong Cork Company and Subsidiaries

Statement of Consolidated Earnings

Year ended December 31, 1970, with comparative figures for 1969

	1970 (000)	1969 (000)
Current Earnings		
Income:		
Net sales	$485,834	$552,349
Other income	4,633	4,760
	490,467	557,109
Costs and expenses:		
Cost of goods sold	333,796	367,735
Selling and administrative	96,995	103,923
Depreciation and amortization	21,891	20,287
Other charges	6,222	3,188
	458,904	495,133
Earnings from operations before income taxes	31,563	61,976
Federal and foreign income taxes (notes 7 and 8)	13,750	30,100
EARNINGS FROM OPERATIONS	17,813	31,876
EXTRAORDINARY GAIN FROM SALE OF CERTAIN BUSINESSES, NET OF INCOME TAXES	—	26,196
NET EARNINGS	$ 17,813	$ 58,072
Per share of common stock:*		
Earnings from operations	$ .67	$ 1.22
Extraordinary gain, net of income taxes	—	1.03
Net earnings	$ .67	$ 2.25
Retained Earnings		
Amount at beginning of year	$297,631	$259,974
Net earnings for the year	17,813	58,072
	315,444	318,046
Deduct dividends:		
Preferred stock—$3.75 per share	443	443
Voting preferred stock: 1970—$2.08 per share; 1969—$2.37½ per share (note 6)	208	238
Common stock: 1970—$.80 per share; 1969—$.77½ per share	20,381	19,713
Common stock of pooled company prior to combination	—	21
	21,032	20,415
Amount at end of year	$294,412	$297,631

*Computed on average number of shares outstanding.

See accompanying notes to financial statements.

* Used by permission of Armstrong Cork Company.

APPENDIX A-2
(Continued)

Armstrong Cork Company and Subsidiaries
Consolidated Balance Sheet
December 31, 1970, with comparative figures as of December 31, 1969

	1970 (000)	1969 (000)
Assets		
Current assets:		
Cash	$ 13,636	$ 15,179
U. S. Treasury and other securities	811	2,097
Accounts and notes receivable (less allowance for discounts and losses: 1970—$3,755,000; 1969—$3,455,000)	64,932	67,010
Current installments on long-term notes receivable (note 2)	327	3,350
Inventories (note 3)	106,315	101,862
Prepaid expenses	5,017	4,332
Total current assets	191,038	193,830
Long-term notes receivable (note 2)	38,958	36,659
Property, plant and equipment, at cost (less accumulated depreciation and amortization: 1970—$159,146,000; 1969—$145,559,000) (note 4)	276,476	253,080
Sundry assets and investments, at cost or less	4,052	4,156
	$510,524	$487,725
Liabilities and Stockholders' Equity		
Current liabilities:		
Notes payable (note 5)	$ 63,188	$ 24,788
Current installments on long-term debt (note 5)	3,477	782
Accounts payable and accrued expenses	38,277	44,684
Federal and foreign income taxes	—	14,733
Total current liabilities	104,942	84,987
Long-term debt (note 5)	13,994	10,802
Deferred income taxes (note 7)	15,404	13,175
Deferred investment credit (note 8)	1,086	1,355
Minority interest in foreign subsidiary	2,240	1,606
Stockholders' equity (notes 6 and 9)	372,858	375,800
	$510,524	$487,725

See accompanying notes to financial statements.

APPENDIX A–2
(Continued)

Armstrong Cork Company and Subsidiaries
Notes to Financial Statements
December 31, 1970

1. Principles of consolidation:

The consolidated financial statements include the accounts of the company and its domestic and foreign subsidiaries. Included in the financial statements are the following data from the company's consolidated foreign subsidiaries at December 31:

	1970 (000)	1969 (000)
Current assets	$40,754	$40,080
Plant and other assets	32,786	31,209
Current liabilities	25,018	25,041
Long-term debt	8,956	7,445
Earnings from operations, net of minority interest	981	2,170

2. Long-term notes receivable:

Long-term notes receivable, including installments due currently, are as follows at December 31, 1970:

	Current (000)	Noncurrent (000)
9½% subordinated note of Kerr Glass Manufacturing Corporation with annual installment payments of $2,500,000 due 1976 to maturity in 1987	$ —	$30,000
8% subordinated note of North Lime Corporation due in annual installments based on earnings of North Lime. Voluntary prepayments by North Lime Corporation have satisfied scheduled payments into 1973. Future minimum annual payments range from $73,000 remaining in 1973 to $1,225,000 in 1984	—	5,000
Other	327	3,958
	$ 327	$38,968

During the year a new subordinated note was negotiated with Kerr Glass Manufacturing Corporation ("Kerr") and substituted for the note of that corporation held by the company, which increased the interest rate from 7% to 9½% but extended the principal payment dates. In addition, the new note provides for mandatory prepayments beginning March 31, 1977, dependent upon Kerr's earnings. Failure of Kerr to meet certain earnings tests may result in deferment of the payment of interest or principal, or both, on the new note.

3. Inventories:

The classification of inventories is as follows:

	1970 (000)	1969 (000)
Finished goods	$ 64,938	$ 60,247
Goods in process	13,456	14,145
Raw materials and supplies	27,921	27,470
	$106,315	$101,862

The inventories are stated at the lower of cost or market. Cost is determined generally under the "first-in, first-out" method except as to certain materials (amounting to $17,686,000 at December 31, 1970) valued under the "last-in, first-out" method.

4. Property, plant and equipment:

The principal categories of property, plant and equipment are as follows:

	1970 (000)	1969 (000)
Land	$ 17,795	$ 17,114
Buildings	124,170	105,092
Machinery and equipment	269,152	237,758
Construction in progress	24,505	38,675
	435,622	398,639
Less accumulated depreciation and amortization	159,146	145,559
	$276,476	$253,080

The unexpended cost of approved capital appropriations amounted to approximately $31,000,000 at December 31, 1970, substantially all of which is estimated to be expended during the year 1971.

5. Notes payable and long-term debt:

Notes payable are as follows at December 31, 1970:

	Current (000)	Noncurrent (000)
Commercial notes payable with interest rates ranging from 5⅝% to 5⅞%	$40,000	
Notes payable to banks and others with interest rates ranging from 6½% to 10%	23,188	
Total notes payable	$63,188	

Long-term debt, including current installments, is as follows:

	Current (000)	Noncurrent (000)
Borrowings of foreign subsidiaries due 1971-1976 with interest rates ranging from 6¾% to 9½%	$ 598	$ 7,979
Mortgages and capitalized lease obligation secured by land and buildings with net book value totaling approximately $8,982,000 due serially to 1991 with interest rates ranging from 5½% to 8½%	688	3,756
Other	2,191	2,259
Total long-term debt	$ 3,477	$13,994

APPENDIX A–2
(Continued)

6. Stockholders' equity:

	1970 (000)	1969 (000)
Preferred stock, $3.75 cumulative, no par value. Authorized 161,821 shares; issued 161,522 shares (at redemption price of $102.75 per share)	$ 16,596	$ 16,596
Voting preferred stock, $2.375 cumulative convertible series, no par value. Authorized 1,500,000 shares; issued 100,000 shares (at $50.00 stated value per share)	5,000	5,000
Common stock, $1.00 par value per share. Authorized 60,000,000 shares. Issued: 1970—25,588,888 shares; 1969—25,568,564 shares	25,589	25,569
Capital surplus	38,876	38,653
Retained earnings	294,412	297,631
	380,473	383,449
Less treasury stock, at cost: Preferred stock, $3.75 cumulative— 43,373 shares	3,986	3,986
Common stock: 1970—104,630 shares; 1969—106,034 shares	3,629	3,663
	7,615	7,649
	$372,858	$375,800

The voting preferred stock is convertible into common stock at the rate of 2.10 shares of common stock for each share of voting preferred and is callable after April 2, 1973, at an initial redemption price of $52.50 a share. At December 31, 1970, there were 210,000 shares of common stock reserved for the conversion of this stock. In 1970, dividends paid on this stock covered the period January 31 to December 1.

Changes in capital surplus for the year 1970 are as follows:

	(000)
Amount at beginning of year	$38,653
Add net excess of proceeds over par value of 20,326 previously unissued shares of common stock and cost of 1,404 shares of treasury common stock sold to employees upon exercise of options	223
Amount at end of year	$38,876

7. Deferred income taxes:
The company generally uses straight-line depreciation for financial reporting purposes and accelerated depreciation as permitted by the Internal Revenue Service for tax purposes. Provision ($2,229,000 in 1970) has been made in the accounts for future income taxes applicable to depreciation and other minor items reported differently for tax and financial reporting purposes.

8. Investment credit:
Investment credits for 1970 and 1969, amounting to $1,468,000 and $1,619,000 respectively, have been taken directly to income as a reduction of provision for income taxes. Credits for 1966 and prior, which were deferred, are being amortized over the lives of the related assets.

9. Stock options:
Under the option plan approved by stockholders in 1952 there were options outstanding for 33,280 shares of common stock at the beginning of the year and 22,620 shares at the end of the year. During the year, options for 10,660 shares were exercised. There were 8,160 shares at the beginning and end of the year available for the granting of options under the plan. The option prices are not less than 95% of the closing market price of the shares on the dates the options were granted.

Under the option plan approved by stockholders in 1964 there were options outstanding for 139,724 shares of common stock at the beginning of the year and 137,500 shares at the end of the year. During the year, options for 564 shares were exercised, and options for 1,660 shares were canceled and thus became available for future granting. There were 140,118 shares at the beginning of the year and 141,778 shares at the end of the year available for the granting of options under the plan. The option prices are not less than the closing market price of the shares on the dates the options were granted.

In addition, there were options outstanding for 52,930 shares of common stock at the end of the year, and options for 10,506 shares were exercised during the year in connection with options originally granted by pooled companies prior to combination.

The average price of all options outstanding at December 31, 1970, was $27.10 per share.

10. Pension plans:
The company and certain of its subsidiaries have pension plans covering substantially all employees. The pension cost charged to operations for the year 1970 was $3,518,000. This includes current service cost and, for the major plans, amortization of prior service cost over periods ranging up to 30 years. The company's policy is to fund these pension costs currently.

APPENDIX A-2
(*Continued*)

Armstrong Cork Company and Subsidiaries

Statement of Consolidated Source and Use of Funds

Year ended December 31, 1970, with comparative figures for 1969

	1970 (000)	1969 (000)
Funds became available from:		
Operations:		
Earnings	$17,813	$31,876
Depreciation and amortization	21,891	20,287
Deferred income taxes	2,229	1,937
Total from operations	41,933	54,100
Working capital generated from sale of businesses	—	27,025
Net long-term borrowings	3,192	3,160
Sale of common stock under option plans	277	1,189
	45,402	85,474
These funds were used for:		
Capital additions to property, plant and equipment	46,013	64,766
Dividends to stockholders	21,032	20,415
Purchases of treasury stock	—	3,339
Other items	1,104	1,902
	68,149	90,422
Net decrease in working capital	$22,747	$ 4,948

See accompanying notes to financial statements.

PEAT, MARWICK, MITCHELL & CO.
CERTIFIED PUBLIC ACCOUNTANTS
1500 WALNUT STREET
PHILADELPHIA, PA. 19102

The Board of Directors and Stockholders,
Armstrong Cork Company:

We have examined the consolidated balance sheet of Armstrong Cork Company and subsidiaries as of December 31, 1970 and the related statements of earnings and source and use of funds for the year then ended. Our examination was made in accordance with generally accepted auditing standards, and accordingly included such tests of the accounting records and such other auditing procedures as we considered necessary in the circumstances.

In our opinion, the above-mentioned financial statements present fairly the financial position of Armstrong Cork Company and subsidiaries at December 31, 1970 and the results of their operations and source and use of funds for the year then ended, in conformity with generally accepted accounting principles applied on a basis consistent with that of the preceding year.

February 16, 1971   *Peat, Marwick, Mitchell & Co.*

APPENDIX A-3

Financial Statements and Opinion of Independent CPA's

From the 1970 Annual Report of Indiana Telephone Corporation*

Statement of Income

	Column A Historical Cost		Column B Historical Cost Restated for Changes in Purchasing Power of Dollar	
	1970	1969	1970	1969
OPERATING REVENUES:				
Local service	$5,384,154	$5,157,024	$ 5,483,761	$5,533,522
Toll service	4,437,918	3,856,564	4,520,019	4,138,120
Miscellaneous	147,557	167,772	150,287	180,021
Total operating revenues	9,969,629	9,181,360	10,154,067	9,851,663
OPERATING EXPENSES:				
Depreciation provision, Note 2	1,541,560	1,441,868	1,950,962	1,854,336
Maintenance	1,427,487	1,152,447	1,466,739	1,236,583
Traffic	1,157,565	1,086,172	1,178,980	1,165,470
Commercial	449,104	411,788	457,412	441,851
General and administrative	1,170,198	967,026	1,230,930	1,047,776
State, local and miscellaneous Federal taxes	648,996	753,037	661,002	808,014
Federal income taxes, Note 2				
Currently payable	1,232,087	1,160,000	1,254,881	1,244,688
Deferred until future years	295,000	328,000	300,458	351,946
Deferred investment tax credit (net)	(14,997)	12,000	(20,237)	9,416
Total operating expenses	7,907,000	7,312,338	8,481,127	8,160,080
OPERATING INCOME	2,062,629	1,869,022	1,672,940	1,691,583
INCOME DEDUCTIONS:				
Interest on funded debt	659,567	663,984	671,769	712,460
Other deductions	21,355	19,872	23,670	22,848
Interest charged to construction (credit)	(30,442)	(21,658)	(31,005)	(23,240)
Other income (credit)	(203,759)	(180,496)	(207,834)	(193,674)
Gain from retirement of long-term debt through operation of sinking fund (credit)	(15,865)	—	(16,158)	—
Price level gain from retirement of long-term debt (credit), Note 1	—	—	(53,126)	(32,885)
Gain from retirement of preferred stock through operation of sinking fund (credit), Note 1	(5,515)	(3,695)	(5,311)	(3,965)
Price level gain from retirement of preferred stock (credit), Note 1	—	—	(11,582)	(9,207)
Price level loss from other monetary items	—	—	113,738	108,910
Total income deductions	425,341	478,007	484,161	581,247
NET INCOME, Note 1	1,637,288	1,391,015	1,188,779	1,110,336
Preferred stock dividends applicable to the period	97,541	98,688	99,346	105,893
EARNINGS APPLICABLE TO COMMON STOCK	$1,539,747	$1,292,327	$1,089,433	$1,004,443
EARNINGS PER COMMON SHARE	$ 3.16	$ 2.65	$ 2.23	$ 2.06
BOOK VALUE PER SHARE	$ 18.29	$ 15.50	$ 17.48	$ 15.63
Stations in service at end of year	72,569	69,220	72,569	69,220

The accompanying notes are an integral part of this statement.

* Used by permission of Indiana Telephone Corporation.

APPENDIX A–3
(*Continued*)

INDIANA TELEPHONE CORPORATION

Statement of Assets—December 31, 1970

	Column A Historical Cost	Column B Historical Cost Restated for Changes in Purchasing Power of Dollar
TELEPHONE PLANT, at original cost, Note 1:		
In service	$30,292,769	$38,010,120
Less—Accumulated depreciation	9,166,697	12,062,598
	21,126,072	25,947,522
Plant under construction	1,068,349	1,088,113
	22,194,421	27,035,635
WORKING CAPITAL:		
Current assets—		
Cash	702,030	702,030
Temporary cash investments accumulated for construction	2,113,653	2,113,653
Accounts receivable, less reserve	1,267,598	1,267,598
Materials and supplies	477,455	486,288
Prepayments	81,764	83,279
	4,642,500	4,652,848
Current liabilities—		
Sinking fund obligations, Note 4	162,000	162,000
Accounts payable	324,622	324,622
Advance billings	300,521	300,521
Dividends payable	109,396	109,396
Federal income taxes, Note 2	280,202	280,202
Other accrued taxes	475,091	475,091
Other current liabilities	368,633	368,633
	2,020,465	2,020,465
Net working capital	2,622,035	2,632,383
OTHER:		
Debt expense being amortized	212,234	263,867
Other deferred charges	69,934	85,547
Deferred Federal income taxes, Note 2	(957,454)	(1,034,603)
Unamortized investment tax credit	(382,070)	(452,242)
	(1,057,356)	(1,137,431)
TOTAL INVESTMENT IN TELEPHONE BUSINESS	$23,759,100	$28,530,587

The accompanying notes are an integral part of this statement.

APPENDIX A–3
(*Continued*)

Statement of Capital—December 31, 1970

	Column A Historical Cost		Column B Historical Cost Restated for Changes in Purchasing Power of Dollar	
	Amount	Ratio	Amount	Ratio
FIRST MORTGAGE SINKING FUND BONDS:				
Series 1, 3% due June 1, 1977 ....$	780,000		$ 780,000	
Series 2, 3⅜% due June 1, 1977	395,000		395,000	
Series 3, 3⅞% due June 1, 1977	415,000		415,000	
Series 4, 3¾% due June 1, 1984	946,000		946,000	
Series 5, 4¼% due September 1, 1986	880,000		880,000	
Series 6, 5⅜% due September 1, 1991	1,860,000		1,860,000	
Series 7, 4¾% due May 1, 1994	2,016,000		2,016,000	
Series 8, 4¾% due July 1, 2005	2,955,000		2,955,000	
Series 9, 6½% due October 1, 2007	2,970,000		2,970,000	
Less—Current sinking funds, Note 4	(142,000)		(142,000)	
Total first mortgage sinking fund bonds	13,075,000	55%	13,075,000	46%
PREFERRED STOCK (no maturity):				
Cumulative, sinking fund, par value $100 per share, 30,000 shares authorized of which 10,000 are unissued:				
1950 Series 4.80%	244,200		244,200	
1951 Series 4.80%	246,700		246,700	
1954 Series 5¼%	339,100		339,100	
1956 Series 5%	261,200		261,200	
1967 Series 6⅛%	693,000		693,000	
Less—Current sinking funds, Note 4	(20,000)		(20,000)	
Total preferred stock	1,764,200	7%	1,764,200	6%
COMMON SHAREHOLDERS' INTEREST:				
Common stock, no par value, authorized 500,000 shares, issued 492,086 shares	4,251,785		6,237,301	
Retained earnings	4,751,675		2,413,070	
	9,003,460		8,650,371	
Less—Treasury stock, 4,336 shares, at cost	(5,192)		(7,590)	
Stock discount and expense	(78,368)		(118,246)	
Total common shareholders' interest	8,919,900	38%	8,524,535	30%
UNREALIZED EFFECTS OF PRICE LEVEL CHANGES, Note 1..	—		5,166,852	18%
TOTAL INVESTMENT IN TELEPHONE BUSINESS...........$23,759,100		100%	$28,530,587	100%

The accompanying notes are an integral part of this statement.

APPENDIX A-3
(*Continued*)

INDIANA TELEPHONE CORPORATION

Source and Disposition of Funds for the Year 1970

FUNDS WERE PROVIDED BY:
  Operations—
    Net income per column A $1,637,288
    Items which did not require current
    expenditure of funds—
      Depreciation—
        Charged to income 1,541,560
        Charged to clearing accounts 52,665
      Deferred Federal income taxes 295,000
      Amortization of investment tax credit .... (14,997)
      Interest charged to construction .... (30,442)
      Amortization of deferred charges 75,849
  Miscellaneous, net .... (15,505)
                                                      3,541,418

FUNDS WERE EXPENDED FOR:
  Gross additions to telephone plant.................................. 3,176,145
  Cash dividends—Common stock..................................... 182,906
                —Preferred stock 97,197
  Redemption of bonds and preferred stock............................. 182,200
                                                      3,638,448
DECREASE IN WORKING CAPITAL .... $ 97,030

The accompanying notes are an integral part of this statement.

APPENDIX A–3
(*Continued*)

Statement of Retained Earnings for the Year 1970

	Column A Historical Cost	Column B Historical Cost Restated for Changes in Purchasing Power of Dollar
BALANCE, December 31, 1969	$3,394,490	$1,509,576
NET INCOME	1,637,288	1,188,779
	5,031,778	2,698,355
DEDUCT:		
Cash dividends declared—		
Common stock, annual rate—$.50 per share	182,906	186,290
Preferred stock	97,197	98,995
	280,103	285,285
BALANCE, December 31, 1970	$4,751,675	$2,413,070

The accompanying notes are an integral part of this statement.

AUDITORS' REPORT

To the Shareholders of Indiana Telephone Corporation:

We have examined the statements of assets and capital of INDIANA TELEPHONE CORPORATION (an Indiana corporation) as of December 31, 1970, and the related statements of income, retained earnings, and source and disposition of funds for the year then ended. Our examination was made in accordance with generally accepted auditing standards and accordingly included such tests of the accounting records and such other auditing procedures as we considered necessary in the circumstances. We have previously examined and reported on the financial statements for the preceding year.

In our opinion, the accompanying financial statements shown under Column A present fairly the financial position of the Corporation as of December 31, 1970, and the results of its operations and source and disposition of funds for the year then ended, in conformity with generally accepted accounting principles applied on a basis consistent with that of the preceding year.

In our opinion, however, the accompanying financial statements shown under Column B more fairly present the financial position of the Corporation as of December 31, 1970, and the results of its operations for the year then ended, as recognition has been given to changes in the purchasing power of the dollar, as explained in Note 1.

ARTHUR ANDERSEN & CO.

Indianapolis, Indiana,
February 19, 1971.

APPENDIX A-3
(Continued)

INDIANA TELEPHONE CORPORATION

Notes to Financial Statements

1. EXPLANATION OF FINANCIAL STATEMENTS

In the accompanying financial statements, costs measured by the dollars disbursed at the time of the expenditure are shown in "Column A— Historical Cost." In "Column B—Historical Cost Restated For Changes in Purchasing Power of Dollar" (where the amounts in A and B differ), these dollars of cost have been restated in terms of the price level at December 31, 1970, as measured by the Gross National Product Implicit Price Deflator. Since 1954, the Corporation has presented supplemental financial information recognizing the effect of the change in the purchasing power of the dollar relating to telephone plant and depreciation expense in the annual report to shareholders.

In computing the amounts set forth in Column B of the accompanying financial statements, the Corporation has followed the methods set forth in Statement No. 3 released in June, 1969, by the Accounting Principles Board of the American Institute of Certified Public Accountants, **except that**, contrary to Statement No. 3, the effects of price level changes on long-term debt and preferred stock have been reflected **as income in the year in which the debt and preferred stock are retired as required by the specific instruments under which they were issued.** The Accounting Principles Board has tentatively taken the position that all such amounts should be taken into income in the year of price level change. **In the opinion of the Corporation's management and of its independent public accountants, such tentative viewpoint of the Accounting Principles Board does not result in a proper determination of income for the period.** "Unrealized Effects of Price Level Changes" recognizes the excess of adjustments on the Statement of Assets over the adjustments of Common Stock and Retained Earnings.

Dollars are a means of expressing purchasing power at the time of their use. **Conversion or restatement of dollars of differing purchasing power to the purchasing power of the dollar at the date of conversion results in all the dollars being treated as mathematical likes for the purpose of significant data.** The resulting financial statements recognize the change in price levels between the periods of expenditure of funds and the periods of use of property. **Accordingly, the earnings, results of operations, assets and other data available for use by management and other readers of financial statements provide important information and comparisons not otherwise available.**

No one would attempt to add, subtract, multiply, or divide marks, dollars, and pounds. The failure to change the title of the monetary unit may be partially responsible for this violation of mathematical principle. This conceals the fact that mathematical unlikes are being used and therefore unfortunate results have been produced by generally accepted accounting methods.

2. RECOVERY OF CAPITAL AND RETURN ON CAPITAL

Under the law of Indiana, the Corporation is entitled to recover the fair value of its property used and useful in public service by accruing depreciation based on the "fair value" thereof and is entitled to earn a fair return on such "fair value." The amount shown in Column B for telephone plant approximates the fair value of the property as determined based on the principles followed by the Public Service Commission of Indiana in an order dated September 1, 1967, authorizing the Corporation to increase its subscriber rates.

In the accompanying financial statements, Column A includes depreciation expense based on historical cost and Column B includes depreciation expense, as well as other expenses, on the basis of historical cost repriced in current dollars to reflect the changes in the purchasing power of the dollar. Also, the annual reports to the Indiana Commission are in the same basic form shown herein.

It must be kept in mind that this determination of depreciation expense is a year-to-year estimate and there are involved the questions of obsolescence, foresight, and judgment giving due consideration to maintenance but the regulatory process does not adjust even to this accurately.

If use of property, obsolescence and current denominators (in the case of monetary inflation) are used accurately by way of keeping the allowable expense of depreciation current and rates sufficient to return it along with a fair return, and the proceeds are immediately invested in property used and useful in the public service, there more likely will be a real return of capital and a fair return thereon. However, if monetary inflation continues, as it usually does, capital is unlikely ever to be truly returned. **It must be observed there is a substantial lag in the regulatory process. In rate making there is no guarantee of recovery of capital or of an adequate rate of return to the Corporation. This is an added risk which should be considered in estimating a fair return.**

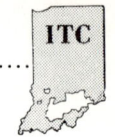

Since the present Internal Revenue Code does not recognize the costs measured in current dollars, they are not deductible for computing Federal income tax payments, **and the Corporation in fact pays taxes on alleged earnings which economically do not exist.** If they were deductible, as they should be, reductions in Federal income taxes as shown in Column B of $229,000 in 1970 and $200,000 in 1969 would result.

For book and financial reporting purposes, the Corporation provides for depreciation on a straight-line basis over the average service lives of the various classes of depreciable plant. In 1970, the overall rate was 5.4%. For Federal income tax purposes, beginning in 1967, an accelerated depreciation method is used and a provision is made in the Statement of Income for the taxes deferred as a result thereof.

3. CREDIT AGREEMENT

The Corporation has entered into a credit agreement which provides for the Corporation to issue unsecured notes not to exceed $3,000,000, bearing interest at ½ of 1% above the lowest prime rate charged by The Indiana National Bank or by Continental Illinois National Bank and Trust Company of Chicago, but not less than 6% or more than 7½%. Such notes may be issued at any time until April 30, 1973, and will be payable in installments to December 31, 1977.

4. SINKING FUNDS

The aggregate annual sinking fund requirement on First Mortgage Sinking Fund Bonds is $142,000. At respective maturity dates, after all required sinking fund payments, including repayments of an assumed borrowing under the bank credit agreement, the remaining balance to be paid will be as follows:

Series	Maturity Date	Balance to be Paid
Bank Note (Note)	December 31, 1973	$ 150,000
Bank Note (Note)	December 31, 1974	240,000
Bank Note (Note)	December 31, 1975	450,000
Bank Note (Note)	December 31, 1976	750,000
1, 2, & 3	June 1, 1977	1,470,000
Bank Note (Note)	December 31, 1977	1,410,000
4	June 1, 1984	803,000
5	September 1, 1986	730,000
6	September 1, 1991	1,460,000
7	May 1, 1994	1,533,000
8	July 1, 2005	1,950,000
9	October 2, 2007	1,890,000

Note: Assumes $3 million is borrowed from bank.

To the annual sinking funds aggregating $142,000 on bonds should be added the annual sinking fund requirement on preferred stock of $20,000. For the year 1971 and thereafter, the total annual sinking fund requirement, exclusive of repayments under the credit agreement (Note 3), on both preferred stock and bonds is $162,000.

5. RETIREMENT PLAN

The Corporation maintains a noncontributory money purchase retirement plan which covers all employees who meet the eligibility requirements based primarily on length of service. The cost under the plan, which is fully funded each year, was $99,000 for the year ended December 31, 1970.

6. CONSTRUCTION COMMITMENTS

Construction expenditures for the year 1971 are estimated at $6,023,000. Substantial commitments have been made in connection therewith.

TABLE B–1
Present Value of $1.00

Periods	4%	6%	8%	10%	12%	14%	16%	18%	20%	22%	24%	30%	40%
1	.962	.943	.926	.909	.893	.877	.862	.847	.833	.820	.806	.769	.714
2	.925	.890	.857	.826	.797	.769	.743	.718	.694	.672	.650	.592	.510
3	.889	.840	.794	.751	.712	.675	.641	.609	.579	.551	.524	.455	.364
4	.855	.792	.735	.683	.636	.592	.552	.516	.482	.451	.423	.350	.260
5	.822	.747	.681	.621	.567	.519	.476	.437	.402	.370	.341	.269	.186
6	.790	.705	.630	.564	.507	.456	.410	.370	.335	.303	.275	.207	.133
7	.760	.665	.583	.513	.452	.400	.354	.314	.279	.249	.222	.159	.095
8	.731	.627	.540	.467	.404	.351	.305	.266	.233	.204	.179	.123	.068
9	.703	.592	.500	.424	.361	.308	.263	.225	.194	.167	.144	.094	.048
10	.676	.558	.463	.386	.322	.270	.227	.191	.162	.137	.116	.073	.035
11	.650	.527	.429	.350	.287	.237	.195	.162	.135	.112	.094	.056	.025
12	.625	.497	.397	.319	.257	.208	.168	.137	.112	.092	.076	.043	.018
13	.601	.469	.368	.290	.229	.182	.145	.116	.093	.075	.061	.033	.013
14	.577	.442	.340	.263	.205	.160	.125	.099	.078	.062	.049	.025	.009
15	.555	.417	.315	.239	.183	.140	.108	.084	.065	.051	.040	.020	.006
16	.534	.394	.292	.218	.163	.123	.093	.071	.054	.042	.032	.015	.005
17	.513	.371	.270	.198	.146	.108	.080	.060	.045	.034	.026	.012	.003
18	.494	.350	.250	.180	.130	.095	.069	.051	.038	.028	.021	.009	.002
19	.475	.331	.232	.164	.116	.083	.060	.043	.031	.023	.017	.007	.002
20	.456	.312	.215	.149	.104	.073	.051	.037	.026	.019	.014	.005	.001
21	.439	.294	.199	.135	.093	.064	.044	.031	.022	.015	.011	.004	.001
22	.422	.278	.184	.123	.083	.056	.038	.026	.018	.013	.009	.003	.001
23	.406	.262	.170	.112	.074	.049	.033	.022	.015	.010	.007	.002	—
24	.390	.247	.158	.102	.066	.043	.028	.019	.013	.008	.006	.002	—
25	.375	.233	.146	.092	.059	.038	.024	.016	.010	.007	.005	.001	—
30	.308	.174	.099	.057	.033	.020	.012	.007	.004	.003	.002	—	—
40	.208	.097	.046	.022	.011	.005	.003	.001	.001	—	—	—	—

TABLE B-2
Present Value of an Annuity of $1.00

Periods	4%	6%	8%	10%	12%	14%	16%	18%	20%	22%	24%	30%	40%
1	0.962	0.943	0.926	0.909	0.893	0.877	0.862	0.847	0.833	0.820	0.806	0.769	0.714
2	1.886	1.833	1.783	1.736	1.690	1.647	1.605	1.566	1.528	1.492	1.457	1.361	1.224
3	2.775	2.673	2.577	2.487	2.402	2.322	2.246	2.174	2.106	2.042	1.981	1.816	1.589
4	3.630	3.465	3.312	3.170	3.037	2.914	2.798	2.690	2.589	2.494	2.404	2.166	1.849
5	4.452	4.212	3.993	3.791	3.605	3.433	3.274	3.127	2.991	2.864	2.745	2.436	2.035
6	5.242	4.917	4.623	4.355	4.111	3.889	3.685	3.498	3.326	3.167	3.020	2.643	2.168
7	6.002	5.582	5.206	4.868	4.564	4.288	4.039	3.812	3.605	3.416	3.242	2.802	2.263
8	6.733	6.210	5.747	5.335	4.968	4.639	4.344	4.078	3.837	3.619	3.421	2.925	2.331
9	7.435	6.802	6.247	5.759	5.328	4.946	4.607	4.303	4.031	3.786	3.566	3.019	2.379
10	8.111	7.360	6.710	6.145	5.650	5.216	4.833	4.494	4.192	3.923	3.682	3.092	2.414
11	8.760	7.887	7.139	6.495	5.988	5.453	5.029	4.656	4.327	4.035	3.776	3.147	2.438
12	9.385	8.384	7.536	6.814	6.194	5.660	5.197	4.793	4.439	4.127	3.851	3.190	2.456
13	9.986	8.853	7.904	7.103	6.424	5.842	5.342	4.910	4.533	4.203	3.912	3.223	2.468
14	10.563	9.295	8.244	7.367	6.628	6.002	5.468	5.008	4.611	4.265	3.962	3.249	2.477
15	11.118	9.712	8.559	7.606	6.811	6.142	5.575	5.092	4.675	4.315	4.001	3.268	2.484
16	11.652	10.106	8.851	7.824	6.974	6.265	5.669	5.162	4.730	4.357	4.033	3.283	2.489
17	12.166	10.477	9.122	8.022	7.120	6.373	5.749	5.222	4.775	4.391	4.059	3.295	2.492
18	12.659	10.828	9.372	8.201	7.250	6.467	5.818	5.273	4.812	4.419	4.080	3.304	2.494
19	13.134	11.158	9.604	8.365	7.366	6.550	5.877	5.316	4.844	4.442	4.097	3.311	2.496
20	13.590	11.470	9.818	8.514	7.469	6.623	5.929	5.353	4.870	4.460	4.110	3.316	2.497
21	14.029	11.764	10.017	8.649	7.562	6.687	5.973	5.384	4.891	4.476	4.121	3.320	2.498
22	14.451	12.042	10.201	8.772	7.645	6.743	6.011	5.410	4.909	4.488	4.130	3.323	2.498
23	14.857	12.303	10.371	8.883	7.718	6.792	6.044	5.432	4.925	4.499	4.137	3.325	2.499
24	15.247	12.550	10.529	8.985	7.784	6.835	6.073	5.451	4.937	4.507	4.143	3.327	2.499
25	15.622	12.783	10.675	9.077	7.843	6.873	6.097	5.467	4.948	4.514	4.147	3.329	2.499
30	17.292	13.765	11.258	9.427	8.055	7.003	6.177	5.517	4.979	4.534	4.160	3.332	2.500
40	19.793	15.046	11.925	9.779	8.244	7.105	6.234	5.548	4.997	4.544	4.166	3.333	2.500

Index

Absorption costing, 443, 444
Accelerated depreciation, 44, 148, 179, 185
Accepted accounting principle, 452
Accounting, accrual basis, 46-47
Accounting, cash basis, 46
Accounting, defined, 1-2
Accounting, interpretive area, 95
"Accounting and Reporting Standards for Corporate Financial Statements: 1957 Revision," 452
Accounting Concepts and Standards Underlying Corporate Supplementary Statement No. 2, 192
Accounting for cost elements, 342
Accounting period, 36
Accounting Research Bulletin No. 43:
  amortization, 205
  fair value, 291
  intangibles, 205
  inventory costs, 453
  inventory pricing, 241
  price level depreciation, 192
  stock split, 293
Accounting Research Bulletin No. 44:
  declining balance, 150
  income tax, 173
Accounting Review, 452
Accounting Terminology Bulletin No. 1:
  accounting defined, 2
  capital, 281
  depreciation accounting, 139
  retained earnings, 287
  stockholders' equity, 284
Accounting Trends and Techniques in Published Corporate Annual Reports:
  contributed capital, 284
  cost of inventories, 243
  intangibles, 204
  pricing inventories, 229
  statement of financial position, 12
  statement of income, 37
  surplus, 287
  treasury stock, 295
Accounts payable, 22
Accounts receivable, 17, 114
Accrual basis of accounting, 46-47
Accumulated depreciation to date, 20
Accuracy of inventory, 229
Acquisition cost, 139
Acquisition of non-current assets, 82
Activity:
  analysis, 395
  measure, 389
  units, 344
  variations, 359
Actual costs, 409
Actual expected standard, 409
Actual expenditures, 139
Actual hours, 423, 425
Addition of specific "assets" to capital base, 105
Additional capital, 284
Additional paid-in capital, 284
Additional shares of stock, 293
Additions to property, 139
Adjustment of specific assets in the capital base, 106
Administrative expenses, 39, 42
Advances, 14
Advertising expense, 39
Agriculture, depreciable assets, 143
AICPA (*see* American Institute of Certified Public Accountants)
  (*see also* Committee on Accounting Procedures of the American Institute of Certified Public Accountants)
Allocation cost, 137, 149, 185
Allocation process, 137
Allowance, overhead, 392
Allowed hours, 424, 425
Alterations, 137
Alternative costing methods, 364
Aluminum Company of America, 282

638 INDEX

American Accounting Association:
  direct costing, 453
  historical dollar cost, 192
  published studies, 199n
American Can Company, 155
American Institute of Certified Public Accountants:
  Accounting Principles Board, 3n
  amortization, 177
  capital, 284
  C.P.A. examination, 7
  income, 196
  income tax, 172
  intangibles, 205
  inventory costs, 453
  inventory pricing, 241
  market figures, 241
  price-level depreciation, 192
  pricing inventories, 229
  surplus, 290
  treasury stock, 295
  (see also Committee on Accounting Procedures of the American Institute of Certified Public Accountants)
American Iron and Steel Institute, 189, 191
Amortization, 204–14
  defined, 135
  emergency facilities, 176
  natural resources, 200
  net carrying value, 21
"Analysis of Manufacturing Cost Variances," 417
Analytical studies, 395
Ancient costs, 115
Annual report to stockholders, 3
Anticipated conditions, standards, 409
Application of funds statement, 73–83
Appraisal of results, 95
Approach of book, 2
Appropriated retained earnings, 298
Argentina, 186n
Armstrong Cork Company, 83, 108, 110, 175n, 621–25
Articles of incorporation, 16, 25
Ashland Oil and Refining Company, 291
Assets:
  addition, 105
  adjustment, 106
  average total, 102
  capital, 100
  carrying value, 135
  classes, 143
  classified, 14–15
  depreciation charges, 148
  disposal, 79, 158–60
  dividends, 289
  guidelines, 142
  intangible, 15
  irregular use, 146
  loss from sale, 39
  necessary for war effort, 176
  non-current, 81, 82
  other, 15
  owned, 105
  physical removal, 200
  reduced base, 178
  sale, 38
  specific, 103, 105
  statement of financial position, 13–14
  total, 97, 102, 114
  understated, 158
Auditing procedures, inventory, 229
Audits, 7
Automobiles, depreciation, 143
Average cost, 226, 236
Average total assets, 102
Avoidable and unavoidable costs, 373

Background of accelerated depreciation, 148
Bad debts, 17
Balance sheet, 12–26
  assets, 13
  classification of assets, 14–15
  classification of liabilities, 15
  condensed statement, 13–16
  detailed statement, 16–23
  liabilities, 13
  stockholders' equity, 13, 16
  uses, 25–26
Base, capital, 100, 103, 105, 106
  future earnings, 291
Basic objectives of inventory management, 251
Basic standard, 408
Basic value, 139

INDEX

Behavior, cost, 358
Behavior of production costs, 358–74
Berkeley Oil Corporation, 200, 203
Bethlehem Steel Corporation, 186, 282
Board of Tax Appeals, 137
Bonded indebtedness factors, 277
Bonds:
   callable, 275
   convertible, 274
   debenture, 273
   income, 274
   interest earned, 3, 39
   issue, 275
   long-term debt, 16
   marketable securities, 16
   mortgage, 273
   payable, 22, 39
   refunding, 275
   serial, 274
   sinking fund, 273
   subordinated debentures, 273
   types, 273
Bonuses, 99
Book value, 21
Bookkeeping, double-entry, 568n
Borrowing:
   long-term, 22
   management control, 305–6
Brand names, 205
Breakdowns, non-personal delays, 414
Break-even tax payments, 176
Break-in expenditures, 139
Breaking-in costs, 137
Bristol-Myers, 196
Britain, 186
Budget:
   comprehensive, defined, 511
   defined, 511
   financial, 514, 516–18, 527–32
   fully coordinated, defined, 511
   operating, 514–16, 520–27
   period, 513–14
   planning techniques, 532–33
Budget allowance, 423–28
   actual hours, 423
   allowed hours, 424
Budget variance, 424
Budgetary control, 6
Budgets, flexible, 387, 396
Building sites, 20

Buildings, 20
   depreciable assets, 142
Bulletin "F" of the Treasury Department:
   replaced, 142
   useful lives, 141
Burden, factory, 334
Bureau of Labor Statistics, 186n
Business expansion, 305
Business failure, 95
Business organization, decentralized, 112
Business organization forms, 25–26
Business receipts, 25
Business success, 95
Business year, 37

Calendar year, 37
Callable bonds, 275
Capacity considerations, 389–91
Capacity hours, 424–25
Capital:
   contributed, 281, 284
   equipment programs, 186
   excess of par, 22, 281, 284, 286, 291
   expenditures, 1, 135–38
   inventory costs, 250
   investment, 180
   recovery and maintenance, 200
   return, 95–117
   stockholders' equity, 281
   surplus, 22, 284
   turnover, 114
   working, 75
Capital base:
   adjustment, 106
   missing assets, 105
   rate of return, 100
   realistic, 103
Capital stock:
   classes, 282
   defined, 286
   illustrations, 79, 80, 81–82
   issuance, 140
   terminology, 281
   value, 140
Capitalization, permanent, 294
Capitalized cost, 136
Carrying costs, inventory, 250

Cash:
  balance, 6
  basis of accounting, 46
  current asset, 14
  defined, 16
  discounts, 228
  dividends, 81
  flow, 6, 73, 75
  position, 73
  statement of application of funds, 73
Caterpillar Tractor Company, 96
Cause analysis, 116
Cause and effect, 117
Certificates of necessity, 176, 177
Change:
  depreciation method, 150
  price level, 186, 188
  resistance, 192
Changing Concepts of Business Incomes, 196n
Charge sales due, 46
Charter:
  corporation, 281
  grant of authority, 25
Chase Manhattan Bank, 117
Chemicals, depreciable assets, 143
Chrysler Corporation, 246, 247
Claims:
  creditors, 13
  income, 304
Classes of assets, 143
Classification of production costs, 358–74
Classifying transactions, 2
Cleared into cost, 424
Closing market price, 291
Code of 1954, depletion, 202
Coin on hand, 16
Commercial paper, 14
Commissions, 39
Committee on Accounting Procedures of the AICPA:
  accelerated depreciation, 149
  amortization, 177
  depreciation, 191
  direct costing, 453
  income tax, 172
  intangibles, 205
  stock split, 294

Committee on Concepts and Standards Underlying Corporate Financial Statements of American Accounting Association:
  direct costing, 452
  historical dollar costs, 192
  stock value, 291
Committee on Terminology of the American Institute of Certified Public Accountants:
  accounting defined, 2
  depreciation defined, 138
  retained income, 287
Common stocks:
  capital stock terms, 282
  explained, 22
  revenue, 39
Company officers, 39
Comparative data, 116, 117
Comparisons:
  absorption and direct costing, 444–47
  principle depreciation methods, 154
Composite rate depreciation, 156
Comptroller General of the United States, 228n
Computers, 254
Concept of depreciation, 138
Condensed financial statements, 48–49
Constant dollar, 200
Construction Cost Index, 187, 191
Continental Can Company, Inc., 135, 225
Contractual interest rate, 277
Contributed capital, 281, 284
Contribution margin, 448
Contribution to fixed costs, 448
Control chart for variables, 590–98
  Lower Control Limit, 595, 596
  Upper Control Limit, 595, 596
Control factor, 303
Control of cost, inventory, 251
Controllable and non-controllable costs, 372
Controller, 5, 6
Conversion cost, 370
Convertible bonds, 274
Co-owners, 25
Copyright, 21, 134, 206

INDEX

Corporate codes, 291–92
Corporate earnings, 290
Corporate tax, 155
Corporate tax liability, 181–82
Corporations, 25
Correlation (*see* Regression analysis)
Cost, 358–74
   allocation, 138, 149, 155
   avoidable and unavoidable, 373
   behavior, 358
   bond issue, 275
   breaking-in, 137
   center, 339
   classification, 372–74
   control, 407–28
   controllable and non-controllable, 372
   conversion, 372
   depletion, 202–4
   depreciation, 145, 192
   determination, 225
   direct and indirect, 372
   direct labor, 342
   direct material, 342
   elements, 342
   experimental, 21
   finished goods, 42
   finished units, 337
   fixed asset, 139
   flow, 360
   goods sold, 39, 41, 331, 337
   historical, 20, 186
   indirect, 334
   inventory, 115, 250
   labor, 414
   manufacturing, 331–47
   opportunity, 373
   organization, 214
   out of pocket, 373
   overhead, 342
   prime, 372
   product standard, 426
   production report, 339
   recently incurred, 47
   replacement, 186
   standard, 427
   unit, 335
   variability, 442
   write-off, 138

Costing:
   absorption, 443, 444
   direct, 441, 451
   job order, 338–42
   process, 338
   rate standard, 419
Credit:
   excess, 182
   investment, 180–85
   issuer, 273
Creditors' equity, 269
Cumulative series stock, 283
Currency on hand, 16
Current assets, 14
   inventories, 225
Current costs, decision-making, 233
   depreciation, 186
Current income, 191
Current liabilities, 15
Current standard, 408, 409
Customer returns, 38
Cyclical fluctuations, 409

Damaged goods, 38
Data comparisons, 116
Data variation, 3–5
Debentures, 22, 271, 273
Debt:
   accounts payable, 22
   accrued expenses, 22
   long-term, 81, 270
   ownership ratio, 304
   reduction, 81
Decentralization, 99, 112
Decision-making:
   current costs, 233
   process, 73
Declaration of cash dividends, 81
Declining-balance depreciation, 150
   acceptance, 186
   AICPA statement, 172
   early years, 150
   income tax, 172
   larger charges, 150
   rental housing, 148
Decrease in working capital, 81
Decreasing annual charges, 149
Deductions granted customers, 39
Deferral of tax payments, 175

Deferred charges, 15, 21
Deferred credit, 278
Deferred tax liability, 172
Deficit, 287
Delivery expenses, 239
Departmental overhead rate, 418
Department of Labor, 186n
Depletion, 200–204
  defined, 135
  rates, 202
  tax history review, 202
Depreciable assets, 142
Depreciable property, 180
Depreciation, 134–62
  accelerated, 148, 153, 154
  accounting purposes, 44
  accumulated, 20
  add-back, 109
  Asset Depreciation Range, 144
  change, 185
  concept, 138, 185
  current income, 192
  declining balance, 150
  defined, 135, 138
  expense, 47, 147
  expense classification, 39
  gradually decreasing, 152
  group and composition rate, 156
  historical cost, 182
  income tax, 172
  initial, 178
  method objective, 145
  method selection, 155
  methods, 145
  original cost, 185
  overhead, 334
  price-level, 185, 192, 194–99
  policy, 155
  replacement cost, 185
  taxation purposes, 44
Depreciation Guides and Rules, 142
Deterioration, 138
Determinable life, 134
Determination of a proper balance, 301
Determination of the capital base, 100
Determination of the profit, 110
Detroit Edison Company, 135, 224, 225

Difference:
  inventory, 448
  margin, 448
  net income, 445
Dillon, C. Douglas, Secretary of the Treasury, 179
Direct and indirect costs, 372
Direct costing, 441–48
  advantages, 451
  defined, 442
  disadvantages, 451
  flow of costs, 368
Direct costs, inventory, 227
Direct labor, 334
Direct labor costs, 334
Direct labor standards, 414
Direct material costs, 334, 342
Direct material standards, 410
Direct material variances, 411
Direct materials, 334
Directors' fees, 39
Directors of corporation, 22
Disbursement, 1
Discount:
  bonds, 277
  cash, 228
  tax credit, 182
Disneyland, 158
Disposal of fixed assets, 158, 162
Disposal of non-current assets, 81
Disposition of funds, 73
Distortion in financial reporting, 172
Distribution expenses, 39
Dividends:
  arrearages, 283
  assets, 289
  cash, 81
  declaration, 81
  net declared, 283
  policy, 300
  received, 39
  rights, 283
  statement of retained earnings, 47
  stock split, 293
  stockholders' equity, 290
Dollar amount of shares, 282
Dollar value equalization, 109
Dollars of cost, inventory, 228
Donated land or building, 140

INDEX

Double declining balance depreciation, 151, 179
Dun and Bradstreet, Inc., 116
Dun's Review, 116
Du Pont(E.I.) de Nemours, 110, 135, 225

Earned surplus:
  restrictions, 297
  retained earnings, 23
  usage of term, 287
Earnings:
  reinvested, 281
  restrictions, 297–99
  retained, 23, 47, 286, 297
  statement, 37
Economic order quantity
  determination, 568–72
Effect of changes in price:
  business income, capital and taxes, 200
  property, plant and equipment, 186
  statement of income, 188
Effect of differing inventory systems, 248
Effect of dividends upon stockholders' equity, 291
Effect of specific factors, 301
Efficiency:
  maximum, 409
  standard, 414
  variance, 423, 425
Electric utilities, 143
Electrical equipment, 143
E.M.Q. (*see* Most economical quantity to manufacture)
Engineering News Record, 187, 191
E.O.Q. (*see* Most economical order quantity)
Equipment:
  acquisition, 134–62
  amortization, 172–214
  depletion, 172–214
  depreciation, 138–54, 172–200
  disposal, 158–62
  price level, 186
Equitable cost allocation, 155
Equity, stockholders', 281–300
  capital in excess of par, 284
  capital stock, 281
  dividends, 289
  restrictions, 297
  retained earnings, 286
  stock split, 293
  treasury stock, 294
Equity of owners, 13
Equivalent unit of production, 340–41
Estimated useful life:
  calculation, 145
  dependent factors, 141
  depreciation, 141, 145
  revision, 157–58
Evolution of cost accounting, 407
Excess profits tax, 177–78
Expected actual standards, 409
Expenditures, 135–38
Expenses, 37, 46–47
  manufacturing, 334
  other, 39
  prepaid, 14
  production, 424
External financing sources, 306

Face value, 276
Factory buildings, 20, 143
Factory burden, 334
Fair return, 196
Fair value, 196, 291
Fairless, Benjamin F., 189, 191
Federal corporate tax, 155
Federal income tax:
  income not taxable, 4
  rates, 111
  statement of income, 39
  trade-in, 161
Federal Trade Commission, 117, 303
Federated Department Stores, Inc., 17, 225
FIFO (*see* First-in, first-out)
Financial costs, inventory, 250
Financial data comparisons, 117
Financial management, 39
Financial measurements viewed, 117
Financial reporting, distortion, 172
Financial review, 36

Financial statements, 3
  condensed, 48–49
  manufacturer, 336
Financial status, 36
Financial structure, 300
Financial structure planning, 300–306
Finished goods:
  costs, 336
  inventory, 332
Finished products, 17
Finished units costs, 337
Fire insurance, 335
Fire loss, 39
First-in, first-out:
  cost determination, 225
  flow of costs, 230
  inventory evaluation, 18–19
  oldest inventory item, 226
  pricing methods, 333
First-year depreciation allowances, 178
Fiscal period:
  accounting period, 36–37
  cost of fixed assets, 138
  future periods, 136
Fiscal year, 37
Fixed assets:
  acquisition, 135–38
  amounts modified, 107–9
  capital base valuation, 108
  classification of assets, 14
  depreciation, 138–58
  diminution, 200
  disposal, 158–62
  intangible, 21, 134
  property, plant and equipment, 134
  sale, 38
  useful life, 154
Fixed budget, 419
Fixed costs, 364–65, 451
Fixed rate of depreciation, 151
Fixtures, depreciable assets, 143
Flexible budget, 387, 396, 419
Flood loss, 39
Flow of cost, 360
  first-in, first-out, 230
  historical cost, 364
  last-in, first-out, 232
  product costs, 339
  production costs, 358–74
Fluctuating dollar, 200

Forbes Magazine, 94
Ford Motor Company, 246
Formosa, 186n
Forms of long-term debt, 270
Franchise, 21, 207
Free retained earnings, 298
Funds:
  application, 81–82
  defined, 74, 75
  property additions, 20
  sources, 79
  statement of application, 73–83
Furniture and fixtures, 20
Future fiscal periods, 136

Gas depletion, 202
General Accounting Office of the
    United States, 8
General Dynamics Corporation, 135, 225
General Electric Company, 135, 220
General Motors Corporation, 135, 225, 282
General tax rates, 191
Generally accepted accounting
    principles:
  financial statements, 3
Generally accepted accounting
    procedure, 454
Glass, depreciable asset, 143
Goal of book, 2
Going business acquisition, 210
Goods:
  cost of finished, 42
  damaged, 38
  returned, 38
  sold, 41
  supplies on hand, 17
Goodwill:
  amortization, 209–14
  intangible assets, 30, 53, 54, 134, 205
  premium paid, 21
Goodyear Tire and Rubber Company, 285
Governmental accounting, 7
Great Britain, initial depreciation, 179
Gross income, 204
Gross margin:
  sales, 114

INDEX

Gross margin (*Continued*)
  statement of income, 40
  variable, 448
Gross profit on sales, 40
Gross sales, 39
Group and composite rate
  depreciation, 156
Guideline lives, 142–44
Gulf Oil Corporation, 135, 225, 282

Handling charges, 331
Handling costs, 227
High-low method, statistical analysis,
  395, 573, 574, 577, 578
Historical cost:
  abandonment criticism, 188
  American Accounting Association
    position, 192
  apparent profit, 188
  asset valuation, 20
  cost flow, 364
  current value variance, 21
  long-term assets, 186
Historical expenses, 395
Hours:
  actual, 423, 425
  allowed, 424, 425

Ideal standards, 409
Identification, judgmental, 395
Illinois Merchants Trust Company
  Case, 137
Illustrative examples:
  absorption costing and direct
    costing-statements of income, 443
  capacity relationships, 391
  comparison of cost methods, 238
  effect of dividends upon
    stockholders' equity, 291
  FIFO versus LIFO, 245
  stockholders' equity, 287
Imperfect goods, 38
Improvements to property, 138
Income:
  advance, 15
  bonds, 274
  generated, 79
  illustration, 443–45
  marginal, 449–51

margin of profit, 96–97
  operating, 137
  price level changes, 188
  single-step statement, 39–40
  sources, 37
  sources of funds, 79
  statement, 36–60
  statement detailed, 40–44
  subject to tax, 155
Income tax:
  corporate, 155
  deferred, 172
  depletion allowance, 202
  depreciation, 172
  overpayment, 189
  planning factor, 304
  trade-in, 161
Increase in long-term debt, 81
Increase in working capital, 82
Independent practitioners, 7
Index number, 108, 188, 407
  land values, 188
  profitability, 449
Indiana Telephone Corporation, 196,
  626–32
Indirect cost, 335, 371
  inventory, 227
Indirect labor costs, 335
Indirect labor expense, 344
Indirect material costs, 335
Inflation, 186, 200
Initial depreciation allowance, 178,
  179, 180
Installment contributions, 279
Installment payment dates, 270
Institutional accounting, 7
Insurance:
  capital expenditures, 137
  classification of expense, 39
Intangible assets:
  amortization, 204
  copyright, 206
  classified, 205
  franchise, 207
  goodwill, 212–14
  leasehold, 207–8
  leasehold improvements, 209–10
  long-term, 206
  organization costs, 214
  patent, 206

Intangible assets (*Continued*)
   trademark, 214
   value, 15, 134
Interest:
   accrued, 22
   bond issue, 275
   earned, 38
   expense, 39, 44
   paid on debt, 304
   periodic payments, 275
Internal analysis, 73
Internal audit, 6
Internal control, inventory, 229
Internal reporting, 4
Internal Revenue Code:
   accelerated depreciation, 149
   direct costing, 453
   maximum depreciation rate, 150
   net income, 44
   non-taxable gain, 295
   section, 453
   trade-in, 160
Internal Revenue Service:
   Bulletin "F", 143
   direct costing, 453
   external financial reporting, 453
   fiscal year, 37
   government accounting, 7
   LIFO, 248
Interstate Commerce Commission, 3
Inventory:
   acquisition costs, 331
   basic objectives, 250
   carrying costs, 250
   change in method, 249
   cost, 250
   current assets, 14
   decreasing, 445
   determination, 568–72
   determination of cost, 225
   differences, 448
   differing methods, 248
   economic order quantity, 568–72
   finished goods, 17, 332
   flow of net working capital, 74
   increasing, 445
   management, 250
   matching concept, 47
   raw materials, 17, 332
   supplies, 18
   systems, 228
   turnover, 95, 115, 117
   type, 224
   valuation, 18, 19
   work in process, 17, 332
Investment:
   affiliated companies, 20
   credit on depreciable assets, 180
   depreciable property, 180
   net effect of credit, 184
   owner's equity, 269
   qualified for credit, 181
   temporary, 14
   treasurer's duties, 6
Iowa-Illinois Gas and Electric Company, 199n, 273

Job order cost sheets, 342
Job order costing, 338, 341–42
Jones, Ralph C., 199n
Judgment of useful life, 142
Judgmental identification, 395

Keller, I. Wayne, 108
Kobler, Eric L., 25
Korean conflict:
   certificates of necessity, 176
   excess profits tax, 111
   rapid amortization, 178

Labor:
   cost of goods, 331
   direct costs, 342
   indirect expense, 344
   mix, 415
   price standards, 409
   productive, 334
   standards, 408, 414
   tight standards, 414
   variances, 415, 416
Land, 20, 134
Last-in, first-out:
   ancient costs, 115
   capital base, 110
   cost of inventory item, 225
   current costs, 189
   flow of costs, 232

Last-in, first-out (*Continued*)
  inventory technique, 232
  inventory valuation, 18, 19
  matching concept, 47
  recent unit sold, 226
  statement of income, 236
Lease:
  financing, 208, 209, 272
  improvements, 205, 209
  intangibles, 205
  leasehold, 207–8
  long-term debt, 271
  operating, 208, 272
  tax credit, 176
Lease-back arrangements, 209
Leasehold, 207–8
Least squares method, 395, 573, 574, 578–81
Legal capital, 300
Legal restrictions on earnings, 299
Leverage factor, 116, 304
Liabilities, 1, 13, 15–16
Lien on property, 273
Life, useful, 141, 145
LIFO (*see* Last-in, first-out)
Liggett and Myers Tobacco Company, 279, 299
Light, heat, and power costs, 335
Linear programming, 253, 598–605
Liquid assets, 279
Liquidity of receivables, 114
Loans, 17, 21
Long-lived assets, 134
Long-run competition, 451
Long-term debt, 269–306
  forms, 270
  increase, 81
  liabilities classified, 15–16
  reduction, 81
  source of funds, 79, 116
Long-term intangibles, 206
Long-term investments, 16
Loss:
  from sale, 39
  net, 48
  not covered by insurance, 39
  of serviceability, 138
Lost sales, 117
Lot size, economical, 253

Lower Control Limit, 595, 596
Lower of cost or market, 240

Maintenance of tangible capital, 200
Management:
  depreciation, 155
  guidance, 155
  inventories, 224–55
  judgment, 117
  marginal income, 449–51
  profit planning, 448
  performance, 95–117
  relationship with accounting, 1–7
  view of accounting, 3–5
Mandatory restrictions on earnings, 299
Manufacturer, financial statements, 336
Manufacturing:
  cost control, 407–28
  costs, 331–47
  expenses, 334
  margin, 448
  overhead allowances, 392
  overhead analysis, 426
  overhead costs, 334, 342
  overhead rate, 420
  overhead standards, 418
  overhead variance, 421
Margin, gross, 448
Margin of profit, 96
Margin on sales, 114
Marginal balance, 448
Marginal income, 448
Marginal profit, 448
Market, meaning, 241
Market forces, 451
Marketable securities, 16, 73–74
Market price, closing, 291
Market value, 291
Marketing expenses, 39
Mason, Perry, 199n
Matching concept, 47
Material costs, direct, 342
Material price standards, 409
Material specifications, 410
Material standards, 408, 410
Material variances, 411
Materials, direct (raw), 334

Maximum efficiency, 408
Measure, activity, 389
Measurement of financial
    management, 116
Measurement significance, 116–17
Measurements in perspective, 117
Merchandise inventories, 17
Military Subsistence Supply Agency,
    D.D., 228n
Mine, depletion, 200
Minerals, depletion, 200
Money orders, 16
Month-end balances, 114
Mortgage, 15, 270
Mortgage bond, 22, 273
Most economical lot size, 253
Most economical quantity to
    manufacture, 253
Motion study, 415
Moving average method, cost
    determination, 236
Multiple-step financial statement, 50
Multiple-step income statement, 39–40

N.A.A. (*see* National Association of
    Accountants)
*N.A.A. Accounting Practice Report
    No. 14,* 113
N.A.A. Bulletin, 108
N.A.A. Research Report No. 35:
    allocation of capital in
        headquarters, 113
    assets revalued, 108
    bibliography, 133
    equity plus long-term debt, 104
    rate of return on assets, 102
    rental payments, 105
N.A.A. Research Series No. 23,
    442, 445
N.A.(C.)A. Bulletin:
    direct costing, 442
    generalizations adapted, 445–46
N.A.(C.)A. Research Series No. 22:
    independent analysis, 417
    direct labor variances, 417
N.A.C.A. Research Series No. 23,
    cost-volume-profit, 368n
National Association of Accountants:
    changing price levels, 108
    labor variance, 417

Natural business year, 37
Natural resources, 134, 200, 202
Negotiable papers, 16
Net carrying value, 21
Net earnings, 16, 95
    reinvested, 281
Net effect of investment credit ,184
Net fixed assets, understated, 177
Net income:
    differences, 445
    direct costing, 451
    generated by operations, 79
    margin of profit, 96–97
    retained earnings, 47
    statement of income, 38
    subject to tax, 155
    taxable, 44
Net loss, 48
Net operating income, 112
Net property, plant and equipment, 20
Net purchases, 337
Net sales, 38, 96–97, 114
Net salvage value, 141
Net working capital, 74
Net worth, 16, 281
Next-in, first-out method, 233n
NIFO (*see* Next-in, first-out method)
Non-controllable costs, 373
Non-cumulative preferred stock, 283
Non-current asset acquisition, 82
Non-current assets, 81, 82
Non-manufacturing costs, 449
Non-perpetual inventory systems, 228
Non-personal tangible property, 181
Non-variable expense, 424
No-par value stock, 282
Norm, practical, 409
Normal capacity, 390
Normal standards, 409
Normal volume, overhead, 419
Note payable to bank, 21
Notes payable, 39
Notes promissory, 22
Notes receivable, 39
Numerical ratios, 116–17

Office buildings, 20
Office force salaries, 39
Office furniture, 143
Office machines, 143

Officers, company, 39
Oil depletion, 200
Omission of specific assets from capital base, 103
One-shot depreciation allowance, 178
Open market, 274
Operating condition, 139
Operating expenses, 146, 148
Operations, analysis, 414
Opportunity costs, 373
Order, cost accumulation, 341
Order quantity, 253
Organization costs, 214
Organization of business, 25
Organizational chart, 5
Organizational structure, 4
Original cost, 107, 186
Original issuance of par-value shares, 284
Other assets, 15
Other basic value, 139
Out-of-pocket and sunk costs, 373
Output, 146
Output record, 339
Outstanding capital stock, 281
Overapplied overhead, 348, 440, 446
Overhead:
    allowances, 393
    analyses, 426
    apportionment, 140
    costs, 342
    costs included, 334
    manufacturing, 334
    rate, 420–21
    standards, 418
    variability, 358
    variances, 421–22
Owens-Illinois Glass Company, 299
Owners' equity, 269
Ownership rights, 15

Paid-in surplus:
    capital in excess of par, 22
    stockholders' equity, 284
Paper profit, 16
Par value:
    callable bonds, 275
    capital in excess, 284
    capital stock, 16, 281
    cost standard, 407
    equity, 17
    price at issue, 276
Participating preferred stock, 283
Partnerships, 25, 179
Past costs, 233
Patents:
    defined, 206
    intangible asset, 134
    limited by law, 205
    rights of ownership, 15
Payroll taxes, 39
Pennsylvania Fruit Company, Inc.:
    profit percentage, 96
    return on capital, 97, 98
    turnover of capital, 98
Per unit cost, 335
Percent of net income to net sales, 96–97
Percent of profit, 96, 113
Percentage depletion, 203–4
Performance:
    measurement of management, 95–117
Period costs, 359, 442
Periodic depreciation expense, 148 157–58
Periodic interest, 275
Periodic inventory system, 228
Periodic net income, 446
Periodic redemption, 296
Permanent capitalization, 290, 294
Perpetual and non-perpetual inventory systems, 228
Personal tangible property, 181
Petroleum and natural gas, depreciable assets, 143
Physical counts, inventory, 229
Physical output record, 339
Physical quantities, inventory, 228
Pittsburgh Brewing Company, 274
Pittsburgh Plate Glass Company:
    diversified, 99
    dividend capitalized, 291
    emergency facilities, 177
Planning:
    accounting data, 4
    factors, 304
    financial structures, 300
    past costs, 233
    profit, 448, 451

Plant:
    acquisition, 134–62
    amortization, 172–214
    depletion, 172–214
    depreciation, 134–62, 172–214
    disposal, 134–62
    price level, 186
Position of direct costing, 451
Practical capacity, 390
Predetermined applicable overhead rates, 347
Predetermined costs, 364
Preferred stock, 16, 22, 39, 116, 282
Premium:
    above par, 275
    on capital, 284
Prepaid expenses, 14, 19
Prepaying the flexible budget, 396
Price:
    decrease, 450
    labor, 415
    material, 409
    reductions, 38
    standards, 408–9
Price levels:
    allowance for change, 186
    conversion to current price, 187
    movement toward price-level depreciation, 194
    no sanction of price-level depreciation, 191–93
    summary of price-level depreciation, 199
Prior claim on assets, 22, 283
Primary metals, depreciable assets, 143
Primary statements of income, 196
Prime cost, 372
Principle depreciation methods, 154
Private accounting, 6
Proctor and Gamble Company:
    capital turnover, 99
    depreciation method selected, 155
    profit percentage, 98
    return on capital, 99
Process costing, 338–42
Product standard cost, 426
Product unit costs, 439
Production:
    continuous process, 338–39
    fluctuation, 446
    sales balance, 445
Production costs:
    avoidable costs, 373
    controllable cost, 372
    conversion cost, 372
    cost behavior, 358–60
    costs classified, 372–74
    cost flow, 360–71
    direct cost, 368–71
    direct costing, 451–52
    indirect cost, 368–71
    opportunity costs, 373
    out-of-pocket costs, 373
    overhead costs, 442
    prime cost, 372
    sunk costs, 373
    unavoidable costs, 373
Productive capital, 189
Productive labor, 334
Profit:
    contribution, 448
    earned, 110
    enterprise objective, 95
    gross, 40
    margin, 96
    marginal, 448
    measurement, 188
    overstatement, 189
    paper, 16
    percentage, 114
    planning, 448, 451
    rate, 115
    undivided, 286
Profitability:
    index, 449
    performance, 95
    ratio, 114
Programming, 253
Progression toward price-level depreciation, 194
Promissory notes, 15, 22, 270
Property:
    acquisition, 19
    amortization, 172–214
    credit for investing, 180–85
    depletion, 200–204
    depreciation, 134–62, 172–76
    disposal, 158–62
    planning, 162

Property (*Continued*)
  plant and equipment, 15
  price level, 186
  rental income, 39
  rented, 105
  statement of financial position, 134
  tax, 335
Proprietorship, sole, 25
Public accounting, 7
Purchase fund, 273
Purchase of outstanding capital stocks, 82
Purchasing:
  department, 410
  power, 196
  timing, 412

Qualified investment, 181
Quality standard, 409
Quantities material, 410
Quantity standard, 414
Quantity to manufacture, economical, 253
Quarterly Financial Report for Manufacturing Corporations, 303
Quarterly Financial Report of Manufacturing Corporations, 117

Radio Corporation of America, 135, 225
  stock dividend effect, 290, 291
Rapid amortization, 176
Rate:
  labor, 414
  standard manufacturing overhead, 420
Rate of profit, 96, 115
Ratio significance, 116–17
Ratios, 96
Raw materials, 17
  inventory, 332
  element of cost, 334
Reacquired stock, 294
Receipts of business, 25
Receivables:
  flow of net working capital, 74
  liquidity, 114
Recorded appreciation of assets, 292
Recording transactions, 2
Records, inventory, 228

Recoverable reserves, 201
Recovery of tangible capital, 200
Recreation and amusements, depreciable assets, 143
Redemption, periodic, 296
Reduction of long-term debt, 81
Reece Corporation, price-level study, 187n
Refunding bonds, 275
Refusal to accredit price-level depreciation, 191
Regression analysis, 572–81
  correlation, 573
  high-low, 573, 574, 577, 578
  least squares, 573, 574, 578–81
  scatter diagram, 574, 575, 576
  visual inspection, 573–77
Reinvested income, 23
Reinvested net earnings, 281
Relationships, capacity, 391
Rental income, 39
Rental payments, 207
Rented assets, 209
Rented property, 105
Repair:
  difference between capital and revenue expenditure, 137
  influences useful life, 142
Repairs and maintenance, 335
Replacement cost:
  price-level depreciation, 186
  Securities and Exchange Commission, 192
Replacement of tangible capital, 200
Reporting, internal, 4
Reserve ration test, 144
Reserved retained earnings, 298
Residual value, 200
Restriction on retained earnings, 298
  bond issue restrictions, 279
Retained earnings:
  assets classified, 14
  restrictions, 297–300
  statement of retained earnings, 47–48
  stockholders' equity, 286–87
Return on capital, 96, 112
  average total assets, 102
  capital base, 100–101
  illustrative case, 100

Return on capital (*Continued*)
   profit earned, 111–12
   turnover of capital, 98–99
Return on stockholders' equity, 115
Revaluation surplus, 292
Revenue:
   accrual basis of accounting, 46–47
   other revenue, 39
   statement of income, 38
Revenue Act of 1913, 200
Revenue Act of 1926, 200
Revenue and expense spread, 97
Revenue expenditures, 135–38
Revenue Procedure 62–21:
   class method of depreciation, 157
   depreciation guidelines, 142
   reasonableness of lives, 145
Revision of estimated useful life, 157–58
Reynolds, R. J. Tobacco Company, 234
Rights, common stock, 22
Rights, preferred stock, 22
Risks costs, 250

Sacramento Municipal Utility District:
   bonded indebtedness, 278
   interest expense on long-term debt, 278
   operating expenses, 198
   sinking fund, 279
Salaries:
   accrued expense payable, 39
   current liabilities, 15
Sale of additional capital stock, 80
Sale of fixed assets, 39
Sales:
   allowances, 38
   discounts, 38
   margins of profit, 96–97
   production balance, 445
   returns, 38
   volume, 446, 448
Salesmen's salaries, 38
Salvage, 138, 140
Salvage value, 139, 145
Sample measurement, inventory, 229
Sampling, 581–90
   Central Limit Theorem, 585, 592

   confidence interval, 588, 589, 594, 596
   defined, 581
   population parameters, 585
   random, 582
   standard error of the mean, 587, 589
   systematic, 582
   Table of Random Numbers, 582, 583n
Savings accounts, 39
Scatter diagram method, 574, 575, 576
Schuylkill County (Penna.) Municipal Authority, 273
SCM Corporation (*see* Smith-Corona Marchant, Inc.)
Scott Paper Company:
   stock outstanding, 282–83
Sears, Roebuck and Co., 291
Seasonal fluctuations, 409
S.E.C. (*see* Securities and Exchange Commission)
Second-hand assets, 154
Secretary of the Treasury Dillon, 179
Section 167 (c) of the 1954 Internal Revenue Code, 152
Section 471 of the Internal Revenue Code, 453
Securities, marketable, 14
Securities and Exchange Commission:
   authority to police financial reports, 192
   figures for industry comparison, 117
   objects to direct costing, 453
   periodic financial statements, 3
   sources used for expansion, 306
   stockholders' equity, 303
Segregated asset, 279
Selection of a depreciation method, 155
Selling expenses:
   classification of expenses, 38
   marginal income, 448
   statement of income, 42
Semi-variable costs, 360
Serial bonds, 273
Service departments, 344
Services, depreciable assets, 143
Set-ups, non-personal delays, 415

Seven percent investment credit, 180
Shareholders' equity, 281
Shipping expenses, 39
Short-run competition, 451
Short-term investments, 14, 16
Single-step financial statement, 50
Single-step income statement, 38
Sinking fund bonds, 273
Small Business Act, 178
Small Business Tax Revision Act of 1958, 178
Smith-Corona Marchant, Inc.:
   consolidated balance sheet, 279
   restriction on retained earnings, 280
   restrictions disclosed by notes to financial statement, 299
Sole proprietorships, 178
Source statement, 73
Sources of capital, 269
Sources of funds, 73, 79
Special amortization of emergency facilities, 176
Specifications, material, 410
Spending variance, 425
Split stock, 293
Stabilized Accounting, 196n
Standard Brands, Inc., 282
Standard cost, product, 426
Standard costing rate, 419
Standard costs, 407–28
   actual hours, 423
   allowed hours, 424–25
   current standards, 409
   direct labor standards, 414–18
   direct material standards, 410–14
   direct labor variance, 415–18
   levels of standards, 408
   manufacturing overhead, 418
   manufacturing overhead variance, 421–23
   material variance, 411–14
   overhead rate, 420
   static standards, 408
Standard manufacturing overhead rate, 420
Standard Oil Company of Indiana, 290
Standard Oil Company of New Jersey, 282, 290
Standard volume, overhead, 419

Standards:
   direct labor, 414
   direct material, 410
Stated capital, 300
Stated value per share, 282, 284
Statement of income:
   absorption costing 443–44
   accounting period, 36–37
   consolidated financial statements, 50–60
   direct costing, 443, 444
   effect of changing price level, 188
   reporting by lines of business, 50
Statement of production, 337
Statement of retained earnings, 47–48
Statements of a manufacturer, 336–38
Static standard, 408
Statistical analysis of the relationship between historical expenses and activity, 395
Statistical Bulletin: Working Capital of U.S. Corporations, 305
Statistical guides, 408
Statistics of Income, 1966, U.S. Business Tax Returns, 25
Steel, depreciation problem, 189–91
Sterling Precison Corporation, 282
Stock:
   certificates, 282
   common, 39
   dividend effect on equity, 291–93
   dividend explained, 289–90
   earnings per share, 44–46
   marketable securities, 16
   outstanding, 82
   payable dividend, 290
   reacquired, 294
   sale of additional, 80
   split, 293, 294
   terminology, 281
   treasury, 294
Stock cards, 254
Stockholders' annual report, 3
Stockholders' equity:
   classified, 16
   current assets, 14
   rate of profit, 96
   rate of return, 114
   retained earnings, 47

654 INDEX

Storage, indirect costs, 227, 250
Straight-line depreciation:
   accounting purposes, 44
   advantages, 146
   disadvantages, 146
   periodic depreciation expenses, 148
   used property, 179
Structure, financial, 300–306
   general factors, 301
   planning factors, 301
   specific factors, 301
Studies, analytical, 395
Study Group on Business Income, 196
Subordinated debentures, 273
Sum-of-the-years' digits method of depreciation, 152
   background of accelerated depreciation, 148
   committee on Accounting Procedure, 149
   European acceptance, 185
Summarizing transactions, 2
Summary:
   price-level depreciation, 199
   total contributed capital, 286
Summary of manufacturing overhead analyses, 426
Summary of standard costs, 427
Sunk costs, 373
Supplies on hand, 18
Surface rights, 200
Surplus, 287
   capital, 16
   earned, 287
Sweden, 186
Sweeney, Henry W., 196n
Swift and Company, 135, 225
System:
   components, 590
   defined, 590
   stable variation, 591
   (*see also* Control chart for variables)

Table of Random Numbers, 582, 583n
Tangible assets:
   accelerated depreciation, 152
   classification of assets, 14–15
   fixed asset, 152

   initial depreciation, 178
   long-lived assets, 134
   personal property, 178
   seven percent investment credit, 180
   summary, price-level depreciation, 199
Tax:
   benefit, 180
   capital expenditure, 137
   corporate rate, 44
   cut, 144
   deferred payments, 172, 175
   depletion allowance, 201
   depreciation, 155, 172
   federal income, 161
   laws, 179
   liability, 182
   payroll, 38
   rates, 110, 191
   savings, 177
Theoretical capacity, 389
Time in depreciation, 145
Time quantity, 414
Time tickets, 342
Time variance recognized, 412
Tobacco, depreciable assets, 143
Total assets versus other bases, 100
Total contributed capital, 286
Total manufacturing overhead, 342
Trade-in, 161
Trademark:
   defined, 214
   existence limited by law, 205
   intangible asset, 134
   net carrying value, 21
Trading company, 332
Trading on the equity, 116
Transition to price-level depreciation, 185
Transportation:
   costs, 227
   equipment, 143
   manufacturing costs, 331
Treasurer, 6
Treasury bond, 280
Treasury Department:
   guide to useful lives, 141
   prohibit write-down, 245
   redetermination complications, 158
   Revenue Procedure 62–21, 142

INDEX

Treasury stock:
    defined, 294–95
    disposal at amount exceeding cost, 286
    reacquired shares, 282
    reasons for acquiring, 296
Trust indentures, 274
Trustee:
    current installment due, 279
    outstanding bonds, 274
    sinking fund, 273
Turnover:
    capital, 98
    explained, 114, 115
    inventory, 115
    measurement of performance, 114–15
Types of bonds, 273

Unavoidable costs, 373
Uncontrollable costs, 372
Underapplied overhead:
    defined, 347
    direct costing, 441
    normal capacity assumed, 446
Undivided profits, 280
Unemployment taxes, 38
Uniform annual depreciation, 145
Uniform Partnership Act, 25
Union Carbide Corporation:
    certificate of necessity, 177
Union contracts, 415
Unissued capital stock, 282
Unit costs, 335, 439
Unit depletion, 200
Unit market price, 294
Unit of activity, 342
United Aircraft Corporation, 135, 225
United States Patent Office, 206
United States Steel Corporation:
    accelerated depreciation, 194
    disadvantage of historic cost, 195
    profit percentage, 97
    return on capital, 98
    stock outstanding, 283
    turnover of capital, 98
    working capital approach, 24
Units of production method, 146
Unproductive hours worked, 425
Upper Control Limit, 595, 596

Usage variance, 412
Use of funds, 73
Used property:
    initial depreciation allowance, 178
    maximum qualified for tax credit, 181
    straight-line depreciation, 179
Useful life:
    depreciation accounting, 138
    new guideline lives, 180
    qualified investment, 181
    revisions, 158
    salvage, 140
    three unknowns, 139
Utilities, expenses, 39

Value:
    fair, 291
    other basic, 139
    par, 17, 284
    residual, 200
    stated, 282
Variability, range, 293
Variability of costs, 359
Variable costs, 364–65
Variable expenses, 424
Variable gross margin, 448
Variation in accounting data, 3–5
Variance:
    cost, 410
    direct material, 411
    manufacturing overhead, 421
    volume, 424
Virginia Electric and Power Company, 275
Volume of operations, 419
Voting power, common stock, 283
Voting rights, 22, 283

Wage:
    direct labor standards, 414
    hourly, 414
    method of payment used, 414
Waste, unavoidable, 411
Wasting assets, 200
Weighted average cost method, 237
Westinghouse Electric Corporation:
    change in inventory method, 250
    changing price level, 195
    goodwill, 212

Weyerhaeuser Company:
  profit percentage, 97
  return on capital, 98
  turnover of capital, 98
Woolworth, F. W., Co.:
  inventory, 224
  leased property, 209
Working capital:
  application of funds, 81
  increase, 82
  ratio, 96
  source of funds, 79
  statement of application of funds, 74
Work in process, 332

Work tickets, 342
World War I, 202
World War II:
  certificates of necessity, 176
  excess profits tax, 111
  increase in costs, 194
  LIFO adopted following war, 232
Write-off:
  amortization of fixed assets, 177
  depreciation, 138

Year, 37
Year's digit method for depreciation, 152